Elaine Mary Wainwright

Towards a Feminist Critical Reading
of the Gospel according to Matthew

Beihefte zur Zeitschrift für die neutestamentliche Wissenschaft

und die Kunde der älteren Kirche

Herausgegeben von
Erich Gräßer

Band 60

Walter de Gruyter · Berlin · New York
1991

Elaine Mary Wainwright

Towards a Feminist Critical Reading of the Gospel according to Matthew

Walter de Gruyter · Berlin · New York
1991

⊗ Printed on acid-free paper which falls
within the guidelines of the ANSI to ensure
Permanence and durability.

Library of Congress Cataloging-in-Publication Data

Wainwright, Elaine Mary, 1948-
    Towards a feminist critical reading of the Gospel according to
Matthew / Elaine Mary Wainwright.
      p. cm. — (Beihefte zur Zeitschrift für die neutestamentliche
Wissenschaft und die Kunde der älteren Kirche, ISSN 0171-6441 ;
Bd. 60)
    Originally presented as the author's thesis (Ph. D.) — University
of Queensland, 1990.
    Includes bibliographical references and index.
    ISBN 3-11-012860-8 (alk. paper)
    1. Bible. N.T. Matthew—Criticism, interpretation, etc.
2. Women in the Bible. 3. Women—Biblical teaching. 4. Bible.
N.T. Matthew—Criticism, Narrative. I. Title. II. Title: Femi-
nist critical reading of the Gospel according to Matthew.
III. Series. IV. Series: Beihefte zur Zeitschrift für die neutestamentliche Wissenschaft und die Kunde der älteren Kirche ;
Beiheft 60.
BS410.Z7 Heft 60
[BS2575.6.W65]
225.6 s—dc20   91-27684
[226.2′06′082]   CIP

Deutsche Bibliothek Cataloging in Publication Data

Wainwright, Elaine Mary:
Towards a feminist critical reading of the gospel according to
Matthew / Elaine Mary Wainwright. — Berlin ; New York : de
Gruyter, 1991
    (Beihefte zur Zeitschrift für die neutestamentliche Wissenschaft
    und die Kunde der älteren Kirche ; Bd. 60)
    Zugl.: Brisbane, Univ., Diss., 1989
    ISBN 3-11-012860-8
NE: Zeitschrift für die neutestamentliche Wissenschaft und die
    Kunde der älteren Kirche / Beihefte

ISSN 0171-6441

Printed in Germany
Printing: Werner Hildebrand, Berlin 65
Binding: Lüderitz & Bauer, Berlin 61

To
my parents
Tom and Kath
with deep love and gratitude

Foreword

This work was accepted by the Department of Studies in Religion of the University of Queensland as a Ph.D dissertation in April, 1990. The text which follows is predominantly the same as that submitted to the University as a contribution to the study of early Christianity and its scriptures, particularly the Gospel of Matthew. I am most grateful, therefore, to Professor Dr. Erich Gräßer who has offered to publish this manuscript as part of the series *Beihefte zur Zeitschrift für die neutestamentliche Wissenschaft*.

Dr. Michael Lattke, Associate Professor in the Department of Studies in Religion, University of Queensland, supervised this project and encouraged its publication, offering his professional support at all stages of the undertaking. Professor Elisabeth Schüssler Fiorenza, Stendahl Professor of Divinity, The Divinity School, Harvard University, Professor Donald Senior, The President, Catholic Theological Union, Chicago, and Dr. Edgar Conrad, Associate Professor, Department of Studies in Religion, University of Queensland, examined the dissertation and their insights and encouragement have assisted in bringing the work to the form in which it is now published. To all of these I am deeply grateful.

Many others have likewise offered academic support to this project. The staff and students of the École Biblique et Archéologique Française, Jerusalem, during the 1984-1986 academic years, provided a stimulating scholarly atmosphere in which much of the initial research was undertaken. A special word of gratitude, however, is due to Drs. Benedict Viviano, O.P. and Jerome Murphy-O'Connor, O.P., both members of the New Testament Faculty of the EBAF, who read various drafts of the manuscript and whose advice helped to refine my own thinking. Other colleagues–Dr. Janice Capel Anderson, and Dr. B. Rod Doyle–also offered valuable insights from their own perspective on Matthean scholarship.

The task of proof-reading is an essential one in the preparation of any manuscript and I offer particular thanks to Gregory Windle and Michael McClure who undertook this. The final stages of the preparation of the text was under the guidance of Felicia Dörfert of Walter de Gruyter & Co., Berlin, whose technical expertise I appreciated.

A work such as this, however, is not simply the result of academic labours. It has been supported and encouraged by both family and friends to whom I owe the deepest gratitude. It has also been nourished and enlivened by women of faith and courage who are undertaking a journey out of patriarchy. I would, therefore, like to acknowledge a final debt of gratitude to all those women with whom I have shared this journey in recent years and who have helped me to ask the critical questions and to be open to new possibilities beyond patriarchy in life and in the biblical text.

Brisbane, Australia   Elaine M. Wainwright
June, 1991

Table of Contents

Technical Preface

Throughout this text, direct quotations from the Bible in English are taken from the Revised Standard Version [*The Holy Bible: Revised Standard Version* (London: Nelson, 1966)], except where an inclusive translation has been made which is marked with an asterisk [*]. The Greek text of the New Testament, referred to throughout as the Christian Scriptures, is that of the 26th edition of the *Novum Testamentum Graece* and in the compilation of the synoptic tables I have been guided by the *Synopsis Graeca Quattuor Evangeliorum* (Leuven/Paris: Peeters, 1986), prepared by M.-E. Boismard and A. Lamouille. Alfred Rahlfs' *Septuaginta* and the *Biblia Hebraica Stuttgartensia* edited by K. Elliger and W. Rudolph are the sources for the Greek and Hebrew texts of the Old Testament, designated as the Hebrew Scriptures in this study.

Quotations from Josephus and Philo are from the translations in the Loeb Classical Library. Rabbinic texts are taken from *The Mishnah: Translated from the Hebrew with Introduction and Brief Explanatory Notes* by Herbert Danby (1933. Reprint. Oxford: Oxford University Press, 1985), and the Soncino edition of *The Babylonian Talmud* (London: Soncino, 1935-1952). All other sources are acknowledged at the appropriate places within the text.

List of Diagrams

Abbreviations

Abbreviations throughout this study adhere for the most part to those proposed by Siegfried Schwertner, *Internationales Abkürzungsverzeichnis für Theologie und Grenzgebiete* (Berlin/New York: de Gruyter, 1974). Where this is silent in relation to an English title, reference has been made to the guidelines proposed for contributors to the *Catholic Biblical Quarterly* ["Instructions for Contributors," *CBQ* 46 (1984): 393-408]. The latter has also been the source for the standard abbreviations used for biblical, pseudepigraphical, and rabbinic texts.

I. Periodicals, Series, and Encyclopaedias

AB	Anchor Bible
AGSU	Arbeiten zur Geschichte des Spätjudentums und Urchristentums
AmJAH	American Journal of Ancient History
AMNSU	Arbeiten und Mitteilungen aus dem neutestamentlichen Seminar zu Uppsala
AnBib	Analecta biblica
AnGr	Analecta Gregoriana
ANRW	Aufstieg und Niedergang der Römischen Welt
AOAT	Alter Orient und Altes Testament
ASeign	Assemblées du Seigneur
AThRS	Anglican Theological Review–Supplement
BA	Biblical Archaeologist
BAGD	W. Bauer, W. F. Arndt, F. W. Gingrich and F. W. Danker, *A Greek-English Lexicon of the New Testament and Other Early Christian Literature*, 2nd ed.(Chicago: University of Chicago Press, 1979).
BWAT	Beiträge zur Wissenschaft vom Alten Testament
BEThL	Bibliotheca ephemeridum theologicarum Lovaniensium

Bib	Biblica
BibOr	Biblica et orientalia
BiTod	The Bible Today
BJRL	Bulletin of the John Rylands Library of Manchester
BLE	Bulletin de littérature ecclésiastique
BNTC	Black's New Testament Commentaries
BTB	Biblical Theology Bulletin
CB.NT	Coniectanea biblica–New Testament Series
CBQ	Catholic Biblical Quarterly
CBQMS	Catholic Biblical Quarterly–Monograph Series
CFi	Cogitatio fidei
CNEB	Cambridge Bible Commentary on the New English Bible
CNT	Coniectanea neotestamentica
CThM	Calwer theologische Monographien
DBS	Dictionnaire de la bible–Supplément
EJ	Encyclopaedia Judaica
EKK	Evangelisch-katholischer Kommentar zum Neuen Testament
EPRO	Études préliminaires aux religions orientales dans l'empire romain
ET	Expository Times
EtB	Études bibliques
EThL	Ephemerides theologicae Lovanienses
ETR	Études théologiques et religieuses
EvTh	Evangelische Theologie
FRLANT	Forschungen zur Religion und Literatur des Alten und Neuen Testaments
HM	Hallische Monographien
HNT	Handbuch zum Neuen Testament
HThK	Herders theologischer Kommentar zum Neuen Testament
HTR	Harvard Theological Review
ICC	International Critical Commentary
IDB	G. A. Butterick, et al, eds., *The Interpreter's Dictionary of the Bible*, 4 Vols. (New York: Abingdon, 1962).
IEJ	Israel Exploration Journal
IJWS	International Journal of Women's Studies

IntB	G. A. Butterick, et al, eds., *The Interpreter's Bible*, 12 Vols. (New York: Abingdon, 1952-1957).
Interp.	Interpretation
IPQ	International Philosophical Quarterly
JAAR	Journal of the American Academy of Religion
JBL	Journal of Biblical Literature
JFSR	Journal of Feminist Studies in Religion
JJS	Journal of Jewish Studies
JQR	Jewish Quarterly Review
JR	Journal of Religion
JRH	Journal of Religious History
JSNT	Journal for the Study of the New Testament
JSNTSup	Journal for the Study of the New Testament–Supplement Series
JSOT	Journal for the Study of the Old Testament
JTS	Journal of Theological Studies
KEK	Kritisch-exegetischer Kommentar über das Neue Testament
LWC	Living Word Commentary
MSSNTS	Society for New Testament Studies Monograph Series
NCB	New Century Bible
Neot	Neotestamentica
NRTh	La nouvelle revue théologique
NT	Novum Testamentum
NT.S	Novum Testamentum–Supplements
NTA	Neutestamentliche Abhandlungen
NTS	New Testament Studies
OBO	Orbis biblicus et orientalis
OTL	Old Testament Library
PNTC	The Pelican New Testament Commentaries
QD	Questiones Disputatae
RAC	T. Klauser, et al, eds., *Reallexikon für Antike und Christentum: Sachwörterbuch zur Auseinandersetzung des Christentums mit der antiken Welt* (Stuttgart: Hiersemann, 1950–)
RB	Revue biblique
RSJB	Recueils de la société Jean Bodin
RSR	Religious Studies Review

RThom	Revue thomiste
SBLMS	Society of Biblical Literature Monograph Series
SBLSBS	Society of Biblical Literature Sources for Biblical Study
SBS	Stuttgarter Bibelstudien
SJLA	Studies in Judaism in Late Antiquity
SJT	Scottish Journal of Theology
SNTU	Studien zum Neuen Testament und seiner Umwelt
SPIB	Scripta pontificii instituti biblici
StANT	Studien zum Alten und Neuen Testament
StEv	Studia evangelica
StTh	Studia theologica
TBT	Theologische Bibliothek Töpelmann
TDNT	G. Kittel, ed.,*Theological Dictionary of the New Testament*, 10 Vols. (Grand Rapids: Eerdmans, 1964-1976).
ThHK	Theologischer Handkommentar zum Neuen Testament
ThLZ	Theologische Literaturzeitung
TICP	Travaux de l'institut catholique de Paris
TS	Theological Studies
TU	Texte und Untersuchungen zur Geschichte der altchristlichen Literatur
UISG	Bulletin of the International Union of Superiors General
USQR	Union Seminary Quarterly Review
VSal	Verbum salutis
VT	Vetus Testamentum
WMANT	Wissenschaftliche Monographien zum Alten und Neuen Testament
YJS	Yale Judaica Series
ZNW	Zeitschrift für die neutestamentliche Wissenschaft und die Kunde der älteren Kirche
ZThK	Zeitschrift für Theologie und Kirche

II. Ancient Documents

A. Classical Texts

Ann.   Tacitus, *The Annals*, 5 Vols., trans. John Jackson, Loeb
                  Classical Library (London: Heinemann/Cambridge,
                  Mass.: Harvard University Press, 1970).
Dig.   P. Bonfante, et al, eds., *Digesta Justiniani Augusti* (Milano:
                  Formis Societatis Editricis Librariae, 1931).

B. Old Testament Pseudepigrapha and Early Christian Literature

Acts Pil.   Acts of Pilate
1 Enoch   Ethiopic Apocalypse of Enoch
T. Jud.   Testament of Judah

C. Josephus

Ag. Ap.   Against Apion
Ant.   Jewish Antiquities

D. Philo

Cong.   De congressu quaerendae eruditionis gratia (On the
                  Preliminary Studies)
De fuga   De fuga et inventione (On Flight and Finding)
Leg. All.   Legum allegoriae (Allegorical Interpretation)
Mut.   De mutatione nominum (On the Change of Names)
Quod Deus   Quod deus immutabilis sit (On the Unchangeableness of
                  God
Virt.   De virtutibus (On The Virtues)

E. Mishnaic, Talmudic and Other Rabbinic Literature

[To distinguish the same-named tractates in the Mishna, Tosepta and Babylonian Talmud, m., t., and b. are used]
ʾAbot   ʾAbot
ʾAbot R. Nat.   ʾAbot de Rabbi Nathan
B. Bat.   Baba Batra

Giṭ.	Giṭṭin
Hor.	Horayot
Ḥul.	Ḥullin
Ker.	Keritot
Ketub.	Ketubot
Mak.	Makkot
Meg.	Megilla
Mek. Ex.	Mekilta Exodus
Menaḥ	Menaḥot
MHG	מדרש הגדול ... ספר בראשית ed. Schechter, Cambridge1902 and מדרש הגדול ... ספר שמור ed. Hoffman, Berlin, 1913-1921.
Midr.	Midraš
Ned.	Nedarim
Nid.	Niddah
Ohol.	Oholot
Peʾa	Peʾa
Qidd.	Qiddušin
Roš. Haš.	Roš Haššana
Sanh.	Sanhedrin
Šabb.	Šabbat
Šebu.	Šebuʿot
Soṭa	Soṭa
Sukk.	Sukka

III. General

AAR	American Academy of Religion
cf.	*confer*, compare
chap.	chapter
col.	column
diss.	dissertation
DSS	Doctor Sacrae Scripturae
ed., eds.	editor/edited by, editors
enl.	enlarged
et al.	*et alii*, and others

etc.	*et cetera*, and so forth
ibid.	*ibidem*, in the same place
idem	the same
LXX	Septuagint
MT	Masoretic Text
N.F.	Neue Folge
p., pp.	page, pages
parl.	parallel
Ph. D.	Doctor of Philosophy
rev.	revised
SBL	Society of Biblical Literature
trans.	translator/translated by
v., vv.	verse, verses
vol., vols.	volume, volumes

Introduction

"The personal is political"--a statement which has provided a significant underpinning for the contemporary Women's Movement and its various expressions over the last twenty or more years--can be adjusted to give expression to a fundamental starting point for feminist theology today: "the personal is political and theological".[1] Therefore, at the outset of this work which shares in many of the goals of contemporary christian feminist theology, it is important to articulate some of the presuppositions that have influenced its shape and content and which have arisen out of my personal and academic history.

I. Personal

As a woman within a mainstream christian church in the second half of the twentieth century, my christian identity and especially my adult faith have

---

1   The importance of experience and especially the experience of a particular theological or biblical scholar as the starting point for her or for his hermeneutical enterprise is borne out by a brief glance at the opening paragraphs of a number of scholarly contributions which have influenced the present work, namely, Mary Ann Tolbert, "Defining the Problem: The Bible and Feminist Hermeneutics," *Semeia* 28 (1983): 113-115; Carolyn Osiek, "The Feminist and the Bible: Hermeneutical Alternatives," in *Feminist Perspectives on Biblical Scholarship*, ed. Adela Yarbro Collins, SBL Centennial Publication 10 (Chico: Scholars, 1985), 93-94; Carter Heyward, "An Unfinished Symphony of Liberation: The Radicalization of Christian Feminism Among White U.S. Women," *JFSR* 1.1 (1985): 99-100; Jean C. Lambert, "An "F Factor"?: The New Testament in Some White, Feminist, Christian Theological Construction," *JFSR* 1.2 (1985): 93; Sharon D. Welch, *Communities of Resistance and Solidarity: A Feminist Theology of Liberation* (Maryknoll: Orbis, 1985), ix; Letty M. Russell, *Household of Freedom: Authority in Feminist Theology.* The 1986 Annie Kinkead Warfield Lectures (Philadelphia: Westminster, 1987), 17-18; and Rosemary Radford Ruether, *Sexism and God-Talk: Toward a Feminist Theology* (Boston: Beacon, 1983), 12-13 and a fuller discussion in her article, "Feminist Interpretation: A Method of Correlation," in *Feminist Interpretation of the Bible*, ed. Letty M. Russell (Philadelphia: Westminster, 1985), 111-116. Also, David Tracy, *The Analogical Imagination: Christian Theology and the Culture of Pluralism* (London: SCM, 1981), 60-61, considers "experience" one of the *constants* in theological discussion.

been profoundly shaped and nourished by the Hebrew and Christian Scriptures. For a number of years, this meant a simple recognition of these scriptures as the word of God, containing truths "for the sake of our salvation",[2] with little adequate understanding of the historical and cultural nature of the text which carried these "truths". However, a growing awareness of oppression and injustice within our global society and involvement within "communities of faithful political resistance"[3] began to pose questions regarding the nature of scripture and both the theory and the practice of its interpretation. It became clear that while the scriptures provided legitimation for the liberation of all who suffered under oppression, they were also used by many within the christian churches as a weapon against the poor and marginalized, as a means of "keeping them in their place". Was there a universally valid set of hermeneutical principles that could solve this dilemma or did each interpretation depend entirely on where the interpreter stood, on the presuppositions that influenced each one's work?[4] On the personal level, what was the influence of my own white, Anglo-Irish, middle-class Australian roots on any hermeneutic of liberation which I was developing in response to the demands of the scriptural text and the situations encountered in our world?

These questions intensified as the contemporary Women's Movement brought me to an awareness of my own invisibility as woman within the legal, theological and liturgical formulations of the christian churches and my exclusion from some sectors of ministerial praxis. Moreover, it became clear that I shared both this invisibility and exclusion with many women of christian faith whatever their racial, socio-economic or cultural situations. I learnt also that this was not only a contemporary phenomenon, but had

---

2   "Dogmatic Constitution on Divine Revelation," § 11, in *Vatican Council II: The Conciliar and Post Conciliar Documents*, ed. Austin Flannery (Dublin: Dominican Publications, 1975), 757.

3   This term is used by Sharon Welch, *Communities of Resistance*, ix, and I have employed it here to designate those small communities around the world which, throughout the seventies and eighties, have been committed to both consciousness raising and political action in the face of a number of local and global situations of oppression and victimization of the poor and marginalized. It includes, therefore, those groups whose motivating principle toward this two-fold objective lies within the paradigm of the christian faith.

4   Rudolf Bultmann asked this question in his now famous article, "Is Exegesis without Presuppositions Possible?" in *Existence and Faith: Shorter Writings of Rudolf Bultmann*, ed. and trans. Schubert M. Ogden, The Fontana Library Theology and Philosophy (London/Glasgow: Collins, 1960), 342-351.

characterized the entire history of the christian church.[5] In a way that was intensely engaging, I found myself struggling with the very tradition that had shaped and formed my identity and whose principles and insights had led me to this present understanding.

In the Bible, I found stories and precepts which placed women together with men at the centre of the story of God's dialogue with and involvement among humanity--the stories of Ruth and Judith, the Canaanite woman (Matt 15:21-28), the woman who anoints Jesus' head (Matt 26:6-13), the woman of Samaria who proclaims her recognition of Jesus (John 4:1-42), the women who encounter and proclaim the risen Jesus (Matt 28:9-10), as well as texts like Gen 1:27 and Gal 3:28. At the same time, however, I saw more and more profoundly that the Bible was the product of a patriarchal culture in which men have power over women, children and slaves (Gen 14:16; Exod 20:17; Num 30:2-12; Judg 11:29-40; 19; Col 3:18-4:1; 1 Pet 3:1-7). This domination, moreover, was legitimated by the androcentric language and reality constructs through which the biblical message found expression, and whereby male existence was considered the norm of human existence, "woman" was subsumed under "man" (Matt 7:24-27; 16:24-28; Luke 24:10-12; 1 Cor 14:34-36). This brought me face to face with the dilemma or the paradox experienced by many women today who choose to stay within the christian tradition and claim its scriptures despite their awareness of the patriarchy and androcentrism intrinsic in these same texts.[6] Mary Ann Tolbert captures the "profoundly paradoxical" nature of this situation when she says that "one must defeat the Bible as patriarchal authority by using the Bible as liberator."[7] This, however, raises significant hermeneutical and methodological questions and it is here that, as biblical scholar and as biblical christian, I find certain points of intersection between personal and academic experience.

---

5   Much has been written which has brought to light this aspect of christian history in recent years. See especially the early ground-breaking works: Mary Daly, *The Church and the Second Sex: With a New Feminist Postchristian Introduction by the Author* (New York: Harper and Row, 1975), especially 74-117; Rosemary Radford Ruether, ed., *Religion and Sexism: Images of Woman in the Jewish and Christian Traditions* (New York: Simon and Schuster, 1974); and Rosemary Radford Ruether and Eleanor McLaughlin, eds., *Women of Spirit: Female Leadership in the Jewish and Christian Traditions* (New York: Simon and Schuster, 1979).

6   Carolyn Osiek in her book, *Beyond Anger: On Being a Feminist in the Church* (New York/Mahwah: Paulist, 1986), addresses the situation of these women.

7   Tolbert, "Defining the Problem," 120.

II. Academic

Within the academic community during recent years, there has been much scholarly research undertaken in the field of hermeneutics generally and of biblical hermeneutics in particular, which seeks to articulate the principles involved when twentieth century interpreters dialogue with ancient biblical texts.[8] My entry into the academic community of scriptural scholarship co-incided with this growing interest in hermeneutical questions, but it was also at a time when the historical-critical method of biblical interpretation dominated the field.

More recently, this method has been challenged from many quarters.[9] At the same time, a number of women, both scripture scholars and theologians seeking a specifically feminist biblical hermeneutics to address the paradoxical situation in which they have found themselves as biblical theologians and biblical christians, have both critiqued and supplemented the

---

8   From among the lengthy list of works that could be cited here, I have simply chosen a representative group of some of the major works--Josef Bleicher, *Contemporary Hermeneutics: Hermeneutics as Method, Philosophy and Critique* (London/Boston/Henley: Routledge & Kegan Paul, 1980); Hans-Georg Gadamer, *Truth and Method*, 2nd ed., trans. William Glen-Doepel (London: Sheed & Ward, 1979); Terence J. Keegan, *Interpreting the Bible: A Popular Introduction to Biblical Hermeneutics* (New York: Paulist, 1985); Hans Küng and Jürgen Moltmann, eds., *Conflicting Ways of Interpreting the Bible*, Concilium 138 (New York: Seabury, 1980); Richard Palmer, *Hermeneutics: Interpretation Theory in Schleiermacher, Dilthey, Heidegger and Gadamer* (Evanston Ill.: Northwestern University Press, 1969); Paul Ricoeur, *Interpretation Theory: Discourse and the Surplus of Meaning* (Fort Worth, Texas: Texas Christian University Press, 1976); idem, *Time and Narrative*, 2 vols., trans. Kathleen McLaughlin and David Pellauer (Chicago: University of Chicago Press, 1984/1985); idem, *Essays on Biblical Interpretation*, ed. Lewis S. Mudge (London: SPCK, 1981); and Anthony C. Thiselton, *The Two Horizons: New Testament Hermeneutics and Philosophical Description with Special Reference to Heidegger, Bultmann, Gadamer and Wittgenstein* (Exeter: Paternoster, 1980).

9   Christian Hartlich, "Is Historical Criticism out of Date?" in Küng and Moltmann, *Conflicting Ways*, 3-8; Archie L. Nations, "Historical Criticism and the Current Methodological Crisis," *SJT* 36 (1983): 59-71; Augustine Stock, "The Limits of Historical-Criticial Exegesis," *BTB* 13 (1983): 28-31; Elisabeth Schüssler Fiorenza, ""For the Sake of our Salvation ...": Biblical Interpretation as Theological Task," in *Sin, Salvation and the Spirit*, ed. D. Durken (Collegeville: Liturgical Press, 1979), 21-39; and idem, "The Ethics of Interpretation: De-Centering Biblical Scholarship," *JBL* 107 (1988): 3-17; Leander Keck, "Will the Historical Critical Method Survive? Some Observations," in *Orientation by Disorientation: Studies in Literary Criticism and Biblical Criticism*, ed. R. A. Spencer, Theological Monograph Series 35 (Pittsburg: Pickwick Press, 1980), 115-127; and finally Walter Wink, *The Bible in Human Transformation: Toward a New Paradigm for Biblical Study* (Philadelphia: Fortress, 1973) and idem, *Transforming Bible Study* (London: SCM, 1981).

expanding field of hermeneutical research.[10] This methodological shift, the development of a feminist biblical hermeneutics, and the questions rising up from the life experience of christian women have brought to light significant problems which face the feminist interpreter of the biblical text.

First, the term "feminism" and related terminology must be clearly defined given the variety of ways in which they are currently employed.[11] Second, awareness of our contemporary and historical silencing and oppression as women has led to a profound shift in our understanding of the interpretive task itself. The context out of which current feminist biblical interpretation arises and toward which it is directed is the "church of women".[12] The adoption, however, of such an advocacy stance as central to a feminist biblical hermeneutics has provided a challenge to the dominant historical paradigm of interpretation. Feminist interpreters participate, therefore, in the current shifting of the paradigm of biblical interpretation and, as a result, a clear articulation of their biblical-historical and theological hermeneutics is essential.[13]

---

10   Much of this literature will be cited during the discussion to follow and it therefore seems inappropriate to simply list it here. I make mention of one article only: Elisabeth Schüssler Fiorenza, "Toward a Critical-Theological Self-Understanding of Biblical Scholarship," in her collection of articles, *Bread Not Stone: The Challenge of Feminist Biblical Interpretation* (Boston: Beacon, 1984), 117-149, in which she discusses contemporary biblical hermeneutics and the points of comparison and contrast between this and feminist biblical hermeneutics which she sees as sharing in the theological goals of liberation theology. Not all feminist biblical hermeneutics would necessarily share all these goals, but her article does point to some of the challenges which the emerging feminist paradigm poses to traditional biblical scholarship.

11   Ruether, *Sexism and God-Talk*, 214-234, discusses what she considers to be three major types of feminism, and Tolbert, "Defining the Problem," 115-117, outlines two perspectives on the goal of the feminist critique that can be found in the work of feminist theologians.

12   I use the term "church of women" or "women-church" in much the same sense as the more general use of the term "church of the poor". It is not intended to be exclusive, referring to a community comprised only of women, but rather it refers to the community of believers, both women and men, which places women at the centre of the life of the community and not on the margins. As Schüssler Fiorenza says clearly, "...to speak of the "church of women" does not advocate a separatist strategy but underlines the visibility of women in biblical religion and safeguards our freedom from spiritual male control. Just as we speak of the church of the poor, of an African or Asian church...without relinquishing our theological vision of the universal catholic Christian church, so it is also justified to speak of the church of women as a manifestation of this universal church." See her article "Emerging Issues in Feminist Biblical Interpretation," in *Christian Feminism: Visions of a New Humanity*, ed. Judith L. Weidman (San Francisco: Harper & Row, 1984), 39; and also her entire article, "Women-Church: The Hermeneutical Center of Feminist Biblical Interpretation," in *Bread not Stone*, 1-22, in which she develops this notion of the church of women as the context of feminist biblical interpretation.

13   Because of the challenge that feminist hermeneutics provides to the "academy", many who use it have sustained and will continue to sustain severe criticism. Moreover, given the marginality of women within the academy, as feminist interpreters they are

This brings us to a third problem, namely, our understanding of the nature of the biblical text. How can a text which supports patriarchy and the androcentric world view which legitimates it function as sacred scripture for contemporary women and the contemporary church? Can it, in fact, be considered canonical, the word of God with attendant authority and truth claims; and if so, how? Or, on the other hand, must it be confined to the status of an historical document?

Similarly, questions arise regarding the methodology or methodologies which will be employed. Are we confined to the standard methodologies of biblical scholarship and the manner in which they are currently applied, or do they too need to be critiqued to determine whether they serve patriarchy and androcentrism or liberation? In the light of a specifically feminist biblical hermeneutics, how will particular methodologies function and be combined?

Out of this intersection of my personal and academic experience has arisen the present undertaking: to begin a feminist reading of the gospel of Matthew. In the opening chapter many of the the key hermeneutical questions and problems raised above will be explored as a way of establishing a theoretical framework for the study, an exploration which will be done in dialogue with contemporary feminist biblical hermeneutics. Subsequent chapters will be given to the application of the established hermeneutical model to the Matthean text with special attention being given to those texts in which women function as characters within the narrative. Within a brief conclusion, some implications of this study for subsequent biblical and Matthean scholarship and the "church of women" will be given.

Such a task shares in many of the presuppositions of feminist criticism generally and of feminist biblical criticism in particular, chief among which is the belief that no scholarship is objective and value-neutral but is "on behalf of".[14] In this case it is on behalf of women; toward the future of the

---

placed in jeopardy as they undertake their interpretive task. Schüssler Fiorenza addresses this in "The Function of Scripture in the Liberation Struggle: A Critical Feminist Hermeneutics and Liberation Theology," in *Bread not Stone*, 43-49. See also Tolbert, "Defining the Problem," 118-119.

14   This point is made forcefully and repeatedly by Schüssler Fiorenza in many of her articles and in her books. See especially, ""For the Sake of Our Salvation...","" 25-28; ""You are not to be called Father": Early Christian History in a Feminist Perspective," *Cross Currents* 29 (1979): 301-303; "Toward a Feminist Biblical Hermeneutics: Biblical Interpretation and Liberation Theology," in *The Challenge of Liberation Theology: A First World Response*, ed. Brian Mahan and L. Dale Richesin (Maryknoll: Orbis, 1981), 93-96; "Feminist Theology and New Testament Interpretation," *JSOT* 22 (1982): 33-35; "Emerging Issues," 33-47; "Critical-Theological Self-Understanding," 128-149; and *In*

"church of women"; for the sake of the transformation of the christian traditions; and for the more careful articulation of the biblical word as the liberating word of God.

Memory of Her: A Feminist Theological Reconstruction of Christian Origins (New York: Crossroad, 1983), 5, 31-33.

1. A Theoretical Framework

The title of this entire study--Towards a Feminist Critical Reading of the Gospel of Matthew--will form the skeleton around which the theoretical framework to be developed in this chapter shall be shaped. In Part I, consideration will be given to the present state of research in the area of feminist biblical exegesis and hermeneutics, and this study will be placed along one of its trajectories. Under the broad banner of "A Feminist Reading", Part II will begin with a detailed analysis of the feminist critique, terms will be defined, and some of the key characteristics of the critique as it will be employed in this study will be outlined. Attention will then be given to hermeneutical and methodological questions which will lead to an outlining of the approach to be followed in the study. Part III will consider the relationship of the above to a study of Matthew's gospel, the text to be analyzed.

I. Towards: Trajectories in Feminist Biblical Hermeneutics

The use of the preposition "towards" as the introduction to the title of this study may suggest a certain tentativeness in the work being undertaken, but such is not the case. Rather, it arises from a two-fold recognition. First, research undertaken from a feminist perspective in all fields of academic endeavour, and especially in biblical studies, is a relative newcomer to the scholarly arena. For this reason, as we shall see below in tracing a brief history of feminist biblical studies, there is no single reigning paradigm of research.[1] Instead, several different models are in dialogue with one another

---

1   In feminist criticism generally, there is a resistance to codification or a master theory. See S. Harding, *The Science Question in Feminism* (Ithaca, New York: Cornell University Press, 1986), 244, quoted in *Gender and Discourse: The Power of Talk*, ed. Alexander Dundes Todd and Sue Fisher, Advances in Discourse Processes XXX (Norwood, NJ.: Ablex, 1988), 12; and Judith Fetterley, *The Resisting Reader: A Feminist Approach to American Fiction* (Bloomington: Indiana University Press, 1978), vii. On the other hand, however, there is a recognition of the need for theory as evidenced in

and new models are being developed according to the skills of individual researchers and the needs of the task being undertaken. It is my hope, therefore, that the model developed in this study may contribute toward the current ongoing conversation.

Second, as one becomes aware of the breadth of a truly feminist reading of a particular biblical text, especially as it is outlined by Schüssler Fiorenza, it is obvious that such an undertaking cannot be completed in one study, but that there will need to be a number of complementary studies over many years.[2] She suggests that a "feminist theological hermeneutics" requires that a developed critique "must be applied to *all* biblical texts, their historical contexts, and theological interpretations, and not just to the texts on women".[3] A comprehensive feminist reading of the gospel of Matthew, therefore, would entail an examination of the gospel as a whole but with particular attention being given to various categories of texts:

- those in which women function as characters;
- teachings regarding women;
- feminine symbolism;
- stories in which women are excluded or subsumed under the male;
- stories clearly bearing the mark of the patriarchal culture of the gospel;
- masculine symbolism; and
- teachings addressed specifically to men.

It would also include a feminist study of their contexts, and the history of their interpretation. Clearly this is impossible in one limited study. The focal point of this study, therefore, will be those stories in which women

---

Elizabeth A. Meese, *Crossing the Double-Cross: The Practice of Feminist Criticism* (Chapel Hill/London: The University of North Carolina Press, 1986), xi. Such theory though must not be allowed to restrict or determine research or creative thought.

2   A comprehensive outline of her feminist biblical hermeneutics is provided in her groundbreaking work, *In Memory of Her*, considered a classic in this field. It will provide one of the strong foundations upon which this study will be built. This will be supplemented by reference to her later collection of essays, *Bread not Stone*. Also, in a 1979 article, "The Study of Women in Early Christianity: Some Methodological Considerations," in *Critical History and Biblical Faith: New Testament Perspectives*, ed. Thomas J. Ryan, College Theology Society Annual Publication Series (Villanova: College Theology Society, 1979), 31-58, especially 30-31, she discussed the types of studies of women in early Christianity which she considered necessary at that time. Some of these have already been undertaken in the intervening years but many still remain untouched.

3   Schüssler Fiorenza, *In Memory of Her*, 33. Elisabeth Moltmann-Wendel, *The Women Around Jesus*, trans. John Bowden (New York: Crossroad, 1982), 10, also indicates that the work of the feminist interpreter is not only to focus on the texts which tell the story of women but on the bible as a whole.

function as characters within the narrative of the gospel. Chosen texts will be set within the context of the gospel as a whole and a number of related texts will be addressed cursorily. Hence the work will offer a contribution toward a feminist reading of the gospel of Matthew. At the outset, however, let us survey the field of contemporary feminist biblical hermeneutics within which the present study finds its place.

A. Feminism: A Newcomer to the Scholarly World

Often one finds that a survey of feminism and its influence on a particular field of academic enterprise will begin with reference to the work of Simone de Beauvoir[4] and Betty Friedan[5], both of whom have had a profound influence on the beginnings of and direction taken by the current Women's Movement. On the other hand, such a survey may confine itself to the last twenty years.[6] In a number of Western countries, however, there was an earlier Women's Movement, beginning in the middle of the nineteenth century and carrying over into the early twentieth century, only to be interrupted by the world wars and then to be revitalized as a result of the revolutionary movements at the end of the sixties to become the Women's Movement as we know it today. While I will not go into detail here regarding the history of this earlier movement and more especially its relationship to Christianity, it is important to claim this history as part of women's history in general and the history of christian women in particular and to note that it was characterized by a struggle for women's equality in education, the professions, and in socio-political life generally as evidenced in the Women's Rights and the Suffragette Movement both in Europe, the United

---

4   Simone de Beauvoir, *The Second Sex*, ed. and trans. H. M. Parshley (New York: Knopf, 1952).
5   Betty Friedan, *The Feminine Mystique* (Harmondsworth, Middlesex: Penguin, 1965).
6   Uwe Gerber, "Feministische Theologie: Selbstverständnis - Tendenzen - Fragen," *ThLZ* 109 (1984): 561-592, especially 565, although the article does make reference to an earlier Women's Movement; Anne Barstow Driver, "Religion: Review Essay," *Signs* 2 (1976): 434-442; and Renate Rieger, "Half of Heaven Belongs to Women, and They Must Win it for Themselves: An Attempt at a Feminist Theological Stock-Taking in the Federal Republic of Germany," *JFSR* 1.1 (1985): 133-144. This is also the beginning point of Hester Eisenstein's *Contemporary Feminist Thought* (London/Sydney: Unwin, 1984), xi and 3. The recent article of Karen Offen, "Defining Feminism: A Comparative Historical Approach," *Signs* 14 (1988): 119-157, undertakes a broader survey.

States of America and Australia.[7] For many women at that time, the goal was a change in the social structures which would gain more access for women and hence allow the voices of women to be heard. Others, however, like Elizabeth Cady Stanton, recognized the interdependence of social structure and ideology as well as the role of the Bible in the construction of that ideology. She wrote in her introduction to *The Woman's Bible* :

> Let us remember that all reforms are interdependent, and that whatever is done to establish one principle on a solid basis, strengthens all. Reformers who are always compromising, have not yet grasped the idea that truth is the only safe ground to stand upon.[8]

As she feared, the greater access that women had acquired in the early Women's Movement to education and to the vote did not change the fabric of society, but rather, in academia for example, left a small group of women struggling in a world which was still dominated by male scholars and their methods of research. Dorothy Bass makes some interesting observations in this regard in her study of women's history in the Society of Biblical Literature. She notes that women's membership of the society in 1920 was better than ten per cent, a figure which decreased over subsequent decades and she goes on to comment parenthetically that "coming at the crest of the "first wave" of American feminism, 1920 marked the high point for women in other professions as well."[9] Later in the same article she observes:

---

7   For a survey of this history and especially its impact within the christian churches, see Elisabeth Moltmann-Wendel, "Christentum und Frauenbewegung in Deutschland," in *Frauenbefreiung: Biblische und theologische Argumente*, ed. Elisabeth Moltmann-Wendel (München: Chr. Kaiser, 1978), 19-62; Elisabeth Schüssler Fiorenza, "Towards a Liberating and Liberated Theology: Women Theologians and Feminist Theology in the USA," *Concilium* 115 (1979): 22-32; Dorothy C. Bass, "Women's Studies and Biblical Studies: An Historical Perspective," *JSOT* 22 (1982): 6-12; Barbara Brown Zikmund, "Feminist Consciousness in Historical Perspective," in Russell, *Feminist Interpretation*, 21-26; and Carolyn De Swarte Gifford, "American Women and the Bible: The Nature of Woman as Hermeneutical Issue," in Collins, *Feminist Perspectives*, 11-33; Anne Summers, *Damned Whores and God's Police: The Colonization of Women in Australia*, Pelican Books (Harmondsworth, Middlesex: Penguin, 1975), especially 347-378; Carol Bacci, "First-wave Feminism: History's Judgement," in *Australian Women: Feminist Perspectives,*, ed. Norma Grieve and Patricia Grimshaw (Melbourne: Oxford University Press, 1981), 156-167; and Barbara Thiering, ed., *Deliver Us from Eve: Essays on Australian Women and Religion* (Sydney: Australian Council of Churches, 1977), and idem, *Created Second? Aspects of Women's Liberation in Australia* (Adelaide: Griffin Press, 1973).

8   Elizabeth Cady Stanton, *The Woman's Bible: The Original Feminist Attack on the Bible*, intro. Dale Spender, 2 parts (Part I, 1895 and Part II, New York: European Publishing Co, 1898; reprint, 2 parts in 1 Edinburgh: Polygon, 1985), 11.

9   Bass, "Women's Studies," 9.

Women SBL members have been active for women's causes, but as far as I can tell they did not combine this commitment with scholarly activity to produce a unified, feminist reading of the Bible.[10]

This would seem to corroborate Cady Stanton's earlier experience in seeking the services of women biblical scholars for the Woman's Bible project:

> Several distinguished women have been urged to do so, but they are afraid that their high reputation and scholarly attainments might be compromised by taking part in an enterprise that for a time may prove very unpopular. Hence we may not be able to get help from that class.[11]

The women who achieved higher education and took their place within it were not yet able to critique the structures of the academic enterprise nor its underlying presuppositions.

Only with the new emerging feminist consciousness as a critique of ideology[12] do we see the pervasive influence of feminist thought not only in society but also in the academy and in almost every field of research--history, anthropology, psychology, literary studies, sociology and theology to mention but a few. No longer is research confined to the search for new material which includes women, but there has been a profound questioning of methods of research and a call for an entirely new interpretive framework.[13] It is this aspect of feminism which makes it a newcomer to the scholarly world, and during the last fifteen to twenty years it has had a significant influence in the field of biblical studies.

---

10   Ibid., 10.
11   Cady Stanton, *The Woman's Bible*, 9.
12   There are a number of definitions provided for the word "feminist" as it is used in contemporary parlance and they will be discussed more fully in the next section, but suffice here to say that its general thrust is political and its concern is with social change not just at the structural level but also at the ideological. See Eisenstein, *Contemporary Feminist Thought*, xii-xiv; Russell, *Household of Freedom*, 17-18; and Phyllis Trible, *God and the Rhetoric of Sexuality*, Overtures to Biblical Theology 2 (Philadelphia: Fortress, 1978), 7-8.
13   Many women scholars have identified this as a "paradigm shift" according to the definition given by Thomas S. Kuhn, *The Structure of Scientific Revolutions* (1962; reprint, Chicago: University of Chicago Press, 1968): Shirley Ann Ranck, "Points of Theological Convergence Between Feminism and Post-Modern Science," *IJWS* 2 (1979): 386-397; Sallie McFague, *Metaphorical Theology: Models of God in Religious Language* (Philadelphia: Fortress, 1982), 67-144; Schüssler Fiorenza, ""For the Sake of Our Salvation ...","" 21-31; idem, "Emerging Issues," 34-40; and Welch, *Communities of Resistance*, 2-14, in which she talks of the "transformation of the modern episteme" in the language of Foucault rather than Kuhn.

A Theoretical Framework

B. Feminism and Biblical Studies[14]

1. A Brief Pre-history

Reviews of the study of women in ancient religions, of women in biblical religion, and of the history of women's research in these fields are beginning to abound.[15] These provide a comprehensive story of the study of women in biblical religion as well as women's study of biblical religion. I do not wish to repeat what these studies have done, but merely to draw some of the broad sweeps of the canvas which will provide a backdrop to the discussion of contemporary feminist biblical hermeneutics to follow.

As Carolyn de Swarte Gifford has pointed out, the question of a specifically feminist interpretation of the biblical text is not a new one, but could be said to have had its beginning, at least in the United States of America, with the essay of Judith Sargent Murray in 1790.[16] It was also a major concern for the abolitionists and emancipationists throughout the nineteenth century--the Grimke sisters, Lucretia Mott, Susan B. Anthony, Elizabeth Cady Stanton, and Frances Willard. In 1889, Frances Willard wrote:

> We need women commentators to bring out the women's side of the book; we need the stereoscopic view of truth in general, which can only be had when woman's eye and man's together shall discern the perspective of the Bible's full-orbed revelation. I do not at all impugn the good intention of the good men who have been our exegetes, and I bow humbly in presence of their scholarship; but, while they turn their linguistic telescopes on truth, I may be allowed to make a correction for the "personal equation" in the results which they espy.[17]

By the late nineteenth and early twentieth century, higher criticism was beginning to make its impact on biblical studies in both Europe and the United States, but as we have seen above, it was not utilized by the small number of women moving into the biblical profession to address the

---

14   This section of Chapter One was published recently as "In Search of the Lost Coin: Toward a Feminist Biblical Hermeneutic," *Pacifica* 2 (1989): 135-150. Certain revisions have occurred, however, in the final editing of the material.

15   The literature in this field has already been cited above: see nn. 6 and 7. The only addition here is Ross S. Kraemer, "Women in The Religions of the Greco-Roman World," *RSR* 9 (1983): 127-139.

16   Swarte Gifford, "American Women and the Bible," 12-13.

17   Frances E. Willard, *Woman in the Pulpit* (Chicago: Woman's Temperance Publication Association, 1889), 21, quoted in Swarte Gifford, "American Women and the Bible," 25.

hermeneutical questions of the women actively engaged in the earlier Women's Movement.[18]

During the first half of the twentieth century, there were occasional studies of women in some aspects of biblical religion, but they were few in number, were in most cases carried out by men, and generally accepted the presuppositions of the historical critical method. Hence, they did little to answer the questions raised previously.[19] As Ross Kraemer points out:

> Articles dating through the 1960s occasionally treat references to women, and issues such as marriage and divorce, normally associated with "women's concerns," but their perspective rarely includes consideration of what these texts reveal either about religious attitudes toward women, or women's actual participation in ancient religions.[20]

The debate over women in contemporary ministries which arose during the 1970s as a result of the impact of the new wave of feminism on the christian churches and the synagogue produced a wealth of material on the roles and status of women in ancient Judaism[21] and Christianity.[22] The religious

---

18   While Swarte Gifford, ibid., 13-31, addresses the situation in the United States during this period, Moltmann-Wendel, "Christentum und Frauenbewegung," 19-62, looks at the women's movement in Germany during this same time-span and how it engages Christianity in general but within that, its relationship to the study of the bible also. I have not been able to find similar surveys for other countries, hence the absence of reference to them here. This, however, is in no way an indication of the status of other histories but rather the current limitations of research.

19   Max Lohr, *Die Stellung des Weibes zu Jahwe-Religion und Kult*, BWAT 1/4 (Leipzig: Hinrichs, 1908), claims that a thorough study of the text will point to women's position in Israelite society and cult while P. Tischleder, *Wesen und Stellung der Frau nach der Lehre des heiligen Paulus: Eine ethisch-exegetische Untersuchung*, NTA 10/3-4 (Münster: Aschendorff, 1923) approaches the Pauline texts from a similar theoretical position. See also, E. A. Leonard, "St. Paul on the Status of Women," *CBQ* 12 (1950): 311-320; David Daube, "Jesus and the Samaritan Woman: The Meaning of συγχράομαι," *JBL* 69 (1950): 137-147; Raphael Patai, *Sex and Family in the Bible and the Middle East* (Garden City, New York: Doubleday, 1959); idem, *The Hebrew Goddess* (New York: KTAV, 1967)--a study which does not draw out the implications for women in Israelite religion; Else Kaehler, *Die Frau in den paulinischen Briefen* (Zürich: Gotthelf, 1960)--a response to G. Delling *Paulus' Stellung zu Frau und Ehe* (Stuttgart: Kohlhammer, 1931) which was not available to the writer; Johannes Leipoldt, *Die Frau in der antiken Welt und im Urchristentum*, (Gütersloh: Gerd Mohn, 1962); and Richard A. Batey, *New Testament Nuptial Imagery* (Leiden: Brill, 1971).

20   Kraemer, "Women in the Religions," 127.

21   Leonard Swidler, *Women in Judaism: The Status of Women in Formative Judaism* (Metuchen, NJ.: Scarecrow Press, 1976); J. H. Otwell, *And Sarah Laughed: The Status of Women in the Old Testament* (Philadelphia: Westminster, 1977); Judith Hauptman, "Images of Women in the Talmud," in Ruether, *Religion and Sexism*, 184-212; J. B. Segal, "The Jewish Attitude toward Women," *JJS* 30 (1979): 121-137; Moshe Meiselman, *Jewish Woman in Jewish Law* (New York: KTAV, 1978); and Roslyn Lacks, *Women and Judaism: Myth, History and Struggle* (New York: Doubleday, 1980).

22   The literature in this field would be too expansive to cite in full but I will name some of the significant contributions: Krister Stendahl, *The Bible and the Role of Women: A*

attitudes toward women revealed in the literature being studied also received attention. The focus of much of this study was on what had previously been ignored or overlooked in the text. Sakenfeld characterized it as a "looking to texts about women to counteract famous texts used "against" women."[23] Such an approach made a significant contribution to the beginning of a consciously feminist biblical hermeneutics. It drew attention to the diversity of biblical testimony to women, much of which had been forgotten. Some of the works reinterpreted previous androcentric readings of certain texts and generally uncovered the influence of the interpreter's presuppositions on exegesis. On the other hand, however, in retrospect, we can detect certain weaknesses. It tended to implicitly simplify complex hermeneutical questions to a presupposition that the Bible contains specific teachings regarding women and that these are be found in texts concerning women. This, in turn, made way for what could be called competing prooftexting around the question of women in minstry. Because of the understanding of the nature of the Bible which characterized this approach, there was a general inability to deal with oppressive texts. Hence there was a tendency to present only a positive attitude to the place of women in the biblical texts, to exalt the position of women in a way that may not have been faithful to the historical reality and in this way to subvert women's struggle for liberation.[24] As Carolyn Osiek says of this approach:

Case Study in Hermeneutics, trans. Emilie T. Sander, Facet Books - Biblical Series 15 (Philadelphia: Fortress, 1966); Franz J. Leenhardt, La place de la femme dans l'église d'après le Nouveau Testament, ETR 23/1 (Montpellier, 1948), which, although written in 1948, already addresses the fact that women are being trained theologically and the implications of this for ministry in the churches; Klaus Thraede, "Frau," RAC 8:227-242; Ruether, Religion and Sexism; Ruether and McLaughlin, Women of Spirit; Roger Gryson, The Ministry of Women in the Early Church, trans. Jean La Porte and Mary Louise Hall (1976; reprint, Collegeville: The Liturgical Press, 1980); Francis J. Moloney, Woman in the New Testament (Sydney: St. Paul Publications, 1981); Evelyn and Frank Stagg, Woman in the World of Jesus (Philadelphia: Westminster, 1978); Leonard Swidler, Biblical Affirmations of Women (Philadelphia: Westminster, 1979); George H. Tavard, Woman in Christian Tradition (Notre Dame/London: University of Notre Dame Press, 1973); Elisabeth M. Tetlow, Women and Ministry in the New Testament (New York/Ramsey: Paulist, 1980); and F. Heiler, Die Frau in den Religionen der Menschheit, TBT 33 (Berlin/New York: de Gruyter, 1977).

23   Katharine Doob Sakenfeld, "Feminist Uses of Biblical Materials," in Russell, Feminist Interpretation, 57-59.

24   The tendency to over-exalt women is not dealt with very much in the literature but I consider it a dangerous subversion of women's struggle for liberation because in "putting woman on a pedestal", it removes her from the concrete historical struggle. In presenting a picture which is falsely positive, it removes the real grounds for liberation, namely, the memory and story of oppression and discrimination.

... it tends to be innocent of the political implications of the types of social interaction and relationships that it advocates on the basis of fidelity to the biblical text as divine revelation.[25]

Awareness of some of these inadequacies, however, together with the influence of other theologies of liberation and the impact of a much more radical feminism which was calling for the rejection of Christianity as intrinsically patriarchal,[26] led women biblical scholars and theologians to a more conscious articulation of a feminist biblical hermeneutics. As a result, new paradigms of feminist interpretation began to emerge.

2. New Paradigms

a. Revisionist

In her article, "Depatriarchalizing in Biblical Interpretation", Phyllis Trible undertook a new task--"to examine interactions between the Hebrew Scriptures and the Women's Liberation Movement"--a task which many said was "impossible and ill-advised".[27] By way of examination of certain texts in the Hebrew Scriptures, however, she uncovered what she called a "depatriarchalizing principle" operating within scripture itself as it moves through history.[28] Using feminism, "a critique of culture in light of misogyny", as an "illustration of involvement between the world and the Bible", Trible developed her feminist hermeneutics more fully in *God and the Rhetoric of Sexuality* [29] and *Texts of Terror*.[30] She acknowledged that the

---

25   Osiek, "The Feminist and the Bible," 100. In the discussion of the above approach, I am indebted to the analyses of Osiek and Sakenfeld.

26   This challenge came especially from Mary Daly, *Beyond God the Father: Toward a Philosophy of Women's Liberation* (Boston: Beacon, 1973); and idem, *The Church and the Second Sex*. In the introduction to her second edition of the latter, she states her case very clearly when she asks the question of the Professor Daly of the earlier edition: "Don't you see that the efforts of biblical scholars to reinterpret texts, even though they may be correct within a certain restricted perspective, cannot change the overwhelmingly patriarchal character of the biblical tradition?" Her approach, with its strengths and weaknesses, is treated in more detail in Osiek, "The Feminist and the Bible," 98-99; Schüssler Fiorenza, *In Memory of Her*, 21-26; and Carter Heyward, "Ruether and Daly: Theologians--Speaking and Sparking, Building and Burning," *Christianity and Crisis* 39 (1979): 66-72.

27   Phyllis Trible, "Depatriarchalizing in Biblical Interpretation," *JAAR* 41 (1973): 30. See also the recent critical article of John W. Miller, "Depatriarchalizing God in Biblical Interpretation: A Critique," *CBQ* 48 (1986): 609-616. His supposedly value-neutral stance in relation to the text demonstrates, in fact, the very support of the entire patriarchal enterprise which Trible critiques. He shows little understanding of her undertaking.

28   Trible, "Depatriarchalizing," 48.

29   Trible, *God and the Rhetoric*, especially 5-8.

scriptural text will never lose its patriarchal stamp,[31] but within a feminist perspective, she used rhetorical criticism to concentrate primarily on the text so as to discover and recover "traditions that challenge the culture",[32] and this challenge to the patriarchal culture of the scriptures she also advanced by her retelling of "biblical stories of terror *in memoriam* ".[33]

The biblical analyses of Trible and of others who work within a similar paradigm[34] are characterized by the recovery of significant textual material for the sake of contemporary biblical women and the future of the church of women. These scholars have contributed to the ongoing dialogue toward a feminist biblical hermeneutics and have provided an alternative to the radical feminist rejection of the medium as the message by illustrating that the patriarchal context is not the message.[35] In this very aspect of their approach, however, one of its weaknesses is detected. The text is extracted from its socio-cultural context and hence a thorough-going critique of the culture it represents and of its patriarchal and androcentric point of view is often not

---

30　Phyllis Trible, *Texts of Terror: Literary-Feminist Readings of Biblical Narratives*, Overtures to Biblical Theology 13 (Philadelphia: Fortress, 1984).

31　Trible, *God and the Rhetoric*, 202.

32　Phyllis Trible, "Feminist Hermeneutics and Biblical Studies," *Christian Century* 99 (1982): 116. The rhetorical criticism used by Trible is derived from the work of James Muilenburg--see his "Form Criticism and Beyond," *JBL* 88 (1969): 1-18. She herself indicates, *God and the Rhetoric*, 26, n. 35, that it does not cover the much broader field of rhetorical criticism as it is understood in literary criticism generally.

33　Trible, "Feminist Hermeneutics," 118. This task is carried out in *Texts of Terror*.

34　Much of the material that has been published in recent years which examines biblical texts from a feminist perspective would share in the two-fold goal of Trible's hermeneutic: the recovery of traditions that challenge culture, and the retelling of texts of terror *in memoriam* , even though the methods may range from literary critical to historical critical. This is seen in a number of articles in *Semeia* 28 devoted to "The Bible and Feminist Hermeneutics": Janice Capel Anderson, "Matthew: Gender and Reading," 3-27; Elizabeth Struthers Malbon, "Fallible Followers: Women and Men in the Gospel of Mark," 29-48; Toni Craven, "Tradition and Convention in the Book of Judith," 49-61; and J. Cheryl Exum, ""You Shall Let Every Daughter Live": A Study of Exodus 1:8-2:10," 63-82. It is also notable in the collection edited by Russell, *Feminist Interpretation*: Sharon H. Ringe, "A Gentile Woman's Story," 65-72; J. Cheryl Exum, ""Mother in Israel": A Familiar Story Reconsidered," 73-85; and T. Drorah Setel, "Prophets and Pornography: Female Sexual Imagery in Hosea," 86-95. Note also Claudia V. Camp, "The Wise Women of 2 Samuel: A Role Model for Women in Early Israel," *CBQ* 43 (1981): 14-29; J. Cheryl Exum, "The Mothers of Israel: The Patriarchal Narratives from a Feminist Perspective," *Bible Review* 2 (1986): 60-67; and Moltmann-Wendel, *Women Around Jesus*, to name but some.

35　It should be noted here, however, that such an approach which can tend to place all the emphasis on the elements in the text which favour women is offset by that of Esther Fuchs, "The Literary Characterization of Mothers and Sexual Politics in the Hebrew Bible," in Collins, *Feminist Perspectives*, 117-136. She questions the possibility of gaining any tradition favourable to women from the patriarchal narrative. Perhaps neither approach, taken independently, allows for the complexity of the text and the diversity within it.

undertaken.[36] Schüssler Fiorenza concludes her discussion of Trible's approach by saying:

> ... a biblical theology that does not seriously confront "the patriarchal stamp" of the Bible and its religious-political legitimization of the patriarchal oppression of women is in danger of using a feminist perspective to rehabilitate the authority of the Bible, rather than to rehabilitate women's biblical history and theological heritage.[37]

b. Liberationist

A second paradigm has been developed predominantly by feminist theologians, especially Letty Russell and Rosemary Radford Ruether. Like Trible, they both consider that the interpretive key lies within scripture itself, not outside it. For Russell this key is "the witness of scripture to God's promise (for the mending of creation) on its way to fulfillment."[38] Ruether, on the other hand, looks to the "prophetic-messianic tradition" which she identifies not simply as "a particular body of texts, which then would be understood as standing as a canon within the canon" but rather as

> a critical perspective and process through which the biblical tradition constantly reevaluates, in new contexts, what is truly the liberating Word of God, over against both the sinful deformations of contemporary society and also the limitations of past biblical traditions, which saw in part and understood in part, and whose partiality may have even become a source of sinful injustice and idolatry.[39]

Both, however, would not see this key as operating in isolation but rather in correlation with the feminist critical principles being developed by contemporary women who are involved in the struggle to free all women from the weight of patriarchal oppression. As Ruether says:

> The Bible can be appropriated as a source of liberating paradigms only if it can be seen that there is a correlation between the feminist critical principle and that critical principle by which biblical thought critiques itself and renews its vision as the authentic Word of God over against corrupting and

---

36 This is the critique made by Schüssler Fiorenza, *In Memory of Her*, 20-21, and Fuchs, "Literary Characterization," 117-118. Osiek, "The Feminist and the Bible," 100-101, discusses this approach under the designation "revisionist hermeneutic" and she critiques it on the basis of its lack of political strategy.

37 Schüssler Fiorenza, *In Memory of Her*, 21.

38 Letty M. Russell, "Authority and the Challenge of Feminist Interpretation," in idem, *Feminist Interpretation*, 139.

39 Rosemary Radford Ruether, "A Method of Correlation," in Russell, *Feminist Interpretation*, 117.

sinful deformations. It is my contention ... that there is such a correlation
between biblical and feminist critical principles.[40]

Even though stated in a different way, this correlation undertaken by Russell
and Ruether closely resembles Trible's use of feminism as the link between
the Bible and the world.

These two paradigms share some common aspects, namely, a recognition of the liberating or depatriarchalizing principles within the scriptures
and an active engagement in bringing these principles into dialogue with
the critical perspectives of contemporary feminism.[41] Their central focus,
however, is   different. While Trible is among those scholars whom
Sakenfeld says are "looking to texts about women to learn from the history
and stories of ancient and modern women living in patriarchal cultures,"
Russell and Ruether share in the liberation approach of those who are
"looking to the Bible generally for a theological perspective offering a
critique of patriarchy."[42]

The feminist liberation hermeneutic, therefore, shares in some of the
presuppositions of other liberation theologies. It challenges the "value-free"
and "objective" claims of historical-critical scholarship[43] while at the same
time proclaiming its own advocacy stance.[44] It looks not only to the biblical
text but also to the transformation of the social order. This approach, however, has begun to raise significant questions for biblical scholars about the
very nature of the biblical text, its revelatory claims and its authority. As

---

40   Ibid., 117. Russell makes a similar point in her introduction to *Human Liberation in a
      Feminist Perspective--A Theology* (Philadelphia: Westminster, 1974) and the principle
      is operative thoroughout the work of both theologians.
41   These same principles are also employed by Diane Bergeant, "Exodus as a Paradigm in
      Feminist Theology," *Concilium* 189 (1987): 100-108.
42   Sakenfeld, "Feminist Uses," 62-63, 59-61. It is Osiek who offers the   designation
      "liberationist hermeneutic" to this approach in "The Feminist and the Bible," 102-104.
43   This challenge comes especially from Schüssler Fiorenza whom I have not included
      among these scholars because her approach differs from theirs in certain aspects and
      hence deserves to be treated separately, but she does share in the liberation perspective
      of Russell, Ruether and others like them. For her detailed treatment of this challenge
      see, ""For the Sake or our Salvation ...","" 25-28; "Remembering the Past in Creating the
      Future: Historical-Critical Scholarship and Feminist Biblical Interpretation," in Collins,
      Feminist Perspectives, 43-63.
44   An advocacy stance for and on behalf of women does not mean an exclusion of men
      from the vision of the new humanity, a point well illustrated by Letty Russell and re-
      vealed even in the titles of two of her earlier works: *Human Liberation*; and *The
      Future of Partnership* (Philadelphia: Westminster, 1979). Rather, for her, the advocacy
      stance which she calls "feminist" is so called "because the women involved are actively
      engaged in advocating the equality and partnership of women and men in church and
      society." See *Human Liberation*, 19. Ruether's advocacy stance is spelt out in *Sexism
      and God-Talk*, 18-20.

early as 1983, Letty Russell recognized "alternative views of biblical authority; and the search for a new biblical paradigm" as two of the three major issues that had emerged from a discussion of feminist hermeneutics during the previous three to four years.[45] She herself takes up the question of authority much more fully in her recent book, *Household of Freedom*, while the issue of a new biblical paradigm has been raised most explicitly by Elisabeth Schüssler Fiorenza in her classical work, *In Memory of Her*. These issues will be discussed more fully below, but it is important to note here their significance for a broad range of feminist biblical scholars.[46]

c. Theological/Reconstructionist

The third paradigm which has emerged within the last fifteen years is that which I have named "theological/reconstructionist" and its chief representative is Elisabeth Schüssler Fiorenza. Her book, *In Memory of Her*, in which she sets forth her feminist biblical hermeneutics in great detail, is subtitled "A Feminist Theological Reconstruction of Christian Origins". Scholars point to the differences between her work and that of others who more clearly belong to one or other of the two groups discussed above.[47] Also, she herself, in the opening chapter of *In Memory of Her*, sets her own hermeneutics off from that of Trible, Russell and Ruether, and Mary Daly.[48] It seems clear, therefore, that her biblical and theological hermeneutics need to be treated in their own right even though she shares a number of the presuppositions of the previous two paradigms.[49]

---

45   Letty M. Russell, "In Search of a Critical Feminist Paradigm for Bibilical Interpretation," (Paper presented to the Working Group on Liberation Theology, AAR/SBL, Feminist Hermeneutic Project, April, 1983), 3.
46   Jean C. Lambert also affirms the centrality of the nature of the authority of scripture in a feminist hermeneutic when she makes it the focal point for her consideration of four contemporary feminist theologians: Sallie McFague, Rosemary Radford Ruether, Carter Heyward, and Elisabeth Schüssler Fiorenza. See her article, "An "F Factor"," 93-113.
47   Ibid., 109, where Lambert shows the difficulties encountered in trying to fit Schüssler Fiorenza's work on the grid she has adopted. Russell, "In Search," 5, points out that Schüssler Fiorenza's canon of feminist interpretation lies outside the scriptures whereas the interpretive key for the two previous paradigms lies within the scriptural text. Rosemary Radford Ruether, perhaps a little cruelly, categorizes her as a "methodological porcupine" in her response to *In Memory of Her* in "Review Symposium," *Horizons* 11 (1984): 147, but also indicates by this comment that Schüssler Fiorenza's work stands alone methodologically.
48   Schüssler Fiorenza, *In Memory of Her*, 14-26.
49   Sakenfeld, "Feminist Uses," 62-63, places both Schüssler Fiorenza's and Trible's hermeneutics in her category "Looking to Texts about Women to Learn from the History and Stories of Ancient and Modern Women Living in Patriarchal Cultures". Osiek, "The Feminist and the Bible," 102-104, on the other hand, places it with that of

As her subtitle above suggests, one of her primary concerns is the theological reconstruction of early Christianity so that it is the history of women as well as men. In the introduction to the book, however, she states clearly that her goal is two-fold:

> The explorations of this book have two goals: they attempt to reconstruct early Christian history as women's history in order not only to restore women's stories to early Christian history but also to reclaim this history as the history of women and men.[50]

Not only is she concerned with the theological reconstruction of early christian origins, but also with the issue of theological hermeneutics which provides a framework for the reclaiming of early christian history for contemporary women and men.

In respect to her focus on reconstruction of origins, she differs from many other feminist biblical scholars in that not only her interpretive key but also her primary focus is outside the text. Her revelatory canon is, as she says, "formulated in and through women's struggle for liberation from all patriarchal oppression,"[51] and the locus of revelation "is not the androcentric text but the life and ministry of Jesus and the movement of women and men called forth by him."[52] In order to reconstruct this locus, she seeks to integrate into her model the "so-called counter-cultural, heretical and egalitarian traditions and texts."[53] Such a model, she claims, must also allow for a reconstruction which draws on methods which are historical-critical and sociological, but these methods must be critiqued from a feminist perspective.[54] Only in this way can we reclaim our foresisters "as victims *and* subjects participating in patriarchal culture."[55]

Key to such an historical reconstruction from a feminist perspective is the application of a hermeneutics of suspicion not only to the context of the

---

the other Liberationists--Russell and Ruether. Also, it should be stated here that even though I have chosen to focus on the work of Schüssler Fiorenza as a New Testament scholar, a reconstructionist approach is being employed by scholars in Judaism such as Bernadette J. Brooten, *Women Leaders in the Ancient Synagogue*, Brown Judaic Studies 36 (Chico: S. holars, 1982), and Ross S. Kraemer, *Ecstatics and Ascetics: Studies in the Function of Religious Activities for Women in The Greco-Roman World* (Ann Arbor: Xerox University Microfilms, 1976), to cite but a few examples.

50   Schüssler Fiorenza, *In Memory of Her*, xiv.
51   Ibid., 32.
52   Ibid., 41.
53   Schüssler Fiorenza, "Femininst Theology and New Testament Interpretation," 44.
54   Ibid., 41, 44; idem, "Remembering the Past," 54-55; and ""You are not to be Called Father"," 302-306. See her own critique of some of these methods in *In Memory of Her*, 68-84.
55   Ibid., 29.

biblical witness but to the text and its history of interpretation. By text, she does not mean "merely the biblical passages on women,"[56] but "*all* biblical traditions and texts."[57] The androcentric nature of the text and the patriarchal culture which it presupposes mean that all biblical texts must be tested according to certain feminist criteria in order to determine how much they have functioned and continue to function to support patriarchal structures and values and, on the other hand, how much they promote liberation.[58] Such a goal begins to determine methodology and the very nature of feminist undertakings.[59] Biblical texts must be considered within the particular book to which they belong and so there need to be studies of individual biblical books from a feminist perspective. Also if such studies are to determine the effect of an entire book and individual texts within it on its historical and contemporary audiences then synchronic and diachronic methodologies must be combined within the feminist biblical hermeneutics which are developing. While Schüssler Fiorenza's primary consideration in *In Memory of Her* was given to diachronic methodologies, she discusses their integration with synchronic methods from a theoretical perspective in *Bread not Stone*,[60] and later develops an integrated model that she applies to the Pauline text of 1 Corinthians.[61]

Taken alone, this goal of theological reconstruction bears within it the inherent danger of the text becoming simply a "window" on the "world behind the text" with insufficient attention being given to the "world in front of the text" and the liberating vision it can present to the church of women. Schüssler Fiorenza, however, has combined her theological

---

56   Schüssler Fiorenza, *In Memory of Her*, 30.
57   Ibid., 32-33.
58   Elisabeth Schüssler Fiorenza, "The Will to Choose or to Reject: Continuing Our Critical Work," in Russell, *Feminist Interpretation*, 131. Here Schüssler Fiorenza contrasts her own "feminist critical evaluation" from the "method of correlation" saying that "such an interpretation must sort through particular biblical texts and test out in a process of critical analysis and evaluation how much their content and function perpetrates and legitimates patriarchal structures, not only in their original historical contexts but also in our contempoarary situation. Conversely, all biblical texts must be tested as to their feminist liberating content and function in their historical and contemporary contexts."
59   Schüssler Fiorenza, "Study of Women," 30-31.
60   Elisabeth Schüssler Fiorenza, "Critical-Theological Self-Understanding," 117-149.
61   Elisabeth Schüssler Fiorenza, "Rhetorical Situation and Historical Reconstruction in 1 Corinthians," *NTS* 33 (1987): 386-403. In this article she uses an approach which she calls "rhetorical criticism" but her use of such a rhetorical approach differs from that of Trible in that she is not only or primarily concerned with the rhetorical arrangement within the text but more particularly with its rhetorical function in a specific sociopolitical situation.

reconstruction with the development of a theological hermeneutics. This second under-taking was begun in the first part of *In Memory of Her*, and extended in a number of the essays in *Bread not Stone*. Within her extended model, a *hermeneutics of suspicion* applied to both biblical texts and their interpretations is a fundamental starting point in a feminist biblical hermeneutics, but it must be supplemented by a *hermeneutics of proclamation* which she says "assesses the Bible's theological significance and power for the contemporary community of faith."[62] This, in turn, is to be "balanced" by a *hermeneutics of remembrance* whereby all biblical texts are reclaimed by means of an "historical-critical reconstruction of biblical history from a feminist perspective". In this way, we remember not only the "history of liberation and religious agency" of our foresisters, but also their suffering and oppression which becomes a *"memoria passionis"* of biblical women.[63] Her final stage is a *hermeneutics of creative actualization* which gives expression to the remembered history in ways that enable contemporary women to creatively and imaginatively enter into it and claim it as their own.

Schüssler Fiorenza's feminist biblical hermeneutics is much more complex than indicated by this brief discussion, but other aspects of it will be considered in Part II below. It is important to emphasize, however, the perspective that she shares with those who interpret the scriptural text from within one or other of the two paradigms discussed above, namely, a feminist critical perspective. This means the articulation of "criteria and principles for evaluating particular texts, biblical books, traditions, or interpretations." She goes on to say that "such criteria or principles must be derived from a systematic exploration of women's experience of oppression and liberation."[64] At no point, however, does she clarify these criteria but rather they seem to be subsumed under the umbrella of "liberation". It appears, therefore, that there is a need to undertake such clarification, a task which will receive consideration in the subsequent discussion of the nature of a feminist reading.[65]

---

62 Schüssler Fiorenza, "Women-Church," 18.
63 Ibid., 19-20.
64 Schüssler Fiorenza, "The Will to Choose or to Reject," 131.
65 Katherine E. Zappone, "A Feminist Hermeneutics for Scripture: The Standpoint of the Interpreter," *Proceedings of the Irish Biblical Association* 8 (1984): 25-38, addresses this issue theoretically in terms of "standpoint of the interpreter" or "reference community".

It will readily be seen in the discussion below that the feminist reading developed there belongs most particularly along the trajectory of Schüssler Fiorenza's theological/reconstructionist paradigm, but it shares a number of insights from the other two contemporary paradigms as well. Within it, a particular method will be developed which seems most appropriate to the study of a gospel text.

II. A Feminist Reading

A. Defining Terminology

It has already been shown that the contemporary Women's Movement is characterized by a feminist critique of culture and ideology. In this section, I will clarify terminology pertaining to this critique as it will be employed throughout this study and will delineate the key characteristics used to evaluate biblical texts, their historical contexts and the presuppositions of the interpreter.

1. Feminism

Uwe Gerber suggests that the term "feminism" was probably coined by the early socialist Charles Fourier at the beginning of the nineteenth century and carried with it certain negative connotations.[66] In the current wave of feminism, however, it is generally used in a positive sense except perhaps by the opponents of the movement. It incorporates activity in every area of human endeavour which seeks to analyze women's experience and to bring about a change in political and social structures for the sake of and on behalf of women.[67] The word is employed, therefore, in a broad political sense

---

66   Gerber, "Feministische Theologie," 566. This is questioned, however, by Karen Offen, "Defining Feminism," 126, who claims that the origins of the term are still uncertain.
67   In support of this definition, see Eisenstein, *Contemporary Feminist Thought*, xii-xx; Joann Wolski Conn, ed., *Women's Spirituality: Resources for Christian Development* (New York/Mahwah: Paulist, 1986), 1-2; Trible, *God and the Rhetoric*, 5; Schüssler Fiorenza, "Women-Church," 5; Tolbert, "Defining the Problem," 115, and Fetterley, *Resisting Reader*, vii.

involving both a critique of reality and strategies for change. It takes on its own unique coloration when used in a particular field of study or area of life, and, in the field of biblical studies or in relation to the christian tradition, such a critique finds its roots in the prophetic tradition of the Hebrew Scriptures and is exemplified most clearly in the life of Jesus of Nazareth.

This prophetic critique rises up out of the "secular" experience of the prophet as it is brought into dialogue with the ancient religious tradition which is often in process of corruption at the hands of the official witnesses to and custodians of that tradition.[68] In the biblical tradition, however, this critique often bore a patriarchal stamp and involved suppression of the religion of the Goddess.[69] In our day, on the other hand, the contemporary Women's Movement and its critique of patriarchy have provided a new level of consciousness and new critical principles which biblical and christian feminists have brought into dialogue with the tradition, resulting in a challenging critique thereof.[70]

In the area of christian feminism, as in other areas of feminism generally, the term itself needs to be distinguished from two other related expressions: female and feminine. "Female" generally functions as a sex-

---

[68] This particular understanding of prophetic ministry in the Hebrew Scriptures and in the life of Jesus is drawn from the work of Carroll Stuhlmueller in *The Biblical Foundations for Mission*, ed. Donald Senior and Carroll Stuhlmueller (Maryknoll: Orbis, 1983), 13-15, 23-26; and Walter Brueggemann, *The Prophetic Imagination* (Philadelphia: Fortress, 1978). The use of the word "secular" in this regard is drawn from Stuhlmueller who states, p. 13, that it "implies nothing derogatory or irreligious; it refers to events and circumstances that are plainly visible and require no special religious insight or any divine revelation to recognize or explain."

[69] Schüssler Fiorenza, *In Memory of Her*, 17; Setel, "Prophets and Pornography," 86-95; and Carol P. Christ, "Heretics and Outsiders," in *Laughter of Aphrodite: Reflections on a Journey to the Goddess* (San Francisco: Harper & Row, 1987), 37-40, to cite but a few who draw attention to this.

[70] Dianne Bergant, "Exodus as a Paradigm," 100-108, discusses this dialectic which is basic to the biblical prophetic critique based on feminism. She claims, p. 105, that "the Exodus-symbol, as the basis of the interpretive approach, and feminism, as the perspective within which it functions, make critical demands on each other. The egalitarian point of view of the symbol calls to account feminism's critique of preunderstanding as well as the agenda that it brings to the dialogue. In turn, the deep convictions that spring from feminist consciousness and feminist critique call to account the content of the core tradition." It is important to acknowledge here also the work of Susanne Heine, *Women and Early Christianity. Are the Feminist Scholars Right?*, trans. John Bowden (London: SCM, 1987). On pp. 46-50 of her work, she speaks of the transcending of the feminist enterprise. As this study proceeds, it will become clear that my use of "inclusion" as a key feminist characteristic shares some elements of this goal but it needs to be very clearly stressed at this point that the feminist project has not yet been adequately incorporated into the total theological process and therefore to seek to transcend it prematurely would be to the detriment of both women and men.

differentiating term carrying with it physical or biological connotations while "feminine", on the other hand, is used in both a simple grammatical or more complex cultural context. As Conn suggests, the cultural referent for the term "feminine" is a "set of abstract qualities that are assumed to be unchanging and universal,"[71] and since these qualities are often those which men have determined and projected onto women, this latter term will be avoided as far as possible throughout this work.

2. Patriarchy / Androcentrism

A term which one could say is almost co-terminus with contemporary feminism is "patriarchy". It is described by Adrienne Rich in general terms thus:

> Patriarchy is the power of the fathers: a familial-social, ideological, political system in which men--by force, direct pressure, or through ritual, tradition, law, and language, customs, etiquette, education, and the division of labor, determine what part women shall or shall not play, and in which the female is everywhere subsumed under the male ...[72]

Throughout this study, however, a distinction will be made between patriarchy and androcentrism, a distinction which Schüssler Fiorenza clarifies. She limits patriarchy to "a sociopolitical system and social structure of graded subjugations and oppressions" and locates its classical expression in Aristotelian philosophy which has profoundly influenced not only Christianity but the whole of western culture and civilization.[73] "Androcentrism", on the other hand, she defines as "a worldconstruction in language, mindset, or ideology that legitimises patriarchy."[74] This is the world-construction which subsumes female existence under male and which is considered the norm for understanding all human existence. Thus

---

71   Conn, *Women's Spirituality*, 1.
72   Adrienne Rich, *Of Woman Born: Motherhood as Experience and Institution* (New York: Norton, 1976), 57-58, quoted by Eisenstein, *Contemporary Feminist Thought*, 5. For more general discussions of the patriarchal system, see Joan Bamberger, "The Myth of Matriarchy: Why Men Rule in Primitive Society," in *Woman, Culture and Society*, ed. Michelle Zimbalist Rosaldo and Louise Lamphere (Stanford: Stanford University Press, 1974), 263-280; Sherry B. Ortner, "Is Female to Male as Nature Is to Culture?" ibid., 67-88; Gayle Rubin, "The Traffic in Women: Notes on the "Political Economy" of Sex," in *Toward an Anthropology of Women*, ed. Rayna R. Reiter (New York/London: Monthly Review Press, 1975), 157-210; and especially Gerda Lerner, *The Creation of Patriarchy*, Women and History 1 (New York/Oxford: Oxford University Press, 1986).
73   Schüssler Fiorenza, "Women-Church," 5.
74   Elisabeth Schüssler Fiorenza, "Breaking the Silence - Becoming Visible," *Concilium* 182 (1985): 4.

patriarchy will be used to refer to the socio-cultural system operative in both the biblical period and our own day while androcentrism will refer to language and ideology as part of an overall world view.

3. Gender

A final term which will be employed repeatedly in the subsequent analysis and which requires brief definition is "gender". It must be distinguished from sexuality which is physical or biological. Gender, on the other hand, belongs to the world of social constructs and belief systems. It encompasses specific cultural roles which are considered appropriate to either men or women in a given society. As Gailey suggests, it "depends on how society views the relationship of male to man and female to woman."[75] When considered in relation to its influence on the creation and reception of literary works, it must be kept in mind that the gender belief system reflected in the literature may not necessarily mirror the historical situation to which it refers or out of which it arose.[76]

B. Key Characteristics

A discussion of key characteristics of the feminist critique takes us into an area of significant exploration at present. For christian and biblical feminists, these characteristics are articulated as a result of the ongoing dialogue between their own human experience of struggle for fulness of personhood and the vision of liberation presented in many and various ways in the biblical text or preserved in communities of biblical witness. As Schüssler Fiorenza so clearly states:

> As the church of women we celebrate our religious powers and ritualize our visions for change and liberation. We bond together in struggling with all women for liberation, and we share our strength in nurturing each other in the full awareness and recognition that the church of women is always the

---

75   Christine Ward Gailey, "Evolutionary Perspectives on Gender Hierarchy," in *Analysing Gender: A Handbook of Social Scientific Research*, ed. Beth B. Hess and Myra Marx Ferree (Newbury Park, Ca.: Sage, 1987), 34.
76   This aspect is treated comprehensively by Kay Deaux and Mary E. Kite, "Thinking about Gender," in Hess and Ferree, *Analysing Gender*, 92-117. Each of the above terms, moreover, together with a number of others are briefly defined by Lerner, *Creation of Patriarchy*, 231-243.

ecclesia reformanda, the church on the way in need of conversion and "revolutionary patience" with our own failures as well as with those of our sisters.[77]

It is, therefore, out of the journey of conversion of the church of women and the ongoing conversation between biblical and other feminists that the following are emerging as key characteristics of the feminist critique which can be applied to biblical texts.

1. Liberation

At the heart of the feminist critique employed by those whose biblical hermeneutics we called "liberationist" and by Schüssler Fiorenza who shares their liberation perspective is, of course, the principle of liberation, and it finds various expressions in their works. Letty Russell begins her early book *Human Liberation in a Feminist Perspective--A Theology* with a chapter entitled "Journey toward Freedom". Within its first page, she points out the difficulty of defining both freedom and liberation, but she suggests that the word liberation draws our attention to the "*process* of struggle with ourselves and others toward a more open future for humanity."[78] This process, she says, will find its own unique expression in the lives of individuals and of communities.[79] Ruether describes her critical principle thus:

> the promotion of the full humanity of women. Whatever denies, diminishes, or distorts the full humanity of women is, therefore, appraised as not redemptive.[80]

---

77 Schüssler Fiorenza, "Emerging Issues," 39. Although the conversion aspect of the nature of the church is stated clearly here, there are places in Schüssler Fiorenza's writing where she runs the risk of placing the entire weight of revelation on the experience of the church of women, thus obscuring its need for conversion and the bible's function in providing a root-model for such conversion in the ongoing struggle toward the vision of fulness of humanity. See Schüssler Fiorenza, *In Memory of Her*, 34. A similar critique to the one made here is found in two responses to her paper "Toward a Feminist Biblical Hermeneutics: Biblical Interpretation and Liberation Theology," (Paper for the Working Group on Liberation Theology, AAR/SBL, Feminist Hermeneutic Project, 1982): Beverly Roberts Gaventa, "Response to Elisabeth Schüssler Fiorenza, "Toward a Feminist Biblical Hermeneutics: Biblical Interpretation and Liberation Theology"," 3; and Bruce C. Birch, "A Response to Elisabeth Schüssler Fiorenza, "Toward a Feminist Biblical Hermeneutics: Biblical Interpretation and Liberation Theology"," 5. In Schüssler Fiorenza's own response to these papers, however, she says of the "locus of revelation" that it is found in the experience of women struggling for liberation but also in "those Biblical texts and visions that reflect the liberating experiences of Biblical women as well as have sustained women in Biblical religion in their struggles for liberation and wholeness."

78 Russell, *Human Liberation*, 25.

79 Ibid., 47.

80 Ruether, *Sexism and God-Talk*, 18; and idem, "A Method of Correlation," 115.

Schüssler Fiorenza, on the other hand, stresses the centrality of an "advocacy stance" to the feminist critical principle of liberation:

> Only when theology is on the side of the outcast and oppressed, as was Jesus, can it become incarnational and Christian. Christian theology, therefore, has to be rooted in emancipatory praxis and solidarity.[81]

While many feminist biblical scholars would share in the goal of "liberation" for all who are oppressed especially all women who bear the pain of restriction, limitation and exclusion, some question its close links with the paradigm of liberation theology. For Drorah Setel, this paradigm is a dualistic or oppositional one based on a separation of oppositional categories and as such would seem to run counter to the emerging feminist paradigm which is looking towards the development of an integrative model for describing human experience.[82] Antoinette Clark Wire also offers a cautionary note when she asks:

> Does a hermeneutic based on "emancipation praxis" find any sure guide in our own yet so partial experience of freedom? Are we building on rock or on shifting sand?[83]

Such critiques are timely and need to be heeded. While they do not destroy the validity of the liberation principle and its goal of fulness of humanity for all, they do, however, warn us that any principle taken in isolation and applied exclusively can rapidly become its own means of oppression.

2. Inclusion

Liberation as a critical principle needs, therefore, to be linked with a second principle which I call "inclusion". One of the profound experiences of women is invisibility because of their exclusion from recorded history as well as from androcentric world views and language systems which have

---

81   Elisabeth Schüssler Fiorenza, "Feminist Theology as a Critical Theology of Liberation," in *Woman: New Dimensions*, ed. Walter Burghardt (New York/Ramsey/Toronto: Paulist, 1977), 40. See also, *In Memory of Her*, 32.
82   T. Drorah Setel, "A Jewish-Feminist Response to Elisabeth Schüssler Fiorenza's "Toward a Feminist Biblical Hermeneutics: Biblical Interpretation and Liberation Theology"," (Unpublished Paper for the Working Group on Liberation Theology, AAR/SBL, Feminist Hermeneutic Project, 1982), 2.
83   Antoinette Clark Wire, "On Elisabeth Schüssler Fiorenza's "Toward a Feminist Biblical Hermeneutics: Biblical Interpretation and Liberation Theology"," (Unpublished Paper for the Working Group on Liberation Theology, AAR/SBL, Feminist Hermeneutic Project, 1982), 1.

shaped much of Western culture and society.[84] This is accentuated for christian women for whom androcentrism and patriarchy have been given divine sanction within a christian framework.[85] Any new feminist model which is developed must be able to include women as well as men at the centre of history and of the christian experience in all its varieties of expression: leadership, discipleship, membership, ministry--in fact all aspects of life.

Simultaneously, women's experience of exclusion can enable them to be more aware of all other forms of exclusion based on hierarchical domination that exist in our society whether it be on the basis of gender, race, religious belief, age or even the domination of humanity over other forms of nature. This critical principle therefore enables the extension of the boundaries of our model beyond gender to other aspects of life. Within this work, however, the concentration will be on gender.

Such a principle, when brought into dialogue with the biblical tradition, finds a resonance in the preaching of Israel's prophets. Amos sees the poor and needy oppressed by those with access to goods and power and he cries out against this (Amos 2:6-7; 4:1; 5:11-12; 8:4-6). For Jeremiah, it is the stranger/alien, the widow and the fatherless whose oppression and exclusion calls out for the justice of God (Jer 7:6; 22:3), and for Isaiah it is the fatherless and the widows who are the symbols of a society whose exclusive policies run counter to their religious tradition (Isa 1:17, 23; 10:2). In the New Testament, the community gathered around Jesus, which is made up of disciples, "tax collectors and sinners", lepers, demoniacs, crippled and sick, many of whom are women, is certainly an inclusive one (Matt 8:16-17; 9:10, 32; Mark 14:3; Luke 8:1-3 and many other passages).[86]

---

84   Mary Milligan in her article ""Give us a Double Share of Your Spirit" (cf. 2 Kings 2:9)," *UISG* 74 (1987): 51, points out that the signs of exclusion in our global society are today many and various. It is this very phenomenon which gives rise to the aspirations for "inclusion" in the hearts of all those excluded and women are one of the many groups of peoples excluded from access to power, wealth, goods and more especially self-determination and self-expression.

85   By way of example of this, see the 1976 Declaration of the Sacred Congregation for the Doctrine of the Faith, *Inter Insigniores: Declaration on the Question of the Admission of Women to the Ministerial Priesthood* (Vatican City: Polygot Press, 1976). The same could perhaps be said of other religious systems also but such an analysis is beyond the scope of this work.

86   Schüssler Fiorenza, *In Memory of Her*, 118-130, treats this aspect of the Jesus movement under the title of "The Basileia Vision of Jesus as the Praxis of Inclusive Wholeness".

I have chosen the principle of "inclusion" rather than "equality" as a necessary correlative to "liberation" since "equality" can function to hide the distinctive experiences of women and men or the distinctive qualities of those experiences in an attempt to show that the same experiences have been or should be available to both.[87] Elisabeth Moltmann-Wendel seems to address a similar issue when she takes as her hermeneutical starting point "a concept of autonomy derived from counselling women" which she says, "does not denote a rationalistic, individualistic self-determination, but self-determination within a context of relationships."[88] For this reason she links the critical principle of autonomy with mutuality in order to be faithful to what she sees as the essentially relational quality of women's experience.[89] Inclusion as a critical principle also takes cognizance of this relational aspect.

My reading suggests that this principle of "inclusion" has not been used explicitly or extensively in the development of a distinctively feminist biblical hermeneutics.[90] It will function, therefore, along with liberation as the conscious feminist agenda which is brought into dialogue with the biblical text.

These two principles are not exclusive nor do they form a complete list.[91] The articulation of experience among *all* women who know oppression, domination, subjugation and exclusion together with the desire for freedom, autonomy and mutual reciprocity will expand and enrich this agenda. For the purposes of this project, however, these two principles will now be brought into dialogue with contemporary biblical hermeneutics toward the articulation of a distinctively feminist biblical hermeneutic and supporting methodologies: a feminist reading.[92]

---

87   In this regard, see John Koenig's review of Schüssler Fiorenza's *In Memory of Her* in "Review Symposium," *Horizons* 11 (1984): 145-146.
88   Elisabeth Moltmann-Wendel, *A Land Flowing with Milk and Honey: Perspectives on Feminist Theology*, trans. John Bowden (London: SCM, 1986), 9.
89   For a much more extensive development of this aspect, see Carol Gilligan, *In a Different Voice: Psychological Theory and Women's Development* (Cambridge, Mass./London: Harvard University Press, 1982). It is also interesting to note that Moltmann-Wendel devotes a later chapter in *A Land Flowing with Milk and Honey* to "Mutuality".
90   Ruether, "A Method of Correlation," 116, briefly discusses "inclusion" within the context of her critical principle of the fulness of humanity in order to warn against women's claiming of their human potential in a way which would denigrate male humanity.
91   For a more complete list, see Bergeant, "Exodus as a Paradigm," 105.
92   I use the term "hermeneutics" to encompass the methodological processes that are applied to a text in order to yield understanding; the hermeneutic or particular frame of reference from which one proceeds to interpretation; and the philosophical underpinning of the interpretation process. "Hermeneutic", therefore, is limited to the inter-

C. A Dialogue with Contemporary Biblical Hermeneutics

> Reading is a highly socialized - or learned - activity. What makes it so excit-
> ing, of course, is that it can be constantly relearned and refined, so as to pro-
> vide either an individual or an entire reading community, over time, with
> infinite variations of the same text.[93]

These words of Annette Kolodny capture the spirit of contemporary feminist
literary criticism which will inform the subsequent development of an appropriate feminist hermeneutic to be applied to the biblical text. I will also
draw on the abundant resources available in the field of biblical hermeneutics, including feminist hermeneutics, and the plurality of biblical
methodologies developed in the past and more recently.

As a starting point, it needs to be acknowledged that contemporary
biblical hermeneutics recognizes two distinct poles around which research
and discussion can be ordered, namely, the text and the interpreter. Wolfhart
Pannenberg stated it rather starkly in 1963 when he said that "the hermeneutical outlook apparently moves solely between the past text and the present
interpreter."[94] The interim debate, however, has extended the parameters of
these two poles to include "the world behind the text" and "the world in
front of the text" as the expressions "texts as windows" and "texts as mirrors"
indicate.[95] It is not my purpose here to enter into this debate but simply to
point out that these key elements in contemporary biblical hermeneutics
will structure the subsequent development of a specifically feminist biblical
hermeneutic.

---

pretive framework of the exegete which will, of course, be shaped by a particular
philosophical perspective.

93 Annette Kolodny, "Dancing through the Minefield: Some Observations on the Theory,
Practice and Politics of a Feminist Literary Criticism," *Feminist Studies* 6 (1980): 11.

94 Wolfhart Pannenberg, "Hermeneutic and Universal History," in *Basic Questions in
Theology*, Vol. I, trans. George H. Kehm (Philadelphia: Fortress, 1970-71), 99.

95 This is the terminology used by Murray Krieger, *A Window to Criticism* (Princeton:
Princeton University Press, 1964), 3-70, and discussed by Norman R. Petersen, *Literary
Criticism for New Testament Critics*, Guides to Biblical Scholarship (Philadelphia:
Fortress, 1978), 24-48. Pannenberg also makes his claim for hermeneutics in the con-
text of a comparison between the hermeneutical outlook and the universal-historical
outlook which "first goes back behind the text, and considers the essential content
[*Sache*], i.e., the event being inquired into behind the text."

A Theoretical Framework

1. The world of the feminist interpreter

To separate the interpreter and the text, the two parties in the hermeneutical dialogue, is a difficult but necessary task for the purpose of analysis. The starting point, however, for any biblical interpretive task is generally the body of questions that the interpreter brings to the biblical text. For the feminist interpreter, these questions are formulated after an attentive listening to the voices of the experience of contemporary women in and under patriarchy. These questions are many and varied and must be continually reviewed and changed because of the changing nature of contemporary reality. They will vary also as one moves into different racial, cultural, religious and socio-economic environments. As Elisabeth Schüssler Fiorenza says:

> Only when we have listened to the many voices of women's experience in patriarchy will we be able to articulate how and through which Biblical texts God speaks to us today.[96]

The questions, therefore, which I bring to the biblical text from a white Anglo-Irish Australian background, many of which were outlined in the introduction, are certainly limited but not invalidated if the feminist principle of inclusion applies at the very outset. Moreover, this work stands with many others as an attempt to hear the biblical witness as it speaks within the contemporary church of women.

The feminist context of the interpreter and its attendant critique leads to a heightened awareness of the androcentric nature of the biblical text and of its patriarchal context. Both text and context must therefore be analyzed to determine to what extent they disclose or conceal the feminist principles of liberation and inclusion. But just as the feminist critique does not consider the autonomy implicit in liberation apart from the mutuality which inclusion implies, so the feminist interpreter together with the church of women finds that the principles of the feminist critique and the feminist context do not function autonomously but are in constant need of reform as a result of the ongoing dialogue with the biblical text. Hence conversion is a significant element in this biblical hermeneutic.[97]

---

96 Elisabeth Schüssler Fiorenza, "Response to Antoinette Clark Wire, Bruce Birch, Beverly Gaventa, Drorah Setel," (Unpublished paper prepared for Discussion at the AAR Meeting, New York City, December, 1982), 3.
97 In her article "Feminist Theology and New Testament Interpretation," 35, Schüssler Fiorenza also talks of the "intellectual conversion" demanded by the shift from an an-

If, however, we acknowledge the necessity of conversion within present-day communities whose lives are shaped by the biblical tradition, our feminist biblical hermeneutic must also allow that such conversion was significant and necessary within   historical biblical communities. It must deal with the fact that there will be texts and traditions within the biblical canon that represent various stages along this journey of conversion. These function in creative tension within the biblical canon, and to seek to remove this tension would destroy the very text itself, which takes us to a consideration of the text which we encounter and a way of understanding it from a feminist perspective.

2. The Nature of the Biblical Text

a. Historico-Literary

"Texts as windows, texts as mirrors, or texts as both!"[98] These words of Norman Petersen characterize one of the fundamental concerns of contemporary biblical criticism: the nature of the biblical text. They also highlight the dynamic or dialectic within which research on the Christian Scriptures has moved during the past two centuries as is indicated by Kümmel in the conclusion to his survey of this research.

> From the very outset New Testament research was confronted with the problem of how the indispensable *historical* task of examining the New Testament could be brought into harmony with the distinctive demand of these documents on the reader for a decision in response to the divine message they contain.[99]

The primary methodological paradigm which has supported this research has been that of historical criticism. It was born of the historicism and positivism of the nineteenth century, and hence gave rise to methods of

---

drocentric to a feminist paradigm. She says that it implies a "transformation of the scientific imagination", and "engenders a shift in perspective and intellectual commitment that allows us to see old "data" and texts in a new light. The "woman's issue" is no longer a marginal topic unworthy of much exegetical or historical attention, but instead it challenges our perception of Christian reality today and in the first centuries."

98   Petersen, *Literary Criticism*, 24.
99   Werner Georg Kümmel, *The New Testament: The History of the Investigation of its Problems*, trans. S. McLean Gilmour and Howard C. Kee (1973; reprint, London: SCM, 1978), 405. The treatment that can be given here to this vast area of research is, by nature of the present undertaking, brief and hence in no way comprehensive. References, therefore, to standard works provide the background which has informed it.

exegesis which have been considered scientific and therefore objective and value-neutral.[100] Ian Howard Marshall describes it as:

> ... the study of any narrative which purports to convey historical information in order to determine what actually happened and is described or alluded to in the passage in question.[101]

Within such a paradigm, the text is viewed as literature as is evidenced by the variety of literary methods which have been developed in order to mine its depths,[102] but it is primarily considered an historical document which provides a window on the historical Jesus, the intention of the original author of a text, and the text's own *Sitz im Leben* or world. This understanding of the historical nature of the text has provided us with various articulations of the objective meaning of the text--"what it meant"[103]--and the reconstruction of the world behind it. Biblical scholars considered it the work of theologians and preachers to bring the historical meaning of the text into dialogue with the contemporary situation of believers.

In recent years, however, there has been a profound shift in historical epistemology and critical hermeneutics whose effect on our understanding of the biblical text and its methods of interpretation is still being determined.[104] In this transitional period, while the use of the historical paradigm continues to provide us with a wealth of information for biblical interpretation and historical reconstruction, scholars have begun to articulate its inadequacies.[105] In fact, Norman Petersen describes the present era in biblical scholarship, using the metaphor of Ricoeur, as a "desert of criticism from which we yearn to be called again".[106] In their attempt to move beyond

---

100 For a brief treatment of the history of this method together with an assessment of its present goals, techniques, presuppositions and achievement, see Edgar Krentz, *The Historical-Critical Method*, Guides to Biblical Scholarship (Philadelphia: Fortress, 1975). For a more extensive analysis of its origin and development through various schools, see Kümmel, *The New Testament*, and Stephen Neill, *The Interpretation of The New Testament. 1861-1961*, The Firth Lectures, 1962 (London: Oxford University Press, 1964).

101 Ian Howard Marshall, "Historical Criticism," in *New Testament Interpretation: Essays on Principles and Methods*, ed. Ian Howard Marshall (Exeter: Paternoster, 1977), 126.

102 These methods are discussed in detail in Raymond F. Collins, *Introduction to the New Testament* (London: SCM, 1983), 75-230; and in Marshall, *New Testament Interpretation*, 126-195.

103 This famous phrase was coined by Krister Stendahl in his article, "Biblical Theology, Contemporary," in *IDB* I:419.

104 Schüssler Fiorenza, "Remembering the Past," 44-55.

105 See n. 9 in the Introduction above for bibliography.

106 Norman R. Petersen, "Literary Criticism in Biblical Studies," in *Orientation by Disorientation: Studies in Literary Criticism and Biblical Criticism*, ed. R. A. Spencer, Theological Monograph Series 35 (Pittsburg: Pickwick Press, 1980), 25.

this desert, therefore, biblical scholars have supplemented their older historico-literary methodologies with some of the newer methods being developed in one of their supporting sciences--literary criticism.

A number of influences both philosophical and literary have led to the development of a variety of literary methods within recent decades-- Structuralism, New Criticism, Narrative Criticism, Reader-Response Criticism and Deconstructionism.[107] Each of these has been taken up and developed in relation to the biblical text with varying degrees of success and/or widespread acceptance.[108] The two, however, which have contributed most to a shifting paradigm in contemporary biblical scholarship are Narrative and Reader-Response Criticism.[109]

According to these approaches, the text is considered the raw material which becomes a literary work in its own right as a result of the activity performed by the reader. When the text is a narrative such as we find in the gospels, then it must be considered in terms of the level of story, which includes events of the plot, characters and settings; and in terms of the level of the discourse involving implied author, narrator, implied reader, point of view and rhetorical strategies.[110] The creative role of the reader consists in attending to the textual signals throughout the narrative.[111] This means that

---

107 For a brief history of this movement in Anglo-American literary criticism, see Elizabeth Freund, *The Return of the Reader: Reader-Response Criticism*, New Accents (London/New York: Methuen, 1987).

108 Keegan, *Interpreting the Bible*, offers a simple overview of these developments together with a good bibliography at the end of the chapter which treats each new methodology.

109 This is seen in a number of recent articles: Petersen, "Literary Criticism in Biblical Studies"; Sean Freyne, "Our Preoccupation with History: Problems and Prospects," *Proceedings of the Irish Biblical Association* 9 (1985): 1-19; Edgar V. McKnight, "The Contours and Methods of Literary Criticism," in Spencer, *Orientation by Disorientation*, 53-69; and Werner H. Kelber, "Gospel Narrative and Critical Theory," *BTB* 18 (1988): 130-137. Those who have applied the new insights to biblical criticism include Robert Alter, *The Art of Biblical Narrative* (New York: Basic Books, 1981); Adele Berlin, *Poetics and Interpretation of Biblical Narrative*, Bible and Literature Series 9 (Sheffield: Almond, 1983); and Meir Sternberg, *The Poetics of Biblical Narrative: Ideological Literature and the Drama of Reading*, Indiana Literary Biblical Series (Bloomington: Indiana University Press, 1985).

110 For a thorough treatment of narrative, see Seymour Chatman, *Story and Discourse: Narrative Structure in Fiction and Film* (Ithaca/London: Cornell University Press, 1978); and Shlomith Rimmon-Kenan, *Narrative Fiction: Contemporary Poetics* (London/New York: Methuen, 1983).

111 Wolfgang Iser, *The Implied Reader: Patterns of Communication in Prose Fiction from Bunyan to Beckett* (Baltimore/London: Johns Hopkins University Press, 1974); idem, *The Act of Reading: A Theory of Aesthetic Response* (Baltimore/London: Johns Hopkins University Press, 1978); and Freund, *Return of the Reader*, to name but a few authors who develop this aspect of narrative. These texts will provide further extensive bibliography.

the text must be considered as an integrated whole, at least initially; for the
world created by the text is just that, namely, a literary construct whose relationship to the real world events to which it refers must be deferred until
the work itself and its narrative world have been fully understood.[112]

In the early stages of the employment of these new literary critical
methodologies in biblical studies, they were adhered to so rigidly by some
scholars that there was a danger that they would be seen to be irreconcilable
with traditional historical criticism. Historical criticism was considered an
extrinsic approach concerned predominantly with the world outside the text
and its historical author and it entailed the use of methodologies which
were diachronic in nature. The new literary criticisms, on the other hand,
entailed an intrinsic approach whose major focus was the literary work itself
as an autonomous system[113] and whose methodologies were therefore
synchronic.

With "inclusion" as one of our feminist critical principles and a two-
fold goal of restoring the stories of women to the biblical texts as well as reconstructing a portion of the history of early Christianity as an inclusive history, the integration of the historical and the literary approaches is essential.
This is a task which has been occupying biblical scholars for a number of
years now and it would seem that there is much work that lies ahead in this
crucial area.[114] As to its importance Stephen Geller says:

> Rivalry between historical and literary approaches to the Bible must there-
> fore be seen as suicidal. It is not a healthy process of dialectical self-
> definition, but intellectual self-destruction. History and aesthetics are not
> either-or, nor are they both-and. It is wrong to think of them as simply co-
> existing or even supplementing each other. If, as the linguistic analogy
> implies, they define each other, they form the obverse and reverse of a
> single sheet of paper, to use Saussure's famous image.[115]

---

112 Petersen, "Literary Criticism in Biblical Studies," 36-42.
113 Petersen, *Literary Criticism*, 26-27.
114 See especially the two collections of essays edited by Spencer, *Orientation by
     Disorientation* and by Bernard C. Lategan and Willem S. Vorster, *Text and Reality:
     Aspects of Reference in Biblical Texts*, SBL Semeia Studies 14 (Atlanta: Scholars, 1985),
     as well as the work of Norman Petersen, *Literary Criticism*, "Literary Criticism in
     Biblical Studies", and most recently *Rediscovering Paul: Philemon and the Sociology of
     Paul's Narrative World* (Philadelphia: Fortress, 1985) in the introduction to which he
     deals with these historical and literary questions.
115 Stephen A. Geller, "Through Windows and Mirrors into the Bible: History, Literature
     and Language in the Study of the Text," in *A Sense of Text: The Art of Langauge in the
     Study of Biblical Literature*, JQR Supplement 1982 (Winona Lake: Eisenbrauns, 1983),
     39.

The integrative model to be used in this work will be developed in detail below but suffice here to indicate that, as Geller suggests, history and aesthetics have worked to define each other and the nature of the biblical text. There has been a profound shift in our understanding of history from the historicist perspective of the nineteenth century to an approach which sees history as available to us already in narrative form.[116] Thus literary works like the gospels mirror aspects of the pluralistic *Sitz im Leben* in which they were created while at the same time they function rhetorically to create the vision contained within them. Such an understanding of the text can then form the basis of our integrative model which allows for the text to function as both mirror and window. This will be important for a feminist reading. It needs to be pointed out, however, in our consideration of the nature of the biblical text that none of the theoretical constructs already treated above specifically deals with the fact that the text is gender-inflected. It is to this aspect of the text that we will now turn.

b. Gender-Inflected

Recent studies by feminist critics in both literary and biblical fields have shown that literary classics including the Bible (that is the contents of the literary canon) are androcentric.[117] There is an assumption that the male norm is co-terminus with the human, an assumption which finds expression in the grammatical and narrative strategies of a text and which results in the marginalization of women. Thus in Matthew's Sermon on the Mount we find the repeated use of terms such as "son(s)", "man/men", "brother", "father" and "he" [5:13, 15, 19, 22, 45; 6:1, 16, 18; 7:3-5, 8, 9, 12, 21] reflecting a narrative world from which women appear to be absent. The experience of sonship, fatherhood and brotherhood is assumed to be universal and hence adequate for the expression of human experience.[118]

---

116 Hayden White, "The Value of Narrativity in the Representation of Reality," *Critical Inquiry* 7 (1980): 5-28; idem, "Historicism, History and the Figurative Imagination," *History and Theory* 14 (1975): 43-67; Fredric R. Jameson, "The Symbolic Inference; or, Kenneth Burke and Ideological Analysis," in *Representing Kenneth Burke*, ed. H. White and M. Brose (Baltimore: Johns Hopkins University Press, 1982), 68-91; Petersen, *Rediscovering Paul*,10-14; Schüssler Fiorenza, "Remembering the Past," 44-55; and idem, "Rhetorical Situation," 386.

117 By way of example, see Patrocinio P. Schweickart, "Reading Ourselves: Toward a Feminist Theory of Reading," in *Gender and Reading: Essays on Readers, Texts, and Contexts*, ed. E. A. Flynn and Patrocinio P. Schweickart (Baltimore: Johns Hopkins University Press, 1986), 40, and Fetterley, *Resisting Reader*, xii.

118 For a more detailed treatment of androcentrism in religious texts and their interpretations, see Rita M. Gross, "Androcentrism and Androgyny in the

Within such a world view, women are spoken about, but rarely are their voices heard except when they are problematic. In the Matthean gospel, we hear the voices of the women characters in only seven verses from the entire gospel and in at least four of these occurrences, their cries or their requests are problematic within the story [15:22, 25, 27; 20:21; 26:69, 71; and 27:19].[119] Such an attitude is reflected not only in the biblical text but also in the history of its interpretation. Women become the object of study, the "other", the "problem to be solved" rather than a participating subject in the biblical drama.[120] In this study, however, even though the focus will be those texts in which the women function as characters in the narrative, the women are not the object of study but rather there is an underlying assumption that they together with the men are subjects in the gospel drama and in the history of early Christianity.

Such an assumption can, in fact, be supported by an understanding of the function of androcentric language within early Christianity. The work of Schüssler Fiorenza has shown that the conventional use of androcentric language in a counter-cultural group like that of the early Christians was inclusive rather than gender specific:

> Masculine terms as for instance *eklektoí, hagioi, adelphoi* or *hyoi* do not characterize males as the elect, saints, brothers or sons over and against women but these terms define *all* Christians over and against the wider society and religion. If this is the case, then *all* titles of the earliest New Testament writings pertain to *all* members, male and female. Androcentric language has to be understood not as gender specific language but as inclusive language since it pertains to an inclusive, egalitarian, counter-cultural group or sect.[121]

This means, however, that texts must be read against the grain in order to bring this inclusion to consciousness, and to counteract the marginalization of women.   As Judith Fetterley says, women must become "resisting

---

Methodology of History of Religions," in *Beyond Androcentrism: New Essays on Women and Religion*, ed. Rita M. Gross, American Academy of Religion Aids for the Study of Religion (Missoula: Scholars, 1977), 7-22.

119 I have not included here 9:21 in which the woman with the haemorrhage speaks within herself nor 20:22 when the mother of the sons of Zebedee presumably answers but with her sons.

120 Ibid., 9; Schüssler Fiorenza, "Women-Church," 16-17 and *In Memory of Her*, 42-48. By way of example of this topical approach, see Swidler, *Biblical Affirmations*, Otwell, *And Sarah Laughed*, and Francis J. Moloney, *Woman First Among the Faithful: A New Testament Study* (Blackburn, Vic.: Dove, 1984).

121 Schüssler Fiorenza, "Study of Women," 46.

readers".[122] Without such a reading, women are left at the mercy of the androcentric texts. They are presumed to be excluded from the male generic language. They are presumed silent or absent from story and history. On the other hand, this new feminist reading must not be allowed to obscure the oppressive nature of the text. A suitable dialectic will be maintained only if the feminist reader continually reads against the grain not just of conventional androcentric texts but also of those texts which explicitly support patriarchy. We see an example of the need for this two-fold reading at the very beginning of the Matthean gospel. The overriding pattern of the genealogy--male ἐγέννησεν male--is androcentric but it also supports the patriarchal traditions of Israelite society whereby the promise is believed to be transmitted from father to son.[123]

Such patriarchal traditions are inherent in the biblical text, its context and the consciousness of its interpreters or, as Schweickart says:

> ... patriarchal constructs have objective as well as subjective reality; they are inside and outside the text, inside and outside the reader.[124]

Like androcentric grammar and narrative strategies, patriarchal constructs also function to marginalize or to obscure women. But the patriarchal text is not a product of an all-male culture. Women have been part of the history that has given rise to the text. They have participated in the making of traditions even if those traditions were intended to suppress, silence or caricature them. Hence a feminist reading must attend to the silences, the gaps, the omissions, the partial truths and the mythologies. A feminist reading against the grain must therefore extend beyond androcentric language and grammar to patriarchal constructs as well.[125]

The above discussion of the androcentric and patriarchal nature of the biblical text leads to the conclusion that it is gender-inflected, a characteristic

---

122   Fetterley, *Resisting Reader*, xxii. Schweickart, "Reading Ourselves," 50, calls this type of reading "reading the text as it was *not* meant to be read, in fact, reading it against itself."
123   This passage will be examined in much greater detail later.
124   Schweickart, "Reading Ourselves," 50.
125   For a more extensive treatment of this aspect of feminist reading, see Gayle Greene and Coppelia Kahn, "Feminist Scholarship and the Social Construction of Woman," in *Making a Difference: Feminist Literary Criticism*, ed. Gayle Greene and Coppelia Kahn (London/New York: Methuen, 1985), 1-36; Adrienne Munich, "Notorious Signs, Feminist Criticism and Literary Tradition," ibid., 238-259; and Schüssler Fiorenza, *In Memory of Her*, 29, 41.

which it shares with all literary productions.[126] Hence a gender reading in which gender functions as a significant analytic category is essential to any reading of the text and especially to a feminist reading. However, in order that such a reading does not abandon the text to the gender hierarchy represented within it or to be shaped by it, it must be accompanied by both the androcentric and patriarchal analyses discussed above. How this can be accomplished will be laid out in more detail below in the unfolding of my own particular methodology.

c. Canonical and Authoritative

Within the believing communities of Judaism and Christianity, the biblical text is considered canonical. Its parameters are the result of a process of selectivity carried on within the communities' liturgical and catechetical life over a long period of time.[127] This entailed the choice of those traditions and texts which, through long years of use and development, reflected a community's religious history and self-understanding as well as the vision which they desired to shape their future. As such, the canon can function as a two-edged sword. It can be perceived as a closed system which contains within itself the totality of divine revelation. As such it can be mined for universally valid truths. This is the mythical archetype paradigm of which Schüssler Fiorenza speaks when she says:

> ... [it] establishes an ideal form for all times that represents unchanging patterns of behaviour and theological structures for the community in which it functions as sacred scripture.[128]

On the other hand, canon can be understood as a dynamic process by means of which the contemporary believing community interacts with its

---

126   This point is made by K. K. Ruthven, *Feminist Literary Studies: An Introduction* (Cambridge/New York: Cambridge University Press, 1984), 9, who says that "gender is a crucial determinent in the production, circulation and consumption of literary discourses." Annette Kolodny, "A Map for Rereading: Or, Gender and the Interpretation of Literary Texts," *New Literary History* 11 (1980): 452, makes a similar point when she claims that "whether we speak of poets and critics "reading" texts or writers "reading" (and thereby recording for us) the world, we are calling attention to interpretive strategies that are learned, historically determined, and thereby necessarily gender-inflected."

127   See James A. Sanders, *Canon and Community: A Guide to Canonical Criticism*, Guides to Biblical Scholarship (Philadelphia: Fortress, 1984), 21-45. When we are speaking of canonical parameters, there is a recognition that a number of biblical canons exist within both Judaism and Christianity.

128   Schüssler Fiorenza, "Emerging Issues," 42. See also "Women-Church," 12-13; and *In Memory of Her*, 33, for a discussion of this issue.

primitive vision and its concrete here-and-now experience in the world in order to shape both present and future traditions as a living word of God.[129] Within this understanding, the Bible functions as historical prototype or "formative root-model" in the language of Schüssler Fiorenza.[130]

Feminist reflection on the canonical process outlined above has brought us to a greater awareness of the androcentric and patriarchal interests influential thereon. One does not find within the canon a simple articulation of the liberating vision of Jesus with regard to women and its successful interpretation in Gal 3:28. Rather, this vision is embedded in a patriarchal context and androcentric language which marginalizes women. Even more so, it contains traditions which betray the liberating vision, traditions which actively oppress women (1 Cor 14:34-35; 1 Peter 3:1-6). Recent scholarship has also discovered that extra-canonical texts often tell the story of women's inclusion in a way that is more in keeping with the vision of the Jesus' movement than is revealed in the canonical story.[131]

From this it is very clear that the canon does not speak with a single voice but is rather the product of many different communities of faith. It tells a partial story of vision, betrayal of vision, and at times return to the original vision. It functions authoritatively within the contemporary christian community when it is brought into dialogue with our experience of faith, our experience of the action of God in our lives as liberating and salvific.[132] In our analysis of Matthew's gospel, we will see that there are stories which inform and support the movement for liberation and inclusion experienced by many in the "church of women". There are tensions in the narrative which are instructive within our contemporary struggle against patriarchy and there are traditions which have been used to oppress women. The subseqent analysis of the text will bring some of these to light. Information will also be drawn from non-canonical texts and non-literary

---

129 William R. Herzog II, "Interpretation as Discovery and Creation: Sociological Dimensions of Biblical Hermeneutics," *American Baptist Quarterly* 2 (1983): 117.

130 Schüssler Fiorenza, "Emerging Issues," 46, *In Memory of Her*, 33-34.

131 Heine, *Women and Early Christianity*, 106-146; Elizabeth A. Clark, *Women in the Early Church*, Message of the Fathers of the Church 13 (Wilmington, Del.: Michael Glazier, 1983), 77-114; Ross S. Kraemer, ed., *Maenads, Martyrs, Matrons, Monastics: A Sourcebook on Women's Religions in the Greco-Roman World* (Philadelphia: Fortress, 1988); Karen L. King, ed., *Images of the Feminine in Gnosticism*, Studies in Antiquity and Christianity (Philadelphia: Fortress, 1988); and Stevan L. Davies, *The Revolt of the Widows: The Social World of the Apocryphal Acts* (Carbondale: Southern Illinois University Press, 1980), to mention but some.

132 For a more comprehensive treatment of authority from a feminist perspective, see Russell, *Household of Freedom*.

sources in order to reconstruct more authentically the Matthean community as it was shaped and experienced by women as well as by men. Such an inclusive reconstruction can then   inform our subsequent reading of the canonical text. We will turn, therefore, to the development of the particular feminist critical method which will support the feminist biblical hermeneutic discussed above, and according to which a feminist reading of Matthew's gospel may proceed.

3. A Feminist Critical Method

The above discussion of the nature of the biblical text has made it clear that an authentic feminist hermeneutics informed by the critical principle of inclusion must begin with a hermeneutics of suspicion aimed at unmasking the androcentric ideology and patriarchal constructs implicit and explicit in the text, in its context and in its history of interpretation. It must also be informed by a hermeneutics of remembrance or reclamation, which then claims the biblical stories and biblical history for women as well as for men. This entails a re-reading which is in fact a revisioning as described by Adrienne Rich:

> Revision--the act of looking back, of seeing with fresh eyes, of entering an old text from a new critical direction.[133]

In order to accomplish this looking back and seeing with fresh eyes, feminist scholars have made use of a variety of methodologies both synchronic and diachronic, literary and historical.[134] The choice and combination depend to a large extent on the nature of the task in hand and the expertise of the interpreter. In the light, therefore, of the brief history of feminist reading already alluded to, I have chosen a model which includes both literary and historical methodologies appropriate for application to a gospel text and ordered in light of the hermeneutical goals discussed above.

---

133   Adrienne Rich, "When We Dead Awaken: Writing as Re-vision," *College English* 34 (1972): 18.

134   A detailed discussion of the variety of methodologies used in feminist biblical critism is not necessary for the sake of this study. Reference has already been made to the different forms of rhetorical criticism used by Trible and Schüssler Fiorenza in the service of each one's particular feminist hermeneutic: see nn. 32 and 61 above. The construction of my own model below will take place in dialogue with the methodologies currently being used by both feminist and non-feminist exegetes, and this model will be considered in relation to the other studies of women in Matthew's gospel in Part III of this chapter.

a. Stage One - Inclusion in the Text

Apart from any academic consideration, experience during the preparation
of this study has convinced me that the beginning point of a feminist reading of Matthew's gospel must be the restoration of the stories of women to
the gospel text. Almost invariably in response to my articulation of the topic
of my research as "Women in Matthew's gospel and community", the reply
would come--are there any? This means that the history of interpretation
and use of the text within the christian community have obscured those
stories of women which are, in fact, included in the text. When one adds to
this a consideration of the patriarchal context in which the gospel was produced as well as the androcentric world view which informs it, then it becomes clear that a reclaiming of women's inclusion in the text is a necessary
starting point. The above discussion has made it clear, however, that this is
only possible by means of a truly feminist re-reading of the text.

The critical approach which will best assist this initial task is literary
rather than historical,[135] and will therefore take account of the insights of
both Narrative and Reader-Response criticism. The gospel will be treated as
a narrative whole[136] and analysis will necessarily take place at the level of
story and discourse.[137] It will be informed by a feminist hermeneutics of
suspicion and of remembrance.

The specifically feminist gender reading undertaken in this study will
focus primarily on those women who function as characters in the narrative.[138] Their stories will be analyzed initially in terms of character presentation which includes physical, social, moral or ideological, and psychological

---

135 Both Petersen, "Literary Criticism in Biblical Studies," 37, 41, and Robert M. Polzin,
     "Literary and Historical Criticism of the Bible: A Crisis in Scholarship," in Spencer,
     Orientation by Disorientation, 104, consider that literary analysis must precede histori-
     cal analysis even though both are important. Polzin says that "scholarly understanding
     of biblical material results from a *circular* movement that begins with a literary analy-
     sis, then turns to historical problems, whose attempted solution then furnishes further
     refinements and adaptations of one's literary-critical conclusions. The priority of
     synchrony ... over diachrony is not in rank but only in operation."
136 Petersen, "Literary Criticism in Biblical Studies," 36, emphasizes that "the form of the
     work is a holistic concept requiring us to start with the whole, rather than with the
     philological and form-critical parts." Note, however, Stephen D. Moore's challenge to
     the concept of the gospels as unified in "Are the Gospels Unified Narratives?" in *SBL
     1987 Seminar Papers*, ed. K. H. Richards (Atlanta: Scholars, 1987), 443-458.
137 This distinction is taken from Chatman, *Story and Discourse*, 19-22.
138 For a general presentation of characterization within narrative, see Chatman, *Story and
     Discourse*, 107-138, and for its relationship to biblical narrative, Berlin, *Poetics and
     Interpretation*, 23-42, and Sternberg, *Poetics*, 321-364.

dimensions.[139] Attention will also be directed to the textual structures or gender codes surrounding the women characters, codes which alert the reader to the ideology the text supports.[140] These codes include the silences in the text, disjunctions, contradictions, gaps and omissions because as Greene and Kahn say:

> ... 'female subcultures' exist in complicated relation to the dominant culture, in collusion with as well as 'counter' to it.[141]

Women's speech or silence may function to serve or critique patriarchy and hence is another significant analytical code[142] as is the presence or absence of their names.[143] Finally, consideration will be given to the comparisons and contrasts made between characters on the basis of gender.[144]

Closely related to, even inseparable from character is an analysis of plot.[145] What characters do, the actions they perform, are constitutive elements in the unfolding of events which constitute the story. From a gender perspective, it will be important to consider the tasks that women are permitted to perform and those which are denied to them. As well, the setting of their actions will be significant. Are they confined to domestic space or do their actions take place in the public arena? At this stage in the analysis, domestic and public space will be considered from the perspective of a gender code but at stage three it will need to be addressed again as a social code.

---

139 Sternberg, *Poetics*, 326.
140 For a discussion of this distinction between the "image" of women presented in the text and the underlying textual codes which accompany it, see Nancy Sorkin Rabinowitz, "Female Speech and Female Sexuality: Euripides' *Hippolytos* as Model," in *Rescuing Creusa: New Methodological Approaches to Women in Antiquity*, ed. Marilyn Skinner (Lubbock, Texas: Texas Tech, 1987), 127.
141 Greene and Kahn, "Feminist Scholarship," 24.
142 See Rabinowitz, "Female Speech"; Betsy Halpern Amaru, "Portraits of Biblical Women in Josephus' Antiquities," *JJS* 39 (1988): 145, 149, 151 and 163; and Mary Lefkowitz, "Influential Women," in *Images of Women in Antiquity*, ed. Averil Cameron and Amélia Kuhrt (Detroit: Wayne State University Press, 1983), 59.
143 The power of this androcentric code is made eminently clear by Sternberg, *Poetics*, 330, when he says that "by analogy to the biblical world, where the absence or the blotting out of a name implies nonexistence, the abstention from naming in biblical discourse thus implies the individual abeyance of the nameless within the otherwise particularized action. If worthy of naming at all, on the other hand, biblical man [sic] receives a proper name in the fullest sense of the word."
144 Although it is not based on a gender analysis, see Sean Freyne's interesting treatment of contrasts set up between characters, "Vilifying the Other and Defining the Self: Matthew's and John's Anti-Judaism in Focus," in *"To See Ourselves as Others See Us": Jews, Christians, Others in Antiquity*, ed. E. Frerichs and J. Neusner, Studies in Humanities (Chico: Scholars, 1985), 117-144.
145 This inseparability is discussed by M. H. Abrams, *A Glossary of Literary Terms*, 3rd ed. (New York: Holt, Rinehart & Winston, 1971), 21, 127.

A comprehensive gender reading is not complete simply as a result of an analysis of the women as characters. This must be accompanied by a search for the symbolic significance of gender, which Annette Kolodny says

> constitutes a second crucial aspect of feminist literary criticism ... crucial because it acknowledges the often subtle distinction between the depiction of male or female characters for their recognizable gender behaviors and the manipulation of gender for symbolic purposes that may have only incidental relation to actual contemporary sex roles. Pursuing this second concern thus sometimes reveals little about the authentic reality of men and women but much about the symbolic terms through which a given cultural group struggles to define the meaning of its most perplexing dilemmas.[146]

An analysis of the point of view of the implied author or narrator can be a valuable tool in the uncovering of character within the narrative and the symbolic significance attributed to it.[147] This aspect of narrative criticism is developed most satisfactorily by Adele Berlin who combines the approaches of Chatman and Uspensky and then applies them to biblical criticism in terms of both the narrator's and an individual character's point of view.[148] Especially significant to our stage one gender reading is the ideological level whereby persons and events are evaluated. This evaluation may be from the perspective of the implied author, narrator or one of the characters. Janice Capel Anderson has pointed out in this regard that in Matthew's gospel the ideological points of view of Jesus and the narrator have been aligned.[149]

Such an alignment can create tension for a female reader of the gospel text who takes on the role of the implied reader. If she responds to all the clues given in the text to the implied reader, then she will be required to accept the androcentric world view and patriarchal constructs implicit therein. If, however, she reads against the grain, combining a gender reading with an androcentric and patriarchal critique which asks where and how androcentricity is at work on us as readers and how gender politics and hierarchy are

---

146   Annette Kolodny, "Turning the Lens on "The Panther Captivity": A Feminist Exercise in Practical Criticism," *Critical Inquiry* 8 (1981): 339.
147   The term "implied author" is used here according to the convention of current narrative criticism to refer to the "author" who is reconstructed from the text and to whom are imputed the norms and social or cultural codes within the text. This construct based on the norms within the text is quite distinct from the real author of the text. See Chatman, *Story and Discourse*, 148-149; and Rimmon-Kenan, *Narrative Fiction*, 86-89.
148   Berlin, *Poetics and Interpretation*, 43-82.
149   Anderson, "Gender and Reading," 22-24.

inscribed in the patriarchal traditions,[150] then she is undertaking a re-
reading which is a seeing of an old text with new eyes.[151]

In order to complete this re-reading and truly reclaim the text as
inclusive of women, other contemporary interpretations will need to be examined in order to determine whether they support the text's liberating vision of the Jesus movement or contribute to the ongoing legitimation of its
patriarchal structures. By way of this analysis, the feminist interpreter will
discover how the rhetorical strategies within the text have functioned for a
variety of readers and how the gender of the reader and the reader's critical
community have influenced interpretations. This means that the androcentric and patriarchal critique of the biblical text is therefore extended to the
history of its interpretation. In this way not only the text but also the history
of its interpretation can be reclaimed as the christian tradition of women and
men.

As was indicated earlier, however, this initial literary approach to the
text is merely the starting point in an ongoing interpretive process.
Questions will be raised at this stage which come from the text itself and
which will lead us into a more specifically historical and diachronic
inquiry.[152] It is to a consideration of this second aspect that we now turn.

b. Stage Two - Inclusion in the Formation of the Text

Having reclaimed the gospel text as an articulation of the Jesus story in
which women and men function at its centre, we will turn to a reclaiming of

---

150 Munich, "Notorious Signs," 240, stresses that feminist criticism cannot ignore this
     aspect of texts.
151 In the field of literary criticism there is a complex debate over the definition of reader
     as is evidenced by the article of Robert M. Fowler, "Who is "The Reader" in Reader
     Response Criticism?" *Semeia* 31 (1985): 5-23, in which he discusses the various posi-
     tions of Booth, Iser and Fish. I do not wish to enter into this debate here but I do wish
     to acknowledge that the position I have taken seems to correspond most closely to that
     articulated by Janice Capel Anderson, "Matthew: Sermon and Story," in *SBL 1988
     Seminar Papers*, ed. David J. Lull (Atlanta: Scholars, 1988), 497, where she says that
     "when I speak of the reader I want to allude to both extremes because I want to hold in
     tension the role the text plays and the role real readers play in creating meaning as in-
     dividuals and as possessors of shared conventions and codes." She links this stance
     particularly to feminist criticism and while she goes on to suggest that it favours Iser's
     definition of reader, it seems that it also allows for Fish's notion of the encounter of
     text and reader within the context of a critical community which in this case may be
     the academic community of feminist biblical and theological scholars or the wider
     community of women-church.
152 See Sean Freyne, *Galilee, Jesus and the Gospels: Literary Approaches and Historical
     Investigations* (Philadelphia: Fortress, 1988), 25-26, where he outlines a similar method
     which begins with a literary approach to the gospel story and then moves to historical
     investigations.

traditions concerning women and women's traditions in the formation of the text. No one would deny that both women and men constituted the Matthean community through its history to the point at which the gospel was written and, of course, beyond. A feminist critique, however, is based on a further claim: that women as well as men participated in the shaping of the traditions of this community. As Munich says, "in the background of patriarchal texts are women trying to escape into readability,"[153] a statement which could be extended to read that not only women but women's traditions are seeking escape from their patriarchal confines.

In order to recover these traditions and their development, the basic methodological tools employed will be those of historical-criticism, but as we noted above in the brief discussion of an inclusive historico-literary paradigm, they have to be redefined in the light of the historical paradigm shift. No longer will the traditional tools for gospel criticism--source, form, tradition and redaction criticism, be used directly by the feminist reader and interpreter to discover the actual historical situation of early Christianity or in particular of the Matthean community, but the data thus obtained will assist toward a reconstruction of the socio-historical situation inscribed within the narrative. By focussing on the stories of women using these diachronic methodologies, the exegete can discover glimpses of the development of the traditions which formed and informed the final rhetorical presentation of these stories in the gospel text. From this, information can be gleaned towards a restructuring of the "historical subtext", the story of women and men within the Matthean community.[154] This information, however, will need to be supplemented at stage three by other historical and sociological data.

The narrative analysis carried out at the previous stage, especially with regard to the attention given to the overall structure of the gospel, the structure of individual sections and their relation to the whole, closely resembles "composition criticism" or "vertical analysis" which in recent years has been seen as a constitutive element of a thorough redaction criticism.[155] This will

---

153 Munich, "Notorious Signs," 257.
154 For a discussion of the textual nature of the "historical subtext", see Jameson, "Symbolic Inference," 73-77.
155 William G. Thompson, *Matthew's Advice to a Divided Community: Mt. 17,22-18,35*, AnBib 44 (Rome: Biblical Institute Press, 1970), 12-13; David E. Garland, *The Intention of Matthew 23*, NT.S 52 (Leiden: Brill, 1979), 5-6; Norman Perrin, "The Evangelist as Author: Reflections on Method in the Study and Interpretation of the Synoptic Gospels and Acts," *Biblical Research* 17 (1972): 15-16; and Graham Stanton, "The Origin and

be supplemented by a horizontal comparison with the other gospels in order to determine whether there are recognizable tendencies in the Matthean redaction of material relating to women.[156] At this point, no particular source theory will be presumed upon but the evidence will be examined in order to determine how the source or sources of a particular text may best be explained.[157] A study of the specifically Matthean language and style will help to determine whether material unique to Matthew belongs to the final redaction or is traditional, that is, it belongs to pre-Matthean material, whether oral or written.[158] Supported by a prior study of both source and form and their adaptation by the final redactor, we will draw some tentative lines of development of the traditions regarding women.[159] Finally, the above analysis will serve the restructuring of the historical sub-text of the Matthean gospel especially from a gender perspective.

Purpose of Matthew's Gospel: Matthean Scholarship from 1945 to 1980," in *ANRW* II.25.3 (Berlin/New York: de Gruyter, 1985), 1895-1896.

156 I use the word "tendencies" here out of a consciousness of the complexity of the redactional process as it is articulated by Stanton, "Origin and Purpose," 1896-1899, and John P. Meier, *Law and History in Matthew's Gospel: A Redactional Study of Mt. 5:17-48*, AnBib 71 (Rome: Biblical Institute Press, 1976), 2-6. In the light of this complexity, the term "final redaction" will be used throughout to refer to the process undertaken by individuals or groups responsible for the compilation of the gospel around the 80s or 90s of the first century of the Common Era. The term "Matthew" will be used to refer to the text resulting from this final redactor. It needs to be acknowledged here, however, that we do not possess this text but that the work of textual critics has sought to present us with a text that approximates this "original text" as closely as possible while acknowledging complex variations.

157 As Stanton, "Origin and Purpose," 1899-1903, points out, the two-source theory has been assumed in Matthean scholarship since 1945, but has come under question in recent years. This theory and its amplifications by various scholars will certainly influence the research undertaken here but it will not be presumed upon in its simple form as the sole source theory. I will also draw upon the work of P. Benoit and M.-E. Boismard, *Synopse des quatre évangiles en français, II: Commentaire par M.-E. Boismard* avec la collaboration de A. Lamouille et P. Sandevoir (Paris: Cerf, 1972), 15-59 and passim, which significantly nuances this theory. The complexity of the field of source criticism needs to be acknowledged here and since this is not the principal focus of this work, I will have to rely on the research already done by scholars who are expert in this field.

158 Stephenson H. Brooks, *Matthew's Community: The Evidence of His Special Sayings Material*, JSNTSup 16 (Sheffield: JSOT Press, 1987), 16.

159 I have avoided using the formal terminology *Tradition Criticism/Traditionsgeschichte/Überlieferungsgeschichte* as its goal would seem to be the tracing of the history of oral traditions whereas here, interest in the history of the transmission of the traditions, especially in written form, is at the service of a clearer understanding of the final redactional stage of transmission. See Richard N. Soulen, *Handbook of Biblical Criticism*, 2nd ed. (Atlanta: John Knox, 1981), 200-201. John H. Hayes and Carl R. Holladay, *Biblical Exegesis: A Beginner's Handbook* (Atlanta: John Knox, 1982), 91-92, point out, however that the goal of tradition criticism is the illuminating of the final form of the text. They also note the hypothetical nature of the results of such an undertaking.

Because this historical-critical study will, of necessity, require a return to the pericopes that were considered in detail in the narrative analysis but from a different perspective, there will be a certain amount of repetition. This will, however, be kept to a minimum while not being able to be completely avoided as a result of the approach taken.

c. Stage Three - Inclusion within History

To this point, our analysis has been directed primarily to the literary text in order to establish the symbolic function of female gender, the role given to women characters in the text and the development of the traditions surrounding these characters to the point of their incorporation into the text. Questions regarding the actual roles of women in the Matthean community and in early Christianity generally still remain and, in fact, are not easily answered;[160] but to fail to address them would leave a feminist reading incomplete. In establishing the theoretical model for this stage of analysis, however, we need to proceed with caution, taking note of the tentative nature of the exploration. As Wayne Meeks says:

> ... our reconstructed worlds will almost certainly be mistaken in many particulars, and the mistakes may have unforeseen consequences. Such flaws belong to the nature of history and to the human condition; they do not negate the importance of the quest.[161]

In her article "Women's Studies and the Hebrew Bible," Jo Ann Hackett outlines five stages at which study of women and history can be located.[162] This final stage of a feminist critical model which I have called "inclusion within history" would seem to be equivalent to her stage four, "women *as* history". It is here that questions are asked regarding what women did in early christian communities, how they participated in the liturgical and catechetical life of the Matthean community, and what they believed. Applying Hackett's final question to the New Testament, however, we must also ask "What, in fact, can we know about what most people actually did and

---

160 Note the caution of Janice Capel Anderson, "Gender and Reading," 6.
161 Wayne A. Meeks, "Understanding Early Christian Ethics," *JBL* 105 (1986): 5.
162 Jo Ann Hackett, "Women's Studies and the Hebrew Bible," in *The Future of Biblical Studies: The Hebrew Scriptures*, ed. Richard E. Friedman and H. G. M. Williamson, SBL Semeia Studies 16 (Atlanta: Scholars, 1987), 145-146.

believed, outside of the edited, relatively pristine theologies and history we confront in the New Testament?"[163]

The answer to this question lies in the area of sources as well as methods and approaches to those sources, and it is here, therefore, that a truly "inclusive-constructive" model is essential. Many of the sources will be literary but they will not be limited to those texts which are considered normative for Judaism or Christianity.[164] Such additional texts must be carefully analyzed according to a gender reading similar to that outlined above so that a true comparison of texts can be made if this is required.[165] Given the ideological or social-communicative nature of literary texts that has already been discussed, it is clear that texts transmit social codes and historical information already present in a given society as well as shaping those codes for the future by means of its socio-rhetorical function. Hence, they all need to be analyzed according to inclusive historical and sociological models.

These models or frameworks, many of which have been developed in the fields of history, anthropology and sociology,[166] have brought to light new categories of analysis. The traditional category of domestic-v-public is

---

163 Ibid., 146. The cautionary note of Phyllis Culham, "Ten Years After Pomeroy: Studies of the Image and Reality of Women in Antiquity," in Skinner, *Rescuing Creusa*, 16, must also be sounded here: "One of the major problems with some current studies of women in ancient literature is mislabeling of the end product. It is entirely legitimate to continue one's analysis to the image of women in a given text as long as one realizes that this is what one is doing. But if one claims to be providing an historically true description of an actual society, one must be held accountable for meeting the standards of historical, not literary methodology, including consulting all available and relevant evidence including material evidence and not generalizing beyond its capacity to support generalization. One should not make claims that from the study of the literary text alone, one is recovering the image of women in the society at large, or, even worse, that one is describing the reality of actual women's lives."

164 Ross S. Kraemer, "Non-Literary Evidence for Jewish Women in Rome and Egypt," in Skinner, *Rescuing Creusa*, 97.

165 This means that a feminist historical-reconstruction of early Christianity or a writing of early christian history as the history of women and men must be a collaborative task and will be continually supplemented over time as more and more scholars study women's lives in various regions of the Graeco-Roman world, in various religions of the time and in its socio-economic life.

166 See Lerner, *Creation of Patriarchy*; Elsie Boulding, *The Underside of History: A View of Women through Time* (Boulder, Colorado: Westview Press, 1976); Bernice A. Carroll, ed., *Liberating Women's History: Theoretical and Critical Essays* (Urbana/Chicago/London: University of Illinois Press, 1976); Reiter, *Toward an Anthropology of Women*; Rosaldo and Lamphere, *Woman, Culture and Society*; and Skinner, *Rescuing Creusa*, to name but a few in these developing fields of study. The use of a variety of methodologies and conceptual frameworks may seem to many to be eclectic but as Gerda Lerner suggests in her article "Placing Women in History: Definitions and Challenges," *Feminist Studies* 3 (1975): 13: "In order to write a new history worthy of the name we will have to recognize that no single methodology and conceptual framework can fit the complexities of the historical experience of all women."

seen in a new light and questions are asked regarding the activity that goes on in the domestic realm and its contribution to society. This is especially important with regard to early Christianity in which the domestic sphere was, in fact, the context of the public life of the christian community.[167] Hackett asks the question of the relationship between periods of social dysfunction and women's status.[168] Carol Meyers' work on the position of women in early Israel points to the influence of urban or rural settings.[169] The social and economic status of women as well as their source of power are further social codes which may be reflected in the text as are kinship and honour/shame. Finally, information gleaned from literary texts analyzed in the above manner must be supported and/or challenged by the study of a wide variety of non-literary evidence.[170]

This area is one which could be much more fully developed but in relation to this study, only some initial signposts can be given regarding the direction in which future studies into the inclusive history of the Matthean community may proceed. Such a choice rests on a number of factors chief among which is the enormity of this type of study if it were adequately completed and the fact that much of the information required is not yet available, and to amass it would amount to a number of other independent studies.[171] The setting up of certain initial signposts, however, will result from

---

167 This is evidenced by Schüssler Fiorenza, *In Memory of Her*, 175-184, and in relation to the Matthean community, Michael H. Crosby's recent work, *House of Disciples: Church, Economics, and Justice in Matthew* (Maryknoll: Orbis, 1988), is significant.
168 Hackett, "Women's Studies," 149-151.
169 Carol Meyers, "The Roots of Restriction: Women in Early Israel," *BA* 41 (1978): 91-103.
170 In this regard I would point to the excellent work of both Ross Kraemer and Bernadette Brooten who exemplify this aspect of women's history in relation to Judaism. See Bernadette J. Brooten, "Jewish Women's History in the Roman Period: A Task for Christian Theology," in *Christians Among Jews and Gentiles: Essays in Honor of Krister Stendahl's Sixty-Fifth Birthday*, ed. George W. E. Nickelsburg with George W. Macrae (Philadelphia: Fortress, 1986), 22-30; "Early Christian Women and Their Cultural Context: Issues of Method in Historical Reconstruction," in Collins, *Feminist Perspectives*, 65-91; *Women Leaders in the Ancient Synagogue*; and Ross S. Kraemer, "Non-Literary Evidence," 85-101; and "Hellenistic Jewish Women: The Epigraphical Evidence," in *SBL 1986 Seminar Papers*, ed. K. H. Richards (Atlanta: Scholars, 1986), 183-200.
171 Brooten, "Early Christian Women," 79-80, says in this regard: "In order to reconstruct this history, one would need to have a good understanding of social, political, and economic conditions of the women of various classes in all parts of the Roman Empire; of women's participation in and the theology of other Greco-Roman religions, including Judaism; of first-century philosophical and religious thinking about women; of the laws affecting women in the various geographical regions; of women's participation in public life, including politics; of sexual behavior and attitudes toward sexuality; and of the physical living conditions of women, that is, architecture, art, ceramics, etc. ... All this requires a new kind of synthesis, drawing upon New Testament and Jewish

the socio-historical analyses of the texts under consideration and other
literary texts and a study of historical and sociological data that is available
from the growing number of studies of women's lives in the Graeco-Roman
world.

The resultant beginning history will, of its very nature, be narrative-
laden, being the product of choices made and arrangement of data. It will,
however, offer a new vision of the Matthean community within early christian history out of which the gospel can be read. As Elisabeth Schüssler
Fiorenza says

> ... we are never able to read a text without explicitly or implicitly
> reconstructing its historical subtext within the process of our reading.[172]

If this reconstruction is consciously inclusive then it points us along the way
toward a truly inclusive history of early Christianity which will inform all
interpretations of the New Testament text.[173]

4. Hermeneutics of Appropriation and Creative Articulation

When all this has been completed, the feminist task is not yet over. It began
with experience and leads through theory back to praxis, a praxis which
must be emancipatory. It must bring about a transformation of theological
reflection and social change.[174]

At the level of theological appropriation, it implies radically new
possibilities for our understanding of discipleship, participation in the community of believers, leadership in that community, the faith traditions of
women as distinct from those of men, the symbolic use of gender, of christology and of ecclesiology. If the inclusive reading suggested above is allowed

---

studies, classics, ancient history, archaeology, art history, papyrology, epigraphy, and
anthropology."

172 Elisabeth Schüssler Fiorenza, *The Book of Revelation: Justice and Judgment*
(Philadelphia: Fortress, 1985), 183.

173 This is the final stage referred to by Hackett, "Women's Studies," 146, and will be the
result of a paradigm shift in mainstream biblical studies which will give consideration
to the above analysis. I would agree with Hackett that this stage is as yet well beyond
our grasp, but it is, in fact, the goal of all our work.

174 D. N. Fewell, "Feminist Reading of the Hebrew Bible: Affirmation, Resistance and
Transformation," *JSOT* 39 (1987): 84. In "Reading Ourselves," 39, Schweickart says that
"the point is not merely to interpret literature in various ways; the point is to *change
the world*. We cannot afford to ignore the activity of reading, for it is here that literature is realized as *praxis*. Literature acts on the world by acting on its readers." See also
Schüssler Fiorenza, "Toward a Feminist Biblical Hermeneutics," 106-110.

to inform this theological appropriation then it will liberate women from the oppression they have suffered within faith communities as a result of the androcentric and patriarchal readings that have abounded. It will enable them to claim their own autonomy towards an inclusive christian community. Such emancipatory praxis will be shaped by the vision of the Jesus movement seen as inclusive.

To assist this new theological appropriation, there is need for a creative and imaginative retelling of the Matthean gospel story. It is this that Schüssler Fiorenza calls a "hermeneutics of creative actualization".[175] Since the stories of the "patriarchs" and the "fathers of the church" have been told in hymns, prayers, ritual and legend to the service of the patriarchal church, then it is necessary that the church of the future, if it is to be a truly inclusive church, must tell new stories to reflect its new vision, stories inspired by the Bible as formative prototype. Such stories will, in their turn, help to create this new vision. Creative articulation, however, is the work of the believing community and the feminist reading of the Matthean gospel undertaken here may simply be of assistance towards it. In conclusion, let us turn to a very brief consideration of my choice of the gospel of Matthew as the text for this initial feminist reading.

III. The Gospel Of Matthew

In the current wave of feminist studies, the Matthean gospel has received little specific attention. Elizabeth Tetlow captures perhaps two attitudes which give rise to this neglect: Matthew simply takes over Markan material; and the gospel is Jewish and hence patriarchal.[176] She says of the author of the gospel:

---

175 Schüssler Fiorenza, "Women-Church," 20-22.
176 Her second characterization represents a commonplace and yet exclusivistic christian bias. A warning against this type of bias is found in Judith Plaskow, "Blaming Jews for Inventing Patriarchy," *Lilith* 7 (1980): 11-12, and "Christian Feminism and Anti-Judaism," *Cross Currents* 28 (1978): 307-309. Elisabeth Moltmann-Wendel, *Women Around Jesus*, 120, also illustrates how easy it is to become prey to this bias when she says of the author of the first gospel: "He was a Jew, and presumably had conservative attitudes."

> [Matthew has] reproduced most of the references to women which were
> found in Mark, although with some editorial alterations. He did not add any
> other references to women from his other sources, whether as disciples or as
> characters ... This reluctance to note the presence of women around Jesus,
> the great rabbi, was consistent with Matthew's method of arguing from
> within the traditions of rabbinic Judaism, which at that time totally
> excluded women from rabbinic schooling. It was also consistent with the
> influence of the Old Testament which warned of the contaminating effect of
> women which could render a man ritually impure.[177]

A similar position has recently been supported by Ben Witherington III who
concludes:

> The Matthean redaction of various Marcan stories involving women gives
> little or no indication of any notable attempts to highlight women or their
> roles beyond what was present in the source ...[178]

Other studies suggest a more creative element in the Matthean gospel's portrait of women.[179] They have not, however, been undertaken from the
feminist perspective already outlined and, therefore, reflect the thematic
study of woman discussed above.[180]

The beginning of a truly feminist reading of Matthew's gospel is
represented by the article of Janice Capel Anderson which appeared in a 1983
edition of *Semeia* devoted specifically to Feminist Biblical Hermeneutics.[181]
In this article she undertakes a gender reading of the narrative together with
a study of the symbolic function of gender. This study, however, is accompanied by little androcentric or patriarchal critique although she does acknowledge the presence of androcentric and patriarchal ideologies. Since her undertaking was literary, she does not analyze the historical dimension of the
narrative but simply approaches the text from a narrative perspective. Later,
she supplemented this work with a second article which focussed in more
detail on the infancy narrative only.[182]

---

177 Tetlow, *Women and Ministry*, 98-99.
178 Ben Witherington III, *Women in the Earliest Churches*, MSSNTS 59 (Cambridge:
     University Press, 1988), 170.
179 Swidler, *Biblical Affirmations*, 235-254; Stagg, *Woman in the World of Jesus*, 215-219;
     Moloney, *Woman in the New Testament*, 33-37; idem, *First Among the Faithful* , 33-
     39; and Josef Blank, "Frauen in den Jesusüberlieferungen," in *Die Frau im
     Urchristentum*, ed. G. Dautzenberg, H. Merklein and K. Müller, QD 95
     (Freiburg/Basel/Wien: Herder, 1983), 29-39, to name a few.
180 Such studies can all too readily be used to undermine women's struggle for liberation
     and inclusion by simply presenting positive aspects of the text divorced from its patri-
     archal and androcentric context. They can lead, therefore, to a false exaltation of
     women.
181 Anderson, "Gender and Reading".
182 Janice Capel Anderson, "Mary's Difference: Gender and Patriarchy in the Birth
     Narratives," *JR* 67 (1987): 183-202.

In the year following Anderson's first article, Marla J. Selvidge, in a short article, analyzed the relationship of the traditions regarding a number of women to the gospel's theme of violence.[183] Although her work is particularly concerned with the theme of violence in the aftermath of the Roman War of 70 CE, she draws attention to three significant stories of women within the gospel and to the Matthean redaction of these stories and analyzes her findings in terms of the traditional family structure. She too supplemented this earlier work in her recent book, *Daughters of Jerusalem* , which is devoted to a study of the portrayal of women in the synoptic gospels and within this a chapter is devoted to the Matthean gospel.[184] Her approach is basically that of redaction criticism with some support from historical research as she points out in her introduction, but she does little to outline her own biblical hermeneutic. Her analysis of the text manifests a positive portrayal of women within the gospel, but it is not accompanied by any critique of the patriarchal and androcentric ideologies that the text enunciates and supports and the effect of these within the community where the stories were told. While my own approach is redactional in part, it is supplemented by a gender reading of the text which critiques its patriarchal and androcentric elements and by a more thorough socio-historical analysis.

The appearance of Jane Schaberg's *The Illegitimacy of Jesus: A Feminist Theological Interpretation of the Infancy Narratives* in 1987 brought with it a very detailed study of the Matthean Infancy Narrative from a feminist perspective. She notes the tension within the Infancy Narrative as the significant naming and presence of women strains the boundaries of the gospel's patriarchal and androcentric perspectives, and she closes her study with this significant statement:

> If my reading of Matthew's Infancy Narrative is regarded as a possible reading, other ears may recognize its echoes in the rest of this Gospel.[185]

It is this challenge that the present study will take up in a similar feminist reading of the entire gospel as a further contribution to the feminist reading of the Matthean gospel which has already been commenced. It will

---

183 Marla J. Selvidge, "Violence, Woman, and the Future of the Matthean Community: A Redactional Critical Essay," *USQR* 39 (1984): 213-223.
184 Marla J. Selvidge, *Daughters of Jerusalem* (Scottdale, Penn./Kitchener, Ont.: Herald Press, 1987).
185 Jane Schaberg, *The Illegitimacy of Jesus: A Feminist Theological Interpretation of the Infancy Narratives* (San Francisco: Harper and Row, 1987), 77.

be limited since the focus will simply be on those stories in which the women function as characters, but these will be examined in the light of the entire gospel. My hope is, however, that others will take up where it leaves off so that our journey towards a truly inclusive reading of the entire biblical story may be accomplished.

2. Inclusion within the Text - A Narrative Critical Reading

"The Gospel of Matthew is a unified narrative, or "artistic whole"."[1]

These words of J. D. Kingsbury characterize the literary critical approach to the gospel to be employed in this chapter which considers the gospel text as an integrated work of the author. Within this unified narrative, the focus of this study will be specifically on the women characters, but they will be considered in the context of the particular moment or movement within the narrative in which their stories occur. At the outset, therefore, it is necessary to delineate the key movements through which the story progresses.[2]

The narrative opens with a prologue or beginning [γένεσις][3] which provides the background to the story of Jesus which is the gospel (1:1-4:16).

---

1   Jack Dean Kingsbury, *Matthew as Story*, 2nd ed. (Philadelphia: Fortress, 1988), 1. This concept of the gospel as an integrated whole is developed by Petersen, *Literary Criticism*, 20-23; idem, "Literary Criticism in Biblical Studies," 36; David Rhoads and Donald Michie, *Mark as Story: An Introduction to the Narrative of a Gospel* (Philadelphia: Fortress, 1982), 2-5; and R. Alan Culpepper, *Anatomy of the Fourth Gospel: A Study in Literary Design*, Foundations & Facets: New Testament (Philadelphia: Fortress, 1983). This is to name but a few of the biblical scholars who have taken over this concept from the field of literary criticism.

2   This is to enter an area of Matthean scholarship in which there is no prevailing consensus as is indicated by Donald Senior, *What Are They Saying About Matthew?* (New York/Ramsey: Paulist, 1983), 20, and David R. Bauer, *The Structure of Matthew's Gospel: A Study in Literary Design*, JSNTS 31 (Sheffield: Almond, 1988), 11. Both these scholars then delineate the various structures that have been proposed especially within the historical- critical paradigm although Senior, 26-27, does go on to suggest the new possibilities for understanding Matthew's structure that a narrative approach to the gospel provides. He then outlines a possible division using such an approach. Recently Frank J. Matera, "The Plot of Matthew's Gospel," *CBQ* 49 (1987): 233-253, has also proposed a different outline based on the notions of narrative "kernels" and "satellites" according to Chatman's *Story and Discourse*. J. D. Kingsbury's proposal in *Matthew as Story*, 40-41, does not differ, however, from that which he proposed earlier in *Matthew: Structure, Christology, Kingdom* (London: SPCK, 1975). I do not want to enter into this area in detail here but merely to indicate the broad movements in the narrative in which individual pericopes will be situated and as I do this, I shall dialogue briefly with the recent studies.

3   According to W. Bauer, W. F. Arndt, F. W. Gingrich and F. W. Danker, *A Greek-English Lexicon of the New Testament and Other Early Christian Literature*, 2nd ed. (Chicago: University of Chicago, 1979), 154, this word may mean "beginning", "origin", or "descent or birth". This variety of possible meanings is one of the reasons for the

At 4:17, the narrator provides the reader with a clear indicator of a new movement in the narrative--Jesus begins his Galilean ministry ['Ἀπὸ τότε ἤρξατο ὁ Ἰησοῦς κηρύσσειν ...]--which continues to 16:20. Within this long section, however, from 11:1, Jesus' teaching, preaching, healing and commissioning of twelve named disciples (4:17-10:42) is supplemented by more significant focus on the response of both disciples and opponents to Jesus within the context of his Galilean ministry (11:1-16:20). The reader is given another signal at 16:21 which is very similar to that of 4:17--Jesus begins instructing his disciples regarding his forthcoming death and resurrection ['Ἀπὸ τότε ἤρξατο ὁ Ἰησοῦς δεικνύειν τοῖς μαθηταῖς αὐτοῦ ...]. There are, however, two significant movements within the long finale. The first is the journey up to Jerusalem (16:21-20:34) and the second takes us through Jesus' last days in Jerusalem to his handing on of his ministerial authority (21:1-28:20).[4]

I. THE PROLOGUE - 1:1-4:16

The opening chapters of Matthew's gospel are very significant in establishing the relationship that the implied author wishes to transact with

---

various scholarly opinions as to the exact reference for this term, a point discussed in n. 7 below.

4   It should be noted here that this outline accepts the significance of the formulaic statements of 4:17 and 16:21, a topic significantly developed by Kingsbury in the two texts cited above. Bauer, *The Structure*, 153, n. 37, cites many other scholars who adopt an outline similar to Kingsbury's. It has been pointed out, however, that there are significant movements within the narrative not encompassed by these two statements and I find, on comparison, that the outline I have proposed is very similar to that of Senior, *What are they Saying*, 27, except for his delineation of 28:16-20 as a separate section. More attention will be given to the structuring of this section of the gospel in a later chapter, but it is sufficient to point out here that 28:16 contains a copulative δέ which links it with what precedes even though it differs from it; hence it would seem more appropriate to allow it to stand as the dramatic climax of the final section of the gospel rather than as a separate movement in its own right. A similar grammatical factor would also seem to raise questions regarding the structure proposed by Matera at the beginning of his Section II, III, IV and VI (Matt 4:12; 11:2; 16:13; and 28:16). A final comment regarding structure is the acknowledgment of its complexity given the variety of what seem to be structural indicators within the text itself. Dan O. Via, "Structure, Christology, and Ethics in Matthew," in Spencer, *Orientation by Disorientation*, 199-201, tries to deal with this complexity by means of what he calls foreground and background patterns, but even this approach shares in the limitations of the entire enterprise of trying to discover an author's structure.

the implied reader by means of the narrator. The reader immediately encounters the narrator in the direct commentary provided in the
superscription and the genealogy,[5] but even when the plot begins in 1:18,
there are a number of intrusions by the narrator in subsequent verses.[6] This
presence of the narrator is intended to guide the reading process.

A. 1:1-17

The superscription introduces the reader to the nature of what is to follow
[βίβλος γενέσεως][7] and to the identity of the chief protagonist ['Ιησοῦ Χριστοῦ
υἱοῦ Δαυὶδ υἱοῦ 'Αβραάμ], linking Jesus to the two great figures through
whom God's promises were given to Israel (2 Sam 7:8-16; Gen 12:1-3).[8] The
genealogy further explicates this identity for the reader by means of the
hero's kinship structure in the form of a patrilineage of Jesus, thirty-nine
repetitions of the pattern--male δὲ ἐγέννησεν male [Pattern 1].[9] From a gender perspective, the reader is immediately invited to share the androcentric
point of view of the narrator according to which Israel's history as the pre-
history of Jesus and vehicle of God's promises is considered ordered and

---

5   Sternberg, *Poetics*, 120, lists "expositional antecedents" and "genealogies and
     catalogues" among a long list of narratorial commentary and Anderson, "Gender and
     Reading," 7-8, points to Matthew's superscription and opening genealogy as belonging
     to this category.
6   Fred L. Horton, "Parenthetical Pregnancy: The Conception and Birth of Jesus in
     Matthew 1:18-25," in *SBL 1987 Seminar Papers*, ed. K. H. Richards (Atlanta: Scholars
     Press, 1987), 175-179, basing his study on Sternberg's *Poetics*, lists four authorial intru-
     sions in 1:18-25 which he claims establishes the author's authority especially as
     "historian" (the inverted commas are mine). Such an analysis can be carried forward
     into the remainder of the opening chapters but since the chief focus here will be Matt
     1, no further indicators will be given.
7   There has been a long controversy in Matthean scholarship as to the precise reference
     of βίβλος γενέσεως: whether it is to the genealogy, the infancy narratives, the prologue
     1:1-4:16, or to the entire gospel. This discussion is well documented by Herman C.
     Waetjen, "The Genealogy as the Key to the Gospel according to Matthew," *JBL* 95
     (1976): 213-215, and Bauer, *The Structure*, 73-77. From a narrative perspective, it intro-
     duces the reader into a story which expands from genealogy through early background
     to entire ministry leading to the denouement.
8   Daniel Patte, *The Gospel according to Matthew: A Structural Commentary on
     Matthew's Faith* (Philadelphia: Fortress, 1987), 18, points out that already the reader is
     alerted to something different or extraordinary here because the biblical genealogies are
     normally headed by the name of the first progenitor whereas this one is named
     according to the descendant in whom it reaches its climax or fulfilment.
9   Philip L. Shuler, *A Genre for the Gospels: The Biographical Character of Matthew*
     (Philadelphia: Fortress, 1982), 53 and 93, points out that such an establishing of the
     family and ancestors of the hero is typical of the beginning of an encomium, the
     ancient genre with which he compares the gospel.

male.[10] This point of view also assumes and affirms a patriarchal view of marriage in which sons are born to and for the male while the woman as simply the means of reproduction is rendered invisible.[11]

The overriding pattern of the genealogy is, however, broken five times by the introduction of the names of women.[12] Four of these breaks form a second pattern[13] while the fifth is unique.

ἐκ τῆς Θαμάρ	1:3	
ἐκ τῆς Ῥαχάβ	1:5	[Pattern 2]
ἐκ τῆς Ῥούθ	1:5	
ἐκ τῆς τοῦ Οὐρίου	1:6	

Μαρίας, ἐξ ἧς ἐγεννήθη ...   1:16.

Diagram 1

The reader is then faced with the question why the narrator has introduced these women into a predominantly male genealogy.

---

10   Michelle Zimbalist Rosaldo, "Woman, Culture, and Society: A Theoretical Overview," in Rosaldo and Lamphere, *Woman, Culture and Society*, 31, points to this as a cultural phenomenon when she says that "men, in their institutionalized relations of kinship, politics, and so on, define the public order." In Israel's sacred story and the Matthean genealogy this cultural phenomenon is sacralized since the narrator's point of view is linked to God's evaluative point of view. For a discussion of such a link in Matthew's gospel, see Anderson, "Gender and Reading," 22-23, and Kingsbury, *Matthew as Story*, 34-37.

11   Fuchs, "Literary Characterization". Within this article, especially pp. 128-129, Fuchs, drawing on the work of Adrienne Rich, makes an important distinction between the legal institution of motherhood which is a powerful patriarchal mechanism and the personal and psychological aspects of motherhood which refer to "the *potential relationship* of any woman to her powers of reproduction and to children." The patriarchal familial structure, which is referred to throughout this study, supports the legal institution of motherhood and it is this aspect which is critiqued. This is not, however, to deny the value of family relationships in which the potential of women, men and children are allowed full development.

12   There are other breaks in the pattern of the genealogy which are discussed in detail by Marshall D. Johnson, *The Purpose of the Biblical Genealogies: With Special Reference to the Setting of the Genealogies of Jesus*, MSSNTS 8 (Cambridge: University Press, 1969), 146-152, 179-184, which shall not concern us here. It should be pointed out, however, that the first four women named in the genealogy are not characters in the Matthean story as such but their stories do belong to the "story-time" of the narrative and since their inclusion is very significant for a gender reading of the text, they will receive careful consideration.

13   The second pattern is also partially broken in the fourth element, ἐκ τῆς τοῦ Οὐρίου which, while retaining the ἐκ τῆς of the original pattern, does not use a personal name but rather the genitive τοῦ Οὐρίου. This will be discussed further in n. 22 below.

1. Present State of Research

That such a question has engaged actual readers down through the ages is
evidenced in the history of biblical scholarship which has been summarized
by Raymond Brown thus:

> The first proposal, already espoused by Jerome ..., is that the four OT women
> were regarded as sinners; and their inclusion foreshadowed for Matthew's
> readers the role of Jesus as the Savior of sinful men ...
>
> The second proposal, one made popular by Luther, has more to recommend
> it, namely, that the women were regarded as foreigners and were included
> by Matthew to show that Jesus, the Jewish Messiah, was related by ancestry
> to the Gentiles ...
>
> The third proposal, which has considerable following today, finds two
> common elements in the four OT women, elements that they share with
> Mary:
> (a)   there is something extraordinary or irregular in their union with
> their partners; ... (and)
> (b)   the women showed initiative or played an important role in God's
> plan and so came to be considered the instrument of God's providence or of
> His Holy Spirit.[14]

Marshall Johnson introduces a fourth explanation: the conscious refuting of
attacks on the legitimacy of Jesus' birth.[15] Each of these explanations, however, needs to be critiqued from both a feminist and a narrative perspective.

a. A Feminist Critique

Beginning with the feminist perspective, it seems clear that the readers' presuppositions regarding women play a significant role in the interpretive
process.[16] That the women are regarded as *sinners* resonates with the

---

14   Raymond E. Brown, *The Birth of the Messiah: A Commentary on the Infancy
      Narratives in Matthew and Luke* (New York: Doubleday, 1977), 71-74.
15   Johnson, *Biblical Genealogies*, 152-159, especially 157-159, and more recently Edwin D.
      Freed, "The Women in Matthew's Genealogy," *JSNT* 29 (1987): 3-19. This point is
      taken up, but developed from a feminist perspective, by Jane Schaberg, who explains
      the presence of the women in the genealogy, not as part of the evangelist's attempt to
      refute accusations of illegitimacy but as an attempt to deal theologically with an illegit-
      imate conception, see *Illegitimacy of Jesus*, 1, 20-34. Her position will not be treated
      separately here but will inform the feminist critique undertaken in this section and the
      following chapter.
16   See Ted Peters, "The Nature and Role of Presuppositions: An Inquiry into
      Contemporary Hermeneutics," *IPQ* 14 (1974): 209-222, for a comprehensive treatment of
      the role of presuppositions generally and Schüssler Fiorenza, "Women-Church," 15-18
      and elsewhere, for her explanation of the hermeneutics of suspicion which must be
      applied to the history of interpretation because of the androcentric perspective of many
      interpreters which, among other factors, influences interpretations and which
      resonates with the same perspective in the text itself.

biblical and cultural linking of women, sexuality and sin,[17] but within the stories of each of these women in the Hebrew Scriptures, while their actions may be presented as anomalous, they are never named as sinful.[18] In fact the opposite is often the case. Tamar, who was deprived of children by the action of Judah, but who took an initiative to right the situation, was about to be condemned for "playing the harlot" and being "with child by harlotry" (Gen 38:24).[19] She is acquitted, however, when all the details of her story come to light and she is proclaimed more righteous than Judah (Gen 38:26).[20] Rahab is called a harlot (Josh 2:1),[21] but the focus of her story (Jos 2:1-21; 6:22-25) is not on harlotry but rather on her acting with חֶסֶד toward the Israelite spies (2:12) and her facilitating their entry into the land. The Book of Ruth also celebrates the חֶסֶד of the woman (Ruth 1:8; 2:20; 3:10) and even though the innuendo of uncovering the feet of Boaz raises questions regarding the anomalous situation this action creates, there is no language of sin in relation to Ruth throughout the book. Finally, the story of "the wife of Uriah", the designation given by the evangelist to Bathsheba, is told in 2 Sam 11-12;[22] but it could hardly be called the story of Bathsheba, nor is she declared guilty of adultery.[23] Rather it is the story of David and the concern

---

17   Anderson, "Gender and Reading," 9. This link is supported by Boismard, *Synopse*, 64; Alfred Durand, *Evangile selon saint Matthieu*, VSal 1 (Paris: Beauchesne, 1924), 4; and Alfred Plummer, *An Exegetical Commentary on the Gospel according to S. Matthew* (London: Scott, 1915), 2.

18   Already at the beginning of this century, M.-J. Lagrange, *Evangile selon saint Matthieu*, EtB (Paris: Gabalda, 1927), 2, made this point and yet the line of interpretation still persists, a fact recognized by Francis Wright Beare, *The Gospel according to Matthew: A Commentary* (Oxford: Blackwell, 1981), 64, when he says, "strange though it may seem to modern commentators, no moral stigma was attached to these women in Jewish tradition."

19   Susan Niditch, "The Wronged Woman Righted: An Analysis of Genesis 38," *HTR* 72 (1979): 147, points to the fact that in the narrative "Tamar, disguised as an ordinary harlot, is not condemned or threatened. When Tamar, the daughter-in-law, is found to be pregnant, however, she is accused of harlotry and is in serious danger of losing her life."

20   A similar explanation of Tamar's story is found in James G. Williams, *Women Recounted: Narrative Thinking and the God of Israel*, Bible and Literature Series 6 (Sheffield: Almond, 1982), 92-93, 102-103; Berlin, *Poetics and Interpretation*, 41; and Alter, *Art of Biblical Narrative*, 3-11.

21   Niditch, "Wronged Woman Righted," 147, and Alice Laffey, *An Introduction to the Old Testament: A Feminist Perspective* (Philadelphia: Fortress, 1988), 86-87, comment on the patriarchal legitimation of prostitution. See also Phyllis A. Bird, "The Harlot as Heroine: Narrative Art and Social Presupposition in Three Old Testament Texts," *Semeia* 46 (1989): 119-132.

22   It is in these two chapters that this same designation is used for Bathsheba. From the time that her identity is made known to David (2 Sam 11:3) until the death of her child (2 Sam 12:23), she is called אֵשֶׁת אוּרִיָּה or simply הָאִשָּׁה. It seems to be this story of Bathsheba and not the subsequent account of 1 Kgs 1:1-31 to which the narrator wants to draw the reader's attention.

of the biblical author is the displeasure of "the Lord" with David (2 Sam 11:27) and his sin (2 Sam 12:7-13).

The classification of the four women as *foreigners* reflects an androcentric perspective which sees women as outsiders to the patriarchal world and culture.[24] While this explanation may have more basis in the Hebrew Scriptures than the former,[25], together with the former, it allows for no link between these four women and Mary, reference to whom also breaks the genealogical pattern (v. 16) even though this final break differs in form.

The third explanation does, in fact, acknowledge links between the four women and Mary, a factor which seems to be in keeping with the hints provided in the narrative by the five-fold breaking of a narrative pattern. In terms of the articulation of those links, however, while a feminist critique may affirm the direction in which they point, it requires a different expression which brings to light the androcentrism in both the text and its interpretation. We have seen above in the discussion of the categorization of the four women as sinners that, on the one hand, such an accusation could not be supported in the text but, on the other hand, each of the women, at some point in her story, is in a situation which renders her dangerous to the patriarchal system, an anomaly.[26] To explain the inclusion of such women

---

23 Berlin, *Poetics and Interpretation*, 25-27, analyzes the story of Bathsheba in 2 Sam 11-12, which, she says, "leads us to view Bathsheba as a complete non-person. She is not even a minor character, but simply part of the plot." She goes on from this to draw a conclusion similar to that which will conclude my line of argument here: "... she is not considered guilty of adultery. She is not an equal party to the adultery, but only the means whereby it was achieved."

24 This classification has found its recent support in Robert H. Gundry, *Matthew: A Commentary on His Literary and Theological Art* (Grand Rapids: Eerdmans, 1982), 14-15; P. Benoit, *L'évangile selon saint Matthieu*, La sainte Bible de Jérusalem, 3rd ed. (Paris: Cerf, 1961), 39; Boismard, *Synopse*, 64; Durand, *Evangile*, 4; Plummer, *Exegetical Commentary*, 2; Lagrange, *Evangile*, 1; Leopold Sabourin, *L'Evangile selon saint Matthieu et ses principaux parallèles* (Rome: Biblical Institute, 1978), 19; and Ernst Lohmeyer, *Das Evangelium des Matthäus*, KEK, rev. W. Schmauch (Göttingen: Vandenhoeck & Ruprecht, 1956), 5.

25 The ancestry of Tamar is unclear from the text, but Ruth and Rahab are clearly designated as outside the nation of Israel--a Moabite and a Canaanite--and the designation of Bathsheba as τοῦ Οὐρίου seems to point to her ethnic background since Uriah was a Hittite. For some of the arguments illustrating the inadequacy of this theory, see Raymond E. Brown, Karl P. Donfried, Joseph A. Fitzmyer and John Reumann, eds., *Mary in the New Testament: A Collaborative Assessment by Protestant and Roman Catholic Scholars* (London: Geoffrey Chapman, 1978), 79-80.

26 This notion of woman as anomaly is discussed from a general anthropological perspective by Rosaldo, "A Theoretical Overview," 31-34, and by Jacob Neusner, "From Scripture to Mishnah: The Origins of Mishnah's Division of Women," *JJS* 30 (1979): 139-140, and idem, "Thematic or Systemic Description: The Case of the Mishnah's Division of Women," in *Method and Meaning in Ancient Judaism*, Brown Judaic Studies 10 (Missoula: Scholars, 1979), 96-100, in relation to Judaism. Woman is

as "extraordinary or irregular" is to support a form of gender politics in which women are recognized only when they are problems. To claim such "problems" as important within "God's plan" especially when that God is identified with patriarchy is to support the androcentric perspective of the biblical stories in which the four women's dangerous situation is brought back under patriarchal control.[27] It is also to fail to recognize that in none of the women's stories does God intervene on behalf of the woman as so often happens in the stories of the male biblical heroes.

The fourth explanation is closely related to both the first and the third and therefore carries much the same critique with the exception that the sin or the irregularity is named as illegitimacy. In attempting to explain the presence of the women, its proponents presume that the women are the vehicles of this illegitimacy, once again anomalies to the patriarchal world.

b. A Narrative Critique

From a narrative perspective, the inclusion of the references to five women within the genealogy must be seen "in function of the whole genealogy."[28] It was noted above that the genealogy is a direct commentary by the narrator under the title βίβλος γενέσεως. As such, it begins to establish the authority of the narrator who draws on a biblical phrase (Gen 2:4a and 5:1) and interprets it by means of the genealogy.[29] It establishes Jesus in the biblical tradition, among the sons of Abraham and the male descendants of David. The reader is surprised, therefore, to find the orderly patrilineage broken by the name of

---

        dangerous to the patriarchal system at those points when she is not properly related to man either in marriage or as daughter.

27   This is the last of four conclusions regarding the four women from the Hebrew Scriptures that is drawn by Schaberg, *Illegitimacy of Jesus*, 33. Anderson, "Mary's Difference," 188, explains the same phenomenon as "domesticating female difference".

28   Brian M. Nolan, *The Royal Son of God: The Christology of Matthew 1-2 in the Setting of the Gospel*, OBO 23 (Éditions Universitaires/Göttingen: Vandenhoeck & Ruprecht, 1979), 62, n. 3, makes this point but goes on to suggest that it must also be seen in function of the Gospel's theology, but this latter criterion is more in keeping with the redaction-critical analysis which will be undertaken in the subsequent chapter.

29   Horton, "Parenthetical Pregnancy," 178. This phrase βίβλος γενέσεως is used in Gen 2:4a either as the close of the Priestly account of creation (Gen 1:1-2:4a) or as the opening of the Yahwist account (Gen 2:4b-3:24). In either case it refers to narrative. In 5:1 it heads a genealogical table of Adam. Robert B. Robinson, "Literary Functions of the Genealogies of Genesis," *CBQ* 48 (1986): 595-608, discusses the complex and reciprocal relationship between genealogy and narrative in the biblical material, indicating that the nature of genealogy is elemental and orderly while narrative contains much more uncertainty. For a more extensive treatment of this relationship, see Robert Wilson, *Genealogy and History in the Biblical World*, Yale Near Eastern Researches 7 (New Haven/London: Yale University Press, 1977).

a woman (1:3), and another two (1:5), another (1:6) and concluded in a completely different form (1:16). Since the narrator is already beginning to be authoritative such breaks also bear the mark of this authority and the reader is alerted to the presence of women in Israel's history and Jesus' ancestry but also to that presence breaking the orderly patterning of that history. In this respect, explanations three and four can be accepted from a narrative perspective since they are in keeping with the very function of the genealogy but the first and second seem to be alien to that function.[30]

That the purpose of the genealogy is the establishing of Jesus, the Χριστός, as υἱός Δαυίδ and υἱός 'Αβραάμ (Matt 1:1) is confirmed for the reader by the repetition in v. 17 of the title Χριστός and the names of 'Αβραάμ and Δαυίδ. Any explanation of the presence of the women which the reader has supplied must be examined in terms of this reaffirmation of purpose.

2. An Inclusive Re-reading

Matthew's gospel opens with an account of Israel's history from an androcentric perspective and as such, it supports patriarchy. This history is also presented, according to the biblical vision, as the vehicle of God's promises to Israel. These promises are, therefore, understood from the same androcentric perspective and in support of patriarchy. With the introduction of the names of five women (vv. 3, 5, 6, 16), however, that exclusive symbolism is broken.[31] The reader must consider the presence and significance of women within Israel's sacred history[32] and hence is invited to read the presence of women into the silences surrounding the thirty-five begettings from which they are absent in the text.

---

30 This is not to deny that the gospel presents Jesus as the saviour of sinners (see already 1:21) or of the Gentiles (witness the gentile response to Jesus in 2:1-12), but it supports the claim that hints and development of these themes seem to belong later in the gospel rather than in relation to the presence of the five women in the genealogy. Their presence serves another function.
31 Dan O. Via, "Narrative World and Ethical Response: The Marvelous and Righteousness in Matthew 1-2," *Semeia* 12 (1978): 132, makes a parenthetical reference to the significance of the femaleness of the women apart from any other explanation given to their presence. François Martin, "Parole écriture accomplissement dans l'évangile de Matthieu," *Semiotique et Bible* 50 (1988): 36, on the other hand, points to the inadequacy of the symbolism which ignores women: "L'écriture, gardant une mémoire insistante des noms symboliquement transmis du père au fils, tend à oublier et à ignorer la chair sur laquelle viennent s'écrire ces traces ... la mère et l'épouse brisent la continuité exclusive et immédiate du père au fils."
32 Except for Bathsheba, each of the women is named and as such is given a specific identity within Israel's history, see Sternberg, *Poetics*, 330.

That the narrator does not name Sarah, Rebekah, Leah and Rachel and the other women who had a place in the messianic lineage raises questions for the feminist reader why only four particular women are specified. It suggests that it is not patriarchal affirmation of motherhood of significant sons which their inclusion encodes. Rather, the anomalous or dangerous situation of each of the women, at a certain point, places her outside of a patriarchal marriage or family structure. Each one's actions threaten this structure further. Tamar puts off her widow's garments and sits by the roadside awaiting Judah (Gen 38:14). Rahab, named harlot, dwells in her own home outside her patriarchal family structure (Josh 2:2). Ruth goes down to the threshing floor where she uncovers the feet of Boaz (Ruth 3:7); and the wife of Uriah comes to David, one of the few actions attributed to her in the entire story (2 Sam 11:4). While the patriarchal narrative quickly domesticates these actions, they can also be seen to encode aspects of women's power. God's messianic plan unfolds in and through such power. The women's presence functions, therefore, as a critique of patriarchy and introduces a point of tension into the narrative that must guide the reader as the story unfolds.[33]

This seems to be even more the case in v. 16--"Ἰακὼβ δὲ ἐγέννησεν τὸν Ἰωσὴφ τὸν ἄνδρα Μαρίας, ἐξ ἧς ἐγεννήθη Ἰησοῦς ὁ λεγόμενος χριστός." Joseph, the male, is not the subject of the verb ἐγέννησεν as is expected, but rather, he is identified in terms of his relationship to a woman [τὸν ἄνδρα

---

33   Schaberg, *Illegitimacy of Jesus*, 32-33, claims "that society was patriarchal, that this caused suffering for women in certain circumstances, and that certain women and men sometimes rectified or manipulated those circumstances in extraordinary ways to lessen the suffering." She says later, p. 211, n. 60, with reference to this statement: "Whether that flash of awareness which some claim to detect in the Bible is sometimes suppressed evidence for what appears to be woman's point of view, or one more literary strategy to promote patriarchal ideology, is one of the most important points to be debated by feminist critics." A number of scholars have, in fact, associated the presence of the women in the genealogy with the Matthean theme of discontinuity within continuity: Donald Senior, "The Ministry of Continuity: Matthew's Gospel and the Interpretation of History," *BiTod* 82 (1976): 670-676; W. G. Thompson in an article co-authored with Eugene LaVerdiere, "New Testament Communities in Transition: A Study of Matthew and Luke," *TS* 37 (1976): 567-582; John P. Meier, *Matthew*, New Testament Message 3 (Dublin: Veritas, 1980), xi-xii, 4-5; and idem, *The Vision of Matthew: Christ, Church, and Morality in the First Gospel*, Theological Inquiries (New York/Ramsey/London: Paulist, 1978), 30. None of these, however, have made reference to the fact that the elements of continuity are heavily linked to patriarchy and that the stories of women provide an element of discontinuity within such a structure. This link has been made most recently, however, by Crosby, *House of Disciples*, 87: "Thus through Joseph the patriarchal line continued. But through the woman, Mary, a new house-ordering would be established in the life and work of Jesus."

Μαρίας].[34] Only Mary, the woman, is associated with the birthing of Jesus, the Messiah. Since she is linked symbolically with the four women from the Hebrew Scriptures, the reader is then faced with many questions. What is the dangerous or anomalous situation of Mary since she is said to have a husband but he is not linked to the birth of Jesus? How does her situation critique patriarchy? How too is it embraced by the patriarchal system and domesticated? How does she give birth to Jesus and how is he incorporated into the messianic line when v. 16 seems to undercut the very purpose of the genealogy? The ambiguity and the tension in the narrative that this verse creates are addressed in 1:18-25.

B. 1:18-25

The narrator continues to address the reader at the beginning of this section, and by the use of γένεσις[35] and Ἰησοῦ Χριστοῦ in the opening phrase the link to the genealogy is clear.[36] The reader is also given information at the outset

---

34 Apart from 1:19 which contains a similar reference, there is no other evidence in the Christian Scriptures of a man being identified in terms of his marital relationship to a woman. Other references occur which contain the phrase "her husband" but in each of these, it is not a phrase used to actually identify the man (Mark 10:12; John 4:16-18; 1 Cor 7:2, 3, 10, 13, 14, 34 and 39). Perhaps the textual variants put forward in some manuscripts for 1:16 stress even further the uniqueness of this identification in Matthew. Several witnesses (θ f^{13} it^a, it$^{(b)}$, c, d, (k), q), change the phrase to "Joseph to whom being betrothed the virgin Mary ..."; and the Sinaitic Syriac manuscript makes a similar change, "to whom was betrothed Mary the virgin." These manuscripts seem to change the identification of Joseph to bring it more into line with the patriarchal character of the genealogy. See Bruce Metzger, *A Textual Commentary on the Greek New Testament*, 3rd ed. (New York: United Bible Societies, 1975), 2-7, and also Boismard, *Synopse*, 64, where it is suggested that the variants originated in order to avoid the phrase which was in the original text.

35 A small number of manuscripts [L f^{13} 𝔐] have the variant reading γέννησις but γένεσις finds the most support. For a discussion of various interpretations of its use, see Waetjen "The Genealogy as Key," 217.

36 Boismard, *Synopse*, 65, describes this pericope thus: "Exposé didactique plus que description pittoresque, cette péricope veut répondre à la question soulevée par le v. 16 ..." Waetjen, "Genealogy as Key," 217, says that "the gospel, however, must be read from 1:1 to 1:16 and then on to 1:18-25 ... 1:16 must be permitted to remain ambiguous ... (such) ambiguity...demands clarification, and ... this is the purpose of 1:18-25." Herman Hendrickx, *The Infancy Narratives* (Manila: East Asian Pastoral Institute, 1975), 15, warns against the scholarly tendency to draw a line between 1:17 and 1:18-25. The link is also stressed by W. Grundmann, *Das Evangelium nach Matthäus*, ThHK I, 2nd ed. (Berlin: Evangelische Verlagsanstalt, 1971), 66; Krister Stendahl, "Quis et Unde? An Analysis of Matthew 1-2," in *The Interpretation of Matthew*, ed. Graham Stanton, Issues in Religion and Theology 3 (Philadelphia: Fortress/London: SPCK, 1983), 60-61; and Meier, *Vision*, 54. Schaberg, *Illegitimacy of Jesus*, 41, extends this to claim that the narrative of 1:18-25 elucidates not only v. 16 but also v.17 of the

that is not available to Joseph, the main character in this section of the narrative: Mary is with child ἐκ πνεύματος ἁγίου.[37] The similarity of this phrase to Pattern 2 above [ἐκ τῆς ...] continues the theme introduced into the genealogy of the presence and power of women which threatens the patriarchal familial structure and which is an essential contributing factor to the unfolding of Israel's history and the maintenance of its messianic line. There is a difference here, however, in that the ἐκ is not followed by a reference to the female partner in a birthing situation. The woman Mary is already named as the one who will give birth to Jesus. Rather the power and presence that it heralds is that of a spirit which is holy and it alerts the reader to the association of the divine with this story of a woman which threatens the prevailing ethos. No mention is made of a male begetting agent.[38] A similar phrase is then repeated within the angelic message (1:20).

At verse 19, however, the focus shifts to Joseph. The narrator tells the reader that Joseph is δίκαιος, just and righteous or living according to the law.[39] The reader is inclined, therefore, to identify with the androcentric perspective despite the information already offered.[40] This perspective is further emphasized by the narrator's providing the reader with Joseph's point of view which involves suspicions of Mary's fidelity and a decision to divorce her quietly to preserve the male system of "justice". Joseph, as male, sees

---

genealogy. I do not think, however, that she has adequately shown that the substitution of a biological father into the third set of 13 generations allows us to count 14 generations unless Joseph as legal father is considered one and the proposed biological father another, but this does not seem to be in accord with the pattern of the genealogy. Nor, therefore, do I think that the text can support her claim that the "narrative *tells* [emphasis mine] us that someone other than Joseph was the biological father of Jesus." The narrative may hint at this as a possibility but it does not seem to *tell* us that.

37   For a survey of the use of this and related phrases in the LXX, see Waetjen, "The Genealogy as Key," 220-224.

38   Horton, "Parenthetical Pregnancy," 179-183, analyzes references in the Hebrew Scriptures to God's involvement in the conception and birth of human persons and the frequent lack of reference to the agency of a human father which does not mean absence of this agency. He says later, p. 188, that for the implied reader the twice repeated ἐκ πνεύματος ἁγίου "in no sense speaks clearly to the issue of unchastity but only argues that the unborn child represents the will of God." Schaberg, *Illegitimacy of Jesus*, 36, also concludes from her study of this phrase that divine and human begetting are not necessarily mutually exclusive. Brown et al., *Mary*, 93, point out that there is also no reference to God as the male partner. See also, Brown, *Birth of the Messiah*, 124: "There is never a suggestion in Matthew or in Luke that the Holy Spirit is the male element in a union with Mary, supplying the husband's role in begetting. Not only is the Holy Spirit not male (feminine in Hebrew; neuter in Greek), but also the manner of begetting is implicitly creative rather than sexual."

39   BAGD, 195.

40   Schaberg, *Illegitimacy of Jesus*, 45, suggests that because of the lack of clarity of meaning associated with the reference to the holy spirit, readers would readily identify with Joseph's dilemma.

himself as authorized to interpret the law in relation to a woman without her participation.[41] He alone receives the divine revelation[42] and in response to it incorporates the woman Mary, who is in an anomalous situation with regard to the patriarchal marriage structure, back into that structure--καὶ παρέλαβεν τὴν γυναῖκα (1:24). Joseph also names the child according to the divine command thus establishing him firmly as υἱὸς Δαυίδ, the culmination of the genealogy. Within this entire story, Mary is marginalized. She is spoken about by either the narrator or the divine messenger, but she is given no speech herself, no independent action of hers is recorded,[43] nor do we gain any insight into her point of view. Her role, however, is crucial; so crucial that this story must be considered a "kernel" within the narrative because without the birth of Jesus from this woman, the story would not proceed.

The narrator directly addresses the reader again in vv. 22-23 providing the reader with a reliable interpretation of the events by means of the first of the fulfilment quotations.[44] Here, in contrast to vv. 19-20, fulfilment is linked to the woman and the child she conceives, and again no reference is made in the text to a male partner. It is the child of this woman (here referred to as παρθένος) who is Ἐμμανουήλ and in whom God is present not just to Israel but to the indefinite multitude who are subject of the verb καλέσουσιν.[45] The introduction of this quotation seems to support not the continuity of patriarchy in and through this birth as vv. 19-20 suggest but rather its rupture or critique in accordance with the counter theme

---

41 Ibid., 42-62, discusses in detail the legal situation that Matthew depicts.
42 In the Hebrew Scriptures, the male is generally the recipient of the divine message. The significant exceptions are Hagar (Gen 16:7-12); the annunciation type-scenes (e.g. Gen 25:22-23); and the unnamed woman who is wife of Manoah and mother of Samson (Jud 13:3-5). Mary is therefore marginalized in the narrative when Joseph is the one to receive the announcement of the birth of a child who is holy to God.
43 Anderson, "Mary's Difference," 189-190. Schaberg, *Illegitimacy of Jesus*, 59, states this even more strongly: "Mary is spoken of by Matthew almost always in the passive. She is never addressed, makes no decision, and performs no action on her own. It is difficult for the reader to identify with her character in this Gospel, without an effort to imagine the horror of her situation, an effort Matthew does not really encourage the reader to make."
44 For an extensive discussion of this first fulfilment or formula quotation, see George M. Soares Prabhu, *The Formula Quotations in the Infancy Narrative of Matthew: An Inquiry into the Tradition History of Mt 1-2*, AnBib 63 (Rome: Biblical Institute Press, 1976), 229-253; K. Stendahl, *The School of St. Matthew and Its Use of the Old Testament* (Philadelphia: Fortress, 1968), 97-99; Robert Gundry, *The Use of the Old Testament in St. Matthew's Gospel with Special Reference to the Messianic Hope*, NT.S 18 (1967; reprint, Leiden: Brill, 1975), 89-90 and 226-227; and Brown, *Birth of the Messiah*, 143-153.
45 The LXX text of Is 7:14 has the second person singular καλέσεις.

introduced in the genealogy and v. 18. Hence within this pericope as in the genealogy, the strong theme of continuity which links Jesus' origin into the patriarchal history of Israel, a history in which God's promises are seen to unfold, is brought into tension with a counter-theme of discontinuity, whereby happenings outside of the traditional patriarchal structure are also named as holy.

1. Present State of Research

The scholarship relating to this section of Matthew's prologue is indeed vast and no attempt will be made here to try to summarize it.[46] Rather, I shall simply highlight two interpretations which form a general consensus and a third more recent explanation.

The first of these focusses on Joseph, his Davidic descent, and his naming of Jesus thus providing him with legal paternity in the line of David. In accord with this emphasis, the formula quotation of v. 23 simply provides another title for the Davidic son ['Ἐμμανουήλ] which underlines further his messianic role.[47] Such an approach also affirms the androcentric perspective of the text itself.

A second emphasis in the history of scholarship has been the virginal conception to which the text is believed to make reference even if obscurely.[48] Most modern commentators would consider the two-fold use of the phrase ἐκ πνεύματος ἁγίου (1:18, 20, with slight variation in v. 20) as an indication of a virginal conception.[49] Also the Matthean use of Isa 7:14 in which the Hebrew הָעַלְמָה is translated into Greek as παρθένος or virgin is considered evidence for belief in a virginal conception which antedated the composition of the Matthean gospel.[50]

A more recent explanation of Matt 1:18-25 has been given by Jane Schaberg. She considers that the Matthean use of ἐκ πνεύματος ἁγίου and the formula quotation from Isa 7:14 is part of an attempt to give a theological explanation to an illegitimate pregnancy that is already hinted at in the

---

46   A bibliography can be found in Brown, *Birth of the Messiah*, 163-164, and its update in idem, "Gospel Infancy Narrative Research from 1976 to 1986: Part I (Matthew)," *CBQ* 48 (1986): 481-482.
47   Stendahl, "Quis et Unde?" 61-62. A more extensive bibliography of this aspect of scholarship is provided in Brown, *Birth of the Messiah*, 512.
48   Brown gives as the heading of this section, "The Conception of Jesus", ibid., 122.
49   Ibid., 124-125, 160-161. In Brown et al, *Mary*, 89-91, however, the phrase is explained in terms of christological reflection moving back from the resurrection through the life of Jesus to the point of his conception.
50   Ibid., 91-97.

references to the four women from the Hebrew Scriptures, and in vv. 16 and
17. She sums up her position thus:

> The virgin betrothed and seduced or raped is, in the great Matthean paradox,
> the virgin who conceives and bears the child they will call Emmanuel. His
> origin is ignominious and tragic. But Matthew's point is that his existence is
> divinely willed and even predicted. That although--or even *because* --he
> was born in that way, the claim of his messiahship was not thereby negated.
> It was, rather, in some strange way strengthened.[51]

Schaberg's approach has already incorporated a feminist critique, but as we
turn now to a similar critique of the other two major emphases within
scholarship, we will also consider aspects of her interpretation.

a. A Feminist Critique

The theological emphasis on Joseph, his Davidic descent and the
incorporation of Jesus into Joseph's patrilineage are all in accord with the
androcentric and patriarchal perspectives within the text itself. Joseph is the
means by which the rupture introduced into the patrilineage by verse 16 is
repaired. Jesus is truly son of David because Joseph who is addressed by that
title names him. He also incorporates Mary and her anomalous conception
into the context of the patriarchal familial structure. It is this structure which
is implicit throughout almost the whole of Matt 2.[52] This stream of scholarship therefore generally fails to take account of the tension introduced into
the narrative in vv. 18 and 23 and simply incorporates these verses into the
androcentric explanation as Joseph did Mary into the patriarchal structure.

In most interpretations, this explanation is closely linked to that of
virginal conception, thus incorporting the latter into the patriarchal framework of the former. From a feminist perspective, however, the account of
Mary's conception of Jesus without reference to male begetting could function as a most profound critique of the androcentric perspective of the
genealogy, which symbolizes woman as vehicle of reproduction and hence
invisible in the sphere of history, and which makes the male the principal

---

51 Schaberg, *Illegitimacy of Jesus*, 72-73.
52 Brief reference is made to Mary in Matt 2, but except for v. 11 where the wise men find
    only the child with Mary his mother, throughout the remainder, Joseph is presented as
    the agent and the mother and child are passive (Matt 2:13, 14, 20, 21). From a feminist
    perspective and in the light of the work of Michael H. Crosby, *House of Disciples*, 11-12,
    who sees "house" as the assumed primary metaphor in the gospel, we find Mary with
    her son who is being worshipped by the foreign wise men in the first "house" context
    within the gospel. Woman is, therefore, linked initially to the house metaphor and its
    function within the symbolic universe of the narrative.

begetting agent. According to the narration, a woman who is named παρθένος is with child and the child is named holy. The reproductive power of woman and her role in the birth of the Messiah is affirmed outside of the patriarchal structure. This would explain the significant break in the genealogy at v. 16 and the anomalous situation of Mary which would link her to the four women from the Hebrew Scriptures. In none of the traditional interpretations, however, do we find this anomalous birth interpreted as a critique of patriarchy or of Israel's support of patriarchy within its unfolding story. Rather the action of God is understood from within the androcentric perspective of the narrative. Mary is simply the vehicle of reproduction.[53]

Jane Schaberg's feminist reading of 1:18-25 also leads her to the conclusion that "God "acts" in a radically new way, outside the patriarchal norm" but for her it is within the normal event of human begetting.[54] She emphasizes the siding of God with the endangered woman and child, a point which is significant for the interpretation of the text even if one does not accept her claim of an illegitimate pregnancy.[55]

2. An Inclusive Re-reading

An inclusive re-reading of 1:18-25, brings to awareness the violence done to the woman, Mary, either by rape or seduction if one accepts the theory of an illegitimate pregnancy and/or by the patriarchal law which assumes her guilty and therefore to be divorced by the just male. It is, however, with this woman who is endangered within patriarchal society and law and with her child that God sides. In fact, her reproductive power is affirmed by its

---

53   This critique is necessarily brief because a thorough feminist critique of the theological doctrine of the virginal conception and birth of Jesus that has emerged as an interpretation of the Matthean text would be an enormous undertaking beyond the scope of this work and out of proportion to the brief Matthean allusions in vv. 18 and 23. This is not to indicate that such an undertaking is not necessary or that it is trivial but rather it is to acknowledge the importance and urgency of it and the enormity of its scope. We find the beginnings of it in Schüssler Fiorenza, "Feminist Theology as Critical Theology," 44-48; Ruether, *Sexism and God-Talk*, 139-158; Mary Daly, *Pure Lust: Elemental Feminist Philosophy* (London: The Women's Press, 1984), 91-121; and Schaberg, *Illegitimacy of Jesus*, 9-14, although each of these focusses on the doctrine generally as it has functioned within christian history rather than on the interpretations specifically arising from the Matthean text.

54   Ibid., 74.

55   The work of Schaberg makes clear the enigmatic nature of the Matthean text and the extreme difficulty of establishing the historicity of either an illegitimate pregnancy or a virginal birth from the text and from its silences. See my brief critique of one of her claims which seems to read more into the silences than they can carry in n. 36 above.

narrative association with a spirit which is named "holy" so that the child to be born of her is to be called "God with us". It is this son of Mary who will later in the gospel be called "son of God".[56]

Such a reading offers a powerful critique of the androcentric perspective of the narrative with its focus on Joseph.[57] It enables the reader to be guided by gender differences which are not only female but male and female. The male and female contributions to the birth of Jesus are different but each is significant.[58] The Holy One whom the narrative claims is present and powerful in this birth is linked with both these contributions.

This reading against the grain of the narrative alerts the reader to the tension within the first chapter of the prologue when traditions which affirm the power and presence of women within Israel's history and the birth of its Messiah are introduced into a narrative which is predominantly androcentric, supportive of patriarchal familial structures and laws and which tends to render women invisible. It recognizes the symbolic significance of female gender whereby woman is considered anomalous and to be brought into the patriarchal order and under patriarchal control; but at the same time, the reader is aware that the narrative affirms a power and presence of women which critiques patriarchal exclusion.[59] Significant narrative clues

---

56 Most scholars hold that Jesus is not called "son of God" until 2:15 in Matthew's gospel but there are hints of it already in 1:18-25. It must also be acknowledged that the child is still son, a male heir and hence a certain ambivalence remains even within the feminist critique.

57 For an excellent summary of the androcentric perspective of this text see Schaberg, *Illegitimacy of Jesus*, 74-75.

58 For a very thorough study of these differences within the language and structuring of the text, see Martin, "Parole," 35-45.

59 This raises again one of the significant points of tension which faces feminist biblical scholars. It is well represented by two articles which are placed side by side in Collins, *Feminist Perspectives*. Nelly Furman, "His Story versus Her Story: Male Genealogy and Female Strategy in the Jacob Cycle," 107-116, illustrates how the stories of women in the Hebrew Scriptures can function like myths to provide acceptable channels for expressing discontent. Her focus is on the element of disruption or discontinuity that such stories introduce into the narrative as a whole. Fuchs, "Literary Characterization," 118, stresses how these stories of discontinuity have been co-opted by the male authors into a predominantly patriarchal narrative so that "the author's point of view determines the ideological framework of the story even when it seems to be altogether absent from it." While each of these positions represents an aspect of the narrative, if pushed to their extremes, they render a cohesive feminist reading impossible. A solution to this dilemma, however, is found in a third essay in the same collection by T. Drorah Setel, "Feminist Insights and the Question of Method," 35-42. Drawing on the feminist concern with "connection and relationship" she seeks the application of these principles to our historical perspective. Practically, this means that rather than positing a separation between patriarchal framework and disruptive/discontinuous story, we seek the relationships between them which will demand "an extension of the text beyond the written word, placing it within a perspective inclusive of female and other non-elite experience," the task already set for this entire study.

are therefore provided which must guide the reader through the rest of the
gospel. Questions are also raised regarding the origin of these counter traditions. From where did the tradition arise which linked the names of the four
women from the Hebrew Scriptures and linked them with Mary? Why
would such traditions be included in a narrative which supports strong
androcentric and patriarchal perspectives? What would such traditions seek
to support ideologically in the Matthean community? These and other
questions which are beyond the scope of this narrative analysis will need to
be addressed in subsequent chapters. We turn now, however, to the next
significant movement within the story.

II. THE PREACHING OF THE BASILEIA - 4:17-10:42

> From that time Jesus began to preach, saying,
> "Repent, for the βασιλεία τῶν οὐρανῶν is at hand."

(Matt 4:17)

These words of the narrator, and the pericope to which they are attached,
which tells of the arrest of John (4:12) and Jesus' withdrawal into Galilee
(4:13),   provide   a transition for the reader from the prologue, which was
concerned with the identity of Jesus in his infancy and preparation for ministry, to the ministry itself. In this section (4:17-10:42), the reading process is
influenced by means of the frames around the narrative section as well as by
plot and character development.

The arrest of John which frames, at its beginning, the section which I
have called "The Preaching of the *Basileia*", continues the *conflict* which
has already characterized the narrative to this point as seen in Herod's
search for the child and slaying of the infants (Matt 2), John's eschatological
preaching (3:7-12), and Jesus' struggle with the devil in the wilderness (4:1-
11).[60] At its closure, the section is also framed by a further reference to John

---

60   Rhoads and Michie, *Mark as Story*, 73, address the significance of conflict in the
     development of plot: "The events and actions of a story often involve conflict, for con-
     flict is the heart of most stories. Without conflict, most stories would be only a
     sequence of events strung together without tension or suspense or struggle on the part
     of the characters." They go on to suggest that the origin of the conflict lies in the very
     nature of God's *basileia*. Schüssler Fiorenza, *In Memory of Her*, 121-122, in a similar
     vein, speaks of the "tension points" of the Jesus movement with the dominant cul-
     ture, noting that these tension points must not be construed as anti-Jewish because

in prison (11:2), which will lead into a portion of the narrative in which the conflict between Jesus and his opponents mounts.[61] Since the presence of Jesus has already brought conflict, the reader is led to expect it also in the preaching of the βασιλεία by Jesus.[62]

Within this frame, the *plot* develops. The section opens with Jesus inviting four fishermen--Peter, Andrew, James and John--to follow him, and the commission given to them in the narrative is to be "fishers" of human persons [ἀνθρώπων] (4:18-22). They are named, called and commissioned, but left aside for the moment while the narrator provides the reader with a summary of Jesus' Galilean ministry (4:23-25) which will be told in full in subsequent chapters.

The activity of 4:18-5:1 gives way to the virtual halt in the narrative from 5:2-7:28 in which the reader is presented with Jesus' teaching of the nature of the βασιλεία.[63] The repetition in 8:1 of a phrase which closed the action in 4:25--"great crowds followed him" [ἠκολούθησαν αὐτῷ ὄχλοι πολλοί]--indicates the resumption of the narrative with Jesus subsequently performing a number of miracles, predominantly the healings already summarized in 4:23-24. The most significant impact of these four chapters on the reader is the establishment of Jesus as an authoritative teacher (7:28) and healer for the sake of the preaching of the *basileia*, a point further emphasized by the inclusion--4:23 and 9:35:

> And he went about all the cities and villages,
> *teaching* in their synagogues
> and *preaching* the gospel of the *basilaía*,

---

they are found similarly in the eschatological preaching of the prophets and John the Baptist. They are the tension points that one would expect of a renewal movement within Judaism.

61 The specific theme of conflict between Jesus and his opponents is treated in full by Jack Dean Kingsbury, "The Developing Conflict between Jesus and the Jewish Leaders in Matthew's Gospel: A Literary-Critical Study," *CBQ* 49 (1987): 57-73.

62 This is seen in the eschatological reversal of the beatitudes (5:10-12); the radical reinterpretation of Torah (5:21-48) and of δικαιοσύνη (6:1-18); various responses to the healing ministry of Jesus (8:11-12; 8:34; 9:3, 11, 34); and in the warnings given to those sent out on mission (10:16-39).

63 We see here one of the literary techniques characteristic of the Matthean narrative in which material of the same kind is gathered together (eg. the teaching of Jesus in 5-7; the miracles 8-9; the parables in 13 etc.). The content of Jesus' sermon will not be treated here but for further reference, see W. D. Davies, *The Setting of the Sermon on the Mount* (1963; reprint, Cambridge: University Press, 1966); idem, *The Sermon on the Mount* (Cambridge: University Press, 1966); Jan Lambrecht, *The Sermon on the Mount: Proclamation and Exhortation*, Good News Studies 14 (Wilmington, Del.: Michael Glazier, 1985); Pinchas Lapide, *The Sermon on the Mount: Utopia or Program for Action?* trans. Arlene Swidler (Maryknoll: Orbis, 1986); and Rudolf Schnackenburg, ed., *Die Bergpredigt: Utopische Vision oder Handlungsweisung?* (Düsseldorf: Patmos, 1982).

and *healing* every disease and every infirmity.

The section closes with Jesus' summoning of twelve male disciples who are subsequently named. He shares with them his own authority to preach and to heal (10:1, 7-8) and proleptically prepares them for a suffering that will be similar to his own.[64] The exclusive nature of this group around Jesus must certainly be given consideration in a feminist reading of the gospel. This will occur progressively as we encounter the group called "the twelve" in the narrative, but also it will be treated more extensively in the final chapter.

In the course of 4:17-10:42, the narrator introduces the reader to many *characters* and more significantly, *character groups* whose boundaries are not clearly defined at this point in the narrative but who are characterized in terms of their relationship to Jesus. The fluidity of character creates a certain suspense for the reader and is intended to guide the reading process especially in Matt 8 and 9, in which individual characters, their response to Jesus, and his response to them are central to the narrative.

The first group to whom the reader is introduced is the group of four fishermen whom Jesus calls and who follow him [ἠκολούθησαν αὐτῷ] (4:18-22). This group is supplemented by the great crowds [ὄχλοι] who also follow [ἠκολούθησαν] (4:25). In 5:1, a group called his disciples [οἱ μαθηταὶ αὐτοῦ] are distinguished from the crowd as the possible audience for the Sermon on the Mount but this distinction is blurred again in 7:28 where it is pointed out that it was the ὄχλοι who "heard all of these teachings".[65]

The reader must deal with the same phenomenon in Matt 8 and 9 which begins with the ὄχλοι continuing to follow Jesus. Out of these crowds, certain individuals and groups emerge: those sick with all kinds of diseases, the demon-possessed, the epileptics and the paralytics who are brought to Jesus in groups (8:16; 9:35; cf. 4:24) or as individuals (9:2, 32), or who themselves come to Jesus for healing (8:2; 9:20, 27). Of this large group whom

---

64   Culpepper, *Anatomy of the Fourth Gospel*, 61-70, discusses the use of prolepses within a narrative.

65   Pierre Bonnard, *L'Évangile selon saint Matthieu*, Commentaire du Nouveau Testament 1, Deuxième Série (Genève: Labor et Fides, 1982), 54, considers that the two groups are "mal défini" and Gundry, *A Commentary*, 66, says that Matthew uses them "interchangeably". Paul S. Minear, "The Disciples and the Crowds in the Gospel of Matthew," *AThRS* 3 (1974): 28-44, on the other hand, presents the two groups as much more clearly defined.

Anderson calls "supplicants",[66] some are lepers, others are blind or dumb, some are Gentiles and they include both women and men. Each person emerges from the crowd and stands before Jesus who responds in a variety of ways. It is this response which guides the reader's reaction to each character and group, and this guidance is enhanced by the implied author's arrangement of episodes and the comparisons and contrasts set up between characters and groupings. These narrative techniques will be very significant as we consider the women characters below.

As the section draws to a close, the reader's attention is directed again to Jesus' μαθηταί. The four fishermen whose call and response was related at the beginning of the section are now named at the head of a list of twelve male disciples [τοὺς δώδεκα μαθητὰς αὐτοῦ] whom Jesus commissions to share in his βασιλεία ministry (10:1-15). This group also includes the tax-collector Matthew, whom Jesus calls during his healing ministry (9:9). Given the fluidity of character grouping already noted in Matt 5-9, however, it is not clear whether these are all the disciples, whether they are the group referred to previously (5:1; 8:21, 23; 9:10, 11, 14, 19, 37), and whether this group is limited by gender.

The juxtaposition of these various groups and the reactions/responses of various people to the miracles of Jesus become the vehicles whereby the narrator's point of view is communicated, particularly in Matt 8 and 9. The early part of the prologue already established that the life of Jesus was an eschatological time, a time of fulfilment, when God was with God's people in a way which brought about, among other things, inclusion of those women marginalized by the dominant patriarchal culture. Jesus' ministry began with an eschatological proclamation: the βασιλεία, the presence and power of God, is at hand (4:17). The subsequent teaching and healing gives substance to this proclamation and the question which faces us here is whether this preaching of the βασιλεία, as it is presented in Matthew, is gender-inflected.

---

66 Anderson, "Gender and Reading," 10-11 and n. 25. Birger Gerhardsson, *The Mighty Acts of Jesus according to Matthew* (Lund: Gleerup, 1979), 43, uses this term for both the sick who come for healing and for those who bring them.

A. The Text

As in the genealogy which introduced the prologue, so too in the story of the
call of the four fishermen which introduces the preaching of the βασιλεία, the
reader is immersed in the androcentric perspective of the narrator. Those
who are first called and respond to Jesus are named and they are male.
Although, as we have seen, the use of μαθητής in Matt 5-9 is ambivalent,
Matt 10 specifically links the designation to twelve males. An underlying
androcentric assumption seems to be being made explicit: membership of
the significant character group called disciples presumes male gender.

The same is not true for the ὄχλοι. When this group is introduced
initially in 4:25, they too follow Jesus as did Peter, Andrew, James and John,
but there is no indication of gender distinctions. This inclusiveness is confirmed when supplicants emerge from the crowd and they are both female
and male as is seen in Diagram 2 below; but in keeping with the androcentric
perspective of the text, seven of the nine stories are concerned with male
supplicants. We find, therefore, indications of gender inflection in relation
to both the μαθηταί and the ὄχλοι. Both, however, seem to be conventional
in the sense that they are reflective of their patriarchal context, but may not
necessarily be explicitly supporting or promoting it.

Within such a perspective, the presence of the stories of three women
and their placement in terms of the structuring of the miracle stories seems
to be very specific. Our attention must now be directed to those stories and
their wider context in order to continue our gender reading.

1. Structure

As Diagram 2 below illustrates, this section of the narrative is structured into
three sections each containing three miracle stories.[67] A collection of small
narrative units and sayings form a "buffer" pericope between each

---

67   This structure emerged from a careful reading of the narrative with particular
     attention to characterization, but after consultation with other scholars, I have discov-
     ered that it most closely parallels the division given by Meier, *Matthew*, 79-101, and
     Beare, *A Commentary*, 201-202, except that both place 8:16-17 with 8:14-15. Both Nestle-
     Aland and Bible Society editions of the Greek text put the healing of Peter's mother-in-
     law together with the healing of the crowds at evening and head the section: "The
     Healing of Many". This acts to shift the focus from the healing of the woman in 8:14-15
     to healing in general and so obscures the woman and her story.

Recipient	Key Character Group Involved	Response	Respondant

Crowds Follow Jesus   (8:1)

* Leper (8:1-4)	Leper - Unclean (male)	"Say nothing to anyone Go - show yourself to the priest"	Jesus
* Centurion's servant (8:5-13)	Gentile/servant (male)	"As you believed - Let it be done to you"	Jesus
* Peter's mother-in-law (8:14-15)	Woman - ill (female)	Rose and served him	Woman

Healing of Many   (8:16-17)

[Buffer Pericope A]

Following Jesus   (8:18-22)

* Storm at Sea (8:23-27)	Disciples (male?)	"Men of Little Faith" "What sort of man is this?"	Jesus Disciples
* Gadarene Demoniacs (8:28-34)	Gentile - possessed (male)	"Go away!"	All the City
* Paralytic (9:1-8)	Sick (male)	Afraid/glorified God "He Blasphemes"	Crowd Scribes

Matthew - called & follows   (9:9-13)

[Buffer Pericope B]

Fasting/new wine-old skins   (9:14-17)

* Ruler's daughter + Woman with haemorr. (9:18-26)	Young girl/dead Woman / unclean (female)	Fame spread "Your faith has made you well"	Jesus
* Blind Men (9:27-31)	Sick (male)	"See no one knows it." Spread his fame	Jesus Men
* Dumb Demoniac (9:32-34)	Demon possessed (male)	Marvel Murmur	Crowd Pharisees

Compassion on the Crowds   (9:35-36)

Diagram 2

section.[68] The two miracle narratives concerning the healing of women[69] occur in strategic positions at the end of the first group of three and at the

---

68   This terminology is taken from Meier, *Matthew*, 80.

beginning of the third. The reader's understanding and interpretation of
these two miracle accounts, therefore, is influenced not only by the group to
which each belongs but also by the "buffer" pericope alongside which it has
been placed.

More specific attention will be given to the Buffer Pericopes A and B in
Chapter Four. Here they will be analyzed simply in terms of their narrative
relationship to their context and their gender inflection.

The first part of Buffer Pericope A (8:16-17) is a combination of a
summary of healings and a fulfilment quotation, both direct commentary by
the narrator. The summary points to Jesus' healing of "all" who were sick,
indicating the inclusive nature of this aspect of Jesus' preaching of the
βασιλεία, while the fulfilment quotation links it to the liberation trajectory
already visible within the prophetic literature of the Hebrew Scriptures and
recalled at the very beginning of the gospel in relation to the birth of Jesus.[70]
The two stories concerning the following of Jesus in 8:18-22 illustrate that
such following of this preacher of the βασιλεία means a break with the
patriarchal household as the basic economic and social unit of society.[71] The
inclusive and liberating nature of the βασιλεία is thereby linked to a break
with a particular patriarchal construct.

Inclusion and liberation are also significant themes in Buffer Pericope B.
The calling of Matthew (9:9) and the table companionship with tax collectors
and sinners (9:10-13) illustrate further the inclusive nature of the βασιλεία.
Not only those who are sick but also those whom the dominant culture considers unclean or pollutants are included in the circles around Jesus. The liberating nature of this activity of Jesus is emphasized for the reader by means
of the recalling of the Hosean text: "I desire mercy, and not sacrifice" (Hos

---

69 The healing of the ruler's daughter and of the woman with a haemorrhage are treated
    as one miracle narrative since the second has been incorporated into the story of the
    first very skilfully and it seems that it is intended to be read as one story. Jack P. Lewis,
    The Gospel according to Matthew, Part I: 1:1-13:52, LWC (Austin: Sweet, 1976), 188,
    notes that these miracles break the symmetry as one is placed in another. It may be that
    we have here another example of a broken pattern similar to what we saw in the
    genealogy, and again it is the stories of women which cause this break, directing the
    reader's attention to something different to the pervading androcentric perspective.

70 This will be developed further in Chapter Three in relation to the Matthean use of Isa
    7:14. The MT version of Isa 53:4 rather than the LXX or Targum Pseudo-Jonathan em-
    phasizes the very concrete nature of the healing action of Jesus as well as its symbol-
    ism. Both the LXX and the Targum present a much more spiritualized or symbolic in-
    terpretation of the text while the Matthean translation of the MT חֳלָיֵנוּ by τὰς
    ἀσθενείας and מַכְאֹבֵינוּ by τὰς νόσους is much more in keeping with the language of
    the gospel (4:23, 24; 9:35; 10:1). For a fuller treatment of this position, see Stendahl,
    School of Matthew, 106, and Gundry, *Use of the Old Testament*, 111.

71 Crosby, *House of Disciples*, 23-31.

6:6; Matt 9:13). The metaphoric language of unshrunk cloth and new wine in relation to old garments and old wineskins suggests that such inclusive and liberating activity brings tension, even rupture or discontinuity in relation to the prevailing ethos.

It seems clear that the two buffer pericopes provide an interpretive key not only for the miracles closest to them but for all the miracles in this section of the narrative. Their highlighting of the inclusive nature of the βασιλεία critiques the androcentric perspective of the narrative generally but also gives particular emphasis to the women's stories to which they are closely linked. Their liberation perspective draws attention to boundary breaking aspects of the miracle stories which bring tension and discontinuity. In relation to each miracle story, we must ask the question regarding the locus of this tension and discontinuity. Our concern, however, is with the three healing stories in which the supplicant is female.

2. 8:14-15

If structure guides reading, then the form of Matt 8:14-15 requires close attention.[72] The narrative is devoid of any unnecessary detail and the repetition of καί five times within two verses linking the five finite verbs focusses the reader's attention on the action and the characters involved. Jesus is the subject of the first two verbs, the healing forms the climax, and the woman who is healed becomes the actor in the final scene and is the subject of the two concluding verbs [see Diagram 3].

---

72 H. J. Held, "Matthew as Interpreter of the Miracle Stories," in *Tradition and Interpretation in Matthew*, 2nd ed., ed. G. Bornkamm, G. Barth and H. J. Held, and trans. Percy Scott (London: SCM, 1982), 167, claims that "one can hardly speak of a real story anymore" in relation to the miracle stories in Matthew. However, Antoinette Clark Wire, "The Structure of the Gospel Miracle Stories and Their Tellers," *Semeia* 11 (1978): 83-113, and Robert W. Funk, "The Form of the New Testament Healing Miracle Story," *Semeia* 12 (1978): 57-96, both propose ways of analysing the structure of the miracle stories which apply equally as well to the Matthean stories as to those of Mark or Luke. For a very clear example of the analysis of the structure of this specific story, see Gerhardsson, *Mighty Acts*, 40.

Καί ...   εἶδεν τὴν πενθερὰν αὐτοῦ ...)
)   Jesus
καὶ   ἥψατο τῆς χειρὸς αὐτῆς,   )

           καὶ   ἀφῆκεν αὐτὴν ὁ πυρετός   Fever

καὶ   ἠγέρθη   )
)   Woman
καὶ   διηκόνει αὐτῷ.   )

Diagram 3

As in the previous two miracle accounts, Jesus stands out as the chief actor and the focus is on his capacity to heal (8:2-3, 5-7). He sees the woman with a fever and touches her hand. The woman is not named but is identified simply in terms of her place in the patriarchal familial structure, she is the mother-in-law of Peter. She is also described as lying sick with a fever and hence is a possible pollutant especially if this sickness is connected to her time of ritual uncleanness. Jesus' simple action in reaching out and touching her breaks open the boundaries which defined "clean" and "unclean" thereby liberating the woman from her infirmity. But it is even more extraordinary that the narrative itself breaks open the pattern the reader expects in a miracle story because here Jesus takes the initiative, whereas normally in miracle accounts the person to be healed approaches Jesus and asks for healing or someone approaches on his or her behalf and makes the request.[73] As we saw in the genealogy, here also, a woman's story breaks a narrative pattern. A brief comparison between this miracle story and the two which precede it may give meaning to this break.

Each of the three characters in the first group of miracles is considered an outsider in terms of the socio-religious patterning of society: the leper is unclean socially and religiously; the Centurion is gentile; and Peter's mother-in-law is a woman and also a possible pollutant in this situation.[74] All three are denied access to the inner sanctuary of the Temple and are marginalized socially and religiously, a marginalization which is represented in the narrative. The leper kneels before Jesus and says, "Lord, if you will, you can make me clean" (8:2). The centurion proclaims, "Lord, I am not

---

73   There is no other miracle account in Matthew's gospel where Jesus takes the initiative and there are only two other accounts of a healing in which this occurs and they are both in Luke's gospel: the raising of the Widow's son at Nain (Luke 7:11-17), and the healing of a crippled woman on the Sabbath (Luke 13:10-13). In each of these examples, it is the plight of a woman which is the object of Jesus' compassion.
74   Christoph Burger, "Jesu Taten nach Matthäus 8 und 9," ZThK 70 (1973): 284.

worthy to have you come under my roof" (8:8). Finally, the woman's two-fold marginalization in a patriarchal culture is represented by her silence and her inability even to approach Jesus.[75]

Jesus, by way of response to each, breaks through the barriers placed around these supplicants. He touches the unclean leper saying, "I will; be clean" (8:3). Regarding the centurion, he makes this scandalous statement to the crowd who follow him, "Truly I say to you, not even in Israel have I found such faith" (8:10). When he sees the woman and recognizes her status, he takes the initiative, reaching out and touching her thereby specifically incorporating the marginalized woman within the liberating wholeness of the βασιλεία. The βασιλεία is being preached indeed. God is present with God's people who are being called to eschatological newness when the marginalized, who include women, are brought into the centre of the group around Jesus and they are liberated from their infirmities.

The brevity of the conclusion to the story of the healing of Peter's mother-in-law serves to focus the reader's attention on the two verbs associated with the woman. First, she arose [ἠγέρθη]. The form of the verb is the aorist passive whose meaning covers both the simple action of rising and also the action of being raised by another (even from the dead).[76] At this point in the narrative, the reader will probably understand the verb in its simple sense. Later, however, in the light of its use in the story of the raising of the young girl to life in 9:18-26, this reading may need to be supplemented by the symbolic sense.[77]

Secondly, the woman serves Jesus [διηκόνει αὐτῷ]. This can be understood to refer simply to the woman's service of Jesus at table.[78] The use of the verb in the imperfect, however, recalls for the reader the angels' service of Jesus after the temptations (4:11) where it suggested both the symbolic and the ongoing nature of the service. In 8:15, therefore, the verb may

---

75   This may be an encoding of an androcentric perspective which silences the voices of women thus rendering them invisible in the narrative.

76   BAGD, 215, 2 a-c.

77   With regard to 8:14-15, Sabourin, L'Evangile, 107, says, "L'interprétation théologique de l'épisode dépend dans une large mesure du sens donné au verbe egeirein, "mettre debout/réveiller". Très probablement, son emploi dans Mc et Mt contient une allusion au pouvoir qu'a Jésus de réveiller de la mort."

78   This is the understanding of Bonnard, Évangile, 117, who acknowledges that while the verb διακονεῖν has a rich christian meaning, in this verse (8:15), it simply means service at table, a service which he calls "service féminin". In such an interpretation we see a scholarly trend which refuses to allow for the possibility of women exercising a religious function in the community of the followers of Jesus and therefore translates διακονεῖν in one way when it refers to men and another when it refers to women.

be understood in a similar fashion and hence on a symbolic level. A glance forward in the story affirms such a reading. As the gospel continues, the verb διακονεῖν is used only three more times but very significantly. In 20:28, it is used by Jesus to characterize his mission and ministry when he says, "The Human One* came not to be served but to serve ..." It occurs in 25:44 in the judgment scene as a question to the Judge: "When did we see you ... and did not minister to you?" Here, it is considered central to the response of those called to and gifted with the βασιλεία of God according to the Matthean gospel.[79] Finally, it is used again of women, this time of those who follow Jesus from Galilee (27:55). Διακονεῖν, therefore, designates the ministry of Jesus and, as a consequence, must characterize the life of the followers of Jesus.[80] This suggests, therefore, a symbolic inference in relation to 8:15, but even without such a glance forward, a similar conclusion suggests itself within the immediate context.

When Jesus cleanses the leper, he instructs him to go and show himself to the priest and to offer the gift that Moses commanded (8:4), thereby acknowledging his restoration to the religious community of Israel.[81] Following Jesus' acknowledgment of the faith of the centurion, he says:

> I tell you, many will come from east and west and sit at table with Abraham, Isaac, and Jacob in the kingdom [βασιλεία] of heaven, while the children* of the kingdom [υἱοὶ τῆς βασιλείας] will be thrown into outer darkness ...
> (Matt 8:11-12)

The centurion represents those who will replace the religious community of Israel in the βασιλεία which Jesus is proclaiming. It would seem, therefore, to be in keeping with this narrative development that we read διηκόνει as indicating a symbolic or religious restoration for the woman also. She ministers to Jesus who is at the centre of the new religious community

---

79   It includes much more than "waiting at table", namely, giving food and drink to those in need, providing shelter and clothing to those without such necessities and visiting the sick and imprisoned.

80   Hermann Wolfgang Beyer, "διακονέω, κτλ.," *TDNT* II:81-93, illustrates how the use of this verb, which did not carry very dignified or acceptable connotations in ordinary Greek usage, gradually moved, within christian contexts both oral and written, from a simple designation of "waiting at table" to refer to the heart of christian discipleship which was a giving of oneself to others in love in a manner similar to Jesus' own gift. See also the analysis of this verb in the Markan gospel by Marla J. Selvidge, "Mark and Woman: Reflections on Serving," *Explorations* 1 (1982): 23-32.

81   Xavier Léon-Dufour, "La guérison de la belle-mère de Simon-Pierre," in *Etudes d'évangile*, Parole de Dieu 2 (Paris: Seuil, 1965), 131.

which he is inaugurating. This symbolic/religious interpretation is confirmed by the setting for the miracle. It is in the "house of Peter".[82]

3. 9:18-26

The second story of the healing of women also breaks the narrative pattern expected in healing stories. The reading of this pericope is guided by its structuring--the story of the healing of the woman with a haemorrhage is placed within the framework of the story of the healing of the ruler's daughter. The frame then provides the interpretive key for the enclosed story [Diagram 4].

As with 8:14-15, the story is streamlined so that the interaction between Jesus and the supplicant(s) is highlighted. The story of the fluteplayers intrudes simply to act as a contrast to the faith of both the ruler and the woman. It underscores the tension between the newness that is possible when people believe in the power of Jesus and the old view of reality that does not allow for the power and presence of God to enter life in this way.

The reader is taken by surprise at the beginning of the story by the extraordinary nature of the ruler's request. It goes far beyond that of any of the other miracles. It is a request to Jesus to come and lay his hands on a child who has already died. The request is even more extraordinary when one realizes that the child is not a son, an heir needed for the continuation of the patriarchal family line, but rather a daughter, a young unmarried girl as the latter part of the story indicates (v. 25 - κοράσιον). Moreover, the request is quite specific: "Come and lay your hand on her and she shall live" (9:18). It is a request that Jesus render himself ritually unclean because the child is dead.[83] Jesus' rising and following the ruler seems to indicate his intention to fulfil the request. Well may the reader ask at this point: is this what was meant by the new wine in fresh skins (9:17)?

---

82   In the Matthean gospel, the house [οἶκος, οἰκία] is one of the places of ministry. It is there that Jesus heals (8:14; 9:23, 28), and also he retires there to instruct his disciples more carefully (13:36; 17:25). When they are sent on a mission similar to Jesus', the apostles are instructed to enter into a house in a village and to use that as their base (10:11-12). Reference has already been made to the work of Crosby, *House of Disciples*, in which he develops the Matthean use of οἶκος, οἰκία as root metaphor. Later in the gospel, the significance of Peter will be further developed.

83   That the ruler would have been conscious of the extraordinary nature of his request is indicated by the suggestion later in the story that his is a Jewish household because of the presence of the traditional fluteplayers and mourners following a death, cf. b. Ketub. 46b.

Introduction - 9:18a

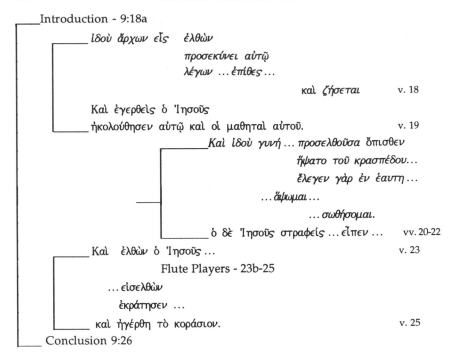

ἰδοὺ ἄρχων εἷς ἐλθὼν

προσεκύνει αὐτῷ

λέγων ... ἐπίθες ...

καὶ ζήσεται   v. 18

Καὶ ἐγερθεὶς ὁ Ἰησοῦς

ἠκολούθησεν αὐτῷ καὶ οἱ μαθηταὶ αὐτοῦ.   v. 19

Καὶ ἰδοὺ γυνή ... προσελθοῦσα ὄπισθεν

ἥψατο τοῦ κρασπέδου...

ἔλεγεν γὰρ ἐν ἑαυτῃ ...

... ἄψωμαι ...

... σωθήσομαι.

ὁ δὲ Ἰησοῦς στραφείς ... εἶπεν ...   vv. 20-22

Καὶ ἐλθὼν ὁ Ἰησοῦς ...   v. 23

Flute Players - 23b-25

... εἰσελθὼν

ἐκράτησεν ...

καὶ ἠγέρθη τὸ κοράσιον.   v. 25

Conclusion 9:26

Diagram 4

There is no time for the reader to answer this question before being
confronted by a second surprising situation. The focus shifts to a woman
who stands alone in the narrative--καὶ ἰδοὺ γυνὴ αἱμορροοῦσα δώδεκα ἔτη. She
is given no name nor is she encountered by the readers in terms of her
human environment.[84] She encounters Jesus in the public arena outside the
confines of the patriarchal household.[85] She is, however, described in terms
of her physical status; she is ritually unclean.[86] With considerable initiative

---

84   Rimmon-Kenan, *Narrative Fiction*, 66, suggests that "human environment" which
     comprises family and social class is one of an author's rhetorical strategies of
     characterization.
85   Anderson, "Gender and Reading," 11, argues that this stark introduction emphasizes
     the woman's double marginality. She appears alone with no indication of an embed-
     ded status in a patriarchal family and she appears afflicted. The ruler, by contrast, has
     the status of father and so is completely embedded in the patriarchal family structure.
     The fact that the woman is outside the patriarchal familial structure may, however,
     allow her more freedom and initiative.
86   The laws of Lev 15 deal with both male and female genital discharges. Lev 15:25-39 is
     the most appropriate to the woman's situation. This law is discussed in much greater
     detail in Tractate Niddah of the Mishnah. For further discussion, see Neusner, "From
     Scripture to Mishnah"; and idem, *A History of the Mishnaic Law of Purities*, SJLA 6,
     pts. 15 and 16 (Leiden: Brill, 1976/1977).

and placing herself at risk, she reaches out and touches Jesus' garment saying to herself: "If I only touch his garment, I shall be made well" (9:21). Here, for the first time in the narrative, we have a woman's point of view. She recognizes Jesus as one who can save her [σωθήσομαι], can free her from her infirmity. Her muted thoughts are in fact a statement of belief, a power which enables her to reach out beyond herself and her infirmity (cf. 1:21).

Structurally, the two accounts, vv. 18-19 and vv. 20-21, are closely parallel [see Diagram 4]. The ἰδού which functions characteristically through-out the narrative to draw attention both to characters and to events[87] here alerts the reader to the parallels between these two stories. More emphatic, therefore, is the difference in content which a few words suggest. The ruler came and knelt before Jesus and made his request that Jesus restore his daughter to life [προσεκύνει αὐτῷ].[88] The woman, because of the inferior status in which society has placed her, is afraid to approach Jesus directly but comes up to him from behind [προσελθοῦσα ὄπισθεν].[89] Her action in touching Jesus' garment and her pondering within herself parallel the ruler's ex-traordinary request. Both have as their goal a restoration to life but one is implicit while the other is explicit.

The cryptic language of the miracle proper reminds the reader of the healing of Peter's mother-in-law. There, Jesus saw the woman, touched her, and the healing was effected. Here, Jesus sees the woman, speaks, and the healing is effected [καὶ ἐσώθη ἡ γυνὴ ἀπὸ τῆς ὥρας ἐκείνης]. It is not necessary for him to touch her because she has already taken that initiative and his words merely confirm her action. There are, however, two elements in the

---

87   Robert Morgenthaler, *Statistik des neutestamentlichen Wortschatzes* (Zürich/Frank-furt am M.: Gotthelf, 1958), 106, lists its use 62 times in Matthew compared with 7 in Mark. Similar figures are given by Frans Neirynck and Frans van Segbroeck, *New Testament Vocabulary: A Companion Volume to the Concordance.* BEThL LXV (Leuven: University Press, 1984), 262.

88   This verb is characteristic of Matthew and indicates the posture before Jesus of both men: the Magi (2:2, 8, 11), a leper (8:2), a ruler (9:18), and the disciples (14:33; 28:17); and women: the Canaanite woman (15:25), the mother of the sons of Zebedee (20:20), and the two Marys at the tomb (28:9). Hubert Frankemölle, *Jahwebund und Kirche Christi: Studien zur Form-und Traditionsgeschichte des "Evangeliums" nach Matthäus,* NTA, N.F. 10 (Münster: Aschendorff, 1974), 166, n. 37, suggests that this verb has a religious connotation. We see reflected in the use of this verb, the implied author's world view with regard to the relationship between divinity and humanity, Jesus being more and more closely linked with divinity in the Matthean narrative. The relationship is pre-sented as one of subservience and self-abnegation which is in tension with the life-affirming attitude to humanity revealed in much of the life and teaching of Jesus (5:43-48; 6:9-15, 25-34).

89   Only twice does this word ὄπισθεν occur in relation to someone approaching Jesus (9:20; 15:23) and each time, the supplicant is a woman.

story of the healing of the woman with the haemorrhage which take the Matthean story of Jesus beyond the point reached with the healing of Peter's mother-in-law. The faith of the woman is mentioned explicitly and salvation is said to be effected by Jesus in response to that faith.

The faith of the woman is such that she takes the initiative and risks crossing religious boundaries in order to come into contact with the healing power of Jesus, which she believes will restore her to life (9:20-22). In the narrative, her faith stands in contrast to the response of the fluteplayers and professional mourners who laugh mockingly at Jesus' attitude to death showing no faith whatsoever in his capacity to heal or to restore to life. Their attitude is representative of the "old garment" or the "old wineskins" which are incapable of receiving the new cloth or the new wine (9:16-17).[90] The story of the woman is therefore representative of the new wine being poured into fresh skins. By her faith, she is saved while the fluteplayers are cast out. The two-fold risk of the woman in crossing both gender and ritual cleanliness boundaries is therefore affirmed by Jesus' turning and saying: "Courage, Daughter, your faith has saved you" (9:22), an acclamation not addressed to the ruler. The woman is therefore explicitly characterized as a person of faith in the words of the most authoritative voice in the narrative, Jesus.[91]

The address, θάρσει, θύγατερ, parallels Jesus' greeting of the paralytic, θάρσει, τέκνον (9:2). Both represent Jesus' response to faith and both the faith of a woman as well as the faith of a man become signs of the manifestation of the βασιλεία, of the power and presence of God in the midst of humanity. Other examples of similar faith in this section of the narrative all occur in the stories of male supplicants: the centurion is praised for his faith (8:10); and the two blind men who share the woman's ritual impurity approach Jesus for healing with a faith comparable to that of the woman (9:27-28).[92]

On the other hand, the faith of the woman is contrasted with that of the disciples who are called "men of little faith" (8:26), and with the lack of response of the scribes who see the healing power of Jesus only as a basis for

---

90   Once again, it must be stressed that this tension between the new and the old is not anti-Jewish but is an expression of a key element of the prophetic critique, namely, the numbness of the dominant consciousness to the newness that the prophet brings. For an excellent exposition of this in relation to the prophets of the Hebrew Scriptures and in relation to Jesus, see Brueggemann, *Prophetic Imagination*.
91   Rimmon-Kenan, *Narrative Fiction*, 60.
92   W. G. Thompson, "Reflections on the Composition of Mt 8:1-9:34," *CBQ* 33 (1971): 384, compares the faith of the woman with that of the two blind men.

an accusation (9:3, 11, 34). The story of this woman of faith stands, therefore, within the narrative of Matt 8 and 9 as an example. Her marginality points to Jesus' healing of those who are most marginal in society, and his restoring of her to new life is a manifestation of the liberating and inclusive nature of the βασιλεία.

Restoration to life is highlighted by the threefold use of σῴζω in 9:20-22. Its interpretation in this pericope is influenced by the story which frames it. In 9:18, the ruler requested:

ἐπίθες   τὴν χεῖρα σου ἐπ' αὐτήν, καὶ ζήσεται.

When Jesus executes the request, it is stated thus:

ἐκράτησεν τῆς χειρὸς αὐτῆς,   καὶ ἠγέρθη ... (9:25).

Ἠγέρθη, as has already been noted, can have both a literal meaning--rising up--and also a symbolic sense--being raised from the dead--and it seems to carry both in 9:25. It is parallel to ζήσεται in the ruler's request which in its turn parallels σωθήσομαι in the woman's implicit request. Since ἠγέρθη can be read here with both a literal and a symbolic meaning, so too its parallels ζάω and σῴζω can be understood on both a literal and a theological level.

Ζάω is used only once to refer to ordinary life (27:63) and there it is followed immediately by a reference to resurrection [ἐγείρομαι]. In all other cases, it is associated with God directly (16:16; 22:32; 26:63) or indirectly (4:4). Hence, it would seem that the word has strong theological overtones in the narrative. In this context, therefore, given the clustering and paralleling of verbs which can be read on two levels of significance, σῴζω too can move between the literal level, "to restore to health", and the theological, "to save or preserve from eternal death".[93] Just as the young girl is clearly seen to have arisen and to have been raised up from death by Jesus (9:25), so too the woman with the haemorrhage is saved from her affliction and restored to life and wholeness in the new religious community around Jesus,[94] a community in which two very significant boundaries have been broken down for women--gender boundaries and ritual cleanliness boundaries.[95]

---

93   BAGD, 798, 1c and 2.
94   Gerhardsson, Mighty Acts, 51.
95   Léon-Dufour, "La guérison," 131, claims that "La guérison de l'hémorroïsse au contact de Jésus qui, loin d'être rendu lui-même impur ... la délivre de son impureté rituelle ... annonce symbolique qu'est abolie dans la Nouvelle Alliance la frontière entre le pur et l'impur." Also, the restoration of a woman to the religious community around Jesus

In each of these stories, the female enters the scene as pollutant, outside the boundaries of ritual cleanliness and the woman with the haemorrhage is also anomalous in relation to gender boundaries. In neither of the stories, however, does restoration entail return to the patriarchal familial structure as a source of salvation. Woman, therefore, as well as man, shares directly in the benefits of the βασιλεία, the saving, life-giving power of Jesus. This is further underlined by the placing of the story of the healing of this woman and the raising to life of a young girl alongside a pericope which speaks most directly of the aspect of discontinuity associated with Jesus' preaching of the βασιλεία.

B. Present State of Research

Recent study of miracle stories, not only in the gospel but in the ancient world generally, has focussed on miracles and miracle stories within their own cultural context or within the world view of the ancient tellers of these stories.[96] This has brought to our attention the radical change in world view between their times and our own and has served as a warning to scholars of the danger of reading back contemporary understandings of reality into the ancient world.[97] Aware of this, scholars have turned their attention more specifically to the function of miracle stories within the ancient world and within primitive Christianity as it developed its kerygma.[98]

The most significant influence on recent study of the miracle stories in Matthew's gospel was the work of H. J. Held. In his ground-breaking article,

---

was one of the tension points created by Jesus' preaching of the βασιλεία in relation to the dominant culture within Judaism. There man stood at the heart of the religious community, fulfilling its obligations since the woman was exempt from all time-bound mitzvot according to b. Qidd. 29a. He was therefore seen as the chief recipient of the spiritual benefits of Judaism. For further discussion of this situation, see Paula Hyman, "The Other Half: Women in the Jewish Tradition," in *The Jewish Woman: New Perspectives*, ed., Elizabeth Koltun (New York: Schocken, 1976), 105-113; and Rachel Adler, "The Jew Who Wasn't There: Halakah and the Jewish Woman," in *On Being a Jewish Feminist: A Reader*, ed., Susannah Heschel (New York: Schocken, 1983), 12-18.

96   This is the goal set by Howard Clark Kee, *Miracle in the Early Christian World: A Study in Sociohistorical Method* (New Haven/London: Yale University Press, 1983), vii.

97   Michael Lattke, "New Testament Miracle Stories and Hellenistic Culture of Late Antiquity," *Listening* 20 (1985): 57.

98   See Gerd Theissen, *Miracle Stories of the Early Christian Tradition*, ed. J. Riches and trans. Francis McDonagh, Studies of the New Testament and its World (Edinburgh: T. & T. Clark, 1983).

"Matthew as Interpreter of the Miracle Stories", he summarized his position thus:

> If one surveys ... the evangelist Matthew's retelling of the miracle stories, it is plain that the miracles are not important for their own sakes but by reason of the message they contain. ...to Matthew the miracle story is the bearer of a doctrine.[99]

As a result, he saw the miracles in Matthew's gospel generally at the service of the "doctrines" of christology, discipleship and faith. This approach has been complemented by subsequent scholars whose work follows a similar method and whose results vary little except in terms of divisions within the structure and theological themes applied to those divisions.[100]

A feminist critique applied to this overriding emphasis among scholars points to the fact that attention to theological themes serves to obscure the characters, their relationship to Jesus and also their gender, all of which we have seen to be of particular significance.[101] Women are simply subsumed under the particular theological theme being discussed and often its androcentric perspective as well. Hence, a feminist reading must give particular attention to characters and the significance of their gender and only then can generalizations regarding theological themes be drawn.

The approach which best serves our goals is that initiated by Gerd Theissen and developed more specifically by Antoinette Clark Wire.[102] Theissen deals with the existential function of the primitive christian miracle stories, both in terms of the human actions giving rise to the

---

99   Held, "Matthew as Interpreter," 165-299, especially 210 and 219.
100 Thompson, "Reflections on the Composition," 365-388, follows a similar structure but specifies the christology as servant christology. K. Gatzweiler, "Les récits de miracles dans l'Evangile selon saint Matthieu," in *L'Evangile selon Matthieu: Rédaction et théologie,* ed. M. Didier, BEThL XXIX (Gembloux: Duculot, 1972), 209-220, does little more than summarize Held's position and praise him for it. Burger, "Jesu Taten," 272-287, points out that the first section focusses on "outcasts" and he sees 9:1-17 presenting characteristics of the new community separating itself from Judaism. Jack D. Kingsbury, "Observations on the "Miracle Chapters" of Matthew 8-9," *CBQ* 40 (1978): 559-573, draws heavily on the work of Burger; and J. P. Heil, "Significant Aspects of the Healing Miracles in Matthew," *CBQ* 41 (1979): 274-287, points to the christological, ecclesiological and soteriological aspects of the healing miracles. A more recent study, Jeremy Moiser, "The Structure of Matthew 8-9: A Suggestion," *ZNW* 76 (1985): 117-118, does not follow Held so closely but still uses a thematic approach which links the themes attached to the three sections in Matt 8 and 9 as well as the two interludes or buffer pericopes to aspects of the Sermon on the Mount.
101 A similar critique is made by Heil, "Healing Miracles," 279-280. His is not offered from a feminist perspective but he sees Held's approach as obscuring the significance of the miraculous healing story.
102 Theissen, *Miracle Stories*, 43-46, gives brief attention to characters in the miracle narratives and this is developed more fully by Wire, "Structure of the Gospel Miracle Stories".

tradition, and the symbolic value of the retelling of the traditional stories. In this way, the characters and their existential situation take on much more significance. As Wire has pointed out, however, in relation to Theissen's work:

> ... he does not differentiate carefully the kinds of interactions in a story (beyond naming the persons interacting), nor does he maintain focus on these interactions as the constructive and hence interpretive key.[103]

In dealing with the healing miracles which she places in a category called "demand story", Wire highlights the oppressive context and the oppositions it offers to the demand as well as the extraordinary breaking out of it as keys to the stories' function.[104] Such an approach allows specific attention to be given to the socio-religious marginalization of women which was overcome in the miracle stories recorded in the gospel and to the function that the retelling of such stories served within the Matthean community.[105] It serves, therefore, the feminist reading which we are undertaking and shall be specifically applicable when these miracle stories are considered further in Chapters Four and Seven.

C. An Inclusive Re-reading

Within the narrative section 4:17-10:42, the ancient androcentric perspective pervades. It finds its expression in various ways, but the two that we have already highlighted are, first, that the recipients of the life-restoring power of the βασιλεία are predominantly male and, second, the assumption which is becoming more explicit that membership of the character group called disciples demands male gender. Within such a perspective, women are presented as marginalized, and as pollutants or possible pollutants. Their voices are silenced or muted.

The stories, however, of two women and a young girl whose healing brings them to the centre of the restored community whose foundation lay in the βασιλεία preaching of Jesus challenge such a perspective. The very stories themselves break the narrative pattern expected of a miracle story.

---

103 Wire, "Structure of the Gospel Miracle Stories," 86.
104 Ibid., 84.
105 Wire, in fact, develops this aspect of the story in relation to women in her article "Ancient Miracle Stories and Women's Social World," *Forum* 2 (1986): 77-84.

Their position within the narrative brings them into close proximity to the two buffer pericopes which point to the tensions inherent in the message which Jesus is inaugurating by his healing action. In terms of the feminist criteria of liberation and inclusion, the stories testify to the presence of these characteristics in Jesus' preaching of the βασιλεία and their application to women.

The feminist reader finds that women's marginalization is critiqued. Women stand out as examples of faith, of risk and initiative, and of service. One woman who is healed serves Jesus in a way that fulfils one of the significant responses to the βασιλεία preaching of Jesus to which he calls recipients of his message, while another experiences the saving power of Jesus because of her faith. This challenges the conventional androcentric perspective of the text. For the feminist reader, therefore, the following of Jesus, the preacher of the βασιλεία, is no longer limited only to men and they are not considered the principal recipients of its fruits. Both women and men share the role of discipleship and both are able to receive the new life which Jesus offers. This is made clear to the reader in the reliable voice of the narrator (8:15) and the authoritative voice of Jesus (9:22).

The reader is aware, however, of the questions and the tensions such a reading creates. Why are these stories of women characters which continually challenge the prevailing perspective of the narrative included in the text? Tension is therefore created around these characters whose gender does not allow them to be named among the twelve or to be among the gender grouping considered principal recipients of the fruits of the βασιλεία and yet they demonstrate the necessary qualities for both. In fact, the qualities which they portray are praised over and above those of the male characters. These questions, insights and tensions must guide the reader into the next stage of the unfolding narrative. It also takes us beyond, however, to the question of the origin of these powerful traditions regarding women, their development within the Matthean community and their influence on that community.

III. CONTINUATION OF THE GALILEAN MINISTRY - 11:1-16:20

As readers move into the next section of the narrative, they are aware of another shift in focus which guides the reading process. While the two central themes of the previous section--Jesus as Teacher and Jesus as Healer--continue (13:1-52; and 12:9-14, 15, 22; 14:14, 34-36; 15:21-28, 29-31), they do not occupy the foreground of the narrative as they did previously, but rather the background. Into the foreground comes Jesus' relationship with the disciples, with the Jewish leaders, with the crowds and with the few supplicants who come to him and their various stances towards him. As the implied readers wait expectantly to see who will be on the side of Jesus and who will be against him, they are faced with the question of their own stance toward Jesus. This shift significantly influences both character and plot development within the narrative and provides the context in which four references to women (12:46-50; 13:55; 14:3-11; 14:21 and 15:38 which are a doublet) and the story of the Canaanite woman (15:21-28) must be read.

The section begins with the question of John: "Are you the Coming One [ὁ ἐρχόμενος] or shall we look for another?" (Matt 11:3), and closes with Jesus charging the disciples not to tell anyone that he is the Christ [χριστός] (16:20).[106] Within this frame, various character groups interact with one another and with Jesus whose identity is becoming clearer, and hence they are compared and contrasted with one another in terms of their response to Jesus as the plot develops.

At the end of the previous section, the μαθηταί were beginning to be distinguished from the ὄχλοι as Jesus called twelve named male disciples to himself (10:1) and shared with them his mission (10:1, 7-8). In this section, the μαθηταί hear Jesus' teaching in parables (13:1-10, 24-30, 31-33, 44-50), he explains the parables to them privately (13:18-23, 37-43), and yet they are still without understanding (15:16). They witness the extraordinary power of Jesus who feeds the multitudes (14:13-21; 15:32-39) and who walks upon the

---

106 In Matt 11, the words of Jesus which follow John's question regarding the Coming One are his answer to that question and they conclude with v. 19 in which Jesus is identified with Wisdom. Susan Cady, Marian Ronan and Hal Taussig, *Sophia: The Future of Feminist Spirituality* (San Francisco: Harper & Row, 1986), 39-42, discuss the interaction between concepts of Messiah and Sophia in early christologies, stating that "almost every major New Testament portrait of Jesus depends on the implicit combination of the Messiah and Sophia figures."

water (14:22-27) and yet they are still without the faith required for discipleship (14:31; 16:8; cf. 8:26). Their lack of understanding and lack of faith become keys to interpreting discipleship in this section of the narrative as other characters are set over against the disciples as foils, the Canaanite woman being one such character.

The tension between Jesus and the Jewish leaders which the reader glimpsed in the previous section of the narrative increases. They question Jesus regarding his actions or those of his disciples (12:2, 10; 15:1-2); they seek for a sign from him (12:38; 16:1); speak condemnations against him (12:24); and even take counsel to destroy him (12:14). It is against the backdrop of one such encounter between Jesus and the leaders that the story of the Canaanite woman is set (see Diagram 5 below).

The elements of the plot in this section also serve the purpose of further developing the web of character interactions that are the central focus within the narrative at this point. The three healings narrated here take place within a discussion or controversy between Jesus and the Pharisees (12:9-14; 12:22-32) or between Jesus and the supplicant (15:21-28), and the interaction between the characters tends to dominate the pericope rather than the miracle itself.[107]

The summary passages (12:15-16; 14:13-14, 34-36; 15:29-31) serve as an economic way of maintaining the narrative theme of Jesus' interaction with the crowds. Within them, we find a repetition of words and phrases from previous summaries (4:23-25; 8:16; 9:35).[108] Two of them (14:13-14; 15:29-31) introduce Jesus' feeding of the multitudes with bread (14:15-21 and 15:32-39) and 12:15-16 precedes the fulfilment quotation of 12:18-21 with its emphasis on the mission of God's servant to the Gentiles. All, therefore, serve to broaden and strengthen the reader's understanding of the healing and life-giving ministry of Jesus and the response of the crowds to this ministry.

Finally, the use of scriptural quotations (12:18-21; 13:14-15; 15:8-9), and future predictions or prolepses (11:21-24; 12:32, 36-37) also serve to focus on the relationships between Jesus and the various character groups who respond to his coming and his proclaiming the βασιλεία in both word and deed.

---

107 In this section of the narrative, we can perhaps give further consideration to the claim of Held, "Matthew as Interpreter," 199, who says of the story of the Canaanite woman "it is not the miracle as such that was important but the conversation which the healing brought forth."
108 This is developed by Janice Capel Anderson, *Over and Over and Over Again: Studies in Matthean Repetition* (Ph.D. diss., University of Chicago, 1985), 199-206, and Boismard, *Synopse*, 120-123 and Annexe II to note 47.

From a gender perspective, however, we are faced with the question of the gender inflection of the response to Jesus which characterizes this section of the narrative.

A. The Text

It has been pointed out that the two key metaphors which dominate this narrative section are Wisdom and Bread.[109] In fact, Matthew identifies Jesus with Wisdom [σοφία] (Matt 11:19), and this identification characterizes 11:1-14:13a.[110] The bread imagery is undeniable given that ἄρτος occurs fifteen times within 14:13-16:12[111] and only six times throughout the rest of the gospel.[112]

At the outset, Jesus who will be revealed as the Wisdom of God is seen with the twelve male disciples (11:1). But as the narrative advances, Jesus-Sophia calls *all* to come to her, to take up her yoke and to learn from her (11:28-29), a call not governed by gender restrictions. This inclusive membership of the community of Jesus-Sophia is not, however, named as discipleship. Subsequently, following a lengthy controversy between Jesus-Sophia and the Pharisaic opponents, membership within a patriarchal family is dramatically replaced by membership within the family of disciples gathered around Wisdom. They are the ones who live out one of the central responses to the βασιλεία preaching--doing the will of the Father (7:21; 12:50)--and the metaphors used for this discipleship are inclusive--brother and sister and mother (12:46-50). Since these words are those of the one who

---

109 B. Rod Doyle, "Matthew's Intention as Discerned by His Structure," *RB* 95 (1988): 42-45, in which he suggests that 11:1-14:13a is characterized by Wisdom and 14:13b-16:12 by the theme of bread. The terminology "section des pains" or "bread section" has, in fact, become common parlance among biblical scholars to refer to Mark 6:30-8:26 and its Matthean parallel 14:13-16:12. See Lucien Cerfaux, "La section des pains: (Mc vi,31-viii,26; Mt xiv,13-xvi,12)," in *Synoptische Studien: Festschrift A. Wikenhauser* (München: Karl Zink, 1953), 64-77; reprinted in *Recueil Lucien Cerfaux*, I (Gembloux: Duculot, 1954), 471-485; Karl Gatzweiler, "Un pas vers l'universalisme: La Cananéenne. Mt 15,21-28," *ASeign* 2/51 (1972): 15; Alice Dermience, "La péricope de la Cananéenne (Mt 15,21-28: Rédaction et théologie," *EThL* 58 (1982): 27; and Meier, *Matthew*, 163.

110 Doyle, "Matthew's Intention," 43, indicates that in Matt 11:1-14:13a, Jesus is presented as the Wisdom of God, a point further developed in idem, *Matthew's Wisdom: A Redaction-Critical Study of Matthew 11:1-14:13a* (Ph.D. thesis, Melbourne University, 1984). See also M. Jack Suggs, *Wisdom, Christology, and Law in Matthew's Gospel* (Cambridge, Mass.: Harvard University Press, 1970), 31-61, and Schüssler Fiorenza, *In Memory of Her*, 134-135.

111 14:17, 19 (twice); 15:2, 26, 33, 34, 36; 16:5, 7, 8, 9, 10, 11, 12.

112 4:3, 4; 6:11; 7:9; 12:4; 26:26.

has become authoritative in the narrative, the reader can presume, therefore, that discipleship of Wisdom is inclusive and that those who are given to know the secrets of the βασιλεία (13:11), who have eyes which see and ears which hear (13:16, 23, 43), who indeed become scribes trained for the βασιλεία (13:52) include both women and men despite the androcentric language in which these passages are cast.

This creates a tension for the reader, however, when those specifically named as members of the character group called disciples and those definitively called, even though the stories of their call may be intended to function paradigmatically, are male. Discipleship, however, is clearly intended to be inclusive as is already clear by way of the imagery used to describe it and also the discipleship qualities exhibited by the women as well as the men who have come to Jesus as supplicants, who have listened to his teaching and who have followed him.[113] This will need further attention later when discipleship is considered in the light of what has been uncovered in this study. For the present, however, it is sufficient to acknowledge the tension created for the reader throughout the remainder of this section of the narrative which gives significant attention to the group called μαθηταί.[114]

Both the wisdom [σοφία] and the mighty works [αί δυνάμεις] of Jesus are questioned by those of his own country (13:53-54). It is in this context that we find a second reference to the mother of Jesus and here she is given her name, Mary. As seen in the infancy narrative, in 12:46-50, and again here, it is not motherhood of a significant son which is of value; nor, for Jesus, belonging to a particular patriarchal family structure. Rather, it is participating in the liberating of humanity, the work of the βασιλεία. What obstructs such work is not one's family status or gender but unbelief (13:58).

The direct opposition to Jesus was noted above. It extends throughout this entire narrative section, is focussed in the Jewish leaders--the scribes, Pharisees, and Sadducees--and is symbolized as predominantly male in the narrative. It extends as well to the political leadership of Herod who is responsible for the death of John the Baptist, the one who is intimately

---

113 Anderson, "Gender and Reading," 16-17, discusses this distinction between character group and discipleship. Many others, however, do not take up the distinction and simply assume the androcentric perspective of the gospel, claiming that the language and imagery of discipleship is without metaphorical significance except when applied to the defined group. This is especially clear in Jack Dean Kingsbury, "The Verb AKOLOUTHEIN ("To Follow") as an Index of Matthew's View of His Community," JBL 97 (1978): 56-73.

114   14:15, 19, 22, 26; 15:2, 12, 23, 32, 33, 36; 16:5, 13, 20.

linked to the ministry of Jesus.[115] Within the story of the death of John, however, there is brief reference to Herodias and her daughter. They are certainly not the focal point of the story. Herod is given centre stage and the reader is given various insights into his thoughts and feelings (14:5, 9). Herodias, on the other hand, is presented as deeply embedded in his patriarchal family structure--"his brother Philip's wife"--and as his property--"it is not lawful for you to *have* her" (14:3-4). She functions behind the scene as murderess and her daughter as seductress, two of the typical depictions of the evil female. Despite the androcentric perspective through which they are viewed in the narrative, their brief appearance creates for the reader an awareness that the opposition to John and hence to Jesus is inclusive of both women and men even though characterized as predominantly male. Later, the brief reference to Herodias will function as a counterpoint to a similar brief reference to the wife of another political leader, Pilate.

The Bread Section, in which the reader finds the final references to women and the story of the Canaanite woman, is carefully structured to guide the reader and this structuring also provides insight into the gender inflection of this section of the narrative.

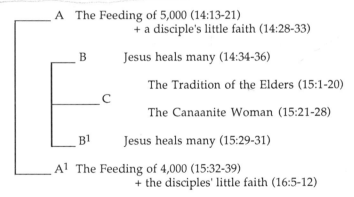

A   The Feeding of 5,000 (14:13-21)
        + a disciple's little faith (14:28-33)

   B   Jesus heals many (14:34-36)

               The Tradition of the Elders (15:1-20)

      C

               The Canaanite Woman (15:21-28)

   B¹   Jesus heals many (15:29-31)

A¹ The Feeding of 4,000 (15:32-39)
        + the disciples' little faith (16:5-12)

Diagram 5

The story of the Canaanite woman together with the discussion regarding the tradition of the Elders with which it is linked[116] form the

---

115 John P. Meier, "John the Baptist in Matthew's Gospel," *JBL* 99 (1980): 383-405.
116 Dermience, in her article, "Péricope," in which she provides an excellent analysis of this pericope from the perspective of redaction criticism, comments on Matthew's use of καί at the beginning of the pericope instead of the δέ which is found at the beginning of the Markan pericope. She gives as the reason for the change: "pour relier le

centre point around which a chiasm is structured. As well as the structural unity, the underlying theme of "bread" gives a thematic unity to this section. The two pericopes which appear least compatible with both the structural and thematic unity, namely, Jesus' walking on the water (14:22-27) and the leaders' demand for a sign (16:1-4), both form a link between the feeding stories and the statements regarding the little faith of one or more of the disciples. They do not, therefore, break the chiastic unity, but rather serve to highlight the "little faith" of the disciples.

This structure can be further extended if we take into account the Double Stories that have been located by Janice Capel Anderson. These double stories extend beyond this section of the narrative, but her structure together with that proposed above may both assist our gender reading of this section of the gospel, especially since she also finds the story of the Canaanite woman at the centre point of a chiastic structure which she outlines thus:[117]

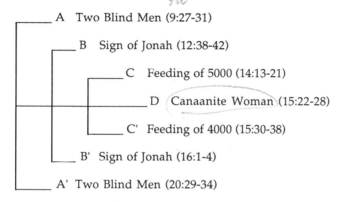

```
┌───── A   Two Blind Men (9:27-31)
│
│   ┌─── B   Sign of Jonah (12:38-42)
│   │
│   │   ┌─── C   Feeding of 5000 (14:13-21)
│   │   │
│   │   │   ┌─── D   Canaanite Woman (15:22-28)
│   │   │   │
│   │   │   └─── C'  Feeding of 4000 (15:30-38)
│   │   │
│   │   └─── B'  Sign of Jonah (16:1-4)
│   │
│   └─── A'  Two Blind Men (20:29-34)
```

Diagram 6

From a gender perspective, the tension that the reader experiences in relation to discipleship is extended here to the crowd as well. The narrator specifies that the 5,000 numbered in the first feeding of the multitude and

---

récit de la Cananéenne au débat qui précède." Gundry, *A Commentary*, 310, also specifically links the two pericopes, as does Frankemölle, *Jahwebund*, 135. Adolf Schlatter, *Der Evangelist Matthäus: Seine Sprache, sein Ziel, seine Selbständigkeit. Ein Kommentar zum ersten Evangelium* (Stuttgart: Calwer, 1948), 488, notes the strong contrast set up between the Pharisees and the Canaanite by placing their stories side by side; and both Krister Stendahl, "Matthew," in *Peake's Commentary on the Bible*, 2nd ed. (London: Nelson, 1962), 787; and David Hill, *The Gospel of Matthew*, NCB Commentary (Grand Rapids: Eerdmans, 1972), 253, note the connection between the question of clean and unclean and the mission to the Gentiles in the Pauline churches. Thus the link between the two stories seems to be generally accepted by scholars.

117   Anderson, *Over and Over*, 249-265, and idem, "Gender and Reading," 14.

the 4,000 in the second are male (14:21; 15:38), but goes on to indicate that the crowd also included women and children. Women, therefore, are recipients of the bread, one of the fruits of the βασιλεία, a point which must be emphasized in a gender reading even though it receives such a cursory mention within the androcentric narrative. The reader assumes also that women are among those healed. The climactic story of the Canaanite woman stands out by way of contrast to the questioning of the elders, a point also made clear in Anderson's structure in terms of the Sign of Jonah stories. As our analysis proceeds, we will find too that her faith will stand out by way of contrast to the little faith of the disciples.[118] This will become clearer in the more detailed study of the narrative of Matt 15:21-28, the only story in this section in which a woman functions as a major character.

1. 15:21-28

Earlier, it was indicated that the discussion between Jesus and the woman in this story seemed to be more significant than the miracle, and now brief attention to the structuring of the story will show that the dialogue does indeed dominate. In the first two verses, the chief characters are introduced: v. 21--καὶ ἐξελθὼν ἐκεῖθεν ὁ Ἰησοῦς; and v. 22--καὶ ἰδοὺ γυνὴ Χαναναία. The dialogue begins in v. 22, a dialogue which is continued within the carefully structured introductions to vv. 24-27: ὁ δὲ ... and ἡ δὲ .... The pericope as well as the dialogue concludes with v. 28 which closely resembles v. 21 in the structuring of its opening phrase. Verse 23, however, intrudes into this narrative as a threat to the dialogue [ὁ δὲ οὐκ ἀπεκρίθη] and to the action [ἀπόλυσον αὐτήν]. It introduces another character group, the disciples; and it seems to break into the dialogue which begins in v. 22 and continues in vv. 24-27.[119]

---

118 Anderson, *Over and Over*, 250, makes the point that the pattern which she has discovered in the central section of the gospel highlights the contrasts between the five major character groups: the outcast supplicants, the Jewish leaders, the crowds, the disciples, and the Gentiles. A gender reading finds women specifically among three of these groups--supplicants, crowds and Gentiles.

119 Lohmeyer, *Evangelium*, 252, supports such a reading when he says: "Dreimal bittet die Frau, dreimal antwortet Jesus in verschiedener Weise." This is contrary to the position of Gundry, *A Commentary*, 311-314, who sees the first ὁ δὲ as indicating a conversation between Jesus and the disciples, a position which seems untenable when one attends to the careful structuring of the text.

Only a detailed analysis of the story contained within this careful structure [Diagram 7 below] can shed further light upon the function of the dialogue and indeed of the entire pericope.

21 Καί + participle ... ὁ Ἰησοῦς + aorist

      22 Καὶ ἰδοὺ γυνὴ Χαναναία ... λέγουσα· ...

                                                          [beginning of dialogue]

           [23 ὁ δὲ οὐκ ἀπεκρίθη ... ἀπόλυσον αὐτήν...]

           24 ὁ δέ ...

      25 ἡ δέ ...   [dialogue]

           26 ὁ δέ ...

     27 ἡ δέ ...

28 Τότε + participle ... ὁ Ἰησοῦς + aorist

                                                    [conclusion of dialogue]

Diagram 7

As the story opens, Jesus withdraws from Galilee into gentile territory to take refuge from the hostility of the Pharisees manifest in the previous pericope (15:1-9). Except for two occasions (9:24; 27:5), the verb ἀναχωρέω in the narrative indicates a withdrawal from a certain place in order to escape the danger of hostile forces (2:12, 13, 14, 22; 4:12; 12:15; 14:13). When it is used with εἰς it signifies entry into a region and not simply moving towards it (cf. 2:12, 14, 22; 4:12).[120] Jesus' entry into gentile territory is not surprising to the reader who recalls that he had to be taken into such territory as a small child

---

120 This position is supported by a similar linguistic analysis in Gundry, *A Commentary*, 310, as well as W. F. Albright and C. S. Mann, *Matthew. Introduction, Translation, and Notes*, AB 26 (Garden City, New York: Doubleday, 1971), 187; Plummer, *Exegetical Commentary*, 214; and Paul Gaechter, *Das Matthäus-Evangelium: Ein Kommentar* (Innsbruck: Tyrolia-Verlag, 1963), 501. It is modified, however, by others in the light of v. 22 and the ambiguity of the phrase τῶν ὁρίων ἐκείνων. This modification centres around the question whether the phrase is to be attached to the subject [γυνή] or to the following participle [ἐξελθοῦσα]. This raises the question whether the woman went out from her region or whether the phrase is simply descriptive and the participle is employed in an absolute sense common to the gospel and not intended to indicate a definite departure. For a full discussion of this question, see Dermience, "Péricope," 31. Dermience chooses the first option with the corollary that Jesus did not go into gentile territory. Her position is similar to that of Meier, *Matthew*, 171; Benoit, *L'évangile*, 105; Grundmann, *Evangelium*, 376; Sabourin, *L'Evangile*, 201; and S. Legasse, "L'épisode de la Cananéenne d'après Mt 15,21-28," *BLE* 73 (1972): 26. In the light of v. 21, however, and given the ambiguity of v. 22, it seems that the narrative actually presents Jesus entering gentile territory.

in order to escape the designs of Herod; and that the narrator has already
proclaimed Jesus as the fulfilment of the Isaian prophecy: "... he shall
proclaim justice to the Gentiles ... and in his name will the Gentiles hope"
(Matt 12:18-21; cf. Isa 42:1-4, 9). The reader also recalls, however, that when
Jesus commissioned his disciples to a mission parallel to his own (10:1, 7-8),
he commanded them:

> Go nowhere among the Gentiles,
> and enter no town of the Samaritans.   (Matt 10:5)

The reader therefore enters this story with conflicting expectations as to its
outcome, and this reflects the conflicting streams within the narrative as a
whole regarding the question of Jesus' mission to the Gentiles. There is a
suggestion, however, that this is a significant aspect of the story at hand.

The reader encounters at the opening of v. 22 the familiar καὶ ἰδού or
simply ἰδού which has been used a number of times previously to separate a
supplicant from the crowd (8:2; 9:18, 32; 12:10). Here, however, it closely
parallels 9:20:

καὶ ἰδοὺ γυνὴ αἱμορροοῦσα ...   (9:20),

καὶ ἰδοὺ γυνὴ Χαναναία ...   (15:22).

In 15:22, the woman does not stand out from the crowd but simply from the
disciples who are with Jesus. Like the woman with the haemorrhage, she is
given no name but she is designated geographically rather than in terms of
an illness from which she seeks a cure. Both women, however, are typed
either by way of uncleanness or by way of ethnic exclusion. Each is doubly
marginalized: as a woman in a male world outside the patriarchal family
structure,[121] and as ritually unclean or gentile.

Ben Witherington III emphasizes even further the narrative's focus on
the gentile status of the woman:

> ... this pericope is the only example in Mark's (and perhaps Matthew's)
> Gospel where the healed patient is definitely a Gentile pagan ... The Roman

---

121 It is interesting to note here that both women encounter Jesus outside the house which
     raises the question for the reader as to what places these women outside. Anderson,
     "Gender and Reading," 11, links the woman with the haemorrhage with the Canaanite
     woman saying of both: "They appear alone with no indication of an embedded status
     in a patriarchal family. The way they are introduced emphasizes their double marginal-
     ity." It was noted earlier, however, that marginality in relation to the patriarchal
     structuring of society can provide opportunity for initiative and freedom for women.

centurion (Mt 8:5-13) was possibly a God-fearer; the Gerasene demoniac (Mk
5:1-20; Mt 8:28-34) lives in a foreign country but his religion is not made
clear.[122]

Regarding the centurion, however, it should be noted that for the reader
"centurion" denotes Roman official and hence gentile and it requires a
guess, not precipitated by the text itself, to indicate that he was possibly a
God-fearer. Apropos of the "Gerasene demoniac", in the Matthean text, the
reference is to two demoniacs in the country of the Gadarenes. There is a textual problem surrounding the name of the region,[123] but it seems clear that it
is gentile territory. Hence, contrary to Witherington's claim, Jesus has
already healed Gentiles; and, it would seem, has entered into gentile territory. In this story, that will become a focal point and an indication as to why
the woman's gentile origin is stressed as she is introduced. Calling the
woman Χαναναία also reminds the reader of another Canaanite woman,
Rahab, who was instrumental in changing the course of Israel's history by
facilitating their entry into the land of Canaan. There is, therefore,
significant expectation raised for the reader regarding the outcome of this
story not only in relation to the narrative theme of mission to the Gentiles
but also in relation to the woman's participation in this outcome and how
her story will be related.

Following the introduction of the woman, the reader is surprised to
hear her voice raised in supplication. This is the first time in the narrative
that a woman has been given speech, and as the story unfolds the importance of that speech will become clear.[124] The woman's request, however,
does not surprise the reader because a similar request has already been heard
on the lips of the two blind men (9:27-31):

---

122 Ben Witherington III, *Women in the Ministry of Jesus: A Study of Jesus' Attitudes to
Women and Their Roles as Reflected in His Earthly Life*. MSSNTS 51 (1984; reprint,
Cambridge: University Press, 1988), 63, 168 n. 87.

123 According to Metzger, *A Textual Commentary*, 23, Γαδαρηνῶν is supported by (א*) B
C[txt] (Δ) Θ syr[s,p,h]; Γερασηνῶν by it vg cop[sa] syr[hmg2]; Γεργεσηνῶν by א[c] C[mg] K L W ƒ[1]
ƒ[13] cop[bo], providing more textual witnesses than those available in the Nestle-Aland
text. Metzger also gives the supporting witnesses for the Markan and Lukan text and
then in relation to the Matthean rendering, argues for the superiority of Gadara over
Gergesa and Gerasa, the second of which is strongly attested in the Markan narrative
but has little attestation in the Matthean account, on external grounds. Geographically
this may represent a difference between the area of the Decapolis in which Gadara is
definitely located and the Tetrarchy of Philip where it is supposed Gergesa may have
been located. Metzger suggests that the latter may have even been first proposed by
Origen. The strongest support, therefore, seems to suggest Gadara. See also Joachim
Gnilka, *Das Matthäusevangelium*, HThK I,1 (Freiburg: Herder, 1986), 321.

124 In 9:21, the readers were merely given an insight into the woman's own thoughts as
she said to herself, "If I only touch his garment, I shall be made well."

κράζοντες καὶ λέγοντες· ἐλέησον ἡμᾶς, υἱὸς Δαυίδ   (9:27),

ἔκραζεν   λέγουσα· ἐλέησόν με, ...υἱὸς Δαυίδ   (15:22).[125]

Both groups make a similar request to Jesus in faith: the first group consists of two Jewish men who are blind; the second, a gentile woman whose daughter is ill. In fact, the request of this gentile woman also closely parallels that of the gentile centurion (8:6) :

ὁ παῖς   μου βέβληται ἐν τῇ οἰκίᾳ παραλυτικός,
                                  δεινῶς βασανιζόμενος   (8:6),

ἡ θυγάτηρ μου
                                  κακῶς δαιμονίζεται   (15:22).

Both are gentile and each requests Jesus for healing on behalf of a dependant who is ill. Thus at the very outset, this story of the Canaanite woman catches up themes already present in the narrative which will be continued as that narrative advances.

    The reader is further surprised by the reaction of Jesus encountered in the subsequent verse--he did not answer her a word [ὁ δὲ οὐκ ἀπεκρίθη αὐτῇ λόγον]. This negative saying is all the more strange in the context of the positive phrase [ἀποκριθεὶς εἶπεν] which characterizes the gospel as a whole.[126] It is also surprising to the reader, given the narrative development of women vis-à-vis Jesus, a movement from a woman's inability to request healing, to another's approaching Jesus from behind, and finally to a woman's direct request to Jesus. The reader is aware of Jesus' initiative in reaching out to heal the woman with the fever and his affirmation of the faith of the haemorrhaging woman. Why this rebuff?

    We have already noted above the tension within the narrative regarding the mission of Jesus to the Gentiles or into gentile territory, and yet Jesus has already healed the centurion's servant. Why not this woman's daughter? Is his silence a narrative device to draw the reader's attention to a ministry within gentile territory? Yet, Jesus has already healed the

---

125 The same request is made in the doublet of the story of the blind men, 20:29-34, see v. 30.

126 A quick survey of W. F. Moulton and A. S. Geden, eds., *A Concordance to the Greek Testament according to the Texts of Westcott and Hort, Tischendorf and the English Revisers*, 5th ed. (Edinburgh: T. & T. Clark, 1978), 93, will indicate the predominance of ἀποκριθεὶς εἶπεν in Matthew's gospel, and Legasse, "L'épisode," 27, n. 29, gives the statistics across the synoptics: 44,10,30. It would seem, therefore, to be a characteristic phrase of the Matthean narrative.

demoniacs in the Gadarene countryside. There is no clear and definitive answer to these questions, but the strangeness of the phrase causes them to rise up before the reader.

From the perspective of a gender reading, however, another possibility also arises, namely, that the ὁ δὲ οὐκ ἀπεκρίθη αὐτῇ λόγον alerts the reader not only to the conflict in the narrative regarding Jesus' mission to the Gentiles but also to a conflict with regard to his ministry to women. That a woman should seek healing from Jesus is not surprising since the reader has already seen Jesus heal Peter's mother-in-law and respond to the desire for healing in the woman with the haemorrhage. Even the presence of a gentile woman, a Canaanite,[127] in the ministry of Jesus has been prefigured in the genealogy in which Rahab appears. We noted above, however, that what is extraordinary here is that a woman approaches Jesus directly and gives voice to her request. It is perhaps at this point that we encounter another of the "tension points" that Schüssler Fiorenza has alerted us to[128] when the preaching of a βασιλεία which is inclusive meets the restrictive points of the dominant patriarchal culture.

The actual freedom or restriction of women in the public arena in Upper Galilee and the region of Tyre and Sidon at the time of Jesus or later within an urban centre at the time of Matthew is not known with any degree of accuracy, but perhaps the conclusion of Jeremias reflects the dominant ethos:

> Eastern women take no part in *public life*. ... accordingly, a woman was
> expected to remain unobserved in public.[129]

In the previous pericope, Jesus challenged the Pharisees and Scribes with the words:

> ... for the sake of your tradition,
> you have made void the word of God   (Matt 15:6).

The silence of Jesus before the spoken request of the woman and the pause in the narrative which it creates would therefore seem to highlight for the reader a similar conflict between the tradition that belongs to God which is

---

127   The Matthean narrative very specifically introduces the woman as a Canaanite whereas in Mark she is referred to as "a Greek, a Syrophoenician by birth" (Mark 7:26).
128   Schüssler Fiorenza, *In Memory of Her*, 121.
129   Joachim Jeremias, *Jerusalem in the Time of Jesus: An Investigation into Economic and Social Conditions during the New Testament Period*, trans. F. H. and C. H. Cave (London: SCM, 1969), 359-360.

preached by Jesus in word and deed (a tradition which the woman invokes) and the cultural tradition, of which Jesus was a part, which would exclude her. By the use of the phrase ὁ δὲ οὐκ ἀπεκρίθη αὐτῇ λόγον, the reader is guided to read the remainder of this story on two levels which touch on the two-fold marginality of the woman--her gentile status and her female status, especially in the public arena--and Jesus' response to both.[130]

The conflict in the narrative regarding the woman's request is strengthened by the remainder of v. 23 which recounts the disciples' request to Jesus to send the woman away. They repeat the verb κράζω of the previous verse, which there had the sense of crying out in supplication.[131] Given the disapproval and dismissal which characterize the second half of v. 23, however, the verb may carry further connotations. Grundmann noted that in the Graeco-Roman world, the verb was used to refer to cries directed to the gods, but that these were generally felt to be unworthy of the gods. Catherine Kroeger, however, in a study which gives more consideration to gender, shows that sacred cries were characteristic of the rituals of Greek women whereas those of the men were characterized by "an auspicious silence."[132] Such public and ritualistic cries of women were seemingly disapproved of by men and so the disciples' use of κράζω suggests their disapproval of the action of this woman in approaching Jesus in public and raising her voice to him in supplication over and above the fact that she is a gentile woman.

Their request to Jesus to send the woman away [ἀπόλυσον αὐτήν] further emphasizes their disapproval.[133] The reader has already heard a similar request on their lips prior to the multiplication of the loaves [ἀπόλυσον τοὺς

---

130 This second level of the narrative finds no mention in commentaries and articles generally, which points to the androcentric perspective that has characteristically governed the interpretation of the pericope.

131 The exact sense of κράζω is difficult to determine. It finds very little attestation in classical Greek or in the papyri of the Hellenistic era but is used frequently in the Psalms where it translates the Hebrew verb קרא; see W. Grundmann, "κράζω," *TDNT* III:898-903. The use of this verb in v. 22 followed by the woman's plea would seem to carry at least the meaning of "to cry out in supplication" even if crying out in prayer may be too developed a notion for the context.

132 Catherine C. Kroeger, "A Classicist Looks at the Difficult Passages," in *Perspectives on Feminist Hermeneutics*, Occasional Papers No. 10, ed. Gayle Gerber Koontz and W. Swartley (Elkhort, Ind.: Institute of Mennonite Studies, 1987), 14. This is developed further by Richard and Catherine Kroeger, "An Inquiry into Evidence of Maenadism in the Corinthian Congregation," in *SBL 1978 Seminar Papers*, ed. Paul J. Achtemeier (Missoula: Scholars, 1978), 331-338. They do not, however, make specific reference to the use of the verb κράζω.

133 Beare, *A Commentary*, 341, suggests that the intervention of the disciples was simply to provide a setting for a saying of Jesus, but this seems too facile given the careful structuring of the pericope that we have already noted above.

ὄχλους] (14:15). There, it was a request to dismiss the crowd without food which was their need at that time so that they could go and search for it themselves. Here too it seems to be a similar request to dismiss without satisfaction.[134]

In the account of the multiplication of the loaves, the reader became aware that the disciples' request in 14:15 stood in contrast to the attitude of Jesus toward the crowd: he had compassion on them and healed their sick (14:14). This attitude is contrasted even more specifically with that of the disciples in the introduction to the second account of the multiplication of the loaves: "I have compassion on the crowd ... and I am unwilling to send them away hungry" (15:32). In both situations, it is only after Jesus has had compassion on the crowd and fed them abundantly that he sends them away (14:22, 23; 15:39). Here too, Jesus ignores the plea of the disciples and his own initial hesitation and enters into dialogue with the woman. He is challenged to reach out beyond the traditional gender boundaries in response to the initiative of a woman. Just as the initiative of both Rahab and Ruth, foremothers of this Canaanite woman, enabled God's חֶסֶד to be made manifest beyond gender and ethnic boundaries, so too the initiative of this woman will become the vehicle whereby the compassion of Jesus will be made manifest beyond the same boundaries. That, however, is seen only later in the story.

The dialogue of vv. 24-27 pertains, at a surface reading, to the theme of Jesus' mission to the Gentiles. This must not, however, be allowed to obscure the reader's attention from the extraordinary nature of the dialogue itself in which a woman debates with Jesus regarding a Jewish tradition (especially vv. 26-27). The impact of this second aspect is clearer in the second part of the dialogue--vv. 26-28--and the narrative thread of Jesus' gentile mission in the first part.

---

134 This argument is based on an understanding of the meaning of ἀπολύω as "send away" or "dismiss", and is supported by Gundry, *A Commentary*, 312; Eduard Schweizer, *The Good News according to Matthew*, trans. David E. Green (Atlanta: John Knox, 1975), 329; Beare, *A Commentary*, 341; Gerhardsson, *Mighty Acts*, 43; and Gnilka, *Matthäusevangelium*, II, 30. Benoit, *L'évangile*, 106, offers an alternative interpretation based on the meaning of ἀπολύω as "set free, release" (See *BAGD*, 96, for the two usages). This second meaning of the verb is found in 18:27 and 27:15 and so it is not foreign to the Matthean narrative. If such were the meaning intended in v. 23, however, then it could be argued that v. 24 was Jesus' response to the disciples. It was shown above that vv. 24-27 form a highly structured dialogue between Jesus and the woman which began in v. 22. Hence, in this story, a number of factors point to the meaning of ἀπολύω being "send away/dismiss".

Jesus' response to the woman in v. 24--"I was sent only to the lost sheep of the house of Israel"-- seems strange in the light of the fact that Jesus has already healed in response to a request by a Gentile.[135] That story, however, served the purpose within the narrative of showing Jesus breaking down the boundaries which separated "outsiders" from the religious community of Israel. Here, the concern within the narrative is with Jesus' mission into gentile territory.[136] At the beginning of this story, Jesus was presented going into gentile territory to seek refuge. His response to the gentile woman's request confirms the reading that for Jesus it was not a missionary journey:

"I was *sent* [ἀπεστάλην] only to the lost sheep of the house of Israel"

(Matt 15:24).

One of the ways in which tension has been created in the narrative around the question of Jesus' mission to the Gentiles has been the placing of the narrator's point of view (12:17-21) into conflict with Jesus' point of view (15:24). The omniscient narrator presents the point of view which is God's, whereas the character Jesus is limited, within the narrative, to a point of view which approaches the divine point of view but only in response to his experience of human situations in which the divine perspective is learnt or discerned. The story must therefore continue for the tension to be relieved.

In spite of Jesus' failure to respond immediately to her request, the woman maintains her role as supplicant,[137] only to meet a refusal similar to that above:

---

135 Even if the "I will come and heal him" of 8:7 is seen as a mild rebuke of the centurion for asking Jesus to enter into a gentile house as has been suggested by Albright and Mann, *Matthew*, 93; Erich Klostermann, *Das Matthäusevangelium*, HNT 4, 3rd ed. (Tübingen: Mohr, 1938), 74, and Boismard, *Synopse*, 115, the remainder of the story shows this barrier being broken down because of the faith of the centurion and the healing is effected.

136 As was indicated earlier in relation to a woman's role in the public arena, so too here in relation to a mission outside Israel, many significant historical questions are raised. What tradition(s) belong to the historical Jesus and what traditions represent the problems and questions facing the Matthean community? These questions will be very significant at the next two stages of analysis. Here, we are concerned with the narrative function of the verse. An indication of the problematic created by the historical questions, however, is gained by reference to Georg Strecker, *Der Weg der Gerechtigkeit: Untersuchung zur Theologie des Matthäus*, FRLANT 82 (Göttingen: Vandenhoeck & Ruprecht, 1962), 107-108; Wolfgang Trilling, *Das wahre Israel: Studien zur Theologie des Matthäus-Evangeliums*, 3rd ed., StANT 10 (München: Kösel-Verlag, 1964), 99-105; Rolf Walker, *Die Heilsgeschichte im ersten Evangelium* (Göttingen: Vandenhoeck & Ruprecht, 1967), 60-63; and Frankemölle, *Jahwebund*, 114-115, 135-137, to mention but a few of the many works which address this question in some detail.

137 The phrase προσεκύνει αὐτῷ λέγουσα· κύριε ... is similar to that used of the leper (8:2) and the ruler (9:18).

ὁ δὲ ἀποκριθεὶς εἶπεν· οὐκ ἀπεστάλην εἰ μή...   v. 24

ὁ δὲ ἀποκριθεὶς εἶπεν· οὐκ ἔστιν καλὸν λαβεῖν...   v. 26

If, as Wire suggests, "the most intense heightening of demand stories is found ... where the miracle worker himself becomes the opposition",[138] then it would follow that a three-fold opposition posed by Jesus to the woman's request, which is unique in the gospel, significantly emphasizes what is at issue in this story, namely, Jesus' mission to the Gentiles and the legitimacy of the woman's request.

The opposition posed by Jesus in v. 26 [οὐκ ἔστιν καλὸν λαβεῖν τὸν ἄρτον τῶν τέκνων καὶ βαλεῖν τοῖς κυναρίοις] shows him drawing on his own Jewish tradition[139] in order to determine his response to this woman and this Gentile. The reader is already familiar with the symbol of "bread" in the context of conflicts surrounding tradition--what is eaten, by whom and how (12:1-8; 15:1-20). On both occasions, Jesus preaches against a human tradition that is contrary to the desires of God:

> ... if you had known what it means, 'I desire mercy and not sacrifice,' you would not have condemned the guiltless. For the Human One* is lord of the sabbath
>
> (12:7-8)

> ... for the sake of your tradition you have made void the word of God ... Well did Isaiah prophesy of you, when he said: 'This people honors me with their lips, but their heart is far from me; in vain do they worship me, teaching as doctrines human* precepts '
>
> (15:6-9).

The symbolic use of "bread" within the parable of v. 26 suggests a similar struggle surrounding tradition and its binding nature, but this time it is Jesus' own struggle.[140] What constitutes "mercy" rather than the

---

138   Wire, "Structure of the Gospel Miracle Stories," 103.

139   There are a number of reasons which suggest that we may be dealing with a traditional statement here. First, it closely parallels Mark but that alone is insufficient. Witherington III, *Women in the Ministry*, 171, n. 106, suggests a possible parallel in Philostratus, *Life of Appolonius of Tyana*, 1.19, but the date of this is uncertain and hence it is difficult to determine whether it pre-dates or post-dates the life of Jesus and/or the early church's compilation of the gospel. Dermience, "Péricope," 40, n. 113, draws attention to the sapiential nature of the introduction to the saying, and to the fact that the diminutive κυνάριον, which is unknown in the LXX, is well attested in Greek classics. All of this would seem to point to the possibility that Jesus makes use of a common wisdom *mashal* which did not belong to the Jewish scriptures but to their oral tradition.

140   This interpretation is supported by Metzger, *Textual Commentary*, 40, who suggests that the introduction of the textual variant ἔξεστιν into some of the ancient

"condemnation of the guiltless", "precepts of men" rather than "word of God" in this situation?

Within the phrase λαβεῖν τὸν ἄρτον, the "bread" symbol recalls Jesus' multiplication of the bread (14:19) and will be repeated again in 15:36. Each forms a prolepsis for the action of Jesus at the last meal that he shares with his disciples (26:26). Hence, bread is not only representative of the tradition, but also of the abundance of gifts associated with the βασιλεία which Jesus inaugurates by his ministry, as well as being representative of Jesus himself. It is these gifts of the abundance of the βασιλεία which Jesus must give in accordance with the merciful designs of God. He searches to know these designs in recalling the parable of v. 26.

The woman, for her part, takes the parable as applying to herself in her two-fold marginality as woman and Gentile as her "Yes, Lord" indicates. She also extends it by directing attention to the possibility for the outsider, the dog in comparison to the child, to receive the crumbs without depriving the children.[141] She thereby continues to claim at least some of the fruits of the βασιλεία preaching of Jesus for herself and for her daughter.

The exclamation of Jesus in response--"O Woman, great is your faith!" (15:28)--indicates his recognition of the fidelity of the woman to her initiative and to her request for life for her daughter. His granting of the woman's request--"Be it done to you as you desire"--represents his response to his own call beyond traditional boundaries of gender and race that came to him through his dialogue with the Canaanite woman.[142]

On the one hand, the authoritative words of Jesus [ὦ γύναι, μεγάλη σου ἡ πίστις] focus the reader's attention on the uniqueness of the faith of the woman,[143] a faith which goes beyond that of the woman with the

---

manuscripts [D it sy[s.c]; Or] in the place of the more original ἔστιν καλόν was to strengthen Jesus' reply from what was appropriate to what was lawful.

141 Patte, *Structural Commentary*, 222, calls the woman's prolongation of Jesus' metaphor "human secular wisdom ... not opposed to the will of God, and thus not to Jesus' vocation."

142 Ibid., 223.

143 While the entire phrase has no parallel elsewhere in Matthew, the address ὦ γύναι has no parallel elsewhere in the synoptics. Regarding the import of this address, Dermience, "Péricope," 43, n. 127, writes: "Le vocatif renforcé par l'interjection ὦ est bien attesté dans la LXX (Gn 27,20; 2 R 6,5; 20,3; Jr 22,18; 4 Ma 15,17: ὦ μόνη γύναι). L'adresse γύναι est des plus respectueuses, comme en témoignent plusieurs textes anciens (e.a. Odysée VI,168: ὡς σέ, γύναι, ἄγαμαί τε, ...) et Jdt 11,1: θάρσησον, γύναι, μὴ φοβηθῇς τῇ καρδίᾳ (σου)." Supporting Dermience's position and yet taking it a step further, Maximilian Zerwick, *Biblical Greek*, SPIB 114, trans. J. Smith (Rome: Biblical Institute Press, 1963), 11-12, § 35, indicates that the use of ὦ with the vocative was very common in classical usage but its omission had become the rule by Hellenistic times

haemorrhage (9:22) and that of the centurion (8:13) whose stories closely parallel her story. This parallel is seen particularly in relation to the story of the centurion, for in both, a Gentile approaches Jesus seeking healing for a dependant and Jesus grants the healing after a dialogue with the supplicant. The centurion approaches Jesus in his own town, Capernaum, and even though Jesus initially questions the granting of the request, the centurion, from his position of power, enters into a dialogue with Jesus regarding authority and the power of a word of authority (8:7-9). The Canaanite woman, on the other hand, approaches Jesus outside his own country. Following Jesus' failure to grant her request, and from a position of powerlessness, she continues with her plea and it is Jesus who enters into a dialogue with her regarding his own authority to extend his healing power to grant the request of a woman and that within gentile territory. Jesus' exclamation therefore draws attention to the extraordinary faith of a woman which has extended the boundaries of the βασιλεία to include active response to the public requests of women. Female power has once again endured against all the barriers which the patriarchal culture has erected against it, and the words of Jesus emphasize this triumph.

On the other hand, Jesus' granting of the woman's request brings his own point of view into line with the narrator's point of view in 12:17-21, but also indicates that the woman already revealed that point of view by way of her initial request and her fidelity to that. It functions in the narrative as a "prophetic exception" which points forward to the mission which will be entrusted to his disciples following his death and the proclamation of his resurrection (28:16-20).[144] This prophetic action of Jesus occurs as a result of a dialogue with a woman. The woman stands, therefore, at one of the pivotal points in the Matthean narrative and in the whole Matthean vision of the

---

and so when it is used there is some specific reason for it. This together with the emphatic positioning of the adjective σου, draws attention to both the woman and her faith.

144 Meier, *Law and History*, 27-30, considers 10:5-6, 15:24 and 28:16-20 as the starting point for reconstructing Matthew's vision of "salvation history". The public ministry of Jesus was restricted in principle to the people of Israel with just a few "prophetic exceptions", 15:21-28 being one of them. Only with the new age following the death and the proclamation of the resurrection of Jesus did the mission become universal. Strecker, *Der Weg*, 101-103, argues that the mission of Jesus included Gentiles directly after his death whereas Walker, *Die Heilsgeschichte*, 60-63, sees the shift in mission from Israel to the Gentiles occurring only after 70 CE. For each, 10:5 and 15:24 act as key verses in determining their understanding of the framework in which the early church understood the Jesus-event and its implications for a particular understanding of history.

Jesus-event. She is the catalyst, and as such, the "foremother" of all gentile christians.[145]

What we see here is the amplification of one of the narrative clues found already in the prologue to the gospel. There, Rahab and Ruth, women from outside Israel whose courageous initiative shaped Israel's history in ways commensurate with the divine plan, were linked to the birth story of Jesus so that they challenged the patriarchal construct in which it was told. Here too, a woman from outside Israel has shown the same courageous initiative and perseverance and this has shaped the Jesus story and the story of the Jesus movement in a way which is similarly commensurate with the divine point of view as it is presented in the narrative. This story, like that of the women in the genealogy, critiques the androcentric perspective revealed in the gospel, especially in the account of Jesus' ministry.

Initially, the faith of the woman serves as a foil for the lack of understanding of the disciples who, without compassion, would have sent her away (15:23); but beyond that, a foil for the lack of faith and understanding of both the disciples and Peter manifest in this section of the narrative. Whereas the woman cries out [ἔκραζεν] in supplication, the disciples who see Jesus walking on the water cry out in fear [ἀπὸ τοῦ φόβου ἔκραξαν] (14:26). She remains faithful to her initial request despite its three-fold rejection by Jesus (15:23, 24, 26) whereas Peter cannot sustain his faith in the face of the winds and waves. His fearful cry:

ἔκραξεν λέγων·   κύριε, σῶσόν με   (14:30),

earns the severe reprimand of Jesus: "O man of little faith [ὀλιγόπιστε]. The similar cry of supplication of the woman,

ἔκραζεν λέγουσα·   ἐλέησόν με, κύριε   (15:22),

sustained even in the face of Jesus' failure to respond immediately to her plea, earns the praise of Jesus: "O woman, great is your faith [μεγάλη σου ἡ πίστις].

Furthermore, Peter's great act of faith, "You are the Christ, the Son of the living God" (16:16) cannot be sustained in the face of the passion predictions, and his attempt to counteract it becomes the catalyst for Jesus' most

---

145 Schüssler Fiorenza, *In Memory of Her*, 138.

severe criticism: "Get behind me, Satan! You are a hindrance to me; for you are not on the side of God, but of men" (16:23). This places Peter alongside the Jewish leaders who put aside the word of God and teach as doctrines their own precepts, human precepts (15:6, 9). The woman, on the other hand, stands out in terms of her relation to Jesus, which is based on a faith that has been able to overcome the obstacle of human precepts.

The great faith of the woman is also set over against the lack of understanding of the disciples. In the previous story, Jesus reprimands the disciples' failure to understand the parable(s) regarding tradition (15:10-14): "Are you still without understanding? [ἀσύνετοί ἐστε;]" (15:16). On the other hand, the woman not only understands Jesus' parable (15:26), but she accepts it and reinterprets it and in this draws forth Jesus' great praise. Immediately following the second multiplication of the loaves (15:32-39), the disciples enter into a discussion with Jesus regarding "leaven" and "bread", and they fail to see the difference between the bread of the Pharisees which represents a tradition which is contrary to the ways of God and the bread with which Jesus feeds the multitude, the bread of compassion, which is in accord with the compassion of God (16:5-12). Their failure to understand is likewise reprimanded by Jesus in words similar to the reprimand given to Peter: "O men of little faith [ὀλιγόπιστοι]" (16:8), a contrast, therefore, to the woman's great faith.

The context for the story of the Canaanite woman is the leaders' question regarding transgression of the traditions of the elders and Jesus' reprimand of their teaching. Subsequently, they test Jesus by asking him for a sign (16:1-4) when he has already indicated that it is evil to ask for such a sign, pointing out that the only sign he can give is that of Jonah (12:38-42).[146] For the reader, this failure to learn from the words of Jesus and opposition to him manifest among the religious leaders are highlighted by and further highlight the faith of a gentile woman who calls Jesus "Son of David" and "Lord".

Finally, according to the structure of Anderson (see Diagram 6 above), the faith of the woman can be compared to that of the Jewish men who are blind and hence outcasts like the gentile woman. While they acknowledge Jesus in words similar to those of the Canaanite woman, the first group fail to comply with Jesus' command following their cure while the woman, on

---

146   See Diagram 6 above.

the other hand, is not granted her request immediately but goes on to kneel before Jesus in worship and continues her plea. She, however, fades from the narrative while the second group of blind men are given a discipleship role as they follow Jesus on the way up to Jerusalem (20:34).

This brings us to a second aspect of the two-edged nature of women's symbolic significance in the gospel story which is manifest in this story as it was in the prologue. We have already seen how a woman who is anomalous, an outsider to the patriarchal system, has significantly advanced Jesus' understanding of his mission and his understanding of the inclusive nature of the βασιλεία, and how her story acts as a foil to those of the male disciples, the male leaders and a number of the male supplicants. Female gender is indeed a power, a strength which enables true recognition of Jesus and a fidelity to that recognition in a way that facilitates participation in the fruits of Jesus' ministry. In the final comparison above, however, it was seen that the androcentric perspective of the narrative acts as a control on this female power and strength.

The two blind men who are healed, follow Jesus along the way (20:34), indicating their ongoing discipleship of Jesus whereas this woman of great faith fades from the narrative as her story closes. She worships Jesus, addressing him as "Lord" (15:25), but the disciples who have been called "men of little faith" give voice to the climactic title "Son of God" (14:33). She understands Jesus and the nature of his ministry, calling him "Lord" and "Son of David" (15:22), but from the lips of Peter who misunderstands Jesus, one hears the title "Christ" and "Son of the living God" (16:16). It is she who initiates or calls forth the action of Jesus which becomes the central prophetic catalyst for a mission beyond the boundaries of Israel, and yet it is the eleven male disciples who will be presented as having been given that mission (28:16-20). Within the androcentric perspective of the narrative and the patriarchal structures which it encodes, female gender also functions symbolically as a limitation which prevents membership of the character group of disciples and hence the intimate knowledge of Jesus which the narrative claims for such membership.

B. Present State of Research

Traditional scholarship has passed over in virtual silence the brief references to women within this section of the narrative, and with regard to the story of the Canaanite woman has focussed solely on the theme of Jesus' mission to the Gentiles.[147] Except for the work of Anderson[148] and Selvidge,[149] there has been no attempt that I am aware of to address the significance of gender in this story and its subsequent significance for the gospel as a whole. We have, therefore, another manifestation of the phenomenon noted in the previous section, namely, that focus on a theological theme functions to assume women under that theme and its androcentric perspective. The gender reading of the text completed above indicates the limitation of such an approach.

C. An Inclusive Re-reading

Within the second half of Jesus' Galilean ministry, it has become clear that membership of various character groups--crowds, opponents and supplicants--must be read as inclusive along with the discipleship of Jesus. Thus the reader understands the responses of these various groups to Jesus as paradigmatic of male and female responses. The group of twelve male disciples stands out, therefore, more clearly as a patriarchal construct, and hence characters are judged by the reader according to the qualities of discipleship that they display rather than according to their membership of this exclusive character group.

For the feminist reader, aware of the androcentric bias of the narrative toward the male response to Jesus, the story of a Canaanite woman is even more climactic than the narrative itself suggests. It highlights the initiative of a woman who crosses both ethnic and gender boundaries, courageously maintaining her stance in the face of a three-fold opposition and thereby influencing the direction of the Jesus story. She becomes the "foremother" of

---

147 Significant works which analyze this story have already been cited above and need not be repeated here. This aspect will also be treated in much greater detail in Chapter Five below.
148 Anderson, "Gender and Reading," 14-17.
149 Selvidge, *Daughters of Jerusalem*, 78-80.

all gentile christians and she stands as the foremost example of faith in the narrative at the climax of the section whose focus is response to Jesus.

Another significant aspect of an inclusive reading of this section of the gospel is the association of both women and men with the theme of bread. They are all participants in the two scenes in which Jesus multiplies loaves and the Canaanite woman appropriates to herself the parable of the children's bread. When the bread theme reaches its climax in the passion narrative, the reader will carry certain expectations regarding the inclusive nature of this theme.

Like the previous stories of women, this too raises the question of the origin of such a tradition and its development within the Matthean community to this point of significance. What type of community would preserve such a tradition and incorporate it into its gospel story of Jesus so that it challenges the perspective of that story as well as advancing it? At this point, however, the story guides the reader into the next stage of the unfolding narrative with greater expectation regarding the narrative theme of women in relationship to Jesus and the community forming around him.

IV. JOURNEY UP TO JERUSALEM - 16:21-20:34

This section will be dealt with very briefly since there is no major story of a significant woman character within it. It does, however, contain the question posed by the mother of the sons of Zebedee and since she is one of the few women characters given a continuing narrative role, her appearance deserves special consideration.

The first passion prediction (16:21), which introduces this section of the gospel, provides the reader with a programmatic statement in the light of which the remainder of the gospel must be read. In fact, the section with which we are now dealing is the first movement in the final great act of the gospel story. Jesus directs his course decisively towards Jerusalem. The narrator conveys this movement by means of geographical references rather than determinative elements in the plot. The events in Galilee (17:22, 24) are followed by Jesus' entry into the region of Judea (19:1), and as the section draws to a close, he is seen leaving Jericho (20:29) on his way up to Jerusalem (20:17).

Against the backdrop of this movement in the plot, the narrator focusses attention on Jesus' teaching of his disciples. They dominate the entire section with only three brief references to the surrounding crowd (17:14; 19:2; 20:29) and one reference to Jesus' opponents (19:3). Questions or misunderstandings give rise to Jesus' teaching of his disciples regarding the nature of discipleship, and within this context he predicts his suffering, death and resurrection three times (16:21; 17:22-23; 20:18-19).

The final question, however, comes not from the character group named "disciples" but rather from a woman, "the mother of the sons of Zebedee". She appears before Jesus with her two sons, which points to the fact that she is a part of the group who are "going up to Jerusalem" with him--an indication perhaps of discipleship.[150] She is identified, however, in terms of her sons. She is embedded in the patriarchal family structure,[151] and her request characterizes her as the typical mother whose sole concern is for her sons.[152]

She presents herself in subservience to Jesus, kneeling before him, and she makes a request which indicates her failure to understand the nature of the messianic βασιλεία which Jesus has been preaching. The opening reference to the patriarchal familial structure reminds the reader of the teachings in this regard earlier in the gospel (10:34-39; 12:46-50), which indicate that family membership is no basis for discipleship of Jesus within the βασιλεία. The true basis for discipleship lies in the receiving of the gifts associated with the βασιλεία and in the consequent doing of the will of God. Hence a mother's request on behalf of her sons can be no guarantee of their place in the eschatological fulfilment of the βασιλεία even though they are members of the group around Jesus called disciples. They too must be open to receive the βασιλεία message of Jesus and to live in accordance with it. On these grounds, Jesus questions the mother and her sons--can you live this discipleship faithfully even if it means suffering? They answer together: "We are

---

150 Schweizer, *The Good News*, 397.
151 Bruce J. Malina, *The New Testament World: Insights from Cultural Anthropology* (London: SCM, 1983), 98, 101, 104, points out that in the Mediterranean region, the mother-son relationship was very significant. As the son grows up, he becomes her ally, and therefore a woman's most important relationship is with her son.
152 Grundmann, *Evangelium*, 444; Schweizer, *The Good News*, 397; and Moltmann-Wendel, *Women around Jesus*, 123-126. From a cultural point of view, the woman is presented as a typical mother protecting the honour of her sons.

able" (20:22). Readers are left in suspense with regard to the outcome of this
affirmation as they move with the group around Jesus toward Jerusalem,
the location foreshadowed in the narrative for Jesus' suffering.

In terms of the gender inflection of this section of the narrative, the
reader finds that it is predominantly male. At the outset, Peter stands out as
spokesperson for the disciples (16:15-16), for Jesus (17:24-25), and on his own
behalf (18:21-22); Peter, James and John witness the transfiguration of Jesus
on the mountain (17:1-8); a man's son and two blind men are healed (17:14-
18; 20:29-34); and a young man with many possessions questions Jesus
regarding the attainment of eternal life (19:16-22). In such a context, the
reader is easily seduced into understanding the references to the disciples
from the androcentric perspective in the text and into hearing the teachings
on discipleship within this section in exclusive rather than inclusive terms.

He or she is therefore quite surprised by the appearance of the woman
who questions Jesus on behalf of her sons. Scholars too have been similarly
baffled by this seemingly strange inclusion. One commonly accepted
explanation is that she was introduced in order to cast the disciples in a more
favourable light.[153] Such an androcentric explanation, however, fails to find
a true resonance in the text itself, since at the beginning of the section Peter,
who is emerging as spokesperson for the disciples, is called "Satan" when he
fails to understand the first passion prediction (16:23). The group of disciples
are reprimanded for their "little faith", which makes it impossible for them
to cast out the demon from the young boy (17:20), and for their readiness to
send the children away from Jesus (19:13-15). The reader would not be
surprised, therefore, if the request which indicates a misunderstanding of
the previous passion prediction came from the two disciples rather than
from their mother. It would be no different from Peter's misunderstanding
following the first prediction.

Elisabeth Moltmann-Wendel explains the appearance of the mother
differently. She considers that the presence of the mother as the one making
the misguided request of Jesus introduces a woman in the typical guise of
mother of significant sons,[154] but also as a mother who leaves "her family,
her husband and her occupation to follow Jesus, the wandering

---

153 Albright and Mann, *Matthew*, 241; Argyle, *The Gospel according to Matthew*, CNEB
     (Cambridge: University Press, 1963), 153; Meier, *Matthew*, 227; J. C. Fenton, *The Gospel
     of St. Matthew*, PNTC (1963; reprint, Harmondsworth, Middlesex: Penguin, 1980), 324;
     Gundry, *A Commentary*, 401; and Schweizer, *The Good News*, 397.
154 Moltmann-Wendel, *Women around Jesus*, 120-127.

preacher."[155] Her portrayal of this woman concludes with an emphasis on the fact that the mother who initially misunderstood Jesus has emancipated herself from the cast or type within whose boundaries she was introduced into the narrative, and she stands with other women followers of Jesus at the foot of the cross (27:56).[156]

The feminist reader who meets this woman as she approaches Jesus is once again reminded that the followers of Jesus include women as well as men and that the teaching of Jesus regarding discipleship that has dominated this section of the gospel is not gender specific. For this reader, the woman is representative of fallible discipleship[157] just as the male disciples are and when she is invited, together with her sons, to a more authentic response, the reader awaits this with anticipation. This and many other prolepses find their fulfilment or completion in the final section of the gospel in which the various narrative streams reach their climax.

V. JESUS' LAST DAYS IN JERUSALEM AND BEYOND
- 21:1-28:20-

Whereas the disciples dominated the previous section of the gospel narrative, the Jewish leaders move into the focal position during the Jerusalem ministry of Jesus (21:1-25:46). On the one hand, they question Jesus' authority to teach and seek ways to trap him in his teaching, while, on the other hand, many of the parables of Matt 21 and 22 are directed against them and the whole of Matt 23 is a denunciation of their practices. The previous section was also characterized by the movement from Caesarea Philippi to Jerusalem, while in this section such movement is dramatically reduced with the action being confined to Jerusalem and, at times, to the Temple itself, until Jesus leaves it definitively (24:1).

---

155 Ibid., 125. This statement cannot be substantiated from the text, but the fact that, within the narrative, the woman emerges from the crowd seems to imply that she was among the followers of Jesus.
156 Ibid., 127.
157 Malbon, "Fallible Followers," 29-48, in which she discusses the way Mark portrays both women and men as fallible and it seems that a similar motivation is operative at this point in the Matthean gospel.

The characteristic trends of the previous section and of the introduction to this last section merge in the passion narrative. The scene opens with Jesus instructing his disciples (26:2) and being plotted against by the Jewish authorities (26:3-5); it closes with the authorities' continuing plot against Jesus even after his death (28:11-15), and with Jesus' final commissioning of the eleven male disciples (28:16-20). Within this frame, the narrative moves from Jesus' last meal and evening with his disciples to his violent death at the hands of the Jewish and Roman authorities.

The gender inflection of this final section of the narrative seems clear; yet a closer examination shows that it is offset by significant stories of women (26:6-13; 26:69, 71; 27:19; 27:55-56, 61; 28:1-10).

A. The Text

Diagram 8 constructed below indicates that the central focus of the passion narrative is the person of Jesus who celebrates with his followers, prays in the garden, is arrested and brought before the Jewish Council and the Roman governor before being condemned to death by crucifixion. The last great moment in the christological development of the gospel is the proclamation of the crucified Jesus having been raised. Interwoven within each of these moments of christological significance is the response of the disciples in the first half of the narrative and the response of both opponents and faithful followers in the second half, some of the latter being women.

The entire passion narrative is framed not only with stories concerning the disciples and the leaders but also with stories of women. Each character group is, therefore, integral to the narrative as a whole.[158] The response of each to Jesus reaches a climax in the passion narrative as does the contrast between them which has been developing throughout the narrative. Against such a backdrop the individual stories of women must be read.

---

158 A number of scholars make the claim with regard to the Anointing at Bethany that it is alien to the passion narrative on the basis of its parallel in Mark's gospel. See Beare, *A Commentary*, 505; Rudolf Bultmann, *The History of the Synoptic Tradition*, trans. John Marsh (Oxford: Blackwell, 1963), 263; J. K. Elliott, "The Anointing of Jesus," *ET* 85 (1973-74): 106; and André Feuillet, "Les deux onctions faites sur Jésus, et Marie-Madeleine: Contribution à l'étude des rapports entre les synoptiques et le quatrième évangile," *RThom* 75 (1975): 364.

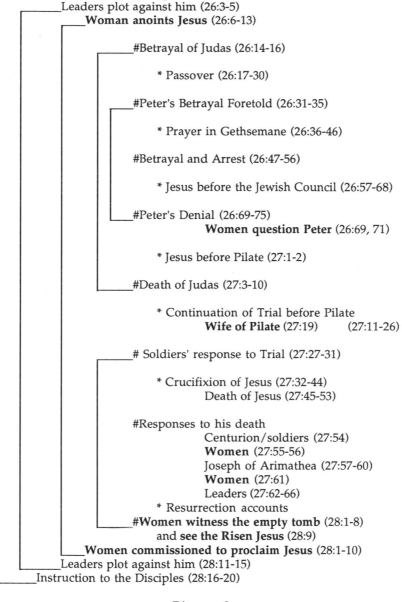

Instruction to the Disciples (26:1-2)
Leaders plot against him (26:3-5)
Woman anoints Jesus (26:6-13)

#Betrayal of Judas (26:14-16)

* Passover (26:17-30)

#Peter's Betrayal Foretold (26:31-35)

* Prayer in Gethsemane (26:36-46)

#Betrayal and Arrest (26:47-56)

* Jesus before the Jewish Council (26:57-68)

#Peter's Denial (26:69-75)
            Women question Peter (26:69, 71)

* Jesus before Pilate (27:1-2)

#Death of Judas (27:3-10)

* Continuation of Trial before Pilate
            Wife of Pilate (27:19)   (27:11-26)

Soldiers' response to Trial (27:27-31)

* Crucifixion of Jesus (27:32-44)
            Death of Jesus (27:45-53)

#Responses to his death
            Centurion/soldiers (27:54)
            Women (27:55-56)
            Joseph of Arimathea (27:57-60)
            Women (27:61)
            Leaders (27:62-66)
* Resurrection accounts
#**Women witness the empty tomb** (28:1-8)
and **see the Risen Jesus** (28:9)
Women commissioned to proclaim Jesus (28:1-10)
Leaders plot against him (28:11-15)
Instruction to the Disciples (28:16-20)

Diagram 8

1. 26:6-13

The clear and concise structuring of individual pericopes within the Matthean narrative that we have already seen is evident here also. As the reader has come to expect, Jesus is introduced by name in the opening verse and becomes the chief actor in the scene (26:6). The action of the woman is directed towards him as is indicated by the two clauses of which she is the subject: προσῆλθεν αὐτῷ ... and κατέχεεν ἐπὶ τῆς κεφαλῆς αὐτοῦ ... These actions become the focal point for the whole scene. They cause the indignant reaction of the disciples (26:8-9); and they are both defended and interpreted by Jesus (26:10-12). This middle section of the pericope is very carefully structured. Both the reaction of the disciples and the reaction of Jesus begin with a question containing the interrogative τί and, in each case, the question is followed by an explanation in the form of an introductory word plus the connective γάρ. This second part of the structure occurs once following the disciples' question and three times following the question of Jesus. Verse 13 provides the conclusion to the story.

This careful structuring can be most clearly seen in diagramatic form.

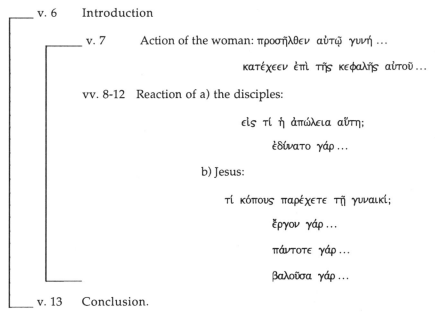

v. 6   Introduction

v. 7   Action of the woman: προσῆλθεν αὐτῷ γυνή ...

κατέχεεν ἐπὶ τῆς κεφαλῆς αὐτοῦ ...

vv. 8-12   Reaction of a) the disciples:

εἰς τί ἡ ἀπώλεια αὕτη;

ἐδύνατο γάρ ...

b) Jesus:

τί κόπους παρέχετε τῇ γυναικί;

ἔργον γάρ ...

πάντοτε γάρ ...

βαλοῦσα γάρ ...

v. 13   Conclusion.

Diagram 9

The scene is set in Bethany on the outskirts of Jerusalem, an oasis in the desert of Jesus' last days in Jerusalem. He retires there after his triumphal entry into Jerusalem is marred by the indignant reaction of the chief priests and scribes; and, following the plotting among the chief priests, elders and the high priest to kill Jesus, the narrator has him again in Bethany, the place of refuge. The setting is even more specific, however, by reference to the house of Simon the leper. Previously, within the narrative, a leper and a woman were brought together within the collection of three miracle stories in 8:1-15. There we saw that the healing power of Jesus restored both the leper and the woman to health and wholeness and hence to the worshipping community of Israel which is symbolized in the Temple. What was implied in Jesus' healing action in Matt 8 was effected indeed in 21:14 when the blind and the lame were actually healed within the Temple itself. Continual rejection by the leaders, however, causes Jesus to turn his back on the Temple definitively (24:1). Hence, the action contained within this story, which parallels the triumphant entry into Jerusalem and the Temple, now takes place in the house of Simon the leper, a place symbolic of the restored community around Jesus, the community which must share with Jesus his rejection of the Temple and its worship.[159]

It is in this situation that a woman approaches Jesus. She does not come as supplicant,[160] but as actor. This comes as a surprise to the reader who is already familiar with the introductory phrase προσῆλθεν αὐτῷ as a way of bringing others into an encounter with Jesus but generally as supplicants.[161]

---

159 Further support for this suggestion of a symbolic reference to a community of restoration around Jesus is gained from a consideration of the use of ἀνάκειμαι in v. 7. Previously in the narrative it has been used to designate reclining at a meal: 9:10 where Jesus is presented eating with tax collectors and sinners; and 22:10 where both the good and the bad share in the banquet of the kingdom. Both symbolize a new and inclusive community.

160 The woman is certainly not a supplicant in the Matthean narrative, but nor is she a prostitute according to the position taken by J. D. M. Derrett in his article, "The Anointing at Bethany and the Story of Zacchaeus," in *Law in the New Testament* (London: Darton, Longman & Todd, 1970), 266-285. Such a trend reflects an interpretation of this story which began with the Lukan narrator. Schüssler Fiorenza, *In Memory of Her*, 128-129, indicates that the woman is designated "sinner" in the Lukan narrative to illustrate more strongly that the kingdom of Jesus is open to sinners. Not all subsequent interpreters make this careful distinction, however, when they call the woman in each gospel a prostitute.

161 They come to hear his teaching (5:1; 13:36; 24:3; 26:17); to make a request (20:20); to seek healing (8:5; 9:28; 14:15; 15:30; 17:14; 21:14); or to find confirmation of suspicions and doubts (19:3; 22:23). In this analysis, I have concentrated on the specific form--aorist of προέρχομαι (singular or plural) plus αὐτῷ. There are many other similar constructions using different forms of the verb which would strengthen further the point made above.

Here, however, the introductory formula is not followed by a request but rather by a definitive action directed towards Jesus: κατέχεεν ἐπὶ τῆς κεφαλῆς αὐτοῦ. Apart from the significance of the action itself, it represents a development in the narration of the stories in which women function as significant characters. First, the mother-in-law of Peter does not even dare to ask anything of Jesus; the woman with the haemorrhage fearfully approaches him from behind merely to touch his garment; the Canaanite woman openly approaches with a request and enters into dialogue with Jesus; and now an unnamed woman not only approaches Jesus but offers him the honourable gesture of anointing his head. The significance of such a gesture must now be examined.

In order to understand the nature of the woman's action within this story, it is necessary to go outside the story and to draw on available historical information. Hence, a brief excursus into the meaning of anointing for the first century reader will follow.

Excursus on Anointing:

The language of this scene is unique to this particular story in the Christian Scriptures,[162] and is not the typical language of anointing whereby the verbs ἀλείφω or χρίω would normally be used; and ἔλαιον (oil) would be found with or replacing μύρον which has more the sense of perfumed ointment.[163] This brief historical survey focusses, therefore, on the linguistic background to κατέχεεν (μύρον) ἐπὶ τῆς κεφαλῆς rather than on anointing generally.

In the Septuagint, μύρον is one of the words used to translate the Hebrew שֶׁמֶן. In Exod 30:25, it is used in a cultic sense, μύρον being equated with "holy anointing oil" [ἔλαιον χρῖσμα ἅγιον] with which the tent of meeting, the ark of the commandments, the table, lampstand, altar and the priests were anointed and in this way consecrated or made sacred (Exod 30:26-31). Its more general usage,

---

162 The word μύρον occurs in Matthew, Mark and John only within the story of the anointing at Bethany (cf. Matt 26:6-13; Mark 14:3-9; John 12:1-8). In Luke, it occurs in a similar anointing which the Lukan narrator places much earlier in the ministry of Jesus at 7:36-50. Luke also refers to the women preparing ἀρώματα καὶ μύρα to take to the tomb of Jesus (Luke 23:56); and the author of the Book of Revelation lists μύρον among the many items in the cargo of the merchants of this earth (18:13). Only in Matt 26:7 and Mark 14:3, however, is it linked to the verb καταχέω and only in those two verses does it state that the oil was poured over the head of Jesus. It is these three items taken together which make the language of this scene unique.

163 Heinrich Schlier, "ἀλείφω," TDNT I:229-232.

however, is as a sign of peace (Ps 133:2), of gladness (Prov 27:9), of prosperity and abundance (Cant 1:3; 4:10, 14; Is 25:6; 39:2; Ps 91:11; Qo 9:8). In the prophets (Amos 6:6), it can stand as a counter-sign of God's generous abundance when its possession and use are set over against neglect for the poor. However, it also functions symbolically as a sign of God's abundant generosity to humanity (Is 25:6; Ps 23:5). Interestingly, the setting for these last two references is a meal.

When a specific part of the body is mentioned as having been anointed, it is always the head (Pss 133:2; 23:5; Qo 9:8). There is only one reference which would link the use of μύρον with burial (2 Chr 16:14), and here it is used in the sense of placing spices on the bier rather than of pouring oil or ointment over the head. Referring to Asa, the Chronicler states:

> They buried him in the tomb which he had hewn out for himself in the city of David. They laid him on a bier which had been filled with various kinds of spices prepared by the perfumers' art [ἀρωμάτων καὶ γένη μύρων μυρεψῶν].

In summary, therefore, the Septuagint could be said to use μύρον as a sign of honour, well-being, or prosperity which particular persons enjoyed, for which they prayed, or which another offered to them, but it also carries certain cultic connotations.

For the Rabbis, the anointing with oil at a meal would have been known as the obscure reference in b. Hul. 94a indicates, but since it required no legislation, it is not mentioned elsewhere. The more common reference in the Talmud is to the preparation and use of the sacred oil in keeping with the precepts of Exod 30:22-33,[164] and these references are generally concerned with those on whom the sacred oils may not be used. Other legislation concerns the use of oil for healing, but the distinction is often made that this oil is smeared on the body and not poured over it.[165] Pouring oil over the head, on the other hand, functioned in specific circumstances as a sign of consecration. Thus b. Ker. 5b states:

> Our Rabbis have taught: In anointing kings one draws the figure of a crown, and with priests in the shape of the letter chi. Said R. Menashia: The Greek [letter] chi is meant. One [Tanna] teaches: The oil was first poured over the

---

164   b. Hor. 11b, 12a; b. Mak. 13a; b. Ker. 2a, 3a, 5a.

165   These references are scarce and much less specific, cf. b. Šabb. 10a; 77b; b. Sanh. 77a.

head and then smeared between the eye-lids whereas another [Tanna]
teaches: The oil was first smeared between the eye-lids and then poured over
the head.

Later in the same tractate, the meaning of anointing is given: "the
consecration of the anointing oil of his God is upon him" (b. Ker
7a). The word used for 'oil' is שֶׁמֶן, which we have already seen is
translated in the Septuagint by μύρον, and the verb יָצַק ("to pour" in
the above passage) is translated in the Septuagint by καταχέω.

In Josephus too, καταχέω and μύρον are used together, and here with
the sense of "giving honour": "after crowning and anointing him
with unguents" (Ag. Ap. 2.36 §256), a symbolic reference to Plato's
treatment of Homer in his writings.

Finally, as has already been noted, καταχέω and μύρον are not used
in the Christian Scriptures outside the story of the anointing at
Bethany, but ἀλείφω is used to refer to the anointing of the head as a
sign of well-being (Matt 6:17), to healing anointing (Mark 6:13), to
the anointing at a meal (Luke 7:46), and to the anointing for burial
(Mark 16:1). This indicates that all of these understandings of the act
of anointing were current in the first century.

In v. 7, the reader encounters a very clear statement of the action of the
woman seemingly without explanation or indication as to its meaning:

προσῆλθεν αὐτῷ γυνὴ
          ἔχουσα ἀλάβαστρον μύρου βαρυτίμου
καὶ κατέχεεν ἐπὶ τῆς κεφαλῆς αὐτοῦ
          ἀνακειμένου.

Hence, it would seem that a number of possible meanings can play in the
reader's mind at this point in the story. The only indicator of a specific
meaning is the use of ἀνάκειμαι immediately following the action of anointing, which would suggest that the setting is not only within the house of
Simon but at a meal.[166] The woman could, therefore, be seen to honour
Jesus by this gesture and to indicate her desire that he be given the peace and

---

166 Donald Senior, *The Passion Narrative according to Matthew: A Redactional Study*,
BEThL XXXIX (1975; reprint, Leuven: University Press, 1982), 32, states that "the verb
ἀνάκειμαι is used consistently by Matthew to designate an attitude of repose at a meal,
while κατάκειμαι seems to be considered more applicable to sick persons."

well-being that come from God.[167] The language itself does not immediately point to the sacred anointing of a king (cf. 1 Sam 16:13; 1 Kgs 1:34, 39; 2 Kgs 9:3) despite the fact that the text indicates that the oil is poured over the head (1 Sam 10:1 combines the language of sacred anointing of kings with a reference to oil being poured over the head).[168]

The broader context, however, makes this last interpretation a possibility. Already in the gospel, Jesus has received messianic acclaim but of a different order from that given to an earthly monarch. He entered Jerusalem as king but "humble and mounted on an ass" (21:5), and was acclaimed by the crowds as "Son of David" (21:9). Jesus' response to this welcome and acclamation was to drive the money-changers and sellers out of the Temple and to claim it for the blind and the lame whom he healed. In response to these actions of Jesus as well as to the acclaim he had received, the chief priests and scribes became indignant:

ἰδόντες δὲ οἱ ἀρχιερεῖς καὶ οἱ γραμματεῖς ... ἠγανάκτησαν

(Matt 21:15).

As Jesus enters into his passion, a woman pours oil over his head, an action which in itself could be construed as further messianic acclaim, the language which differs from the expected language for sacred anointings being an indication that a different type of kingship is understood here.[169] The use of language other than the typical language of messianic anointing may also result from an androcentric perspective which will not allow a woman to assume the role of anointing which was reserved for men and for specifically designated men at that. In response to such a messianic acclaim at the hands of a woman, the disciples are indignant as were the chief priests and scribes at the strange kingly acclaim Jesus received from the crowd on his entry into Jerusalem:

---

167 The use of the *hapax legomenon* βαρύτιμος meaning "very expensive" or "precious" underscores the lavishness of the woman's gesture and also the honour which she wishes to bestow on Jesus as a recognition of his person.

168 This is contrary to the argument of Elliott, "The Anointing," 106, who claims reference to kingship simply on the basis of the pouring of oil over the head without any other exploration of linguistic evidence. The investigations above indicate that pouring oil over the head is used in a number of situations that are not royal or cultic anointings. Selvidge, *Daughters of Jerusalem*, 82, suggests, in her redaction critical study that Matthew chose not to use the typical language of anointing which was associated with power and dominion but rather the language associated with kindness.

169 This theme of kingship is further developed as the passion narrative unfolds; see 27:11, 29, 37, 42.

ἰδόντες δὲ οἱ μαθηταὶ ἠγανάκτησαν ...   (Matt 26:8).

Both groups misunderstand the person and the mission of Jesus and react with a question to Jesus: "Do you hear what these are saying?" (21:16) and "Why this waste?" (26:8).

The misunderstanding of the disciples is further emphasized when they give the reason for their question: "For this ointment might have been sold for a large sum and given to the poor."[170] They have completely missed the significance of this moment in Jesus' life, a moment which he has just indicated to them is two days before his being delivered up to be crucified. Simon offers Jesus the hospitality of his house and his table. The woman pours ointment over Jesus' head with a sensitivity whose full import is still not yet clear to the reader. The disciples are sensitive neither to the time in Jesus' unfolding life story nor to the action of the woman. They simply interpret the outpouring of the ointment as "waste".

That they have focussed on what is secondary rather than what is primary at this moment is further exemplified when we look at the theme of "the poor" [πτωχός] in the Matthean narrative as a whole. The first Matthean beatitude is addressed not only to the materially poor, but to the poor in spirit (5:3). It is not physical poverty which is a cause for rejoicing in the Matthean community, but rather an attitude of mind and heart which knows the giftedness and limitation of one's own humanity. The preaching of the gospel to the poor is, however, one sign among many which Jesus gives to the disciples of John to indicate that he is the Coming One (11:5); and the call which Jesus offers to the rich young man (19:21) indicates that giving to the poor is constitutive of discipleship of Jesus. In fact, in his last great sermon, Jesus identifies himself with those in need of compassion amongst whom the poor could be numbered (25:40). The disciples have left everything and followed Jesus (19:27), but at this unique moment when he faces suffering and death, they become concerned with giving to the poor whereas the action of the woman shows a recognition of Jesus' own need.

For the reader, the indignation of the disciples and their question are a reminder of their reaction to the Canaanite woman's persistent approach to

---

170 F. Blass, A. Debrunner and R. W. Funk, *A Greek Grammar of the New Testament and Other Early Christian Literature* (Chicago: University of Chicago Press, 1961), 235-236 § 452 (1), suggest that this construction [ἐδύνατο γὰρ τοῦτο πραθῆναι πολλοῦ καὶ δοθῆναι πτωχοῖς] with γάρ may indicate the reason for a reproach (expressed or unexpressed). This seems to be the sense in which it is used in this pericope.

Jesus (15:23). The contrast established between the group called disciples and the women characters is strengthened.[171] Also, their misunderstanding and failure to recognize this final moment of Jesus' journey is in keeping with a dominant theme in this section of the narrative, namely, the disciples' ultimate failure in spite of all that they have both heard and seen while they were with Jesus. In fact, a contrast seems to be set up between this scene and the two previous ones.

At the beginning of the passion narrative, Jesus speaks plainly to his disciples of his approaching passion: "You know that after two days the Passover is coming, and the Human One* will be delivered up to be crucified", and the stage is set for all that follows. On the one hand, the chief priests and the elders gather in the palace of the high priest and plan how they can kill Jesus. Jesus, on the other hand, gathers with his disciples in the house of a leper at Bethany and here is anointed by a woman. The action of the woman is set, therefore, in direct contrast to the action of Jesus' opponents. The reaction of the disciples puts them also in direct contrast to the woman. The irony of their reaction ("Why this waste?") is further emphasized when, immediately following this scene, Judas, one of the disciples, goes to the chief priests asking for money in return for the betrayal of Jesus whereas the woman has poured out expensive ointment for his anointing.

Jesus' question turns the focus of the narrative back to the woman. The use of the noun γυνή is clearly a narrative device used for this very purpose. Jesus then, in giving reasons for his reproach of the disciples, also offers an interpretation of the woman's act from three different perspectives.

The first interpretation calls the action of the woman ἔργον καλόν (a good work or deed). Ἔργον standing alone in the Matthean narrative simply refers to a deed or action (11:2; 11:19; 23:3, 5). The context allows the reader to determine whether such deeds are in line with the point of view of the narrator or not. When καλός is added, however, it brings the actions referred to into the Matthean ethical realm. What is good is set over against what is bad or evil.[172] What the disciples have interpreted as waste [ἀπώλεια] and

---

171 From 10:1 onwards when the character group called "disciples" have been more clearly defined as male, they have appeared in each of the stories in which women have functioned as central characters in conflict with or contrast to the women.

172 This ethical distinction is established primarily by way of imagery: the good tree/good fruit and the bad tree/bad fruit (3:10; 7:17-20; 12:33); the good seed and good earth (13:8, 23, 24, 27, 37, 38); good pearls (13:45); and good fish (13:48).

therefore put in the category of bad or evil,[173] Jesus interprets as good. But
even more importantly, he acknowledges the significance of the action as being done to himself [εἰς ἐμέ]. Good deeds directed towards the person of Jesus
are rare in the Matthean narrative: the angels minister to him (4:11) as do
Peter's mother-in-law (8:15) and the women who follow Jesus from Galilee
(27:55), and Joseph of Arimathea takes his body and buries it (27:57-60). Of all
these deeds, however, only the anointing action of this woman is given over
to Jesus for interpretation. His εἰς ἐμέ recalls the great eschatological discourse which has just preceded in which Jesus proclaimed: "as you did it to
one of the least of these my brethren [τῶν ἀδελφῶν μου], you did it to me"
(25:40).[174] The eschatological judge, the triumphant messiah (25:31) will
consider as done to himself those good deeds which are done to the least
among humanity. The woman has anticipated this coming when she performs her good deed directly for Jesus. The earlier suggestion of messianic
symbolism is confirmed in the first interpretation given to the woman's
action.

The significance of the εἰς ἐμέ is even further emphasized by the second
interpretation given by Jesus: "for you always have the poor with you, but
you will not always have me." This would seem to be Jesus' response to the
objection raised by the disciples. It calls to mind for the reader a similar
statement made earlier in the narrative which also compared the time of
Jesus' presence with his disciples with the time beyond his death: "Can the
wedding guests mourn as long as the bridegroom is with them? The days
will come when the bridegroom is taken away from them, and then they
will fast" (9:15). The woman, in performing this anointing of Jesus rather
than selling the ointment and giving the money to the poor, is said to have
anticipated the imminent delivery of Jesus into the hands of those who will
crucify him (26:2). She has recognized what Jesus now gives voice to,
namely, the importance of the time that he is with his followers, when their
attention should be directed towards him rather than towards performing
good deeds.[175] This is particularly so in the present context in which the
imminence of Jesus' departure has been made explicit.

---

173   It is significant here that the only other use of ἀπώλεια is at 7:13 which has strong
      ethical connotations: "Enter by the narrow gate for the gate is wide and the way is easy
      that leads to destruction [ἀπώλεια]."
174   In the eschatological discourse, the dative ἐμοί is used rather than the εἰς ἐμέ of v. 10
      but the sense of a good action directed towards Jesus is the same in each case.
175   This importance and uniqueness of Jesus' presence is further emphasized by the use of
      πάντοτε for the first and only time in the narrative. However, this verse does not deny

In the third interpretation, the exact language of the narrator (v. 7) is changed in the mouth of Jesus so that he can give his own symbolic interpretation to the woman's action. The allusion-filled ἔχουσα ἀλάβαστρον μύρου βαρυτίμου καὶ κατέχεεν ἐπὶ τῆς κεφαλῆς αὐτοῦ[176] is changed to the very simple βαλοῦσα γὰρ αὕτη τὸ μύρον τοῦτο ἐπὶ τοῦ σώματός μου which is without allusion.[177] Jesus then gives a further amplification: "she has done it to prepare me for burial", and so shifts the attention from head [κεφαλή] to body [σῶμα]. Again her act is interpreted as one of anticipation.[178] This time, it is said to anticipate the fact that Jesus' death by crucifixion will deny him the normal burial customs.[179]

By means of this three-fold interpretation, Jesus points to the prophetic nature of the woman's action.[180] She herself, however, does not interpret her prophetic action as do the prophets of old, a fact which denies her a voice. This woman who performs one of the most significant acts within the gospel story and whose action functions as a powerful critique of those patriarchal structures whereby significant acts of history are reserved for males is denied a voice. Her story is brought back into the patriarchal order by the androcentric narrator who denies her this voice. Her action is interpreted in the male voice of Jesus. His is certainly the authoritative voice at this point in the narrative but it is still a male voice. The action itself, however, cries out with its own voice which cannot be silenced. The woman has recognized

---

the importance of good deeds towards the poor but rather seeks to focus on the importance of this time with Jesus before his death. See Bonnard, *Évangile*, 372: "l'opposition de ces deux oeuvres n'est pas principielle mais temporelle: tant que le Christ est là et surtout le Christ souffrant toute acte d'amour ou d'adoration à son égard est plus urgent que les aumônes aux pauvres."

176   Much of the significance of this phrase has already been explored. It should be noted, however, that the linking of μύρον and καταχέω also has significant attestation in classical Greek writings. See "καταχέω" in *BAGD*, 420.

177   In the discussion of "βάλλω" in *BAGD*, 130-131, there is no classical attestation for the verb when it has the sense of pouring ointment on the body.

178   Derrett, "The Anointing," 274.

179   Under Roman Law, the body of a criminal was given for burial only as a result of the good-will of the competent authority (see Tacitus, *Ann.* 6,29 and Ulpian, *Dig.*, 48,24,1). Many of those crucified outside the walls of Jerusalem were possibly buried in a common grave in the Valley of Gehennah.

180   While Elliott, "The Anointing," 105, calls the action of the woman "a symbolic act of acknowledging a king's consecration", Senior, *The Passion*, 28, takes up the explanation of Lagrange, *Évangile*, 492, who calls the action "une prophétie en action de la passion prochaine" and makes it more explicit as "a symbolic act of preparation for burial." Witherington III, *Women in the Ministry*, 115, combines these two aspects and draws out the significance for the early gospel communities: "It is possible that Mary's [?] act of anointing is presented by the first and second and even the fourth evangelist as a coronation ritual, but it is more probable that it is seen as a prophetic burial rite. The Gospel writers may be implying that it was acceptable for women to take on the role or tasks of a prophet."

the uniqueness of this moment in the life of Jesus. She focusses her whole being on him, undistracted by other ethical considerations. In pouring out costly oil on his head, she honours him while praying for his peace and strength and well-being as he enters into his passion. Her action also acknowledges him as Anointed One, but of a different order which will be accomplished only through the passion. Finally, she prepares his body for burial, a task which loved ones do for their beloved or disciples for their teacher (14:12; 27:57). It is the power of this action which draws forth the concluding declaration of Jesus.

As in the conclusion to the story of the Canaanite woman, the authoritative voice of Jesus directly characterizes a female participant in the gospel story. The solemnity of his declaration in v. 13 is revealed in its careful structuring. It begins with the familiar statement used repeatedly in Matthew to alert the reader to an important saying by Jesus: ἀμὴν λέγω ὑμῖν.[181] The saying itself falls into two carefully paralleled clauses, each of three parts: verb, subject and adverbial phrase. It seems, therefore, that each part of one clause is intended to assist in the interpretation of its parallel in the other.

ὅπου ἐὰν κηρυχθῇ   τὸ εὐαγγέλιον τοῦτο   ἐν ὅλῳ τῷ κόσμῳ,

λαληθήσεται καὶ ὃ ἐποίησεν αὕτη   εἰς μνημόσυνον αὐτῆς.
                                              (Matt 26:13)

One clue to the interpretation of this verse lies in the clear paralleling of κηρυχθῇ and λαληθήσεται. Both have a future passive sense even though κηρυχθῇ is in the aorist subjunctive form as is determined by the conjunction ὅπου ἐάν. Their meaning is almost interchangeable and hence they help to guide the interpretation of each clause. Whenever the gospel is preached, the story of the woman's action will be told in the whole world as a remembrance of her. But also, the gospel will only be preached fully when the action of this woman is included in its retelling and in the community's remembering.

---

181 This phrase occurs 31 times in Matthew's gospel. Gerhard Ebeling, "Jesus and Faith," in idem, *Word and Faith*, trans. James W. Leitch (London: SCM, 1963), 237, says of Jesus' use of ἀμήν: "It gives expression to the fact that Jesus understood his statements, and wished to have them understood, as statements made before God, in which God ... is the Guarantor of what is said and watches over the authentication of this word, i.e. sees to it that it comes about."

The most surprising phrase for the reader is the concluding one εἰς μνημόσυνον αὐτῆς and hence we will turn to it first. The use of the noun μνημόσυνον is unique in the Matthean narrative.[182] The verb μνημονεύω, however, is used in Matt 16:9 and may provide some clues to the interpretation of the noun. In 16:8-9, Jesus asks with surprise of his disciples:

> O men of little faith, why do you discuss among yourselves the fact that you have no bread? Do you not yet perceive? Do you not remember [οὐδὲ μνημονεύετε] the five loaves of the five thousand, and how many baskets you gathered?

"To remember" is not only to call to mind, but to understand and to believe in the works of Jesus, works which are not just the multiplication of loaves to feed the hungry but are those enumerated in response to John's question: "Are you the Coming One [ὁ ἐρχόμενος] or shall we look for another?" (11:3). Jesus replies that the blind receive their sight, the lame walk, lepers are cleansed and the deaf hear, the dead are raised up and the poor have the good news [εὐαγγέλιον] preached to them (11:5). These are the signs of the Coming One, these are the signs of a different messianic order as the interplay between ὁ ἐρχόμενος, Son of David and King in the triumphal entry into Jerusalem indicate (21:1-11). These are, therefore, the signs of the βασιλεία; and in this narrative, the gospel is the gospel of the βασιλεία. The three times that εὐαγγέλιον is used in the narrative other than here in 26:13, it is always εὐαγγέλιον τῆς βασιλείας.[183] In Matthew, therefore, "to remember" is to see, to understand, and to participate in the power of the βασιλεία manifest in the deeds of Jesus. This remembering is constitutive of the proclaiming of the gospel of the βασιλεία.

Here, however, an extraordinary shift has been made. It is not the action of Jesus which will be remembered,[184] but rather a woman's action. Her good work which was a recognition of the impending suffering which Jesus faced is recognized as parallel to the works of Jesus on behalf of broken and suffering humanity. Together they are to be proclaimed as gospel. But even more extraordinarily, Jesus does not claim the story in his memory but in

---

182 The only other times that it is used in the entire New Testament is in the Markan parallel (Mark 14:9), and in Acts 10:4.

183 4:23; 9:35; 24:14.

184 Within the early christian communities, the remembrance of Jesus was highlighted in the celebration of a meal which recalled his final meal with his own followers before his death. This is reflected in Paul's letter to the Corinthians as a conclusion to the account of this meal in 1 Cor 11:25: "Do this, as often as you drink it, in remembrance of me [εἰς τὴν ἐμὴν ἀνάμνησιν]."

hers. No such statement is made in relation to any other person within the Matthean narrative, nor within the entire gospel tradition; and the remembering is not simply by God at the eschaton as some scholars claim in a way which detracts from the extraordinary honour given by Jesus to this woman,[185] but it is a remembrance in the concrete human world which moves towards the eschaton.[186] As Michel states:

> What Jesus has said and done has been for remembrance by the community, just as the anointing in Bethany was authoritatively dedicated to the remembrance of the woman.[187]

This unique prophetic action of the woman at Bethany takes its place, therefore, alongside of and complementary to the actions of Jesus. The preaching and the telling of both comprise the gospel which will be proclaimed in the whole world. To hear this gospel is not only to hear the stories of Jesus and to remember him by means of them, but it is also to hear the story of a woman's prophetic action and thereby to remember her.

The story of a woman at the beginning of the passion narrative is a story of female power, a power which recognizes suffering and reaches out courageously to bring the touch of mercy and compassion to the one suffering. As the words of Jesus at the end of her story indicate, it is the most extraordinary story of one of the followers of Jesus and hence is to be continually proclaimed as gospel. Female gender therefore symbolizes faithful discipleship at this point in the narrative. The force of this symbol is, however, blunted by the androcentric narrative. This woman of compassion is given no name nor is she given a voice in the narrative. Her prophetic action is interpreted by the male voice of Jesus. Also, like the Canaanite woman, there is no story of her call within the narrative and she is excluded from among the group called "disciples" because of its patriarchal construct. Her action, however, stands as a powerful critique of the response of both the patriarchally structured group of disciples and of leaders as the passion begins. Moreover, her story has been foreshadowed in the narrative by that of Tamar, Rahab and

---

185 This position was first put forward by J. Jeremias, "Beobachtungen zu neutestamentlichen Stellen an Hand des neugefundenen griechischen Henoch-Textes," *ZNW* 38 (1939): 116-117. J. Harold Greenlee, "Εἰς μνημόσυνον αὐτῆς, 'For her Memorial': Mt xxvi. 13; Mk xiv. 9," *ET* 71 (1959-60): 245, also argues against the common interpretation of Jesus' words as indicating a remembering of the woman. He claims, on the other hand, that it is a memorial to Jesus.

186 When we look at all the Matthean references, it is clear that the word κόσμος is always used with the primary meaning of the concrete world of human history, cf. 4:8; 5:14; 13:35, 38; 16:26; 18:7; 24:21; 25:34; 26:13.

187 Otto Michel, "μνημονεύω," *TDNT* IV:682.

Ruth, whose extraordinary initiative was also domesticated in the service of patriarchy.

As the story moves on, all those who symbolize patriarchy are set over against Jesus. Members of the group of male disciples betray Jesus, deny any association with him and eventually all flee leaving Jesus in the hands of the Jewish and Roman authorities who bring about his death. At brief moments, however, women stand out from these groups.

Two of these brief moments occur during Peter's denial of Jesus (26:69, 71) and Jesus' trial before Pilate (27:19). In the first, two women recognize Peter as being with Jesus and their affirmation of this is set over against Peter's vigorous denial. While their affirmation symbolically places them on the side of Jesus so that they symbolize the truth, Peter, on the other hand, symbolizes falsehood and is characterized as unfaithful to Jesus at this crucial moment. In the second brief moment, Pilate's wife is referred to by the narrator. Like Herodias, she does not appear on the scene, but her words of warning, which claim Jesus as a righteous man, stand out in stark contrast to the sea of accusations surrounding him. Like the two women who recognized Peter, she is given a voice in the narrative even though she is introduced as embedded in the patriarchal structure. Her words, like theirs, place her on the side of Jesus and of the truth; but like them, she has no power in or against the male world which surrounds her and which claims power over life and death even on the basis of falsehood. In the narrative, these female voices are drowned out by the male voices of denial and condemnation, a point which is illustrated by the many interpretations which pass over these verses in silence. In a gender reading, however, they are significant especially in terms of their symbolic function. This symbolic function will receive more attention at the end of this section. We turn, therefore, to the final stories of significant women characters, those who remain with Jesus at the foot of the cross and at the tomb.

2. 27:55-56, 61; 28:1-10

A significant factor in this section of our study is the question of the validity of treating these three stories or references together as part of the same movement in the narrative. A brief glance at scholarly opinions indicates

that they are divided on this issue.[188] The analysis of the text above
[Diagram 8] showed that there was a clear parallel between the three opening
and closing stories of the passion-resurrection narrative so that they function as a frame for the entire narrative from 26:1-28:20, supporting the claim
that it be treated as a narrative unit.[189] Here, I will argue further that a
recognition of the interrelationship between the stories of the women who,
together with Jesus, are central characters in this final part of the narrative,
will reveal a very skilfully interwoven conclusion to the passion-
resurrection account which began in 26:1.

With regard to 27:55-56, Senior is correct when he says:

> The adverb [ἐκεῖ] serves an important linking function with the previous
> portion of the pericope, thus helping identify the women (even though they
> look on "from afar") with the centurion and the guards as believing
> witnesses to the manifestation of God's power.[190]

Moreover, the verb θεωρέω as a transitive verb implies an object, and here
that object is the cross, the crucified one and the events surrounding the crucifixion. Hence, the two short verses, 27:55-56, certainly look back toward the
preceding scene. They are linked linguistically, however, with the scenes
which follow. The verb θεωρέω is associated with the women who come to
the tomb (28:1) and makes reference to the reason for their visit.[191] Ἐκεῖ is repeated again in 27:61 in a sentence which is structured according to a similar
pattern to that of 27:55.[192] Finally, the two women at the tomb (Mary

---

188   Senior, The Passion, 328, sees 27:55-56 as a terminal point in the passion narrative;
      Charles Homer Giblin, "Structural and Thematic Correlations in the Matthean Burial-
      Resurrection Narrative (Matt. xxvii.57-xxviii.20)," NTS 21 (1974-75): 406-420, omits
      27:55-56 from his structuring of the final stage of the gospel; and Beda Rigaux,
      Témoignage de l'évangile de Matthieu, Pour une histoire de Jésus 2 (Louvain: Declée
      de Brouwer, 1967), 142, places it together with the burial and the placing of the guard as
      the last stages of the passion narrative. Gundry, A Commentary, 578-582, also places vv.
      55-56 together with vv. 57-61 as does Meier, Matthew, 353-354; but for Meier, these
      verses are considered within the wider section 26:1-28:20 as they are for Gnilka,
      Matthäusevangelium, II, 478-497; and Patte, Structural Commentary, 390-402. Norman
      Perrin, The Resurrection Narratives: A New Approach (London: SCM, 1977), 43-60,
      begins his treatment of Matthew's resurrection narrative at 27:55. This is simply an
      indication of some of the different opinions among scholars and is in no way an
      attempt to list all opinions.
189   See also the work of S. J. P. K. Riekert, "The Narrative Coherence in Matthew 26-8,"
      Neot 16 (1982): 118-137, who considers the three chapters a coherent narrative unit after
      employing a number of features of discourse analysis.
190   Senior, The Passion, 330.
191   The only time this verb is used in the entire gospel is at 27:55 and 28:1.
192   This will be discussed in more detail below.

Magdalene and the other Mary) are also two of the three specifically named at the cross.[193]

Not only are there verbal and character links between the scenes in which the women function as characters in this final stage of the narrative but the same links exist between other surrounding scenes as well.[194] In two different scenes there are representations made to Pilate and there are also two scenes in which the chief priests are concerned about the guard set up to prevent the stealing of the body from the tomb. This interlocking of pericopes according to character can be seen below:

	Women	Pilate	Chief Priests & guards	Disciples
1. 27:55-56	Many women [Among whom were Mary Magdalene and another Mary] *			
2. 27:56-60		To Pilate		
3. 27:61	Mary Magdalene and other Mary *			
4. 27:62-66		To Pilate	Chief priests/ a guard	[his disciples]
5. 28:1-10	Mary Magdalene and other Mary *			[his disciples]
6. 28:11-15			Chief priests/ a guard	[his disciples]
7. 28:16-20				Eleven disciples

Diagram 10

Further verbal links are also in evidence. The parallel use of θεωρέω has already been noted above; here we can see that it links Scene 1 and 5 (27:55; 28:1). Similarly, προσκυνέω links Scene 5 with Scene 7 (28:9; 28:17). These same scenes (1, 5 and 7) are linked by references to Galilee (27:55; 28:7, 10; 28:16). The verb μαθητεύω links Scenes 2 and 7 and secondary links include ἐκεῖ in Scenes 1 and 2; λίθος in 2 and 5; and τάφος in 2, 4, and 5. The most significant links, however, seem to be between Scenes 1, 5 and 7. This further

---

193 For Giblin, "Structural and Thematic Correlations," 407, the specifying of only two women in 27:61 and 28:1 is seen as a redactional technique to separate 27:55-56 from the subsequent pericopes. It is argued here, however, that the linguistic links work to unite the pericopes rather than to separate them one from the other.

194 Riekert, "Narrative Coherence," 122, notes the important role that characters (whom he calls actants or participants) play in clustering material.

strengthens the argument above that the stories of the women at the cross, at
the tomb and at the resurrection belong to the same movement within the
narrative which begins to direct the reader's attention away from the cross
through the burial of Jesus to the resurrection account.

a. 27:55-56, 61

The structuring of 27:55-56 and 27:61 suggests that they be treated together.
First, 27:55-56 consists of three clauses, two of which are structured around a
finite verb and a participle thus:

Finite verb [ἦσαν] ...   participle [θεωροῦσαι]

Finite verb [ἠκολούθησαν] ...   participle [διακονοῦσαι].

The third clause simply lists the names of some of the women. Second, 27:61
closely parallels 27:55:

Imperfect of εἰμί [ἦσαν]   + δέ + ἐκεῖ + ... participle [θεωροῦσαι]

Imperfect of εἰμί [ἦν]   + δέ + ἐκεῖ + ... participle [καθήμεναι].

The opening of vv. 55 and 61, ἦσαν/ἦν δὲ ἐκεῖ, focusses the reader's
attention very definitely on the scene and on the characters who are subsequently named. The first scene is the crucifixion of Jesus, which was accompanied by an earthquake and other eschatological phenomena [τὰ γενόμενα]
and followed by a centurion and other guards at the foot of the cross proclaiming Jesus to be son of God [θεοῦ υἱός]. It is this that the women look
upon or witness.The Matthean use of the verb θεωρέω only in 27:55 and 28:1
would seem to indicate that it is used here with a specific purpose. Both the
crucifixion account and the story surrounding the proclamation of Jesus'
having been raised are amplified by a recording of extraordinary cosmic
phenomena indicating that they are of extraordinary significance in the life
story of Jesus in which a power greater than simple earthly power is operative. The reader, therefore, understands the women to be witnesses to the
divine power which surrounds the crucifixion and the manifestation of
Jesus' resurrection.[195] The use of θεωρέω only in these two places links the

---

195 See Donald Senior, "The Death of Jesus and the Resurrection of the Holy Ones (Mt
     27:51-53)," *CBQ* 38 (1976): 312-329, for a detailed interpretation of these events. Patte,

two accounts and points to the uniqueness of women's witness.[196] Unlike the centurion and the guards, however, who appear in and disappear from the narrative within a few short verses (27:36, 54; 28:4), the women have been with Jesus prior to these last days, and they shall be missioned subsequent to their witnessing these manifestations (28:7,10). In this way, the reader is assured of their authenticity as witnesses.[197]

The second half of v. 55 directs the reader's attention to the long-term association of the women with Jesus. They have followed him from Galilee [ἀκολουθέω] ministering to him [διακονέω]. It has already been suggested that the Matthean διακονέω functions on two levels: the literal level referring to service of physical needs; and the symbolic level of service within the new religious community which Jesus is inaugurating.[198] Kingsbury has also pointed out that ἀκολουθέω must be understood on both a literal and metaphorical level.[199] In 27:55, the literal meaning of these verbs is clear but the question remains whether the symbolic or metaphorical meaning also functions for the reader. On this point, the opinion of scholars is divided.[200] It seems necessary, therefore, to go beyond the immediate context in order to seek further clues which may assist our interpretation.

The phrase ἀπὸ μακρόθεν used in 27:55 is already familiar to the reader. Earlier, it was used in relation to Peter who followed Jesus at a distance in order to see the end (26:58), but who fled when threatened by the questions of the servants and in remorse at his own denial of Jesus (26:69-75). The context, therefore, suggests that Peter keeps his distance from Jesus in order not

---

       Structural Commentary, 389-390, links the signs of 27:51-53 with the apocalyptic and eschatological imagery of Matt 24-25.

196   Wilhelm Michaelis, in his long article, "ὁράω κτλ.," *TDNT* V:315-381, especially pp. 318-319, 328, and 345-346, discusses the possible origins of the verb θεωρέω in terms of θεωρός/a spectator of cultic or religious festivals. It still retained some of this sense in the LXX extending, in some cases, to include the notion of participation. In his interpretation of Matt 27:55, however, he limits its meaning to simply watching something as a spectator. The presence of this verb only in these two related pericopes in the gospel narrative suggests, however, that it may retain some of its religious connotations.

197   While Josephus points out that neither women nor slaves were allowed to testify as witnesses (Ant. 4.8.15 §219), he also indicates that the credibility of witnesses is established by their past life. V. 55 serves to establish the women's credibility as does their subsequent missioning.

198   See pp. 85-86 above.

199   Kingsbury, "The Verb *AKOLOUTHEIN*," 56-73.

200   Sabourin, *L'Evangile*, 384; Bonnard, *Évangile*, 407; and Kingsbury, "The Verb *AKOLOUTHEIN*," 61, all state very clearly that discipleship is not meant in this verse. On the other hand, Witherington III, *Women in the Ministry*, 122; Herman Hendrickx, *The Passion Narratives of the Synoptic Gospels* (Manila: East Asian Pastoral Institute, 1977), 125; and Gundry, *A Commentary*, 578, all suggest that the two verbs in v. 55 are to be read as an indication of discipleship.

to be associated with him. The women, however, have followed Jesus from
Galilee and have remained with him faithfully until the end. Their presence
at the scene of the execution of their teacher and friend rules out fear as a
contributing factor in their standing at a distance. Given the context, the
presence of the soldiers at the foot of the cross seems to offer a more plausible explanation. The women's presence, however, is in contrast to the absence of Peter and the other disciples. In the light of Jesus' explicit teaching
on discipleship (especially 16:24-26), the reader would have expected the
group of named disciples to be faithful even to the foot of the cross. The fact
that a group of women demonstrate such fidelity and that their fidelity is
referred to in discipleship terminology indicates that discipleship is clearly
intended here.

This is further affirmed for the reader by the naming of one of the
women as "mother of the sons of Zebedee", which recalls the earlier scene
(20:20-22) in which Jesus invited this woman and her sons to drink the cup
of suffering with him, an invitation to faithful discipleship which they
accepted verbally. The woman has remained faithful to her previous
affirmation and stands, therefore, at the foot of Jesus' cross. Her presence
confirms the reading of the two verbs as symbolic of discipleship, true
discipleship. Furthermore, she and the other women are linked to Joseph of
Arimathea by the phrase ὃς καὶ αὐτὸς ἐμαθητεύθη τῷ Ἰησοῦ (27:57) in which
the language is clearly discipleship language.[201]

Two other women from among those standing at the cross are also
identified by name--Μαρία ἡ Μαγδαληνὴ καὶ Μαρία ἡ τοῦ Ἰακώβου καὶ Ἰωσὴφ
μήτηρ (27:56). Other than in the prologue and 14:3, these are the only women
who are identified by name in the entire gospel. They are linked to the cross
(27:56), to the tomb (27:61), and to the symbolic narrative of 28:1-10. Women
characters emerge from anonymity and their very naming emphasizes their
significance in the narrative at this point.[202]

The second scene to which the reader's attention is clearly directed by
the opening ἦν δὲ ἐκεῖ is that of the burial of Jesus (27:61). In this verse, it is
two of the women who take up their position opposite the tomb. Giblin suggests that the specifying of two women in this and the resurrection story is a
redactional technique to separate the two stories from that situated at the

---

201   Anderson, "Gender and Reading," 18-20.
202   Sternberg, *Poetics*, 330.

foot of the cross.[203] It has already been shown, however, that these two women formed part of the group at the foot of the cross and hence point to a continuity rather than discontinuity with it. Longstaff's thesis that the women came to inspect the tomb to ensure that premature burial had not taken place is an attractive one,[204] but the reference to the great stone rolled across the door (27:60) makes this less plausible. The verse seems simply to link the stories of the death, burial and resurrection of Jesus by means of the women characters and to underline their role as authentic witnesses in each. It is to the last of these stories that we now turn.

b. 28:1-10

The opening verse links the resurrection scene with the burial and crucifixion by means of the women characters who are named. The time phrases at the beginning of the verse have received much scholarly attention and, since they do not directly affect our topic, will not be discussed further.[205] The construction of the second half of the verse may have been an attempt to parallel the opening of the previous two pericopes (27:55-56 and 27:61), namely, a finite verb followed later by a supporting participle. Here, however, the finite verb [ἦλθεν] is followed later by the aorist infinitive [θεωρῆσαι] in place of the future participle which had virtually dropped out of use by the time of the writing of the gospel.[206] The use of the verb θεωρέω continues the theme of the women's witness.[207]

The phraseology of v. 2 recalls 8:24: καὶ ἰδοὺ σεισμὸς μέγας ἐγένετο, and reflects a significant Matthean interest. The clearly eschatological imagery of

---

203 Giblin, "Structural and Thematic Correlations," 407.
204 Thomas R. W. Longstaff, "The Women at the Tomb: Matthew 28:1 Re-examined," *NTS* 27 (1981): 277-282, examines evidence in the Jewish tractate Ṣemaḥot [8:1] which is of late origin but which is believed to contain much older material. He concludes that as early as the first century there existed the custom of watching the tomb of a loved one until the third day after death in order to ensure that premature burial had not taken place. On p. 281, n. 18, he says: "It would undoubtedly strengthen our argument here if there were clear evidence that women could carry out the inspection described in Ṣemaḥot 8:1. Unfortunately, this is the only text known which describes the practice in any detail. Accordingly, in the absence of any evidence to indicate that women could not perform this inspection and since they did perform many other tasks associated with burial (anointing etc.) it seems safe to assume that they could perform this particular task as well."
205 G. R. Driver, "Two Problems in the New Testament," *JTS* 16 (1965): 327-337, gives detailed attention to this question and provides adequate bibliographical references.
206 Zerwick, *Biblical Greek*, 95, §282.
207 Matthew has no mention of the women coming to anoint the body. For Matthew, the anointing has been performed by the anonymous woman (26:6-13). Also the appointment of a guard would make such anointing impossible.

24:7 is extended in Matthew to 8:24; 27:54; and 28:2--the accounts of the storm at sea; of the crucifixion and of Jesus' being raised from the dead. In 8:23-27, the σεισμὸς μέγας is contrasted with the γαλήνη μεγάλη as a prelude to the crucifixion and resurrection accounts. In these later accounts, however, the imagery is much more sophisticated. The earthquake is accompanied by other eschatological phenomena and would seem to point to the breaking in of the new age which accompanied Jesus' death and the proclamation of his resurrection.[208] This is further substantiated in the account of Jesus' having been raised from the dead in which the angel of the Lord is said to accompany the earthquake.

In the Matthean gospel, quite apart from allusions to the Hebrew Scriptures and the apocalyptic literature,[209] the angel of the Lord is clearly the bearer of a divine message and, at times, mission. In the infancy narrative, Joseph encounters the angel of the Lord three times in a dream (1:20; 2:13; 2:19) and is commissioned with a task. There, the angel is linked with the patriarchal understanding of Jesus' coming and mission, symbolized by Joseph's role in the narrative. In the symbolic narrative of Jesus' resurrection, it is the two women who encounter the angel and they too are commissioned. The first commission is to witness the signs of the resurrection: "He is not here; for he has risen, as he said. Come, see the place where he lay." The second is that of proclaiming the resurrection to the disciples: "Go quickly and tell his disciples that he has risen from the dead." Contrary to the patriarchal structuring of society whereby men carry out the significant tasks, the divine message and mission is here given to women rather than men.

---

208 Senior, *The Passion*, 313, indicates that the earthquake is a traditional element of eschatological imagery and later, p. 325, he goes on to say that this, together with the other signs of 27:51-53, is the immediate result of Jesus' death and serves as a symbolic description of God's seal of approval on the life-giving death of Jesus as son of God. In his article, "The Death of Jesus," 312-329, he points to the significance of a "resurrection sign" accompanying the death of Jesus to indicate that it functions as a turning point in the history of salvation. Hendrickx, *Passion Narratives*, 125, also suggests that it is the death of Jesus which marks the end of the old dispensation and the beginning of the new. Edward Lynn Bode, *The First Easter Morning: The Gospel Accounts of the Women's Visit to the Tomb of Jesus*, AnBib 45 (Rome: Biblical Institute Press, 1970), 57; and Meier, *Matthew*, 352 and idem, *Vision*, 204-205, both claim that the earthquake is intended to point to the beginning of the new age, the eschatological age inaugurated by the death of Jesus and the proclamation of his resurrection. Although there may be slight differences in interpretation, each interpreter draws on the link between the death and resurrection of Jesus indicated by the common eschatological imagery, and points to the symbolic nature of these events.

209 Dan 7:9; 10:6; 1 Enoch 14:20; 71:1; and 4 Ezra 10:25, all of which speak of the divine messenger(s) in apocalyptic terms similar to that of 28:3.

The reversal of expectations regarding character roles within this scene is accompanied by other reversals. Those who stand guard over the dead man's tomb become like dead men themselves at the appearance of the angel (28:4). The message to the women who come seeking the crucified one is that he has been raised [ἠγέρθη] (28:5-6). To these, Marin adds other reversals.[210] These reversals are signs of the new age, and one of those signs is the role assumed by women which the narrative affirms. They are faithful followers of Jesus whose fidelity enables them to witness the signs of the resurrection and to be commissioned with its proclamation.

The response of the women is two-edged. Their fear recalls the guards' response to the earthquake and presence of the angel (28:4) and Peter's response to the winds and the waves around him as he walks toward Jesus on the sea (14:30). As a result of this fear, the guards become like dead men and Peter begins to sink, but the women's fear is accompanied by great joy which points beyond fear in the face of eschatological manifestations to a joy that comes from understanding their meaning. Their fear and great joy are also accompanied by a fulfilling of the command.

Within the scene, the point of view changes with the phrase καὶ ἰδοῦ or ἰδοῦ (28:2, 7, 9).[211] In the first half of the scene, the reader's and narrator's attention is focussed on the angel and the tomb (vv. 2-6). At v. 7a, the words of the angel shift the focus to the journey of the risen Jesus into Galilee, including the women as addressees among those who will see him there, but the reader's attention is returned to the tomb in the last part of that verse. The scene closes with attention directed once again to the risen Jesus who meets the women, not in Galilee but as they depart the scene of the empty tomb. His greeting [χαίρετε] continues the reversal motif. The word used by Judas to betray Jesus (26:49) and by the soldiers to mock him (27:29) now becomes the first word used by the risen Jesus to greet the women. The great joy of the women (28:8) meets the joyful greeting of Jesus (28:9) and their response is worship. It is only after this encounter as indicated by the correlative adverb τότε that Jesus reiterates the mission given to the women.

These final verses of the pericope deserve consideration from a gender perspective. The women who encounter the risen Jesus worship him

---

210 L. Marin, "Les femmes au tombeau: Essai d'analyse structurale d'un texte évangélique," *Langages* 22 (1971): 39-50.
211 See Berlin, *Poetics and Interpretation*, 62-63, for her treatment of the term <u>hinneh</u> in biblical narrative.

[προσκυνέω], which may be seen as an act of subservience, but is also symbolic of faith, the power to see beyond the confines of human limitations and human boundaries (cf. 9:22; 15:28). When the eleven male disciples encounter the risen Jesus on a mountain in Galilee they too worship [προσκυνέω], but the narrator goes on to say that certain ones doubted [οἱ δὲ ἐδίστασαν]. To the very end, the contrast between the women characters and the character group of male disciples continues.

On the other hand, however, within the narrative, the commission given to the women by the angel to proclaim the resurrection is limited in the words of Jesus to a proclamation of his journeying to Galilee in order to meet them there. In each case, furthermore, it is a proclamation for the absent μαθηταῖς or ἀδελφοῖς. As the gospel closes, however, the commission to make disciples of all nations is given to the eleven male disciples even though they have failed to manifest the qualities of true discipleship. Once again, the androcentric perspective of the implied author supports the patriarchal structure, which limits membership of the character group called disciples to males and makes them the most significant actors in the continuation of the mission of Jesus despite their infidelity to the call to discipleship throughout his own ministry, an infidelity which is especially manifest in the concluding scenes of the passion narrative in which they are continually referred to in their absence until the final scene [see Diagram 10 above].[212] As we turn now to a brief survey of the trends in recent research, we shall see that on the whole the androcentric perspective encoded in the text often influences the gospel's interpreters, as well as their own perspectives obscuring further the significant stories of women characters that appear in the narrative itself.

---

212 Such an analysis needs to be held in tension with the exposition of Jesus' reconciliation with the followers who have deserted him which is inherent in this scene in order not to obscure the community's understanding of the inexhaustible nature of God's forgiveness and grace which may have also shaped the formation of this section of the narrative. The feminist critique, however, questions the androcentric perspective which presents this grace and forgiveness as manifest primarily in the lives of the male characters and in the restoration of a non-inclusive model of missionary activity.

B. Present State of Research

To try to summarize contemporary scholarship on the Matthean passion-resurrection narrative would be extraneous to our present task,[213] as would be a similar attempt to summarize the scholarship which addresses the pericopes under consideration. In fact, some of this has already been incorporated into the previous discussion and additional material will be considered in Chapter Six. In the light of the final statement above, however, it seems more appropriate to illustrate, by way of a few examples, how the androcentric perspective in the text can influence the interpreter or coincide with his or her own perspective.

It was seen earlier that one of the questions which faces interpreters of the Matthean passion-resurrection narrative is that of its structuring and, hence, of the divisions within the text. In none of the studies, however, has any consideration been given to the possible influence of the pericopes in which women function as significant characters on the structuring of the final chapters of the gospel. In fact, the characters' female gender can mean that their story or stories are easily overlooked as is illustrated by the following analysis of the opening verses of the passion (26:1-16):

> These three short pericopes: the prediction of the Passion (XXVI, 1-5), the anointing at Bethany (XXVI, 6-13) and the betrayal by Judas (XXVI, 14-16) serve as an overture to the entire passion and offer a rich example of Matthew's redactional activity. Within these first sixteen verses, Matthew presents the *dramatis personae* (the Jewish leaders, the betrayer, the apostles, Jesus).[214]

If, however, one takes up this statement of Senior as a starting point and adds to the final sentence the *dramatis persona* whom he has omitted, namely, the woman who anoints Jesus' feet, then it is possible that a different analysis of the passion-resurrection account will emerge especially in the light of the other female characters who function significantly in the narrative as it draws to a close [see Diagram 8 above].

---

213 Senior, *The Passion*, provides a comprehensive dialogue with much of the scholarship to 1975. This dialogue is continued in two of his later works: *The Passion of Jesus in the Gospel of Matthew* (Wilmington, Del.: Michael Glazier, 1985); and "Matthew's Special Material in the Passion Story: Implications for the Evangelist's Redactional Technique and Theological Perspective," *EThL* 63 (1987): 272-294.

214 Donald Senior, "The Passion Narrative in the Gospel of Matthew," in *L'évangile selon Matthieu: Rédaction et théologie*, ed. M. Didier, BEThL XXIX (Gembloux: Duculot, 1972), 349.

Reference was also made earlier to Charles Giblin's analysis of the final verses of the gospel.[215] He established the unity of 27:57-28:20 by way of the inclusion formed by the verb μαθητεύω in 27:57 and 28:19, and then claimed that the entire section was built concentrically around 28:1-10 with each of the parallels containing a reference to the disciples, the focus of the central section being the relationship between Jesus and the disciples. This arrangement is seen more clearly in his diagram which I shall repeat below to facilitate discussion [Diagram 11]:

xxvii. 57-61	A	Burial of Jesus by Joseph who has also been *made a disciple* of Jesus
xxvii. 62-66	B	Placing of a guard at the grave to prevent deception *by the disciples*
xxviii. 1-10	C	Fulfilment of Jesus' words. Focus--Jesus and *his disciples*
xxviii. 11-15	B'	Bribing of the guard, to say *the disciples* stole the body
xxviii. 16-20	A'	Jesus' commission to the *eleven disciples to make disciples* of all nations.

Diagram 11

The first critique that needs to be brought to such a structure is the fact that in only the last part of Giblin's five-part structure do the disciples function as active characters. In the other pericopes, they are referred to in their absence. Giblin's androcentric perspective, however, is certainly in keeping with that of the narrator who keeps them before the reader's mind even when they are absent because of their infidelity.

Also of interest to our study is the fact that he considers the focal point of 28:1-10 the relationship between Jesus and his disciples. This relationship is certainly an element in the pericope but to consider it central suggests an androcentric perspective even beyond that of the narrator. In the first part of the pericope, the angel as representative of God plays a central role. It is this angel who invites the women to come and see the place where Jesus lay and hence to be witnesses to the resurrection, recalling for the reader the opening of the pericope where they are referred to in terminology which suggests

---

215   See n. 188 above.

their subsequent role. Only then are the women commissioned to go and tell the disciples of the resurrection (vv. 6-7). If the absent disciples are to encounter the risen Jesus, it can only be through the women's faithful carrying out of the commission given them. In the second part of the pericope, v. 9 is concerned with the women's encounter with the risen Jesus subsequent to their witnessing the signs of his resurrection. Only after this encounter are they given, from Jesus this time, a commission which concerns the disciples. This suggests, therefore, that not only is Giblin influenced by the androcentric perspective within the text but his own androcentric perspective allows him to read the last section of the gospel with virtually no account being taken of the significant role played by the women characters.

Other examples could be drawn upon but those considered above provide sufficient evidence of the claim being investigated, namely, that the androcentric perspectives of interpreters often co-incide with the same perspective that is evidenced in the text itself. Their own perspectives have also led them to gloss over or ignore the evidence of women's significant participation in the final movement of the gospel narrative.

C. An Inclusive Re-reading

For the feminist reader, the stories considered within this section are climactic in the gospel narrative as a whole. Firstly, an unnamed woman performs a prophetic sign acknowledging Jesus as the anointed messiah as he enters into his passion. She not only performs a task normally reserved for significant and appointed males but she demonstrates by her action true discipleship of Jesus. Although her story has been obscured down through the centuries by the stories of Judas who betrayed Jesus and Peter who denied him, in an inclusive reading it must be allowed to stand in all its radicality according to the prophecy made by Jesus, who affirmed the woman's action (26:13).[216] It will function, therefore, as a witness to female discipleship and as a critique of all those stories in the first part of the passion-resurrection narrative in which the male disciples are principal actors, especially the

---

216 Schüssler Fiorenza, *In Memory of Her*, xiv, calls this a politically dangerous story.

story of Jesus' celebration of the feast of Unleavened Bread with the twelve male disciples.[217]

Of significance in this re-reading are the two minor references to the women who symbolize truth and fidelity over against the force of arms and deceit arrayed against Jesus. They prepare the reader for the final scenes in which the women characters emerge as faithful disciples and hence as reliable witnesses: the first to encounter the risen Jesus. Furthermore, they are the first to proclaim the gospel message that Jesus is risen, the founding members therefore of the christian communities who gather around this message. Women therefore emerge from the narrative as paradigms of discipleship and as foundational to the early church's mission of proclaiming that Jesus whom they saw crucified has indeed been raised from the dead.

✓   VI. CONCLUSION

A narrative reading of the gospel of Matthew with specific attention being given to gender has enabled the reader to see clearly the androcentric perspective encoded within the text. At times, this led to the explicit support of patriarchal social structures manifest in patrilineage as the vehicle of divine promise at the beginning of the narrative; in the male membership of the group called "the twelve"; and in this group being presented as constitutive of the universal commission at the close of the narrative. This same androcentric perspective was seen to be implicit in the narrative which presumed on significant acts being performed by males and on male participation in the βασιλεία ministry of Jesus so that the presence and action of women was seen as exceptional.

Such a perspective, however, was found to be in tension with a well-developed narrative theme, namely, women's participation in the βασιλεία ministry of Jesus. This theme began as the gospel opened and continued, by way of a progressive development through to the very close of the gospel,

---

217 Ibid., xiv, where Schüssler Fiorenza points to the "reclaiming (of) the supper at Bethany as women's Christian heritage in order to correct symbols and ritualizations of an all-male Last Supper that is a betrayal of true Christian discipleship and ministry."

indicating its significance in the Jesus story. A woman participated in a most extraordinary way in the birth of Jesus drawing into her story memories of women's participation in Israel's history, but there were but brief references to her in the text and her story was eclipsed by the patriarchal context in which it is set. Women were open to the healing power of Jesus which in turn empowered them for that faith-filled response which exemplified discipleship, but their approach was characterized by an inability to make a request of Jesus and an indirect approach to him from behind. Later, however, an unnamed woman debated with Jesus in the public arena in a way which profoundly influenced his own culturally-conditioned perspective in relation to women's participation in the public forum and in relation to the extension of the βασιλεία mission beyond the confines of Israel to the Gentiles. A woman outside the confines of the patriarchal familial structure, like the woman with a haemorrhage, was able to push back the boundaries regarding membership within the βασιλεία community, manifesting its inclusive nature which Jesus preached. She represented the turning point in the narrative as women characters moved from being silent recipients to vocal actors in the unfolding story. In the conclusion of the narrative, therefore, the women are courageous participants in the climactic last days of Jesus' ministry. A woman prophetically anoints Jesus in recognition of his messianic ministry and his approaching death. Others stand faithfully at the foot of the cross of Jesus and two of their members are named in the narrative as the first witnesses of God's power manifest in the raising up of Jesus and as the first commissioned with a resurrection proclamation.

In tracing the development of this theme, we also noted the symbolic function of female gender which was two-edged. Female power, whether it be reproductive power or the power of faith-filled seeing, understanding and acting, was many times affirmed by the authoritative voice of the narrator or Jesus but within the androcentric perspective of the gospel it was also intended to function as a limitation preventing the women characters' participation in the character group called "the twelve" or perhaps even "the disciples". As with the stories of the four women from the Hebrew Scriptures, so too with the stories of women in the Matthean gospel, female power, which is viewed as anomalous within the androcentric perspective which supports patriarchy, was brought within the confines of this perspective in the narrative. It also functioned, however, as a threat to that perspective which the narrative could not silence.

A reading of these stories, however, from the perspective of a feminist hermeneutics of suspicion allowed them to stand as a powerful critique of the androcentric perspective and the patriarchal structures which the narrative supports. This made possible the hermeneutics of remembrance and reclamation which lead to an inclusive reading of the gospel text. Within such a reading, women together with men stand at the heart of the gospel story. Both Mary and Joseph are active participants in the birth of Jesus. Women together with men receive the fruits of the βασιλεία with a faith that calls forth the life-restoring power of Jesus. This healing brings both together in the inclusive community around Jesus. Both women and men struggle toward full discipleship of Jesus and both manifest it in various ways just as both groups are presented in opposition to Jesus. Finally, women, together with men, are central to the mission of resurrection proclamation both within Israel and beyond its geographic confines. The stories of women are restored to the biblical text so that it must now be read as the story of women and men who participated in the Jesus story.

Such a reading, however, raises further literary and historical questions that could not be answered in the above analysis but which have risen up out of it.

**** Does the tension within the narrative which a gender reading has brought to light reflect a similar tension within the Jesus' movement itself or within the Matthean community?

**** If the tension existed within the Matthean community, can further analysis of the text and a reconstruction of its historical situation make manifest the traditions which may have been in conflict within the community?

**** What was the source of such conflict within the community and why did it find expression in the gospel story?

**** What light does a further study of the stories of women within the context of the Matthean community bring to bear on theological questions regarding faith, community, discipleship and leadership as they were reflected upon within that community and given expression in its gospel story?

**** Will further literary and historical analyses enable us to discover and restore women's place not only in the text but within the reconstructed Matthean community as well?

These and other questions give shape now to stage two of our investigation: an historical-critical analysis of the text whose goal is the inclusion of women within the formation of the text.

3. The Prologue

A narrative reading of Matthew's prologue has already alerted us to the presence of a predominant theme as well as a significant counter theme in the opening chapter which could suggest that there are different traditions underlying the final redaction by the evangelist. Gospel scholarship itself also lays claim to the presence of such traditions.[1] Below we will search for these traditions, indications of their formation, the possible contribution of women and men to their development, and the hints they provide toward a reconstruction of an "historical subtext".

This search will draw heavily on the many studies of the Matthean prologue--especially of Matt 1 and 2--undertaken by source, redaction and tradition critics in recent years.[2] The feminist critique of scholarship already begun must continue at this stage of analysis since most of the material drawn upon will reflect the general androcentric perspective of contemporary biblical scholarship.[3]

At the outset, it is necessary to acknowledge the difficulties inherent in uncovering traditions and sources especially within the infancy narratives of the gospels, but these difficulties cannot be allowed to obscure the task itself. As most scholars indicate, the final form of the Matthean infancy narrative

---

1   Charles Thomas Davis, "Tradition and Redaction in Matt 1:18-2:23," *JBL* 90 (1971): 404-421; Brown, *Birth of the Messiah*, 45-232; and many of the other studies which will be cited throughout this chapter.

2   Some of these have already been mentioned in Chapter Two, but I will list them again with other booklength studies. Significant articles will be cited when needed. Brown, *Birth of the Messiah*; Jean Daniélou, *Les évangiles de l'Enfance* (Paris: Seuil, 1967); Hendrickx, *Infancy Narratives*; Johnson, *Biblical Genealogies*; Nolan, *Royal Son of God*; André Paul, *L'Evangile de l'enfance selon saint Matthieu*, Lire la Bible 17 (Paris: Cerf, 1968); Soares Prabhu, *Formula Quotations*; Schaberg, *Illegitimacy of Jesus*; and Anton Vögtle, *Messias und Gottessohn: Herkunft und Sinn der matthäischen Geburts- und Kindheitsgeschichte* (Düsseldorf: Patmos, 1971).

3   A very clear example of this is found in Paul, *L'Evangile*, 30. He begins with a very significant insight into the role of the women in the genealogy: "Si des femmes ont été introduites dans la généalogie, elles sont là avant tout en tant que femmes." He does not follow through the full implications of this insight, however, but simply reduces the women to mere instruments within the patriarchal system: "... plus précisément, puisqu'il s'agit d'une succession de générations, elles sont là en tant que mères: mères de certains ancêtres du Messie, et mères du Messie en personne."

and also its various parts are heavily redacted by the final editor of the gospel, making the task of separating tradition from redaction extremely difficult.[4] A study, however, which proceeds through the stage of redaction criticism to a reconstruction of possible traditions whose exact verbal form may not be able to be determined is certainly a legitimate enterprise. Such a study will be applied in detail to the genealogy (1:1-17); and less extensively to the narrative 1:18-25.[5]

I. The Genealogy - 1:1-17

A. In General

The Genealogy is structured within the inclusion formed by v. 1:

Βίβλος γενέσεως Ἰησοῦ Χριστοῦ υἱοῦ Δαυίδ υἱοῦ Ἀβραάμ;

and v. 17:

Πᾶσαι οὖν αἱ γενεαὶ ἀπὸ Ἀβραάμ ἕως Δαυίδ γενεαὶ δεκατέσσαρες,

καὶ ἀπὸ Δαυίδ ἕως τῆς μετοικεσίας Βαβυλῶνος γενεαὶ δεκατέσσαρες,

καὶ ἀπὸ τῆς μετοικεσίας Βαβυλῶνος ἕως τοῦ Χριστοῦ γενεαὶ δεκατέσσαρες.

The Christ is specifically related to Abraham and David. Even if the final text has been influenced by the superscription of the Markan gospel [Ἀρχὴ τοῦ εὐαγγελίου Ἰησοῦ Χριστοῦ ⟨υἱοῦ θεοῦ⟩],[6] it has been edited according to the theological purposes operative in the compiling of this gospel. We have

---

4   This is shown by Davis, "Tradition and Redaction"; and is commented on by Brown, *Birth of the Messiah*, 111 and 119. Soares Prabhu, *Formula Quotations*, 2, makes a more radical statement: "An attempt to investigate the redactional history of the Infancy Narrative of Mt, to distinguish, that is, its redactional from its "traditional" elements, must appear a rash if not a hopeless enterprise." A further witness to this difficulty is the variety of results illustrated by various scholars: Soares Prabhu, *Formula Quotations* on the attached sheet at the end of his book titled "Tradition and Redaction in Matthew 1-2"; Nolan, *Royal Son of God*, 21-22; Brown, *Birth of the Messiah*, 109; and Davis, "Tradition and Redaction," 421.

5   Attention has already been drawn to the brief references to women characters in Matt 2 and no further analysis needs to be done here.

6   Johnson, *Biblical Genealogies*, 225, discusses this possibility in the light of his thesis that Matt 1 is a "midrash" on Mark 1:1. I do not want to discuss here the literary relationship between Matthew and Mark but shall address it in the following chapter where it will be more relevant.

already noted that the use of βίβλος γενέσεως to open verse 1 seems to recall
Gen 2:4a and 5:1 which make reference to the generations (חולדה) of both the
heavens and earth (2:4a) and of the human creature, Adam (5:1). The
threefold repetition of γενεαί in verse 17 confirms the genealogical structure
at its close. The designation of Ἰησοῦ Χριστοῦ as υἱοῦ Δαυίδ and υἱοῦ Ἀβραάμ
and the recalling of this again in the summary verse (v.17) begins to point to
a theological interest which links Jesus' story to the history of Israel and
especially its patriarchs[7] and Davidic king.[8] This suggests, therefore, that
verses 1 and 17 belong to the final redaction.[9]

Within the frame provided by verses 1 and 17, we have already
observed a carefully constructed patrilineage of Jesus extending from
Abraham through David and the exile to Joseph. This patrilineage serves to
establish Jesus, the Messiah, firmly within Israel's sacred history, a function
accomplished by the patterned repetition--male δὲ ἐγέννησεν male.[10] The
pattern is broken, however, by a number of incidental references (2c, 6a,
11),[11] the structured references to four women from the Hebrew Scriptures
(3, 5a and b, 6b), and significantly at v.16.

The question which faces us here is whether the content of the genealogy is completely Matthean or whether there are pre-Matthean elements
that have been worked into the final patterning and structuring.[12] We turn

---

7   In the Matthean narrative, the patriarchal history finds its fulfilment or completion in
     the history of Jesus and hence Abraham is linked with the eschatological theme in
     Matthew; see Johnson, Biblical Genealogies, 208, 219-223. Matthew 22:32 contains the
     reference to the God of Abraham, Isaac and Jacob (cf. Mark 12:26) in the context of a dis-
     cussion on the resurrection. The logion regarding the raising of children to Abraham
     from the stones (3:9; cf. Luke 3:8) is included in the text; and the eschaton is equated
     with reclining with Abraham, Isaac and Jacob (8:11). This theme receives more
     attention in Luke, however, than in Matthew: ibid., 219; and Gundry, A Commentary,
     14-15.
8   E. L. Abel, "The Genealogies of Jesus Ο ΧΡΙCΤΟC," NTS 20 (1973-74): 205; and Gundry, A
     Commentary, 19. Nolan, Royal Son of God, 13-14, argues that royal Davidic theology
     integrates all the christological titles in Matthew.
9   Gnilka, Matthäusevangelium, 6-8. Ulrich Luz, Das Evangelium nach Matthäus, 1,
     Teilband: Mt 1-7, EKK I,1 (Zürich: Benziger, 1985; Neukirchen-Vluyn:
     Neukirchener,1985), 91, n. 24, indicates that verse 17 contains significant Matthean
     vocabulary [οὖν, πᾶς οὖν, ἀπό ... ἕως].
10   This position is supported by Brown, Birth of the Messiah, 80-81; Nolan, Royal Son of
     God, 28; Daniélou, Evangiles de l'Enfance, 16-17; and Benoit, L'évangile, 39. Johnson,
     Biblical Genealogies, 76, speaks of the "legitimating function" of biblical genealogies in
     relation to the Davidic line (and one could add the patriarchal history), but he does not
     go on to address their legitimation of an androcentric view of reality and their support
     of the patriarchal family structure.
11   Luz, Evangelium, 91-92, suggests that these references belong to the Matthean
     redaction.
12   As was discussed in Chapter One, such a search for tradition and redaction in the
     Matthean gospel would normally involve a comparison with other synoptic texts but

first to one of the clearest possible sources for at least part of the genealogy, namely, the genealogies of Ruth 4:18-22 and 1 Chr 1:34; 2:1-13; 3:9,10-19. The formula "male ἐγέννησεν male" is visible here but not in the very regular pattern employed in the Matthean genealogy.[13] Similar progressions of generations appear, but we do not find in these genealogies the carefully numbered blocks of generations that are characteristic of Matthew's final genealogy (cf. v. 17).[14] There are references to women occasionally in these genealogies (1 Chr 2:3, 4; 3:5) but not in the patterned form of the Matthean genealogy and the only correspondence between the two is a reference to Tamar (1 Chr 2:4; Matt 1:3).[15]

Since the biblical genealogies do not supply all the information necessary for the construction of the Matthean genealogy, additional information must have been drawn from other sources. Johnson suggests a variety of possible extra-biblical sources and also the influence of both biblical and rabbinic sources on the final structuring of the genealogy.[16] His own arguments, however, illustrate the tenuous nature of these suggestions.

It was noted above that vv. 1 and 17 introduce themes that characterize the final redaction. In the previous chapter, we saw the verbal and thematic links between the references to the four women from the Hebrew Scriptures, the reference to Mary in v.16, and elements of the subsequent story (1:18-25) which suggest a tradition that may have been separate from the genealogy at a certain point. Leaving aside for the moment the clear Matthean redaction of vv. 1 and 17 and the possible tradition surrounding the women, we are left, it seems, with the patrilineage of Joseph who will later be designated the legal father of Jesus, and hence with the patrilineage of Jesus. There does not seem to be sufficient evidence available to us to determine exactly whether this patrilineage was the product of final redaction or community tradition.[17]

---

in the area of the Infancy Narratives, it is generally accepted that these narratives in both Matthew and Luke developed independently of one another even though they may have been based on shared traditions. See Brown, *Birth of the Messiah*, 33-37. No comparison with the Lukan text will therefore be carried out in this chapter.

13   The exception is Ruth 4:18-22 where the pattern is clear.

14   For a summary of the scholarly explanations for the seeming discrepancy between v. 17 and the number of generations in the 3 sections (vv. 2-16), see Schaberg, *Illegitimacy of Jesus*, 37-38, and her own explanation pp. 38-41.

15   1 Chr 3:5 refers to Bathsheba thus: τῇ Βηρσαβεε θυγατρὶ Αμιηλ, but there is no use of the Matthean reference τοῦ Οὐρίου.

16   Johnson, *Biblical Genealogies*, 179-184, 189-208; and Hendrickx, *Infancy Narratives*, 26.

17   Brown, *Birth of the Messiah*, 70, argues that "the end product (1:1-17), then, is very much a Matthean product in all its important theological and structural emphases",

It is clear that the weight of scholarship is on the side of Matthean
redaction, and it would seem that the careful structuring does belong to the
final redactional stages. If, however, we take up Bonnard's suggestion that
the material in the genealogy represents the faith of the community, it could
be argued, especially in the light of our suggestion that the tradition regarding the women may have existed in the community prior to the gospel formation, that the patrilineage of Jesus also existed in some form in the
Matthean community. If this were so, it would give witness to a strong tradition within the community which sought to firmly establish the legitimacy of the Messiah, Jesus, within Israel's history and which stressed the
continuity between his story which follows and that of Israel which had
passed.[18] It would also acknowledge the influence of the Hebrew Scriptures
and rabbinic genealogical interests on certain sectors of the community.[19]
Finally, it would suggest that the preservation and legitimation of a patriarchal history was very significant. This may point to a strong patriarchal
culture, but it may also indicate that the social systems which supported patriarchy were under threat within the community because of the Jesus
movement and because of the circulation of the stories of this movement
that were giving shape to the community's lifestyle. If the latter were the

---

an argument in line with the redactional structuring we have indicated above, but he
also suggests that the genealogy was neither created in full nor was an existing genealogy of Jesus found. The weight of his emphasis, however, lies on the final redaction
rather than on community tradition. Johnson, *Biblical Genealogies*, 210, argues
strongly for Matthean redaction which Luz, *Evangelium*, 91, critiques. Bonnard,
Évangile, 15, considers the genealogy a literary composition and hence of Matthean
redaction but claims that it expresses the faith of the early community.

18   Nolan, *Royal Son of God*, 28, calls the genealogy a "hymn to the continuity and
invincibility of the grace of Yahweh." Both Daniélou, *Evangiles de l'Enfance*, 16; and
Beare, *A Commentary*, 65, make reference to the theme of continuity underlying the
genealogy.

19   Johnson, *Biblical Genealogies*, 3-138. In two short summary statements, pp. 189 and 208,
he draws together the threads of his analysis of the Matthean genealogy, and what he
attributes to a Matthean redactor could also be attributed to sectors of the community:
"... the details of Matt 1:1-17 reveal a close knowledge of both the Old Testament and
also current Rabbinic biblical interpretation. ... the Matthean genealogy, we may
therefore suggest, was written by a scribe acquainted with Pharisaic Judaism who believed that the Messiah had come." It should be pointed out here, however, that the
Matthean genealogy differs radically from that of m. ʾAbot 1:1ff which may well have
been circulating in oral form around the time of the Matthean redaction of the gospel
[for reference to dating of this section of m. ʾAbot see Benedict T. Viviano, *Study as
Worship: Aboth and the New Testament*, SJLA XXVI (Leiden: Brill, 1978), 1-2)]. Jesus is
clearly linked to a Davidic and Abrahamic ancestry in Matthew whereas m. ʾAbot is
concerned with the succession through which Torah passed.

case then the genealogy could be explained in terms of a strong symbolic re-affirmation of patriarchy.[20]

At this point, nothing further can be claimed for the tradition. The incorporation, however, of such a strong patriarchal tradition as the opening of the gospel narrative certainly sets a tone for what follows.[21] The full effect of this is broken only by a counter theme introduced at the beginning of the narrative and it is to this that we now turn.

B. The Four Women from the Hebrew Scriptures

We have already seen that the naming of four women from the Hebrew Scriptures breaks the overall pattern of the Matthean genealogy. At the outset, it seems strange that in the final redaction a pattern that is so clearly established would be broken. Reference, however, to the remainder of the gospel shows that this is not the only occurrence of this phenomenon.[22] Only the subsequent analysis will suggest the reasons for this.

As we begin this analysis of the references to the four women in the first section of the genealogy, it is necessary to highlight that the first thing that they share in common is their womanhood and it is this that begins to break open the overriding patriarchal mould.[23] This does not, however, answer the question why these particular women would have been included and so

---

20   Jane Tompkins, ed., *Reader-Response Criticism: From Formalism to Post-Struct-uralism* (Baltimore/London: The Johns Hopkins University Press, 1981), xxv, points to the two-fold aspect of discourse: its responsibility for reality as well as its reflection of it. Kolodny, "The Panther Captivity," 339, also speaks of the "manipulation of gender for symbolic purposes that may have only incidental relation to actual contemporary sex roles." Schüssler Fiorenza, *In Memory of Her*, 56-59, looks at the question of "descriptive" and "prescriptive" language in her discussion of Neusner's analysis of the Mishnaic system of "reality building". She points out that certain texts that seem to reflect a patriarchal view of reality may, in fact, be seeking to bring about that reality in response to its being undermined by an alternative tradition. She offers a similar analysis of the household codes in "Discipleship and Patriarchy," in *Bread Not Stone*, 70-79.

21   The narrative closes on a similar note with the commissioning of the eleven male disciples.

22   Matt 6:2-18; 13:18-23; 23:8-10 and 23:13-29, to name but a few examples. Floyd V. Filson, "Broken Patterns in the Gospel of Matthew," *JBL* 75 (1956): 227-231, considers some of these patterns, but argues that they found their origin in the early oral tradition rather than in the creative activity of a Matthean author.

23   Via, "Narrative World," 131, calls this a possible "threat to God's purpose" which he says turns out not to be so. His analysis, however, points to the disruptive nature of the broken pattern.

we look to how they were characterized in the traditions available to the Matthean community for clues which may help us to determine why they were brought together.

A recognition of the importance of the fulfilment of scripture that we see in the Matthean gospel[24] will indicate that the primary source to which we must look in order to understand the significance of the four women is the Hebrew Scriptures. This source needs to be supplemented by reference to the intertestamental literature and the thinking of the early rabbis as it is found in the vast body of later rabbinic literature.[25] Some of this latter material, however, needs to be used with caution because of our lack of knowledge of its influence on early christian communities.

1. Tamar

The story of Tamar in the Hebrew Scriptures (Genesis 38) is set against the backdrop of the law of the levirate:

> If brothers dwell together, and one of them dies and has no son, the wife of the dead shall not be married outside the family to a stranger; her husband's brother shall go in to her, and take her as his wife, and perform the duty of a husband's brother to her. And the first son whom she bears shall succeed to the name of his brother who is dead, that his name may not be blotted out of Israel.

(Deut 25:5-6)

It was a law intended to support the patriarchal family structure and its concomitant property rights[26] and also to maintain patriarchal protection for the

---

24 Within the gospel itself we find the specific use of the formula quotations--1:22; (2:5); 2:15, 17, 23; 4:14; 8:17; 12:17; 13:35; 21:4--and allusions to the Hebrew Scriptures are scattered throughout. This may have been the work of a Matthean redactor but as Stendahl, *School of Matthew*, 30-35, suggests, a wider group of the community were involved in the study of scripture. We do not have the information that will tell us how widely some of this knowledge was disseminated but we can presume upon a knowledge of the Hebrew Scriptures among some members of the community and perhaps some sharing of this as the community developed traditions about Jesus.

25 This *religionsgeschichtlich* approach has already been used by Johnson, *Biblical Genealogies*, 152-179; Renée Bloch, "'Juda engendra Pharès et Zara, de Thamar" Matt., 1.3," in *Mélanges bibliques rédigés en l'honneur de André Robert*, TICP 4 (Paris: Bloud & Gay, 1957), 381-389; Paul, *L'Evangile*, 28-37; Yair Zakowitch, "Rahab als Mutter des Boas in der Jesus-genealogie (Matth. I.5)," *NT* 17 (1975): 1-5. Such an approach is fraught with the difficulties of dating rabbinic material and while Johnson and Bloch acknowledge this, it seems to be largely ignored by Paul and Zakowitch, thus rendering their results less plausible.

26 Gerhard von Rad, *Genesis*, 3rd rev. ed., OTL (1961; reprint, London: SCM, 1972), 358; and Claus Westermann, *Genesis 37-50: A Commentary*, trans. John J. Scullion (Minneapolis: Augsburg, 1986), 52.

childless widow.[27] When Judah fails to give his son Shelah to Tamar in marriage, he places her in the anomalous situation of being a childless widow in her father's house.[28] He also sets himself above the law and prevents its accomplishment.

At this point in the story, Tamar takes the initiative to right this situation. She tricks Judah into having intercourse with her while she is disguised as a harlot (Gen 38:14-19).[29] When her pregnancy is discovered, Judah is quick to condemn her in keeping with the protection of one of the most sensitive areas in ancient Israel's patriarchal power-and-honour system: the sexual morality of women.[30] She is an endangered woman in the hands of the patriarchal law. Because of Tamar's foresightedness, however, it becomes clear that the child Tamar bears is of Judah and she is therefore reincorporated into the patriarchal clan but in a way that has challenged its structures.[31] Judah does not lie with her again (v. 26) and the text does not say that she is given to Shelah. She has made possible the accomplishment of the levirate law, the continuation of the male line to the house of Judah;[32] but she has also protected her own right to exercise her reproductive power and to bear children. As such, her story breaks into the saga of the patriarch Joseph and the genealogy of Jacob,[33] and it challenges the patriarchal understanding of generation and the continuity of the male name. It is a two-edged story in which female power's critique of patriarchy is acknowledged, but that same female power is incorporated into patriarchal structures and androcentric perspectives.

---

27   Niditch, "The Wronged Woman Righted," 144-146, does a careful sociological analysis of this passage. She points to the fact that an Israelite woman must pass through various categories of protection and that those who find themselves outside one of these categories are social misfits or anomalies. See also Fuchs, "Literary Characterization," 130, n. 24.

28   Niditch, "The Wronged Woman Righted," 146. Here she notes that "Judah's attempt to send Tamar back to her father's home appears highly irregular. She no longer belongs there. The social fabric as a whole is weakened by her problem."

29   Von Rad, *Genesis*, 359, suggests that after the death of his wife (Gen 38:12), Judah himself could have fulfilled the duty of the levirate.

30   Patai, *Sex and Family*, 133.

31   If von Rad's suggestion above is correct, that Judah could have fulfilled the duty of levirate, then Schaberg's claim that we have here a "legitimated illegitimacy", *Illegitimacy of Jesus*, 23, is not as firm. It is rather a legitimate pregnancy achieved by illegitimate means which pushes back patriarchal norms and boundaries. Note also, however, Niditch's discussion of the incest law, "The Wronged Woman Righted," 148. Our lack of knowledge of the dating of these laws seems to render it impossible to know the exact legal situation.

32   Fuchs, "The Literary Characterization," 130, claims that Tamar is seen as a biblical heroine because of her support of the patriarchal institution of the levirate law.

33   Furman, "His Story versus Her Story," 107-116.

Tamar's story is recalled at a later point in Israel's history and her name is used by the people of Bethlehem in the patriarchal blessing they bestow on Boaz for his fulfilment of the levirate law in regard to Ruth (Ruth 4:12). She is mother of Perez, the ancient ancestor to David (Ruth 4:18-22). She is also designated "daughter-in-law" of Judah in the genealogy of 1 Chronicles (1 Chr 2:4).

In one of the earliest Jewish interpretations of this story, the Palestinian Targum, the action of Tamar is understood as part of God's unfolding history:

> A voice emerged from heaven: "You are both innocent,
> the matter came about from before me."[34]

In fact, it is a constant tendency in the Palestinian Targums to emphasize the role of God in the story of Tamar, a role which Schaberg calls an "intervention of a sort."[35] Although there is no mention of the action of God in the Genesis story, it seems that by the first century, God is explicitly linked to the Tamar story and hence to its double-edged power. Also Tamar is clearly pronounced righteous.

Positive references to Tamar are also found in the Book of Jubilees (Jub. 41:1) and The Testament of the Twelve Patriarchs (T. Jud. 10:1, 6; 12:1-10 and 13:3); and her story is used allegorically by Philo (Leg. All. 3.24.74; Quod Deus 29.36-137; Cong. 23.124-126; Mut. 23.134-136; Virt. 40.220-222; and especially De fuga 27.149-156), but the influence of these on the Matthean tradition seems to be minimal or even non-existent. Other rabbinic references are too late to have been able to provide a source.

We find, therefore, in Jewish tradition, a story of a woman within a patriarchal society whose actions and story functioned both to support the

---

34   "Targum Pseudo-Jonathan on Genesis Chap. 38" in *The Fragment-Targums of the Pentateuch according to their Extant Sources*, Vol. 2, ed. Michael L. Klein, AnBib 76 (Rome: Biblical Institute Press, 1980), 25. I am indebted to the excellent article of Bloch, ""Judah engendra Pharès et Zara, de Thamar"," 382-389, for the background to this reference. Not only does she discuss the Targumic reference and its context but she goes further to illustrate how the thinking displayed in the Targum is further amplified in later rabbinic material but these are too late to have been influential in the Matthean community. Louis Ginzberg, *The Legends of the Jews*, Vol 2, trans. H. Szold (Philadelphia: Jewish Publication Society of America, 1910), 32-36, also provides further rabbinic references but an examination of these traditions and also those referred to by Bloch reveal that the linking of Tamar with the ancestry of the Messiah seems to be a late development built on Ruth 4:12. Johnson, *Biblical Genealogies*, 160, would date it to the third century.

35   Schaberg, *Illegitimacy of Jesus*, 24, and Bloch, ""Judah engendra Pharès et Zara, de Thamar"," 386-387.

values of that society but also to challenge or critique it, especially its familial structure. Her action, undertaken alone and outside the established societal boundaries for women, is later understood as one of the points where God was involved in Israel's history.

2. Rahab

The biblical story of Rahab (Jos 2; 6:22-25) stands out from the midst of the military campaign of Israel against the land of Canaan.[36] Within this story, the woman Rahab, designated as a harlot but whose profession receives no more attention in the story,[37] stands out by way of contrast to the male world of conquest (represented by the two Israelite spies) and the world of power (represented by the King of Jericho and his men).[38] She also stands out as a woman outside of the patriarchal familial structure, dwelling alone within her own house in the city of Jericho as Niditch has pointed out:

> Rahab lives apart from her family, in contrast to normal kinship arrangements; for in order to save her family from the conquering Hebrews, she is told to gather them into *her* house. She lives outside the family unit, beyond the normal social structure and its boundaries.[39]

She is neither virginal daughter nor non-virginal wife and hence represents a danger to the patriarchal social structure, but as professional harlot she is also an endangered woman in the hands of this same system.[40]

---

36 Alfred Marx, "Ecriture et prédication. 25 - Rahab, prostituée et prophétesse. Josue 2 et 6," *ETR* 55 (1980): 72-73.

37 Patai, *Sex and Family*, 146, notes that "no moral judgment of any kind is passed by the Biblical narrative on either the *ad hoc* harlotry engaged in by Tamar, or on the professional prostitution of Rahab." The same could be said of the early christian tradition represented by Heb 11:31; James 2:25 and 1 Clement 12:1, each of which mention that Rahab was a harlot but praise her for her faith, her works and her hospitality respectively. Similarly in the rabbinic tradition, she is designated as harlot but here also the focus of the text is elsewhere: eight prophets and priests were descended from her (b. Meg. 14b); she became a proselyte (Mek. Ex. 18:1); and the divine spirit rested upon her (Midr. Ruth 2:1). Such references to Rahab of Jericho within the tradition and the traditional association of Ῥαχάβ in Matt 1:5 with this Rahab (see R. E. Brown, "Rachab in Mt 1,5 Probably is Rahab of Jericho," *Bib* 63 (1982): 79-80; and Zakowitch, "Rahab als Mutter") seem to counteract the hypothesis of J. D. Quinn, "Is ῬΑΧΑΒ in Mt 1,5 Rahab of Jericho?" *Bib* 62 (1981): 225-228, who would consider the ῬΑΧΑΒ of Matthew as an unknown woman and not the Rahab of Jericho.

38 Laffey, *An Introduction*, 86.

39 Niditch, "The Wronged Woman Righted," 147.

40 Laffey, *An Introduction*, 86, notes that professional harlots were tolerated in a patriarchal society to satisfy men's physical needs when neither wife nor concubine was available, but there is no mention in the text of the ramifications of this for the woman.

Within the story, however, Rahab is the chief actor. She thwarts the search for the spies, secures the promise of the spies to contravene the rule of *ḥērem* [חֵרֶם] (Josh 6:17)[41] and thereby guarantees a place for herself and her family in the history of Israel (Jos 6:22-23, 25). The woman who is outsider to the patriarchal culture generally and outsider to the ethnic culture of Israel is incorporated into both (6:25). The "profession of faith" of Rahab (Jos 2:9-11) is linked closely to her securing a promise of safety from the spies (vv. 12-13) and hence it would seem that the ancient text is already hinting at the power of God which is associated with the extraordinary initiative taken by Rahab in the face of the powers of the patriarchal world. Again we have a double-edged story of a woman whose actions provide a powerful critique of the patriarchal world view as well as its familial structure, but who is incorporated into that world view and structure. There is an implication in the narrative also that God is associated with both.

Subsequently, Josephus (Ant. 5.1.2 §12) will make this point more explicit:

> ... and she bade them depart to their own place, after swearing that they would verily save her and all that was hers, when, on taking the city, they should destroy all its inhabitants as had been decreed by their people, for of this (she said) she knew through certain signs which God had given her.

There is, however, no mention of Rahab in the intertestamental literature nor in Philo, but other early Jewish traditions also link the action of Rahab with the action of God and in this way incorporate her even more fully into Jewish history than did the book of Joshua:

> The same [i.e. because she drew near to God, God drew her near to himself] is true of Rahab the harlot. R. Eliezer [c. A.D. 80-120] says: 'The words, "of the house of Asheba" [1 Chron. 4:21] refer to Rahab the harlot who was an innkeeper. Eight priests and eight prophets descended from her! They are Jeremiah, Hilkiah, Seraiah, Machsaiah, Baruch, Meraiah, Hanamel, and Shallum.' R. Jehuda [b. Elai, c. 150] says: 'Also Hulda the prophetess was a descendant of Rahab.' Now if she, who came from a people of whom it is said [Deut 20:16]: 'Thou shalt not leave alive any soul,' because she drew near [to God], God drew her near [to himself], much more so with Israel ...[42]

---

41 François Langlamet, "Rahab," *DBS* IX, Fasc. 52 (Paris: Letouzey et Ané, 1979), 1074, discusses this aspect of the Rahab tradition. For an extensive study of Rahab in the tradition of the Hebrew Scriptures, intertestamental and rabbinic literature and early christian tradition with comprehensive bibliography, see the entire article, 1065-1092.

42 Mid. Sifre on Numbers, 78; parl. b. Meg. 14b and Ruth R. 2:1 quoted in Johnson, *Biblical Genealogies*, 163-164.

It does not seem, on the other hand, that there is any linking of Rahab with the ancestry of David and the messianic line;[43] and, at present, we have no sources for a tradition which identifies Rahab as the mother of Boaz since, according to the biblical tradition, Rahab lived at least two hundred years before Boaz.[44] This suggests that she did not find her way into the tradition because of her motherhood of a male ancestor of the Messiah. Rather, this emphasis comes from her incorporation into the Matthean genealogy. We are still left, therefore, with the question: what caused the names of the four women from the Hebrew Scriptures to be incorporated into the genealogy?

3. Ruth

If the story of Rahab could be said to stand out from its context within a patriarchal narrative, then the same claim can be made for the book of Ruth. It is, as Trible rightly says,

> ... a woman's story ... women in culture, women against culture and women transforming culture.[45]

It stands as a critique of patriarchy which structures society so that woman is always under the protection of a male. Three women who are childless widows, anomalies within the social structure, make independent choices. The focus of the story is on the choice of Ruth who leaves her own country to go with her mother-in-law, Naomi. As Trible states so clearly:

> Not only has Ruth broken with family, country, and faith, but she has also reversed sexual allegiance. A young woman has committed herself to the life of an old woman rather than to the search for a husband, and she has made this commitment not "until death us do part" but beyond death. One

---

43   Johnson's attempts, ibid., 164-165, to forge such a link are tenuous indeed and he seems to stretch the data to fit his particular scheme. It is at places like this that Nolan's critique of his work is most applicable. Nolan, *Royal Son of God*, 62, n. 3, says: "The weakness of *Biblical Genealogies* is that the four women are discussed in relation to Pharisaic disputation rather than in function of the whole genealogy, Mary and the Gospel's theology." A similar critique is made by Waetjen, "The Genealogy as Key," 205, n. 1.

44   Later rabbinic and christian interpretations (see Langlamet, "Rahab," 1074-1086 and M. A. Beek, "Rahab in the Light of Jewish Exegesis," *AOAT* 211 (1982): 37-44), indicate that Rahab had become a figure of theological significance in both christian and jewish exegesis but these interpretations do not throw further light on the link made in the genealogy between herself and Boaz.

45   Trible, *God and the Rhetoric*, 166, 196.

female has chosen another female in a world where life depends upon men. There is no more radical decision in all the memories of Israel.[46]

The story is set, however, in a patriarchal context. It begins within a patriarchal family (1:1-5). In Ruth 3, the emphasis shifts from the radical choice made by Ruth to her obedience to her mother-in-law in seeking out a relative of her deceased husband who may perform the duties of the levirate law in her regard (3:1-13). The independent woman who attached herself to another woman unto death and even beyond (1:16-17) is incorporated into the patriarchal family structure (4:1-13). The book closes with an ancestry of David (4:18-22).[47]

Although this story deals predominantly with the initiative of the young woman Ruth, there are hints within the text that her actions are linked with the חֶסֶד of God (1:8; 2:20; 3:10). This is more explicit in Josephus who also makes clear Ruth's place in David's ancestry:

> This story of Ruth I have been constrained to relate, being desirous to show the power of God and how easy it is for Him to promote even ordinary folk to rank so illustrious as that to which he raised David, sprung from such ancestors. (Ant. 5.9.4 § 337)

Her story finds no mention, however, in other intertestamental literature and the rabbinic references to her are much later.[48]

Of the three stories, that of Ruth is certainly most clearly two-edged or a story of discontinuity within continuity. It may well have functioned as an acceptable vehicle for the expression of women's discontent within a patriarchal culture as Trible's words above suggest. The androcentric ideological framework of the narrator remains, but within this is a tradition which may

---

46 Ibid., 173. Such, however, has not been the emphasis in most recent exegesis. For Jack M. Sasson, *Ruth: A New Translation with a Philological Commentary and a Formalist-Folklorist Interpretation*, The Johns Hopkins Near Eastern Studies 11 (Baltimore/London: Johns Hopkins University Press, 1979), 242-243 and 246-247, the book of Ruth is a lesson in family solidarity and universalism. Others focus on theological questions to the detriment of the characters and their story, see Edward F. Campbell, *Ruth: A New Translation with Introduction, Notes, and Commentary*, AB 7 (Garden City, New York: Doubleday, 1975), 28-32 and throughout his commentary. A shift in focus has occurred, however, among a few scholars who would supplement the views of Trible: see Alter, *Art of Biblical Narrative*, 48-60; and Williams, *Women Recounted*, 84-88, 109, 112.

47 That such a framework has influenced interpretations of the entire story is illustrated by Moshe Weinfeld, "Ruth, Book of," in *EJ* 14 (Jerusalem: Macmillan, 1971), 518-524: "The book concludes with the genealogy of David (4:17-22) which seems to have been the ultimate purpose of the author. His aim was to present in an idyllic way the origin of the great king David." Schaberg, *Illegitimacy of Jesus*, 28, notes a very curious point in this genealogy: four of the men listed are associated with the four women in Matthew's genealogy: Perez, Salmon, Boaz, and David.

48 Johnson, *Biblical Genealogies*, 165.

well have been expressive of the women in the community, a tradition which "turns the order of the world upside down without giving up the establishment that provides protection," in the words of Judah Goldin.[49] The patriarchal order emerges as the divine order and within that tradition, the action of the woman is associated with the action of God; but aspects of the story remain subversive.

4. The Wife of Uriah

The fourth reference which breaks Pattern 2 in the genealogy does not name Bathsheba but uses the designation τοῦ Οὐρίου which is that used in 2 Sam 11 and 12 up to the point of the death of the child born of her union with David while still the wife of Uriah (2 Sam 11:3, 26; 12:9, 10, 15). Although the text of 2 Samuel lays the fault very clearly at the feet of David (11:27) and Bathsheba is presented as passive throughout the story, the manner of referring to her points to the anomalous situation in which David's action places her. She is a danger to the patriarchal family structure, a danger which David removes by murdering Uriah and making Bathsheba his wife legally, thus incorporating her into that structure. It is important to note here that, according to the biblical tradition, it is not as wife of Uriah but as legal wife of David that Bathsheba becomes the mother of Solomon, her link into the Matthean genealogy. At this early stage of the tradition, however, it is difficult to determine whether there may have been a two-edged aspect to this story.[50]

If we turn to the Jewish traditions more contemporaneous with the emergence of early Christianity, we find some answers to our difficulties. The sin of David, while not being overlooked, has certainly been exonerated and Bathsheba is seen more positively as the mother of Solomon. Josephus recounts the David saga stressing the righteousness of David despite his sin, since its final outcome is the birth of Solomon.

> Now David, although he was by nature a righteous and godfearing man and one who strictly observed the laws of his fathers, nevertheless fell into grave

---

49 Judah Goldin, "The Youngest Son or where Does Genesis 38 Belong," *JBL* 96 (1977): 44, uses these words to refer to the revenge of the weak against the strong in terms of fraternal rivalry; but they are used by Furman, "His Story versus Her Story," 113, in relation to the story of Tamar (Genesis 38).

50 Alter, *Art of Biblical Narrative*, 61, asks a similar question of this and other betrothal type-scenes which he calls "betrothals by violence". His answer is as tentative as ours here when he says: "perhaps ... from this distance in time it is hard to be sure."

error ... for he was, as all agreed, a god-fearing man and never sinned in his life except in the matter of Uriah's wife (τὴν Οὐρία γυναῖκα).[51] ... Then David lay with his wife Beethsabē and she conceived and bore a son, whom he named Solomon, at the bidding of the prophet Nathan (Ant. 7.7.1 §130, 7.7.3 §153, and 7.7.4 §158).

In the early rabbinic tradition, the anomalous woman, Bathsheba, is associated with the divine guidance of Israel's unfolding history and with the action of God. Echoes of this are found in a tradition believed to be early:

Our Rabbis taught: Three beheld but did not see, viz, Nebat, Ahitophel, and Pharoah's astrologers. Nebat - he saw fire issuing from him. He interpreted it [as signifying] that he would reign, yet that was not so, but that Jeroboam would issue from him. Ahitophel - he beheld leprosy breaking out in him. He thought that it meant that he would reign[52] but it was not so but referred to BathSheba, his daughter,[53] from whom issued Solomon.

(b. Sanh. 101a)

It is more explicit in a tradition coming from possibly the early to middle second century:

It is revealed and known to thee that Bath-sheba was held ready for me from the six days of Creation, yet she was given to me for sorrow.

(Midr. Ps 3:5)[54]

Finally, it it is very explicit in the following century:

Raba (d. ca. 247) expounded: ... BathSheba, the daughter of Eliam, was pre-destined for David from the six days of Creation, but that she came to him with sorrow. And the school of R. Ishmael taught likewise: She was worthy [i.e. predestined] for David from the six days of Creation but that he enjoyed her before she was ripe.

(b. Sanh. 107a)

These last two texts represent, therefore, a fuller expression of a tradition which may well have existed in Jewish circles in the latter part of the first century.

The story of Bathsheba, like the previous three but not so clearly, is one of a woman whose action or being acted upon places her in an anomalous

---

51   Josephus uses a similar designation for Bathsheba as does the author of 2 Sam up to the point of the death of her son.

52   At this point, the footnote in the Soncino Talmud states: "According to legend, David was smitten with leprosy for six months on account of his sin with Bathsheba. Ahitophel therefore interpreted the outbreak on his own person as shewing that David's leprosy would bring him to the throne."

53   A further footnote states: "I.e. his granddaughter. Her father Eliam (2 Sam 11) being identified with the son of Ahitophel (2 Sam 23:34)."

54   This text is quoted by Johnson, *Biblical Genealogies*, 174, and linked with the exoneration of David.

position vis-à-vis the patriarchal family structure. She is incorporated back into the structure, however, and in the course of the traditioning process, her story is more explicitly associated with the action of God in Israel's history, an action which supports patriarchy but which must also be linked with the counter-cultural elements in the story.

The above survey has made it clear that there are no sources that are available to us which linked the names of these four women prior to their incorporation into the Matthean genealogy or tradition.[55] There are, however, certain thematic links in the biblical and later traditions which may suggest why they were brought together either within the Matthean community or at the stage of final redaction, but a polemic regarding the ancestry of the Messiah does not appear to be one of these as Johnson claims.[56] Within the Matthean genealogy, on the other hand, they are made to serve its purpose which is the establishment of the ancestry of the Messiah, but at times there is a clear shaping of the tradition to this purpose especially with regard to Rahab and to the linking of "the wife of Uriah" to the birth of Solomon. This suggests that it is possible that a tradition that already existed within the community and that needed to be shaped to fit the final purpose of the genealogy was incorporated. To test out this possibility, we will turn now to consider the above traditions in relation to verse 16 which provides a further break in the genealogical pattern and which concerns a woman.[57]

---

55   There are links between one or other of the women in a number of sources. Tamar and Bathsheba appear in the genealogies of 1 Chr 2-3; Tamar and Ruth in the Book of Ruth; then in later rabbinic tradition, Ruth and Bathsheba appear in Midr. Ruth 2:2; Ruth and Tamar in Midr. Ruth 9:1; and Ruth and Rahab in Sifre on Num 78. Rahab, Ruth and Bathsheba are listed among the twenty-two women of valour in MHG 1.334-339, see Ginzberg, *The Legends*, vol. V, 258, but Tamar is absent from this list.

56   Johnson, *Biblical Genealogies*, 156-179. Much of the material he uses refers to what seems to be a later rabbinic polemic regarding the ancestry of the Messiah but, as noted above, this polemic does not bring together the names of these four women.

57   Such a link is questioned by Hartmut Stegemann, ""Die des Uria": Zur Bedeutung der Frauennamen in der Genealogie von Matthäus 1,1-17," in *Tradition und Glaube: Das frühe Christentum in seiner Umwelt, Festgabe für Karl Georg Kuhn zum 65. Geburtstag*, eds. G. Jeremias, H.-W. Kuhn and H. Stegemann (Göttingen: Vandenhoeck & Ruprecht, 1971), 246-276, especially 255, who claims that the different wording of v. 16 suggests a different role for Mary and so the women from the Hebrew Scriptures must be treated separately. For him the designation τοῦ Οὐρίου becomes significant for interpretation because of its value as a commentary, something missing from the other three references. Gaechter, *Matthäus-Evangelium*, 36, also claims that Mary's role is unique and has no relation to the other four women named but the text does not seem to support this.

C. Verse 16

The reference to Mary in v. 16 breaks Pattern 1 which is repeated throughout
the genealogy as well as Pattern 2 which was used in relation to the other
four women. Where the reader expects to read Ἰωσήφ δὲ ἐγέννησεν τὸν
Ἰησοῦν, one finds instead that Joseph is identified not as the father of Jesus
but as the husband of Mary [τὸν ἄνδρα Μαρίας], and the birth of Jesus who is
called the Messiah [Χριστός] is linked to Mary, his mother, and not to Joseph.
The intricate patriarchal family structure with its emphasis on the male seed
or male adoption as the necessary legitimating factor is challenged at this
very point by means of this reference to Mary. The phrase, however, is
extremely enigmatic and can only be understood in the light of its
explanation in 1:18-25.

Whether this extraordinary verse is the result of the final redaction is
uncertain at this point. If, however, this process shaped Pattern 1 which is
used at the beginning of the verse and the concluding phrase ὁ λεγόμενος
χριστός,[58] then it is difficult to argue otherwise than that the same process
governed the entire verse even if community tradition was incorporated.
Since, however, verse 16 is explained further in the narrative following, we
must turn to an investigation of 1:18-25 in order to come to any final
conclusions regarding tradition and redaction in Matt 1.

II. The Narrative - 1:18-25

This narrative has been the object of extensive research which it is not my
purpose to repeat. Rather, I shall approach this section with the question
whether there is a link between the naming of the four women in the genealogy, v. 16 and elements of this story which may suggest a tradition that
existed in the community and has been incorporated into the overall
narrative thus providing a counter theme to its central focus.

We have already noted the pervasive androcentric perspective which
characterizes the genealogy and this provides a possible explanation for the

---

58   Luz, *Evangelium*, 92.

author's need to amplify the obscure reference to Joseph in 1:16. Hence Joseph dominates the narrative as the one who has control over the destiny of Mary (v. 19), as recipient of the divine message (v. 20), the one who can give legal paternity to Jesus because he himself is υἱὸς Δαυίδ (vv. 20, 21), and as the one who is obedient to the divine command in this situation (vv. 24-25).[59] Mary too is described initially within the patriarchal framework assumed here--she is betrothed to Joseph (v. 18). Thematically, at least, this suggests a strong link between the tradition underlying the genealogy and the Joseph tradition within this story.[60]

Within the same narrative, however, a counter-theme exists. It is linked to the unique role of Mary which continues to be treated enigmatically. While she was simply named as the one who gave birth to Jesus in the genealogy, although her naming did break the genealogical pattern, she is introduced to this section of the narrative as one who is in an anomalous situation in relation to patriarchal familial structures--πρὶν ἢ συνελθεῖν αὐτοὺς εὑρέθη ἐν γαστρὶ ἔχουσα ἐκ πνεύματος ἁγίου (v. 18). This is explained to Joseph by the angel (vv. 20-21) and it is presented as the fulfilment of the Isaian prophecy (Is 7:14):

> Behold, ἡ παρθένος shall conceive and bear a son,
> And his name shall be called Emmanuel.   (Matt 1:23)

Within this counter-theme, it is suggested that the conception of Jesus took place in an anomalous situation outside the patriarchal familial order, but that it was according to the creative plan of God.[61] This raises the possibility of a separate tradition that may have been linked in the final redaction or linked within the community so that the "endangered" woman and child

---

59   Soares Prabhu, *Formula Quotations*, 229-253, analyzes vv. 18-25 in terms of a dream narrative which he claims was pre-Matthean and which has been shaped into the present command-execution pattern by a Matthean redactor.

60   Nolan, *Royal Son of God*, 46, emphasizes this aspect of the narrative when he says: "The twin narrative of 1:18-25 depicts Joseph almost as another patriarch, receiving in a dream the assurance of a son and the continuance of blessing. The annunciation legitimizes the child as the spirit-generated Son of David and Jesus-Emmanuel. The activity of the holy spirit is recognizable from the divine creative power seen at work in scripture. The faithful compliance of Joseph follows the standard religious pattern of the obedience formula. From Matt 1:18 onward may be detected a certain patriarchal climate of interest in wife and heir, dreams, the angel of the Lord, threat to life, and migration within and outside the Promised Land."

61   Extensive reference has already been made to Schaberg, *Illegitimacy of Jesus*. She analyzes the reference to conception by the Holy Spirit and the use of the Isaian quotation in terms of her thesis on pp. 62-73.

are re-incorporated into the patriarchal order.[62] At this point I should like to allow the two possible traditions which are in tension within the narrative to stand together as they do in the narrative rather than to argue for the superiority of one over the other in order that we may gain insight into their formation.[63]

The best point to begin a brief analysis of the formation of the traditions underlying 1:18-25 seems to be vv. 22-23. These verses are held almost universally by scholars to be redactional, in fact, to belong to the final redaction of the gospel.[64] Opinions differ, however, as to the origin of the quotation.[65] Brown, therefore, raises significant questions for consideration here when he says,

> Reflection on the LXX of Isa 7:14 (cited in Matt 1:22-23) might have caused a Christian to compose a story about Jesus' mother being a virgin, but it could scarcely have led him [sic] to compose a narrative wherein Joseph was the main figure.[66]

This suggests that the use of the Isaian quotation may have led to the composing of a story but, if a tradition was developing in the community regarding the birth of Jesus of the woman Mary separate from the Joseph tradition, it may have been linked more naturally to this tradition regarding Mary and her son. Given the anomalous situation attributed to Mary in v. 18 and Soares Prabhu's suggestion that the verse is "substantially pre-redactional",[67] it seems that the purpose of the Isaian text is to underscore that the child to be born of Mary, the endangered woman within the patriarchal social structure, is, in fact, the child in whom God is with God's people. It

---

62   Meier, *Law and History*, 3, suggests that the bulk of the fulfilment quotations existed in the tradition before the time of the final redaction.
63   Schweizer, *The Good News*, 31, does make a choice: "The form of address "descendant of David" shows that legal fatherhood alone is all that matters: as the acknowledged son of Joseph, Jesus is a descendant of David. This is more important to Matthew than the virgin birth." Daniélou, *Evangiles de l'Enfance*, 45, also places the emphasis on Joseph as the object of the narrative.
64   Soares Prabhu, *Formula Quotations*, 45; Brown, *Birth of the Messiah*, 104; and Hendrickx, *Infancy Narratives*, 13, who goes so far as to suggest that the whole story is directed toward the quotation.
65   Strecker, *Der Weg*, 82-85, suggests a written collection of passages from the Hebrew Scriptures interpolated by a Matthean redactor. Soares Prabhu, *Formula Quotations*, 189, claims that a final redactor inserted the quotations into the text but he stresses the complex interaction between context, quotation and Matthean theology. Brown, *Birth of the Messiah*, 104, allows for two options: a Matthean redactor first recognized the applicability of a specific quotation; or that it already existed in a pre-Matthean tradition and it was then used within the gospel.
66   Ibid., 100.
67   Soares Prabhu, *Formula Quotations*, 246.

could be argued, therefore, that within the Matthean community as christians reflected on the birth of Jesus, on accusations made in relation to this
birth, and their growing belief in the action of God in Jesus' birth, life and
ministry, the Isaian text was recalled.[68] Its links, therefore, with the tradition
behind v. 18 and v. 16b may also have been pre-redactional.

Such reflection on Mary's role in the birth of Jesus could also have led
to the recalling of the stories of Tamar, Rahab, Ruth and Bathsheba, the wife
of Uriah. Like Mary, the mother of Jesus, who conceived her child in a
situation that the prevailing patriarchal culture regarded as anomalous, each
of these women too, at a certain point in her history, found herself in a similar position vis-à-vis that culture. It is this aspect of each of their stories that
is a disruptive element, which critiques the prevailing culture and its androcentric world view and which threatens its continuity and control. It is also
this aspect of the tradition which may well have originated among or at least
been supported by women in the community who sought to keep alive the
inclusive and liberating vision of Jesus which was in tension with the prevailing culture especially in their regard.[69] Their traditions preserved the
memory that God was present in their midst as the one whose inclusive vision incorporated women who were endangered by a patriarchal culture into
the divine unfolding of history, not as patriarchal vessel but as active participant. This aspect of the earlier traditions surrounding the four women was
already becoming explicit at this stage of their development, and so they
were linked to the story of Mary and became a significant tradition for
women within the Matthean community. Perhaps this tradition also functioned for them as a counter to the strong patriarchal tradition surrounding
the birth of Jesus which seemed to prevail within the community. As such

---

68   Brown, *Birth of the Messiah*, 149, links this reflection to a belief in virginal conception:
     "reflection on Isa 7:14 colored the expression of an already existing Christian belief in
     the virginal conception of Jesus."
69   Schüssler Fiorenza, *In Memory of Her*, 118-130, discusses the *Basileia of Jesus* as
     inclusive of women. I would also draw attention here to the fact that the majority of
     the formula quotations used throughout the gospel are drawn from what Walter
     Brueggemann, "Trajectories in Old Testament Literature and the Sociology of Ancient
     Israel," *JBL* 98 (1979): 161-185, calls the "liberation trajectory" in the Hebrew Scriptures.
     The two exceptions are Matt 2:23, whose very origin is obscure, and Mt. 13:35, which is
     drawn from the Psalms and is general in nature. This suggests that a tradition linking
     the liberation of women to the birth of Jesus may well have belonged within a much
     broader stream of traditions within the community which supported a christology with
     a strong liberation perspective.

we may have here a glimpse of what Schüssler Fiorenza calls "the egalitarian-inclusive practice and theology of early Christians."[70]

If such a tradition had developed within significant sectors of the Matthean community, it would have been difficult to suppress it completely in the final redaction of the gospel. It has been incorporated, however, into the predominantly androcentric perspective of the narrative and been overshadowed by the Joseph tradition into which it has been set, but its traces have not been able to be obliterated.[71] It gives rise, however, to a tension in the narrative surrounding its women characters.

III. Conclusion

Within the first chapter of Matthew's gospel which addresses the question "Quis" or "Who" in relation to Jesus as an introduction to his story which is to follow,[72] we have seen two major streams of tradition which have been incorporated into the gospel. These traditions seem to have different origins within the community and to reflect different theological emphases. The tradition which predominates in the text and which has claimed the attention of most exegetes is that which is summarized by Nolan:

> ... the royal, Davidic theology integrates all the forenamed roles (Lord, Christ, King, Son of God, Son of Man, Son of David, Shepherd, Servant and Prophet), without necessarily exhausting their meaning. The Christ of Matthew is Lord of the heart. Only through immersion in the Gospel's royalist faith-vision can the various colours of the christological spectrum, as caught by the titles, coalesce into the glory that captivated the evangelist.[73]

It supports, as divinely legitimated, the patriarchal tradition and the incorporation of the Jesus story into that tradition.

---

70   Schüssler Fiorenza, "Remembering the Past," 59.
71   Much work has already been done on discovering the sources behind the Joseph tradition which I will not repeat here. See especially Waetjen, "The Genealogy as Key," 225-227, and Brown, Birth of the Messiah, 111-113.
72   Stendahl, "Quis et Unde," suggests this focus and Brown, Birth of the Messiah, 133-134, extends it by attaching the "Quis" to the genealogy and "Quomodo" or "How" to the following narrative.
73   Nolan, Royal Son of God, 13.

There is a second tradition, however, which does not emphasize a royal theology but is linked to a liberation christology. Jesus is Emmanuel, "God with us", and God's unfolding history in Israel, which reaches a climax in Jesus, is a history incorporating and intimately linked to the lives and actions of women, women endangered by patriarchal laws and social structures. The incorporation of this tradition into the opening of the gospel critiques the royal theology and its support of patriarchy.[74] As the story continues especially into Matt 2 and the remainder of the prologue, the patriarchal tradition dominates the narrative almost to the exclusion of the alternative but as this study proceeds, it will become clear that the voice of the tradition which speaks for an alternative is never entirely silenced.

---

74 At this point, I find that what has emerged in regard to the prologue of Matthew's gospel seems to place elements of it along each of the trajectories discovered by Brueggemann within the Hebrew Scriptures. In his study, "Trajectories", he examines "the structure of liberation faith vis-à-vis a religion of legitimated order." His work provides an excellent base for a critique of Nolan's exclusive emphasis on royal Davidic theology which Brueggemann claims was used as a legitimation of the status quo. Unfortunately no study comparable to Brueggemann's has been undertaken in relation to the Christian Scriptures but even the limited findings here point to the value of such a study. See also in this regard two later articles of his: "A Shape for Old Testament Theology, I: Structure Legitimation," CBQ 47 (1985): 28-46; and "A Shape for Old Testament Theology, II: Embrace of Pain," CBQ 47 (1985): 395-415.

4. The Miracle Stories - 8:14-15; 9:18-26

Already, the reader is aware of the carefully constructed narrative in Matt 8-9 containing nine miracle stories divided into three groups of three[1] and interspersed with two interpretive buffer pericopes. Even a brief comparison with the gospels of Mark and Luke suggests that Matthean redaction has shaped the collection of miracle stories and buffer pericopes in Matthew since similar material is scattered throughout the Markan and Lukan texts. Such a suggestion is confirmed by recent scholarship which, even though it may reveal differences in its claims regarding the purpose of the redaction, nevertheless acknowledges the overwhelming evidence of it.[2] Here, I intend merely to recall that the emphasis within this scholarship has been on the theological themes believed to have guided the final redaction and that this was critiqued earlier from a feminist perspective. It was also suggested that an approach which focusses more specifically on the characters in the story, their interaction and the function of the story in the community will better serve our purposes. This is especially so since our major concern in this chapter is with the origin of the traditions regarding women in three healing stories, their development within the community or sectors of the community, their possible links with other traditions within the text and finally their influence on the theology of the community which led to their incorporation into the Matthean text.

---

1   Such a claim runs contrary to the theory that we have in Matthew's gospel ten miracle stories which parallel Moses' ten miracles in Egypt. This is found in Klostermann, *Matthäusevangelium*, 73; Grundmann, *Evangelium*, 245-246; Sabourin, *L'Evangile*, 100; and Lagrange, *Evangile*, 161, all of whom link the Matthean miracle collection with m. 'Abot 5:4f. Davies, *The Setting*, 86-90, accepts the number ten but argues against Moses' typology. It seems, however, that the account of the healing of the ruler's daughter and of the woman with the haemorrhage must be considered one story even though two miracles are recounted within the one story.
2   The works cited p. 93, n. 100 comprise the majority of recent studies of Matt 8 and 9 from a redaction-critical perspective.

I. 8:14-15

A. Comparison of Synoptic Texts

2 Matt 8:14-15	Mark 1:29-31	Luke 4:38-39
¹⁴ Καὶ	²⁹ Καὶ εὐθὺς ἐκ τῆς συναγωγῆς ἐξελθόντες ἦλθον	³⁸ Ἀναστὰς δὲ ἀπὸ τῆς συναγωγῆς εἰσῆλθεν
ἐλθὼν ὁ Ἰησοῦς εἰς τὴν οἰκίαν Πέτρου	εἰς τὴν οἰκίαν Σίμωνος καὶ Ἀνδρέου μετὰ Ἰακώβου καὶ Ἰωάννου.	εἰς τὴν οἰκίαν Σίμωνος.
εἶδεν τὴν πενθερὰν αὐτοῦ βεβλημένην καὶ πυρέσσουσαν·	³⁰ ἡ δὲ πενθερὰ Σίμωνος κατέκειτο πυρέσσουσα, καὶ εὐθὺς λέγουσιν αὐτῷ περὶ αὐτῆς.	πενθερὰ δὲ τοῦ Σίμωνος ἦν συνεχομένη πυρετῷ μεγάλῳ καὶ ἠρώτησαν αὐτὸν περὶ αὐτῆς.
	³¹καὶ προσελθὼν	³⁹ καὶ ἐπιστὰς ἐπάνω αὐτῆς
¹⁵ καὶ ἥψατο τῆς χειρὸς αὐτῆς,	ἤγειρεν αὐτὴν κρατήσας τῆς χειρός·	
		ἐπετίμησεν τῷ πυρετῷ
καὶ ἀφῆκεν αὐτὴν ὁ πυρετός,	καὶ ἀφῆκεν αὐτὴν ὁ πυρετός,	καὶ ἀφῆκεν αὐτήν·
καὶ ἠγέρθη καὶ διηκόνει αὐτῷ.	καὶ διηκόνει αὐτοῖς.	παραχρῆμα δὲ ἀναστᾶσα διηκόνει αὐτοῖς.

It has already been noted that the Matthean account of the healing of Peter's mother-in-law is a carefully structured unit[3] and I will simply reproduce Diagram 3 here for ease of reference.

Καί ...		εἶδεν τὴν πενθερὰν αὐτοῦ ...	)) Jesus
	καὶ	ἥψατο τῆς χειρὸς αὐτῆς,	)
		καὶ ἀφῆκεν αὐτὴν ὁ πυρετός	Fever
	καὶ	ἠγέρθη	)) Woman
	καὶ	διηκόνει αὐτῷ.	)

Comparison with the parallel accounts in Mark 1:29-31 and Luke 4:38-39, shows that these accounts are not carefully structured around verb and subject as is the Matthean version. In Luke, there is certainly no evidence of a careful linking of main verbs by means of the particle καί and even if one

---

3   See p. 84.

would argue that such a structure is a possibility behind the Markan account, it is broken at least once at the beginning of v. 30 by ἡ δὲ πενθερὰ Σίμωνος. Also, in both Mark and Luke, there is not the clear focus on the subjects of the main verbs that we find in Matthew.[4] The subject changes from Jesus to the woman, to the group in the house, back to Jesus, the fever, and finally to the woman again. Thus the careful structuring observed by way of a narrative-critical study of the Matthean gospel is now seen to be peculiar to this synoptic text.

The question arises, therefore, whether within the Matthean redaction process a story that was found in the Markan text which Luke has taken over almost intact with only minor alterations has been altered, or whether a tradition which had a different history of development from that found in Mark and Luke has been used. The most common scholarly response to this question is simply that Matthew depends on Mark but that the Matthean account has been more carefully structured, removing extraneous details in a way that is common to all the miracle stories in this gospel.[5] There are, however, a small number of scholarly voices expressing dissent and therefore further investigation is necessary.[6] A closer examination of the structure of these three accounts and hence of their basic form will constitute the beginning of this investigation.

Using the compositional structure of motifs common to miracle stories that Theissen has developed,[7] an analysis of both Mark and Luke indicates that they clearly belong to this category of story.

---

4   Gerhardsson, *Mighty Acts*, 40, suggests a slightly different structure but it too points to the emphasis on Jesus and the woman.

5   This is the underlying assumption which informs the work of Held, "Matthew as Interpreter," especially 169-171. It is the position argued by Rudolf Pesch, "Die Heilung der Schwiegermutter des Simon-Petrus: Ein Beispiel heutiger Synoptikerexegese," in *Neuere Exegese - Verlust oder Gewinn?* (Freiburg: Herder, 1968), 143-176; and Albert Fuchs, "Entwicklungsgeschichtliche Studie zu Mk 1:29-31 par Mt 8:14-15 par Luke 4:38-39. Macht über Fieber und Dämonen," *SNTU* A/6-7 (1981-82): 21-76. It is also generally accepted in commentaries: see Bonnard, *Évangile*, 116; Gundry, *A Commentary*, 148; Klostermann, *Matthäusevangelium*, 75; Grundmann, *Evangelium*, 254; Sabourin, *L'Évangile*, 109; and Gnilka, *Matthäusevangelium*, 306.

6   Lagrange, *Evangile*, 167, suggests that Matthew writes a well-known memory without the use of Mark. Léon-Dufour, "La guérison," 142, argues for 2 separate traditions; and Boismard, *Synopse*, 97, suggests two different forms of the story in Matthew and Mark/Luke. Lohmeyer, *Evangelium*, 159 also suggests a different source for the Matthean account other than the Markan gospel.

7   Theissen, *Miracle Stories*, 72-74.

COMPOSITIONAL MOTIFS	Matt 8:14-15	Mark 1:29-31	Luke 4:38-39
INTRODUCTION Coming of miracle worker	Καὶ ἐλθὼν ὁ Ἰησοῦς εἰς τὴν οἰκίαν Πέτρου	Καὶ εὐθὺς ἐκ τῆς συναγωγῆς ἐξελθόντες ἦλθον εἰς τὴν οἰκίαν Σίμωνος	Ἀναστὰς δὲ ἀπὸ τῆς συναγωγῆς εἰσῆλθεν εἰς τὴν οἰκίαν Σίμωνος.
Appearance of crowd		καὶ Ἀνδρέου μετὰ Ἰακώβου καὶ Ἰωάννου.	
Appearance of distressed person	εἶδεν τὴν πενθερὰν αυτοῦ	ἡ δὲ πενθερὰ Σίμωνος	πενθερὰ δὲ τοῦ Σίμωνος
EXPOSITION Description of distress	βεβλημένην καὶ πυρέσσουσαν·	κατέκειτο πυρέσσουσα,	ἦν συνεχομένη πυρετῷ μεγάλῳ,
Approach of miracle worker		καὶ εὐθὺς λέγουσιν αὐτῷ περὶ αὐτῆς.	καὶ ἠρώτησαν αὐτὸν περὶ αὐτῆς.
Behaviour of miracle worker		καὶ προσελθὼν	καὶ ἐπιστὰς ἐπάνω αὐτῆς
MIDDLE Miraculous action	 καὶ ἥψατο τῆς χειρὸς αὐτῆς,	ἤγειρεν αὐτὴν κρατήσας τῆς χειρός· 	 ἐπετίμησεν τῷ πυρετῷ
Recognition of miracle	καὶ ἀφῆκεν αὐτὴν ὁ πυρετός,	καὶ ἀφῆκεν αὐτὴν ὁ πυρετός,	καὶ ἀφῆκεν αὐτήν· παραχρῆμα δὲ ἀναστᾶσα
CONCLUSION Demonstration	καὶ ἠγέρθη καὶ διηκόνει αὐτῷ.	καὶ διηκόνει αὐτοῖς.	διηκόνει αὐτοῖς.

Diagram 12

The Matthean account, on the other hand, is seen to be briefer in some sections by comparison. There are also a number of differences. There is no crowd present in the Matthean account and the verb εἶδεν introduces the "Appearance of the distressed person" motif, a feature not found in other healing miracle stories in the gospels.[8] The miracle worker (Jesus) is not

---

8   In one of the summaries of Jesus' healings (14:14), however, we do find the use of εἶδεν but it refers to Jesus seeing the crowds on whom he has compassion and then he heals the sick out of the crowd so the εἶδεν does not necessarily refer to the supplicants specifically. The participle ἰδών is used in John 5:6 but not in terms of the "Appearance

approached, but rather he himself takes the initiative on seeing the woman who is ill with fever. This means that the behaviour of the miracle worker in response to the approach is also absent. The use of the verb εἶδεν, the absence of others and the initiative of Jesus therefore suggest that we explore another story-type, namely, the vocation story.[9]

The features of this story-type can be organized into four divisions similar to those of the miracle story but with different motifs as seen below. In examining Matt 8:14-15 according to these motifs, I will compare it with Matt 9:9 which is clearly a vocation story.[10]

COMPOSITIONAL MOTIFS   **Matt 8:14-15**   **Matt 9:9**

INTRODUCTION
Coming of the caller   Καὶ ἐλθὼν ὁ Ἰησοῦς   Καὶ παράγων ὁ Ἰησοῦς
                              εἰς τὴν οἰκίαν Πέτρου   ἐκεῖθεν

Sees one to be called   εἶδεν τὴν πενθερὰν αὐτοῦ   εἶδεν ἄνθρωπον ...
                                                          Μαθθαῖον

EXPOSITION
Description of one to be
called   βεβλημένην καὶ   καθήμενον ἐπὶ τὸ τελώνιον
                              πυρέσσουσαν

MIDDLE
Call - word or action   καὶ ἥψατο τῆς χειρὸς   καὶ λέγει αὐτῷ ἀκολούθει
                              αὐτῆς   μοι.

                              (καὶ ἀφῆκεν αὐτὴν ὁ
                              πυρετός)

CONCLUSION
Response to call   καὶ ἠγέρθη   καὶ ἀναστὰς
                              καὶ διηκόνει αὐτῷ.   ἠκολούθησεν αὐτῷ.

Diagram 13

Thus it would seem that, while Mark and Luke recount the story of Peter's mother-in-law as a healing story, Matthew presents it within the basic structure of a vocation story including, however, a healing motif: καὶ ἀφῆκεν αὐτὴν ὁ πυρετός. This would seem to support the minority position noted above, namely, that there were two different sources, one of which influenced the Matthean story and the other the Markan and Lukan stories.

_____

of the distressed person" motif but following this and introducing a conversation between Jesus and the supplicant.

9   These features are found in a number of stories--Matt 4:21; 9:9; Mark 1:16, 19; 2:14--all of which are clearly vocation stories.

10   Such a comparison was suggested in Boismard, *Synopse*, 97.

This is the position argued by Boismard who illustrates that the vocation story-type used in Matt 8:14-15, 9:9, and the calling of the first four disciples (Mark 1:16-20; Matt 4:18-22) had its origin in one of the earliest written collections of gospel traditions in which there were a number of stories composed on the model of similar stories in the Hebrew Scriptures. There, the parallel for the vocation story was the calling of Elisha in 1 Kgs 19:19-21.[11] On the basis of Boismard's analysis[12] and the data investigated above, it can be argued that the earliest written form of the story of Peter's mother-in-law was a vocation story. The earliest memory, therefore, that influenced the Matthean community was the vocation of a woman, and it was this memory that was preserved by the community during the course of the story's development. It is difficult to establish whether the healing motif belonged to the story in its origin or whether it was inserted later under the influence of the story as preserved in the Markan and Lukan traditions. The most likely possibility seems to be that it belonged to the origin of the story,[13] and that the Matthean community has maintained its two-fold aspect: vocation and healing.[14]

---

11   Boismard, *Synopse*, 97. A similar position is held by Francis Martin, *Encounter Story: A Characteristic Gospel Narrative* (DSS Dissertation, Pontifical Biblical Institute, Rome, 1977), 62, who bases his analysis of this pericope on the work of Boismard. Pesch, "Die Heilung," 166, also notes elements of a vocation story in the pericope. None of these scholars, however, have followed through the theological and ecclesiological implications of the use of this form of story in relation to a woman. Other scholars too have recognized the difficulty of explaining the form and source of this story. Léon-Dufour, "La guérison," 148, calls it a "récit catéchetique" and Bonnard, *Évangile*, 166, an "effort pédagogique" as they seek to explain its structure and brevity. Still others recognize the peculiarity of the initiative of Jesus; see Gundry, *A Commentary*, 148 and Schweizer, *The Good News*, 217, but neither gives an adequate explanation for this.

12   It should be acknowledged that what we have here is an hypothesis but as with much Source Criticism, some hypothetical judgments are necessary to provide a starting point. In this particular instance, Boismard's hypothesis seems to offer the best explanation of the material available to us in the text.

13   One argument that may support this claim is that in the four clear vocation stories in the Synoptic gospels: Mark 1:16-20; 2:14; Matt 4:18-22 and 9:9, the description of the one called is introduced by a participle--ἀμφιβάλλοντας (Mark 1:16); καθήμενον (Mark 2:14); βάλλοντας (Matt 4:18); and καθήμενον (Matt 9:9). The MT of 1 Kgs 19:19 uses a participle also--חֹרֵשׁ--but the LXX of the same verse, however, uses the imperfect ἠροτρία. If the MT shaped the form of the vocation stories in the early christian period, then the use of the participle in the description of the one called could well have been a common feature in those stories. The use of βεβλημένην and πυρέσσουσαν in 8:14 may well have belonged, therefore, to the story in its origin which would mean that the illness of the woman formed part of the original vocation story.

14   Patte, *A Structural Commentary*, 116, who analyzes the gospel according to structural exegesis, wonders "whether this third type of healing initiated by Jesus--without request from anyone and thus without expression of a prior faith on the part of the patient--is not comparable to the calls to discipleship (cf. 4:18-22; 9:9); they too are fully initiated by Jesus." He goes on to ask "But would this mean that a call to discipleship is to be viewed as comparable to a healing?"

B. Redaction

We return now to the final form of the miracle story. A study of some of its clearly redactional features will enable us to suggest the stages which linked the original story to the form it now has in the Matthean gospel.

The redactional introduction to both the Markan[15] and Lukan[16] accounts suggests a common source in which the healing of Peter's mother-in-law was linked with the exorcism of an unclean spirit and the multiple healings, and together the three were set in Capernaum, beginning in the synagogue and concluding outside Simon's house. The fact that Matthew's gospel does not contain this same arrangement of material suggests two possibilities. The first is that the introduction is omitted because the miracle account was taken from Mark and used in a different context.[17] Given the overall simplicity of the Matthean account, however, and its retention of elements of an early form of the story as seen above, it seems more in keeping with this information to suggest that in the final redaction, the story was incorporated as it existed in the tradition of the community where it was not linked to the exorcism story as in the Markan tradition. In the Matthean redaction, however, the story is followed by the summary passage as found in Mark but it forms part of Buffer Pericope A rather than being a conclusion to the "day in Capernaum" as in Mark and Luke.

The final redactions that are specifically Markan and Lukan suggest that a unique emphasis has been added to an already existing healing story. Luke adds ἐπετίμησεν τῷ πυρετῷ, giving the story the quality of an exorcism. Also, the use of ἠρώτησαν, ἐπιστάς and παραχρῆμα[18] adds a Lukan distinctiveness

---

15   The Markan account begins with καὶ εὐθύς which is a typical Markan phrase (1:10, 12, 20, 23, 30, 42). The following phrase ἐκ τῆς συναγωγῆς ἐξελθόντες ἦλθον is intended to link this miracle with the one which precedes and, together with the summary verses of 1:32-34, it forms a unit—a day in Capernaum. Léon-Dufour, "La guérison," 135, calls this day a "composition théologique". Pesch, "Die Heilung," 159-161, also points to the Markan redactional activity in this construction.

16   Luke's opening Ἀναστὰς δέ is a typical Lukan semiticism, see Boismard, Synopse, 96. Ἀπὸ τῆς συναγωγῆς then links the story to the previous account and, parallel to Mark, the story is joined to a concluding summary which brings to a close a "day in Capernaum".

17   This is the argument of Fuchs, "Entwicklungsgeschichtliche Studie," 28-29; it is an underlying presumption in Gundry, A Commentary, 148; and is stated explicitly by Willoughby C. Allen, A Critical and Exegetical Commentary on the Gospel according to S. Matthew, ICC (Edinburgh: T. & T. Clark, 1907), 79.

18   That such vocabulary belongs predominantly to the Lukan redaction is seen readily by comparison with the other two Synoptics: ἐρωτάω (4,3,16); ἐπίστημι (0,0,7); and παραχρῆμα (2,0,10).

to an already existing story form. The Markan emphasis, on the other hand, seems to be on the resurrectional aspect of the story. The expected order, κρατήσας τῆς χειρός ἤγειρεν αὐτήν, is changed so that ἤγειρεν αὐτήν appears at the very beginning of the miraculous action giving it a place of emphasis. This change is clear when Mark 1:31 is compared with 5:41-42 (καὶ κρατήσας τῆς χειρός ... καὶ εὐθὺς ἀνέστη ...) and 9:27 (κρατήσας τῆς χειρὸς αὐτοῦ ἤγειρεν αὐτόν), the raising of Jairus' daughter and the healing of the epileptic boy, one of whom was dead and the other of whom seemed as if he were dead.[19] In these two stories, the resurrectional emphasis is clear. The vocabulary used in Mark 1:31 and the reversal of word-order seem to point to a strong resurrectional emphasis in the account of the healing of Simon's mother-in-law. Both the Markan and Lukan final redactions, therefore, suggest that minor distinctive changes were made by each evangelist to a story which already had the quality of a healing miracle story. Hence, we can argue that in the early stages of the Markan tradition, the story had the common characteristics of a healing account.

When we turn to the final Matthean redaction, there are three items which demand our attention. First, it seems clear that the use of the name of Jesus in 8:14 to draw attention to Jesus as the one who has the power to heal, belonged to this stage since this explicit use of Jesus' name is a common characteristic of the entire Matthean gospel and it often appears in places where the third person pronoun is used explicitly or implicitly in the other two Synoptics.[20] Secondly, the use of Πέτρου where the Markan and Lukan accounts both have Σίμωνος points towards Matthean redaction.[21] Further investigation confirms this when it is seen that in contrast to Mark, Matthew contains the name of Peter together with Simon in the account of his call (Matt 4:18; Mark 1:16) and Peter in contrast to Simon in the account of the healing of his mother-in-law, both prior to the choosing of the twelve where the name Peter is first used by Mark (Matt 10:2 and Mark 3:16). Later in the gospel, Matthew also includes a number of stories which highlight

---

19   Boismard, *Synopse*, 96-97.
20   By way of example, see Matt 8:18; 9:9, 19, 23, 27, and 35 within the miracle chapters under examination, and also 15:21; 26:6; 27:55; and 28:9 in the pericopes to be examined subsequently. Gundry, *A Commentary*, 148, gives the statistics as 80 times in Matthew for this particular characteristic. It is mentioned by Sabourin, *L'Evangile*, 107, and Fuchs, "Entwicklungsgeschichtliche Studie," 32. Fuchs, however, argues that it has no special significance but is simply a necessary grammatical construction to bring the reader's focus back onto Jesus after the end of the previous narrative.
21   There are only two syriac texts of the fourth century [sy [s.c]] which contain the variant reading Σίμωνος Κήφα and hence it seems that the most authentic reading is Πέτρου.

the role of Peter and which are not included in the other gospels (14:28-33; 15:15; 16:18-19; 17:24; and 18:21-22). This suggests that the use of the name Peter is not haphazard but develops the theme of the representative and leadership role of Peter which extends through the entire gospel and has definite theological implications for the interpretation of the stories in which it occurs.[22] This will receive more attention when the results of this investigation are interpreted, but it may be suggested here that this aspect of Matthean redaction reflects a strong patriarchal tradition within the community, a tradition which included the patrilineage of Jesus seen in Matthew's genealogy and emphasis on the leadership function of Peter, both of which significantly influenced the final redaction.

The last sign of Matthean redaction is possibly the use of ἥψατο (ἅπτω) in 8:15 (cf. Mark 1:31). When we look at the Markan form κρατήσας τῆς χειρός, we find that it occurs three times in that gospel with the sense of taking hold of someone's hand (Mark 1:31; 5:41; and 9:27). We have already seen that in each of these cases, it is linked with the verb ἐγείρω and the theme of resurrection from the dead. Matthew contains this phraseology only once in 9:25, the raising of the ruler's daughter. The Matthean account of the cure of the epileptic boy contains no parallel to his seeming dead (Mark 9:26), nor to the healing action found in Mark 9:27. Moreover, the predominant use of the verb κρατέω in both Matthew and Mark is that of laying hands on to arrest and hold captive (Matt 14:3; 21:46; 26:4, 48, 50, 55, 57 and Mark 6:17; 12:12; 14:1, 44, 46, 49, 51). The question arises, therefore, whether a typical resurrection formulation was changed so as not to overemphasize this aspect of the story or whether the use of ἅπτω belonged in the original form of the story. The use of ἠγέρθη in v. 15 has already been discussed and its possible symbolic/resurrectional overtones indicated. It would seem, therefore, that there was no desire to avoid resurrection symbolism and language and hence the second option must prevail. Further study of the use of ἅπτω in the Synoptics, however, may point to any

---

22   Scholarly interpretations differ in regard to the significance given to the name Peter in this story. Beare, *A Commentary*, 210, claims that "the fact that the woman is the mother-in-law of Peter is immaterial to the miracle". Gundry, *A Commentary*, 148, argues that the emphasis falls on Peter because of the establishing of a representative role for Peter. For a more detailed discussion of a similar position, see Fuchs, "Entwicklungsgeschichtliche Studie," 33-35. Paul Lamarche, "La guérison de la belle-mère de Pierre et le genre littéraire des évangiles," *NRTh* 87 (1965): 523, considers the replacement of Simon by Peter to have ecclesial significance while Pesch, "Die Heilung," 165, although not giving it this significance, does acknowledge that it is a carefully thought out change in the Matthean text.

particular significance in the Matthean retention of this phrase from an original source.

The most common use of ἅπτω in Mark and Luke is in relation to Jesus' healing activity (Mark 1:41; 3:10; 5:27-31; 7:33; 8:22; Luke 5:13; 7:14; 8:44-47; 22:51). It is also used in the blessing of children (Mark 10:13; Luke 18:15).[23] This usage is paralleled in Matthew only in the healing of the leper (Matt 8:3; Mark 1:41; Luke 5:13) and the woman with a haemorrhage (Matt 9:20, 21; Mark 5:27, 28, 30, 31; Luke 8:44, 45, 46, 47). The verb is used, however, in the Matthean account of the healing of Peter's mother-in-law which, as we have seen, is in the form of a vocation story; and it is also found in the two accounts of the healing of blind men (Matt 9:29 and 20:34) in which the motif of discipleship is suggested by the use of ἀκολουθέω (9:27 and 20:34); and in the account of the transfiguration in which Jesus touches the disciples and invites them to "Rise and have no fear" (17:7). There seems to be a strong link, therefore, in the Matthean gospel between the touch of Jesus and the discipleship motif. If, as suggested above, this verb was found in the source used for this story in which healing and discipleship motifs were combined, it is understandable that it would be retained in a story in which these two motifs were also to be maintained.

The remaining two items which require consideration here and which add weight to the argument that the Matthean account originated as a vocation story are the use of εἶδεν (v. 14) and the singular pronoun in the final phrase διηκόνει αὐτῷ. As we have already seen in the comparison of 8:14-15 and 9:9 and as has been discussed above, the typical vocation story begins with the movement of the one who calls toward the place where he or she *sees* the one to be called. One possible explanation of the use of this verb in 8:14 is that the wording of an original vocation story was retained in the redactional process. This seems more plausible than the suggestion that a typical healing story was changed to a form that differs from every other

---

23   Johannes Behm, *Die Handauflegung im Urchristentum nach Verwendung, Herkunft und Bedeutung* (Leipzig: Deichert, 1911), in his first chapter entitled "Die Handauflegung bei Jesus," 8-15, discusses the laying on of hands as it was associated with Jesus and this action is seen by him to connote healing and blessing similar to what has been claimed here for the Synoptic use of ἅπτω. In his discussion, however, it is the phrase ἐφίστημι τὰς χειράς which receives most attention. In Matthew, this latter phrase is never used for Jesus' healing activity as it is in Mark and Luke where it occurs in both summary statements of healing and healings of individuals. It is used only for the blessing of children. The one exception is Matt 9:18 but here the words are not those of the Matthean narrator but rather of the ruler who comes to Jesus with a request.

healing story in the gospel in that Jesus takes the initiative. The gospel evidence of care about structure and form tells against the second explanation as does the emphasis on the prior faith of the recipient common to many of the miracle stories.[24]

The singular αὐτῷ can certainly be explained in terms of a Matthean removal of extraneous characters and the focus on the woman and Jesus if one follows the interpretation given by Held.[25] In the light of what has already been argued, however, the singular form is a natural conclusion to a vocation encounter which involves simply Jesus as caller, and the woman as the one called. Διηκόνει αὐτῷ parallels ἠκολούθησεν αὐτῷ of Matt 9:9 and both parallel וַיְשָׁרְתֵהוּ/ἐλειτούργει αυτῷ in 1 Kgs 19:21.[26]

We can argue, therefore, from the redactional study of Matt 8:14-15 that an early vocation story has been preserved by the community relatively intact. Some of the vocabulary (ἥψατο, ἠγέρθη, διηκόνει) which may well have been in the original story has also been influenced by the theology of the gospel. The only significant redactional features are the use of Jesus' name and the name of Peter.

C. Development of the Tradition

We are now in a position to draw together some of the threads of the above investigation, to point to the possible development of the tradition until its destination within the Matthean gospel text, and to highlight the

---

24 Held, "Matthew as Interpreter," 178-181, 239-241, and 284-296, discusses the theme of faith in relation to the Matthean miracle stories and on pp. 215, 222 and 225, lists some of the characteristics of Matthean structuring of these stories. For further discussion of the faith motif see Theissen, *Miracle Stories*, 129-140, and Ebeling, "Jesus and Faith," 223-246. Wire, "The Structure of the Gospel Miracle Stories," 99-108, discusses opposition to the demand which is a common element in healing stories together with the necessity of the supplicant to struggle against this opposition.

25 Held, "Matthew as Interpreter," 169-170.

26 The use of διακονέω has already been discussed above pp. 85-86. To this discussion should be added the comment made by Fuchs, "Entwicklungsgeschichtliche Studie," 58: "Der kirchliche Klang von διακονεῖν läßt auf dem Hintergrund der ausdrücklichen christologischen Konzentration in dieser Wundergeschichte mit der Möglichkeit rechnen, daß Mt auch hier mehr als die Überlieferung einer für den Glauben wenig bedeutsamen historischen Episode im Sinn hat und dem Leser ein Bild der urkirchlichen Nachfolge, im besonderen der Frau, vor Augen stellt, das Nachahmung finden soll." The ecclesial dimension of the verse is also noted by Lamarche, "La guérison," 520, and Pesch, "Die Heilung," 167, who says that christology and parenesis hang together. Schweizer, *The Good News*, 217, also considers that discipleship is significant in this verse.

interpretive process within the Matthean community that may have supported this development.[27]

The clearest point emerging from our study of 8:14-15 is that the beginning of the literary history of this tradition regarding Peter's mother-in-law was the inclusion of a primitive christian memory or story within an early Jewish-christian collection of stories and sayings of Jesus,[28] and that this story was cast in the form of a vocation story but with a healing motif inserted. This seems to have been a unique combination of elements from two traditional story-forms which leads us to question the possible intention behind such a combination.

Two statements of Theissen help to guide this stage of our investigation. First, he states that "traditions are the product of human actions,"[29] and second, that "traditions can be understood only in terms of the real context of social and historical life."[30] This suggests, therefore, that behind the story as it has been recounted within the tradition may lie a human action of Jesus, an action of healing and calling to membership in the new community that was developing around him. The exact understanding of the nature of πυρετός at the time of Jesus is difficult to determine[31] but the use of the two participles βεβλημένην and πυρέσσουσαν may, within the story, be the intensification of the problem that is to be overcome.[32] Jesus reaches out across the religious and social boundaries, heals the woman with a touch and invites her into the new community that is developing around him.[33] The preservation of this early memory may suggest that

---

27   Wire, "Structure of the Gospel Miracle Stories," 87, calls this the "story's intention".
28   Boismard, *Synopse*, 48-50. Theissen, *Miracle Stories*, 246-249, suggests the possibility of a Galilean origin for the miracle stories even though he opposes the theory that they were aetiologies for Galilean churches.
29   Ibid., 26.
30   Ibid., 231.
31   K. Weiss, "πυρέσσω/πυρετός," *TDNT* VI:956-959, points to the belief in the Hebrew Scriptures that it was the result of a divine curse (Deut 28:22; Lev 26:16) and to the rabbinic understanding that equated it with demonic possession (b. Ned. 41a; b. Giṭ. 70a) against which elaborate incantations and magical practices were developed (b. Giṭ. 67b; b. Šabb. 66b). Given the wide range of historical eras which his analysis covers and its lack of grounding in any particular region, it is difficult to determine from his work the understanding that prevailed in Galilee at the time of Jesus.
32   Wire, "Structure of the Gospel Miracle Stories," 102.
33   Theissen, *Miracle Stories*, 242, draws attention to the distinction between magicians and charismatic miracle workers and his statement helps to throw light on the nature of the community which grew up around Jesus: "Magic is an individualistic reaction to social disintegration. The magician has no need to be integrated into society. He remains in the dark. It is quite different with the charismatic miracle-worker. He seeks followers quite openly, starts up missionary movements or founds 'schools'--not because he wants to be integrated into the existing pattern of social life (that is what dis-

within the Jesus movement itself discipleship of Jesus was inclusive and not dependent on male gender distinctions. This would be one new form of social integration, expressing a new social awareness and it would certainly have led to the unavoidable conflict with the surrounding world.[34]

Wire points out that opposition to be overcome is key to the functioning of the demand or healing story.[35] There has been no analysis similar to hers carried out in relation to vocation stories but the story we have in Matt 8:14-15 would seem to suggest that the illness of the woman was the opposition to discipleship which Jesus overcomes. The story would then be used within the community to celebrate a woman's encounter with Jesus which is good news.[36] It called the hearers beyond the gender boundaries which limited participation in both social and religious aspects of life within their community to males. It gave legitimating power to women's active participation in the extension of the Jesus' movement into the early christian community and to a possible struggle for this participation. A new paradigm was developing for women's religious and social participation in the early christian community based on the praxis of Jesus which recognized that gender boundaries could indeed be crossed in order that women might be invited to discipleship.

Such a story would certainly have been told among women within the community. Perhaps too it was they who preserved the story's vocational aspect down through the history of their community's developing theology. The story would also seem to belong with the liberating tradition surrounding women found in the prologue to the gospel and hence further corroborates the suggestion made in Chapter Three that there may have been a body of tradition preserved within some sectors of the community that supported a vision and practice based on the Jesus movement that was an alternative to the predominant androcentric vision. The use of the name Peter may, however, represent an attempt to bring the discipleship of women within the confines of patriarchal leadership and it may be the legacy of another body of tradition which was strong within the community.

---

tinguishes him from the healing sanctuaries), but because he is looking for new patterns of life applicable to society ... the charismatic miracle-workers and their followers feel themselves to be distinct from magicians. They are looking for new forms of social integration, expressing a new social awareness, and thus come unavoidably into conflict with their world, whereas a magician would tend to avoid this conflict."

34 Ibid., 242.
35 Wire, "Structure of Gospel Miracle Stories," 84.
36 Ibid., 107.

At the stage of final redaction, the story of the healing of Peter's mother-in-law is included in its vocational form and not only that, but it is placed at the climactic point of the first three miracle stories in Matt 8. It is also followed by the summary passage and fulfilment quotation of vv. 16-17 which link it to the motif of Jesus' liberating activity. It is also placed in close relationship to the discipleship sayings of 8:18-22 thus emphasizing this motif further. At the end of the story, the woman healed stands alone outside the patriarchal family structure with a ministry that is central to the gospel--she serves Jesus.[37] Finally, even though we noted above the possible influence of a patriarchal tradition in the naming of Peter, this Matthean redaction places the service of the woman in the community called church.[38] This gives further impetus to the claim that the story served a legitimating function in regard to the participation of women in active ministerial service within the Matthean community.

The clues provided by a narrative-critical study of the text have been more than adequately substantiated by the redaction-critical investigations and the study of the development of the tradition. The initiative of Jesus which, at the narrative-critical stage of investigation was thought to be a breaking of a narrative pattern in order to point to the crossing of gender boundaries so that women could be incorporated into the new community forming around Jesus, has now been shown to be a typical element in a vocation story. It is, on the other hand, the statement of healing which breaks the structural pattern of a vocation story but toward the same end--to illustrate the need for Jesus to cross gender boundaries in order to incorporate women into the community around him. The tension which such a story creates in an androcentric narrative has been seen to be a possible reflection of a tension within the community between two bodies of tradition which have been finally incorporated into the gospel. It suggests a struggle to keep

---

37   In a number of passages in Luke (10:40; 12:37; 17:8), the verb διακονεῖν clearly refers to service at table but this meaning is absent from both Mark and Matthew; see Selvidge, "Mark and Woman". Pesch, "Die Heilung," 167, also states clearly that more than table service is meant: "Der Dienst der Frau is kein bloßer Tischdienst mehr, sondern Dienst gegenüber dem göttlichen Kyrios, der ihr die Gesundheit, die Heilung geschenkt hat, der ihr das Heil gebracht hat. Das ekklesiologisch-paränetische Anliegend des Evangelisten wird in der hier durchschimmernden symbolischen Bedeutung erkennbar."

38   Elisabeth Schüssler Fiorenza, "'Waiting at Table': A Critical Feminist Theological Reflection on Diakonia," *Concilium* 198 (1988): 84-94, discusses the reappropriation of this term from a feminist perspective.

alive the memory of the new religious and social status given to women by Jesus as a legitimation for the ongoing participation of women within the community. All of these factors are at play within this first story of a woman to be recounted within the gospel proper.

At this point, we are now ready to proceed to an examination of the story of the woman with the haemorrhage which parallels the healing of Peter's mother-in-law in many ways, and this story will be considered within the context of the healing of the ruler's daughter.

II. 9:18-26

An examination of 9:18-26 in the context of this study will need to proceed by two stages: the first, a detailed investigation of 9:20-22; and the second, an examination of those aspects of 9:18-19, 23-26 which are significant in terms of the context they give to 9:20-22 and for their own contribution to an understanding of the function played by stories involving females in the unfolding Matthean narrative as well as in the community out of which and for which the narrative was written. Only when these two aspects have been considered separately will they be interpreted as a unit and that within the wider context already established.

A. 9:20-22

1. Comparison of Synoptic Texts

Matt 9:20-22	Mark 5:25-34	Luke 8:43-48
20 Καὶ ἰδοὺ γυνὴ αἱμορροοῦσα δώδεκα ἔτη	25 Καὶ γυνὴ οὖσα ἐν ῥύσει αἵματος δώδεκα ἔτη	43 Καὶ γυνὴ οὖσα ἐν ῥύσει αἵματος ἀπὸ ἐτῶν δώδεκα, ἥτις
	26 καὶ πολλὰ παθοῦσα ὑπὸ πολλῶν ἰατρῶν καὶ δαπανήσασα τὰ παρ' αὐτῆς πάντα	ἰατροῖς προσαναλώσασα ὅλον τὸν βίον οὐκ ἴσχυσεν
	καὶ μηδὲν ὠφεληθεῖσα	ἀπ' οὐδενὸς θεραπευθῆναι
	ἀλλὰ μᾶλλον εἰς τὸ χεῖρον ἐλθοῦσα,	

Matt	Mark	Luke
	27 ἀκούσασα περὶ τοῦ Ἰησοῦ,	
προσελθοῦσα	ἐλθοῦσα ἐν τῷ ὄχλῳ	44 προσελθοῦσα
ὄπισθεν	ὄπισθεν	ὄπισθεν
ἥψατο	ἥψατο	ἥψατο
τοῦ κρασπέδου		τοῦ κρασπέδου
τοῦ ἱματίου αὐτοῦ·	τοῦ ἱματίου αὐτοῦ·	τοῦ ἱματίου αὐτοῦ,
21 ἔλεγεν γὰρ ἐν ἑαυτῇ·	ἔλεγεν γὰρ ὅτι	
ἐὰν μόνον ἅψωμαι τοῦ	ἐὰν ἅψωμαι κἂν τῶν	
ἱματίου αὐτοῦ	ἱματίων αὐτοῦ	
σωθήσομαι.	σωθήσομαι.	
	29 καὶ εὐθὺς	καὶ παραχρῆμα
	ἐξηράνθη ἡ πηγὴ τοῦ	ἔστη ἡ ῥύσις τοῦ
	αἵματος αὐτῆς	αἵματος αὐτῆς.
	καὶ ἔγνω τῷ σώματι ὅτι	
	ἴαται ἀπὸ τῆς μάστιγος ·	
22 ὁ δὲ Ἰησοῦς	30 καὶ εὐθὺς ὁ Ἰησοῦς	45 καὶ
	ἐπιγνοὺς ἐν ἑαυτῷ τὴν ἐξ	
	αὐτοῦ δύναμιν ἐξελθοῦσαν	
στραφεὶς	ἐπιστραφεὶς ἐν τῷ ὄχλῳ	
	ἔλεγεν·	εἶπεν ὁ Ἰησοῦς·
	τίς μου ἥψατο	τίς ὁ ἁψάμενός μου;
	τῶν ἱματίων;	
		ἀρνουμένων δὲ πάντων
	31 καὶ ἔλεγον αὐτῷ	εἶπεν
	οἱ μαθηταὶ αὐτοῦ·	ὁ Πέτρος·
		ἐπιστάτα,
	βλέπεις	
	τὸν ὄχλον	οἱ ὄχλοι
		συνέχουσίν σε
	συνθλιβοντά σε	καὶ ἀποθλίβουσιν.
	καὶ λέγεις·	46 ὁ δὲ Ἰησοῦς εἶπεν·
	τίς μου ἥψατο;	ἥψατό μού τις,
		ἐγὼ γὰρ ἔγνων δύναμιν
		ἐξεληλυθυῖαν
		ἀπ' ἐμοῦ.
	32 καὶ περιεβλέπετο	
καὶ ἰδὼν αὐτὴν	ἰδεῖν τὴν τοῦτο ποιήσασαν.	
		47 ἰδοῦσα δὲ
	33 ἡ δὲ γυνὴ	ἡ γυνὴ
		ὅτι οὐκ ἔλαθεν
	φοβηθεῖσα	
	καὶ τρέμουσα,	
	εἰδυῖα ὅ γέγονεν αὐτῇ,	τρέμουσα
	ἦλθεν καὶ προσέπεσεν	
	αὐτῷ	ἦλθεν καὶ προσπεσοῦσα
		αὐτῷ
		δι' ἥν αἰτίαν ἥψατο αὐτοῦ
	καὶ εἶπεν αὐτῷ	ἀπήγγειλεν
		ἐνώπιον παντὸς τοῦ λαοῦ
	πᾶσαν τὴν ἀλήθειαν.	
		καὶ ὡς ἰάθη παραχρῆμα.
εἶπεν·	34 ὁ δὲ εἶπεν αὐτῇ·	48 ὁ δὲ εἶπεν αὐτῇ·
θάρσει,		
θύγατερ· ἡ πίστις σου	θύγατηρ, ἡ πίστις σου	θύγατηρ, ἡ πίστις σου
σέσωκέν σε.	σέσωκέν σε·	σέσωκέν σε·
	ὕπαγε εἰς εἰρήνην	πορεύου εἰς εἰρήνην.
	καὶ ἴσθι ὑγιὴς ἀπὸ τῆς	
καὶ ἐσώθη ἡ γυνὴ	μάστιγός σου.	
ἀπὸ τῆς ὥρας ἐκείνης.		

When one comes to consider the form of the story of the woman with the haemorrhage, one finds that it has been so closely woven into the account of the raising of the ruler's daughter that the transitional verse (Matt

9:19; Mark 5:24; Luke 8:42) belongs to both stories. Hence, this verse will be included below as the structure of the story is examined according to Theissen's compositional structure of motifs for miracle stories which has already been used above. From this structuring of motifs, some clues will begin to emerge as to the relationship between the three accounts and their possible sources.

Compositional Motifs	Matt 9:19-22	Mark 5:24-34	Luke 8:42-48
INTRODUCTION			
Coming of miracle worker	¹⁹καὶ ἐγερθεὶς ὁ Ἰησοῦς		⁴²Ἐν δὲ τῷ
	ἠκολούθησεν αὐτῷ	²⁴καὶ ἀπῆλθεν μετ' αὐτοῦ	ὑπάγειν αὐτὸν
Appearance of crowd	καὶ οἱ μαθηταὶ αὐτοῦ	καὶ ἠκολούθει αὐτῷ ὄχλος πολὺς καὶ συνέθλιβον αὐτόν.	οἱ ὄχλοι συνέπνιγον αὐτόν.
Appearance of distressed	²⁰Καὶ ἰδοὺ γυνὴ	²⁵Καὶ γυνὴ	⁴³Καὶ γυνὴ
EXPOSITION			
Description of distress	αἱμορροοῦσα δώδεκα ἔτη	οὖσα ἐν ῥύσει αἵματος δώδεκα ἔτη ²⁶ καὶ πολλὰ ... ²⁷...	οὖσα ἐν ῥύσει αἵματος ἀπὸ ἐτῶν δώδεκα, ἥτις ...
Approach of miracle worker	προσελθοῦσα ὄπισθεν ἥψατο τοῦ κρασπέδου τοῦ ἱματίου αὐτοῦ·	ἐλθοῦσα ἐν τῷ ὄχλῳ ὄπισθεν ἥψατο τοῦ ἱματίου αὐτοῦ·	⁴⁴ προσελθοῦσα ὄπισθεν ἥψατο τοῦ κρασπέδου τοῦ ἱματίου αὐτοῦ,
Expression of trust	²¹ ἔλεγεν γὰρ ἐν ἑαυτῇ· ἐὰν μόνον ἅψωμαι τοῦ ἱματίου αὐτοῦ σωθήσομαι.	²⁸ ἔλεγεν γὰρ ὅτι ἐὰν ἅψωμαι κἂν τῶν ἱματίων αὐτοῦ σωθήσομαι.	
Behaviour of miracle worker	²² ὁ δὲ Ἰησοῦς στραφεὶς καὶ ἰδὼν αὐτὴν	(³⁰ Καὶ εὐθὺς ὁ Ἰησοῦς ἐπιγνοὺς ἐν ...³³ ...)	(⁴⁵ καὶ εἶπεν ὁ Ἰησοῦς· τίς ὁ ...⁴⁷...)
MIDDLE			
Miraculous Action	εἶπεν· θάρσει, θύγατερ· ἡ πίστις σου σέσωκέν	²⁹ καὶ εὐθὺς ἐξηράνθη ἡ πηγὴ τοῦ αἵματος αὐτῆς ... (v.34b καὶ ἴσθι ὑγιὴς ἀπὸ τῆς μάστιγός σου.) ...	⁴⁴ καὶ παραχρῆμα ἔστη ἡ ῥύσις τοῦ αἵματος αὐτῆς

Recognition   καὶ ἐσώθη ἡ γυνὴ   καὶ ἔγνω τῷ σώματι
                     ἀπὸ τῆς ὥρας   ὅτι ἴαται ἀπο τῆς
                     ἐκείνης.   μάστιγος·
                                        ** vv. 30-33   ## vv. 45-47

CONCLUSION
Dismissal   34 ὁ δὲ εἶπεν ...**   48 ὁ δὲ εἶπεν αὐτῇ
                                        ὕπαγε   ... πορεύου
                                        εἰς εἰρήνην ...   εἰς εἰρήνην.

Diagram 14

It is clear from the above that each of the accounts is in the form of a miracle story. Some of the motifs of this story-type, however, have been combined differently in the three accounts. This is especially clear in the Markan account in which a reason for the appearance of the distressed [ἀκούσασα περὶ τοῦ Ἰησοῦ--v. 27] not found in Matthew or Luke has been added. The long section which describes Jesus' response to the woman's touch (Mark 5:30-33; Luke 8:45-47),[39] in fact follows the miracle itself in each of these accounts (see Mark 5:29; Luke 8:44b). This section is absent in the Matthean account. In Mark, there is a repetition of the miraculous action at the very end of the pericope [καὶ ἴσθι ὑγιὴς ἀπὸ τῆς μάστιγός σου--5:34c]. Finally, the Matthean account stands out, by way of contrast to both Luke and Mark, in terms of its simplicity and its basic accord with the pattern of miracle stories.

Vernon Robbins has called attention to another structural feature in the Matthean account other than its fidelity to the compositional motifs of a healing story: the repetition of key words--ἥψατο ... τοῦ ἱματίου αὐτοῦ/ἅψωμαι τοῦ ἱματίου αὐτοῦ; σωθήσομαι/σέσωκέν/ἐσώθη. He goes on to point out, using the analysis of Robert Alter, that such repetition reflects a characteristic of storytelling in the Hebrew Scriptures, especially in relation to the link between speech and narration.[40] This may suggest, given the simplicity of the Matthean account and its exhibiting of features characteristic of the narrative style of the Hebrew Scriptures, that the account in Matthew's gospel relies very much on an early source. This may well be the same source noted behind the story of the healing of Peter's mother-in-law, in which the patterns of the Hebrew Scriptures influenced the early versions of the stories

---

39   "Behaviour of Miracle Worker" and "Expression of Trust" according to Theissen's motifs.

40   Vernon K. Robbins, "The Woman who Touched Jesus' Garment: Socio-Rhetorical Analysis of the Synoptic Accounts," *NTS* 33 (1987): 505-506. See also Alter, *Art of Biblical Narrative*, 67-68, for a more detailed study of repetition in biblical narrative, and Sternberg, *Poetics*, 365-440, especially 387-390, for verbal repetition.

contained therein.[41] We need, however, to give further attention to literary relationships between the three accounts to test out this hypothesis and draw firmer conclusions.

An examination of the Mark/Luke literary relationship yields evidence of possible dependency which can be seen in the synopsis of the texts above without a detailed listing. Even where exact verbal similarity is not obvious, there is similarity of content and structuring. The Mark/Matthew comparison, on the other hand, shows fewer signs of literary dependency. It is all the more surprising, therefore, that we notice evidence of possible literary dependence at precisely that point where Mark differs from Luke (Matt 9:21; Mark 5:28). This, together with the Matthean/Lukan parallel [προσελθοῦσα ὄπισθεν ἤψατο τοῦ κρασπέδου τοῦ ἱματίου αὐτοῦ (Matt 9:20; Luke 8:44)] where Mark has ἐλθοῦσα ἐν τῷ ὄχλῳ in place of προσελθοῦσα and does not have τοῦ κρασπέδου, points to a rather complex history of transmission.

A comparison of content may shed further light. In this regard, both Matthew and Mark have Jesus turning and seeing the woman (Matt 9:22b; Mark 5:30b), but in Matthew this action introduces the miraculous action of Jesus whereas in Mark it follows it and leads into the questioning of the crowd, which is absent from Matthew. Both have the healing mentioned at the end, but in Mark this is a doublet (cf. Mark 5:29 and 5:34). The content parallels between Mark and Luke are more numerous: the extension of the description of the distress to include the reference to the fact that the woman had not been able to be healed by doctors; the immediate healing of the haemorrhage following the woman's touching of Jesus' garment; Jesus' questioning regarding who touched him; a statement that power had gone out from him; acknowledgment by the woman of her action; and a command to go in peace.

If one accepts a simple version of the Two-Source Theory, this complexity is explained in terms of a Matthean "taking over" and "tidying up" of the complex Markan account, omitting the many items included in

---

41 Boismard, *Synopse*, 211, places the origin of this story in his Document A, the same source he argued for the healing of Peter's mother-in-law and he characterizes this document as relying on patterns from the Hebrew Scriptures, but in regard to the healing of the woman with the haemorrhage, he does not illustrate the pattern of narration highlighted by Robbins. Held, "Matthew as Interpreter," 237-239, on the other hand, argues for these "catchwords", as he calls them, as signs of the Matthean redaction. He does not, however, deal with the presence of this technique within the Hebrew Scriptures and it seems more difficult to argue that an evangelist would change an existing story to return to such a technique especially as the stories moved out of their origin in Palestine and into the Graeco-Roman world.

Luke that are common to Mark.[42] This would also explain a Matthean dependence on Mark even at the point where Luke differs, but it does not explain the Matthean/Lukan parallel that differs from Mark. We also noted above that this explanation does not offer the most satisfactory explanation for the structuring of the narrative around speech and action in which words are repeated, although it must be acknowledged that these phrases, except the last, do occur in the Markan narrative but not in the same pattern of alternating speech and action.

A more satisfactory explanation which seems to deal with the above information together with a consideration of the text variants is given by those who recognize the complexity of the literary relationships in this story and see in it an indication of independent sources for Matthew and for Mark/Luke.[43] If we take up the positions of Sabourin and Boismard as offering the most concrete working hypotheses, we may outline the following possibility: the Markan account has combined two different sources of the healing of the woman with a haemorrhage which have influenced Matthew and Luke respectively. From evidence already discussed above, it may be argued that the source behind the final Matthean account was a very concise story similar to the present form which was contained in the same collection of stories as the healing of Peter's mother-in-law. The Lukan story, on the other hand, is based on a source containing a more picturesque miracle story. These two accounts were edited most successfully in the Markan

---

42 Gerard Rochais, *Les récits de résurrection des morts dans le Nouveau Testament*, MSSNTS 40 (Cambridge: University Press, 1981), 100, 110-111, whose argument applies particularly to the account of the raising of the ruler's daughter into which the healing of the woman with the haemorrhage has been inserted. See also J. T. Cummings, "The Tassel of his Cloak: Mark, Luke, Matthew - and Zechariah," in *Studia Biblica 1978: II. Papers on the Gospels*, ed. E. A. Livingstone, JSNTSup 2 (Sheffield: JSOT Press, 1980), 47-61; Argyle, *Matthew*, 75; Allen, *A Critical Commentary*, 94; Alexander Jones, *The Gospel according to St. Matthew: A Text and Commentary for Students* (London: Geoffrey Chapman, 1965), 32; Schweizer, *The Good News*, 228; Meier, *Matthew*, 97; Grundmann, *Evangelium*, 273; Held, "Matthew as Interpreter," 167; Hill, *The Gospel*, 178; Klostermann, *Matthäusevangelium*, 81; and most recently Gnilka, *Matthäusevangelium*, 339-340. All but Cummings argue thus for the entire pericope 9:18-26.

43 Lagrange, *L'Evangile*, 185, warns against pretending that there is the same relationship between Matthew and Mark as there is between Mark and Luke. Lohmeyer, *Evangelium*, 175-178, especially 178, argues for an independent tradition behind Matt 9:18-26 but he does not discuss the source for the Markan and Lukan account. Bonnard, *Évangile*, 134, on the other hand, argues that Matthew and Luke have the same source, a position that will be shown to be untenable in the light of the evidence discussed in this section and in what is to follow. Sabourin, *L'Evangile*, 125, suggests that Mark is secondary and combines different sources and Boismard, *Synopse*, 211, makes this more specific by claiming that the two different sources are those followed in the Matthean and Lukan redaction respectively.

redaction, except that the actual healing at the end of the story is repeated according to the Matthean source even though its occurrence had already been stated earlier in accord with the Lukan source. From here we can now proceed to a study of the redactional elements especially in the Matthean account.

2. Redaction

The typically Matthean introduction of a supplicant--καὶ ἰδού--and the close parallel between 9:18 and 9:20-21 have already been discussed in Chapter Two but it may assist our investigation to detail the parallels below.

9:18	A¹	ἰδοὺ ἄρχων εἷς[44]	
9:20	B¹	ἰδοὺ γυνὴ	αἱμορροοῦσα δώδεκα ἔτη
	A²		ἐλθὼν
	B²		προσελθοῦσα ὄπισθεν
	A³	προσεκύνει αὐτῷ	
	B³	ἥψατο τοῦ κρασπέδου τοῦ ἱματίου αὐτοῦ·	
	A⁴	λέγων ὅτι	
	B⁴	ἔλεγεν γὰρ ἐν ἑαυτῇ·	
	A⁵		ἡ θυγάτηρ μου ἄρτι ἐτελεύτησεν
	A⁶	ἀλλὰ ἐλθὼν ἐπίθες τὴν χεῖρα σου ἐπ' αὐτήν	
	B⁶	ἐὰν μόνον ἅψωμαι τοῦ ἱματίου αὐτοῦ	
	A⁷	καὶ ζήσεται.	
	B⁷	σωθήσομαι.	

Diagram 15

Such careful structuring would seem to belong to the redactional process in order to highlight various aspects of the story, but that needs further exploration below. As part of that exploration we will seek to determine how much of the material so structured was source and traditional material and how much belonged to the final redactional stage.

The opening of each pericope (A¹ and B¹) focusses attention on the supplicant: ἄρχων εἷς (who is later qualified by his own statement--ἡ

---

44   This is the reading as given in the 26th Nestle-Aland edition of the Greek New Testament and it is the most widely attested. The variants are discussed by Rochais, *Récits*, 89.

θυγάτηρ μου ἄρτι ἐτελεύτησεν)[45] and γυνὴ/αἱμορροοῦσα δώδεκα ἔτη.[46] Although Rochais claims that the Matthean redaction does not demonstrate an interest in the characters but their attitudes,[47] we have already noted that both Theissen and Wire question this and the text itself seems to confirm their position.[48] As Wire says in regard to the woman with the haemorrhage and other women healed:

> The healing is for the woman, not the woman for the healing. Whatever her experience once was, and we cannot reach back to that, the teller calls the hearer to break out of a closed world and to demand, struggle and realize miracle in human life.[49]

The character and the situation of oppression that each represents for the hearers is, therefore, central to the miracle story and the simplicity of the Matthean story under consideration emphasizes this focus. The ruler [ἄρχων] is introduced as male and is representative of official authority whether it be that of the synagogue[50] or of socio-political life generally.[51] He is also head of a patriarchal family. The woman, on the other hand, appears alone,

---

45   The young girl is identified by means of her position in the patriarchal family. She is her father's daughter and m. Ketub. 4:4 speaks of her status thus: "The father has control over his daughter (n. 3 Not yet twelve and a half years old) as touching her betrothal whether it is effected by money, by writ, or by intercourse [whereby betrothal is effected]; and he has the right to aught found by her and to the work of her hands. ... When she is married the husband exceeds the father in that he has the use of her property, during her lifetime, and he is liable for her maintenance and for her ransom and for her burial." It is interesting that this paragraph of the Mishnah concludes with the statement: "R. Judah says: Even the poorest in Israel should hire not less than two flutes and one wailing woman," a tradition which is set in contrast to the action of Jesus at the conclusion of the story of the raising of the ruler's daughter. This young girl, by way of a premature death, is cut off from the fulness of her womanhood which, in the Jewish tradition to which she belonged, was to bear children (cf. Judges 11:37-40).

46   Both the young girl and the woman, by reason of their respective conditions as presented in the story, are outside the boundaries of control which the later Mishnaic traditions would set for women and girls. See Neusner, "Thematic or Systemic Description," 79-100, for a discussion of the points where women cross established boundaries.

47   Rochais, Récits, 90. Gerhardsson, Mighty Acts, 43, also claims that Matthean interest in the supplicants is slight.

48   Theissen, Miracle Stories, 287, claims that "the character field is crucial to an understanding of the inner dynamics of the miracle story."

49   Wire, "Structure of the Gospel Miracle Stories," 108.

50   In the Matthean account, in contrast to that of Mark and Luke, the ruler is not designated as head of the synagogue. From the evidence available to us, it is difficult to know whether the simple title "ruler" belonged to the miracle story as it appeared in its source or whether Matthean redaction has simplified it to "ruler" because of a desire to dissociate this man of faith from the synagogue which, in Matthew's gospel, is always presented as over against Jesus (4:23; 9:35; 10:17; 12:9; 13:54; 23:34 in which the reference is to *their* or *your* synagogue; and 6:2, 5 and 23:6 which contain reprimands of conduct within the synagogue).

51   BAGD, 113-114, contains both meanings.

excluded from the patriarchal world and the explanation of her illness underlines this exclusion further. She represents women cut off socially and religiously and is in direct contrast to the ruler.[52]

The starkness of the participle αἱμορροοῦσα (B¹) closely parallels the ἄρτι ἐτελεύτησεν (A⁵) descriptive of the young girl. Both are female, both can be considered as dead (one socially and religiously, the other physically), and both therefore have the capacity to contaminate life and hence need to be carefully controlled.[53] Both situations, therefore, deal with very clear boundaries as they refer to women. Whether this participle belonged to the source or is the work of Matthean redaction is difficult to determine. The verb αἱμορροέω is a New Testament *hapax legomenon* (cf. the more descriptive οὖσα ἐν ῥύσει αἵματος of Mark and Luke). The twelve years which is common to each evangelist, and which, therefore, probably belongs to the original story, functions to emphasize even further the severity of the

---

52   The Levitical rules regarding such an extraordinary flow of blood were severe. Lev 15:25-27 states: "If a woman has a discharge of blood for many days, not at the time of her impurity, or if she has a discharge beyond the time of her impurity, all the days of the discharge she shall continue in uncleanness; as in the days of her impurity, she shall be unclean. Every bed on which she lies, all the days of her discharge, shall be to her as the bed of her impurity; and everything on which she sits shall be unclean, as in the uncleanness of her impurity. And whoever touches these things shall be unclean, and shall wash his clothes, and bathe himself in water, and be unclean until the evening." It is clear that this debars the woman not only from participation in the religious community but from normal human social relationships and especially from sexual relations with her husband. Her unavailability for sexual intercourse or fertility could well have produced a divorce and would certainly have prevented her from remarrying. See R. Grob, "ἅπτω," in *The New International Dictionary of New Testament Theology*, vol. 3, ed. Colin Brown (Exeter: Pater Noster, 1978), 861; and J. Duncan M. Derrett, "Mark's Technique: The Haemorrhaging Woman and Jairus' Daughter," *Bib* 63 (1982): 474-505. For a discussion of such sexual boundaries from an anthropological point of view, see the two essays of Mary Douglas, "External Boundaries," and "The System at War with Itself," in *Purity and Danger: An Analysis of the Concepts of Pollution and Taboo* (London/Boston/Henley: Routledge & Kegan Paul, 1966), 114-128 and 140-158.

53   As a corpse, the young girl renders all unclean (Num 19:11-13) just as the woman does (Lev 15:25-27). In terms of the woman's ritual uncleanness, it is linked to death in Lev 15:31. It would seem that the person who first linked these two gospel stories certainly intended the interaction of themes which we see operating here both in the gospel stories and in the scriptural texts which form their backdrop. The laws of scripture regarding corpse uncleanness are commented on by the rabbis in m. Ohol. (especially 1:1-4; 2:1) and regarding a haemorrhaging woman in m. Nid. both of which belong to the Order of Purities of which Neusner claims that "the principal and generative ideas of the system as a whole are to be located at its very beginnings, some time before the turn of the first century," Neusner, *Method and Meaning*, 121, n. 22. Hence, it seems reasonable to argue that the principles behind the commentary were operative as elements of the oral law during the time of Jesus' ministry and certainly during the era of the christian community which produced the Matthean gospel. These did not change the scriptural laws in any way but added extra burdens especially upon women in terms of determining exactly the time of menstruation, the type of extraordinary flow and various other minute details.

woman's condition and the inhuman restrictions and suffering placed upon her by the law over and above the suffering due to her illness itself.

The explanation of the approach of both the ruler (A[2], A[3]) and the woman (B[2], B[3]) underline the boundaries that apply to the woman and the contrast indicated above is further emphasized. The ruler simply approaches Jesus (ἐλθών), the woman approaches him from behind (προσελθοῦσα ὄπισθεν) indicating her recognition of the boundaries society has placed upon her. Προσελθοῦσα could well belong to the final Matthean redaction given the verb's predominant use in Matthew;[54] but the notion of approaching from behind seems to have belonged to the original sources (cf. Mark 5:27; Luke 8:44). The fact, however, that the phraseology προσελθοῦσα ὄπισθεν ἥψατο τοῦ κρασπέδου τοῦ ἱματίου αὐτοῦ is the one parallel common to Luke and Matthew over against Mark needs further consideration.

Where Matthew and Luke have ἥψατο τοῦ κρασπέδου τοῦ ἱματίου αὐτοῦ, Mark simply has ἥψατο τοῦ ἱματίου αὐτοῦ. The explanation that both Matthew and Luke have been influenced by Mark 6:56 (τοῦ κρασπέδου τοῦ ἱματίου αὐτοῦ) while Mark has omitted the τοῦ κρασπέδου here in 5:27 seems unconvincing.[55] A more satisfactory explanation seems to be found in the search for the history of the transmission of the story itself. Within the Matthean story, the phrase ἥψατο τοῦ κρασπέδου τοῦ ἱματίου αὐτοῦ is parallel to προσεκύνει αὐτῷ (A[3], B[3]). Προσκυνέω has already been shown to belong to Matthean redactional vocabulary and to carry certain religious connotations.[56] It could be argued that the original story of the ruler's request contained a phrase similar to that now in Mark's account: πίπτει πρὸς τοὺς πόδας αὐτοῦ.[57] The Matthean account, on the other hand, employs a verb from redactional vocabulary in order to strengthen the parallel with ἥψατο τοῦ κρασπέδου τοῦ ἱματίου αὐτοῦ which, I shall argue below, was found in the source.

The background which can give meaning to this phrase is located in two different places and perhaps the two were commonly known in early

---

54   Across the synoptics the occurrence of this verb is 51,5,10, according to Neirynck and van Segbroeck, New Testament Vocabulary, 311.

55   This is the position held by Cummings, "The Tassel," 48.

56   See p. 89, n. 88. Statistically across the synoptic gospels it appears thus: 13,2,3; see Neirynck and van Segbroeck, New Testament Vocabulary, 312.

57   This is very similar to the phraseology of a resuscitation story in the Hebrew Scriptures (2 Kgs 4:27) which may well have provided a model for the christian story. This strengthens the argument which shall follow, namely, that the story was in the form of a resuscitation story in its source, a position which differs from Rochais, Récits, 102-103. This, however, will receive further consideration below.

Judeo-christian Palestine. Manfred Hutter, in a recent article, illustrated that in the ancient Orient this gesture often accompanied by similar words, was part of a prayer formula and that its presence in Israel is implied by 1 Sam 15:24-27.[58] Another possible influence is Zech 8:23 where the LXX translates כְּנַף (cf. Num 15:38, 39; Deut 22:12) by κρασπέδος. Here it is not used in relation to ritual requirements connected with the *mitzvot* as found in the Torah but rather is used in a worship context (Zech 8:20-22) and it is the Gentiles (δέκα ἄνδρες ἐκ πασῶν τῶν γλωσσῶν τῶν ἐθνῶν) who take hold of the robe of a Jew saying that God is with them. Well may the original storyteller have used this same phrase for the action of the woman whose illness rendered her an outsider;[59] but who reached out to Jesus, Emmanuel, God with us. Either influence or the interaction of both point to the petitionary and worship aspect of the action and hence to the reason behind the Matthean use of προσκυνέω to form a parallel with it.[60]

We can argue, therefore, that the full formulation ἥψατο τοῦ κρασπέδου τοῦ ἱματίου αὐτοῦ belongs to the Matthean source and it was at a later stage of Matthean redaction that it was linked with the phrase προσελθοῦσα ὄπισθεν. The Lukan account must have been influenced, at a late stage of redaction also, by the Matthean formulation, possibly because of the prayer formula connotations which may have been known in the Lukan commu- nity.[61] Mark, on the other hand, retained the formulation, ἐλθοῦσα ἐν ... ὄπισθεν ἥψατο τοῦ ἱματίου αὐτοῦ, as it was found in the second source.

Matthew 9:21 and Mark 5:28, except for the ἐν ἑαυτῇ in the Matthean text, are drawn from the story as found in the Matthean source and in the

---

58   Manfred Hutter, "Ein altorientalischer Bittgestus in Mt 9:20-22," *ZNW* 75 (1984): 133-
     135. He sums up his argument in these words: "Wenn wir zusammenfassen: Für Mt
     9:20-22 ließ sich zeigen, daß es Mt in seiner Darstellung der Heilung der blutflüssigen
     Frau nicht um die Schilderung des Wunders geht, sondern um den Glauben der Frau.
     Daher ist es für des Gesamtverständnis der Perikope angemessener, im Erfassen des
     Gewandsaums nicht eine magische Handlung zu sehen, wodurch die Heilung
     'erschlichen' wird, sondern eine Geste äußerst intensiven Bittens. Die Wurzeln dieser
     Geste liegen bereits im Alten Orient."
59   According to the Mishnah, the Samaritans were considered unclean as a nation
     because their women were considered menstruants from birth or perpetual
     menstruants (m. Nid. 4:1). Like them, this woman, therefore, becomes excluded from
     religious and social life within Judaism because of her illness.
60   Derrett, "Mark's Technique," 495, suggests sexual implications in the woman's action,
     arguing that ἄπτω has sexual connotations; but the parallel with προσκυνέω and the pe-
     titionary nature of the action seem to provide a strong argument against this. From a
     feminist perspective, one needs to apply a hermeneutics of suspicion to his argument
     since it can too easily reflect an androcentric ideology in which women's role in a
     narrative is considered simply sexual.
61   Boismard, *Synopse*, 210, whose theory of synoptic interaction allows for an
     intermediate stage of Matthean influence on Luke.

final Matthean redaction ἐὰν μόνον ἄψωμαι τοῦ ἱματίου αὐτοῦ is both paral-lel and in contrast to the ruler's ἀλλὰ ἐλθὼν ἐπίθες τὴν χεῖρά σου ἐπ' αὐτήν. Both represent a request for healing. The Matthean introduction of ἐν ἑαυτῇ emphasizes even further the boundaries experienced by the woman. She cannot make a direct request to Jesus and yet the ruler makes the most extraordinary request--to come and lay hands on a young girl who is already dead.[62] The significance of σώζω in this context will be discussed later.

The close parallels which we have seen between the introductions to both the story of the raising of the ruler's daughter and the healing of the woman with the haemorrhage, highlighted and enhanced in small ways by later redaction, would seem to suggest that the stories were placed together at the beginning of their written transmission precisely to emphasize the contrast between the woman and the ruler and yet the similarity of their re-quests for salvation and life.[63] This linking of the two stories seems to have been present in both the Matthean and Lukan sources even though the content of the stories differed in parts so that the two stories found their way into Mark and Luke in a much more picturesque form. I shall not deal, in this analysis, with the additional elements found in Mark 5:26-27 and Luke 8:43b, 44b-47 but rather shall continue the analysis of the Matthean form of the story.

The simplicity of Matt 9:22a, ὁ δὲ Ἰησοῦς στραφεὶς καὶ ἰδὼν αὐτήν, and hints of it in Mark 5:30a (ὁ Ἰησοῦς ... ἐπιστραφεὶς) and v. 32 (ἰδεῖν) suggest the simple construction of the Matthean source. The exact agreement across the three gospels in the words: θύγατερ, ἡ πίστις σου σέσωκέν σε points to their

---

62   Grundmann, Evangelium, 274-275, points out that the possibility of raising from the dead was already part of the tradition in both the Hebrew Scriptures (1 Kgs 17:17ff and 2 Kgs 4:33ff) and in the Hellenistic world with regard to the θεῖος ἀνήρ.

63   Boismard, Synopse, 211, sees a similar motivation for their being joined but for him the contrast is not that between the request of a man and of a woman but rather be-tween the great and the poor or humble. Jean Potin, "Guérison d'une hémorroïse et résurrection de la fille de Jaïre. Mc. 5,21-43," ASeign 2/44 (1969): 38-47, suggests three reasons for the linking of the stories: the number of years is 12 in each (this is the same argument as that of Sabourin, L'Evangile, 124, who cites Lohmeyer's commentary on Mark); each healing takes place by way of physical contact; and in each there is a play between the words "save" and "believe". O. Lamar Cope, Matthew: A Scribe Trained for the Kingdom of Heaven, CBQMS 5 (Washington: Catholic Biblical Association of America, 1976), 71, suggests that the two stories are linked because they both deal with matters of serious defilement. This last aspect and also the parallel between the ruler and the woman seem to be more clearly visible in the text itself. It could also be argued that the stories were joined because they both involve women, or more accurately, a woman and a young girl on the threshold of womanhood, and that it was this which caused the stories to be joined so that they functioned to interpret one another.

presence in both sources.[64] The Matthean θάρσει may well have been found
in the original source as it is not a common Matthean term (9:2; 14:27; par.
Mark 6:50, 10:49). Its retention in the final Matthean redaction may have
been a further emphasis on the woman's faith (cf. 9:2 in which it follows the
phrase: ἰδὼν ὁ Ἰησοῦς τὴν πίστιν αὐτῶν; and 14:27 in which it is an
invitation to faith issued to the disciples).

Attention needs to be given to the address θύγατερ/θυγάτηρ since it is the
only time that we find this address in its simple form without qualification
being used by Jesus in relation to a woman in the gospels.[65] Its presence in
each of the accounts suggests that it was common to the sources and hence
represents early christian tradition. Its inclusion here highlights further the
relationship between the two stories which have been linked. In the first, we
have a father imploring aid for his daughter who is embedded in the patriarchal familial structure. Here, a woman who has entered the story without
connections with such a structure is healed by Jesus and is called
"Daughter", thus establishing a new possibility for women within the
βασιλεία. It is not a βασιλεία of sons but of daughters and sons.[66] In this regard, it is important to note that the Matthean account does not include the
dismissal of the woman (cf. Mark 5:34c and Luke 8:48c). Given the significance of ἅπτω in terms of the discipleship motif in the Matthean redaction,
there may be a hint of that same motif here. The healed woman is discipled
within the community of the preacher of the βασιλεία. It is significant also
that at the end of the healing of the ruler's daughter in Matthew, the young

---

64   Both the Markan and Lukan accounts contain the nomative θυγάτηρ while the
      vocative θύγατερ is found in Matthew. This may further substantiate the argument
      above that the source for Mark and Luke differs from that of Matthew. It also gives
      weight to the suggestion that the Matthean account relied heavily on an early memory
      or written account of the story since Blass, Debrunner and Funk, A Greek Grammar, 81,
      §147, suggest that there was a tendency for the nominative to usurp the vocative in
      New Testament usage.
65   Luke 13:16 contains the phrase "Daughter of Abraham" and we find at 23:28,
      "Daughters of Jerusalem" with "daughter" in the vocative in the second instance, but
      in each of these cases Θύγατερ/θυγάτηρ is qualified and not the direct address of 9:22.
66   Twice Matthew makes reference to "sons" of the βασιλεία (8:12; 13:38); once to "sons"
      of God (5:9); and once to "sons" of your heavenly father (5:45). There is no similar ref-
      erence to "daughters". Crosby, House of Disciples, 51, notes that "'son' is essentially a
      house-connected word; the line of house-based authority was extended from the head
      of the house through the sons." It could be that the title "daughter" suggests a change
      in the traditional line of authority in some of the Matthean house-churches. On the
      other hand, it could be argued that "daughter" is a diminutive term which could be
      seen as illustrative of the androcentric perspective dominant in a patriarchal culture
      which failed to accord to women their full adulthood. The subsequent words of Jesus,
      however, do not seem to be in accord with this second reading.

girl who parallels the woman in terms of her healing is not returned to the patriarchal family structure as in Mark and Luke (Mark 5:43; Luke 8:55).

The καὶ ἐσώθη ἡ γυνὴ ἀπό τῆς ὥρας ἐκείνης which concludes the Matthean account is most certainly the result of redaction, possibly during the stage of the final redaction. The phrase ἀπό τῆς ὥρας ἐκείνης is typically Matthean (cf. 8:13; 15:28; 17:18), and emphasizes the authoritative power of Jesus which is characteristic of the Matthean redaction of the miracle stories generally. The first half of the phrase, καὶ ἐσώθη ἡ γυνή, points to a redactional connection with the linking word σώζω found in the source as a way of emphasizing a significant aspect of the healing, namely, salvation,[67] and reminding the reader that the one saved is a woman. The notion of salvation is common within the traditions of the early christian communities.[68] Here, however, it takes on a particular coloration given the nature of the miracle. The woman's faith opens up for her a direct channel of salvation. Given that this last verse is Matthean redaction, it may suggest an attempt to counteract trends within the christian community which may have sought to limit women's access to the saving power of Jesus within that community.[69] The Matthean redaction specifies clearly that the woman received the saving power of Jesus directly as did men who were healed.

In summary, a concise story of the healing of a woman with a haemorrhage structured around the progressive repetition of ἅπτω and σώζω, a technique found in narratives within the Hebrew Scriptures, has been altered little by the Matthean redaction. This redaction has explicitly paralleled elements of this story with its frame, 9:18 commencing with a typically Matthean introduction καὶ ἰδού. The conclusion also belongs clearly to the redaction as does the participle προσελθοῦσα. The remainder seems to be preserved from the original source.

---

67 Heil, "Healing Miracles," 281-282, sees the salvation experience as being central to the miracle stories. He summarizes thus: "Healings ... do not only guarantee that the kingdom is on its way, but actually usher in the kingdom as saving experiences in themselves. They are more than mere signs which point to the kingdom. They have a saving or healing effect on the people in the gospels who experience them. They are the means by which the kingdom is made present and actual in these people's lives."

68 Statistically across the synoptics the verb is used 15,15,17 times.

69 This may have paralleled a similar trend within Rabbinic Judaism, reflected in the Mishnah, whereby women were excluded from the channels of salvation open to men, namely, sacrifice in the temple and fidelity to the *mitzvot* (m. Qidd. 1:7-8; m. Menaḥ. 9:8). Her salvation, or more specifically sanctification, came through her husband. As Neusner has pointed out such may not have reflected the actual situation within Judaism but the vision that a few men desired for it.

3. Development of the Tradition

For the Matthean account, this history is relatively simple. A concise form of the story, closely resembling the present Matthean account, was linked, prior to the written transmission of the story, with the story of the resurrection of a ruler's daughter in order to set up the contrast between the ruler and the woman, highlighting the boundary crossing nature of her request and also establishing a comparison between the ruler's daughter and the woman. It is impossible to go back behind the stories to the community in which they originated but it may well be that these stories were preserved among women who desired to keep alive their memories of the healing power of Jesus in their own regard. Little was added to this simple story during the course of its transmission, but it seems, in the light of our findings with regard to the healing of Peter's mother-in-law, that we have evidence of a small collection of stories based on patterns from the Hebrew Scriptures which were preserved in their early simplicity within the Matthean community. Again, it can be argued that such a story would have been significant to the women within the community especially if they were struggling with attempts to exclude them socially or religiously, and that they may have been responsible for its preservation in its original stark simplicity. As such it allowed them to celebrate their direct access to the saving power of Jesus no matter what the obstacles that needed to be overcome, and also to legitimate their full membership in the βασιλεία.

The final redactional process has retained the story in its traditional simplicity adding little. Significantly, however, the woman is not dismissed but the story is concluded by a highlighting of the salvific aspect of the healing with regard to a woman. There is no co-opting of this story within the patriarchal structure. In fact, the redactional process seems to counteract such a trend. Only, however, when we have examined more closely some of the redactional elements of the story of the resurrection of the ruler's daughter can we make conclusive comments on this story and its place within the gospel structure. We turn, therefore, to a more detailed analysis of 9:18-19, 23-26.

1. Comparison of Synoptic Texts

Matt 9:18-19,23-26	Mark 5:21-24,35-43	Luke 8:40-42,49-56
	²¹ Καὶ διαπεράσαντος τοῦ Ἰησοῦ ἐν τῷ πλοίῳ πάλιν εἰς τὸ πέραν	
		⁴⁰ Ἐν δὲ τῷ ὑποστρέφειν τὸν Ἰησοῦν ἀπεδέξατο αὐτὸν ὁ ὄχλος·
	συνήχθη ὄχλος πολὺς ἐπ᾽ αὐτόν,	ἦσαν γὰρ πάντες προσδοκῶντες αὐτόν.
	καὶ ἦν παρὰ τὴν θάλασσαν.	
¹⁸ Ταῦτα αὐτοῦ λαλοῦντος αὐτοῖς, ἰδοὺ	²² Καὶ ἔρχεται	⁴¹ Καὶ ἰδοὺ ἦλθεν ἀνὴρ ᾧ ὄναμα Ἰάϊρος
ἄρχων εἷς	εἷς τῶν ἀρχισυναγώγων, ὀνόματι Ἰάϊρος, καὶ ἰδὼν αὐτὸν	καὶ οὗτος ἄρχων τῆς συναγωγῆς ὑπῆρχεν,
ἐλθὼν προσεκύνει αὐτῷ	πίπτει πρὸς τοὺς πόδας αὐτοῦ ²³ καὶ *παρακαλεῖ αὐτὸν* πολλὰ	καὶ πεσὼν παρὰ τοὺς πόδας τοῦ Ἰησοῦ παρεκάλει αὐτὸν εἰσελθεῖν εἰς τὸν οἶκον αὐτοῦ,
λέγων· ἡ θυγάτηρ μου	λέγων ὅτι τὸ θυγάτριόν μου	⁴² ὅτι θυγάτηρ μονογενὴς ἦν αὐτῷ ὡς ἐτῶν δώδεκα
ἄρτι ἐτελεύτησεν· ἀλλὰ ἐλθὼν ἐπίθες τὴν χεῖρά σου ἐπ᾽ αὐτήν,	ἐσχάτως ἔχει, ἵνα ἐλθὼν ἐπιθῇς τὰς χεῖρας αὐτῇ	καὶ αὐτὴ ἀπέθνῃσκεν.
καὶ ζήσεται.	ἵνα σωθῇ καὶ ζήσῃ.	
¹⁹ καὶ ἐγερθεὶς ὁ Ἰησοῦς ἠκολούθησεν αὐτῷ καὶ οἱ μαθηταὶ αὐτοῦ.	²⁴ καὶ ἀπῆλθεν μετ᾽ αὐτοῦ.	Ἐν δὲ τῷ ὑπάγειν αὐτὸν
	καὶ ἠκολούθει αὐτῷ ὄχλος πολὺς καὶ συνέθλιβον αὐτόν.	οἱ ὄχλοι συνέπνιγον αὐτόν.
....	....	....
	³⁵ Ἔτι αὐτοῦ λαλοῦντος ἔρχονται ἀπὸ τοῦ ἀρχισυναγώγου λέγοντες ὅτι ἡ θυγάτηρ σου ἀπέθανεν· τί ἔτι σκύλλεις τὸν διδάσκαλον;	⁴⁹ Ἔτι αὐτοῦ λαλοῦντος ἔρχεταί τις παρὰ τοῦ ἀρχισυναγώγου λέγων ὅτι τέθνηκεν ἡ θυγάτηρ σου· μὴ σκύλλε τὸν διδάσκαλον.
	³⁶ ὁ δὲ Ἰησοῦς παρακούσας τὸν λόγον λαλούμενον λέγει τῷ ἀρχισυναγώγῳ· μὴ φοβοῦ, μόνον πίστευε.	⁵⁰ ὁ δὲ Ἰησοῦς ἀκούσας ἀπεκρίθη αὐτῷ· μὴ φοβοῦ μόνον πίστευσον,

Matt	Mark	Luke
		καὶ σωθήσεται.
		⁵¹ ἐλθὼν δὲ εἰς τὴν οἰκίαν
	³⁷ καὶ οὐκ ἀφῆκεν οὐδένα μετ' αὐτοῦ συνακολουθῆσαι εἰ μὴ τὸν Πέτρον	οὐκ ἀφῆκεν εἰσελθεῖν τινα σὺν αὐτῷ εἰ μὴ Πέτρον καὶ Ἰωάννην
	καὶ Ἰάκωβον καὶ Ἰωάννην τὸν ἀδελφὸν Ἰακώβου.	καὶ Ἰάκωβον
		καὶ τὸν πατέρα τῆς παιδὸς καὶ τὴν μητέρα.
²³ Καὶ ἐλθὼν ὁ Ἰησοῦς εἰς τὴν οἰκίαν τοῦ ἄρχοντος καὶ ἰδὼν τοὺς αὐλητὰς καὶ τὸν ὄχλον θορυβούμενον	³⁸ καὶ ἔρχονται εἰς τὸν οἶκον τοῦ ἀρχισυναγώγου, καὶ θεωρεῖ θόρυβον καὶ κλαίοντας καὶ ἀλαλάζοντας πολλά,	
	³⁹ καὶ εἰσελθὼν	⁵² ἔκλαιον δὲ πάντες καὶ ἐκόπτοντο αὐτήν,
²⁴ ἔλεγεν·	λέγει αὐτοῖς· τί θορυβεῖσθε	ὁ δὲ εἶπεν·
ἀναχωρεῖτε,	καὶ κλαίετε; τὸ παιδίον	μὴ κλαίετε,
οὐ γὰρ ἀπέθανεν τὸ κοράσιον ἀλλὰ καθεύδει. καὶ κατεγέλων αὐτοῦ.	οὐκ ἀπέθανεν ἀλλὰ καθεύδει. ⁴⁰ καὶ κατεγέλων αὐτοῦ.	οὐ γὰρ ἀπέθανεν ἀλλὰ καθεύδει. ⁵³ καὶ κατεγέλων αὐτοῦ εἰδότες ὅτι ἀπέθανεν.
²⁵ ὅτε δὲ ἐξεβλήθη ὁ ὄχλος,	ὁ δὲ ἐκβαλὼν πάντας παραλαμβάνει τὸν πατέρα τοῦ παιδίου καὶ τὴν μητέρα καὶ τοὺς μετ' αὐτοῦ,	⁵⁴ αὐτὸς δὲ
εἰσελθὼν	καὶ εἰσπορεύεται ὅπου ἦν τὸ παιδίον.	
ἐκράτησεν τῆς χειρὸς αὐτῆς,	⁴¹ καὶ κρατήσας τῆς χειρὸς τοῦ παιδίου λέγει αὐτῇ· ταλιθα κουμ, ὅ ἐστιν μεθερμηνευόμενον· τὸ κοράσιον, σοὶ λέγω, ἔγειρε.	κρατήσας τῆς χειρὸς αὐτῆς ἐφώνησεν λέγων· ἡ παῖς, ἔγειρε.
		⁵⁵ καὶ ἐπέστρεψεν τὸ πνεῦμα αὐτῆς,
καὶ ἠγέρθη τὸ κοράσιον.	⁴² καὶ εὐθὺς ἀνέστη τὸ κοράσιον καὶ περιεπάτει· ἦν γὰρ ἐτῶν δώδεκα.	καὶ ἀνέστη παραχρῆμα,
		καὶ διέταξεν αὐτῇ δοθῆναι φαγεῖν.
	καὶ ἐξέστησαν εὐθὺς ἐκστάσει μεγάλῃ.	⁵⁶ καὶ ἐξέστησαν οἱ γονεῖς αὐτῆς·
²⁶ καὶ ἐξῆλθεν ἡ φήμη αὕτη εἰς ὅλην τὴν γῆν ἐκείνην.		
	⁴³ καὶ διεστείλατο αὐτοῖς πολλὰ ἵνα μηδεὶς γνοῖ τοῦτο,	ὁ δὲ παρήγγειλεν αὐτοῖς μηδενὶ εἰπεῖν

Matt	Mark	Luke
		τὸ γεγονός.
	καὶ εἶπεν δοθῆναι αὐτῇ	
	φαγεῖν.	

Once again, we see readily the simplicity of |the Matthean narrative. Rochais has argued that this story is well-structured into four parts with each part commencing with the verb ἔρχομαι:[70]

The ruler's request vv. 18-19	v. 18	ἰδοὺ ἄρχων εἷς ἐλθὼν ...
The arrival of Jesus and		
entry into the house vv. 23-25a	v. 23	καὶ ἐλθὼν ὁ Ἰησοῦς
The miracle v. 25b	v. 25b	... εἰσελθών ...
The outcome v. 26	v. 26	καὶ ἐξῆλθεν ...

Because of the numerous occasions on which some form of this verb may occur in any given story it is not as easy to argue here for the repetition characteristic of early biblical narrative as we did above.[71] A glance at the Markan and Lukan narratives confirms this since it would seem clear that this verb does not structure their narratives and that, in these two accounts, the interest is more in details of the story than in style of narration.[72] Structurally, therefore, there seems to be a relationship between Mark and Luke, and Matthew stands out alone.

In trying to locate sources, we must look beyond the structure of the story to the literary relationships. A possible literary dependence between Mark and Luke is much stronger than that between Matthew and either of the other two gospels. At the precise point, however, where Luke differs from Mark, the Matthean and Markan accounts are parallel although with slight variations (Matt 9:18/Mark 5:23: ἐπίθες τὴν χεῖρά σου ἐπ' αὐτήν/ἐπιθῆς τὰς χεῖρας αὐτῇ). This information, together with the detailed source analysis already undertaken in relation to 9:20-22 which was presumably linked to this story at the stage of its being written, suggests a similar source analysis of 9:18-19, 23-26 as has already been argued for 9:20-22. This means that a simple story from the Matthean source and a much more picturesque one from the Lukan source have been combined in the Markan redaction.[73] The

---

70 Rochais, *Récits*, 89, and for his discussion of the history of the formation of this structure, see pp. 104-110.
71 Ibid., 89, where Rochais compares this structure with Matt 8:2, 3a, 3b; 9:21, 22a, 22b; and 14:28, 29a, 29b.
72 Bonnard, *Évangile*, 135.
73 This is basically the argument of Boismard, *Synopse*, 208-211. Bonnard, *Évangile*, 134, recognizes the difficulties raised by the text and proffers three possible solutions: Matthew is independent of Mark; is a simplification of Mark; or that Matthew and Luke share a common narrative source. In the face of the various solutions, however,

presence of Mark 5:35-36 and Luke 8:49-50 in their respective narratives implies that the early Lukan source was once simply a healing story that developed into a resurrection story in the course of its transmission, while in the Matthean source the story seems to have had the form of a resurrection story from the point at which it was included in the written transmission.[74]

Such an argument has been strongly criticized by Rochais[75] and some attention must be given to his critique without allowing it to take the investigations too far afield into the long-debated arena of gospel source criticism. First, he uses as his foundational hypothesis the Matthean dependence on Mark but his method of establishing this is by counting words which are similar in each account.[76] Word agreements, however, form only one element in determining literary relationships. Structure is another, variations in use and arrangement of compositional motifs is another, as is the complex of relationships between the three synoptic accounts that we have already discussed above. It is these elements which Rochais' foundational hypothesis seems to ignore. Other elements of his study will be taken into account in the course of the discussion to follow.

2. Redaction

As with the previous story, so too here, only those items which are significant for the subsequent interpretation of the Matthean text will be considered.

---

74 one is still left with a decision as to which fits the evidence best and it seems that Boismard's solution fulfils this requirement.
74 This is further strengthened by Bonnard's claim, ibid., 136, that the Matthean form of the story is the most Palestinian, the most biblical and hence the earliest form, and it is supported by Grundmann's claim (see n. 62 above) that resurrection was already part of the tradition.
75 Rochais, *Récits*, 102, argues that there is stronger evidence of an Aramaic background to the Markan form of the story and that this brings into question Boismard's thesis that the original concise form of the story was found in the Matthean source. His position will be dealt with throughout the discussion of this pericope.
76 Ibid., 88, where Rochais claims that out of Matthew's 89 words compared with Mark's 191, there are 38 words in common and 24 synonyms giving 62 words in common out of 89. Even on the basis of this quantitative analysis, Rochais' evidence would need to be questioned because there are no more than 12 words which correspond exactly while there are, in other words and phrases, similar root words but differences in tense, case, number etc. This may suggest an original oral source in common into which variations have been introduced giving rise to different forms of words and to the 24 synonyms which Rochais counts, but the evidence of direct literary dependence is slight: 12 words out of the 191 of Mark's account is very slight. Grundmann, *Evangelium*, 273, counts words in agreement but not so minutely as does Rochais.

It has already been discussed elsewhere and simply needs to be reaffirmed here that the ἰδού and προσεκύνει of Matt 9:18 is Matthean redaction whose intention seems to be to draw attention to the parallel between the request of the ruler and that of the woman with the haemorrhage. The Matthean retention of the simplicity of the story has served to highlight the stark parallel between the description of the woman--αἱμορροοῦσα δώδεκα ἔτη, and the young girl--ἄρτι ἐτελεύτησεν.

Some attention must also be given to the very close parallel between the ruler's request (v. 18) and Jesus' later action (v. 25) in fulfilling this request as seen in the Matthean account:

v. 18   ἐπίθες   τὴν χεῖρά σου ἐπ' αὐτήν, καὶ ζήσεται

v. 25   ἐκράτησεν τῆς χειρὸς   αὐτῆς, καὶ ἠγέρθη τὸ κοράσιον.

Beginning with the request of v. 18 above, we find that it closely parallels the Genesis Apocryphon of Qumran Cave 1, (20.21-22), a request sent by Pharaoh to Abraham that he come and lay hands on him that he might live:

די אנה ... ואסמוך ידי עלוהי ויחה[77]

Such a statement, translated almost directly into the words of the Matthean account as given above, suggests that the laying on of hands to restore to life/health, especially in the face of severe affliction, was a practice known to at least some sectors of the Jewish community around the time of Jesus. The request of the ruler reflects this knowledge. That such a statement would find its way into an early Palestinian collection of stories of Jesus is quite understandable. The slight change in wording in relation to Jesus' carrying out of the request may have functioned to suggest that the healing action of Jesus differed from other healings and given the peculiar use of κρατέω that has already been discussed above, it may well have been the author's way of pointing to the uniqueness of this healing in that it was a raising to life. This is further substantiated by ἠγέρθη which follows.

---

77   This text and translation is taken from Joseph A. Fitzmyer, *The Genesis Apocryphon of Qumran Cave I: A Commentary*, 2nd ed., rev. BibOr 18A (Rome: Biblical Institute Press, 1971), 64-65. See also Klaus Beyer, *Die aramäischen Texte vom Toten Meer* (Göttingen: Vandenhoeck & Ruprecht, 1984), 176. This same passage is discussed by David Flusser, "Healing through the Laying-on of Hands in a Dead Sea Scroll," *IEJ* 7 (1957): 107-108; and by Rochais, *Récits*, 104, 58-59.

In terms of the Markan parallel to the text considered above, Rochais argues that the Aramaic background in the Genesis Apocryphon and what he claims is a more direct translation of the Aramaic די אתה by the Markan ἵνα ἐλθών point to the fact that the Markan account is earlier than the Matthean. The similarity between the two renderings and the close relationship between the Matthean account and the Genesis Apocryphon as argued above calls his claim into question. With respect to ἵνα ἐλθών, it is common in the New Testament for this phrase to be used absolutely with the sense of an imperative (see Eph 5:33; 2 Cor 8:7; Mark 5:12; 10:51; 12:15, 19; 1 Cor 16:15f; 2 Cor 13:17; Tit 3:13).[78] Hence its use here in this way in the Markan account may not necessarily indicate a more primitive and therefore more exact rendering of the Aramaic.

Similarly, Rochais claims that the Markan double ἵνα σωθῇ καὶ ζήσῃ which concludes the request was an attempt to include the nuances of the two verbs used to refer to healing or curing in the Genesis Apocryphon (אסי and חיה),[79] but אסי is used in relation to the cure which could not be effected by the physicians and magicians of Pharaoh, while חיה is used when speaking of the gesture of laying on of hands and the healing effect of such a gesture. The doublet is, therefore, better explained by the fact that the Markan redaction has taken over σωθῇ from an earlier Lukan source (cf. σωθήσεται in Luke 8:50) and ζήσῃ from an earlier Matthean source of the story (cf. Matt 9:18).

We can argue, therefore, that the request (9:18) and its fulfilment (9:25b) preserved in the Matthean account are based on a Jewish petition as found in the Genesis Apocryphon. In order to point to the fulfilment of the ruler's request in response to his faith, v. 25b closely parallels v. 18c but the words describing the action of Jesus differ from those describing the request, perhaps suggesting that the healing power of Jesus is not confined to traditional gestures and formulae. Moreover, the phrase ἐκράτησεν τῆς χειρὸς αὐτῆς seems to have been used in the transmission of the early christian tradition to speak of the extraordinary power of Jesus to raise to new life.[80] Similarly,

---

78 Zerwick, *Biblical Greek*, 141-142, §415.
79 Rochais, *Récits*, 58-59.
80 At this point, Rochais' argument works against him. He claims that an indirect account often came before a direct account of words spoken in the history of the tradition, ibid., 106, 109. It could be argued in this respect that the simplicity of the action of Jesus, as recorded in the Matthean account, reflects the simplicity of the primitive form of the story as found in the Matthean source document and that it was a later amplified form of the story as found in the Lukan source which influenced Mark who included Jesus'

ἠγέρθη is used parallel to ζήσεται in the request, carrying with it the two-fold sense of rising up but also of being raised to new life from death.[81]

In the context of the combined stories of 9:18-26, this new life is such that it extends the social and religious boundaries within which this young girl's life would be contained. In the Matthean account, there is no instruction to the parents to give her something to eat (Mark 5:43; Luke 8:55), indicating her return to the patriarchal family. Rather, the young girl stands alone in the narrative at the end of the account. In breaking the taboo of death, in reaching out and touching the young girl, Jesus has symbolically broken through all the taboos which would have oppressed the young girl as she grew into adult life, taboos symbolized by the infirmity of the woman with the haemorrhage. For her, as for the woman, channels of salvation and life have been opened through contact with Jesus outside the structure of patriarchal family and religion.

3. Development of the Tradition

Even though all the minute details of this story have not been treated fully here, the broad outline of the history of the transmission of this unit can be drawn.

The simple and concise story of the raising of a ruler's daughter[82] was linked with the story of the healing of a woman with a haemorrhage in an early Matthean source because the two stories interacted to draw attention to the boundaries placed upon women because of their gender, which excluded them from the religious and social life of the community. At an early stage of the tradition, this pericope was possibly linked with the chain of miracle stories--Calming of the Storm, Exorcising of the Gadarene Demoniacs and the Raising of a ruler's Daughter--as found in Mark and Luke. In the Lukan source, the stories of both the ruler's daughter and the woman with the haemorrhage were much more descriptive and greatly influenced the Markan redaction which combined elements of both stories from the two sources. Thus in both the Markan and Lukan accounts, the stories appear

---

direct command to the young girl to rise (5:41). Thus, once again, it can be seen that it is not necessary to argue for the priority of Mark as Rochais would have us do.

81   Zerwick, *Biblical Greek*, 81-82, §250.

82   Even the adding of the name "Jairus" as seen in Mark and Luke represents a later stage of the transmission of a tradition, see Beare, *A Commentary*, 283.

with many more descriptive elements which have been shaped according to each evangelist's own redactional perspective and techniques. In the Matthean account, on the other hand, the simple form of the story, as it appeared in its source, has been preserved with very few redactional additions save for perhaps a heightening of the faith aspect of the story by rendering the parallel between request and fulfilment very clear.

Once again, we see that the Matthean redaction has preserved a story in the simplicity in which it was transmitted within the community. This points perhaps to the centrality of such a story or stories within the community or within certain sectors of the community. The preserving intact of the ancient memory must have been significant for the ongoing life of this group, and this significance led to its inclusion as it was retained in the community tradition with little redaction.

C. 9:18-26

This brings us to a point where we can now consider the work of the final Matthean redaction which has placed these two miracle stories into the context of the final group of three miracles within the structuring of the miracle chapters and alongside the second buffer pericope.

In each miracle story, Jesus confronts powerful taboos relating to women and uncleanness. In each story, he reaches out across the boundaries set up to control these areas of taboo and he opens up channels of salvation and life to women outside of the channels offered in the context of patriarchal religion and family, these latter being ultimately ways of controlling women. This action of Jesus in the face of death and the possibility of ritual uncleanliness is seen in Matthew as climactic. The stories are placed, therefore, at the head of the final three miracles. Because the stories are concerned with new parameters which must be shaped by the preaching of the βασιλεία, they are placed alongside of the parables of the new and old.[83] Just as Jesus called a tax-collector and ate with sinners, thus breaking down the categories for inclusion or exclusion set up by religious leaders (9:9-13), so too he breaks down the boundaries which exclude women and girls from

---

83   The significance of this positioning is noted by Bonnard, *Évangile*, 135; and Plummer, *Exegetical Commentary*, 141.

active participation in the salvation and life offered by God through the preaching and action of Jesus.

The stories are much more than examples of faith. They are stories of a woman and a young girl oppressed by religious, social and human boundaries and of Jesus as the one who reaches out across these boundaries offering new expectations for life and wholeness. The telling of these stories not only recalls but generates hope, expectation and a vision of new possibilities for all females of whatever age. The stories are powerful christologically and ecclesiologically in that they speak to the community of the channels of salvation which Jesus opens to women as well as men beyond the boundaries of gender,[84] and of life offered to young women beyond the confines of the patriarchal family.

III. Conclusion

Within Matt 8 and 9, the Matthean redaction has retained three stories involving women taken from early written sources. Each of these stories has been preserved with the simplicity and directness that reflect the early christian memory preserved within the Matthean community. By means of the interaction of miracle and teaching, the interplay of christological, soteriological and discipleship motifs and focus on the interaction between Jesus and supplicant, a paradigm for women within the community has been presented. They are recipients of the fruits of the βασιλεία, serve as disciples of Jesus within its parameters and believe, beyond all manner of obstacles, that Jesus has the power to cross the boundaries established by various forms of human limitation. This paradigm seems to reflect a vision that had been kept alive by the community itself, but its preservation and its skilful incorporation into the text would also function to challenge other paradigms of discipleship, and of participation in the fruits of the kingdom which were present in the community and were reflected in the gospel. This explains something of the tension that we find in the gospel surrounding

---

84   It is interesting to note in this regard that it is the faith of the woman rather than that of the ruler which is praised (9:22).

these stories, a tension which the redactional process does not avoid. In fact, the Matthean redaction claims that this tension is at the heart of the stated purpose in redacting--to bring out the new and the old. The parables of 9:16-17 symbolize this tension.

At this stage also, within the Matthean redaction, we note that the sources did not control the final text but rather there is a careful structuring of material for a particular purpose. It could be argued, therefore, that the progressive nature of the motif of liberation in respect to women has influenced the redaction. The brief mention of the names of four women from the Hebrew Scriptures and of Mary's role in the birth of Jesus gives way to a story in which Jesus takes the initiative in healing a woman, calling her to discipleship. Subsequently a request is made on behalf of a young girl and a woman displays extraordinary courage and faith in reaching out to touch Jesus' cloak, careful, however, to approach from behind.

5. The Canaanite Woman - 15:21-28

In Chapter Two, it was shown by way of a narrative-critical analysis that the story of the Canaanite woman stood at the centre point of a chiastic structure or structures which highlighted the comparison and contrast between her story and others relating to the disciples, supplicants and opponents of Jesus. As we turn now to a redaction-critical study of this same text, it is important to note that it is also situated within a major section of the Matthean gospel in which the order of pericopes is very closely related to that in the Markan gospel (Matt 12:22-20:34; Mark 3:22-10:52). Within this chapter, the redaction-critical study of the central pericope, 15:21-28, will enable conclusions to be drawn regarding the development of this tradition within the Matthean community. Subsequently, attention will be directed to other brief references to women within this section of the gospel from a redaction-critical perspective in order to determine their relationship to the developing understanding of the traditions relating to women that seem to have been shaped in this gospel community.

I. 15:21-28

A. Comparison of Synoptic Texts

Matt 15:21-28	Mark 7:24-30
21 Καὶ ἐξελθὼν ἐκεῖθεν ὁ Ἰησοῦς ἀνεχώρησεν εἰς τὰ μέρη Τύρου καὶ Σιδῶνος.	24 Ἐκεῖθεν δὲ ἀναστὰς ἀπῆλθεν εἰς τὰ ὅρια Τύρου. καὶ εἰσελθὼν εἰς οἰκίαν οὐδένα ἤθελεν γνῶναι, καὶ οὐκ ἠδυνήθη λαθεῖν·
22 καὶ ἰδοὺ γυνὴ Χαναναία	25 ἀλλ' εὐθὺς ἀκούσασα γυνὴ

Matthew	Mark
	περὶ αὐτοῦ,
ἀπὸ τῶν ὁρίων ἐκείνων ἐξελθοῦσα ἔκραζεν λέγουσα· ἐλέησόν με, κύριε υἱὸς Δαυίδ· ἡ θυγάτηρ μου κακῶς δαιμονίζεται.	
	ἧς εἶχεν τὸ θυγάτριον αὐτῆς πνεῦμα ἀκάθαρτον,
23 ὁ δὲ οὐκ ἀπεκρίθη αὐτῇ λόγον. καὶ προσελθόντες οἱ μαθηταὶ αὐτοῦ ἠρώτουν αὐτὸν λέγοντες· ἀπόλυσον αὐτήν, ὅτι κράζει ὅπισθεν ἡμῶν. 24 ὁ δὲ ἀποκριθεὶς εἶπεν· οὐκ ἀπεστάλην εἰ μὴ εἰς τὰ πρόβατα τὰ ἀπολωλότα οἴκου Ἰσραήλ.	
25 ἡ δὲ ἐλθοῦσα προσεκύνει αὐτῷ	ἐλθοῦσα προσέπεσεν πρὸς τοὺς πόδας αὐτοῦ· 26 ἡ δὲ γυνὴ ἦν Ἑλληνίς, Συροφοινίκισσα τῷ γένει·
λέγουσα· κύριε, βοήθει μοι.	
	καὶ ἠρώτα αὐτὸν ἵνα τὸ δαιμόνιον ἐκβάλῃ ἐκ τῆς θυγατρὸς αὐτῆς.
26 ὁ δὲ ἀποκριθεὶς εἶπεν,	27 καὶ ἔλεγεν αὐτῇ,
Οὐκ ἔστιν καλὸν λαβεῖν τὸν ἄρτον τῶν τέκνων καὶ βαλεῖν τοῖς κυναρίοις. 27 ἡ δὲ εἶπεν· ναί κύριε, καὶ γὰρ τὰ κυνάρια	Ἄφες πρῶτον χορτασθῆναι τὰ τέκνα, οὐ γάρ ἐστιν καλὸν λαβεῖν τὸν ἄρτον τῶν τέκνων καὶ τοῖς κυναρίοις βαλεῖν. 28 ἡ δὲ ἀπεκρίθη καὶ λέγει αὐτῷ, κύριε, καὶ τὰ κυνάρια ὑποκάτω τῆς τραπέζης
ἐσθίει ἀπὸ τῶν ψιχίων	ἐσθίουσιν ἀπὸ τῶν ψιχίων τῶν παιδίων.
τῶν πιπτόντων ἀπὸ τῆς τραπέζης τῶν κυρίων αὐτῶν. 28 τότε ἀποκριθεὶς ὁ Ἰησοῦς εἶπεν αὐτῇ· ὦ γύναι, μεγάλη σου ἡ πίστις· γενηθήτω σοι ὡς θέλεις. καὶ ἰάθη ἡ θυγάτηρ αὐτῆς ἀπὸ τῆς ὥρας ἐκείνης.	29 καὶ εἶπεν αὐτῇ·
	διὰ τοῦτον τὸν λόγον ὕπαγε, ἐξελήλυθεν ἐκ τῆς θυγατρός σου τὸ δαιμόνιον. 30 καὶ ἀπελθοῦσα εἰς τὸν οἶκον αὐτῆς εὗρεν τὸ παιδίον βεβλημένον ἐπὶ τὴν κλίνην καὶ τὸ δαιμόνιον ἐξεληλυθός.

The earlier narrative-critical analysis of this pericope showed that its central focus was the dialogue of vv. 24-27. There I suggested that this dialogue began in v. 22 with the woman's request, was interrupted by the comment on Jesus' silence and the intervention of the disciples (v. 23), only to be resumed in v. 24, which constituted Jesus' response to the woman's request and not a reply to the disciples.[1] The dialogue then continues to the

---

1 The difficulty raised by the presence of v. 23 and the influence it has had on the interpretation of the story especially in regard to v. 24 and the question to whom it is addressed, is clear from the two general lines of interpretation that one encounters: 1) that Jesus responds to the woman, supported by Daniel J. Harrington, *The Gospel according to Matthew*, Collegeville Bible Commentary New Testament Series 1 (Collegeville: Liturgical Press, 1983), 64; and 2) that the words of v. 24 are directed to the disciples, supported by Held, "Matthew as Interpreter," 198; Witherington III, *Women in the Ministry*, 65; Floyd V. Filson, *A Commentary on the Gospel according to St. Matthew*, BNTC (London: Black, 1960), 180; Plummer, *Exegetical Commentary*, 216; and Gundry, *A Commentary*, 312. Few, however, address the anomaly of v. 23 directly with

conclusion of the pericope in v. 28. Diagramatically this was represented according to the format below but to this diagram has now been added some of Theissen's miracle motifs to allow for better comparison with the Markan account to follow.

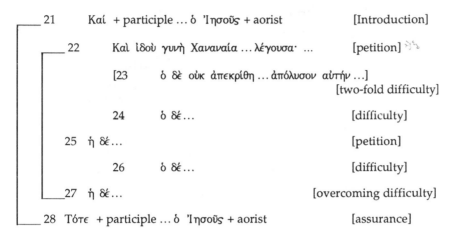

21   Καί + participle ... ὁ Ἰησοῦς + aorist   [Introduction]

22   Καὶ ἰδοὺ γυνὴ Χαναναία ... λέγουσα· ...   [petition]

[23   ὁ δὲ οὐκ ἀπεκρίθη ... ἀπόλυσον αὐτήν ...]
                                                         [two-fold difficulty]

24   ὁ δέ...   [difficulty]

25 ἡ δέ...   [petition]

26   ὁ δέ...   [difficulty]

27 ἡ δέ...   [overcoming difficulty]

28 Τότε + participle ... ὁ Ἰησοῦς + aorist   [assurance]

Diagram 16

When one compares this structure with that of the Markan account, it is clear that they differ radically. For Mark, the first three verses (7:24-26) are introductory and are at the service of the miracle rather than the dialogue (cf. Matt 15:21-22a). Mark 7:27 operates, according to Theissen's classification of miracle motifs, as a "difficulty" which highlights the 'boundary-stressing' aspect of the encounter while the reply of the woman, v. 28, constitutes the overcoming of the difficulty and functions in terms of 'boundary-crossing'. The latter aspect is further underlined by the words of assurance offered in v. 29.[2] Thus Theissen states that "in Mark the order of motifs is: petition, difficulty, overcoming of difficulty, assurance."[3] He goes on to argue that in Matthew the Markan pattern of petition/difficulty has been reproduced

---

the exception of Theissen, *Miracle Stories*, 182, who comes to no conclusion: "It is not clear to whom the answer is directed: ἀποκριθείς strictly refers to the woman's plea, but in the story it is a reply to the disciples intervention." Lohmeyer, *Evangelium*, 253, also highlights the difficulty: "Er ... antwortet ihnen, aber Seine Antwort ist nicht für sie. ... Er antwortet nicht auf das Verlangen der Jünger ... sondern auf das flehen der Frau. ... in Seiner Antwort sieht Er nur die Mutter, trotzdem sie an die Jünger sich richtet."

2   Theissen, *Miracle Stories*, 74-80, discusses these motifs. Wire, "Structure of the Gospel Miracle Stories," 103, places this miracle in the group where the miracle worker himself becomes the opposition.

3   Theissen, *Miracle Stories*, 181.

four times. For ease of comparison I shall reproduce here the table he constructs to explicate this repetition.

1. **Petition**:

'Have mercy on me, O Lord,
Son of David; my daughter
is possessed by a demon.'

           1. **Rejection**:

             'But he did not answer.'

           2. **Rejection** (by the disciples):

             'Send her away.'

2. **Continued petitions**:

'... for she is crying after us.'

           3. **Rejection**:

             'I am sent only to the lost sheep
             of the house of Israel.'

3. **Petition**:

'Lord, help me.'

           4. **Rejection**:

             'It is not fair to take the
             children's bread and throw it

4. **Petition**:
             to the dogs.'

'Yes Lord, but even the dogs ...'

Diagram 17[4]

Reference to the table he constructs shows that the actual petitions of the woman are only three; he uses as the fourth petition the statement of the disciples "for she is crying after us", whose rejection is their statement "send her away", which, in fact, precedes the supposed petition in v. 23b. Hence, for Theissen, the woman's first petition: "Have mercy on me ..." is followed by two rejections, that of Jesus not answering her and that of the disciples who request that she be sent away. In order to avoid the heaping up of rejections contained in vv. 23-24, he calls the explanation of the disciples, "she is crying

---

4   Ibid., 182. See also John Meier, "Matthew 15:21-28," *Interp.* 40 (1986): 397-399, who reads a four-fold verbal encounter but he sees the disciples' intervention as a second petition which is rejected by Jesus in v. 24. The conclusion to the fourth encounter is Jesus' granting of the woman's request.

after us," a second petition which is followed by the rejection of Jesus in v. 24. The petition of v. 25 is followed by the rejection of v. 26 and he then adds v. 27 as his fourth petition, for which there is no rejection. Diagram 16 above seems to offer a better explanation of v. 27 as the expression of a concluding 'boundary-crossing' motif initiated by the woman and not by Jesus. This is then followed by the words of assurance of Jesus in v. 28.

The difficulties which arise from Theissen's explanation of what seems to be a valid observation, namely, that Matthew contains a structural pattern found in Mark, add further weight to the narrative-critical claim that v. 23 intrudes into a highly structured narrative. Returning to Diagram 16 above, and omitting, for the moment, v. 23 and its two-fold difficulty, we find that the pericope can be structured according to an initial petition (v. 22) followed by the difficulty raised by v. 24, a pattern which is repeated in vv. 25-26 of the dialogue. The woman's statement contained in v. 27 constitutes a crossing of the boundaries which have been stressed by the two-fold rejection and it is this which opens the way for the words of assurance of v. 28.

This repetition of a structural pattern in order to highlight the dramatic tension within the story suggests that the Matthean narrative is subsequent to that of Mark. A further underpinning for this suggestion is the Matthean use of direct speech given to the woman, which parallels an indirect request in Mark (Mark 7:25b parl. Matt 15:22b; and Mark 7:26 parl. Matt 15:25b),[5] together with an emphasis on the dialogue rather than the miracle.[6] These factors alone, however, are insufficient indicators of the Matthean source. Hence we must turn to the literary relationships between the two accounts.

It is surprising to find that the only evidence of direct literary dependence is Mark 7:27-28 paralleled in Matthew 15:26-27. Within these two verses, there is a slight reversal of word order in Mark 7:28 and Matthew 15:27. Whereas in Mark the two verses conclude with τῶν παιδίων, in Matthew we find τῶν κυρίων αὐτῶν. Tyre is also mentioned in the opening verse of each account, but in Matthew this has been supplemented to become the biblical designation "Tyre and Sidon".

While direct literary dependence may not be strong, there are, however, certain content relationships. The woman intercedes on behalf of her

---

5   Bultmann, *History*, 312, discusses the change from indirect to direct speech, noting that it serves the function of "reproducing motives and feelings" and generally appears to be a sign of a later development of a tradition.

6   Held, "Matthew as Interpreter," 199, and Hill, *The Gospel*, 253.

daughter who has an unclean spirit, prostrating herself before Jesus, only to be rebuffed by an apparently familiar parabolic saying about throwing the children's bread to the dogs. She extends the parable to include herself and her daughter and thus wins Jesus' admiration and his compassion which extends to her daughter through her.

Another factor that is significant in determining the Matthean source for this pericope is the fact that it finds its place within a section of the gospel where there is direct paralleling of episodes in Matthew and Mark.[7] All this evidence and the absence of strong evidence to the contrary point to Matthean use of an earlier Markan text as source, supplemented, however, by significant elements of tradition from the community and/or from the evangelist's own theology. It is this conclusion which shall form the basis of the subsequent redactional analysis and the outlining of a possible development of the tradition.[8]

B. Redaction

At the outset, the words of McNeile in relation to the story of the Canaanite woman highlight the challenge that this story provides for the redaction critic:

> If Matthew had no other source than Mark, he contributes an unusual amount from his own pen, and that of a highly artistic and dramatic character. The incident must have possessed a profound interest for him.[9]

---

7   It has already been noted above that there is a distinct paralleling of episodes in the long section Matt 12:22-20:34; Mark 3:22-10:52. This pericope, however, finds its place within a shorter section where the parallels are clear, a section which we have already seen is often designated the "Bread Section"--Matthew 14:13-16:12 and Mark 6:30-8:21 (or 8:26 if one includes the Healing of the Blind Man of Bethsaida which is not in Matthew). See Cerfaux, "Section des Pains," and Albert-Marie Denis, "La section des pains selon s. Marc (6,30 - 8,26), une théologie de l'eucharistie," *StEv* IV=*TU* 102 (1968): 171-179.

8   Dermience, "Péricope," 26, takes this position but in her discussion, pp. 25-26 and nn. 1-4, she gives the bibliographical references not only for the position which she accepts (add also Allen, *A Critical Commentary*, 168-169; Hill, *The Gospel*, 253; Witherington III, *Women in the Ministry*, 169, n. 88; D. C. Duling, "The Therapeutic Son of David: An Element in Matthew's Christological Apologetic," *NTS* 24 (1977-78): 402; E. A. Russell, "The Canaanite Woman and the Gospels (Mt 15:21-28; cf. Mk 7:24-30)," in Livingstone, *Studia Biblica 1978*, 291; Gnilka, *Matthäusevangelium*, II, 29; and Ringe, "A Gentile Woman's Story," 67); but also for an alternative position which considers Matthew anterior to Mark and a third which suggests a source common to both.

9   Alan Hugh McNeile, *The Gospel according to St. Matthew. The Greek Text with Introduction, Notes, and Index* (London: Macmillan, 1915), 229.

One of the first signs of Matthean redaction in this pericope is the use of both words and phrases which seem to be drawn directly from or are at least parallel to other material in the gospel story. They are used here to construct the story around the two sayings that relate directly to the Markan version. Such activity is seen first in the opening verse where the typically Matthean addition of the name of Jesus focusses the reader's attention on him as the chief actor. More significantly, however, the verb ἀναχωρέω is used (Mark has ἀπέρχομαι). This verb occurs ten times in Matthew's gospel as compared to its occurrence only once in Mark. Six of these refer to Jesus, two during his infancy (2:14, 22) and four during his public ministry (4:12; 12:15; 14:13; and 15:21). The last three are found within the section of the gospel under consideration as the immediate context for this pericope. They point to the growing opposition to Jesus from both the political and religious leadership and his periodic moving away from it to continue his ministry.[10]

Following a controversy with the Pharisees over the question of healing on the Sabbath (12:9-13), Jesus simply withdraws (12:15). After John has been put to death by Herod, the withdrawal is stated in more dramatic terms: "he withdrew from there in a boat to a lonely place apart" (14:13). Finally, there occurs the most dramatic withdrawal of all. After the controversy with the Pharisees over the question of cleanness and uncleanness, Jesus withdraws "to the district of Tyre and Sidon" which is considered gentile territory.[11]

The first withdrawal is followed by the prediction of a mission to the Gentiles according to the vision of Isaiah (Isa 42:1-4, 9; 11:10 LXX):

> Behold, my servant whom I have chosen, my beloved with whom my soul is well pleased. I will put my Spirit upon him, and he shall proclaim justice to the Gentiles. He will not wrangle or cry aloud, nor will any one hear his voice in the streets; he will not break a bruised reed or quench a smoldering wick, till he brings justice to victory; and in his name will the Gentiles hope.
>
> (Matt 12:18-21).

---

10   Dermience, "Péricope," 27, calls attention to the Septuagintal character of this verb which is used 14 times and generally in contexts of harassment or violence. Both Gundry, *A Commentary*, 641, and Luz, *Evangelium*, 36, point to this verb as redactional.

11   Already above, p. 103-105, we discussed the question whether the Matthean text showed that Jesus entered gentile territory or merely approached its borders and the conclusion was drawn that he actually entered into gentile land. A redactional study of the Matthean use of τὰ μέρη instead of the τὰ ὅρια in v. 21 and then the return to τῶν ὁρίων in v. 22 throws no further light on this question for it is soon discovered that the two terms seem to be used interchangeably within the Matthean redaction; see Russell, "Canaanite Woman," 272. Such a conclusion is confirmed when immediately following this pericope, Matthew contains εἰς τὰ ὅρια (Matt 15:39) where Mark has εἰς τὰ μέρη.

The third, which is also from the Pharisees, is concerned precisely with the question of the fulfilment of this prophecy, namely, Jesus' actual mission to the Gentiles.[12]

We noted above the Septuagintal flavour of the Matthean use of ἀναχωρέω and as we move forward in the text, the use of scriptural allusions continues. Where Mark has simply "Tyre" as the destiny of Jesus, in Matthew we find the typically biblical ensemble "Tyre and Sidon" which has already been used in 11:21-22.[13] The exact import of the Matthean designation is difficult to determine but it seems to be theological.[14] In an earlier part of the gospel, reference to a great multitude from about Tyre and Sidon hearing all that Jesus did and coming to him (Mark 3:8; cf. Matt 4:25), is omitted from Matthew so that the first Matthean reference to the twin cities is in 11:21-22 where they are presented in parallel with Sodom as cities under judgment (11:20-24). Galilean cities, however, which had been the direct object of Jesus' ministry of teaching and healing, are placed under a more severe judgment. In 15:21, when the controversy with the leaders of the people who have been offered the fruits of Jesus' βασιλεία ministry is mounting, he turns away from these Galilean cities and moves toward Tyre and Sidon. Such a setting will be very significant with regard to the outcome of the story. Significantly, that same region parallels that of Elijah's encounter with the widow of Zarephath, but there seems to be little else which would point to a parallel between the two stories.[15]

Finally, in relation to v. 21, it is significant that in the Matthean redaction, mention of Jesus' entry into a house and his not wanting anyone

---

12   The significance of the "withdrawal" motif is shown by Jerome Murphy-O'Connor, "The Structure of Matthew XIV-XVII," *RB* 82 (1975): 372-375, but since his analysis is limited to Matt 14-17, he does not consider the first reference in 12:15 and its close relationship to 15:21.

13   The Markan references to "Tyre" in 7:24 and 7:31 are the only places in the Christian Scriptures where Tyre is mentioned alone, and the second is followed in the next phrase by reference to Sidon. All other references are the typically biblical designation "Tyre and Sidon". See Dermience, "Péricope," 28, n. 17, for a list of such references in the Hebrew Scriptures and n. 18 for a similar list drawn from the Christian Scriptures.

14   Boismard, *Synopse*, 235-236, suggests that already in the earlier Markan version of the story, the placing of the miracle in Tyre was an addition in order to highlight the theme of Jesus' mission to the gentiles which is central to the Markan story. J. Duncan M. Derrett, "Law in the New Testament: The Syro-Phoenician Woman and the Centurion of Capernaum," *NT* 15 (1973): 163, also suggests that the Markan setting is an appendage. Gundry, *A Commentary*, 310, makes this point even more strongly in relation to the Matthean gospel when he says: "The stereotyped pairing of the cities conforms to the language of the OT ... and makes them typical of the whole world of Gentiles. ... for Matthew "the districts of Tyre and Sidon" are literarily and theologically Gentile, whatever the historical character of their population."

15   Gnilka, *Matthäusevangelium*, II, 29.

to know of it (Mark 7:24) is suppressed. Rather, the encounter with the woman takes place in a public place which may direct the attention of the readers outside the household of believers to the public arena where those designated outsiders were seeking entry into the community. From a feminist perspective, such a setting is also significant because in the words of Elisabeth Schüssler Fiorenza:

> ... in those societies in which the boundaries between the household and the public domain are not so sharply drawn, women's positions and roles are more equal to those of men.[16]

The typically Matthean introduction to v. 22, καὶ ἰδοὺ γυνή, which calls to mind the introduction of the woman with the haemorrhage (9:22), is followed by the archaism Χαναναία.[17] This word is a *hapax legomenon* in the Christian Scriptures, and hence we are faced with a difficulty when seeking to understand its rhetorical use in Matthew in place of the Markan "Greek, Syrophoenician by birth." The most thorough study of this has been done by Dermience, who links it with the introduction which she sees as also drawing on allusions from the Hebrew Scriptures. Even though the feminine term Χαναναία is never found in the Septuagint, she considers that by the time of the writing of the Christian Scriptures, the term Χανανάιος had acquired a global meaning within Judaism comprising any outsiders whether by way of race, creed or trade.[18] Such a reading would then be in keeping with what seems to be a Matthean tendency to set the woman over against the "lost sheep of the house of Israel" to whom Jesus refers in v. 24.[19] With regard to this designation, however, it is difficult to determine whether its origin is with the evangelist or whether it had developed within the community during the story's transmission.

The fact, too, that she is a gentile *woman* is very significant in this context for it was by way of women that the Gentiles were considered unclean since their women were considered "menstruants from the cradle" (m. Nid. 4.1). On the other hand, the designation of the woman as Χαναναία

---

16   Schüssler Fiorenza, *In Memory of Her*, 86.
17   Both Dermience, "Péricope," 29, and Légasse, "L'épisode," 26, refer to this designation of the woman as an "archaism" as do McNeile, *Matthew*, 230; Meier, *Matthew*, 172; and Stendahl, "Matthew," 787 while Klostermann, *Matthäusevangelium*, 133, calls it 'biblisch und archaistisch'.
18   Dermience, "Péricope," 29-30. S. T. Lachs, *A Rabbinic Commentary on the New Testament: The Gospels of Matthew, Mark and Luke* (Hoboken, NJ.: KTAV, 1987), 248, also notes that in early rabbinic sources, it was a common term for a non-Jew.
19   Held, "Matthew as Interpreter," 200; Grundmann, *Evangelium*, 376; Gaechter, *Matthäus-Evangelium*, 501; Lagrange, *Evangile*, 308.

recalls another Canaanite woman, Rahab, who is one of the four women named in the Matthean genealogy. By her initiative, she was able to cross ethnic and gender boundaries and thus secure a place for her family within Israel's unfolding history. Her story was kept alive within some sectors of the Matthean community to provide the scriptural foreshadowing for the role which women would play in the Jesus movement. In such a sector of the community, the designation γυνὴ Χαναναία would act as a reminder not only of the boundaries constructed by patriarchal society which made women outsiders but also of the initiative and boundary-crossing power of women. This latter is confirmed by the following phrase--ἐξελθοῦσα ἔκραζεν λέγουσα--which indicates that the woman does take the initiative. As has been noted, for the first time in the Matthean gospel, a woman addresses Jesus directly.

At this point, it may serve subsequent analysis to recapitulate the Matthean redaction of the introduction to the pericope. By means of two very clear allusions from the Hebrew Scriptures, one of which may have been developed within the community, the boundaries which separate both gentile territory and the gentile people from Israel as land and nation have been clearly underlined. Significantly, it is a woman who exemplifies these boundaries with the ἰδοὺ γυνή used to introduce her drawing attention to this. The redaction process, therefore, which has been responsible for most of the introduction, has highlighted at the beginning of this story two streams of narrative tension already encountered in the gospel--the place of Gentiles and of women within the Jesus movement--both of which will reach a climactic point as this story unfolds.

The initiative of the woman in addressing Jesus and the cry on her lips do nothing to alleviate this tension but rather emphasize it. For some within the community, her initiative and her prayer would strike at a number of their socio-religious boundaries. First, she is gentile and hence a source of uncleanness, but secondly, she is a woman alone, outside the structures of the patriarchal family, who approaches a man in public, an action which ran counter to the patriarchal structures of the society to which she belonged. It is the cry itself, however, which is most extraordinary.

The cry is one familiar within the gospel and therefore, it could be suggested, familiar within the Matthean communities especially in their liturgies. In other words, it may have been a liturgical formula.[20] The plea ἐλέησόν με (or equivalent) is that of the two blind men in 9:27 and in 20:30, 31, and of the father of the epileptic boy (17:15), but it is strange on the lips of a gentile woman unfamiliar with the Jewish traditions.[21] To all of these requests, except the first, is added the title κύριος which is a significant Matthean (and Lukan) title[22] used in situations of healing or discipleship (8:2, 6; 9:28; 15:22, 25, 27; 17:15; 20:30, 31; and 8:21, 25; 14:28; 16:22; 17:4; 18:21; 26:22).[23] The combination ἐλέησόν με, κύριε also recalls the Septuagint, especially the psalms.[24] The redactional process then attributes to this gentile woman the title υἱὸς Δαυίδ (Son of David), a title used by the blind men (9:27 and 20:30, 31) and by the children of Israel who greet Jesus on his entry into the Temple (21:9, 15).[25] Both titles point to the christological reflection taking place within the Matthean community since κύριος is used only once as a title within the Markan gospel (7:28), and then with little christological import,[26] and υἱὸς Δαυίδ accompanies only the request of the blind Bartimaeus in Mark 10:47-48 and hence provides little evidence of theological development. Its more extensive use, however, in Matthew's gospel

20 Dermience, "Péricope," 34. Frank J. Matera, *Passion Narratives and Gospel Theologies: Interpreting the Synoptics through Their Passion Stories*, Theological Inquiries (New York: Paulist, 1986), 115, points out that the verb κράζω which introduces the woman's plea is frequently used in the Septuagint to indicate "deep and heartfelt prayer". It too indicates a liturgical function.

21 It is significant that when the father of the epileptic boy pleads for his son in 17:15 (a similar situation to that of 15:22), he uses the prayer ἐλέησόν μου τὸν υἱόν rather than simply ἐλέησόν με as used by the woman. This would seem to suggest, as I have mentioned previously, that the story of the Canaanite woman is the story of a woman's plight and not so much a concern for a miracle for her daughter. Gundry, *A Commentary*, 311, suggests this also: "The borrowing from the other story shows itself not only in the phraseology, absent in Mark's present parallel, but also in the woman's seeking mercy for herself rather than for her daughter, as though she, like the blind men, needed healing." The argument here is not that she requested healing for herself but that she was certainly making a request on her own behalf.

22 Comparison across the synoptics shows the statistics as 80,18,104; see Neirynck and van Segbroeck, *New Testament Vocabulary*, 273.

23 For a more detailed discussion of the Matthean use of this title, see J. D. Kingsbury, "The Title "Kyrios" in Matthew's Gospel," *JBL* 94 (1975): 246-255. Grundmann, *Evangelium*, 376, calls it an address of discipleship.

24 Pss 6:3; 9:14; 26:7; 30:10; 40:5, 11; 55:2; 85:3; 122:3 and Pss 26:7; 50:3; 56:2; 85:16; 118:29, 58, 132 where the plea occurs alone or followed by the title ὁ Θεός. Here the title is generally a translation of יהוה.

25 For a more thorough analysis of this title, see Christoph Burger, *Jesus als Davidssohn: Eine traditionsgeschichtliche Untersuchung*, FRLANT 98 (Göttingen: Vandenhoeck & Ruprecht, 1970), 72-91 and especially 79-81; and Duling, "Therapeutic Son," 392-410.

26 Dermience, "Péricope," 33.

indicates the possibility of a strong Jewish influence on the christological and theological reflection within the Matthean communities.[27]

What we see, therefore, in v. 22, especially in the words placed on the lips of the woman, is evidence of developing liturgical formulae and of christological reflection. These words are augmented by the explicitly theological statement of the woman ἡ θυγάτηρ μου κακῶς δαιμονίζεται, which takes the place of the indirect requests of Mark 7:25-26. It is clear, therefore, that the cries of the woman in the Matthean account reflect the communities' theological tradition. On the lips of a woman who is clearly presented as an outsider is placed their developing liturgical and theological formulations. This suggests, therefore, that the dynamic involved in this pericope is not only that which concerns the extension of Jesus' healing power to the Gentiles, which the Markan text reveals, but also the role of women in the liturgical and theological life of the community.

To what extent this latter aspect confronted boundaries which already existed or were in process of being constructed to prevent women's active participation in those aspects of the life of the community to which they belonged is difficult to determine but some broad outlines can be suggested. As is evidenced within the Christian Scriptures whose composition extended over at least a century, so too in the Mishnaic and Talmudic literature which spans a number of centuries, the information regarding such participation is scattered, fragmentary and at times contradictory.

Within the Christian Scriptures, there is little information regarding leadership within liturgical assemblies, but we can assume the active participation of women from some of the prescriptions proposed by Paul (e.g. 1 Cor 11:2-16, which concerns the attire of both women and men at worship; and 1 Cor 14:34-35 which seeks to prohibit women speaking in the assembly but which thereby carries with it the assumption that they had been participating actively).[28] Furthermore, it is clear that women shared in the missionary

---

27   Beare, *A Commentary*, 341; and Bonnard, *Évangile*, 230. Hill, *The Gospel*, 254, passes over the significance of these titles and maintains that the point of the story lies in the fact that the woman won acceptance with Jesus, not because of her recognition of his Messiahship but because of her strong and humble faith. It would seem strange that such significant liturgical and theological language would be placed on the lips of a gentile woman not only in v. 22 but also in v. 25, just to point to the woman's strong faith.

28   Schüssler Fiorenza, *In Memory of Her*, 45, illustrates that these passages indicate that 1 Cor 11-14 refers to female and male prophets despite their androcentric language. See also pp. 226-233. Text-critically, there is also a question as to whether 1 Cor 14:34-36 is a later addition to the Pauline text.

activity of Paul,[29] a mission which was predominantly that of teaching and preaching the gospel (Phil 4:2; Rom 16:1-16). Later prescriptions, however, tried to curtail this teaching role of women (1 Tim 2:11-15), a role which in fact would have involved them in the theological reflection within their christian communities.

A similar ambiguity is found within rabbinic Judaism. M. Ned. 4:3 presumes the religious duty of teaching scripture to both daughters and sons.[30] Certain prescriptions, however, such as m. Sot. 3:4 would limit this.[31] As Judith Wegner points out, it is difficult to determine whether the references to "the law" in the prescriptions are to scripture generally or to a specific rule; but she goes on to indicate that their social commentary reveals the ambivalence of the framers of the Mishnah to women's study of the sacred texts.[32] She also points out that the exempting of women from much of the cultic obligations that were performed at specific times led to a discouraging of their entering the public domain of religious practice.[33] In Judaism as in Christianity, the women whose stories are told stand out by way of exception from the androcentric contexts of those stories. The stories surrounding Beruriah, who was well versed in Torah, provide examples of such an exception within Judaism,[34] but, like the references to women in the ministry of Paul and the early church, these stories may point to a wider involvement of women in cultic activities than the prescriptions would indicate.[35]

---

29   Ibid., 168-175.
30   "[He that is forbidden by vow ... the other] ... may teach him [his fellow] *Midrash*, *Halakoth*, and *Haggadoth*, but he may not teach him Scripture, though he may teach Scripture to his sons and to his daughters."
31   "Ben Azzai says: A Man ought to give his daughter a knowledge of the Law so that if she must drink [the bitter water] she may know that the merit [that she has acquired] will hold her punishment in suspense. R. Eliezer says: If a man gives his daughter a knowledge of the Law it is as though he taught her lechery."
32   Judith Romney Wegner, *Chattel or Person? The Status of Women in the Mishnah* (New York/Oxford: Oxford University Press, 1988), 161-162. Her concluding paragraph highlights the ambiguity: "These statements convey the general impression that the sages think it socially undesirable, if not actually prohibited, to teach women the sacred texts. Certainly they would not countenance men and women studying *together*. As Israelites, women theoretically must study Torah (since this is not a time-contingent precept). Yet the assumption that women as a gender should not engage in study leads first to their exemption and then, inexorably, to their exclusion."
33   Ibid., 148-156.
34   David Goodblatt, "The Beruriah Traditions," *JJS* 26 (1975): 68-85; and Leonard Swidler, "Beruriah: Her Word Became Law," *Lilith* 1.3 (1977): 9-13.
35   An androcentric reading of these stories, however, limits the scope of their application as is seen in Zvi Kaplan's interpretation of Beruriah in the article "Beruryah," *EJ* IV:70l: "... she is famous as the only woman in talmudic literature whose views on halakhic matters are taken seriously."

What can be seen, therefore, from the above analysis is the ambivalence which existed within both Christianity and Judaism during the first two centuries of our era in relation to women's active participation in public ritual and related religious activity. In the light of this, the plea placed on the lips of the woman--ἐλέησόν με, κύριε υἱὸς Δαυίδ--may well reflect a stage in the development of this story beyond the writing of the Markan gospel. It may have developed within some of the Matthean communities as a legitimation of women's participation in liturgical and theological life. Its affront to the socio-religious boundaries of other sectors of the community or other communities is reflected in the response to the woman's request in v. 23.

The opening phrase of v. 23--ὁ δὲ οὐκ ἀπεκρίθη αὐτῇ λόγον--is one of the most radical 'boundary-stressing' phrases in any miracle story within the gospels and it magnifies for the hearers of the story their sensitivity to the opposition that the supplicant must overcome. The only other occurrence of a similar phrase in relation to Jesus is during his trial before Pilate when he gives no answer to Pilate's question, and in that instance the Matthean phrase closely parallels that of Mark 15:5.[36] The phrase would, therefore, seem to be part of the tradition but its final form in the Matthean gospel reflects the redactional of style.[37] Hence, it could be argued that this phrase was introduced into the story by those within the community who saw the woman's plea in the words of v. 22 as a radical threat to their understanding of the person and ministry of Jesus, a threat similar to that of the trial before Pilate.[38] It was retained in the Matthean redaction but revised according to the particular style characteristic of the gospel.[39]

---

36 Mark's ὁ δὲ Ἰησοῦς οὐκέτι οὐδὲν ἀπεκρίθη (15:5) is rendered in Matthew as καὶ οὐκ ἀπεκρίθη αὐτῷ πρὸς οὐδὲ ἓν ῥῆμα (27:14).

37 Two factors govern this conclusion, namely, the positive use of ἀποκριθεὶς εἶπεν that has already been noted as Matthean redaction (see p. 106, n. 126 above and also Luz, *Evangelium*, 37); and also the phrase καὶ οὐδεὶς ἐδύνατο ἀποκριθῆναι αὐτῷ λόγον (Matt 22:46) where the evangelist links ἀποκρίνεσθαι and λόγον. Dermience, "Péricope," 35, says the phrase reflects the influence of Mark's gospel but also bears stylistic indications of Matthean redaction.

38 That the pericope is concerned with community problems is confirmed by Bonnard, *Évangile*, 230, who says: "..les paroles et les gestes de Jésus sont racontés pour guider les communautés chrétiennes dans leurs options historiques, et non point pour alimenter des souvenirs sentimentaux sur Jésus." However, he, like many other exegetes would confine the community question(s) to that of the mission to the gentiles.

39 The difficulty of this phrase has caused interpreters to pass over it in silence--Grundmann, *Evangelium*, 376, and Lagrange, *Evangile*, 309--or to explain it in general terms which often add little to our understanding of its function within this specific Matthean narrative. Gatzweiler, "Un pas," 19, highlights the biblical resonance of the phrase while Légasse, "L'épisode," 27, calls it the departure point for a didactic gradation in the story--both equally evasive. Others call it a testing of the woman's faith--Gundry, *A Commentary*, 312 and Witherington III, *Women in the Ministry*, 64.

This harsh response is then extended in the second half of the verse to include the disciples who request Jesus to send the woman away.[40] There is no mention of the disciples in the Markan pericope and hence it would seem that their introduction arises as a result of Matthean redaction, drawing perhaps on a tradition within the community as was seen with regard to the beginning of this verse.[41] Thus, we can argue that v. 23b may have belonged to the same tradition as v. 23a and had its origin within those same sectors of the Matthean community that were opposed to the entry of foreigners into the community,[42] but were also opposed to the active participation of women, and perhaps even more so of foreign women, in the public liturgical and theological life of the community.[43] It may, however, belong solely to the final redaction. As a unit, therefore, v. 23 reflects a strong tradition within the Matthean community which has been maintained and

---

40   The different meanings given to the disciples' statement have already been discussed above in Chapter Two, p. 108-109. Here, however, attention needs to be given to the argument of Murphy-O'Connor, "The Structure," 382, who follows the line of the Jerusalem Bible and considers that ἀπολύω in this context means "to release" in order to make sense of the reply of Jesus which follows in v. 24. According to what I have argued, however, v. 24 formed the immediate response to v. 22 and as such made quite good sense and with the introduction of v. 23 an imperfect redactional link failed to be corrected. Such an argument is quite plausible given similar examples in the gospel, e.g. 21:1-7 in which the Matthean account of the disciples' obtaining two animals for Jesus' entry into Jerusalem in order to fulfil the scripture is followed by the statement that he sat thereon, a statement which seems "nonsense". Xavier Léon-Dufour, "Vers l'annonce de l'église: Etude de structure (Mt 14,1-16,20)," in idem, *Etudes d'évangile*. Parole de Dieu 2 (Paris: Seuil, 1965), 243-244, also claims that the disciples intercede on behalf of the woman but his arguments are purely theological: "On reconnaît aisément le sens ecclésial et la portée universaliste du rôle des disciples", but he gives no literary evidence to support this statement and hence his position stands challenged by the literary arguments already put forward.

41   Russell, "Canaanite Woman," 278, shows that there are only two occasions when Matthew actually introduces the disciples as a character group into a received narrative where there is no Markan mention of them--at 15:23 and 17:6-7 in the story of the transfiguration where the disciples fall on their faces in fear and hear the heavenly voice. He goes on to question whether this addition is redactional or whether it is drawn from oral tradition. Bonnard, *Évangile*, 230, considers the phrase Matthean redaction indicative of the evangelist's pastoral and ecclesial preoccupations. Witherington III, *Women in the Ministry*, 170, n. 97, suggests that Matthew had access to oral tradition not available to Mark but does not go on to address the development of such an oral tradition within the community or the question of whose interests were served by its preservation.

42   This is supported by a number of scholars including Bonnard, *Évangile*, 231-232; Hill, *The Gospel*, 254; Schweizer, *The Good News*, 329; Russell, "Canaanite Woman," 279; and Mark C. Thompson, "Matthew 15:21-28," *Interp*. 35 (1981): 282.

43   Note should be taken of a comment by Gundry, *A Commentary*, 312: ""After us" sets the scene outside as opposed to Mark's setting the scene in a house (Mark 7:24, omitted in Matthew). It may also imply that the woman is following Jesus as a disciple, for she has confessed him as Lord and Son of David (v 22)." This is the only explanation that I am aware of which approaches anything similar to what I am proposing here, namely, that the Matthean development of the Markan story points to a concern within the Matthean community over and above that of mission to the gentiles.

probably strengthened to highlight dramatically the final outcome of the story and to enable the different factions within the community to hear their own position in relation to that outcome.

Attention can now be directed to the dialogue or debate (vv. 24-27) which forms the heart of the Matthean pericope, a debate which is built on the dialogue taken from the Markan narrative but extended to include vv. 24 and 25 of the Matthean account. Initially these verses will be considered as a unit since it has already been argued that they form the central unit of the Matthean structure. It will become clear, however, that they also represent a significant development or even corrective of the Markan perspective.

When one compares the Matthean dialogue with the actual exchange in Mark (7:27-28), it is quickly noted that the Markan text has been augmented so that the exchange between the woman and Jesus takes on the quality of a debate especially given the negative introductions to each of the replies of Jesus to the woman's requests which set forward her position. She then appropriates the argument of Jesus (v. 27) and extends it, and it is only then that Jesus affirms her stance. The dialogue is certainly the most extensive in any of the miracle stories in Matthew.[44] Except for a brief exchange between Jesus and the mother of the sons of Zebedee, it is the only dialogue between Jesus and a woman within the gospel. It stands, therefore, alongside that of 16:13-20 between Jesus and the disciples and 19:16-22 between Jesus and the rich young man. Hence, we are faced with the question why the Markan account has been so extended. Is it merely to emphasize further the significance of the mission to the Gentiles or are there other factors involved?

Comparison with encounter stories in the rabbinic literature in which a dialogue often does take place between a rabbi and a woman indicates that at times the rabbi himself may initiate the dialogue, but generally it is the woman who approaches with a question which the rabbi answers by way of the dialogue.[45] In none of the stories does the woman come with a request

---

44   The only possible parallel is that in the healing of the Centurion's servant (8:5-9) where the concern is also for Jesus' mission beyond Israel. See Légasse, "L'Episode," 23, and Held, "Matthew as Interpreter," 193, for a discussion of the relationship between the two accounts.

45   Martin, *Encounter Story*, has gathered together a number of such stories in the Appendix to his Thesis. Those most relevant for our consideration here include the account of R. Yoḥanan's meeting with the daughter of Naqdimon b. Gurion in which the rabbi initiates the dialogue [*Abot of Rabbi Nathan*. Version A, ed. Schechter (Vienna, 1887), 65, and *The Fathers according to Rabbi Nathan*, YJS X (New Haven: Yale University Press, 1956), 88-89]; and a series of encounters between a Rabbi and a Roman

such as that of the Canaanite woman and in none does the dialogue move
with the clarity and precision of the Matthean dialogue, nor does it function
to resolve a situation of intense conflict. Thus we may well agree with the
statement of Martin:

> ... in regard to the gospel material, we are more likely to find encounter sto-
> ries in those narratives which present something to be overcome, that is in
> accounts of conflict situations. This is generally but not exclusively the case
> in rabbinic literature as well, though ... rabbinic encounter stories tend to be
> less intense than their gospel counterparts.[46]

These stories, therefore, do not provide us with an adequate model to
explain the Matthean redaction, so we must turn to a careful analysis of the
dialogue within its Matthean context.

The Matthean addition of v. 24 has given rise to extensive controversy
and discussion among scholars, which can be addressed here only briefly.
Jeremias has defended its authenticity[47] as have a number of other scholars;[48] but Dermience provides a thorough refutation of this position.[49]
Bultmann, on the other hand, places this verse among the "I-sayings" of
Jesus which he considers to be a product of the Hellenistic churches,
although he does acknowledge that many of these sayings may have had
their origins in the Palestinian church. He considers that 15:24 belongs to the
latter category and would have arisen out of "missionary debates."[50] This
position has influenced a number of exegetes and we find it expressed in two
slightly different ways. For many, this verse's inclusion is considered part of
the Matthean redaction, but its content arose from discussions in the early
church regarding the mission to the Gentiles.[51] For others, however, it is a
little more nuanced; they consider that the saying arose within a Jewish-
christian milieu which wished to oppose the now-evident mission to the

---

matron which illustrate the second type of story where the woman is initiator. See
Martin, *Appendix to the Thesis*, R 124-131.

46   Martin, *Encounter Story*, 277.
47   Joachim Jeremias, *Jesu Verheissung für die Völker* (Stuttgart: Kohlhammer, 1956), 22-
     24, whose contention is that it has a significant Aramaic substrata similar to 10:5b-6.
48   Bonnard, *Évangile*, 232; Grundmann, *Evangelium*, 375; Hill, *The Gospel*, 254; and
     Gundry, *A Commentary*, 313.
49   Dermience, "Péricope," 36-38.
50   Bultmann, *History*, 153, 155, 165.
51   This is the position taken by Dermience, "Péricope," 39; Strecker, *Der Weg*, 107-108; and
     Trilling, *Das wahre Israel*, 99-100, who sees the logion of 10:5b-6 as providing the source
     for the Matthean construction of 15:24. Beare, *A Commentary*, 342, calls it a
     "retrojection into the life of Jesus of the controversy over the propriety of extending
     the Christian mission beyond Israel, with echoes of the bitterness of the struggle within
     the early church."

Gentiles.[52] It is this latter position which seems to accord best with the development of the tradition or traditions behind this pericope which are beginning to emerge from our explorations. We will, therefore, give it further consideration.[53]

It seems that during the redactional process, the mild statement of Mark 7:27 [ἄφες πρῶτον χορτασθῆναι τὰ τέκνα], has been omitted, and in its place a much more particularist saying: "I was sent *only* to the lost sheep of the house of Israel" has been included. The question which faces us initially is the origin of this saying. It is readily seen that it contains both language and allusions from the Hebrew Scriptures. In Jer 50:6 (LXX--27:6), the people of Israel and Judah, namely, the whole nation of Israel, are called lost sheep [πρόβατα ἀπολωλότα], while Num 27:17; Jdt 11:19; 2 Chr 18:16 and 1 Kgs 22:17 compare Israel to sheep without a shepherd. The influence of this imagery on Matthean theology is clear when one notes that the mission of Jesus in 2:6 is placed under the rubric of Mic 5:1--Thus he shall shepherd [ποιμανεῖ] my people Israel. Moreover, prior to Jesus' commissioning his disciples to go to "the lost sheep of the house of Israel" (10:6), he is said to have compassion on the multitude because they are like sheep without a shepherd (9:36). Thus the linking of the two allusions from the Hebrew Scriptures, "lost sheep" and the more frequent "house of Israel", points to a clear distinction between Israel and the other nations.[54]

In the story of the Canaanite woman, this particularist statement in v. 24 stands in sharp contrast to the outcome of the story in v. 28.[55] It is in tension also with the finale of the gospel which is a commissioning of the disciples to a universal mission (28:18-20), a mission already predicted in 12:18-21.

---

52   Boismard, *Synopse*, 236; Légasse, "L'épisode," 31; and also Gatzweiler, "Un pas," 20.
53   Reference should be made here to the excellent studies of Schuyler Brown, "The Matthean Community and the Gentile Mission," *NT* 22 (1980): 193-221; "The Mission to Israel in Matthew's Central Section (Mt 9,35-11,1)," *ZNW* 69 (1978): 73-90; and "The Two-fold Representation of the Mission in Matthew's Gospel," *StTh* 31 (1977): 21-32, in which he discusses the tension within the gospel at this point as reflecting the tension between different understandings of mission within the community. He considers that the incorporation of the saying was the Matthean redactor's way of teaching the community.
54   In this respect, I agree with Bonnard, *Évangile*, 232, who reads the genitive οἴκου Ἰσραήλ as a epexegetic genitive, making the phrase synonymous with "lost sheep" over against Jeremias, *Jesu Verheissung*, 22, who considers it a partitive genitive. For further discussion of this difference see T. A. Burkill, "The Syrophoenician Woman: The Congruence of Mark 7:24-31," *ZNW* 57 (1966): 26.
55   This is the position taken by Boismard, *Synopse*, 236, who says of v.24: "... en l'insérant dans l'épisode de la Cananéenne, Mt a voulu montrer que Jésus lui-même avait fait une entorse à cette règle, puisqu'il avait finalement exaucé la prière de la Cananéenne!"

This same tension is reflected in the scholarly debate surrounding v. 24 and related verses. One of the commonly held opinions is that the particularist saying of Matt 10:5-6 and 15:24 originated among Jewish christians, and the reliance on imagery from the Hebrew Scriptures contained therein would seem to confirm this.[56] Opinions differ, however, as to its function within the Matthean gospel. For Strecker,[57] Walker,[58] Trilling[59] and Meier,[60] it is seen as part of a Matthean "schema of salvation-history" even though each may conceive of that schema quite differently as well as representing a stage that has been superseded by the time of the writing of the gospel. These positions are very adequately critiqued by Schuyler Brown[61] especially in light of the fact that often the texts are examined outside their immediate context in the gospel. Brown himself proposes that the particularist saying represents a tradition born in the Jewish-christian sector of the Matthean community when it had to deal with the gentile mission as a result of its expulsion from Palestine after 70 CE and the growing Pharisaic restriction on Jewish christians' participation in Judaism.[62] The emphasis on a universal mission is the work of the Matthean redaction which seeks to affirm the wider community's extension of its mission to include the Gentiles.

In the light of this debate and its conclusions, we can argue that in the story of the Canaanite woman, the Matthean redaction includes v. 24, a tradition developed and preserved in at least one sector of the community, as

---

56   Strecker, *Der Weg*, 108; Trilling, *Das wahre Israel*, 105; Meier, *Law and History*, 27; and
      Brown, "Two-fold Representation," 25, 49; contrary to Frankemölle, *Jahwehbund*, 114,
      137, who considers that the verse is solely Matthean redaction. For his fuller treatment
      of mission in Matthew, see "Zur Theologie der Mission im Matthäusevangelium," in
      Mission im Neuen Testament, QD 93, ed. Karl Kertelge (Freiburg/Basel/Wien: Herder,
      1982), 93-129.
57   Strecker, *Der Weg*, 107-109, for whom 10:5-6 and 15:24 point to the historical mission of
      Jesus which was restricted to Israel but after the death of Jesus, the mission was
      extended to the gentiles as reflected in 28:18-20.
58   Walker, *Die Heilsgeschichte*, 60-63, sees 10:5-6 and 15:24 as particularist statements
      representative of the mission to Israel which extended up to 70 CE but, after 70, the
      mission extended to the gentiles. He calls 10:5f. (see pp. 62-63) a foundation "für das
      große geschichtliche Mosaik der Jesuszeit."
59   Trilling, *Das wahre Israel*, 99-105, sums up his analysis of the relationship between
      these verses in terms of 15:24 being programmatic for Jesus' relationship to Israel while
      28:19 was programmatic for the disciples' relationship to the nations. They offer, for
      him, a key to the correct christological understanding of the culpability of Israel and
      also to the topographical structure of the gospel.
60   Meier, *Law and History*, 27-40, claims that Matthew quite consciously orders an
      "economy" of salvation: to the Jews first and then to the gentiles. For him the death-
      resurrection of Jesus is the great turning point.
61   Brown, "Two-fold Representation," 21-23.
62   Ibid., 24-32 and also idem, "Matthean Community and Gentile Mission," in which he
      reconstructs the *Sitz im Leben* of the verses in tension.

one of the difficulties which the supplant must overcome in order to highlight the outcome of the story. The request of the woman, which by its very nature indicates that the gentile woman has in fact encountered Christianity, is opposed by a statement which would seek to prevent such contact. The remainder of the pericope, however, and especially its conclusion indicate that v. 24 has been included here so that the context might temper or soften its particularist nature.[63]

The obstacle presented by this statement does not, however, deter the woman who renews her petition. The question which faces us here is whether this renewed petition and Jesus' response to it are included simply to strengthen the dynamic already present in vv. 22-24 or whether the repetition adds nuances absent from the previous exchange but significant for the reader's understanding of the pericope as a whole.

Previously, the woman entered the story as an outsider to the circle of Jesus and the disciples, but v. 25 brings her into a more direct encounter with Jesus. She kneels before Jesus and continues her plea: Κύριε, βοήθει μοι. It seems at this point that the introduction to this plea is taken from the Markan text but Mark's phrase, ἐλθοῦσα προσέπεσεν πρὸς τοὺς πόδας αὐτοῦ, to ἐλθοῦσα προσεκύνει αὐτῷ is changed. The verb προσκυνέω is used thirteen times in the Matthean gospel as compared with twice in Mark (5:6; 15:19), and even these two are suppressed in Matthew (cf. 8:29; 27:29). This points to its redactional nature in Matthew's gospel and we find that it is used to indicate a person's recognition of Jesus' authoritative power,[64] and that it is applied even to those who are considered outsiders (a gentile ruler, a leper, and women). The two times that the disciples are the subject of the verb, it is linked to a reference to their little faith or their doubt. Thus in 14:31, Jesus rebukes Peter with the words: "O man of little faith, why did you doubt?" and the description of the Eleven worshipping the risen Jesus is followed by the statement οἱ δὲ ἐδίστασαν, translated variously as "some/all doubted"

---

63   Brown, "Two-fold Representation," 32: "Matthew has softened the particularist conception not by limiting it temporally but rather by removing the unconditional character of Jesus' prohibition through the context in which he has placed it."

64   Both Luz, *Evangelium*, 49-50, and Gundry, *A Commentary*, 647, point to this verb as redactional, Luz suggesting its Septuagintal nature. The verb is used in Matt 2:2, 8, 11 to refer to the Magi's attitude before Jesus; in 8:2 in relation to the leper who requests healing; in 9:18 in relation to the ruler who interceded on behalf of his daughter. At 20:20 the mother of the sons of Zebedee kneels before Jesus as she intercedes on behalf of her sons. The disciples are the subject of the verb in 14:33 and 28:17 as are the women at the tomb in 28:9. Its use in 4:9, and 10 is also within the context of Jesus' authoritative power. Only in 18:26 is the verb used apart from its reference to Jesus.

(28:17). Here, therefore, the woman's kneeling, which indicates her recognition of Jesus' authoritative power, can be contrasted with the attitude of the disciples who would have sent her away. Her request underlines her belief in Jesus' power while their action of "sending away" has already appeared in the gospel in a context which points to their failure to believe in this power.

The request itself is unique in Matthew's gospel whereas it occurs twice in Mark in the story of the father's request to heal his epileptic son (9:22, 24). Both these are omitted in Matthew and replaced by the request: κύριε, ἐλέησόν μου τὸν υἱόν. We already noted above that when the father's request was compared with that of the Canaanite woman in 15:22, it was clear that he was specifically interceding for his son, whereas in v. 22a, her request seems to be for herself and only in 22b is mention made of her daughter. Here also, the request seems to be solely on her own behalf and there is no mention of her daughter. This adds further weight to the claim made above that this pericope, in its final form, is more concerned with the plight of the woman than with a miracle to be accomplished for her daughter. Thus her request stands out in the first gospel by way of its uniqueness, a request on the lips of a woman interceding on her own behalf. The request itself has Septuagintal overtones (Pss 43:27; 69:6; 78:9; 108:26; 118:86, 117) and may have been used in the liturgy as a liturgical formula.[65]

The close relationship between the two-fold request of the woman (15:22a and 15:25) and the petition of Ps 108:26,

> Βοήθησόν μοι, κύριε ὁ Θεός μου,
> σῶσόν με κατὰ τὸ ἔλεός σου,

suggests a possible influence on the development of the Matthean story. An examination of the Psalm shows that it is the cry of the oppressed person in the face of severe adversaries. It is significant, therefore, that it is the same cries for "help" and "mercy" that are given to the woman who cries out to Jesus from a position of exclusion and oppression. To this second cry is attached the title κύριε only, the title developed within Hellenistic christian circles, while the title υἱὸς Δαυίδ used in her first plea was more likely to be of Jewish-christian origins.[66] Together her pleas incorporate the theology

---

65   Dermience, "Péricope," 40; Grundmann, Evangelium, 377; Gundry, A Commentary, 314; and Lohmeyer, Evangelium, 255.
66   Dermience, "Péricope," 40, says of her pleas that "la prière semble plus spécifiquement chrétienne, sa portée est plus universaliste."

and/or liturgical formulae from two possible sectors of the community, the Jewish-christian and the more diverse gentile christian.

A first glance at v. 26 suggests that it simply reproduces the saying of Jesus found in Mark 7:27. It is soon realized, however, that the relativizing statement of Mark regarding the feeding of the children *first* has been omitted together with the conjunction γάρ, so that the parabolic statement regarding the throwing of the children's bread to the dogs stands out in all its absoluteness and recalls 15:24. Many commentators consider this saying to be a *mashal* or wisdom saying,[67] but its enigmatic nature leaves its meaning unclear. The commonly accepted position is that "dogs" was a derogatory term used by the Jews to speak of Gentiles.[68] There is no doubt that it was intended as insulting or degrading as the use of the term in scripture suggests,[69] but whether its referent was necessarily or solely the Gentiles is difficult to determine from scripture although there are such specific references in later rabbinic writings.[70] The general understanding of the Markan use of this *mashal* is that it functions to emphasize the difficulty faced by Jesus in terms of the question of a mission to the Gentiles and therefore "dogs" is understood to have a restricted referent in this case. To this saying, however, Markan redaction has added the relativizing comment of 7:27a indicating that the children must be fed first and then the Gentiles so that the story might speak less shockingly to the gentile church which was Mark's audience.[71]

---

67   Argyle, *The Gospel*, 120; Gundry, *A Commentary*, 314; Filson, *The Gospel*, 180; Gaechter, *Matthäus-Evangelium*, 503; Cerfaux, "Section des pains," 78; Russell, "Canaanite Woman," 264 and Dermience, "Péricope," 40-41 and n. 113, where she points to the sapiential nature of the saying and the fact that such a form occurs nowhere else in the Christian Scriptures.

68   Derrett, "Law in the New Testament," 165, who considers both the scriptural and rabbinic use of the word.

69   See for example 1 Sam 24:14; 2 Sam 9:8; 16:9; 2 Kgs 8:13; Isa 56:10. Lefkowitz, "Influential Women," 53, points out that "dogs" were disliked in the Greek world also and the use of this term with reference to persons was hence derogatory. D. Winton Thomas, "Kelebh 'Dog': Its Origin and Some Usages of It in the Old Testament," *VT* 10 (1960): 410-427, illustrates by means of a study of the word across Semitic and non-Semitic cultures that the term can certainly be used as an invective when applied by the speaker to someone else.

70   Gnilka, *Matthäusevangelium*, II, 31, asks this same question and goes on to suggest that the *am ha-aretz* were also identified by this word but gives no supporting evidence. For rabbinic references which make this connection, see H. L. Strack and P. Billerbeck, *Kommentar zum Neuen Testament aus Talmud und Midrasch* I (München: Beck, 1922), 724-725.

71   Cerfaux, "Section des pains," 68 and T. A. Burkill, "The Syrophoenician Woman: Mark 7,24-31," *StEv* IV=*TU* 102 (1968): 168-171, who outlines a four-phase development of the tradition.

Regarding the function of this *mashal* in the Matthean account, we have already noted that the initial relativizing comment is missing and the statement stands therefore as a possible parallel to the very particularist statement of v. 24. It has also been suggested, however, that in Matthew's gospel the story deals not only with the question of Jesus' mission to the Gentiles but also with the role of women within the christian community, and this together with the indeterminancy of the referent for the term "dog" suggests that we explore it further. In Isaiah 56:10, those who are blind and without knowledge are likened to "dumb dogs" and, as we saw above, it may also have been a term used for the *am ha-aretz* , those without knowledge of the Torah and hence unable to keep its precepts. They were thereby ritually unclean. In later rabbinic writings we also find that the term is used to refer to those not versed in the Torah (Midr. Lev 9:3 and b. B. Bat. 8a).[72] Whether such an understanding was known to the Matthean community is difficult to determine with any degree of accuracy especially given the late date of the

---

72   Midr. Lev 9:3: "There is a story that R. Jannai when once walking in the road, saw a
      man who said to him: 'Would you, Rabbi, care to accept my hospitality?' R. Jannai an-
      swered: 'Yes,' whereupon he brought him to his house and entertained him with food
      and drink. He tested him in [the knowledge of] Talmud, and found [that he possessed]
      none, in *Haggadah*, and found none, in Mishnah, and found none, in Scripture, and
      found none. Then he said to him: 'Take up [the wine-cup of benediction] and recite
      Grace.' The man answered: 'Let Jannai recite Grace in his own house!' Said the Rabbi to
      him: 'Are you able to repeat what I say to you?' 'Yes,' answered the man. Said R. Jannai:
      'Say: A dog has eaten of Jannai's bread.' The man rose and caught hold of him, saying:
      'You have my inheritance which you are withholding from me!' Said R. Jannai to him:
      'And what is this inheritance of yours which I have?' The man answered: 'Once I
      passed a school, and I heard the voice of the youngsters saying: *The Law which Moses
      commanded us is the inheritance of the congregation of Jacob* [Deut. XXXIII,4]; it is
      written not 'The inheritance of the congregation of Jannai', but *'The inheritance of the
      congregation of Jacob '*. Said R. Jannai to the man: 'How have you merited to eat at table
      with me?' The man answered: 'Never in my life have I, after hearing evil talk, re-
      peated it to the person spoken of, nor have I ever seen two persons quarrelling without
      making peace between them.' Said R. Jannai: 'That I should have called you dog, when
      you possess such good breeding [*derek-eres*]!"
      [From *Midrash Rabbah. Leviticus*, chs. 1-9, trans. J. Israelstam (reprint; London:
      Soncino, 1961), 108-109].
      b. B. Bat. 8a: "Rabbi once opened his storehouse [of victuals] in a year of scarcity, pro-
      claiming: Let those enter who have studied the Scripture, or the *Mishnah*, or the
      Gemara, or the *Halachah*, or the *Aggada* ; there is no admission, however, for the igno-
      rant. R. Jonathan b. Amram pushed his way in and said, 'Master, give me food.' He said
      to him, 'My son, have you learnt the Scripture?' He replied, 'No.' 'Have you learnt the
      Mishnah ?' 'No.' 'If so,' he said, 'then how can I give you food?' He said to him, 'Feed
      me as the dog and the raven are fed.' So he gave him some food. After he went away,
      Rabbi's conscience smote him and he said: Woe is me that I have given my bread to a
      man without learning!"
      [From *The Babylonian Talmud. Seder Nezikin II. Baba Batra*, Chs. 1-4 trans. Maurice
      Simon and Chs. 5-10 trans. Israel W. Slotki (London: Soncino, 1935), 33-34.]

rabbinic writings, but further analysis of the Matthean changes in v. 26 may add weight to the possibility of its being so.

A slight change in the order of words in the parable itself has been made so that a parallelism focuses the reader's attention on τέκνων and κυναρίοις:

οὐκ ἔστιν καλὸν λαβεῖν τὸν ἄρτον τῶν τέκνων

καὶ   βαλεῖν   τοῖς κυναρίοις.

According to the parable, the children have a right to the bread whereas the dogs do not. If the plea of the woman is intended to be a request to Jesus to help her as she struggles to maintain her role in the religious life of her community, then the absoluteness and the emphases in this response of Jesus may well be expressive of a counter-tradition. The parable can be read as a claiming of the bread of Torah and the work of public worship solely for men who consider themselves the rightful recipients of these salvific benefits. They indeed are the τέκνων.[73] Used in this way, the parable therefore precludes women who are considered unlearned and hence deserving of the designation "dog". These words then on the lips of Jesus represent not only a community tradition opposed to the mission to the Gentiles but also one opposed to the active participation of women in the liturgical and theological life of the community. Like v. 24 , however, its exclusiveness is softened and tempered by means of the context in which it is placed. It suggests also that this participation of women was a part of the theology and teaching of the final redactional stage of the gospel just as was the notion of a universal mission.

The reply of the woman (v. 27), in which she takes up the words of Jesus but extends their application, confirms more strongly the claim that the dialogue is presented in terms of a legal debate,[74] and it authenticates the suggestion that the Matthean pericope, as well as being concerned with the mission of Jesus to the Gentiles, is also concerned with the right of a woman to dialogue on theological issues.[75] The slight change from the Markan κύριε,

---

73   In such a parabolic saying τέκνον need not be gender specific but could symbolically point to those who belong to the family and have a right to its bread. It could, however, be used in a particular situation with gender specific connotations.

74   Derrett, "Law in the New Testament," 183. That this legal aspect was recognized and even highlighted in the early church is evidenced in the textual amendment in some of the Western witnesses in which ἔστιν καλόν of v. 26 is changed to ἔξεστιν. See Metzger, *Textual Commentary*, 39-40.

75   It is interesting to note in this regard that Thomas' investigation, "Kelebh," 414 and 427, led him to two significant conclusions for our purposes. First, when the speaker

καὶ τὸ ναί κύριε, καὶ γάρ suggests a change from the adversative position of Mark to an assent followed by a positive line of reasoning in Matthew.[76] The more significant change, however, is from παιδίων[77] to κυρίων thus appropriating the full force of the twice-repeated title, κύριε, of vv. 22 and 25.[78] The woman claims for herself as Gentile the right to receive the benefits of the βασιλεία which Jesus preaches directly from himself and not secondarily from those who have claimed for themselves the right to these benefits.[79] As a woman within the christian community, she claims the right to learn and to scrutinize the scriptures and the teachings of Jesus, a benefit not reserved solely for the male members of the community but available to all from the table of the Lord.[80] It is the woman who in fact begins to cross the barriers erected to exclude her, barriers which are attributed to Jesus himself. The final words of Jesus, however, affirm all that is implied in her requests and in her appropriation of the parable of the bread.

Jesus' greeting ὦ γύναι calls attention to the uniqueness of all that has gone before. It is the only time that such an address is offered to a woman in the first gospel in contrast to its use twice in Luke (13:12; 22:57) and five times in John (2:4; 4:21; 19:26; 20:13; 20:15) although without the exclamatory ὦ in those instances. The use of the exclamatory ὦ in Matthew gives expression, therefore, to the strong emotion involved in this culmination of an

---

applies the term "dog" to herself, it can function as an expression of deference before the addressee. Second, it was an expression which, when used in religious circles of prayer and worship, was not without honour.

76   Dermience, "Péricope," 41, discusses the change from the adversative to assent; but the phraseology is further discussed by Anton Fridrichsen, "Einige sprachliche und stilistische Beobachtungen: 2. Marc. 7,28 = Matth. 15,27," AMNSU 2 (1936)/CNT 1 (1936): 10-13, in which he argues that ναί + καὶ γάρ prepares for a positive line of reasoning and not a rejection or fundamental modification. Grundmann, Evangelium, 377, argues similarly: "Das γάρ begründet ihre Bitte mit der Wendung, die sie dem Bilde gibt."

77   Used in Mark as an equivalent to τέκνων in the previous verse.

78   Gundry, A Commentary, 316.

79   Thus it seems clear that within the Matthean redaction the mission of Jesus is not understood as Jews first and then gentiles but rather the gentile mission is an extension of the Jewish mission while also inclusive of it.

80   Bonnard, Évangile, 233, recognizes the eucharistic allusions here but only in terms of the question of openness to the inclusion of the gentiles and not of women. He also interprets this verse as the woman's recognition of the priority of Israel claiming that this is the faith that Jesus praises but it seems that the Matthean change from παιδίων to κυρίων precludes such an interpretation. Gundry, A Commentary, 316, also recognizes in the verse a symbol of the Lord's table and links it with Matthew's eucharistic editing of 14:13-21. (It should be noted that in Matthew reference is made to women and children at the two feedings of the multitudes even though they are not within the official count--14:21; 15:38). Hence it is clear that the Matthean understanding of eucharist was that it was inclusive. That the allusion is not limited to participation in Eucharist or liturgy but also extends to a study of "the Lord's" teaching is stengthened by way of reference to 16:12 in which bread is symbolic of teaching.

emotionally charged story and it has also been suggested that its force "is not confined to the following vocative but dominates and colors the whole sentence."[81] The greeting also represents a development in relation to θύγατερ, the address given to the woman with the haemorrhage in 9:22.[82] As to the quality of this address, Dermience says that in antiquity it was "des plus respectueuses" according to the witness of several ancient texts.[83] It acknowledges Jesus' unconditional acceptance of the woman in contrast to the barriers that have been placed on his lips during the course of the story.

The greeting itself is followed by an equally extraordinary exclamation: μεγάλη σου ἡ πίστις. Although μέγας is used twenty times throughout the Matthean text, nowhere else is it attached to πίστις. In every other instance where faith is considered quantitatively, it is in terms of "little faith" [ὀλιγόπιστος] rather than "great faith". Hence, it would seem that Jesus' acclamation of the woman's faith sets her in contrast to those addressed in each of the other instances (6:30--the general group of disciples who are the recipients of the Sermon on the Mount; 8:26--the disciples who are in the boat with Jesus; 14:31--Peter as he walks toward Jesus on the sea and fails to believe; 16:8--the disciples who discuss the question of failure to bring bread; and 17:20--the disciples who fail to be able to cast out the demon from the epileptic boy).[84] In each of these examples, the referents are the members of the character group called "disciples" over against whose failure in faith the great faith of the woman is set. This contrast is further authenticated by the fact that Matthew's gospel includes the tradition attributed to the disciples in v. 23. The woman also exemplifies the mode of faith proposed to the disciples who could not cast out the demon from the boy:

> For truly I say to you, if you have faith as a grain of mustard seed, you will say to this mountain, 'Move from here to there,' and it will move; and nothing will be impossible to you.
>
> (Matt 17:20)

---

81   Blass, Debrunner and Funk, A Greek Grammar, 81, §146.
82   Some could suggest that the use of the title "daughter" in addressing a woman was demeaning, keeping her in a position of inferiority. Within the gospel text, however, it can function to specifically highlight the inclusion of women in the βασιλεία offsetting the androcentric υἱός which is used by way of reference to all participants in the βασιλεία, whether male or female (5:9, 45; 8:12; 13:38).
83   Dermience, "Péricope," 43, n. 127.
84   Gundry, A Commentary, 316. Gaechter, Matthäus-Evangelium, 501, considers this story as a highpoint and contrasts it with the little faith of the people of Nazareth and the lack of faith of the disciples.

Her faith was such that it refused to be moved by the harshest of rejections even from Jesus himself. Jesus' affirmation of this faith functions as an affirmation of female power which was able to overcome extraordinary obstacles. Within the Matthean community, this story would therefore have affirmed the contribution of gentile women to the life of the community[85] as well as legitimating women's participation in its liturgical and theological life. If Jesus so affirms the questioning of this woman who extended his understanding of his mission, so too must the community accept the active participation of women in its deliberations regarding its understanding of its mission and life-style.

Just as the first half of Jesus' final statement reveals the Matthean redaction, so too does the second half, which finds no echo in the Markan text. The use of γενηθήτω σοι recalls the concluding words of Jesus to the centurion whose servant was healed (8:13) and to the two blind men likewise healed (9:29). In each case, it was attached to a reference to their faith. Here, it is not linked directly to the proclamation of the woman's faith, but rather to the phrase ὡς θέλεις. Such a link recalls the twice repeated phrase γενηθήτω τὸ θέλημά σου of 6:10 and 26:42: the prayer of Jesus in the garden (26:42) echoing the words of the prayer he taught his disciples (6:10), and both prayers linking the will of the "Father in heaven" with those who beseech God on earth as a means of bringing in the βασιλεία. Here it would seem that Jesus is acknowledging that the desire of the woman [ὡς θέλεις] functions as a means of bringing in the βασιλεία in accordance with the will or purpose of God. With such a proclamation on the lips of Jesus, the woman's approach to him is vindicated over against each of the accusations or lines of opposition levelled against it. As Schüssler Fiorenza suggests, she stands as "foremother" of all gentile christians and even more so in Matthew's gospel as paradigm of female leadership within the christian community.

In conclusion, attention turns once again to the woman's daughter [καὶ ἰάθη ἡ θυγάτηρ αὐτῆς ἀπὸ τῆς ὥρας ἐκείνης]. It appears that in the Matthean gospel that this is an adaptation of 8:13; 9:22 or 17:18, a point which affirms an earlier claim that the dialogue between Jesus and the woman has obscured the miracle in Matthew.[86] However, the miracle is not obscured entirely and so the conclusion reminds the reader of the faith of this woman

---

85   Selvidge, *Daughters of Jerusalem*, 80.
86   In this regard, note that the last verse of Mark (7:30) refers solely to the miracle aspect of the pericope and its accomplishment in contrast to Matthew where the major part of the last verse is concerned with the conclusion of the dialogue.

which was able to bring healing for her daughter. The story is concerned, therefore, not only with the woman but also with her daughter and the participation in the βασιλεία of Jesus which is obtained for her through the pleading of her mother. The woman's plea is not for herself alone but for her daughter and her future participation in the community of faith. We turn, therefore, to a consideration of the lines of development of the complex traditions that stand behind the final Matthean rendition of this gentile woman's story.

C. Development of the Tradition

Behind the Markan pericope (7:24-30) lay a simple miracle story. Into this story were introduced the saying regarding bread being thrown to dogs (v. 27)[87] and the response of the woman to this saying in v. 28, both of which were intended to highlight Jesus' mission to the Gentiles. The story was then given a geographical setting that further emphasized this theme, namely, the district of Tyre (v. 24), and the designation of origin of the woman as "Greek, a Syrophoenician by birth" (v. 26a).[88] The Markan redaction added to this story the brief introduction in v. 24a and also sought to soften for a gentile audience the harshness of the parabolic statement by introducing v. 27a which referred to the children being fed first.[89]

Within the Matthean community, the Markan story seems to have provided a basis around which two groups of counter traditions developed. A natural development from the Markan story would have been the highlighting of the extension of Jesus' mission to the Gentiles by doubling the pattern of petition and difficulty. Hence the woman's request is made in direct speech--ἡ θυγάτηρ μου κακῶς δαιμονίζεται (v. 22c), and a strong community tradition against such a mission is introduced in response to it (v. 24). If, as our analyses of previous pericopes have indicated, there also existed within the Matthean community traditions in conflict surrounding the

---

87   Burkill, "Mark 7:24-31," 168, calls this phase 1 of his 4-phase development of the Markan tradition. He, however, reverses the order claiming that the saying of Mark 7:27b is dramatised in a miracle story.
88   Boismard, *Synopse*, 236. This stage is the pre-Markan composition that Schüssler Fiorenza refers to; see *In Memory of Her*, 137.
89   Burkill, "Mark 7:24-31," 170, sees this as phase 3.

question of women's role and contribution, then it is reasonable, in the light of the exegesis above, to argue that this story which involved a woman whose contribution to the extension of Jesus' mission was significant, would be developed to highlight this role. The story could then function paradigmatically within the community in relation to these points of tension. Hence the woman's request in v. 22c was extended so that one of the liturgical formulae of the community was placed on her lips indicating her significant participation in the community's life. The fact that it is a cry for help points to that participation being under threat. It was perhaps also at this point that the second cry was placed on the lips of the woman (v. 25b). In the light of this development, the particularist statements of vv. 24 and 26, and especially v. 26, took on a new significance, namely, a counter to those traditions which supported the active participation of women in the community's religious life. At this stage, I would suggest that v. 23 or at least v. 23a was introduced as a more specific counter tradition to this second level of the story's development.[90]

It was this story containing tradition and counter-tradition that was taken up and edited in order to preserve both groups of traditions, but also, by contextualizing them within the gospel story, to incorporate them into the gospel's teaching. Thus, the beginning and end of the pericope (vv. 21 and 28) and the introduction of the woman as Canaanite link the story into various gospel themes already unfolding. The concluding verse, however, suggests that both the extension of Jesus' mission to the Gentiles and support for the active participation of women in the public religious life of the community belonged to the theology of the final redaction as well as to sectors of the community. The careful structuring of the story as a debate, a structuring which also seems to belong to this final stage, further authenticates the above suggestion.

Within the community's gospel story, this pericope could have functioned not only as an authentication of the community's extended mission among the Gentiles but also as a legitimation of women's active role in liturgy, their participation in the community's theological reflection on the life and ministry of Jesus in the light of their scriptures, and their leadership role.

---

90   Verse 23b regarding the disciples may have been the work of the final redaction.

The Matthean redaction has also maintained this story in its significantly revised form in a context which, although closely following the Markan story, has been structured according to redactional purposes. Hence, the beginning of the story presents Jesus withdrawing from the Pharisees, who have been characterized in the previous chapters as being concerned with the external law (12:2) and human traditions (15:2) rather than the commands of God (15:4-9) or the plight of the person in need (12:9-14). Their distinctions between clean and unclean according to types of food, ethnic background or blood taboos may be considered "human precepts" (15:9). In the previous story, it was emphasized that God is concerned with the heart of the human person, the relationship with oneself and with one's neighbour (15:19).[91]

The narrative which follows 15:1-20 is illustrative of Jesus' withdrawal from these narrow distinctions. Jesus encounters a woman in public and not only a woman but a gentile woman, an immediate source of impurity according to cultural and religious taboos. He enters into a debate with her which centres on two significant questions: the right of this woman and her daughter as Gentiles to receive the benefits of the messianic era present in the ministry of Jesus,[92] and also her right as woman to engage with a man in a debate over religious matters in the public arena. The outcome of the dialogue ("Be it done for you as you desire") indicates that the pleas of this woman are according to the mind of God even though they run contrary to the "human precepts" exemplified in the rebukes offered to her.

We have seen too that the disciples have been introduced into the story as opponents of the woman and her request. They are the ones who received the missionary commission to preach and to heal among the lost sheep of the house of Israel (10:5-8); but they also heard Jesus' reply to Peter's request to explain the parable regarding clean and unclean to them (15:11). These distinctions are not dependent on being Jew or Gentile, male or female, but on what comes from the heart. As the story unfolds, the disciples are representative of those whose boundaries regarding clean and unclean remain unchallenged by the parable of Jesus. The woman, on the other hand, risks crossing ethnic, gender and religious boundaries and remains faithful to this

---

91   Grundmann, *Evangelium*, 375, links the story of 15:21-28 with the previous parable (vv. 17-20) and its concern with the human heart and the gift of God.

92   For many scholars, this link between mission to the gentiles and distinctions between clean and unclean is the sole focus of this pericope. See Gundry, *A Commentary*, 310; Hill, *The Gospel*, 253; and Stendahl, "Matthew," 787.

risk. For this, Jesus praises her fidelity in contrast to that of the male disciples who have been privy to more constant and intimate exposure to the teaching of Jesus and yet have demonstrated little faith (14:31; 16:8; 17:20).

Given that the Matthean redaction of the story of the Canaanite woman has brought the narrative theme of women in the Jesus movement to a high point of development which will climax in the passion narrative, we will do well now to turn to the brief references to women which surround it in its immediate narrative context. The analysis of these references will be in terms of their redactional nature and their possible sources within the community.

II. Minor References

The first of these minor references occurs in 12:46-50 and the second in 13:54-58. In both instances the reference is to the mother of Jesus in the context of the patriarchal family. She could scarcely be designated a character in each of these stories but rather a character type symbolizing the familial structure. The two references also frame the parable chapter.[93]

Turning first to 12:46-50, we find that it is necessary to go back to two other passages in the gospel which seem to prepare for it. Toward the end of the missionary discourse addressed to the disciples, Jesus sets out the demands of discipleship, demands which are specifically inclusive:

> Do not think that I have come to bring peace on earth; I have not come to bring peace, but a sword. For I have come to set a man against his father, and a daughter against her mother, and a daughter-in-law against her mother-in-law; and a person's foes will be those of their own household. The one who loves father or mother more than me is not worthy of me; and the one who loves son or daughter more than me is not worthy of me; and whoever does not take their cross and follow me is not worthy of me. The one who finds their life will lose it, and the one who loses their life for my sake will find it.   (Matt 10:34-39*).

---

93 Crosby, *House of Disciples*, 56-59, sees the relationship between these two passages as significant in terms of the understanding of discipleship developed in 12:46-13:58. Doyle, *Matthew's Wisdom*, 339, also notes the frame but sees 13:53-58 as a parallel to the rejection by the Galilean towns in 11:20-24.

To the Q saying in v. 34 (cf. Luke 12:51), a much closer rendering of Micah 7:6 has been added (v. 35; cf. Luke 12:53), with the conclusion of this quotation forming v. 36: "a person's foes will be those of their own household." If, as Schüssler Fiorenza suggests,

> ... the apocalyptic destruction and dissolution of the family announced for the cataclysmic last days before the end of the world in Micah 7:6 and Mark 13:12, characterize, according to the Q traditions, the present time of discipleship,[94]

then this has been highlighted by the Matthean redaction.

Discipleship, as well as being inclusive (it was addressed to both men and women--ἄνθρωπον, θυγατέρα, νύμφην), also entails a break with the patriarchal family structure. The radical nature of this break is expressed in v. 36 where one's own household will become one's enemies.[95] This Matthean redaction is in keeping with the challenge to accepted family structures already visible in the prologue and the miracle accounts as analyzed above. In this pericope and its context, the call to discipleship is specifically linked to the necessary break with traditional family structures. It points, however, toward the establishment of a new type of household.[96]

Linked to 12:46-50 because of its placement within the Wisdom section of the gospel is 11:28-30 in which Jesus-Sophia calls *all* to herself so that they may learn wisdom. Discipleship of Jesus as Sophia is inclusive and it entails learning. This passage is strictly Matthean redaction and foreshadows 12:46-50. Moreover, its symbolic language provides a backdrop for the interpretation of the debate in 15:21-28. Jesus-Sophia has invited all to her to learn from her and to find the rest and restoration that they seek. The debate of 15:21-28 highlights for the reader the forces within the community opposed to this ideal.

The concern of 12:46-50 is precisely with the nature of the community of discipleship and its relationship to the patriarchal family. Matthean redaction draws on the Markan pericope (Mark 3:31-35), which also introduces the parable chapter, and makes those changes necessary to incorporate the material into the developing Matthean theology.[97] The most significant Matthean

---

94 Schüssler Fiorenza, *In Memory of Her*, 146.
95 Benoit, *L'Evangile*, 92; Filson, *The Gospel*, 134; Harrington, *Matthew*, 47; and Meier, *Matthew*, 113.
96 Grundmann, *Evangelium*, 300.
97 Matthew has no parallel to Mark 3:19b-21 which links the family of Jesus with those who consider him "beside himself".

redaction occurs in v. 49. Where Mark has Jesus "looking around on those who sat about him" (3:34a), in Matthew Jesus is described as "stretching out his hand towards his disciples" (12:49a). Matthew's gospel specifically relates the pericope, therefore, to the group called disciples.[98]

The new household comprises those who "do the will of the heavenly Father".[99] At this point, the Markan phraseology is retained, but within the first gospel the phrase "doing the will of the heavenly Father" has taken on its own particular meaning. In the prayer of Jesus, the coming of the βασιλεία of God is paralleled to the doing of the will of God (6:10), and the metaphor used for God is that of father. The parable of 7:24-27 likens the wise one to the one who does the will of God and hence enters into the fulness of the βασιλεία (7:21). The centrality of this theme to the Sermon on the Mount in the Matthean gospel links it to the Matthean teaching on discipleship and this is further highlighted by its re-appearance in 12:50.[100]

We see at work here a Matthean redactional technique similar to that operative in 15:21-28. Just as there the particularist statements which limited Jesus' mission to Israel were softened in order to extend the mission but in a way which was still inclusive of Israel, so too in this pericope the harshness of the Markan rejection of family (3:21; 31-35) is softened to extend the boundaries of the new household to include all those women and men who live out a faithful response to the call inherent in Jesus' preaching of the βασιλεία. One element of this response is participation in the βασιλεία in a way which is in keeping with the intention and purpose of God, symbolized in the gospel as a doing of God's will.[101]

The theology supported here is similar to that of the final redaction noted in the conclusion to 15:21-28. There the desire and the will of the Canaanite woman was in keeping with the commandment of God and the

---

98   Allen, *A Critical Commentary*, 142; and Meier, *Matthew*, 140.
99   Bruce J. Malina, "Patron and Client: The Analogy behind Synoptic Theology," *Forum* 4 (1988): 24, in his analysis of the Jesus-movement as a "faction" which he describes as "a coalition of persons (followers) recruited personally, according to structurally diverse principles by or on behalf of a person in conflict with another person(s) with whom they (coalition members) were formerly united over honor and/or control of resources and/or "truth"," suggests that Jesus' break with his mother and brothers points to his seriousness about his special personal obligations within the new coalition which he has established.
100 Crosby, *House of Disciples*, 57 develops these links more fully.
101 Lagrange, *Evangile*, 375, points out that 15:4 and 19:19 are indicative of the importance of the command to honour one's parents and so the gospel does not support an outright rejection of family structures. See also Benoit, *L'Evangile*, 92; and Filson, *The Gospel*, 134. The gospel message, however, challenges family structures which are specifically patriarchal.

word of God and it was accomplished. Her membership and that of her daughter within the βασιλεία and their sharing in its resources are in keeping with the theology of this pericope. In the new community, men and women will participate as equals since the same obligation is laid on both: the doing of God's will and purpose. The words of Jesus indicate that, in fact, this command pertains to women as well as men by naming the disciples "sister" as well as "mother and brother". Membership of the new household includes women not just as "mothers of sons", a view in keeping with the patriarchal vision of reality, but extends to women who become "sisters", co-equal sharers.

We have already seen that in the story of the Canaanite woman, this principle of inclusion of women was under threat. The story concerns the actual possibility of a woman receiving the benefits of the βασιλεία as well as participating as disciple in the household of the faith, especially listening to Jesus' teachings and dialoguing about these. As her story unfolds, Jesus recognizes the "will of the Father" in the faith of the woman. To her could be extended the title "sister". She and her daughter appear in the story outside the patriarchal family structure. The woman is neither "wife of a man", nor "mother of a son". Rather, she is mother of a daughter, a model of true discipleship in the βασιλεία of Jesus; and her daughter is beneficiary of the fruits of the βασιλεία. Together they are members of the new household.

In 13:55, the Markan reference to Jesus as "son of Mary" is changed to the question--Is not his mother called Mary? The change is slight and the reason for it difficult to determine, but in the light of the theology that we have seen developing in the gospel and supported by the final redaction, we might suggest that the linking of the name Mary to the phrase "his mother" is intended to recall the tension in the prologue surrounding Mary. There her motherhood of Jesus functioned as a profound critique of the patriarchal family structure and yet her story was co-opted back into that structure. The residents of Nazareth completely overlook the first aspect and look to Mary's role in the patriarchal family as argument against the wisdom and mighty works of Jesus. As 12:46-50 has warned, they will not find the explanation they seek in that arena.

With regard to 14:1-12, there are two significant redactional changes made in the Matthean gospel, but they seem to be at the service of the contrast set up between this pericope and 27:11-26 and will be best considered in the context of the passion narrative. In passing, it will simply be pointed out that in the Matthean story, Herodias never appears as a character on the scene as she does in Mark (cf. Mark 6:19, 24), but is merely the voice behind the scene (Matt 14:8). Also, Herod rather than Herodias is the one who desired the death of John (Matt 14:5; Mark 6:19). It would seem, therefore that the Matthean redaction sought to minimize without eliminating the role of Herodias because it ran contrary to the theme of women's response to Jesus. Their response in the narrative to this point illustrates their inclusion in the βασιλεία and it is such inclusion that is one particular concern in this section of the gospel .

The two references to women and children as participants in the feeding of the multitudes (14:21 and 15:38) are Matthean redaction and, in the light of the specifically inclusive references already noted in this section of the gospel, it seems that here also it is made absolutely clear that both women and men as well as children participate in the fruits of the βασιλεία. Their inclusion stands as a critique of the androcentric perspective which counts only men.[102]

III. Conclusion

The Matthean redaction is clearly visible in the narrative section which concludes the Galilean ministry of Jesus. In the context of various responses to Jesus and at a climactic point in the narrative, the story of the Canaanite woman stands as a paradigm of the faith required of the true disciple of Jesus, a faith in the universality of the blessings of the βασιλεία which are available beyond all the ethnic, religious, gender and patriarchal-familial barriers that the human community can construct. The broader framework in which this story is to be interpreted is provided in part by the redactional emphasis on discipleship as inclusive, based not on familial relationships but rather on the radical call to do the will of God in response to the gift of the βασιλεία, a call to which all can respond.

In this context whose focus is response to Jesus, the Wisdom and the Bread, this woman's story functions as a foil for both the character group

---

102 Crosby, *House of Disciples*, 114-115, discusses these references in terms of the question whether women were considered disciples in Matthew's gospel.

called disciples and for the leaders. As the narrative advances, their stories will be further developed and their responses further highlighted and the contrast will appear even greater. Although the Canaanite woman does not appear again in the story, other women's stories will function similarly to hers and it is to these and to their function and formation within the community that we now turn.

6. Stories of Women in The Journey to Jerusalem, Passion and Resurrection

In parts IV and V of Chapter Two, consideration was given to a number of stories in which women characters were significant participants in the story of Jesus' journey to Jerusalem, his passion and resurrection. These stories will now be examined from a redaction-critical perspective in order to gain some insights into the development of the traditions preserved within them and their rhetorical function within the Matthean community. Each story will be treated in greater or lesser detail depending on the significance of its function within the narrative.

I. 20:20-22

Matt 20:20-22

20 Τότε προσῆλθεν αὐτῷ

ἡ μήτηρ τῶν υἱῶν Ζεβεδαίου
μετὰ τῶν υἱῶν αὐτῆς
προσκυνοῦσα

καὶ αἰτοῦσά τι ἀπ' αὐτοῦ.

21 ὁ δὲ εἶπεν αὐτῇ·
Τί θέλεις;
λέγει αὐτῷ·
εἰπὲ ἵνα καθίσωσιν
οὗτοι οἱ δύο υἱοί μου
εἷς ἐκ δεξιῶν σου καὶ εἷς ἐξ εὐωνύμων σου

ἐν τῇ βασιλείᾳ σου.
22 ἀποκριθεὶς δὲ ὁ Ἰησοῦς εἶπεν·
οὐκ οἴδατε τί αἰτεῖσθε.

Mark 10:35-39a

35 Καὶ προσπορεύονται αὐτῷ
Ἰάκωβος καὶ Ἰωάννης
οἱ υἱοὶ Ζεβεδαίου

λέγοντες αὐτῷ· διδάσκαλε,
θέλομεν ἵνα
ὃ ἐὰν αἰτήσωμέν σε
ποιήσῃς ἡμῖν.
36 ὁ δὲ εἶπεν αὐτοῖς·
Τί θέλετέ [με] ποιήσω ὑμῖν;
37 οἱ δὲ εἶπαν αὐτῷ·
δὸς ἡμῖν ἵνα

εἷς σου ἐκ δεξιῶν καὶ εἷς ἐξ ἀριστερῶν
καθίσωμεν
ἐν τῇ δόξῃ σου.
38 ὁ δὲ Ἰησοῦς εἶπεν αὐτοῖς·
οὐκ οἴδατε τί αἰτεῖσθε.

Matthew	Mark
δύνασθε πιεῖν τὸ ποτήριον	δύνασθε πιεῖν τὸ ποτήριον
ὃ ἐγὼ μέλλω πίνειν;	ὃ ἐγὼ πίνω
	ἢ τὸ βάπτισμα ὃ ἐγὼ βαπτίζομαι
	βαπτισθῆναι;
λέγουσιν αὐτῷ·	39 οἱ δὲ εἶπαν αὐτῷ·
Δυνάμεθα ...	Δυνάμεθα ...

A comparison of the Markan and Matthean texts reveals a number of minor differences in the opening of this pericope which tells of the request made of Jesus that two of his disciples be given seats at his right and left hand in the messianic fulfilment of his mission. Whereas Mark begins with the phrase καὶ προσπορεύονται αὐτῷ, the Matthean introduction points to redactional activity. The adverb τότε is clearly redactional,[1] as is the phrase προσῆλθεν αὐτῷ to introduce someone into the presence of Jesus.[2] In the Matthean account, however, the person introduced is ἡ μήτηρ τῶν υἱῶν Ζεβεδαίου to which is added μετὰ τῶν υἱῶν αὐτῆς. In the Markan text it is Ἰάκωβος καὶ Ἰωάννης οἱ υἱοὶ Ζεβεδαίου. We have seen that the introductory phrase reveals Matthean redaction, but with regard to the naming of the characters involved, we shall have to search further.

In the early part of the gospel, Matthew can be said to parallel Mark in relation to the use of the designation "sons of Zebedee" and the naming of the two James and John (cf. Matt 4:21 parl. Mark 1:19-20; Matt 10:2 parl. Mark 3:17). At Matt 20:20, however, where Mark in the parallel story names "James and John, the sons of Zebedee" as the ones who approach Jesus with the question regarding a place in the messianic fulfilment of the βασιλεία which Jesus preached, the Matthean redaction has the question come from the "mother of the sons of Zebedee ... with her sons". Later in the garden scene, Mark names James and John as two of the disciples who accompany Jesus (14:33), whereas Matthew omits the names, and simply uses the designation "sons of Zebedee" (26:37). Finally, at the cross, the third woman who is named "Salome" by Mark (15:40), is given the title "mother of the sons of Zebedee" in Matthew (27:56). This seems to suggest a redactional linking of mother and sons in the second part of the Matthean gospel. Whether such a link was made during the final redaction of the gospel or within the

---

1 Luz, *Evangelium*, 52, and Neirynck and van Segroeck, *New Testament Vocabulary*, 324, both give the statistical occurrence of this word across the synoptics as 90,6,15. In Luz' analysis, he considers more than 80 of the Matthean occurrences to be redactional.
2 This formula or a slight variation of it is found 30 times in Matthew's gospel to introduce a character or characters into the presence of Jesus whereas it occurs only twice in Mark.

community traditioning process is difficult to determine accurately, but whatever its origin, it has been carefully incorporated into the final text.[3]

Verse 21 of the Matthean text is clearly a conversation between Jesus and the woman as the second person singular of the verb θέλω [θέλεις] indicates. When we come to v. 22, however, the texts parallel one another quite closely as is indicated by the verbs in the second person plural [οἴδατε, αἰτεῖσθε, δύνασθε] and the reply [δυνάμεθα]. It would seem, therefore, that in the Matthean account, the disciples are included in the conversation from this point onward.[4] In subsequent verses, the close parallel between the Markan and Matthean texts continues. This suggests that traditional or redactional material regarding the mother of the sons of Zebedee as the questioner of Jesus has been introduced and that this material merely changes the opening verses of a story whose source is the Markan text.

The mother of the sons approaches Jesus, kneeling before him with a request as did the Canaanite woman (15:25),[5] an approach which suggests that women were among the company of Jesus as he moved toward Jerusalem.[6] The contrast, however, between the Canaanite woman and the mother of the sons of Zebedee is clear from the beginning. Whereas the Canaanite woman cries out her request at the outset regardless of societal barriers, the mother of the sons of Zebedee who is presented within the confines of the patriarchal familial structure, approaches Jesus, but does not present her request until after Jesus initiates the dialogue: τί θέλεις; (20:21). It is then that she makes her request, not on her own behalf but on behalf of her sons: "Command that these two sons of mine may sit, one at your right hand and one at your left, in your kingdom [βασιλεία]." What she asks is not healing but rather "authority" (v. 25) and "greatness" (v. 26) for her sons.

---

3   Lagrange, *Evangile*, 392, and Lohmeyer, *Matthäus*, 291, both consider that a separate tradition had developed in the Matthean community which was combined with the Markan story. Schweizer, *The Good News*, 398, considers that Matthew corrected Mark in the opening verses but then went on to borrow the Markan account unchanged.

4   For most scholars, the addressees of v. 22 are the disciples only, see McNeile, *Matthew*, 289; Meier, *Matthew*, 228; Klostermann, *Matthäusevangelium*, 163; Hill, *The Gospel*, 288; Jones, *Matthew*, 225; Grundmann, *Matthäus*, 444; Filson, *The Gospel*, 216; and Beare, *A Commentary*, 405. Only Plummer, *Exegetical Commentary*, 277, considers the addressees to be the woman and her sons. Both Gundry and Hill point to the addition of the mother as secondary on the very grounds that Matthew reverts to the plural verbs, but they do not advert to the possibility that the woman may well be included in the address.

5   In this way, she can certainly be seen in the line of Israelite mothers, cf. Grundmann, *Matthäus*, 444. In this regard, Schweizer, *The Good News*, 397, cites 1 Sam 1 and 2 Mac 7. Meier, *Matthew*, 227, sees her request as being reminiscent of Bathsheba who pleads with David for her son Solomon (1 Kgs 1).

6   McNeile, *Matthew*, 287; and Schweizer, *The Good News*, 397.

The Markan reply, οὐκ οἴδατε τί αἰτεῖσθε, which is taken up in Matthew in v. 22, clearly refers to the mother and her sons. The three do not understand the implications of the request. To the three, Jesus addresses his question: δύνασθε πιεῖν τὸ ποτήριον ὃ ἐγὼ μέλλω πίνειν; This is an invitation to enter into a new stage of discipleship which will lead to a sharing in Jesus' own journey as v. 28 indicates. To this request, both mother and sons answer: δυνάμεθα.

As the story unfolds, however, the sons, who are invited to join Jesus in his last agonizing prayer that the cup [ποτήριον] pass him by (26:36-46), fail to respond to this invitation and, in fact, immediately following upon Jesus' arrest, they flee (26:56). Only the mother remains faithful to her affirmation and stands with Jesus at the foot of his cross. Within the Matthean redaction she is presented as misunderstanding the nature of the mission of Jesus, but as she goes on with her sons to listen to the remainder of Jesus' teaching (vv. 23, 25-28), she comes to an understanding which leads to the cross.[7] She stands, therefore, within the Matthean narrative, as a model of the woman who is identified first according to her place within the patriarchal family structure but who moves beyond this, as a result of her encounter with Jesus, to become a faithful member of the community around Jesus, recognized not according to patriarchal role models, but according to signs of discipleship--following and serving (27:55).

Such a tradition may well have had its origin, as some have suggested, in an attempt to present the disciples in a favourable light;[8] in a cultural presentation of a mother preserving the honour of her sons;[9] or in the preservation of a typical portrayal of woman as mother of significant sons.[10] Whatever its origin, however, it seems that this tradition developed around the theme of discipleship and was linked with the women around the cross in order to present a model of women's discipleship which acclaimed their capacity to be free of the bounds of the patriarchal familial structure in response to the teachings of Jesus, in order to be disciples. It may well have been shaped, therefore, in that sector of the community

---

7   As such, she becomes a model of discipleship in the community, which, according to Grundmann, *Matthäus*, 443, is without hierarchy, this pericope forming the conclusion to the section 17:24-20:28 which he sees as addressing the question of order within the community.

8   See p. 120, n. 153 above.

9   See p. 119, nn. 151 and 152.

10 See p. 120, n. 154.

that supported women's inclusion and liberation from oppressive structures
in line with the teaching of Jesus. As such a tradition developed, it seems
that it highlighted the contrast between the response of the mother and her
sons. This is incorporated into the narrative in the final redactional process
in which the designation of James and John as "sons of Zebedee" in the
garden scene links that scene with 20:20-28. The final redaction would seem,
therefore, to support the inclusive nature of discipleship which the tradition
regarding the mother of the sons of Zebedee affirms together with its
liberating claims for women.

II. 26:6-13

It was argued in the narrative analysis in Chapter Two that the context of
26:6-13 is the entire passion-resurrection narrative (26-28), which is a well-
structured narrative unit. Among redaction critics, however, there exists a
variety of opinions regarding this structure. For some, Matt 26 and 27 comprise the passion account and Matt 28 the resurrection account, and the two
are considered separately.[11] Others take a more nuanced and yet related position. Gaechter, for example, makes a division at 27:62, calling 26:1-27:61
"Leidensbericht", and 27:62-28:20 "Auferstehungsbericht".[12] Donald Senior
argues that 27:55-56 represents the "terminal point" in the passion narrative
and that "a clean break in tempo and context separates the burial account
from the previous sequence."[13] His position has already been given consideration above where it was argued that the account of the women at the
cross (27:55-56) certainly does look back towards the crucifixion as he
suggests, but that it also looks forward to the resurrection and thus forms a
transition pericope which links the accounts of the passion and

---

11   Beare, A Commentary, 498; and Benoit, L'Evangile, 170. Albert Descamps, "Rédaction
      et christologie dans le récit matthéen de la Passion," in Didier, L'Evangile, 360, defends
      the omission of Matt 28 from his work on the grounds that the resurrection accounts
      reveal distinct traditions and are less "synoptic" than those of the passion.
12   Gaechter, Matthäus-Evangelium, 827, 942-945.
13   Senior, The Passion, 328-329. Grundmann, Matthäus, 563, also considers 27:56 as the
      close of the "Bericht von der Passion" but does not take it as a break in the overall
      structure of Matt 26-28.

resurrection.[14] Other variations on the structuring of Matt 26-28, especially its conclusion, have been discussed previously and it will suffice here to point out that, despite these variations, the unity of the three chapters is supported by a large number of scholars, often in their commentaries where structure is simply presumed without further discussion.[15]

The narrative structure illustrated above in Diagram 8[16] can be further verified from a redactional perspective. The opening verse of the passion narrative in Matthew is purely redactional. The formula καὶ ἐγένετο ὅτε ἐτέλεσεν ὁ Ἰησοῦς πάντας τοὺς λόγους τούτους of 26:1a follows a similar pattern to that used in 7:28; 11:1; 13:53; and 19:1. Each time it is used, it provides a transition from discourse material to the narrative which follows. Since 26:1 is the last occurrence of the phrase, πάντας is added in order to conclude all the discourse material and to lead into the final narrative.[17] Thus, there is a hint at the outset that we are moving into the concluding narrative. This is even further substantiated when one notices the similarities between the vocabulary of 26:1a and the LXX rendition of Deut 31:1-2; 32:44b, 45-46, the conclusion of Moses' discourse before ascending Mount Nebo prior to his death.[18] The transition formula in Matthew, however, leads not into the time indication of Mark 14:1, but rather into a direct address by Jesus to his disciples which includes the time indication in Jesus' words but which also contains a further prediction of the passion.

In a manner typical of the Matthean redaction, the name of Jesus is introduced at the very beginning of the passion account so that he stands out as the chief actor, whereas in Mark the first characters to be mentioned are the chief priests and scribes (cf. Matt 26:1a; Mark 14:1b). In these opening

---

14   Gaechter, *Matthäus-Evangelium*, 935, also argues for the transitional nature of 27:55-61 which refers back to 27:38-54 and forward to 28:1, 5-8.

15   Argyle, *The Gospel*; Bonnard, *Évangile*; Filson, The *Gospel*, 22-23; Grundmann, *Matthäus*, xii-xiii; Lagrange, *Evangile*, 490; Loymeyer, *Matthäus*; McNeile, *Matthew*; Meier, *Matthew*; Sabourin, *L'Evangile*, 333; and Schweizer, *The Good News*, 483. N. A. Dahl, at the conclusion of his article, "Die Passionsgeschichte bei Matthäus," *NTS* 2 (1955-56): 17-32, does give reasons for his conclusion that Matt 26-28 as a unity brings to a close the account of the teaching activity of Jesus, and he cites several links with the concluding chapters of Deuteronomy. His position is based on the division of Matthew's gospel into five books with a prologue and epilogue according to the plan of Benjamin Bacon. Albert Vanhoye, on the other hand, argues for the unity of the passion and resurrection in Matthew's gospel on theological grounds in his article, "Structure et théologie des récits de la passion dans les évangiles synoptiques," *NRTh* 89 (1967): 135-163, especially pp. 136, 138.

16   See p. 123.

17   Senior, *The Passion*, 9-13, provides a very detailed study of the various scholarly interpretations of this phrase.

18   Ibid., 14-15, and Dahl, "Passionsgeschichte," 29, n. 3.

verses, Jesus speaks with authority to his disciples regarding his impending death. Similarly, the gospel closes with the same voice of authority being heard as Jesus commissions the disciples to a universal mission--to make disciples, to baptize and to teach all [πάντα] that Jesus had commanded (28:18-20). The narrative states that, prior to his passion, Jesus concluded πάντας τοὺς λόγους τούτους, and it is these words which the disciples are commissioned to pass on subsequent to his passion and resurrection. Hence Jesus' own words of authority addressed to his disciples and reference to his authoritative teaching frame the account of the passion and resurrection.[19]

In the second scene of the opening overture (26:3-4), Matthew contains an expanded reference to the plotting of the chief priests and scribes (in Matthew, "elders of the people" rather than "scribes") in comparison with the opening of the Markan passion account. Matt 26:4 closely parallels Mark 14:1b-2 except for the naming of the Jewish leaders who are included in the opening verse of this scenario in Matthew. The language of vv. 3-4a--the naming of the leadership group [ἀρχιερεῖς and πρεσβύτεροι], their gathering together [συνήχθησαν], and their taking counsel [συνεβουλεύσαντο]--parallels that of Matt 28:11b-12, the opening verses of the second last scene of the gospel in which the chief priests and elders continue to plot against Jesus even after his death. The names of the leaders are the same as is the use of the verb συνάγω, and where the verb συμβουλεύω is used in 26:4a, the corresponding noun [συμβούλιον] is used in 28:12. It seems, therefore, at least at the level of the final redaction, a clear parallel was made between these two scenes, thereby strengthening the relationship between the beginning and end of the passion-resurrection account and pointing towards a unified narrative encompassing Matt 26-28.

The third scene in Matthew's overture parallels very closely the second scene in Mark, namely, the anointing of Jesus by the woman at Bethany. While there are no direct literary parallels between this scene in Matthew and that just prior to the plotting of the chief priests and elders at the end of

---

19 A question arises here regarding the source of this Matthean redaction. If 28:16-20 was drawn from the traditions within the Matthean community, then it could be argued that 26:1b-2 may have belonged to a similar tradition or was developed in the final redaction to parallel the closing verses of the gospel. However, since many exegetes argue for the redactional quality of both passages, it could be concluded, contrary to Senior, *The Passion*, 20, that 26:1b-2 was inspired by the final redaction of the conclusion of the gospel rather than that it was based on a reference to the plotting of the scribes in Mark 14:1b-2. For a fuller discussion of the opinion of various scholars as to the origin of 28:16-20, see Pheme Perkins, *Resurrection: New Testament Witness and Contemporary Reflection* (Garden City, New York: Doubleday, 1984), 146, n. 71.

the gospel, namely, the appearance of Jesus to the women (28:9-10), it could be argued that a parallelism exists, as in the previous two parallels discussed above, on the level of characters. In both we find a woman or women in direct relationship with Jesus. In the first, a woman pours ointment over the head of Jesus as a sign of recognition of his impending passion and death, while in the second the two women fall at the feet of the risen Jesus and worship him in recognition of his resurrection. A cursory glance would seem to suggest that the tradition behind Matt 28:9-10 is clearly Matthean, and has its place here by virtue of the final redaction.

This brief redactional survey of the opening and closing scenes of the Matthean gospel suggests that the structure determined earlier from a narrative-critical perspective was a result of the final redaction. Around the account of the passion and resurrection of Jesus, Matthean redaction has placed a three-pronged inclusion: Jesus instructing his disciples, the leaders plotting against him, and women recognizing and acknowledging Jesus' death and resurrection. Within the overture, the chief *dramatis personae* (Jesus, the disciples, the Jewish leaders and a woman) enter the scene for the final scenario, which will be played out within the last chapters of the gospel until members of each of these character groups leave the scene in the reverse order from which they entered, bringing the gospel to a close.

A brief glance at Diagram 8 will show further that a number of narrative threads which are highlighted within the frame surrounding the passion-resurrection narrative are then played out within the broader narrative thus strengthening the unity established by way of the frame itself. One of the disciples betrays Jesus, another denies him and all flee until they are presumably summoned by the women to the mountain in Galilee to receive their final commission. The leaders continue their plotting against Jesus throughout the entire scene even beyond the resurrection. Women are sensitive to Jesus' impending death, are present at the crucifixion and burial of Jesus, witness the empty tomb and finally encounter the risen Jesus.

In concluding this brief survey of the context of 26:6-13, it should be noted, that a feminist analysis which draws attention to the women characters has enabled us to see that it was not only the accounts of the two character groups, disciples and leaders, which influenced the structuring of the Matthean passion-resurrection account. The stories of women have also significantly shaped the narrative. In the light of this, the Matthean redaction of the individual pericopes in which they function as characters will be significant.

A. Comparison of Synoptic Texts

Matt 26:6-13	Mark 14:3-9	Luke 7:36-50	John 12:1-8
6 Τοῦ δὲ Ἰησοῦ γενομένου	3 Καὶ ὄντος αὐτοῦ		1 Ὁ οὖν Ἰησοῦς πρὸ ἓξ ἡμερῶν τοῦ πάσχα ἦλθεν
ἐν Βηθανίᾳ	ἐν Βηθανίᾳ		εἰς Βηθανίαν,
		40 καὶ ἀποκριθεὶς ὁ Ἰησοῦς εἶπεν πρὸς αὐτόν,	
ἐν οἰκίᾳ Σίμωνος τοῦ λεπροῦ,	ἐν τῇ οἰκίᾳ Σίμωνος τοῦ λεπροῦ,	Σίμων ...	
			ὅπου ἦν Λάζαρος, ὃν ἤγειρεν ἐκ νεκρῶν Ἰησοῦς.
		36 ἠρώτα δέ τις αὐτὸν τῶν Φαρισαίων ἵνα φάγῃ μετ’ αὐτοῦ,	2 ἐποίησαν οὖν αὐτῷ
			δεῖπνον ἐκεῖ, καὶ ἡ Μάρθα διηκόνει, ὁ δὲ Λάζαρος εἷς ἦν ἐκ
	κατακειμένου αὐτοῦ	καὶ εἰσελθὼν εἰς τὸν οἶκον τοῦ Φαρισαίου κατεκλίθη.	τῶν ἀνακειμένων σὺν αὐτῷ.
7 προσῆλθεν αὐτῷ γυνὴ	ἦλθεν γυνὴ	37 καὶ ἰδοὺ γυνὴ ἥτις ἦν ἐν τῇ πόλει ἁμαρτωλός, καὶ ἐπιγνοῦσα ὅτι κατάκειται ἐν τῇ οἰκίᾳ τοῦ Φαρισαίου,	3 ἡ οὖν Μαριὰμ
ἔχουσα ἀλάβαστρον μύρου βαρυτίμου	ἔχουσα ἀλάβαστρον μύρου νάρδου πιστικῆς πολυτελοῦς, συντρίψασα τὴν ἀλάβαστρον	κομίσασα ἀλάβαστρον μύρου	λαβοῦσα λίτραν μύρου νάρδου πιστικῆς πολυτίμου
καὶ κατέχεεν ἐπὶ τῆς κεφαλῆς αὐτου ἀνακειμένου.	κατέχεεν αὐτοῦ τῆς κεφαλῆς.		
		38 καὶ στᾶσα ὀπίσω παρὰ τοὺς πόδας αὐτοῦ κλαίουσα τοῖς δάκρυσιν ἤρξατο βρέχειν τοὺς πόδας αὐτοῦ καὶ ταῖς θριξὶν τῆς κεφαλῆς αὐτῆς ἐξέμασσεν	ἤλειψεν τοὺς πόδας τοῦ Ἰησοῦ
		καὶ κατεφίλει τοὺς πόδας αὐτοῦ καὶ ἤλειφεν τῷ μύρῳ. ...	καὶ ἐξέμαξεν ταῖς θριξὶν αὐτῆς τοὺς πόδας αὐτοῦ·

Matt	Mark	Luke	John
			ἡ δὲ οἰκία ἐπληρώθη ἐκ τῆς ὀσμῆς τοῦ μύρου.
8 ἰδόντες δὲ	4 ἦσαν δέ		4 λέγει δὲ Ἰούδας ὁ Ἰσκαριώτης εἷς [ἐκ]
οἱ μαθηταὶ	τινες		τῶν μαθητῶν αὐτοῦ, ὁ μέλλων αὐτὸν παραδιδόναι·
ἠγανάκτησαν	ἀγανακτοῦντες πρὸς ἑαυτούς·		
λέγοντες· εἰς τί ἡ ἀπώλεια αὕτη;	εἰς τί ἡ ἀπώλεια αὕτη τοῦ μύρου γέγονεν;		5 διὰ τί
9 ἐδύνατο γὰρ τοῦτο πραθῆναι πολλοῦ	5 ἠδύνατο γὰρ τοῦτο τὸ μύρον πραθῆναι ἐπάνω δηναρίων τριακοσίων		τοῦτο τὸ μύρον οὐκ ἐπράθη τριακοσίων δηναρίων
καὶ δοθῆναι πτωχοῖς.	καὶ δοθῆναι τοῖς πτωχοῖς· καὶ ἐνεβριμῶντο αὐτῇ.		καὶ ἐδόθη πτωχοῖς;
			6 εἶπεν δὲ τοῦτο οὐχ ὅτι περὶ τῶν πτωχῶν ἔμελεν αὐτῷ, ἀλλ' ὅτι κλέπτης ἦν καὶ τὸ γλωσσόκομον ἔχων τὰ βαλλόμενα ἐβάσταζεν.
10 γνοὺς δὲ ὁ Ἰησοῦς εἶπεν αὐτοῖς· τί κόπους παρέχετε τῇ γυναικί; ἔργον γὰρ καλὸν ἠργάσατο εἰς ἐμέ·	6 ὁ δὲ Ἰησοῦς εἶπεν, ἄφετε αὐτήν· τί αὐτῇ κόπους παρέχετε; καλὸν ἔργον ἠργάσατο ἐν ἐμοί·		7 εἶπεν οὖν ὁ Ἰησοῦς· Ἄφες αὐτήν,
			ἵνα εἰς τὴν ἡμέραν τοῦ ἐνταφιασμοῦ μου τηρήσῃ αὐτό.
11 πάντοτε γὰρ τοὺς πτωχοὺς ἔχετε μεθ' ἑαυτῶν,	7 πάντοτε γὰρ τοὺς πτωχοὺς ἔχετε μεθ' ἑαυτῶν καὶ ὅταν θέλητε δύνασθε αὐτοῖς εὖ ποιῆσαι,		8 τοὺς πτωχοὺς γὰρ πάντοτε ἔχετε μεθ' ἑαυτῶν,
ἐμὲ δὲ οὐ πάντοτε ἔχετε·	ἐμὲ δὲ οὐ πάντοτε ἔχετε. 8 ὃ ἔσχεν ἐποίησεν·		ἐμὲ δὲ οὐ πάντοτε ἔχετε.
12 βαλοῦσα γὰρ αὕτη τὸ μύρον τοῦτο ἐπὶ τοῦ σώματός μου πρὸς τὸ ἐνταφιάσαι με ἐποίησεν.	προέλαβεν μυρίσαι τὸ σῶμά μου εἰς τὸν ἐνταφιασμόν.		

Matt	Mark
13 ἀμὴν λέγω ὑμῖν,	9 ἀμὴν δὲ λέγω ὑμῖν,
ὅπου ἐὰν κηρυχθῇ	ὅπου ἐὰν κηρυχθῇ
τὸ εὐαγγέλιον τοῦτο	τὸ εὐαγγέλιον
ἐν ὅλῳ τῷ κόσμῳ,	εἰς ὅλον τὸν κόσμον,
λαληθήσεται καὶ	καὶ
ὃ ἐποίησεν αὕτη	ὃ ἐποίησεν αὕτη
	λαληθήσεται
εἰς μνημόσυνον	εἰς μνημόσυνον
αὐτῆς.	αὐτῆς.

The earlier narrative-critical analysis of this pericope showed that the Matthean text was carefully constructed around the action of the woman who anointed Jesus and the reactions to this on the part of the disciples and Jesus. That structure was represented diagramatically and it will serve the purpose of our analysis to repeat the diagram here for easier reference.

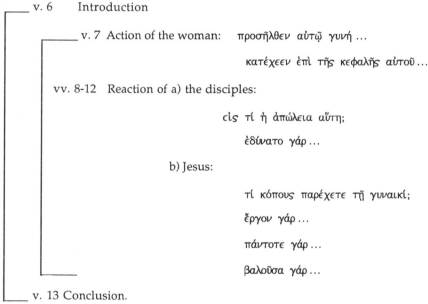

v. 6   Introduction

v. 7 Action of the woman: προσῆλθεν αὐτῷ γυνή ...

κατέχεεν ἐπὶ τῆς κεφαλῆς αὐτοῦ...

vv. 8-12   Reaction of a) the disciples:

εἰς τί ἡ ἀπώλεια αὕτη;

ἐδύνατο γάρ ...

b) Jesus:

τί κόπους παρέχετε τῇ γυναικί;

ἔργον γάρ ...

πάντοτε γάρ ...

βαλοῦσα γάρ ...

v. 13 Conclusion.

Diagram 9

When the Matthean story is compared with the similar accounts in Mark 14:3-9; John 12:1-8; and perhaps Luke 7:36-50,[20] a brief glance shows

---

20   The question of the relationship between the four accounts of the anointing is complex and can certainly not be summed up as facilely as does Elliott, "The Anointing," 105, when he claims that "it is generally agreed among scholars that all four accounts relate the same episode." M.-J. Lagrange, "Jésus a-t-il été oint plusieurs fois et par plusieurs femmes? Opinions des anciens écrivains ecclésiastiques (Luc, 7,36-50; Matthieu, 26,6-13; Marc, 14,3-9; Jean, 12,1-8), cf. Jean, 11,2," *RB* 9 (1912): 504-532, reviews in detail the opinions of the early church writers on this question and discovers that there was no agreed upon position among them and that none of them calls on a traditional memory, but

that, in terms of the structuring of the story and literary dependence, the closest relationship exists between Mark and Matthew.[21] Therefore, as Matthew's structuring is discussed in more detail, it will be done in relation to the Markan story.

In the introduction to the story, the Matthean text typically names Jesus so that the focus of the story is on him as the chief actor from the outset [Τοῦ δὲ 'Ιησοῦ γενομένου ἐν Βηθανίᾳ ...]. Furthermore, there is not the double genitive absolute of Mark 14:3, so that the action moves immediately from the location in the house of Simon to the entry of the woman.[22] As can be seen in the diagram above, the two main verbs of v. 7 are oriented towards Jesus.[23] Matthew contains αὐτῷ after the first verb [προσῆλθεν] emphasizing this orientation and also there is no descriptive detail in the participial phrase describing the ointment. The connective καί before the second main verb [κατέχεεν] draws attention to the verbs so that they stand out clearly in the text.

Two principles seem to have guided the final Matthean redaction in vv. 8-12. First, there is no descriptive detail which would distract from the clear focus of the pericope. There is no interaction between the disciples and the woman (cf. Mark 14:5c, καὶ ἐνεβριμῶντο αὐτῇ; and 14:6a, ἄφετε αὐτήν) so that the words of Jesus and of the disciples are all directed towards the action. Repetition of μύρον is avoided (cf. Mark 14:4b, 5a), and details like the price of the sale are absent (cf. Mark 14:5a). Second, what could be seen as minor

that in the popular memory, the stories were united. Robert Holst, "The One Anointing of Jesus: Another Application of the Form-Critical Method," *JBL* 95 (1976): 435-446, argues for one incident with changes occurring in the developing tradition as does Claus-Peter März, "Zur Traditionsgeschichte von Mk 14, 3-9 und Parallelen," *SNTU* A/6-7 (1981-82): 89-112, with both offering significantly nuanced arguments. A. Legault, "An Application of the Form-Critique Method to the Anointings in Galilee (Lk 7.36-50) and Bethany (Mt 26.6-13; Mk 14.3-9; Jn 12.1-8)," *CBQ* 16 (1954): 131-145, argues for two distinct scenes, and in this, he relies on the position of Benoit, *L'Evangile*, 157, who says of Luke 7:36-50, that it is "foncièrement différent", and of Feuillet, "Deux onctions". Boismard, *Synopse*, 371, considers that there were two events as do Meier, *Matthew*, 312, and Plummer, *Exegetical Commentary*, 385; while Durand, *Evangile*, 422, speaks of two events but a single woman.

21 Beare, *A Commentary*, 504, notes that Matthew keeps closely to the Markan *form* of the story. Gundry, *A Commentary*, 519, says explicitly that Matthew follows Mark, but also that "discussion of the great differences in Luke 7:36-50 belongs in commentaries on Mark and Luke"; and that John 12:1-8 offers little if anything for the elucidation of the Matthean text. I must concur with him on his second point and also limit the following discussion to a detailed analysis of the relationships between the Markan and Matthean forms of the story with little further reference to either Luke or John.

22 The second genitive absolute in Mark, κατακειμένου αὐτοῦ, occurs at the end of v. 7 in Matthew and has been changed to ἀνακειμένου.

23 Gnilka, *Matthäusevangelium*, II, 386, understands the entire Matthean redaction as a concentration on Jesus.

structural elements in the Markan text seem to be used very intentionally in favour of structure in the Matthean account. This is clear in relation to the τί ... γάρ phrase. It appears in both Mark 14:4-5 and 6-7; but it comes into much clearer focus in Matthew because, in 26:8-9, there is no intervening phrase between the εἰς τί ἡ ἀπώλεια αὕτη and ἐδύνατο γάρ. Moreover, in vv. 10-12, γάρ is repeated three times following the τί κόπους question so that Jesus' threefold interpretation of the woman's action is clearly delineated.[24] Mark, on the other hand, has only one of the three interpretations introduced by γάρ, leaving the second part of the pericope much less structured than the parallel in Matthew. Finally, in both the Matthean and Markan accounts, the final verse functions as a conclusion to the entire pericope.

The above analysis suggests that the more biographical and descriptive account in Mark[25] has been given a tighter structure in the Matthean redaction rather than *vice versa*. This, together with a recognition of the strong literary dependency which exists between the two accounts, suggests that the primary source for the Matthean account is Mark's text. Such a position is simply accepted by a number of scholars without comment.[26] Boismard, however, claims that there are two shorter stories which lie behind the Markan text, one of which influenced an earlier redaction of Matthew but whose only trace now is in the phrase τί κόπους παρέχετε τῇ γυναικί.[27] With little concrete evidence for such a claim, it seems simpler to accept the single Markan source as the basis for an analysis of the Matthean story. Boismard's position, however, acts as a reminder that, even though the final account in Matthew may be drawn primarily from the Markan text, more than one account of this story and others may have been transmitted orally in the community over a number of years and that traces of these different memories may be seen in their final rendition alongside the simple redaction of the Markan text.[28]

---

24 Lohmeyer, *Matthäus*, 349, notes this three-fold usage but does not make any interpretive comment with regard to it.
25 Bultmann, *History*, 37, 263.
26 Feuillet, "Deux onctions," 368; März, "Traditionsgeschichte," 90; and Elliott, "The Anointing," 107, all dismiss the relationship between Matthew and Mark in a sentence although they give detailed attention to the possible literary connections between Mark, Luke and John. See also Lagrange, *Evangile*, 505; Bonnard, *Évangile*, 370; Gundry, *A Commentary*, 519; Gnilka, *Matthäusevangelium*, II, 385; and Grundmann, *Matthäus*, 537, who says that "Matthäus übernimmt Stellung und Inhalt des Textes von Markus."
27 Boismard, *Synopse*, 373.
28 This is the position taken by Dahl, "Passionsgeschichte," 18, 20; and Descamps, "Rédaction," 39, whereas Senior, *The Passion*, would argue for a strictly Matthean

Matthean dependence on Mark is further substantiated when one considers the claim that the story of the anointing is misplaced in Mark and Matthew.[29] It is true that in both gospels, the account of the betrayal by Judas could be read immediately following the plotting of the high priests without any break in the narrative, suggesting that the story of the anointing may have been inserted into an already existing narrative at a certain point in its development. A consideration, however, of the integral part played by the anointing story in the overall structure of the passion-resurrection account in Matthew's gospel would seem to indicate that the impressive framework evidenced in the previous narrative analysis was built on the foundations of the Markan text rather than that the Markan redaction broke down such a structure omitting many of its elements.[30] Hence our argument for Matthean dependence on Mark is further strengthened. Should there have been a different ordering of the opening pericopes, it must have occurred prior to the Markan text with little evidence of it remaining in the Matthean narrative. From this position, we can turn now to a more detailed redactional analysis of the text.

B. Redaction

Matthew's pericope opens with the adversative δέ plus a genitive absolute in contrast to Mark's καί (Matt 26:6; Mark 14:3). Supported by a lengthy discussion in a footnote, Senior concludes that such a change is "habitual on the part of the redactor."[31] While the evidence certainly supports this, a closer examination may reveal that considerations other than simply literary habit may have governed the Matthean change here. Following Jesus'

---

redaction of the Markan text. This question will need to be considered again when the tradition history of the individual pericopes within the passion-resurrection account is examined after the detailed analysis of each text which is to follow.

29 Beare, *A Commentary*, 505; McNeile, *Matthew*, 374; and Elliott, "The Anointing," 106. For a detailed discussion, see Senior, *The Passion*, 28, n. 1.

30 Gaechter, *Matthäus-Evangelium*, 827, points to the careful structuring of 26:1-35, which links the introductory scenes into the passion proper. In his structure, the meal at Bethany and Jesus' final meal with the disciples (26:6-13 and 26:26-30) are parallel, and constitute the centre-point in their respective sections: An Introduction to the Paschal Meal (26:1-19) and the Paschal Meal (26:20-35). Lagrange, *Evangile*, 492, also recognizes that both Matthew and Mark integrate this pericope into their passion accounts, but he goes on to say that "cela se comprehend mieux dans Mt. après la prophétie de Jésus car l'onction est comme une prophétie en action de la passion prochaine."

31 Senior, *The Passion*, 29, and especially n. 4.

prediction of his sufferings in vv. 1-2, two scenes of plotting (3-5) and betrayal (14-16) are introduced by the connective τότε, thus providing a significant link between the three scenes.[32] Within this movement of events, however, stands the account of the anointing of Jesus by the woman at Bethany, a scene which is in direct contrast to those introduced by τότε, and hence the adversative δέ may have been used to highlight this contrast.[33] Similarly, in the closing scenes of the gospel, the appearances of Jesus to the women and to the Eleven are contrasted with the final plotting of the leaders, and this contrasting pericope is introduced by δέ. In both segments of the frame around the passion-resurrection narrative, therefore, contrasting pericopes are set off from those surrounding them by the adversative δέ,[34] and this would seem to be the result of the final redaction.

We have already noted the typical introduction of the name of Jesus at the beginning of the scene in contrast to Mark, and here it seems most appropriate when the remaining characters are highlighted as they enter the scene--γυνή (v. 7), and οἱ μαθηταί (v. 8).[35] The location of the scene at Bethany in the house of Simon the leper is taken over directly from Mark, but in the context of the Matthean gospel may be intended to symbolize the restored community of believers gathered around Jesus.

The second genitive absolute, κατακειμένου αὐτοῦ is moved to the end of the sentence, and changed to ἀνακειμένου.[36] This change of position of the phrase highlights the approach of the woman at this point in the narrative, and the change of word may suggest a Matthean link between this supper and that which Jesus will celebrate immediately before his arrest. In the Matthean account of the second supper, the scene opens with Jesus seated at table [ἀνέκειτο] (26:20).[37] The verb ἀνάκειμαι also refers to the restored

---

32   Ibid., 22-23, and n. 6.

33   Gundry, A Commentary, 519; and Meier, Matthew, 312.

34   Gnilka, Matthäusevangelium, II, 388, says of the passion narrative generally that "die Frauen schneiden in der Passion weitaus besser ab als die Männer. Sie sind tapferer und treuer."

35   Most commentators give slightly different nuances to this aspect of the Matthean redaction: Senior, The Passion, 30, says it gives the scene "more intrinsic coherence"; Gundry, A Commentary, 519, points to "a Christological emphasis"; and Descamps, "Rédaction," 373, sees the name of Jesus "comme sujet de l'action principale". All, however, point towards the central focus which Matthew gives to the person of Jesus throughout the entire passion narrative.

36   Senior, The Passion, 32, notes that "the verb ἀνάκειμαι is used consistently by Matthew to designate an attitude of repose at a meal, while κατάκειμαι seems to be considered more applicable to sick persons."

37   In the Markan account of the supper, Jesus comes with the twelve (14:17) and in the subsequent verse is seated with them at table (14:18). The Markan text does not seem to highlight the parallel between the two accounts as does the Matthean.

community around Jesus since it was used in 9:10, where Jesus sits at table with taxcollectors and sinners, and in the symbolic or parabolic language of 22:10, the good and the bad sit down at table at the marriage feast of the king's son. This Matthean redaction would seem to suggest both these links.

The typical phrase προσῆλθεν αὐτῷ introduces the woman into the scene where Jesus is present;[38] but the description of the woman [γυνὴ ἔχουσα ἀλάβαστρον μύρου βαρυτίμου] is taken over from the Markan text and in its simplicity, it prepares the reader for the action to follow.[39] The woman anoints the head of Jesus with the perfumed ointment [καὶ κατέχεεν ἐπὶ τῆς κεφαλῆς αὐτοῦ].

In a lengthy discussion above it was shown that the language used in both Mark and Matthew is not typical of cultic anointings but that the action itself has strong overtones of such.[40] Hence, two possible lines of argument begin to emerge. On the one hand, it could be argued that even by the time the story found its way into the Markan gospel, the traces of an historical memory of a woman's anointing of Jesus at a meal, thus acknowledging prophetically and symbolically his Messiahship, are presented in the less threatening language of showing honour and love and praying for his prosperity as he faces death. On the other hand, it is possible that the historical memory was simply that of an anointing which paid homage to Jesus.[41]

---

38   Senior, *The Passion*, 30-31, and especially n. 5. Normally this phrase introduces supplicants to Jesus.

39   The Matthean redaction simplifies the Markan text by removing the duplicate expression νάρδου πιστικῆς and the Markan *hapax legomenon* πολυτελοῦς is replaced by another *hapax legomenon* βαρυτίμου. It should be noted here that several witnesses--ℵ A D L Θ 33. 565. 892. 1010. 1424 *al* sy^hmg --read πολυτίμου in place of βαρυτίμου but this would seem to be a harmonization with Mark. See Senior, *The Passion*, 31, n. 4.

40   See pp. 126-128 above. Scholars have readily interpreted the action of the woman as a prophetic anointing of Jesus acknowledging his messiahship, see Beare, *A Commentary*, 506; Argyle, *The Gospel*, 196; and Schüssler Fiorenza, *In Memory of Her*, xiv. An interesting point is made by Sherman E. Johnson, "The Gospel according to St. Matthew. Introduction and Exegesis," *IntB* VII: 568, when he compares this pericope with that of Jesus' entry into Jerusalem (21:8) and other acclamations (16:16; 20:30-31), which he says indicate that "the common people wished Jesus to take over political control of the nation. The woman may even have hoped to force Jesus' hand. The anointing was in private, as in the case of Saul (1 Sam 10:1), Solomon (1 Kgs 1:38-39) and Jehu (2 Kgs 9:4-10); and this suggests the hope of a revolt or *coup d'etat*. Jesus, however, does not accept the acclamation and says, somewhat wryly, that it is an anointing for burial, not kingship. The evangelist did not understand the story." What Johnson has highlighted here is what shall be argued below, namely, that there are layers of development and interpretation of this story, some of which perhaps obscure the original political nature of the action as both he and Schüssler Fiorenza argue, even if from different perspectives.

41   Boismard, *Synopse*, 372, argues that--"A l'origine de ces récits, il y eut un événement très précis. Au cours d'un repas à Béthanie, une femme vint répandre sur la tête de

Since the first possibility is the least explored and the second offers less potential for explaining the strong indignation of the disciples or those present,[42] then we will do well to follow the line of the first suggestion.

We shall take as our working hypothesis that an extraordinary historical memory of a cultic anointing of Jesus by a woman is rendered in the language of honorific anointing as the story develops to the point of the Markan redaction. It is this which the Matthean redaction has taken over and highlighted by omission of supporting descriptive elements so that the action stands out in all its simplicity and directness. It is also reasonable to presume that the strong indignation of those present preserves an historical memory of the reaction to the woman's deed.

We must ask why those present at the meal were scandalized by the action of the woman. If the action of the woman were simply honorific or what would have been expected of a woman in an eastern home, then there seem to be fewer grounds for an indignant reaction from those present at the meal. Indignation, however, would have been the expected response if she, as a woman, had undertaken the prophetic function reserved for men, namely, that of anointing, thereby violating one of their "sacred" roles. If, as Boismard argues, this reaction was followed by a word of defense of the woman's action by Jesus, a word whose exact composition it is difficult to reestablish,[43] then we could argue that at the core of this pericope lies an historical memory which confirms earlier discoveries, namely, that the historical Jesus crossed social and religious boundaries in order to include women in the community developing around him and to establish that they were full participants in the βασιλεία which he was proclaiming and inaugurating. We could argue, further, however, that Jesus also confirmed the initiative and actions of those women who courageously crossed those same boundaries.

If such an historical memory lay behind this tradition then it most certainly was, as Schüssler Fiorenza points out, "a politically dangerous

---

Jésus un vase de parfum"--and he suggests that it was an honorific sign--"C'était là une marque d'honneur attestée dans la Bible (Ps 23:5; 92:11; 133:2; Qo 9:8; Am 6:6), et dont parlent les écrits rabbiniques." März, "Traditionsgeschichte," 94, also rules out the possibility of an early understanding of the event as an anointing of a King, anointing for burial or an aspect of cult and calls it simply an act of veneration.

42   Hill, The Gospel, 334, and Bonnard, Évangile, 371, both claim that the gesture of the woman would not have been extraordinary in an eastern home, but they do not provide any evidence to support such a claim.

43   Boismard, Synopse, 372.

story".[44] It is not surprising, therefore, that the language may have been modified and the reaction tempered by concern for the poor in order to distract from the volatile nature of that memory. It may then have been a modified form of the story that was taken over from Mark, but elements of the original memory are still retained in the action of pouring perfumed ointment over the head of Jesus. It is this form of the story that is incorporated into a theological context which repeatedly proclaims Jesus as the Χριστός, the Anointed One, the Messiah.[45]

Returning now to the work of Matthean redaction, we note that, at the beginning of v. 8, ἰδόντες δέ replaces ἦσαν δέ (ἦσαν being part of the periphrastic phrase ἦσαν ἀγανακτοῦντες), so that the attention of the disciples is directed onto the woman's action. Also the vague τινές (some) is changed to μαθηταί (disciples). For Senior, this

> attribution to the disciples of the mildly derogatory question about the waste of the ointment helps illustrate Matthew's balanced portrait of the disciples as representative Christians. The redactor's intent may well be to enable the words of Jesus to take on a more defined ecclesial dimension.[46]

While this is a valid analysis, it does not address the question which is of concern in this study, namely, did the fact that this story centred upon a woman character influence the change. Already, we have seen in our analysis of 15:21-28, that the disciples were introduced into that pericope as the ones who objected to the plea of the Canaanite woman, and it was suggested that this element of the tradition developed within a sector of the community that was opposed to the claim that the new participation of women in the social and religious life of the community was based on the praxis of Jesus. The same could also be claimed here, although it is less clear from the text whether we are dealing with community tradition or Matthean redaction. Even if it is the latter, however, it could be argued that the redactional process was influenced by the tension and conflict in the community that has already been discussed in previous chapters. Another element which may have influenced the change to "disciples" in this pericope is the close relationship that has been established between the beginning and end of the

---

44   Schüssler Fiorenza, *In Memory of Her*, xiv.
45   Matt 1:1, 16, 17, 18; 2:4; 11:2; 16:16, 20; 22:42; 23:10; 24:5, 23; 26:63, 68; 27:17, 22.
46   Senior, *The Passion*, 32-33. For a more detailed treatment of the theme of οἱ μαθηταί in Matthew, see his excursus, pp. 14-17. For Beare, *A Commentary*, 505, and Sabourin, *L'Évangile*, 338, the disciples are representative of the christian community while for Bonnard, *Évangile*, 371, and Hill, *The Gospel*, 333, they specifically represent the Matthean community.

passion-resurrection narrative. In the account of the resurrection, the women are given the commission to proclaim the resurrection to the disciples who are absent from the scene of the burial of Jesus because they have fled (26:56). Perhaps here, the way is being prepared for the great contrast between the response of the women and the response of the disciples to the passion of Jesus which will be illustrated throughout the narrative to follow.

The disciples' question εἰς τί ἡ ἀπώλεια αὕτη; is simplified, thus omitting Mark's τοῦ μύρου γέγονεν. A similar simplification occurs in v. 9 with the result that the τί ... γάρ construction in vv. 8b-9 stands out clearly:

εἰς τί ἡ ἀπώλεια αὕτη;
    ἐδύνατο γὰρ τοῦτο πραθῆναι πολλοῦ
    καὶ δοθῆναι πτωχοῖς.

Here, it appears that a Markan tradition whose origins are obscure has been taken over in the Matthean redaction. The linking of the question [εἰς τί ἡ ἀπώλεια αὕτη;] to the command to give to the poor has no attestation in the Hebrew Scriptures. Each time ἀπώλεια is used in the LXX, it carries the sense of destruction, loss, calamity, but never means a wasting of resources contrary to the command to care for the poor. Plummer notes also that in the Christian Scriptures generally, "waste" is hardly an adequate translation. "Destruction" is nearer to the meaning.[47] Hence, the question [εἰς τί ἡ ἀπώλεια αὕτη;] may have been attached to the indignation of those present in the early stages of the development of the tradition to capture something of the horror of the onlookers at the woman's supposedly presumptuous behaviour. Only later was the explanation regarding the poor added as a way of softening their indignant response and directing attention away from the extraordinary action of the woman.

Scholars argue for various origins of the concern for the poor. For Jeremias, it was Palestinian because of the Semitic distinction between almsgiving (*Almosen*) and good deeds (*Liebeswerk*).[48] Senior suggests that such a distinction may have been a matter of concern within the Matthean community, an explanation which, in fact, does not contradict Jeremias given the Jewish if not Palestinian influence on many sectors of the

---

47   Plummer, *Exegetical Commentary*, 355.
48   Joachim Jeremias, "Die Salbungsgeschichte Mc 14:3-9," *ZNW* 35 (1936): 75-82.

community.[49] Boismard, on the other hand, suggests that the concern for distribution to the poor within this story originated among gentile christians,[50] and we have already seen that such a concern is not alien to the theology of the final redaction.[51] Its origin, therefore, may have to remain obscure, but its incorporation into this story may well have been an attempt to temper a lavish and politically volatile action and response with a more "traditional" theological concern.

At the beginning of v. 10, Matthew has γνοὺς δέ referring to Jesus, a phrase which is difficult to explain, especially in the light of the redactional changes that were made in the previous two verses. Whereas Mark has those present speaking indignantly among themselves [πρὸς ἑαυτούς], in the Matthean text, the πρὸς ἑαυτούς is omitted and λέγοντες has been added so that it seems clear that Jesus would have known what the disciples were saying. Given this redactional activity, it is difficult, therefore, to agree with Senior who claims that the use of γνούς might imply "that Matthew considers the disciples' murmuring to have been kept to themselves, even though he has eliminated Mark's ambiguous πρὸς ἑαυτούς."[52] Rather, I would suggest that since the preceding verse seems to render the use of γνούς redundant, its presence prepares for what follows, namely, Jesus' prophetic interpretation of the woman's action. It therefore highlights Jesus' prophetic knowing.[53]

In light of the omission of καὶ ἐνεβριμῶντο αὐτῇ (and they rebuked her) from the previous verse, a similar omission of ἄφετε αὐτήν from v. 10 is easily explained in terms of the avoidance of any interaction or reference to interaction between the disciples and the woman which would distract from focus on the action which is central to the pericope. Jesus' question [τί κόπους παρέχετε τῇ γυναικί;] is taken over from Mark but the Matthean redaction replaces the pronoun αὐτῇ by τῇ γυναικί. This brings the focus of

---

49   Senior, *The Passion*, 33.
50   Boismard, *Synopse*, 372-373.
51   A brief survey of the justice aspect of Matthean theology especially with regard to "the poor" was undertaken earlier, see p. 130.
52   Senior, *The Passion*, 35, n. 2. Lagrange, *Evangile*, 492, calls it simply Matthean style and not an allusion to supernatural knowledge which is contrary to Meier, *Matthew*, 312, who sees it as indicating divine knowledge, but this seems to be too exaggerated. When it has been used previously in the gospel, it has, however, indicated Jesus' knowledge of some private or hidden fact (Matt 12:15; 16:8; 22:18).
53   There is no Septuagintal use of this phrase which would help to throw light on its use here. It appears only four times (Gen 38:9; 2 Esdr 5:17; Job 24:14; Wis 8:20) and it refers to knowledge that results from the law and from historical fact (Gen 38:9; 2 Esdr 5:17); or from one's experience of life and one's perception (Job 24:14; Wis 8:20).

Jesus' words not only onto the woman's action but onto the woman herself. She stands alone and unnamed but her action will receive the highest praise offered by Jesus in the entire gospel tradition. It is to Jesus' three-fold interpretation of her action that we now turn.

Into the phrase καλὸν ἔργον ἠργάσατο of Mark 14:6 is introduced the connective γάρ, and the order in the phrase καλόν ἔργον is reversed, so that it is the word ἔργον which stands out in the position of emphasis before the γάρ. Many times in Matthew γάρ is used as a link between a command or prohibition and an explanatory word which follows.[54] Here, however, it does not follow a command, but rather a question, but it still functions in the same way in that it links the question and the subsequent explanation.[55] The three-fold use of γάρ in this way was perhaps suggested by a single occurrence in Mark 14:7. It serves to highlight the three aspects of the interpretation which Jesus gives.

The first of these refers to the woman's action as a "good work" done to Jesus. Jeremias argues that καλὸν ἔργον refers to the *Liebeswerk* of *Spätjudentum* among which was included the burying of the dead.[56] März, on the other hand, refutes this position on a threefold basis. First, he claims that "good work" has a more general reference than *Liebeswerk*, pointing out that there is no distinction between almsgiving and good work in the Christian Scriptures as Jeremias claims.[57] Second, he shows that anointing was not necessarily considered a part of the command to bury the dead and so was not directly considered a *Liebeswerk*; and finally, he claims that the καλὸν ἔργον of Mark 14:6b is not a reference forward to the *Liebeswerk*

---

54 Senior, *The Passion*, 80, especially n. 3.
55 Blass, Debrunner and Funk, *A Greek Grammar*, 236, § 452.
56 Jeremias, "Die Salbungsgeschichte," 77-81. A modification is made to Jeremias' position by Lohmeyer, *Matthäus*, 349, for whom the core of the story lies in v. 11 and the differentiation which is made between a good work done to Jesus and almsgiving which he claims is obscured by focussing on the rabbinic distinction between "good works" and "almsgiving".
57 März, "Traditionsgeschichte," 97. His argument could be extended into Judaism also because in ᵓAbot R. Nat. 20a, with reference to the words of R. Johanan b. Zakkai (end of 1st century CE), we read:
    What then were the acts of loving-kindness in which
    he (referring to Daniel) was engaged?
    He used to outfit the bride and make her rejoice,
    accompany the dead,
    give a pĕruiah to the poor,
    and pray three times a day.
    See Judah Goldin, trans., *The Fathers according to Rabbi Nathan*, YJS X (New Haven: Yale University Press, 1956), 35. Only much later did the distinction arise that we find in b. Sukk. 49b and t. Peᵓa 4.19.

referred to in Mark 14:7, but simply an acknowledgment of the woman's attendance on Jesus.[58] This last point will be taken up and developed in more detail, especially since it seems to be more clearly the case in the Matthean text.

Initially, it appears difficult to explain the origin of the expression καλὸν ἔργον. The phrase does not appear in the LXX and it is used in Mark only at 14:6. The only other time that the word ἔργον appears in Mark is in 13:34 where it refers to the ordinary work of a servant. The phrase ἐν ἐμοί, especially in relation to Jesus, is unique in the Markan text. Since März has shown the weaknesses in Jeremias' argument which explained καλὸν ἔργον in terms of the category of the *Liebeswerk* of *Spätjudentum*, the evidence therefore suggests that the phrase καλὸν ἔργον ἠργάσατο ἐν ἐμοί may have been a strong historical memory of the interpretive words of Jesus as he defended the woman's action. This argument is strengthened by a consideration of the Matthean redaction. The phrase καλὸν ἔργον is used only one other time in Matthew in special Matthean material (5:16) where its reference is very general, the context providing no specific interpretive key. This gives further weight to März' argument that the term had a more general reference than that indicated by Jeremias. Second, the Matthean insertion of γάρ into v. 10b and v. 12a would seem to point to the distinctiveness of each interpretation, rather than to the fact that καλὸν ἔργον was linked to the notion of preparation for burial which is to follow. It could be further argued that, given the strong Jewish flavour of many of the Matthean traditions, if the link between καλὸν ἔργον and Jesus' reference to his burial had been operative in the development of the story, then this link would have been highlighted rather than reduced or eliminated as it seems to be in the final redaction. This point, together with Matthean fidelity to the Markan text except for the slight change to εἰς ἐμέ which is almost impossible to explain,[59] further substantiates the suggestion above that we have preserved here words which are close to those of the historical Jesus.

The second interpretation given to the woman's action is closely linked to the objection to it raised earlier (v. 9); it was suggested above that this objection was a later development in the tradition.[60] As such, it is secondary

---

58   März, "Traditionsgeschichte," 97.
59   Senior, *The Passion*, 36, discusses this change and considers it presumptuous to attempt to give a specific reason for it.
60   Plummer, *Exegetical Commentary*, 355, on the other hand, suggests that "its originality stamps it as authentic. Considering the teaching of Christ and of the Old Testament

to the καλὸν ἔργον of the previous verse.[61] When the very specific objection regarding the sale of the ointment for giving to the poor was raised, then the action of the woman needed to be defended against it in line with the defense offered in the previous verse--she has done a good work to me. The words of Jesus needed to address the objection specifically. This was done by contrasting an action done to Jesus with an action done to the poor not in general, but at this particular moment in Jesus' life.

When one examines Mark 14:7, Matt 26:11 and Jn 12:8, the line of development in the tradition becomes clear. In Mark, the antithetic parallelism is obscured by the statement καὶ ὅταν θέλητε δύνασθε αὐτοῖς εὖ ποιῆσαι. Matthew omits this phrase, highlighting the parallelism:

πάντοτε   γὰρ   τοὺς   πτωχοὺς   ἔχετε   μεθ' ἑαυτῶν

ἐμὲ   δὲ   οὐ   πάντοτε   ἔχετε·   (Matt 26:11)

The Johannine text renders the parallelism even more sharply, suggesting the possibility of a literary dependence existing between the Johannine text and the Markan or Matthean text.[62] Thus we have in John:

τούς   πτωχοὺς γὰρ   πάντοτε   ἔχετε   μεθ' ἑαυτῶν,

ἐμὲ   δὲ   οὐ   πάντοτε   ἔχετε.   (Jn 12:8)

When one recognizes the significance of the time indicator [πάντοτε/οὐ πάντοτε] within this statement,[63] it could be argued that, if the story of the anointing existed prior to its incorporation into the passion narrative then, the addition of Mark 14:7 must have coincided with or been subsequent to such incorporation since the statement seems most intelligible in relation to the imminent departure of Jesus from their midst. Such a development also

---

respecting the poor, we may be sure that He alone would have used this argument; no one would have invented it." As our argument proceeds below, however, there will be evidence supplied to counter this position.

61   Such an interpretation runs counter to the claim of Bultmann, *History*, 36, for whom the point of the story lies in v. 7 of Mark (i.e. Matt 26:11), and also to that of Lohmeyer, *Matthäus*, 349, who considers that the sense of the story lies in the alternative raised by v. 11--a good work done to Jesus *or* to the poor.

62   It may, however, be more correct to say that a relationship existed not at the literary but at the oral tradition level. In the objection of Jn 12:5, one can also see evidence of a relationship especially between the Markan and Johannine traditions. Lagrange, *Evangile*, 493, says of this dependency that it is not literary but existed in the living memory (tradition).

63   Bonnard, *Évangile*, 372, says that the distinction in this verse is temporal rather than between good works and almsgiving.

raises further questions in relation to Jeremias' distinction between *Almosen* and *Liebeswerk*.

The saying itself, when closely examined, has little or no actual reference to the action of the woman, another fact which points to its later insertion into an existing tradition. The Matthean redaction, however, seems to try to incorporate it more closely into the story by taking up the connective γάρ which is used in this statement and repeating it in relation to the other two interpretations. The change in the previous verse of the Markan ἐν ἐμοί to εἰς ἐμέ may also have been to facilitate this incorporation so that the pronoun ἐμέ, which belonged to the statement regarding the presence of the poor and the presence of Jesus, was used in the first interpretive statement as well.

The time reference used here in relation to the poor offers further insight into a possible background to this aspect of the tradition, namely, Deut 15:11:

> For the poor will never cease out of the land;
> therefore I command you,
> You shall open wide your hand to your brother,
> to the needy, and to the poor in the land.

This, however, still leaves the exact origin of the tradition difficult to determine. It is clear though that when the challenge to the woman's action was introduced, it then needed to be defended by Jesus and hence the insertion of 14:7 into the Markan text.

Finally, we come to the third interpretation highlighted by the Matthean use of γάρ. This is the prophetic interpretation of the prophetic action,[64] and it is here that the Matthean redaction most significantly changes the Markan text. This then provides us with the best clue to the desired Matthean emphasis in this pericope. Already we have seen that the Matthean text contains nothing that would distract from the woman's action in relation to Jesus. Thus the καὶ ὅταν θέλητε δύνασθε αὐτοῖς εὖ ποιῆσαι has been omitted from Matthew in order to highlight the imminence of Jesus' departure and the significance of the woman's action in this regard. The Markan clause ὃ ἔσχεν ἐποίησεν (she has done what she could), which suggests certain limitations in the woman's action has also been omitted and in Matthew

---

64   März, "Traditionsgeschichte," 98, refers twice to Mark 14:8 as "Todesprophetie".

Jesus directly interprets the action according to the pattern of the two previous interpretations.

In order to understand the Matthean redaction better, brief attention should be given to Mark 14:8. Both Bultmann and März consider this verse to be secondary in the development of the tradition, and März goes on to show its redactional links with vv. 6-7.[65] Daube provides arguments for a possible context for the growth of this element of the narrative which, while strengthening the claim for its secondary character, may call into question its link with vv. 6-7. He sees the origin of this interpretation in the concern in the early christian community with the question of *niwwul*, the disgrace of a criminal burial, which may have historically been the lot of Jesus or certainly was the Jewish accusation against him.[66] Indeed, the early christian tradition does not seem to have known of an anointing of Jesus just prior to burial (cf. Mark 15:46ff. and 16:1), and therefore it is easy to imagine how a story recounting the anointing of Jesus by a woman during his public ministry could have been incorporated into the passion narrative and then the interpretation added which rendered this anointing as an anticipation of Jesus' burial anointing so that the disgrace was avoided. This is seen first in Mark 14:8 where the words describing the action of the woman (cf. 14:3) are radically changed in the interpretation. It is no longer the head but the whole body which is anointed. The phrase προέλαβεν μυρίσαι (she has come beforehand to anoint) lacks the concreteness of συντρίψασα τὴν ἀλάβαστρον κατέχεεν αὐτοῦ τῆς κεφαλῆς (v. 3). Finally, εἰς τὸν ἐνταφιασμόν, introduces the notion of preparation for burial which is absent from the earlier description of the action. In Mark, the tentativeness or sense of inadequacy of such an action and explanation is further underlined by the phrase ὃ ἔσχεν ἐποίησεν (she has done what she could).[67]

In the Matthean redaction, on the other hand, the tentative phrase of Mark 14:8a has been omitted, providing us with the first hint that the

---

65   Bultmann, *History*, 263; and März, "Traditionsgeschichte," 97-98. März uses the argument that neither the burial of Jesus by Joseph of Arimathea (Mark 15:46-47) nor the opening verse of the resurrection narrative (16:1) recognizes an anticipated anointing of Jesus. Hence, v. 8 is secondary and has not been completely incorporated into the overall gospel. Influenced, however, by the arguments of Jeremias, he claims that by means of the redactional activity of Mark, v. 8, with its reference to anointing for burial, is clearly linked with vv. 6-7.

66   D. Daube, "Anointing at Bethany," in idem, *The New Testament and Rabbinic Judaism*, Jordan Lectures in Comparative Religion 2 (London: Athlone Press, 1956), 312-324. See also Sabourin, *L'Evangile*, 337.

67   Beare, *A Commentary*, 504, calls this a "doubtful phrase".

tradition is rendered more definitely.[68] Also the statement in v. 12 is introduced with the connective γάρ indicating a third interpretation. Together these indicate a two-fold purpose. First, they render the Markan text more definitely and second, they are linked to the action of the woman (v. 7) in order to provide a further interpretation of κατέχεεν (μύρον) ἐπι τῆς κεφαλῆς.

The phrase βαλοῦσα ... τὸ μύρον τοῦτο is much more concrete than Mark's προέλαβεν μυρίσαι and provides a clear link by means of the noun μύρον with the action of the woman in v. 7. The Matthean inclusion of αὕτη renders not only the action but also the actor more concretely present in Jesus' interpretation. As well as providing a parallel with ἐπί τῆς κεφαλῆς of v. 7, the adverbial phrase ἐπι τοῦ σώματός μου directs attention to the action more specifically than the Markan accusative--το σῶμά μου. Finally, the Matthean use of ἐποίησεν at the end of the sentence rather than attached to ὅ ἔσχεν at the beginning indicates that the action of the woman is presented not as a second-best, but as the very act of anointing which prepared for burial. This is exemplified most clearly in the use of the purpose clause--πρὸς τὸ ἐνταφιάσαι με--which carries with it more finality than Mark's εἰς τὸν ἐνταφιασμόν.[69] The woman's action in pouring out the ointment upon the body of Jesus was an actual anointing in anticipation of his burial and hence no further consideration is given to the need for anointing (cf. Matt 28;1 which differs from Mark 16:1 in this respect).

Whereas, as März argues, Mark redactionally links v. 8 with vv. 6-7, it seems that the Matthean link exists between the interpretation of v. 12 and the action of the woman in v. 7, so that v. 12 stands as the climactic prophetic interpretation of the woman's action and not as an explanation of καλὸν ἔργον. Jesus' simple defense of the woman as seen in v. 10, has, in the course of the development of the tradition, been supplemented by two later interpretations, each establishing more clearly the focus of the entire pericope--Jesus, the woman and her action done to him. The ultimate significance, however, is only realized when one considers the concluding verse (v. 13).[70]

---

68   Daube, "Anointing," 320-321; and Senior, *The Passion*, 37.
69   See Zerwick, *Biblical Greek*, 135, § 391, for a discussion of this type of phrase. Lagrange, *Evangile*, 493, says of this phrase that it "indiquerait que déjà la femme a procédé à l'ensevelissement."
70   März, "Traditionsgeschichte," 98, calls the final verse the highpoint of the pericope, especially because of its introduction.

The potential in this verse (v. 13) for the legitimation of women's socio-religious activity is enormous, not only historically but also in the present as Schüssler Fiorenza's selection of its final words as the title for her recent ground-breaking work on a feminist reconstruction of christian origins indicates. It is not surprising, therefore, that there exists a counter-tradition which undermines the power of the text.[71] A thorough redaction-critical analysis of the text may, however, help to reclaim its potential.

A brief glance shows that the Markan text has been used with few alterations and, as with the previous verse, a study of Mark may help to throw light on these alterations. Mark 14:9 opens with the phrase ἀμὴν δὲ λέγω ὑμῖν which Jeremias includes as one of the identifying characteristics of the *ipsissima vox Jesu*.[72] We shall take, therefore, as a starting point the possibility that these opening words at least may point to authentic words of the historical Jesus, and shall use our analysis to determine whether it is possible that at least some of the final verse of the pericope may belong to that category. Mark has introduced the connective δέ into this phrase; the only time in the thirteen occurrences of the phrase in the gospel that it has been broken in this way. Perhaps this was the evangelist's way of setting the words of Jesus off from the traditional material which was introduced into the story in vv. 7-8. When one considers the subsequent phrase ὅπου ἐὰν κηρυχθῇ τὸ εὐαγγέλιον εἰς ὅλον τὸν κόσμον, however, there seem to be significant reasons to suggest that it belongs to Markan tradition rather than to the historical Jesus.[73] The absolute use of εὐαγγέλιον is recognized as typically

---

71   This stream of interpretation has its origin in the work of Joachim Jeremias, "Beobachtungen," 116-117; and is followed up in his article "Mc 14:9," *ZNW* 54 (1952-53): 103-107. He gives the verse a purely eschatological interpretation indicating that it is God who is reminded of the deed: "so oft von der Tat der Jesus salbenden Frau geredet werden wird, wird Gott an diese Tat erinnert." Similarly, both Gaechter, *Matthäus-Evangelium*, 836, and Grundmann, *Matthäus*, 532, refer to her being remembered by God at the eschaton, an explanation which undermines the present socio-religious potential of the story. Greenlee, "Εἰς μνημόσυνον," 245, argues that "consideration should be given to the possibility that the intended meaning of these verses is that this unknown woman's humble deed served as her memorial *to Jesus* [italics mine] in view of His coming death."

72   Joachim Jeremias, *The Prayers of Jesus* (Philadelphia: Fortress, 1978), 112-115. In his earlier work, "Die Salbungsgeschichte," 76, he discounted this introduction merely with the words "trotz des einleitenden ἀμήν = אָמֵן" and went on to argue for the secondary nature of the verse because of its lack of semitisms. Later, he reviewed this position in the light of the work of Hahn and his own further research, and came to recognize the verse as eschatological and hence possibly at least a part of the original pericope even though he contends with Hahn that perhaps the phrase ὅπου ἐὰν κηρυχθῇ τὸ εὐαγγέλιον ... was redactional.

73   This is the position taken by Ferdinand Hahn, *Das Verständnis der Mission im Neuen Testament*, WMANT 13 (Neukirchen-Vluyn: Neukirchener, 1963), 101, which is taken up by Jeremias as noted above, and by März, "Traditionsgeschichte," 101-102.

Markan,[74] and the aorist passive form of the verb κηρύσσω occurs only here and in the apocalyptic discourse (13:10) compared to its active use each of the other 10 times that it occurs in the gospel. These two factors together suggest the influence of a later church tradition as does the phrase ὅλον τὸν κόσμον, which also occurs in Mark 13:10.[75]

A different picture arises, however, when we turn to the final half of the verse: ὃ ἐποίησεν αὕτη λαληθήσεται εἰς μνημόσυνον αὐτῆς. The most extraordinary element is the last phrase εἰς μνημόσυνον αὐτῆς (in memory of her) in which we find μνημόσυνον preceded by the preposition εἰς and followed by the genitive of a personal pronoun referring to a human person and not to God. When one examines the possible background of this phrase in the Septuagint, one discovers that μνημόσυνον plus the genitive of the personal pronoun is used either to speak of God's being remembered (Pss 6:6; 134:13; 101:13; Hos 12:6), of the righteous being remembered by God (Hos 14:8; Num 31:54), or of the remembrance of the wicked being blotted out from God's memory (Job 18:17; Deut 32:26; Pss 33:17; 108:15). At other times, it is followed by the dative of either a noun or pronoun and again it refers to God's deeds being remembered (Ex 28:12, 29; 30:16; Num 17:5; Jos 4:7). Only twice do we find the phrase εἰς μνημόσυνον. In Ex 17:14, it is not followed by a pronoun but refers to a remembrance of the deeds of God, while in Ps 111:6, εἰς μνημόσυνον αἰώνιον ἔσται δίκαιος (the righteous will be remembered [as a memorial] forever) seems to refer to remembrance by God, although this is not perfectly clear from the text. The αἰώνιον, however, suggests eschatological inference.

We find a similar picture when we examine the material from Enoch cited by Jeremias.[76] In none of the places where μνημόσυνον occurs is it in a construction completely parallel to that which we find in Mark's gospel. Either μνημόσυνον stands alone (1 Enoch 97:7; 103:4) or we find εἰς μνημόσυνον without the subsequent genitive (1 Enoch 99:3). Even within the Christian

---

74   Senior, *The Passion*, 39, nn. 2 and 3; Rudolf Pesch, *Das Markusevangelium*, Teil I, HThK (Freiburg/Basel/Wien: Herder, 1976), 74-75; Wilfrid Harrington, *Mark*, New Testament Message 4 (Dublin: Veritas, 1979), 2; Vincent Taylor, *The Gospel according to Mark. The Greek Text with Introduction, Notes, and Indexes* (London: Macmillan, 1952), 152; and Eduard Schweizer, *The Good News according to Mark: A Commentary on the Gospel*, trans. Donald H. Madvig (Atlanta: John Knox, 1970), 30, who recognizes the origin of the use of the term in Paul.

75   McNeile, *Matthew*, 376; Pesch, *Das Markusevangelium*, II, 334-335; Taylor, *Mark*, 534; and Bultmann, *History*, 37.

76   Jeremias, "Beobachtungen," 116-117.

Scriptures, we find that the complete phrase is unique to this pericope.[77]
Jeremias, from his analysis of the above material, argues that the phrase as
used in Mark 14:9 must mean that God will be reminded of the woman's action. It could be argued, however, that the uniqueness of the entire phrase
with its specific link to the gracious action of the woman [ὅ ἐποίησεν αὕτη]
may indicate that its origin lay with the historical Jesus.[78] Furthermore, it is
difficult to explain how the later tradition could have created these
extraordinary words to refer to the action of a woman when the tendency
was to minimize the significance of women.[79] One could indeed even be led
to speculate whether possible discipleship language which may have been
used in relation to this woman and other women in the early tradition has
all but disappeared in the course of the transmission so that we are left with
only slight hints like that contained in Mark 14:9/Matt 26:13, in which the
action of a woman who performed an extraordinary prophetic sign in
relation to Jesus was given the highest praise offered to any human person
in the gospel record.

In summarizing the minor Matthean changes in the final verse, we
note first the omission of the connective δέ from the phrase ἀμὴν λέγω ὑμῖν
which gives little insight into the redaction. The Matthean reversal of the
phrases λαληθήσεται and καὶ ὅ ἐποίησεν αὕτη can be explained simply in
terms of a clearer structuring which is typical of the Matthean redaction. The
only other significant change is the addition of τοῦτο to εὐαγγέλιον, again a
clear sign of Matthean redaction because each time εὐαγγέλιον is used in the
gospel, it is qualified: τῆς βασιλείας (4:23; 9:35); τοῦτο ... τῆς βασιλείας (24:14)
and εὐαγγέλιον τοῦτο (26:13). Whether the reference is to the teaching of
Jesus, the entire proclamation of his life and message, or to the events of the

---

77   Εἰς μνημόσυνον occurs only one other time in the Christian Scriptures (Acts 10:4) but
      without the accompanying pronoun and it seems that we could argue from its context
      that it is based on the model from the LXX, especially Ex 17:14; and Num 31:54. We
      have already noted, however, the similar phrase εἰς τὴν ἐμὴν ἀνάμνησιν (1 Cor 11:25)
      which refers to the remembering of Jesus in the celebration of the eucharist. This act of
      remembering the deeds of the woman in the preaching of the gospel seems to parallel
      the remembering of Jesus in the eucharistic celebration.
78   Taylor, *Mark*, 534, suggests that the absence of the woman's name represents an early
      tradition. Its uniqueness may also point to a tradition belonging to the historical Jesus.
      Ernst Käsemann, "The Problem of the Historical Jesus," in *Essays on New Testament
      Themes*, trans. W. J. Montague (London: SCM, 1964; Philadelphia: Fortress, 1982), 15-47,
      especially, 44, highlights the criterion of distinctiveness as a significant element in
      determining what can be attributed to the historical Jesus.
79   Winsome Munro, "Women Disciples in Mark?" *CBQ* 44 (1982): 237, makes this point
      but with regard to Mark 16:8. However it is also the trend which Schüssler Fiorenza
      uncovers in the second part of *In Memory of Her*.

passion,[80] it is clear that it is not intended to refer to some final eschatological moment but to the ongoing concrete proclamation of the life and message of Jesus in the christian community. It is in such a context that the
proclamation will have a political and religious effect similar to that of the
original act. Thus the Matthean text skilfully blends words of the historical
Jesus with the developing tradition of the early christian community, both
of which had been preserved in the Markan text, in order to bring a particular emphasis in the story of the anointing of Jesus to its fitting climax. This
analysis also brings us to the point where we can draw some conclusions
regarding the development of the tradition within the Matthean
community.

C. Development of the Tradition

Behind the text itself lies an historical memory of an anointing performed
for Jesus by a woman, an action which was prophetic by nature, and which
demonstrated the initiative and courage of the woman. Those around Jesus
who witnessed such an act were indignant, but the woman's action was
defended and approved of by Jesus.

In the course of the transmission of this historical memory, whether at
the oral or written tradition level, the words chosen to describe the anointing were those of a general act of anointing rather than those of the
prophetic act itself, thus reducing the impact of its radicality. The reference to
those present being indignant was retained in the story as were the words of
Jesus' defence--the woman had performed a good or beautiful deed for him
and it would be told in her memory.

When the pericope was incorporated into the Markan text, it would
seem that to the words of indignation of those present had been added the
question of giving to the poor, the addition constituting an attempt to discredit the action of the woman. These accusations were countered with
words given to Jesus and his defense became a second interpretation of the
action, added to the original καλὸν ἔργον. Also, the incorporation of the story
into the passion narrative gave rise to the third interpretation of the

---

80   For examples of this variety of positions, see Senior, *The Passion*, 39-40; Lohmeyer,
      Matthäus, 349; McNeile, *Matthew*, 376; and Meier, *Matthew*, 313.

woman's action, namely, that it was an anointing for burial, a tradition which perhaps arose in the face of Jewish criticism of the "disgrace" of Jesus' criminal burial. Both of these secondary interpretations could be seen as attempts to give a specific christological focus to the story because the original christological significance of the woman's act had been blurred in the transmission of the story.

In incorporating this story into the gospel, the Matthean redaction has made minor changes which served to direct the focus of the pericope onto Jesus, the woman and her action. Because of what seems to be close reliance on the Markan text, however, it is difficult to determine the exact history of the tradition in the Matthean community. The contrast set up by naming those indignant as the disciples may reflect the tension already noted within the Matthean community regarding women's participation, the disciples representing, for some, authoritative tradition opposed to that participation. As in 15:21-28, so here also, the impact of the entire story seems to counter that opposition. The redaction has focussed the entire attention onto the action of the woman by way of the structuring of the pericope, has offered a three-fold interpretation of this action in the words of Jesus, has presented the action as the anointing of Jesus for burial, an act of discipleship, and has rendered v. 13 as the climax of all that precedes.

This story like that of the Canaanite woman draws attention to a woman's recognition of Jesus: the one of his healing power and the other of the true nature of his mission and ministry (his messiahship). It celebrates women's prophetic ministry and could well have functioned in the community to legitimate and authenticate this activity as it was already being performed by women and/or to encourage its performance. It also proclaims the initiative and courage of women in the face of opposition and misinterpretation of their actions. It provides a fitting introduction to the theme of women's role in the passion narrative.

III. The Minor Stories

Within the passion narrative prior to the crucifixion scene, the Matthean text retains one reference to women characters (26:69, 71), and adds another (27:19). In the account of Peter's denial of Jesus (26:69-75), the focus of the story is certainly on Peter,[81] with the questioners simply highlighting the fact of Peter's association with Jesus. This is especially so with regard to the two women characters. Matthew introduces a second woman (26:71) so that the reference is to μία παιδίσκη (26:69) and ἄλλη (26:71) whereas Mark has μία τῶν παιδισκῶν τοῦ ἀρχιερέως (14:66) and ἡ παιδίσκη (14:69). This seems to be simply a redactional technique which serves to highlight the women's recognition of Peter's association with Jesus. There is also, however, a significant symbolic quality to the presence of these women in the narrative[82] which has been maintained and even augmented by the Matthean redaction. In light of the consistent development of the narrative thread of women's participation in the Jesus story, it could be suggested that the retention of this story and the introduction of a second woman as questioner continues this development especially within the passion narrative, where a woman appeared in the introduction as representative of a significant character group who would be participants in the drama of the passion, namely women.

In the light of this, it is not surprising that the final redactional process has introduced another woman into the passion narrative: the wife of Pilate (27:19). The verse which makes reference to her activity is often dismissed simply as a rhetorical device to fill in the time gap while the chief priests incite the people.[83] Senior, however, basing his analysis on the study made by Trilling, undertakes a detailed analysis of the language and structure of this verse which I will not repeat here. He concludes that it has all the signs of Matthean compilation, or at least heavy redaction of an already existing tradition.[84] When he comes to interpret it, however, he places his emphasis on the content of the verse because he finds no parallel for the intercessory role of Pilate's wife, but he does draw attention to the intercessory role given

---

81 See the extensive treatment of the Matthean redaction of the entire pericope in Senior, *The Passion*, 192-209.
82 See p. 137.
83 Grundmann, *Matthäus*, 554; Lagrange, *Evangile*, 524; Lohmeyer, *Matthäus*, 384; McNeile, *Matthew*, 412; and Meier, *Matthew*, 341.
84 Senior, *The Passion*, 242-246.

to the mother of the sons of Zebedee in Matthew. This last pericope has already been examined in detail and nothing came to light which would link it in any way with the appearance of Pilate's wife in the story. If, however, we consider the account of the death or rather condemnation of John the Baptist (14:1-12), then some parallels appear which may throw light on 27:19.

In the earlier pericope (14:1-12), Matthean redaction has made two redactionally significant changes. First, in Mark 6:19-20, it is Herodias, whom Herod has taken as his wife, who wants to put John to death but cannot because Herod fears John to be a prophet. In Matthew, on the other hand, it is Herod himself who wants to put John to death (14:5) but cannot because he fears the people who consider John to be a prophet.[85] His opportunity to carry out his desire comes through the instrumentality of Herodias. In the Matthean redaction of the story, however, she never appears as a character on the scene as she does in Mark (cf. Mark 6:19, 24), but is the voice behind the scene (Matt 14:8) who brings about the condemnation of this innocent man. Thus Herod is the one who has both the power and the desire to condemn John, but is unwilling to do so. He is given the opportunity to carry out his desire by way of his wife who is portrayed, however briefly, as the deceitful adultress, one of the stereo-typical roles given to women.

When we turn to 27:11-26, the trial and condemnation of Jesus before Pilate, we find parallels and contrasts. Similar to Herod, Pilate has the power to condemn Jesus, but there are hints in the narrative that he is unwilling to do so, not because he fears the people but rather because he considers Jesus to be an innocent man (27:14, 18, 23, 24). While Herod sought to kill John, Pilate seeks for a way to release Jesus. His opportunity to carry out his desire also comes by way of the instrumentality of his wife. She too is behind the scene as was Herodias, but whereas Herodias' intervention for the death of John came from her own designs, the intervention of Pilate's wife for the release of Jesus is inspired by what she hears in a dream. In Matthew, the dream is the means for conveying a divine message: what to do or what to avoid.[86] In the case of Pilate's wife it is the second: "Have nothing to do with

---

85 Grundmann, *Matthäus*, 361, considers that the Matthean redaction intends to highlight the parallel between the fate of Jesus and the fate of John.

86 Κατ' ὄναρ appears only five other times in Matthew apart from 27:19, and each occurrence is in the infancy narrative: 1:20; 2:12, 13, 19, 22, and each time Joseph is the recipient of the divine message. Each time it is a divine message designed to save either Jesus or his adherents from danger to their lives. See Grundmann, *Matthäus*, 554, and Hill, *The Gospel*, 350. This position is contrary to Gaechter, *Matthäus-Evangelium*, 911, who claims that dreams are not characteristically Matthean because they are

that righteous man, for I have suffered much over him today in a dream" (Matt 27:19). The stereotypical role given Herodias is here reversed when an unknown gentile woman,[87] the wife of Pilate, becomes a prophetic messenger not to bring about the condemnation of Jesus but to save him from condemnation. Where Herodias was successful in her designs, however, Pilate's wife was unsuccessful.

Additional comparisons and contrasts could be made, but the above suffice to enable some conclusions to be drawn regarding the redactional activity operating in Matt 27:19. First, in the light of the passion narrative and its development, we find here, within the narrative proper, another step forward in the development of the narrative thread regarding the role of women. In the introduction to the passion narrative, a woman performed the prophetic act of anointing Jesus, recognizing his messiahship. As the narrative moves to a climax, we encounter another woman who also plays a prophetic role, this time being given a revelation as to the righteousness and innocence of Jesus at the very time when her husband, the governor, is about to condemn him, despite the fact that he recognizes his innocence. Like the woman who anoints Jesus, she too is made to stand out by way of contrast to the surrounding male characters: the Jewish leaders and her husband. Her word alone, in the midst of the condemnations, acknowledges the truth of Jesus' innocence, but it is unable to change the course of androcentric history. It is as if she had not spoken.[88]

It seems clear from the above that Matthean redaction has shaped the compositional aspect of the inclusion of 27:19. Senior summarizes his detailed analysis of the language of this verse in these words: "The preceding survey reveals that the language of 27:19 contains a mixture of undeniable Matthean words and common synoptic or traditional vocabulary."[89] The

---

confined to Matt 1-2. This, however, seems to be contrary to the redactional principle which claims that the key characteristics of an author or redactor are to be found in the special material (Matthean *Sondergut*).

87 Jones, *Matthew*, 309, interprets this incident as the evangelist's way of underlining the malice of Israel since a pagan woman pleads the cause of Jesus against his own people. His interpretation may be too harsh but it does seem that the woman who is considered an "outsider" to Israel stands in contrast to the male leaders of Israel who condemn Jesus or incite the crowds to condemn him.

88 Gaechter, *Matthäus-Evangelium*, 911, discusses the reasonable nature of such a request from the wife of a Roman official and points to similar references in Josephus, as does Bonnard, *Évangile*, 397. Johnson, "The Gospel," 596, gives the parallel example of Caesar's wife, Calpernia, who tried to keep him from going to the Forum on the day of his death because she had been warned by a dream (Appian, *Civil Wars* II.480).

89 Senior, *The Passion*, 246.

above information makes it difficult to determine whether the inclusion of the reference to the wife of Pilate comes purely from the final redaction or is drawn from already existing tradition. Given the extraordinary nature of the verse, some see its origin in legend.[90] Argyle suggests a Palestinian source for 27:19, 24-25, 62-66 and 28:11-15, all of which concern Pilate;[91] while Meier sees the Matthean church as the context for the development of the tradition which may have had its origin in an oral legend.[92] It is clear from the scholarship that the exact origin and development of the tradition regarding the wife of Pilate is difficult to establish. In terms of our study, however, and the evidence which seems to point to the preservation and development of traditions within the Matthean community which authenticate the role of women in the Jesus movement in the later believing community, it seems reasonable to argue that the community preserved this tradition which may have been of early origin in order to highlight the role played by women during Jesus final suffering. Such a tradition would have also served the final redaction well, especially in terms of the development of the narrative thematic of women's participation in the death-resurrection event. It becomes a narrative link which prepares the way for the presence of women at the foot of the cross.

---

90 Erich Fascher who investigates this aspect in his short monograph, *Das Weib des Pilatus (Matthäus 27,19). Die Auferweckung der Heiligen (Matthäus 27,51-53). Zwei Studien zur Geschichte der Schriftauslegung*, HM 20 (Halle: Niemeyer, 1951), 5-31; Beare, *A Commentary*, 530; and Grundmann, *Matthäus*, 554 who recognizes only elements of a legend in the verse.
91 Argyle, *Matthew*, 211.
92 Meier, *Matthew*, 341.

IV. 27:55-56, 61; 28:1-10

A. Comparison of Synoptic Texts

An examination of the pericopes below which recount the presence of women at the cross and at the tomb indicates that there appear to be basic traditions common to all four evangelists behind them; but the variations in the texts suggest different histories of development and also the possibility of the influence of additional traditions as well.

Matt 27:55-56	Mark 15:40-41	Luke 23:49	John 19:25
55 Ἦσαν δὲ ἐκεῖ	40 Ἦσαν δὲ	49 εἱστήκεισαν δὲ πάντες οἱ γνωστοὶ αὐτῷ ἀπὸ μακρόθεν	25 εἱστήκεισαν δὲ παρὰ τῷ σταυρῷ τοῦ Ἰησοῦ
γυναῖκες πολλαὶ ἀπὸ μακρόθεν θεωροῦσαι, αἵτινες ἠκολούθησαν τῷ Ἰησοῦ ἀπὸ τῆς Γαλιλαίας διακονοῦσαι αὐτῷ·	καὶ γυναῖκες ἀπὸ μακρόθεν θεωροῦσαι,	καὶ γυναῖκες αἱ συνακολουθοῦσαι αὐτῷ ἀπὸ τῆς Γαλιλαίας, ὁρῶσαι ταῦτα.	
56 ἐν αἷς ἦν	ἐν αἷς		ἡ μήτηρ αὐτοῦ καὶ ἡ ἀδελφὴ τῆς μητρὸς αὐτοῦ, Μαρία ἡ τοῦ Κλωπᾶ
Μαρία ἡ Μαγδαληνὴ καὶ Μαρία ἡ τοῦ Ἰακώβου καὶ Ἰωσὴφ μήτηρ καὶ ἡ μήτηρ τῶν υἱῶν Ζεβεδαίου.	καὶ Μαρία ἡ Μαγδαληνὴ καὶ Μαρία ἡ Ἰακώβου τοῦ μικροῦ καὶ Ἰωσῆτος μήτηρ καὶ Σαλώμη, 41 αἳ ὅτε ἦν ἐν τῇ Γαλιλαίᾳ ἠκολούθουν αὐτῷ καὶ διηκόνουν αὐτῷ, καὶ ἄλλαι πολλαὶ αἱ συναναβᾶσαι αὐτῷ εἰς Ἱεροσόλυμα.		καὶ Μαρία ἡ Μαγδαληνή.

Matt 27:61	Mark 15:47	Luke 23:55-56	John

Matt 27:61

61 ἦν δὲ ἐκεῖ
Μαριὰμ
ἡ Μαγδαληνὴ
καὶ ἡ ἄλλη Μαρία

Mark 15:47

47 ἡ δὲ Μαρία
ἡ Μαγδαληνὴ
καὶ Μαρία ἡ
Ἰωσῆτος

Luke 23:55-56

55 Κατακολουθήσασαι
δὲ αἱ γυναῖκες,
αἵτινες ἦσαν
συνεληλυθυῖαι ἐκ τῆς
Γαλιλαίας αὐτῷ,
ἐθεάσαντο

ἐθεώρουν

καθήμεναι
ἀπέναντι
τοῦ τάφου.

ποῦ τέθειται.

τὸ μνημεῖον
καὶ ὡς
ἐτέθη τὸ σῶμα αὐτοῦ,
56 ὑποστρέψασαι δὲ
ἡτοίμασαν ἀρώματα
καὶ μύρα. Καὶ τὸ μὲν
σάββατον ἡσύχασαν
κατὰ τὴν ἐντολήν.

Matt 28:1-8	**Mark 16:1-8**	**Luke 24:1-11**	**John 20:1-18**

Matt 28:1-8

1 Ὀψὲ δὲ σαββάτων

Mark 16:1-8

1 Καὶ διαγενομένου
τοῦ σαββάτου Μαρία ἡ
Μαγδαληνὴ καὶ Μαρία
ἡ [τοῦ] Ἰακώβου καὶ
Σαλώμη ἡγόρασαν
ἀρώματα
ἵνα ἐλθοῦσαι
ἀλείψωσιν αὐτόν.

τῇ ἐπιφωσκούσῃ
εἰς μίαν
σαββάτων,

2 καὶ λίαν πρωῒ
τῇ μιᾷ τῶν
σαββάτων

Luke 24:1-11

1 τῇ δὲ μιᾷ τῶν
σαββάτων
ὄρθρου βαθέως

John 20:1-18

1 Τῇ δὲ μιᾷ τῶν
σαββάτων

ἦλθεν
Μαριὰμ
ἡ Μαγδαληνὴ
καὶ ἡ ἄλλη Μαρία

ἔρχονται

Μαρία
ἡ Μαγδαληνὴ

ἔρχεται
πρωῒ σκοτίας ἔτι
οὔσης

θεωρῆσαι τὸν τάφον.

ἐπὶ τὸ μνημεῖον

ἀνατείλαντος τοῦ
ἡλίου.

ἐπὶ τὸ μνῆμα
ἦλθον

εἰς τὸ μνημεῖον

φέρουσαι ἃ ἡτοίμασαν
ἀρώματα.

3 καὶ ἔλεγον πρὸς
ἑαυτάς, Τίς
ἀποκυλίσει ἡμῖν
τὸν λίθον ἐκ τῆς
θύρας
τοῦ μνημείου;

2 καὶ ἰδοὺ σεισμὸς
ἐγένετο μέγας·
ἄγγελος γὰρ κυρίου
καταβὰς ἐξ οὐρανοῦ
καὶ προσελθὼν

4 καὶ ἀναβλέψασαι

Matt	Mark	Luke	John
	θεωροῦσιν	2 εὗρον δὲ	καὶ βλέπει
		τὸν λίθον	τὸν λίθον ἠρμένον
ἀπεκύλισεν	ὅτι ἀποκεκύλισται	ἀποκεκυλισμένον	ἐκ τοῦ
τὸν λίθον	ὁ λίθος·	ἀπὸ τοῦ μνημείου,	μνημείου ...
	ἦν γὰρ μέγας σφόδρα.		
	5 καὶ εἰσελθοῦσαι	3 εἰσελθοῦσαι δὲ	11b παρέκυψεν
	εἰς τὸ μνημεῖον		εἰς τὸ μνημεῖον
		οὐχ εὗρον τὸ σῶμα	
		τοῦ κυρίου Ἰησοῦ.	
		4 καὶ ἐγένετο ἐν τῷ	
		ἀπορεῖσθαι αὐτὰς	
		περὶ τούτου	
	εἶδον	καὶ ἰδοὺ	12 καὶ θεωρεῖ
	νεανίσκον	ἄνδρες δύο	δύο ἀγγέλους
		ἐπέστησαν αὐταῖς	
			ἐν λευκοῖς
καὶ ἐκάθητο ἐπάνω	καθήμενον ἐν τοῖς		καθεζομένους,
αὐτοῦ.	δεξιοῖς		
3 ἦν δὲ ἡ εἰδέα αὐτοῦ		ἐν ἐσθῆτι	
ὡς ἀστραπὴ		ἀστραπτούσῃ.	
καὶ τὸ ἔνδυμα αὐτοῦ	περιβεβλημένον στολὴν		
λευκὸν	λευκήν,		
ὡς χιών.			
			ἕνα πρὸς τῇ κεφαλῇ
			καὶ ἕνα πρὸς τοῖς
			ποσίν, ὅπου ἔκειτο
			τὸ σῶμα τοῦ Ἰησοῦ.
4 ἀπὸ δὲ τοῦ	καὶ		
φόβου αὐτοῦ	ἐξεθαμβήθησαν.	5 ἐμφόβων δὲ	
		γενομένων αὐτῶν	
ἐσείσθησαν οἱ			
τηροῦντες καὶ			
ἐγενήθησαν ὡς νεκροί.			
		καὶ κλινουσῶν τὰ	
		πρόσωπα εἰς τὴν	
		γῆν	
5 ἀποκριθεὶς δὲ	6 ὁ δὲ		13 καὶ
ὁ ἄγγελος			
εἶπεν	λέγει	εἶπαν	λέγουσιν
ταῖς γυναιξίν·	αὐταῖς·	πρὸς αὐτάς·	αὐτῇ
μὴ φοβεῖσθε ὑμεῖς,	μὴ ἐκθαμβεῖσθε·		
οἶδα γὰρ ὅτι			
Ἰησοῦν	Ἰησοῦν		
τὸν ἐσταυρωμένον			
		Τί	ἐκεῖνοι· γύναι, τί
ζητεῖτε·	ζητεῖτε	ζητεῖτε	κλαίεις;
	τὸν Ναζαρηνὸν		
	τὸν ἐσταυρωμένον·	τὸν ζῶντα μετὰ	
		τῶν νεκρῶν;	λέγει αὐτοῖς ὅτι
	ἠγέρθη,		
6 οὐκ ἔστιν ὧδε,	οὐκ ἔστιν ὧδε·		ἦραν τὸν κύριόν μου,
ἠγέρθη γὰρ			
καθὼς εἶπεν·			καὶ οὐκ οἶδα
δεῦτε ἴδετε	ἴδε		ποῦ
τὸν τόπον ὅπου	ὁ τόπος ὅπου		ἔθηκαν αὐτόν.
ἔκειτο.	ἔθηκαν αὐτόν.		...17 λέγει αὐτῇ
			Ἰησοῦς· μή
			μου ἅπτου, οὔπω
			γὰρ ἀναβέβηκα πρὸς
			τὸν πατέρα·

Matt	Mark	Luke	John
7 καὶ ταχὺ πορευθεῖσαι	7 ἀλλὰ ὑπάγετε		πορεύου δὲ πρὸς τοὺς ἀδελφούς μου καὶ εἰπὲ αὐτοῖς·
εἴπατε τοῖς μαθηταῖς αὐτοῦ	εἴπατε τοῖς μαθηταῖς αὐτοῦ καὶ τῷ Πέτρῳ		
ὅτι ἠγέρθη ἀπὸ τῶν νεκρῶν,	ὅτι		Ἀναβαίνω
			πρὸς τὸν πατέρα μου καὶ πατέρα ὑμῶν καὶ θεόν μου καὶ θεὸν ὑμῶν.
		6μνήσθητε ὡς ἐλάλησεν ὑμῖν ἔτι	
καὶ ἰδοὺ προάγει ὑμᾶς εἰς τὴν Γαλιλαίαν, ἐκεῖ αὐτὸν ὄψεσθε· ἰδοὺ εἶπον ὑμῖν.	προάγει ὑμᾶς εἰς τὴν Γαλιλαίαν· ἐκεῖ αὐτὸν ὄψεσθε, καθὼς εἶπεν ὑμῖν.	ὢν ἐν τῇ Γαλιλαίᾳ	
		7 λέγων τὸν υἱὸν τοῦ ἀνθρώπου ὅτι δεῖ παραδοθῆναι εἰς χεῖρας ἀνθρώπων ἁμαρτωλῶν καὶ σταυρωθῆναι καὶ τῇ τρίτῃ ἡμέρᾳ ἀναστῆναι. 8 καὶ ἐμνήσθησαν τῶν ῥημάτων αὐτοῦ.	
8 καὶ ἀπελθοῦσαι	8 καὶ ἐξελθοῦσαι	9 καὶ ὑποστρέψασαι	18 ἔρχεται Μαριὰμ ἡ Μαγδαληνὴ
ταχὺ ἀπὸ τοῦ μνημείου	ἔφυγον ἀπὸ τοῦ μνημείου, εἶχεν γὰρ αὐτὰς τρόμος καὶ ἔκστασις· καὶ οὐδενὶ οὐδὲν εἶπαν·	ἀπὸ τοῦ μνημείου	
μετὰ φόβου	ἐφοβοῦντο γάρ.		
καὶ χαρᾶς μεγάλης ἔδραμον			
ἀπαγγεῖλαι		ἀπήγγειλαν ταῦτα πάντα	ἀγγέλλουσα
τοῖς μαθηταῖς αὐτοῦ		τοῖς ἕνδεκα	τοῖς μαθηταῖς
		καὶ πᾶσιν τοῖς λοιποῖς.	
			ὅτι ἑώρακα τὸν κύριον, καὶ ταῦτα εἶπεν αὐτῇ.

Matt 28:9-10	Matt 28:5,7	Mark 16:6-7	John 20:17
⁹ καὶ ἰδοὺ Ἰησοῦς ὑπήντησεν αὐταῖς λέγων· χαίρετε. αἱ δὲ προσελθοῦσαι ἐκράτησαν αὐτοῦ τοὺς πόδας καὶ προσεκύνησαν αὐτῷ. ¹⁰ τότε			¹⁷ λέγει αὐτῇ Ἰησοῦς· Μή μου ἅπτου, ...
λέγει αὐταῖς ὁ Ἰησοῦς· μὴ φοβεῖσθε·	⁵ ἀποκριθεὶς δὲ ὁ ἄγγελος εἶπεν ταῖς γυναιξίν, μὴ φοβεῖσθε ὑμεῖς, ... ⁷ καὶ ταχὺ πορευθεῖσαι	⁶ ὁ δὲ λέγει αὐταῖς· μὴ ἐκθαμβεῖσθε ...	
ὑπάγετε		⁷ ἀλλὰ ὑπάγετε	πορεύου δὲ πρὸς τοὺς ἀδελφούς μου
ἀπαγγείλατε τοῖς ἀδελφοῖς μου	εἴπατε τοῖς μαθηταῖς αὐτοῦ ὅτι ἠγέρθη ἀπὸ τῶν νεκρῶν, καὶ ἰδοὺ προάγει ὑμᾶς	εἴπατε τοῖς μαθηταῖς αὐτοῦ καὶ τῷ Πέτρῳ ὅτι προάγει ὑμᾶς	καὶ εἰπὲ αὐτοῖς· ἀναβαίνω πρὸς τὸν πατέρα μου καὶ πατέρα ὑμῶν
ἵνα ἀπέλθωσιν εἰς τὴν Γαλιλαίαν, κἀκεῖ με ὄψονται.	εἰς τὴν Γαλιλαίαν, ἐκεῖ αὐτὸν ὄψεσθε· ἰδοὺ εἶπον ὑμῖν	εἰς τὴν Γαλιλαίαν· ἐκεῖ αὐτὸν ὄψεσθε, καθὼς εἶπεν ὑμῖν.	

As with the account of the anointing of Jesus, it seems that the closest literary relationship exists between Mark and Matthew. There is no significant indication of a literary relationship between Matthew and Luke over against Mark, nor between the Johannine and the Markan/Matthean accounts. Any minor similarities will be treated individually as they arise in the analysis of the text. The best working hypothesis, therefore, for an examination of the pericopes under consideration is that within the Matthean redaction, the Markan text is used as a primary source.[93]

---

93   This is the position argued by Senior, *The Passion*, 328-334, and Boismard, *Synopse*, 427-428, with regard to 27:55-56, a pericope which, in fact, receives little attention in the literature. Boismard's position in relation to 27:61 (p. 434) is a little more nuanced and in terms of 28:1-10 (p. 443), he suggests that the final Matthean redaction follows Mark, but that redaction is clearly evident in the final text. Perkins, *Resurrection*, 124, also argues that Matthew has adapted Mark's story of the empty tomb. When one considers the literature on 28:1-10 more closely, one finds that opinions are more nuanced and more complicated. This aspect will receive more detailed attention at the beginning of the redactional analysis of 28:1-10 below.

B. Redaction

1. 27:55-56

From a redactional point of view, Matthew's account of the women at the foot of the cross is, as Senior remarks, "simpler but more compact" than that of Mark.[94] The descriptive material (Mark 15:41) is linked to the statement regarding the women's presence at the cross (Matt 27:55), and it was clear from the earlier narrative analysis that this verse is carefully structured around the two finite verbs and their qualifying participles, which are carefully placed at the beginning and end of the two clauses in order to highlight the presence and the activity of the women. Diagramatically this structure appears thus:

Finite verb [ἦσαν] ...   participle [θεωροῦσαι]

Finite verb [ἠκολούθησαν] ... participle [διακονοῦσαι].[95]

Verse 56 then simply names three women who are members of the group and whose activity is described in the previous verse. Although it could be argued that the content of the two pericopes is the same, it will be seen that the structuring and redaction brings a unique Matthean emphasis to the tradition.

First, Mark's opening phrase, ἦσαν δὲ καὶ γυναῖκες is changed to ἦσαν δὲ ἐκεῖ γυναῖκες πολλαί. Ἐκεῖ, which has been used a number of times in the passion account to direct attention to a place and the characters present, is introduced here as part of the Matthean redaction. In 26:36, it points to Jesus praying at a distance from the disciples, and at 27:36 it directs the readers attention to the scene of Jesus' crucifixion and the presence of the soldiers who are keeping watch. The ἐκεῖ of 27:55 retains the same spatial focus, but the characters change from soldiers to the women at the cross. Finally, it is introduced in 27:61 where the scene changes to the tomb and it is once again the women who are present. It seems that the initial use of ἐκεῖ in the passion narrative highlights the distance which will separate Jesus from his

---

94 Senior, The Passion, 330. He notes, p. 329, that Mark's two verses have a four-point structure: A. Presence at the cross; B. Identifying activity; A' Presence of other women; and B' Identifying activity. This is simplified to a two-point structure in Matthew: 1. Presence of many women and identifying activity; and 2. List of names. Plummer, Exegetical Commentary, 405, suggests a "smoother arrangement of clauses".

95 See p. 140, for further discussion of the Matthean structuring of v. 55.

disciples during the passion, but the subsequent use of the word brings into focus those who were present at the foot of the cross, namely, the soldiers and the women. These are the ones who witness both the death and the signs of divine power surrounding the raising of Jesus, and the skilful Matthean use of vocabulary seems to indicate this.

The verb τηρέω (27:36, 54 and 28:4) links the soldiers to the cross and the tomb whereas ἐκεῖ (27:55, 61) functions in the same way for the women. The language of 27:36 and 27:61 also seems to point to the witness value of both groups. Of the soldiers at the cross it is said, καθήμενοι ἐτήρουν αὐτὸν ἐκεῖ, and of the women at the tomb, ἦν δὲ ἐκεῖ ... καθήμεναι ἀπέναντι τοῦ τάφου. This is further substantiated by the Matthean redaction of 27:54. Whereas in Mark it is a centurion who witnesses Jesus' death and proclaims him a son of God, the Matthean redaction adds the phrase οἱ μετ' αὐτοῦ τηροῦντες τὸν Ἰησοῦν. The soldiers who keep guard witness the crucifixion and the phenomena which surround it and they proclaim Jesus as son of God. This immediately precedes the witness of the women which the Matthean redaction seems to highlight, a witness further substantiated by the transference of πολλαί, which Mark has in a dangling phrase at the end of 15:41, to the beginning of the Matthean pericope. Just as a number of soldiers witness the death of Jesus, so too do many women.

The use of the participle θεωροῦσαι which concludes the first half of v. 55 could be readily dismissed as a simple borrowing from Mark. Further investigation reveals, however, that of the seven times that the verb is used in Mark, this is the only place where Matthew retains it; and it is significant here that the only other time that the verb is used in the entire Matthean gospel is in 28:1 describing the purpose for the women's visit to the tomb. It would seem, therefore, that the Matthean redaction gives the verb a particular nuance in the gospel over and above the general usage in Mark (3:11; 5:15, 38; 12:41; 15:40, 47; 16:4). The context may provide us with the best place to begin to understand the particular sense in which this verb is used.

In both situations (27:55; 28:1), the women's witness is linked to what became central to the early christian kerygma: Jesus' death on the cross and his resurrection as evidenced by the empty tomb and subsequent appearances. The situation was not one requiring legal witnesses and so the witness of the women was not told in the language of legal witness found in the Hebrew Scriptures (Num 35:30; Deut 17:6; 19:15). In the context of the development of the early christian kerygma, however, the proclamation of the death of Jesus and belief in his having been raised became more and more central. Matthean use of the verb θεωρέω only in relation to these two aspects of the Jesus story may suggest that it carries some of the sacral character of its origin, namely, the witnessing of sacred or religious events, rather than the more general sense of simply looking at or observing.[96] The women are presented as witnesses to the two central elements that constitute the christian kerygma.[97] They will also be the first to proclaim these.[98]

The Matthean presentation of the women as witnesses to what was central to the community's kerygma may point to certain tensions which this tradition created for the community. Biblical law contains nothing concerning the qualifications of witnesses;[99] but by the time of Josephus (Ant. 4.8.15 §219) certain restrictions had begun to appear:

> Put not trust in a single witness but let there be three or at least two whose evidence shall be accredited by their past lives. From women let no evidence be accepted, because of the levity and temerity of their sex.

Later Rabbinic traditions also severely restricted the witness value of women,[100] and their similarity to the text of Josephus suggests that, at least within the sector of the Matthean community where Jewish tradition prevailed, the credibility of the women as witnesses may have been questioned.[101] According to Roman law, however, women could act as witnesses in legal proceedings, but this right was also limited in particular circumstances.[102] This may have meant that for others within the Matthean community, the women's witness was accepted and affirmed. The Matthean use of θεωρέω only in relation to the women's witness of the cross

---

96 Michaelis, "θεωρέω," TDNT V:318.
97 Within Judaism, witnesses were required not only for legal matters but also in religious matters, e.g. witnesses to the first appearance of the new moon regulating Rosh Ha-Shanah. It is in the context of such religious witness (m. Roš. Haš. 1.7-8) that the witness of women is compared to that of a dice-player, a usurer, pigeon-flyers, traffickers in Seventh Year produce, and slaves. Despite Moshe Meiselman's claim that the feminist categorizing of women with the above groups is absurd, it seems that the evidence rests with the text itself. See Meiselman, Jewish Women in Jewish Law, 73; also Hyman, "The Other Half," 106; and Adler, "The Jew Who Wasn't There," 16.
98 Gaechter, Matthäus-Evangelium, 935: "Sie waren Augenzeugen der letzten Stunden des Meisters."
99 Haim Hermann Cohn, "Witness," EJ 16:585.
100 See b. Roš. Haš. 22a; b. Soṭa. 47b; b. Šebu. 29b; and m. Ketub. 2.5-6.
101 Gaechter, Matthäus-Evangelium, 936.
102 One of the limiting cases was adultery as seen in the Lex Julia de Adulteriis. For further discussion, see Julia O'Faolain and Lauro Martines, Not in God's Image: Women in History from the Greeks to the Victorians (New York/Hagerstown/San Francisco/London: Harper & Row, 1973), 62-63, and Jane F. Gardner, Women in Roman Law and Society (London/Sydney: Croom Helm, 1986).

and in the account of the empty tomb may, therefore, be an attempt to present the women's witness in unique terminology which highlights the
nature of their action, but which is also in terminology acceptable to the
entire community.[103]

The structuring of the verse, however, emphasizes the validity of the
women's witness. As cited above, Josephus claims the past lives of witnesses
as validating their testimony. Immediately following the simple statement
of the women's observing the crucifixion and the events surrounding it,
therefore, the Matthean text describes the women in terms of their past activity: they followed Jesus from Galilee ministering to him (27:55b). The two
verbs used here--ἀκολουθέω and διακονέω--have been taken over from the
Markan text but have been highlighted by the Matthean structuring. The
verb ἀκολουθέω is used to describe the response of the group called
"disciples" or to explicitly designate discipleship in Mark's gospel (Mark 1:18;
2:14; 6:1; 8:34; 10:21, 28). It is also used to describe others who accompany
Jesus in response to being healed or hearing his preaching. They too display
discipleship characteristics (2:15; 3:7; 10:52; 11:9). In the Matthean redaction,
the word is employed in a similar fashion so that it is clearly a discipleship
term, but it occurs more frequently in relation to the crowds (Matt 8:1, 10;
14:13; 19:2; 20:29), the group called "disciples" (4:22; 8:23; 19:28), and in teaching on discipleship (8:19, 22; 10:38) so that the redactional activity augments
its discipleship significance.[104] It seems, therefore, that the women are
designated as disciples, and this is further emphasized by the use of διακονέω,
the verb used in both the Markan and Matthean gospel to characterize Jesus'
own ministry (Mark 10:45; Matt 20:20) and by extension, therefore, that of his
disciples (Matt 10:24-25). These two verbs are associated with all the women
according to the Matthean redaction rather than simply with three from the
group (Mark 15:41), increasing, therefore the number of women who are
witnesses just as the number of soldiers were also increased.

The use of the phrase ἀπὸ τῆς Γαλιλαίας seems to reflect a tendency that
is typical of Matthean redaction, namely, the streamlining of the Markan

---

103   Michaelis, "θεωρέω," TDNT V:318-319, indicates that while θεωρέω may have had
       certain sacral connotations in its origin, it quickly passed over into general usage with
       the sense of "to look at" or "to view something". The language generally used with
       regard to official witnesses is that of μαρτυρέω and cognates.
104   Luz, Evangelium, 36, in his analysis of Matthean vocabulary lists the redactional uses
       of the word as approximately 10, and also calls the verb a "Leitwort" in Matt 8-9, and
       19:2-20:34 since it occurs 9 times in the first section and 6 in the second.

text into concise form.[105] Here the two Markan phrases--ἐν τῇ Γαλιλαίᾳ as the locus of the discipleship of the three named women and εἰς Ἱεροσόλυμα as the destination of the many woman who accompanied Jesus--are combined in order to focus on the women's discipleship of Jesus especially in terms of accompanying him to Jerusalem and the cross, the great test of discipleship. Such a phrase functions retrospectively to include women disciples in the entire journey narrative. They hear the teaching of Jesus along the journey, receive the passion predictions, and perhaps it is one of their number who, in the light of all that she has heard, recognizes the critical nature of the days in Bethany for Jesus and anoints him as a sign of prophetic recognition as well as for his strengthening in the face of the danger that they all sensed lay ahead. These women, therefore, are valid witnesses to the crucifixion precisely because they have shown themselves faithful disciples of Jesus.[106]

In v. 56, Matthew closely follows Mark and names three women, perhaps in keeping with the Jewish requirement of at least two witnesses but better still three (Ant. 4.8.15 §219 cited above). The only significant change is in relation to the third name. Where Mark refers to Σαλώμη, Matthew has μήτηρ τῶν υἱῶν Ζεβεδαίου.[107] That change has already been discussed above and its significance for the theme of women's faithful discipleship noted.

An analysis of the redactional activity in this pericope, seems to indicate that the Markan text has been significantly refined in the Matthean redaction in order to give greater emphasis to certain aspects of the account. Typically Matthean language links the scene very closely to the cross and to the witness of the soldiers, while both the structuring of the verse and the

---

105 Senior, The Passion, 331, explains the Matthean phrase in this way, contrary to Lohmeyer, Matthäus, 398, who claims that it represents a more primitive notion of discipleship, namely, the following of Jesus from Galilee to Jerusalem.
106 Senior, The Passion, 331; Gundry, A Commentary, 578; and Gnilka, Matthäusevangelium, II, 478-479, understand the reference to the women in discipleship terms. Sabourin, L'Evangile, 384, represents another position which considers discipleship a category reserved for the twelve and so even in the face of the evidence in the text, he cannot allow that the women were disciples. He argues, therefore, that they did not follow Jesus habitually but only on the journey to Jerusalem, yet surely this was the most significant journey of all and the real test of discipleship in the gospel story.
107 Whether or not these two names were synonymous in the tradition is almost impossible to determine, but this is a commonly accepted position among scholars. See Durand, Evangile, 332; Grundmann, Matthäus, 444; Gundry, A Commentary, 401; Lagrange, Evangile, 392; and Plummer, Exegetical Commentary, 405. Meier, Matthew, 354, on the other hand, claims that there are no grounds for identifying the two.

vocabulary retained from the Markan account point to the faithful discipleship of the women and therefore their credibility as witnesses to the death of Jesus. It was suggested that the particular emphasis given to the Matthean text may have been a response to questions or tensions in the community regarding the validity of women's testimony.

Before leaving this pericope, brief attention will be directed to the tradition which has been used in each of the gospels according to particular redactional purposes. In Matthew, Mark and John, Mary Magdalene is mentioned as being present at the foot of the cross together with one or more other women. Luke specifically mentions that women were among those at the cross (Luke 23:49) but names them only later in the account of the resurrection (24:10), and there Mary Magdalene is the first named. This seems to suggest a strong historical memory of women at the cross among whom was Mary Magdalene.[108] The authenticity of such a memory is made more plausible when one considers how difficult it would be in the patriarchal societies within which the gospel stories were recounted to create such a scandalous story: that women were the ones who remained faithful to Jesus to the point of his death and beyond, while the male disciples were absent, having deserted him. Such a position is reiterated from a slightly different perspective by Witherington III:

> The passion narrative, it is generally agreed, was one of the first pieces of tradition to become relatively fixed in the course of transmission. Accordingly, few would doubt that the reporting by the Evangelists of the betrayal, failure or desertion of Jesus' trained male leadership, the Twelve, during the crucial events of the last days of Jesus' ministry is historically accurate. It is not something that the post-Easter community was at all likely to invent.[109]

What, in fact, is much more likely is that the community would later compile stories to rehabilitate the male disciples and rectify the scandalous

---

108 See Norman Perrin, *Rediscovering the Teaching of Jesus*, (London: SCM, 1967), 45-47, for a discussion of the criterion of "multiple attestation". See also Acts Pil. 11:3a. Luise Schottroff, "Maria Magdalena und die Frauen am Grabe Jesu," *EvTh* 42 (1982): 5, points to the dire consequences of such presence near a crucified criminal within the Roman empire. The recent article by Susanne Heine, "Eine Person von Rang und Namen: Historische Konturen der Magdalenerin," in *Jesu rede von Gott und ihre Nachgeschichte im frühen Christentum: Beiträge zur Verkündigung Jesu und zum Kerygma der Kirche. Festschrift für Willi Marxsen zum 70. Geburtstag*, ed. Dietrich-Alex Koch, Gerhard Sellin and Andreas Lindeman (Gütersloh: Gerd Mohn, 1989), 179-194, came to my attention too late to be incorporated.
109 Witherington III, *Women in the Ministry*, 118-119.

memory, and reference will be made to this tendency when we consider the traditions surrounding the resurrection narrative.

2. 27:61

The structural link between 27:61 and 27:55 has already been noted, and the significance of ἐκεῖ discussed above. Similarly to Mark, Matthew reduces the number of women to two. Whatever of the Markan reasons for this reduction, it could be argued that Matthew, as well as being influenced by the Markan text, was also influenced by the change in 27:56 from Salome to "the mother of the sons of Zebedee". Her symbolic function reaches a climactic point at the foot of the cross when she, who earlier misunderstood the nature of the βασιλεία proclaimed by Jesus now stands with him at his death. The two Marys continue to witness to the final event--the burial of Jesus. They provide the link with the presence of the women at the cross and in this way, are presented as witnesses to the one who died, was buried and was raised.[110]

A more fundamental change from the Markan text occurs in the second half of the verse where Mark's ἐθεώρουν ποῦ τέθειται (they saw where he was laid) is changed to καθήμεναι ἀπέναντι τοῦ τάφου ([they were] sitting in front of the tomb).[111] Clearly Mark's statement is linked to the visit of the women to the tomb on the following morning to anoint the body of Jesus, hence their need to know exactly where the tomb was located. Matthew, on the other hand, has already provided for the anointing of Jesus, and the sealing of the tomb (27:66) will render such action impossible.[112] As already suggested above, the language of the Matthean redaction provides the clue to understanding this passage. Linguistically it is linked to 27:36. There the soldiers sat keeping guard over Jesus and in witnessing the crucifixion and

---

110 Albright and Mann, *Matthew*, 355, interpret the stories of the women as witnesses to the 3-fold event at the heart of the creed--death, burial and resurrection (cf. 1 Cor 15:3-4)--as emphasizing its veracity. Filson, *Matthew*, 298-299, and George A. Buttrick, "The Gospel according to St. Matthew. Exposition. Text," *IntB* VII:611, both consider that Matthew presents the women as the source and guarantors of the crucifixion/resurrection traditions.

111 Gaechter, *Matthäus-Evangelium*, 940, gives the reason for the women's presence as their coming to mourn, but notes that this is not mentioned in the text. A similar reason is given by Grundmann, *Matthäus*, 568, and Lagrange, *Evangile*, 535. If this were so, it seems strange that it is not mentioned directly in the text (cf. 9:23; Jn 20:11). Rather, the language used, especially in 28:1, is that of witnessing.

112 This same action of sealing the tomb would render implausible Longstaff's suggestion that the women came to the tomb to watch over it in order to ensure that premature burial had not taken place. See Longstaff, "Women at the Tomb," 277-282.

the events surrounding it, they acknowledged Jesus, the crucified, as son of God. The women who sit opposite the tomb, having witnessed the burial of Jesus will also be those who, on visiting the tomb again in the early morning, will witness that it is empty, will encounter the risen Jesus, and will be given the mission of proclaiming the resurrection. For both groups, the use of the verb κάθημαι with reference to their activity prepares for their role of believing witnesses and it is perhaps this which has governed the choice of expression here.[113] It is interesting to note, however, that the Matthean redaction does not have the verb θεωρέω in this pericope but will introduce it in 28:1. This may suggest that this verse is simply seen as a bridging between the events at the cross and the symbolic narrative of the raising up of the crucified one.

Both passages, 27:55-56 and 27:61, are closely linked by virtue of their structure and vocabulary, both place women at a most significant moment in the unfolding story of Jesus, and both function to establish the women as faithful witnesses to the events they observe. This tradition is absent from John, and Luke 23:54-56 has developed it quite differently with virtually no linguistic similarities to Mark or Matthew. This may suggest that the historical memory of the women at the foot of the cross was gradually elaborated in the light of the developing tradition regarding the burial of Jesus.

3. 28:1-10

In the Matthean composition of 28:1-10, it appears that the entire scene is divided into two very distinct sections [Diagram 18], whose careful structuring and relationship, particularly in terms of the commission given to the women at the end of each, point to a final redaction and indicate that the entire scene must be understood as a unit. In the Matthean account, the experience at the tomb is completed by the encounter with the risen Jesus.

---

113   Sabourin, *L'Evangile*, 377.

v. 1   Setting the scene

vv. 2-8   Καὶ ἰδοὺ σεισμός................Angel and the women

                                    Response

vv. 9-10   Καὶ ἰδοὺ Ἰησοῦς................Jesus and the women

                                    Response.[114]

Diagram 18

Into this structure, has been introduced material that is either community tradition or redactional (28:2-4, 9-10), while the basic outline is that of the Markan story of 16:1-8.[115] The story is also framed by the accounts of the guard at the tomb (27:62-66; 28:11-15), and fragments of this story are included in 28:1-10 itself. It is clear, therefore, that the Matthean redactional

---

114 Subsequent to my own analysis of the Matthean composition of 28:1-10, I discovered that by H. Bloem, *Die Ostererzählung des Matthäus: Aufbau und Aussage von Mt 27:57-28:20* (Rome: Zeist, 1987), 24-25, in which he makes similar divisions but points to more similarities between the two major sections. I shall repeat his structure here for ease of reference.

Themavers:	V. 1	ἦλθεν ... θεωρῆσαι τὸν τάφον
		mit Namen der Frauen und Zeitangaben
1e Sequenz:	V. 2	καὶ ἰδοὺ ... ἄγγελος γὰρ κυρίου
	V. 5	εἶπεν
		Ἰησοῦν ... ζητεῖτε· οὐκ ἔστιν ὧδε (Frauen)
	V. 7	εἴπατε τοῖς μαθηταῖς (+ Auftrag)
	V. 8	ἀπελθοῦσαι ...
2e Sequenz:	V. 9	καὶ ἰδοὺ Ἰησοῦς
		λέγων
		χαίρετε. αἱ ... προσεκύνησαν (Frauen)
	V. 10	ἀπαγγείλατε τοῖς ἀδελφοῖς μου (+ Auftrag)
	V. 11	πορευομένων δὲ αὐτῶν

115 This is the generally accepted position taken by scholars. See F. Neirynck, "Les femmes au tombeau: étude de la rédaction matthéenne (Matt. xxviii. 1-10," *NTS* 15 (1968-69):168, especially n. 2, but he also draws attention to contrary opinions and others that are more nuanced. Also, Bultmann, *History*, 288, for whom vv. 9-10 are an appendix; Reginald H. Fuller, *The Formation of the Resurrection Narratives* (Philadelphia: Fortress, 1980), 72, for whom vv. 2-4 are legendary; Perkins, *Resurrection*, 124; Bode, *First Easter Morning*, 57; Filson, *Matthew*, 301; Grundmann, *Matthäus*, 567; Hill, *The Gospel*, 358; and John E. Alsup, *The Post-Resurrection Appearance Stories of the Gospel Tradition*, CThM A:5 (Stuttgart: Calwer, 1975), 109, who thinks that Matthew follows Mark to v. 8 and then constructs vv. 9-10, a position which resembles that of Boismard, *Synopse*, 443, 446-447. S. Dockx, *Chronologies néotestamentaires et vie de l'église primitive: Recherches exégétiques* (Paris/Gembloux: Duculot, 1976), 233, on the other hand, claims that Mark's original story did not contain 16:1-8 but that three successive interpolations were included at the end of the Matthean text: 28:9-10, which led to the alterations in 27:61 and 28:1b; 28:5-8; and 27:56. The Markan version was then supplemented according to the Matthean interpolated version. Such a position is difficult to support in the face of the argument for the development of the tradition which placed women at the foot of the cross as the result of a strong historical memory as outlined above.

process has shaped this story, and a careful study of that activity will help to uncover the significance of the story in itself and within the entire gospel, especially in terms of the women as characters.[116]

The pericope opens with a time indication, ὀψὲ δὲ σαββάτων τῇ ἐπιφωσκούσῃ, which has given rise to much scholarly discussion but which need not concern us here.[117] Of greater importance for this study is 28:1b, in which we find the names of the two women who come to the tomb: Mary Magdalene and the other Mary, the same two who sat opposite the tomb (27:61). Mark, on the other hand, has only two women who see the burial place (Mary Magdalene and Mary the mother of Joses), but in 16:1, returns to the group named at the cross: Mary Magdalene, Mary the mother of James, and Salome. The Matthean redaction seems, therefore, to provide a much more specific link with the women at the tomb, as does the use of τάφον instead of μνημεῖον (Mark 16:2).[118] Finally, in the opening verse, the purpose given in Matthew for the visit to the tomb is simply to see the tomb [θεωρῆσαι τὸν τάφον]. In this way, the Matthean text continues the theme of the women's witness which began in 27:55, but also reaffirms the validity of the anointing in Bethany as the authentic preparation for burial.[119]

Verses 2-4 shall be considered together since they are Matthean tradition or redactional material inserted into the account of the resurrection. Some

---

116 Meier, *Matthew*, 360, points out that, like the infancy narratives, the resurrection accounts offer a fine opportunity to understand the particular message of the evangelist. It is important to observe that women are significant in both sections.

117 See Driver, "Two Problems," 327-337, who gives detailed attention to this question: his article contains references to other bibliographical material on the subject. See also Dockx, *Chronologies*, 235, n. 5.

118 A study of the use of τάφος/μνημεῖον in Mark and Matthew does little to explain the difference. The word τάφος never appears in the Markan gospel but is used six times in Matthew (23:27, 29; 27:61, 64, 66; 28:1), the last example being the only one which has a Markan parallel in the use of the term μνημεῖον. Μνημεῖον, on the other hand, is used seven times in Mark and six times in Matthew, three of those being parallels (Matt 8:28 parl. Mark 5:2; Matt 27:60 parl. Mark 15:46; Matt 28:8 parl. Mark 16:8. See also Matt 23:29; 27:52, 53; Mark 6:29; 16:2, 3, 5). Since it appears that Matthew uses the two words interchangeably, the use of τάφος in 28:1 must be explained by virtue of the link between 27:61 and 28:1ff.

119 The Matthean avoidance of any mention of anointing as a purpose for the women's visit to the tomb together with the arguments presented by Daube, "Anointing," 312-324, regarding the development from Mark to Matthew in terms of the assurance of the adequacy of the anointing at Bethany, call into question the position put forward by Dockx, *Chronologies*, 232-237. He claims that the Markan text of 16:1-8 is compiled from Matthew and Luke. It is difficult to explain how Markan redaction could move from the very clear position presented in Matthew to a much more tentative one as presented in the Markan text, and one which is also difficult to explain historically--would the women come to anoint a body which has already been in the tomb for at least one day? The problematic regarding the reason for the women's visit is discussed at length by Gaechter, *Matthäus-Evangelium*, 951-952.

scholars consider that these verses are to be interpreted in relation to 27:62-66 and 28:11-15.[120] It is certainly clear that 27:62-66 and 28:11-15 provide a frame in which 28:1-10 is to be interpreted,[121] but one notes that the language referring to the guards is different in 28:4 [οἱ τηροῦντες] as compared with 27:66 and 28:11 [κουστωδίας]. Rather, the language of 28:2-4 is much more closely related to that of 27:51-54. The guards are referred to as τηροῦντες in both sections, the verb τηρέω occurring only in the Matthean gospel.[122] The word σεισμός occurs in a key position in v. 2 immediately following the Matthean phrase καὶ ἰδού and picks up the nuances of the verb σείω from 27:51, the verb being used again in 28:4 in relation to the guards who shake from fear.[123] In both situations, the response to the phenomena is fear (27:54; 28:4); and in each, the subsequent verses indicate that there are women present also and that they too observe the phenomena. It seems clear, therefore, that 28:2-4 is more closely linked to 27:51-54 than to 27:62-66 and 28:11-15, which may, in fact, be a separate tradition.[124]

---

120 Nikolaus Walter, "Eine vormatthäische Schilderung der Auferstehung Jesu," *NTS* 19 (1972/73): 415-429, argues that the links between the three sections--27:62-66; 28:2-4 and 28:11-15--are the remnants of an original narrative of the type found in Acts which relates the extraordinary opening of doors of prisons to free the prisoner. Walter sees this as a third type of early Easter story alongside that of the empty tomb and resurrection appearances. Hubert Ritt, "Die Frauen und die Osterbotschaft. Synopse der Grabesgeschichten (Mk 16,1-8; Mt 27,62-28,15; Lk 24,1-12; Joh 20,1-18," in Dautzenberg et al., *Die Frau im Urchristentum*, 124-125, interprets the whole of 28:1-10 within the framework of 27:62-66 and 28:11-15.

121 Bloem, *Ostererzählung*, 3, extends this frame further to include 27:57-61 and 28:16-20. Then what he calls the "Anti-Jesus Front" is further enclosed within elements of the "Pro-Jesus Front" with 28:1-10 as a climactic and pivotal point also belonging to the latter.

122 Luz, *Evangelium*, 52, considers four or more of the six times that it is used in Matthew to be redactional.

123 This language seems also to reflect Matthean redaction. Σεισμός occurs only once in Mark (13:8) in the eschatological discourse which is paralleled in Matt 24:7 and Luke 21:11. It is not used again in the other gospels but is found in Matt 8:24; 27:54; and 28:2. Σείω is unique to Matthew among the gospels (Mt 21:10; 27:51; 28:4). Luz, *Evangelium*, 50, classifies from one to three of the occurrences of each of these two words as redactional.

124 Perkins, *Resurrection*, 127-128, places emphasis on the links between 27:51-54 and 28:2-4 on the basis of apocalyptic legendary material. Senior, "The Death of Jesus," in which he examines 27:51-53 specifically and contests Hutton's thesis that it is merely a transposed resurrection account, does himself recognize its links with the resurrection account when he says, p. 326: "By his inclusion of a resurrection sign as one of the immediate results of the *death* of Jesus, Matthew has underlined the importance of the crucifixion of Jesus as a turning point in the history of salvation. The choral confession by gentile soldiers and the believing presence of the women (later to be witnesses of the resurrection) point to the new community who will be bearers of the Risen Lord's message to the world."

The distinctly Matthean language suggests further that these verses are Matthean redaction.[125]

The earthquake [σεισμός] as eschatological symbol[126] has been discussed earlier along with the apocalyptic imagery surrounding the appearance of the angel of the Lord.[127] Both point to the divine power believed to be at the heart of resurrection faith, a power already seen to be associated with the crucifixion. This eschatological and apocalyptic emphasis is much stronger in Matthew than in Mark, for whom the one at the tomb is simply a νεανίσκον and is not considered responsible for the rolling back of the stone. It further substantiates the link between the cross and resurrection that was posited earlier on the basis of the references to the women [see Diagram 10]. A final observation in relation to these verses concerns the guards. At the crucifixion, those keeping watch became the first to proclaim the crucified Jesus as son of God, whereas those who witnessed the events surrounding the resurrection become like dead men [ὡς νεκροί], no longer standing with the women as witnesses, but rather in contrast to them. While they become like dead men, the women receive the message that the crucified one lives.[128] Hence, only the women both receive and positively respond to both extraordinary manifestations. The Matthean redaction of these verses has, therefore, significantly emphasized and more closely connected an original historical memory and an early tradition, namely, that women were the veritable witnesses to the cross and were the first to believe in Jesus' resurrection.

---

125 Boismard, *Synopse*, 440, 443; Neirynck, "Les femmes," 171-176; and Herman Hendrickx, *The Resurrection Narratives of the Synoptic Gospels* (Manila: East Asian Pastoral Institute, 1978), 35-37. Senior, "The Death of Jesus," 314-318, uses similar redactional arguments together with a contrasting of both form and function to illustrate that it is highly unlikely that the Matthean redaction drew on an early resurrection tradition that was shared by the author of the Gospel of Peter. For him, the Markan source and Matthean redaction best explain Matt 27:51-54 to which 28:2-4 is closely connected.

126 See p. 144. Hill, *The Gospel*, 358, and Grundmann, *Matthäus*, 569, make the point that the earthquake is not an attempt to describe the resurrection as such, a position contradicted by Gundry, *A Commentary*, 587; but, in the face of the eschatological nature of the language and also its use surrounding the crucifixion, Gundry's position is difficult to support.

127 Hill, *The Gospel*, 359; Grundmann, *Matthäus*, 568; and Lohmeyer, *Matthäus*, 408, all point to the part played by the angel in both the infancy narrative and resurrection account, the beginning and end of Matthew's gospel. Lagrange, *Evangile*, 538; Meier, *Matthew*, 361; and Bonnard, *Évangile*, 412, are all at pains to point out that the angel is not instrumental in the actual resurrection of Jesus but that the rolling back of the stone is simply to enable the women to enter and to see the place where he was laid.

128 Marin, "Femmes au tombeau," 41-42, points to this literary opposition together with many other such oppositions in the resurrection account.

With v. 5, Matthew follows the Markan story, but introduces the verse with a typical opening phrase--ἀποκριθεὶς δὲ ὁ ἄγγελος εἶπεν ταῖς γυναιξίν.[129] The following verses (vv. 5-8) closely follow Mark 16:6-8, but within the Matthean construction of the conclusion to the gospel, vv. 5-7 constitute a centre point, and hence are highly significant.[130] Some of the minor changes need not concern us here, but attention will be directed to those changes which highlight the Matthean redaction.

The words of the angel open with a typically biblical greeting accompanying a divine manifestation, μὴ φοβεῖσθε. The Matthean redaction changes the Markan phrase μὴ ἐθαμβεῖσθε, which is uniquely Markan, the verb ἐκθαμβέομαι occurring nowhere else in the entire Christian Scriptures,[131] and uses instead φοβέομαι which is linguistically connected to the redactional use of the verb in 27:54 and of the noun φόβος in 28:4, both in reference to the guards. It is also the same greeting which will be used by Jesus in his encounter with the women (28:9). Matthew then has the angel speaking authoritatively: οἶδα γὰρ ὅτι Ἰησοῦν τὸν ἐσταυρωμένον ζητεῖτε, a reiteration and perhaps even an extension of the women's purpose in coming to the tomb--Θεωρῆσαι τὸν τάφον. This is to prepare the women and hence the readers for the divine origin of the resurrection proclamation to follow with Matthew specifying that this divine revelation is given specifically to the women, ταῖς γυναιξίν.[132]

When we come to the words of the central proclamation that Jesus has been raised, we notice a significant shift in the Matthean account. In the Markan account, this proclamation is surrounded by references back to the crucifixion, ἐσταυρωμένον in A and ἔθηκαν in A' below:

A   Ἰησοῦν ζητεῖτε τὸν Ναζαρηνὸν τὸν ἐσταυρωμένον·

B   ἠγέρθη, οὐκ ἔστιν ὧδε·

A'   ἴδε ὁ τόπος ὅπου ἔθηκαν αὐτόν.   (Mark 16:6b-d)

---

129 Boismard, *Synopse*, 443.
130 This is argued by Bloem, *Ostererzählung*, 7-9, 23, who considers these verses the centre point of the chiastic structure within 27:57-28:20. See also Schottroff, "Maria Magdalena," 23.
131 It is used four times in Mark--9:15; 14:33; 16:5, 6.
132 Bloem, *Ostererzählung*, 11: "Die Auferstehungsproklamation kommt von Gott." See also Ritt, "Die Frauen," 125. Grundmann, *Matthäus*, 569: "Matthäus macht diesen Unterschied in der Weise kenntlich, daß die Wächter wohl durch das Geschehen in Furcht und Schrecken versetzt werden, aber keine Botschaft des Engels empfangen; nur die beiden Frauen werden angeredet, die nach seiner Darstellung auch als Zeugen des Geschehens zu denken sind."

In the Matthean account, on the other hand, there is a reversal of the phrases ἠγέρθη and οὐκ ἔστιν ὧδε, so that the central proclamation is structured thus around two negative statements with which it is contrasted:

A   οὐκ ἔστιν ὧδε

B   ἠγέρθη γὰρ καθὼς εἶπεν

A' δεῦτε ἴδετε τὸν τόπον ὅπου ἔκειτο.   (Matt 28:6)

Significantly, the phrase καθὼς εἶπεν is detached from its place in Mark (16:7) where it referred to Jesus going into Galilee as a fulfilment of his earlier prediction (Mark 14:28); and is attached here to the angel's proclamation of Jesus' resurrection (v. 6)--ἠγέρθη γὰρ καθὼς εἶπεν. It now indicates that the three predictions made by Jesus (16:21; 17:23; 20:19) have been fulfilled. The one who has been raised is linked to the earthly Jesus. The women who were faithful witnesses to the crucifixion of Jesus, and whose fidelity brings them to the grave, hear that the words Jesus spoke to them during his lifetime have indeed been fulfilled and that he has been raised. Their mission in coming to see the grave is accomplished when they are invited to come and see the place where he lay.

Turning now to the commission given to the women, we see that Matthean redaction has changed the verb of command from ὑπάγω to πορεύομαι so that this commission parallels that given later to the disciples:

πορευθεῖσαι   εἴπατε   τοῖς μαθηταῖς   (28:7)

πορευθέντες οὖν μαθητεύσατε πάντα τὰ ἔθνη.   (28:19)

Furthermore, Matthew omits καὶ τῷ Πέτρῳ so that the commission is to the disciples generally. Such a change is difficult to explain in the face of the tendency in Matthew's gospel to single out Peter as representative of the disciples (14:28-32; 15:15; 16:18-19; 17:24; 18:21-22).[133] Here, however, there is no question of leadership or representative function, but rather all the disciples have failed and have abandoned Jesus and hence all need to

---

133 Both McNeile, *Matthew*, 432; and Sabourin, *L'Evangile*, 390, explain this difficulty by assigning the reference to Peter to a later edition of Mark. This may be in line with the tendency to rehabilitate Peter seen in the work of Luke and John. For Klostermann, *Matthäusevangelium*, 229, it is omitted because Matthew does not want to report an appearance to Peter alone which seems reasonable in the light of the attention to Peter already evidenced in this gospel, but Gundry, *A Commentary*, 589, rejects this line of reasoning and argues for the omission of the reference to Peter on the grounds that he apostatized.

receive the message of the resurrection. Therefore, the Markan phrase is omitted.

An even more extraordinary change has been made to the actual message which the women are given. They are first to proclaim the resurrection [ἠγέρθη ἀπὸ τῶν νεκρῶν] and not just the rendez-vous in Galilee. They are commissioned to be the first apostles to witness to the raising up of Jesus, the oldest christian kerygma.[134] An explanation often given for Matthew's inclusion of this kerygmatic statement is that it continues the apologetic of 27:64 and is an exact repetition of the words which the chief priests claim that the disciples will use falsely.[135] Bloem, however, offers another motive for its inclusion which better addresses the context, namely, that the commission of 28:7 is a fulfilment of the prediction of Jesus in 26:32 in which he follows a reference to his being raised from the dead [μετὰ δὲ τὸ ἐγερθῆναι] by a promise to go into Galilee [προάξω ὑμᾶς εἰς τὴν Γαλιλαίαν]. The commission of the angel, therefore, is a fulfilment of these words of Jesus and that they are authoritative is stressed by the concluding words of the angel--ἰδοὺ εἶπον ὑμῖν.[136]

One cannot deny that the Matthean text like the Markan limits the women's commission by sending them to the disciples. This point is taken up and emphasized even further by Gaechter who claims that the Easter message was not meant for the women but for the disciples; for had the reverse been the case, it would have been a humiliation for the Twelve.[137] An historical-critical as well as a feminist reading, however, questions whether the tradition found in Mark and taken over in Matthew, which limits the women's commission, was not, in fact, a later tradition intended for that very purpose. It may well have been that an early tradition was preserved within the Matthean community which linked the ancient Easter kerygma to the angel's commissioning of the women. Only later were the

---

134 Cf. 1 Cor 15:4, 12; 1 Thess 1:10; Rom 4:24; 6:4; 7:4; 8:11, 34; 10:9; Acts 3:15; 4:10 by way of example.
135 Boismard, *Synopse*, 444; and Gundry, *A Commentary*, 589.
136 Schottroff, "Maria Magdalena," 22, says that this is not an "angelus interpres", but divine message given with full divine power.
137 Gaechter, *Matthäus-Evangelium*, 955: "Die Osteroffenbarung war in erster Linie nicht für die Frauen bestimmt, sondern die für Zwölf, welche die offiziellen Boten Jesu an die Welt sein sollten. Darum war auch der Auftrag des Engels letzlich ein Auftrag Jesu. Nicht von irgend einer Tendenz der Evangelisten, sondern von der Natur der Sache kam es her, daß mit der von Frauen überbrachten Botschaft eine gewisse Demütigung der Zwölf verbunden war." Such an interpretation would seem to go beyond the text itself and to be the product of a dogmatic hermeneutic and androcentric perspective in interpretation.

would-be recipients of their proclamation limited to the disciples. This would be in line with the development that one sees within the stories surrounding the resurrection to rehabilitate the disciples (Mark 16:7; Matt 28:16-20; Luke 24:12; John 20:3-10). It was perhaps this older tradition that the Matthean redaction skilfully incorporated into the women's commissioning. Furthermore, the Matthean introduction of καὶ ἰδού before the statement προάγει ὑμᾶς εἰς τὴν Γαλιλαίαν may well point to the inclusion of the women within the ὑμᾶς of this prediction.

The most significant change in this section, however, is made with respect to the response of the women (v. 8).[138] Many scholars have already discussed the difficulty inherent in the Markan ending,[139] which perhaps was recognized in the Matthean redaction. Our task here, however, is to search for possible reasons for the Matthean change, but in order to facilitate this, attention must be given to the Markan text and its import for the presentation of women in that gospel. I shall use as the beginning point for my discussion, the recent articles of Elizabeth Struthers Malbon and Winsome Munro.[140] Munro, in her article, sees the mention of the women at the cross and the tomb as reminiscent of an historical memory that was so powerful that it was not able to be suppressed, but that the ending in Mark 16:8 manifests that tendency toward suppression.[141] Part of her evidence for such a claim is the preservation of an actual or implied ongoing oral tradition of the Easter message in each of the other three gospels, from which she argues that, even though Mark may be considered the earliest written version of the gospel, it does not necessarily preserve the earliest tradition. This adds strength to the line of argument already pursued earlier which suggests that some of the earliest memories of the role of women during the last days of Jesus' life were incorporated in the Matthean gospel because of a specific concern within the community to preserve these memories. The Matthean

---

138 The following considerations run contrary to the analysis of Dockx, *Chronologies*, 245, who argues that Mark 16:1-8 depends on Matthew rather than the reverse. However, he makes no attempt to explain why Mark would change the response of the women but merely says that he has.

139 Norman Petersen, "When is the End not the End? Literary Reflections on the Ending of Mark's Narrative," *Interp.* 34 (1980): 151-166; and Malbon, "Fallible Followers," 29-48. For a brief discussion of the history of research surrounding this problem, see Thomas E. Boomershine, "Mark 16:8 and the Apostolic Commission," *JBL* 100 (1981): 225, n. 2.

140 Malbon, "Fallible Followers", and Munro, "Women Disciples".

141 This is but a brief summary of Munro's position with regard to 16:8 as found on pp. 235-237. There are many statements in the remainder of her article which would require more lengthy comment in a critical analysis of all her material, but that is not my purpose here.

intention, therefore, is different from that of Mark who, Malbon claims, presents both men and women as fallible followers of Jesus. For her, it is especially in 16:8 that the fallibility of the women disciples is most evident, but this verse also leaves the way open for the reader to continue the story which seems to be the purpose of the final Markan redaction.[142] For the Matthean community in which the traditions regarding women were often in tension with the traditions of a more patriarchal sector of the community, and where the tendency of the redaction seems to be to reflect those tensions rather than posit a solution to them, it is understandable that the Matthean redaction would preserve the full impact of the women's response. This is not to deny, however, that the verse also bears the mark of redactional activity.

The women are presented as responding faithfully to the command of the angel accomplished by the repetition of the adverb ταχύ. The only element of the Markan description of the women's response that is retained in Matthew is μετὰ φόβου in place of the verb φοβέομαι. This has been qualified, however, by καὶ χαρᾶς μεγάλης, in order to signify an appropriate response to a divine manifestation. Previously in the gospel when the disciples saw the manifestation of divine power which enabled Peter to walk upon the water, they cried out in fear [ἀπὸ τοῦ φόβου ἔκραξαν] (14:26); and the guards trembled with fear [ἀπο δὲ τοῦ φόβου] before the divine power manifest in the earthquake and descent of the angel (28:4). For each, though, it was a fear before a power whose source was not recognized and acknowledged. The story of the wise men from the East who saw the star rest over the place of Jesus' birth tells, however, of how they rejoiced with exceedingly great joy [ἐχάρησαν χαρὰν μεγάλην σφόδρα] (Matt 2:10). It is these two responses which are combined to describe the women's recognition of the power of God manifest in the resurrection and also of the authority of the angel's command.

Finally, our attention must turn to the climax of the Matthean resurrection pericope, vv. 9-10, verses which also form the climax or denouement of the thematic which we have been following, namely, the Matthean presentation of the role of women in the pre-history, life and death-resurrection of Jesus. These verses are manifestly Matthean[143] or the

142 Malbon, "Fallible Followers," 43-46.
143 Schweizer, The Good News, 523; and Sabourin, L'Evangile, 391. Boismard, Synopse,
     446-447; and Neirynck, "Les femmes," 176-184, also argue that the final redaction is

tradition of the community.[144] Only a careful examination will enable us to posit one or other of these positions more definitely.

This final section opens as did the first with the phrase καὶ ἰδού,[145] and so provides a smooth transition from 28:5-8 to vv. 9-10, which suggests Matthean redaction.[146] The phrase is also typical of a Matthean introduction to an epiphany (Matt 1:20; 2:13, 19; 3:16, 17; 4:11; 17:3, 5; 27:51). The greeting χαίρετε which Jesus gives to the women is often simply passed over as a typical Greek greeting possibly replacing the Hebrew or Aramaic *shalom*.[147] This same greeting is used two other times in the Matthean passion account (26:49: the greeting of Judas when he comes to betray Jesus which has no parallel in Mark; and 27:29: the greeting of the soldiers who mock Jesus as king which parallels Mark 15:18). Both are in situations of infidelity or lack of understanding of Jesus. Here, it seems that the evangelist uses profound irony by placing this same greeting on the lips of Jesus in his first encounter following his death and resurrection. The women, therefore, who have remained with Jesus through his passion and death become the representatives of those who are to be forgiven their role in that death. This seems to point to final redaction.

The response of the women to the greeting is presented in language typical of the Matthean gospel.[148] Of the eight times that ἔρχομαι or προσέρχομαι is followed by προσκυνέω, it has been used twice in relation to

---

clear in these verses. McNeile, *Matthew*, 432; and Gaechter, *Matthäus-Evangelium*, 944-945, on the other hand, see it as a later addition.

144 Plummer, *Exegetical Commentary*, 413, considers that at this point Matthew does not rely on Mark but on additional material that was available to him. For a number of scholars there exists a link between the story preserved in Matt 28:9-10 and Jesus' appearance to Mary Magdalene in John 20:14-18. See Benoit, *L'Evangile*, 174 and idem, "Marie-Madeleine et les disciples au tombeau selon Jn 20,1-18," in *Exégèse et Théologie* 3, CFi 30 (Paris: Cerf, 1968), 274; Grundmann, *Matthäus*, 568; Lagrange, *Evangile*, 541; Lohmeyer, *Matthäus*, 409; Meier, *Matthew*, 363; and Hill, *The Gospel*, 359. At this point I will not discuss the relationship between Matthew and John, but rather simply note that there may have been a direct borrowing or an early tradition that influenced each other.

145 Many ancient manuscripts [A C L 0148 *f*[1] (1424) 𝔐 f (q) sy[h]] contain the introduction ὡς δὲ ἐπορεύοντο ἀπαγγεῖλαι τοῖς μαθηταῖς αὐτοῦ, but as Metzger, *A Textual Commentary*, 72, points out, it is more likely that this phrase was added as a natural expansion of the preceding verse to make a smooth transition from v. 8 rather that it was omitted due to scribal error. Neirynck, "Les femmes," 176, argues against the added reading on the basis of Matthean style.

146 Ibid., 176-177, where Neirynck discusses the lack of artificiality in this transition contrary to those who would argue otherwise.

147 Boismard, *Synopse*, 446, says simply that "c'est la formule classique de salutation pour des Grecs." Neirynck, "Les femmes," 177, gives a similar but more nuanced explanation.

148 Hendrickx, *Resurrection Narratives*, 41; and Boismard, *Synopse*, 446.

women (15:15; 20:20). The verb προσκυνέω is also used repeatedly throughout Matthew in epiphanies (2:2, 8, 11; 14:33; 28:17). What is a little more difficult to explain, however, is the phrase ἐκράτησαν αὐτοῦ τοὺς πόδας (they took hold of his feet). It is not, however, to be contrasted with the command of Jesus, μή μου ἅπτου (don't touch me), of John 20:17 which occurs in the encounter between Mary Magdalene and the risen Jesus. Rather it is seen simply as an amplification of the verb προσκυνέω in the context of an epiphany of the risen Jesus.[149] Verse 9, therefore, seems to point to Matthean redaction.

Verse 10 opens in a manner common to the gospel with the use of τότε.[150] Jesus' words to the women, μὴ φοβεῖσθε, are not surprising as they are typical of a situation of epiphany, having occurred already in 28:5 in the words of the angel to the women. His subsequent command, however, is often understood as a doublet of the angel's message in 28:7.[151] A brief glance at the synoptic chart above will confirm such an observation, but closer examination also shows that, whereas the words of the angel are in the form of a command and a promise, the words of Jesus form a two-fold command: ὑπάγετε ἀπαγγείλατε ... ἵνα ἀπέλθωσιν. The first is a direct command to the women to go and to announce to the disciples, and the second is an indirect command to the disciples to go into Galilee. Both are fulfilled in accordance with the typical Matthean command-execution pattern. The execution of the women's command is recorded in the opening of 28:11 [πορευομένων δὲ αὐτῶν];[152] and of the disciples' in 28:16 [οἱ δὲ ἕνδεκα μαθηταὶ ἐπορεύθησαν εἰς τὴν Γαλιλαίαν]. As many have indicated, it is a Matthean preparation for the appearance of Jesus to the disciples,[153] but this is to miss the fact that it is the women who, at the command of Jesus, make possible the disciples' meeting with Jesus in Galilee. This commission is not based simply on the words of the angel and the experience of the empty tomb, but on an encounter with the risen Jesus. As Bloem suggests, the women model a resurrection faith which moves from seeking Jesus in the tomb (27:61; 28:1-5), to the

---

149 Hendrickx, Resurrection Narratives, 41; and Neirynck, "Les femmes," 179, who gives examples illustrating that the combination of such a phrase with προσκυνέω is typical biblical language.

150 It occurs ninety times in Matthew compared with six in Mark and fifteen in Luke. Luz, Evangelium, 52, considers eighty of these as redactional.

151 Boismard, Synopse, 446; Neirynck, "Les femmes," 183; and Meier, Matthew, 363, make this point but proceed to qualify it with other considerations. Bloem, Ostererzählung, 26, on the contrary compares vv. 9-10 with v. 8.

152 The women no longer have to go to Galilee to see Jesus (v. 7) because they have encountered him as they leave the graveside.

153 Boismard, Synopse, 446; Alsup, Appearance Stories, 113; Hendrickx, Resurrection Narratives, 43; and Neirynck, "Les femmes," 182.

recognition that the tomb is merely an empty gravesite (28:8), and finally to an encounter with the risen Jesus (28:9-10).[154] In Matthew's gospel the women are the first to encounter the risen Jesus. In this encounter, they neither fail to recognize Jesus which is common in the traditions surrounding the resurrection appearances (Luke 24:16, 37; Jn 20:14; 21:4), nor do they doubt as do some of the disciples (Matt 28:17). They are worshipping believers. The task given them is to make possible the necessary reconciliation between the risen Jesus and his unfaithful disciples.

In this regard, the Matthean redaction uses the title ἀδελφοῖς in v. 10 rather than μαθηταῖς as used by the angel in v. 7. For Hengel, it is an indication of a common source for the Matthean and Johannine story,[155] but more and more scholars are seeking to explain the change in terms of the Matthean gospel itself.[156] Often, its use in 28:10 is linked to its four-fold occurrence in 12:46-50.[157] This argument, however, does not seem consonant with the present scene. In 12:46-50, the "brothers" are those who do "the will of the Father" and, therefore, this sense of the term scarcely applies to the disciples at the very point of their absolute infidelity to Jesus during his suffering. A more appropriate link within the Matthean gospel seems to be 23:8, the one reference not treated by Hendrickx in his analysis of Matthean use of the term.[158] Within the condemnation of the Scribes and Pharisees, Jesus, addressing the "crowds and his disciples" says: "You are not to be called rabbi for you have one teacher and you are all brothers." It is not to a hierarchically-structured community that the universal mission is to be given, but to those who have experienced their solidarity in failure and are now reconstituted as the "brothers of Jesus". Such an explanation is further exemplified by the Matthean omission of the reference to Peter as separate from the disciples in 28:7.[159]

---

154   Bloem, *Ostererzählung*, 27.
155   See John 20:17. Martin Hengel, "Maria Magdalena und die Frauen als Zeugen," in *Abraham unser Vater: Festschrift für Otto Michel zum 60. Geburtstag*, AGSU V (Leiden/Köln: Brill, 1963), 255. See also the discussion of Alsup, *Appearance Stories*, 113.
156   Bode, *First Easter Morning*, 56; Neirynck, "Les femmes," 183; and Hendrickx, *Resurrection Narratives*, 43.
157   Bode, *First Easter Morning*, 56; and Trilling, *Das wahre Israel*, 29-31 who links it to the parallel reference in Mark 3:31-35.
158   Hendrickx, *Resurrection Narratives*, 43.
159   Perkins, *Resurrection*, 131; Bonnard, *Évangile*, 413; and Rik Hoet, *"Omnes autem vos fratres estis": Etude du concept ecclésiologique des "frères" selon Mt 23,8-12*, AnGr 232 (Roma: Università Gregoriana, 1982), 171.

Although it has been shown that Matt 28:9-10 is no mere doublet simply repeating the message of the angel, it does seem clear that the text that we have here results almost exclusively from Matthean redaction. Consideration needs to be given, therefore, to whether an early Easter appearance to women was created during the Matthean redactional process or whether an early tradition that has been completely shaped to fit this gospel scene was used. Before we leave the final redaction process, however, 28:1-10 needs to be considered in the context of the entire passion-resurrection narrative, given its function in the composition of this narrative that has already been discussed.

Most scholars agree on the apologetic and polemical nature of 27:62-66 and 28:11-15, which is closely related to it. What they do not consider, however, is the claim made early in this chapter of the close relationship between this final section and the opening section of the passion-resurrection narrative, and the fact that at both the beginning and end of this narrative, the chief *dramatis personae* are presented side by side. It is in the light of this that we need to consider the framing of 28:1-10 by the apologetic material and the commissioning of the eleven.

The dramatic irony in this section of the narrative is high and is played out between the character groups. The Jewish leaders who wanted to put Jesus to death, but who were afraid to do so because of the crowd (26:3-5), have now achieved their purpose, and yet they continue to plot against Jesus because of their fear of Jesus' disciples' claiming he had been raised in fulfilment of his predictions. Ironically, the disciples, whose deceit they fear are completely absent from the subsequent scene and the two-fold reference to them as recipients of the women's commission underscores this absence. Rather, the very thing the leaders fear is accomplished by means of a divine messenger who proclaims to the women at the tomb the same message that the leaders feared the disciples would proclaim (27:64; 28:7). This message, the women in their turn are to proclaim to the absent disciples. Furthermore, the disciples who are portrayed as absent from the raising up of Jesus are given an active role in it according to the false story which the Jewish leaders circulate among their own people. Only the two women, who stand in direct contrast to both the Jewish leaders together with their guard and also the disciples are linked within the narrative to the description of Jesus' having been raised.

In 28:1-10, the women were presented as faithful followers who remained through the crucifixion and burial to become the first to encounter the risen Jesus and to bring to the disciples the message of his resurrection together with that of his going into Galilee. While the women believe and worship the risen Jesus, some of the Eleven doubt (28:17). To them, however, is given the universal mission. By placing the two appearance pericopes at the end of the gospel, separated only by the final plotting of the Jewish leaders, traditional and redactional material has been used[160] to bring together what may well have been traditions in tension within the community, namely, the commissioning of male and female disciples. Within the final structure, however, the commissioning of the eleven male disciples dominates and the women's commission is made to serve this.[161]

In the midst of these three stories stands Jesus, raised from the dead.[162] His prediction that he would be raised lives on beyond the crucifixion, not in the faith of his male disciples but in the fear of his opponents and in the fidelity of the women disciples. He is encountered first by these women who, without fear, return to the tomb and not by the male disciples or leaders both of whom were dominated by fear. The risen Jesus stands over against the false story circulated by his opponents and finally, as the one with authority, restores the unfaithful eleven to their discipleship role through the reconciling ministry of the women disciples. They are then given the universal mission. It is this picture that is painted by bringing together different traditions--polemical, patriarchal and alternative. A brief look now at the history of at least the traditions that have been our concern here will bring this section to a close.

C. Development of the Traditions

The above study has revealed that the development of the traditions behind the stories of the cross, tomb and resurrection is a little more complex than a simple redaction of the Markan text, although this, in fact, does occupy a

---

160 Perkins, *Resurrection*, 131, for a discussion of Matt 28:16-20 and its possible relation to 1 Cor 15:5 or of its redactional nature.

161 That such an androcentric perspective in the text itself influences exegetes is seen in the work of Bloem, *Ostererzählung*, 27-28, who considers the progressive role given to the women in 27:61-28:10 as catechetical and liturgical; but that of the male disciples as fundamentally ecclesial. He too employs a dogmatic hermeneutic similar to that seen earlier in the work of Gaechter.

162 Meier, *Matthew*, 364, notes that Matthew uses no titles but simply the designation "Jesus" in the resurrection accounts.

significant part of that history. Rather, it would seem that the traditions preserved in the Markan text developed around a strong historical memory of
women at the cross and tomb of Jesus, a memory which was supplemented
as the kerygma and traditions associated with it developed.

It also appeared highly likely that the Matthean community preserved a
tradition regarding the intervention of Pilate's wife. The tradition regarding
Jesus' appearance to Mary Magdalene and the other Mary is readily considered a creation of the Matthean redaction process, but its similarity to the
Johannine account of an appearance solely to Mary Magdalene suggests an
earlier tradition from which both communities borrowed, especially since
any linguistic similarities can be explained in terms of redactional activity
rather than direct borrowing from one another.[163] This would indicate that a
trend is operative here similar to what we have seen in relation to a
number of other traditions concerning women, namely, that the Matthean
community has preserved early traditions that represented more closely the
historical memory of women in the ministry of Jesus, traditions that generally incorporated a more liberating and inclusive vision of women within
the community. Such traditions could well have supported a liberating and
inclusive vision of women within the sectors of the community where
these traditions were preserved and constantly recounted.

In the final text, the Markan and the community traditions have been
integrated, with both being edited so that they are incorporated into the
Matthean passion-resurrection account. It becomes clear that these traditions
are in tension with those regarding the male disciples' role within the
passion-resurrection story. The women whose fidelity led them along a
journey of faithful discipleship to Jerusalem and the cross are presented
much more convincingly in the Matthean redaction, by way of language and
structuring of material, as credible witnesses to both the cross and
resurrection, possibly in response to those who were challenging this
tradition. The Matthean redaction also supplements the Markan account
with the community tradition of the appearance of Jesus to the women and
his commissioning of them. This sets up a contrast between the women
disciples and Jewish leaders/male disciples. The use of the patriarchal
tradition of the universal commission being given only to the eleven male

---

163 Hengel, "Maria Magdalena," 255-256, shows how an early tradition of an appearance to
Mary Magdalene has been developed differently by both the Matthean and Johannine
evangelists.

disciples represents, however, the developing tendency within the early christian communities to rehabilitate the male disciples and thereby to undermine the witness role and commissioning of the women disciples. Their stories are made to serve the final commissioning of the eleven. This conclusion to the gospel would seem to represent, therefore, a strong tension within the community and the final redaction represents a bias toward the patriarchal traditions.

This brings us to a point where we can draw together the threads of this long analysis which has taken us from Jesus' journey to Jerusalem through his passion to his resurrection and the commissioning of female and male disciples to proclaim first and foremost the resurrection and then what Jesus had taught during his lifetime.

V. Conclusion

The question of discipleship in the face of Jesus' predicted passion and death dominated the journey of Jesus and his disciples to Jerusalem. This narrative theme was brought to a climax in the passion-resurrection account. In the final composition of the gospel, that account was framed by a three-pronged inclusion making reference to the disciples, the leaders and women disciples. Thus the three major character groups who interact with Jesus during the passion enter the scene one after the other and leave the scene in the reverse order at the end. The stories of each are then played out during the course of the narrative itself.

Our particular focus has been the narrative thread which links the stories of women stretching from the conclusion of the journey narrative to Jesus' appearance to two women at the end of the gospel. Two major themes have characterized this narrative thread, namely, the recognition of Jesus by women--both who he is and/or the significance of this climactic moment or moments in his life--and the contrast established between them and the male characters.

Toward the end of the journey narrative, a female disciple misunderstands Jesus' βασιλεία message and the nature of its fulfilment, but she hears the invitation of Jesus to move beyond misunderstanding to faithful discipleship which means a journey to the cross and she responds to this invitation, standing with other women at the cross while her two sons who have heard the same invitation have fled. As the passion account itself opens, another female disciple anoints Jesus, acknowledging him as the Anointed One as he enters his passion. Her action is discredited by the male disciples, but vindicated by the prophetic words of Jesus. Later, a woman receives the divine message as to the innocence of Jesus, but her voice is ignored in the face of the power of the male Jewish leaders and the lack of courage of her own husband, leading to Jesus' conviction. At the climax of the movement of the narrative, women stand at the cross with the gentile soldiers as the principal credible witnesses over against the Jewish rulers who have condemned Jesus and the twelve who have betrayed and deserted him. Some of these same women stay on to the very end and watch at the tomb and, by their fidelity, are the first to receive the Easter message--the one whom they saw crucified has been raised. What they have witnessed, they are to proclaim--Jesus has been raised. They are also to mediate between the risen Jesus and his faithless disciples. The climax of this narrative thread is reached, however, when the risen Jesus appears to the women as they go from the tomb.

Such traditions and the story into which they had been embedded must have been a scandal to those sectors of the Matthean community who disclaimed the validity of the witness of women and developed traditions which would rehabilitate the discredited disciples. The powerful historical memory which surrounded the presence of women at the cross and the tomb meant, however, that their stories could not be reduced to simply a service of Jesus' physical needs, but that, in sectors of the community which faithfully preserved the early memories of women in the ministry of Jesus, these stories were more clearly developed as stories of the women who were the sole credible witnesses to the cross and and to the power of God manifest in the resurrection of Jesus. They were remembered, therefore, as the foundation members of the believing community which developed around these memories.

The Matthean redaction, however, is two-edged. On the one hand, the final redaction has retained and enhanced these stories by way of the redactional activity carried out. The woman who questions Jesus regarding places for her son stands faithfully at the foot of the cross. The woman who anoints Jesus has, in fact, performed the actual anointing for his burial, and the final group of stories is so structured that the women's credible witness is highlighted and they encounter the risen Jesus. On the other hand, however, the conclusion of the gospel represents symbolically the power of the patriarchal traditions and the role played by the final redactional process in maintaining that power.[164]

The story of the woman who anoints Jesus is not told in the language of discipleship as is that of Joseph of Arimathea who performs a similar action in burying the body of Jesus. How much more poignant and striking would the story have been had the woman's relationship with Jesus in the community which accompanied him been indicated in her own story, especially if she was one of the women who followed Jesus, ministering to him. The word of Pilate's wife goes unheeded in the male world which clamours for Jesus' death, and it is this second voice which Pilate heeds rather than the prophetic voice of a woman. At the foot of the cross, the words of confession are those of the male gentile soldiers, while the women are presented as silent and looking on from a distance. Even as the scene draws to a close, the story of their encounter with the risen Jesus is framed by the deceitful plotting of the Jewish leaders and is overshadowed by the universal commission given to the eleven male disciples who have previously deserted Jesus.

We have seen the possibility previously that the very power of the individual stories and the undermining of them by counter traditions which were patriarchal in nature may have reflected a similar tension within the community which profoundly influenced the final redaction. The stories could have provided the continuing legitimation for the new role of women within the community grounded in the praxis of Jesus. The attempts to counter this power would have rendered even more urgent the preservation and re-telling of the stories. However, this would also have provoked stronger opposition to women's roles within the community and traditions would have developed which gave expression to this, grounding them also in the life of Jesus. The Matthean redaction seems to have preserved many of these tensions in the final editing of the gospel story in an attempt to preserve faithfully what was new and what was old in the community's developing tradition as it sought to keep alive the memory of Jesus in a very different environment from that in which he lived and ministered.

---

164   Anderson, "Gender and Reading," 18-21.

7. Inclusion within History

Our previous analysis has been limited almost exclusively to the text of the Matthean gospel either as an integral narrative or as the product of community tradition and final redaction. In this chapter, a brief summary of the final redaction and the development of community traditions regarding women will constitute the first stage of a movement towards the inclusion of women within the history of the Matthean community and hence of early Christianity.

In the next stage of this movement, the text will still be our basic document, but it will be analyzed in terms of the "world" that it textualizes and the "world" that it seeks to create by this textualization;[1] or, in other words, the "inscribed historical situation and rhetorical function of the story."[2] In this regard, Jameson says that "language and the texts of language carry the real within themselves as their own "intrinsic" subtexts",[3] and it is therefore the construction of this subtext as it involves women that is our major concern at this stage of analysis. Such an analysis must be accompanied, however, by a hermeneutics of suspicion that questions what is not textualized because of the androcentric world view of the author. What are the hints that the text supplies of a world that is perhaps being suppressed rather than being created by the text? Even this, however, is an acknowledgment that women as well as men are central to the narrative world of the author.

Fundamental, also, to this stage of analysis is a recognition that the text itself is a poetic text in narrative form. This is the rhetorical strategy that has been chosen by the author as the means of communication with the audience. Such a text does not have a one-to-one correspondence with the "real" world of the audience but rather invites them into the world of the text in

---

1 Jameson, "Symbolic Inference," 74, for a fuller treatment of this two-fold function of texts.
2 Elisabeth Schüssler Fiorenza, "A Feminist Critical Interpretation for Liberation: Martha and Mary: Lk. 10:38-42," *Religion and Intellectual Life* III:2 (1986), 30.
3 Jameson, "Symbolic Inference," 74.

order to explore new possibilities for understanding life.[4] One of the
difficulties that we face in relation to the Matthean gospel, however, is that
the narrative is not explicitly about the evangelist's community. Its subject
matter is the life of Jesus. His story is told, however, within a new historical
setting, namely, that of the evangelist and the evangelist's community.[5]
Thus, there are at least two different levels of the narrative, or what Lategan
calls, "stages of reception of a text": that of the historical Jesus and that of the
Matthean community. He goes on to say, with regard to these levels of
reception, that

> ... reference in the final text functions *by virtue* of the previous receptions.
> These previous receptions, each with its own "world" or frame of reference,
> are presupposed in the final text and form the foil against which the final
> text sets itself off.[6]

Our focus will be predominantly on the final stage of reception within the
Matthean community and the world that is created in the narrative for that
community in order to reflect its present and to shape its future. Some attention, however, will need to be given to the world of the historical Jesus
to which the narrative refers.

Much of the material for this analysis has already been brought to light
in the narrative and redactional studies already completed. Of particular concern is the function of the implied author, the construct whereby the symbolic universe or ideological point of view and the values by which the
community lives or desires to live are inscribed in the narrative. Attention
must also be given to the signifying codes and social conventions represented in the text since these too contribute to the establishment of the world
of the text but are also drawn from the world of the author and audience.
This stage of the analysis will enable us to begin to give expression to what I
have called "Women in the Narrative World of Matthew".

In the light of this articulation of the world that is textualized and the
world that the text seeks to create, we will move to the final stage of our
analysis. Here, we will be concerned with the reconstruction of the socio-
ecclesial situation of women which the Matthean gospel addresses. Our

---

4   Bernard C. Lategan, "Some Unresolved Methodological Issues in New Testament
    Hermeneutics," in Lategan and Vorster, *Text and Reality*, 21, where he distinguishes
    between descriptive text and narrative world (erzählte Welt).
5   Willem S. Vorster, "Meaning and Reference: The Parables of Jesus in Mark 4," ibid.,
    57-58.
6   Bernard C. Lategan, "Reference: Reception, Redescription and Reality," ibid., 77.

presupposition will be that this finds expression not only in the pastoral-theological concerns of the evangelist in relation to women, but even more so in the concerns of women themselves that are captured in the traditions that we have studied, concerns expressed directly by their contribution to the shaping of the gospel story or indirectly through their participation in the life of the house-churches which constituted the Matthean community.[7] The analysis carried out in the previous stage will allow us to draw certain inferences regarding the "real-world" of both the author and the audience because of the interaction between the "real-world" and the narrative world. As Greene and Kahn point out,

> In their creation of fictions, writers call upon the same signifying codes that pervade social interactions, re-presenting in fiction the rituals and symbols that make up social practice. Literature itself is a 'discursive practice' whose conventions encode social conventions and are ideologically complicit. Moreover, since each invocation of a code is also its reinforcement or rein-scription, literature does more than transmit ideology: it actually creates it-- it is 'a mediating, moulding force in society' that structures our sense of the world.[8]

This stage of our analysis will be called, therefore, "Women in the Matthean Communities", and there will be a constant dialogue with the many other studies which have sought to reconstruct the contextual history of the Matthean community from a variety of perspectives.

The analysis carried out in this chapter must involve dialogue with the information that is available to us regarding women's participation in the socio-religious life of the Graeco-Roman world in the first century. As more and more detailed information becomes available, however, it is clear that the conditions of women's lives often varied from region to region and from era to era. Therefore, broad general comparisons will be avoided, but the information available will be used to support or critique conclusions arrived at from a literary analysis where this is possible. We turn, first, however, to a summary of the previous redactional analysis, namely, the inclusion of women within the history of the text.

---

7   Schüssler Fiorenza, *In Memory of Her*, 70, points out that "theoretical frameworks adequate to a feminist historiography must not only elucidate what it meant for women to become active members and leaders in early Christianity but also highlight the historical significance of women's active involvement in early Christian beginnings." Later, pp. 85-86, she points out that the theoretical framework chosen by feminist historians must "maintain the dialectical tension of women's historical existence as active participants in history as well as objects of patriarchal oppression."

8   Greene and Kahn, "Feminist Scholarship," 4.

I. Redaction and Community Traditions

The final redaction of the gospel was responsible for its overall structure or final composition.[9] As John Meier indicates, this redaction drew on the work of a christian scribal school whose reflections and study gave rise to certain citations from the Hebrew Scriptures being used as the basis for some of the community's developing christology.[10] It was also noted above that the majority of the citations used in the gospel text belong to the "liberation trajectory" of the Hebrew Scriptures. As well, the final redaction incorporated the traditions that were preserved in the various sectors or house churches which constituted the total community,[11] with the Markan gospel, and possibly with Q.[12]

Both the narrative-critical analysis and the redaction-critical study already undertaken have shown that within this final composition, there is a well-developed narrative theme of the discipleship of women which has been shaped during the final redaction. A community tradition, which remembered four women from the Hebrew Scriptures as foremothers of those women who were participants in the life of Jesus in a way that was anomalous in the patriarchal world into which he was born and in which he lived and ministered, was incorporated during the final redaction into the patrilineage of Jesus as the gospel opened. Three stories which told of the healing of female supplicants were retained in the simple early form in which they were remembered in the community and were then incorporated into the highly structured section containing nine miracle stories so that they functioned as paradigms of women's reception of the fruits of the βασιλεία, of women's faith, and of women's discipleship of Jesus. Another story of a woman's faith was significantly developed within the Matthean redaction to

---

9   There is no evidence that would indicate that the overall structure of the Matthean gospel was significantly altered beyond the time of what I have called its "final composition" between the years 80 and 90 of the first century CE.
10 Raymond E. Brown and John P. Meier, *Antioch and Rome: New Testament Cradles of Catholic Christianity* (New York/Ramsey: Paulist, 1983), 56-57.
11 This notion is developed most fully by Crosby, *House of Disciples*, especially 21-75.
12 See Werner Georg Kümmel, *Introduction to the New Testament*, rev. ed., trans. Howard Clark Kee (London: SCM, 1975), 106-110, for a discussion of the sources of the Matthean gospel; and Jean Zumstein, "Antioche sur l'Oronte et l'évangile selon Matthieu," *SNTU* A/5 (1980): 131-132, in which he discusses the sources used by Matthew and pp. 132-138 in which he situates the resultant gospel in a possible community setting.

incorporate conflicting streams of tradition within the community around
the question of a mission to the Gentiles and the question of women's participation in the liturgical life of the community. This story is resolved in a
way that points to the woman's role as foremother to the gentile mission
and her story becomes a paradigm for women's inclusion within the liturgical and theological life of the community. This is reinforced by the redactional emphasis on the inclusive nature of discipleship in the same section
of the narrative.

While the final redaction presents one woman as an opponent of Jesus'
message and mission and another as one who misunderstands it, these two
images of women are reversed in the latter part of the gospel when a woman
stands out from among the ultimate opponents of Jesus and proclaims his
innocence, and the woman who misunderstands shows a shift in both understanding and fidelity which takes her to the foot of Jesus' cross. In fact, the
Matthean redaction of the passion-resurrection narrative makes women one
of the significant groups in the unfolding of this last great movement in the
narrative, and the only group who remain faithful. One prophetically recognizes the imminence of the death of Jesus, proclaiming him as The
Anointed One as he enters his passion. Others stay as faithful disciples
through the death and burial of Jesus so that they are the authentic witnesses
to these events for the early christian communities. They also see the empty
tomb and encounter the risen Jesus.

This significant narrative thread, however, finds its place within an
androcentric narrative which, at times, explicitly supports patriarchy. This is
most clearly apparent at the beginning and end of the gospel story, in the patrilineage of Jesus and his commissioning of the eleven male disciples to a
universal mission. It is seen throughout, however, in that the most significant christological titles are found on the lips of men, the group called
"disciples", who when named, are male, while it is clear that both women
and men followed Jesus. Moreover, the male characters who are often given
a voice in the narrative certainly dominate, at least in number, the female
characters who are often left voiceless. The result is that the narrative thread
of women's discipleship has become submerged in the androcentric narrative to the point of being almost silenced by it, as the history of research into
the Matthean gospel has shown. Thus, the androcentric perspective in the
final redaction has prevailed despite an attempt at a certain point in the
redaction, to record faithfully a counter tradition. Like the women from
Israel's story whose memory was preserved in the genealogy, the women in

the life of Jesus were anomalous within an androcentric world view. Their stories were retained because of their potential for empowerment within some sectors of the community and because of their strong roots in its historical memory, but they were finally incorporated into a patriarchal narrative which succeeded in domesticating them and rendering them silent.

Going behind the final redaction, we find the preservation and development of community traditions that significantly influenced the final form of the gospel. Some of these traditions, especially the three miracle stories of Matt 8 and 9, were maintained in an early form, which suggests that they were based on women's experience of the Jesus movement and that their preservation in this form was an attempt to remain faithful to the vision contained therein. Others, like the memory of the four women from the Hebrew Scriptures, may well have been developed within some sectors of the community where the memory of the historical Jesus' inclusion of women within his group of followers was reflected upon in the light of the scriptures. Within these same sectors, the traditions which critiqued patriarchal familial structures may have been kept alive and augmented--the tradition surrounding Mary that is incorporated into the infancy narrative, aspects of the miracle stories, and minor references to inclusive discipleship not based on familial structures. Another tradition which also seems to have been significantly augmented, this time in both the sectors of the community that supported the full inclusion of women and those opposed to it, was that of the Canaanite woman. Finally, there was notable amplification of the various traditions which linked women to the last journey of Jesus to Jerusalem, to his death and to the proclamation of the resurrection. Many of these traditions also served to maintain powerful historical memories.

Thus, it seems clear that within the Matthean community there has been a significant development of the traditions relating to women which would suggest that these traditions were important in that they either addressed the real-life situation of that community or that they were intended to shape its vision of the future. In the light of the final redaction and the development of certain community traditions that significantly influenced this work, we turn now to an analysis of the subtext contained within the text of the gospel.

II. Women in the Narrative World of Matthew

> It can safely be concluded that the house churches at Antioch and elsewhere found Matthew's gospel both constitutive and normative for their life and apostolic witness.[13]

These words of Crosby indicate what is the commonly accepted opinion of scholars, namely, that the inscribed historical situation of the Matthean gospel is that of the Matthean community or communities and not that of the historical Jesus. Hence, what follows will be an attempt to narrate the story of women in the Matthean community that is reflected in the gospel text as well as the future of women in that community that the text seeks to establish. At the heart of the Matthean gospel, however, is the story of Jesus as that story has been remembered and shaped by generations of believers from the time of the death of Jesus until the writing of the gospel. It is this story which the final redaction of the gospel has also shaped to speak to the situation of the communities for which it was written and to form their christian vision for the future.[14] Therefore some attention will need to be given to women in the world of the Jesus' movement as the originating vision and impetus that was at least one of the significant elements forming the symbolic universe of the Matthean community, but our major focus will be this community and its constitutive "house churches".

The Matthean story of Jesus opens with a genealogy, a patrilineage of Jesus, and thereby introduces the readers to one of the primary rhetorical strategies to be employed throughout the gospel, namely, the presentation of a history-like narrative.[15] By way of the genealogy, Jesus is situated within Israel's history. But the genealogy is much more than an historical statement. As Wilson suggests:

> The genealogies may therefore provide the modern historian with valuable insights into the domestic, political, and religious perceptions of the people who use the genealogies.[16]

---

13 Crosby, *House of Disciples*, 49.
14 Ibid., 131: "By telling the story of Jesus, Matthew demonstrated how the pattern of Jesus' life could be reflected in the lifestyle or ethos of his house churches."
15 Robert M. Fowler, "Reading Matthew Reading Mark: Observing the First Steps toward Meaning-as-Reference in the Synoptic Gospels," in *SBL 1986 Seminar Papers*, ed. K. H. Richards (Atlanta: Scholars, 1986), 13-16; and Horton, "Parenthetical Pregnancy," 176-178.
16 Wilson, *Genealogy and History*, 200.

The genealogy of Matthew's gospel is no exception.

Initially, it gives us an insight into the favourable economic perceptions that were presupposed within the community, for, as Robert Smith points out,

> ... genealogies were especially safeguarded as the historical records of the urban elite. They served to record a family's pedigree and defended its prestige.[17]

Sociologically, genealogies functioned as "household histories" (Gen 6:9; 37:2). Hence, the opening of the gospel provides a foundation for the Matthean community's consideration of itself as the household of Jesus, whose own origin lay in a particular family, that of Abraham and David.[18] This image of the community as a household of faith seems to be a theological amplification of a social situation, namely, the community's foundation within the homes of believers and its continued existence as house communities or house churches.[19] The genealogy may also have functioned socially as an instrument of propaganda,[20] whose major purpose was to establish the honour lines of Jesus, especially in the face of questions regarding his legitimacy.[21] As such it points to community awareness of opposition which sought to discredit Jesus and the Jesus traditions.[22]

When we consider, however, that the genealogy is in the form of a patrilineage, we gain further insight into the symbolic universe which it seeks to create. It, together with the Joseph tradition of Matt 1:18-25 and 2, affirms patriarchy as the foundational ethos of the Matthean communities and the patriarchal familial structure as its social expression.[23] It may have been intended to function ideologically within the communities to re-establish and legitimate such a world view with its attendant social structures in

---

17   Robert H. Smith, "Were the Early Christians Middle-Class? A Sociological Analysis of the New Testament," *Currents in Theology and Mission* 7 (1980): 266.
18   Crosby, *House of Disciples*, 85.
19   Floyd V. Filson, "The Significance of the Early House Churches," *JBL* 58 (1939): 105-112. Also Crosby, *House of Disciples*, 11-12, considers *oikos/oikía* to be the "assumed primary metaphor" in Matthew's gospel, like the air the community breathed.
20   D. E. Nineham, "The Genealogy in St. Matthew's Gospel and Its Significance for the Study of the Gospels," *BJRL* 58 (1975-76): 424.
21   See Malina, *New Testament World*, 27, and also Schaberg, *Illegitimacy of Jesus*, which has been discussed extensively.
22   David M. Bossman, "Authority and Tradition in First Century Judaism and Christianity," *BTB* 17 (1987): 8.
23   That such values were supported within Graeco-Roman sectors of the community as well as those who drew on the Hebrew Scriptures is confirmed by E. A. Judge, "St. Paul as a Radical Critic of Society," *Interchange* 16 (1974): 191-203, especially 201, who discusses the influence of Greek humanism on first century Graeco-Roman society.

the face of the grave crisis that faced the patriarchal family in the Roman Empire of the first century of the Common Era;[24] and also in the face of the teachings of Jesus regarding a new kinship structure based on fidelity to the βασιλεία vision and the Jesus traditions rather than on family ties and bloodlines. This trend favoured continuity within the tradition, grounding this in the Hebrew Scriptures, and it would have been supported by many of the cultural and political values in the surrounding society.

The patrilineage and its context within the infancy narrative are punctuated, however, by a counter tradition. Four women are named in the genealogy; the woman, Mary, is the one through whom the Isaian prophecy is fulfilled; and it is she together with her son whom the wise men from the East find in the house (2:11). Since none of these stories function symbolically in support of patriarchy or its attendant family structures, it can be proposed that a certain ambivalence or tension in relation to gender characterized the community's symbolic universe. One of the values that is associated with the advent of Jesus, the Christ, which challenges household membership according to familial blood ties, is that of inclusion. Women as well as men, Gentiles as well as Jews, were significant in Jesus' family history and in his birth. They are all found within the household. This suggests that the gospel seeks to clearly affirm this inclusion as a characteristic of the future vision which it creates.[25] The valuing and preservation of inclusion must continue to punctuate any vision or implementation of the patriarchal household as a model for the christian community.

Within such a world, women participated not according to their status in a patriarchal family but on the basis of their inclusion within the βασιλεία vision of Jesus. Accordingly, it appears that both the Jesus movement and the later christian communities were not based on family ties, but they reflect certain kinship structures which were a necessary element in Mediterranean societies of the first century. The particular model which

---

24   Jo Ann McNamara, "Wives and Widows in Early Christian Thought," *IJWS* 2 (1979): 575-578; Selvidge, "Women and the Future," 218; and idem, *Daughters of Jerusalem*, 63. Selvidge argues that the War of 70 CE was the cause of family disruption in Palestine and surrounding Jewish communities. Raoul Mortley, *Womanhood: The Feminine in Ancient Hellenism, Gnosticism, Christianity, and Islam* (Sydney: Delacroix, 1981), 46, points to Celsus' concern that Christianity was in fact causing the collapse of familial and societal authority.

25   Smith, "Early Christians," 275, who proposes: "Matthew's was itself a comprehensively mixed community, including many well-educated and well-heeled persons, because that community was inclusive rather than exclusive and practiced ecumenicity up and down the social and cultural ladder. At least Matthew had such a vision of inclusion and ecumenicity and his gospel was received and preserved by his community."

Malina proposes to explain both movements as they are represented in the early christian narratives is that of patron and client with its attendant establishment of factions.[26] According to Malina's model, however, the patron-client relationship is established with and by "adult males";[27] but within the Jesus' movement and the subsequent christian communities, women were also a significant part of this new kinship structure. They were certainly members of the group which accompanied Jesus as the strong historical memory of their presence at the foot of the cross indicates and they responded to the invitation to become part of his core group as is shown by the preservation of the early memory of the vocation story of Peter's mother-in-law.[28] They also became clientele by way of their reception of the teaching and healing of Jesus as many of the stories already analyzed have illustrated, especially that of the woman with the haemorrhage who is not dismissed in the Matthean narrative but is given an invitation: "Take heart!"[29]

The symbolization of the Matthean community as a group-centred faction or coalition (Matt 23:8-12) would have supported new kinship structures. Women were not considered members of the households because of their place in familial kinship structures but rather because of their participation in the community gathered around Jesus Messiah as leader. The women who ·symbolized this for them were Tamar, Rahab, Ruth, Bathsheba, and Mary, and the tradition which gathered together their stories is included in the final gospel. That such a vision and its implementation.created conflicting value systems seems clear from the stories which we

---

26   Malina, "Patron and Client," 2-32. Of special import for an understanding of the Matthean symbolic universe is the short section he calls "God as patron", pp. 9-10, where he shows how the Matthean language of God as "father" and of "kingdom of heaven" can be explained well according to the patron-client model. I will not take this up further here as it is outside the scope of this study, but this aspect of Malina's work supports the use of the patron-client model in relation to the Matthean symbolic universe.

27   Ibid., 5.

28   Ibid., 18. Malina illustrates that Jesus moves from his connection with John the Baptist to establish his own faction by recruiting his own core group.

29   Ibid., 12. Luise Schottroff, "Women as Followers of Jesus in New Testament Times: An Exercise in Social-Historical Exegesis of the Bible," in *The Bible and Liberation: Political and Social Hermeneutics*, ed. Norman K. Gottwald (Maryknoll: Orbis, 1983), 419-423, discusses women's following of Jesus in Palestine before 70 CE. She considers that they were partners of the men because of two factors: first, the economic, social and political situation which rendered both women and men poor; and second, "the collective life" which resulted from the "hope for the impending kingdom of God". See also Schüssler Fiorenza, *In Memory of Her*, 118-151, who discusses the inclusive nature of the *basileia* vision of Jesus and the "discipleship of equals" which this called forth.

have analyzed. If the mother of the sons of Zebedee was introduced into the story to present a woman within the typical role of mother within the patriarchal familial structures in order to support the belief system of some sectors of the community, then that intention has been subverted by the context of her story within the entire gospel. As mother, the woman misunderstands the role of the Messiah as she seeks new positions of honour and power for her sons, and it is only when she stands apart from her sons and with the other faithful women at the cross that she represents the true discipleship of women. Similarly, the mother-in-law of Peter is introduced to the audience as a woman embedded within the family structure, but it is by way of her encounter with Jesus and her sharing in the healing power he offers that she becomes a minister of the gospel, symbolic of women's ministerial leadership within the community whatever their own family history.

Such participation on the basis of new kinship structures receives further symbolic affirmation in the story of the Canaanite woman: a foreign woman who dialogues with Jesus on her own behalf and on behalf of her daughter in an attempt to gain, to legitimate, or to retain their participation in the healing power of Jesus that resided in the community's remembering and retelling of the Jesus story and in its breaking of the bread. The words given to her signify a valuing of foreign women's participation in the liturgy and in the communities' theological reflection, while the arguments set up against her support strong opposition to this participation. It seems that the inclusive vision of the βασιλεία which the gospel promoted did not go unopposed at the ideological level, and perhaps also at the level of implementation, a consideration for the subsequent section.

The women remembered in the passion-resurrection story of Jesus most represent the new kinship structures envisioned for the living out of the βασιλεία vision of Jesus. Each of them acts independently of any familial bonds. They are prophets and missionaries entrusted with the Easter message, representatives of the new roles that were available as the early christian communities formed and grew. One is an independent woman, perhaps of significant wealth, who brings this to the service of Jesus in his time of need and in this way symbolizes a faithful response to the gospel message.[30] Others courageously remain faithful to Jesus, the condemned criminal, and are entrusted with the message of his resurrection. They are

---

30 See Crosby, *House of Disciples*, 117-119, for a more detailed treatment of this aspect of the story.

women who act alone, but whose actions stand at the very centre of the
ethos of the communities. Their stories affirm the centrality of women
among the clientele of Jesus, the patron, around whom the groups that
formed the Matthean community coalesced in their struggle against an
often hostile environment (10:16-22).

This points, therefore, to a visioning of the community as ἐκκλησία, a
gathering of free individuals, and not as a patriarchal household.[31] One
finds, however, that this ἐκκλησία is variously symbolized in the narrative
world. In the first instance, it is said to be founded on the male leadership of
Peter (16:18), and yet later it is imaged as the gathering of two or three in the
name of Jesus (18:20) regardless of ethnic or gender qualifications. The
twelve male disciples are its foundational representatives (10:2-4; 28:16-20)
and yet the followers of Jesus both within the Jesus movement and in the
later Matthean communities included women as well as men. In order to
understand more fully the symbolic universe created by way of these tensions or ambiguities which are at the heart of the function of gender within
the narrative, we must give brief attention to the redactional nature of the
special Petrine material in the Matthean gospel as well as the Matthean presentation of the character group called "disciples", both of which have
received detailed attention in recent scholarship.[32]

The term μαθητής reflects Hellenistic linguistic traditions, according to
the studies of Luz and Wilkins,[33] which suggests that it came into

---

31   Ibid., 33-35, for a discussion of ἐκκλησία and its relation to οἶκος within the Christian
      Scriptures. See also Wayne A. Meeks, *The First Urban Christians: The Social World of
      the Apostle Paul* (New Haven/London: Yale University Press, 1983), 74-110.
32   Raymond E. Brown, Karl P. Donfried, and John Reumann, *Peter in the New Testament*
      (Minneapolis: Augsburg/New York: Paulist, 1973), 75-107; Gerhard Barth's discussion
      of the essence of discipleship in his essay, "Matthew's Understanding of the Law," in
      Bornkamm, Barth and Held, *Tradition and Interpretation*, 58-164, especially, 105-125;
      Eduard Schweizer, *Matthäus und seine Gemeinde*, SBS 71 (Stuttgart: KBW Verlag,
      1974), 151-155, 159-163; Ulrich Luz, "The Disciples in the Gospel according to Matthew,"
      in Stanton, *Interpretation of Matthew*, 98-128; Jean Zumstein, *La condition du croyant
      dans l'évangile selon Matthieu*, OBO 16 (Fribourg Suisse: Éditions Universi-
      taires/Göttingen: Vandenhoeck & Ruprecht, 1977); Kingsbury, "The Verb *AKOLOU-
      THEIN* "; idem, "The Figure of Peter in Matthew's Gospel as a Theological Problem,"
      JBL 98 (1979): 67-83; Minear, "Disciples and Crowds"; Richard A. Edwards, "Uncertain
      Faith: Matthew's Portrait of the Disciples," in *Discipleship in the New Testament*, ed.
      Fernando F. Segovia (Philadelphia: Fortress, 1985), 47-61; and the most recent and
      comprehensive work of Michael J. Wilkins, *The Concept of Disciple in Matthew's
      Gospel as Reflected in the use of the Term Μαθητής* (Leiden: Brill, 1988).
33   Luz, "Disciples," 115-119; and Wilkins, *Concept of Disciple*, 11-125, in which he investi-
      gates in detail the background to the term; this investigation is summarized on pp. 217-
      221. He suggests: "In the late Hellenistic period μαθητής continues to be used with gen-
      eral connotations of a "learner" and "adherent." The type of adherency was determined

prominence as a designation for the followers of Jesus as the Jesus story formed the foundation for early christian communities. The term occurs rarely in Q material and hence is rarely found on the lips of Jesus.[34] It is difficult to establish, therefore, whether this term was used either by Jesus himself or by others to refer to his followers during his earthly ministry. This is not impossible, however, since Wilkins shows that the terms μαθητής and its Hebrew equivalent *talmîdh* "were popular terms at the time of Jesus to designate a follower who was virtually committed to a teacher/leader and/or movement." He goes on to say that "the terms themselves did not determine the type of discipleship; the type [of] discipleship was determined by the type of leader or movement or teaching to which the disciple was committed."[35] The occurrence of the term most predominantly in the narrative material of the gospel means, however, that it may reflect the perspective of the compilers of the Q material or the evangelists, hence early christian communities, rather than Jesus himself.

Further evidence which may substantiate an argument for the origin of the term μαθητής within early christian communities who preserved and developed memories of the historical Jesus is the fact that this term was not used by Paul and is found only within the Gospels in which the Jesus story is central and in Acts. It does not designate a particular office, function or mission, but rather is a general term for the following of Jesus or being an adherent to him and to the movement which developed around him. This seems to confirm that the term possibly belongs to the early narrative traditions of the Jesus story.

The phrase οἱ δώδεκα [The Twelve], on the other hand, does belong to a Pauline or even a pre-Pauline tradition[36] and is found in 1 Cor 15:5. This suggests, therefore, an early origin for this tradition, but as Schüssler Fiorenza points out, it is no guarantee of the historicity of the Twelve:

> ... the traditional formula of 1 Cor 15:3-5 does not indicate whether this group of the Twelve existed already before Easter as a definite circle of

---

by the master, but it ranged from being the pupil of a philosopher, to being the follower of a great thinker and master of the past, to being the devotee of a religious figure."

34   In Matthew: 10:24-25, whose source is Q; 10:42, an interpretation of Mk 9:41; and Mt 26:18 which parallels Mk 14:14.

35   Ibid., 221.

36   C. K. Barrett, *A Commentary on the First Epistle to the Corinthians*, 2nd ed., BNTC (1971; reprint London: Black, 1979), 341.

disciples in the ministry of Jesus or whether it was constituted by the resurrection appearances and commission of the Lord.[37]

There was no connection, however, between οἱ δώδεκα and μαθητής in the Pauline traditions.

The possible Q saying[38] which has been preserved in Matthew at 19:28 does not include the term μαθητής, but it refers to the disciples indirectly as those who have followed [οἱ ἀκολουθήσαντές μοι]. In this saying which is clearly eschatological, the followers of Jesus are promised judgment seats over the twelve tribes of Israel; but such a saying is in tension with Jesus' response to the request that James and John be granted seats in his eschatological kingdom (20:20-28). With regard to 19:28, Schüssler Fiorenza points out that it

> does not underline the historical existence of a group of twelve men but the function of the disciples of Jesus in the eschatological future vis-a-vis Israel.[39]

Burnett, on the other hand, may come close to explaining the origins of this reference when he suggests that the saying supported moves among second generation Hellenistic-Jewish communities who preserved a memory of the Twelve in order to legitimate distinctions within their communities.[40] Whether such distinctions were along gender lines is uncertain, but Schüssler Fiorenza seems to be correct when she says that in the early traditions, the Twelve were conceived of as "eschatological-symbolical" rather than "historical-masculine."[41]

It is unclear, therefore when, where or why the link was made between μαθητής and οἱ δώδεκα, but they are certainly linked in the Markan tradition. Here the Twelve are the named male disciples of 3:13-19, a text generally

---

37   Elisabeth Schüssler Fiorenza, "The Twelve," in *Women Priests: A Catholic Commentary on the Vatican Declaration*, ed. Leonard and Arlene Swidler (New York: Paulist, 1977), 116.

38   Ivan Havener, *Q: The Sayings of Jesus. With a Reconstruction of Q by Athanasius Polag*, Good News Studies 19 (Wilmington, Del.: Michael Glazier, 1987), 145, includes this among the Q sayings according to his source, Athanasius Polag, *Fragmenta Q. Textheft zur Logienquelle* (Neukirchen-Vluyn: Neukirchener, 1979). For Polag, however, its inclusion is questionable, see p. 78. Fred W. Burnett, "Παλιγγενεσία in Matt. 19:28: A Window on the Matthean Community," *JSNT* 17 (1983): 69, also questions whether 19:28 actually is Q material, but goes on to affirm, however, that Matthew seems to receive the idea of the eschatological role of the twelve from traditional sources.

39   Schüssler Fiorenza, "The Twelve," 116.

40   Burnett, "Παλιγγενεσία," 64-65.

41   Schüssler Fiorenza, "The Twelve," 117.

considered to be redactional,[42] and throughout the gospel they are almost synonymous with the character group called οἱ μαθηταί. They are appointed to be with Jesus and to do as he did--to preach and to exorcise (3:14-15). Hence the two terms οἱ μαθηταί and οἱ δώδεκα are closely linked to the historical Jesus in the Markan narrative. These fail, however, to understand his mission (6:52; 8:17, 21) and hence to fulfil their own, but the gospel indicates that the mission, at least the preaching mission, goes on in and through the Markan community (13:10; 14:9). There is a divergence of opinion among scholars, therefore, as to the exact referent for the group called disciples within the Markan community, but it seems generally agreed that they had a representative function.[43] Such a representative function is shared, however, by another group of characters who, in fact, are foils for the disciples in that they represent true discipleship values,[44] and among this group women are included. This literary technique of the use of foils suggests that for the Markan church, the twelve were not considered the only representatives of discipleship nor was leadership confined to them or to their successors. The gender of the twelve was not, therefore, constitutive of discipleship or ministerial functions within the community.

Within the Matthean gospel, the historicizing tendency in relation to the terms μαθητής and οἱ δώδεκα visible in the Markan redaction is considered to be accepted as established tradition.[45] The μαθηταί are, therefore, generally seen as identified with the Twelve [οἱ δώδεκα] although this does not exclude the existence of other disciples.[46] By way of a variety of redactional techniques, however, which have been analyzed in great detail

---

42   Ibid., 117 and 121, n. 6 for references. Some manuscripts add the phrase οὒς καὶ ἀποστόλους ὠνόμασεν to οἱ δώδεκα in 3:14 but as Metzger, A Textual Commentary, 80, points out, this may be an interpolation from Luke. The linking of οἱ δώδεκα and ἀπόστολος is clearly a Lukan tradition which has had little influence on Mark or Matthew and so shall not be considered further here.

43   Regarding the complexity of the characterization of the disciples in Mark's gospel, see Theodore J. Weeden, Mark: Traditions in Conflict (Philadelphia: Fortress, 1971); Werner Kelber, ed., The Passion in Mark: Studies on Mark 14-16 (Philadelphia: Fortress, 1976); Augustine Stock, Call to Discipleship: A Literary Study of Mark's Gospel, Good News Studies 1 (Wilmington, Del.: Michael Glazier, 1982); Ernest Best, Following Jesus: Discipleship in the Gospel of Mark, JSNTSup 4 (Sheffield: JSOT Press, 1981); and idem, Disciples and Discipleship: Studies in the Gospel according to Mark (Edinburgh: T. & T. Clark, 1986).

44   Rhoads and Michie, Mark as Story, 129-136.

45   Luz, "Disciples," 98-102, discusses this tendency, but points out that it is no more developed in the Matthean gospel than in the Markan tradition used by the Matthean redactor. Zumstein, Condition du croyant, 45, considers the technique stylization rather than historicization.

46   Wilkins, Concept of Disciple, 132-133, 166-167. Luz, "Disciples," 99, suggests that Matthew took this identification for granted as part of the tradition.

by Wilkins,[47] the term μαθηταί is seen to be employed in the Matthean gospel to link those named "disciples" with the teaching of Jesus so that the disciple hears and understands the words of Jesus, lives this teaching, and is able to teach others.[48] The group called "disciples" are therefore character-ized, within the gospel narrative, according to their performance or lack of performance of these tasks in the life of the historical Jesus. Within the symbolic universe of the narrative, therefore, the μαθηταί are presumed to function rhetorically as "examples" for the Matthean communities.[49] Furthermore, in the Matthean narrative, the μαθηταί are considered to be represented by Peter who as a "first among equals"[50] is exemplary of both positive and negative discipleship along with the other disciples.[51] Wilkins proposes, therefore, that the special Petrine material in the Matthean gospel serves to identify Peter as "a very real disciple whom Jesus has personally taught, corrected, and established as a rock to carry on his work"[52] in order to make the group called "disciples" more accessible to the members of the Matthean communities.

In the studies considered above, little attention has been given to gender.[53] The analysis carried out in Chapters Two to Six above has shown, however, that within the gospel of Matthew, the term μαθητής seems to function as a patriarchal construct since only males are ever named as members of the group designated by this term,[54] although it occurs often with an indefinite refererent.[55] The effect of this within the symbolic world of the narrative is to characterize the group called "disciples" as male. That gender, however, created ambiguity in this symbolic universe precisely in

---

47   Ibid., 126-172. See also Zumstein, *Condition du croyant*, 22-46.
48   Barth, "Matthew's Understanding of the Law," 105-112, examines the Matthean use of συνιέναι in relation to discipleship. See also Crosby, *House of Disciples*, 44-45; and Luz, "Disciples," 102-105.
49   Luz, "Disciples," 110-114, says that they are "transparent for the present situation" and indicates that the historicizing tendency is a necessary pre-requisite for this trans-parency. Both Zumstein, *Condition du croyant*, 40, and Wilkins, *Concept of Disciple*, 169, refer to the disciples as "examples" or to their function as "exemplaire" for the Matthean community.
50   Kingsbury, "Figure of Peter," 69-76; and Wilkins, *Concept of Disciple*, 210-211.
51   Ibid., 211.
52   Ibid., 210.
53   One of the few exceptions is Schüssler Fiorenza, "The Twelve". Also Anderson, "Gender and Reading," 23-24, considers it very briefly in the conclusion to her study of the Matthean gospel.
54   Matt 10:1-4; 11:1; 17:6, 1; 27:57. Note the later tradition (Acts 9:36) in which Tabitha is called μαθήτρια, but she is not necessarily considered one of the followers of the historical Jesus.
55   Matt 5:1; 9:10, 37; 14:15; 15:33, 36; 16:21; 18:1 by way of example, as well as the indefinite reference for the verb μαθητεύω in 13:52 and 28:19.

relation to the question of the following of Jesus is clear. There is no specific terminology used in the gospels for "discipleship" or the following of Jesus as there is for the character group called "disciples", although the gospel tradition provides a composite picture of it by way of the use of verbs such as ἀκολουθέω and διακονέω, teachings of Jesus, and examples of faithful following of Jesus, many of which have been previously analyzed. It has also been shown conclusively in relation to the Matthean gospel, that the women characters demonstrate much greater fidelity to this following of Jesus and adherence to him and his way than do many male characters, especially the twelve called disciples. An attempt must be made, therefore, to explain how this ambiguity functioned within the symbolic framework of the narrative.

It seems that the Matthean community received a tradition which held to the historicity of a distinctively male discipleship group and that this tradition profoundly coloured the narrative. The placing of this tradition in the gospel context alongside stories of women's fidelity to Jesus and sayings of his regarding the inclusive nature of discipleship tended to modify its possible exclusive character. For this reason it can be argued that the term μαθηταί functioned rhetorically and symbolically within the Matthean narrative as inclusive of all adherents to Jesus and the Jesus movement within the communities. Both women and men who had heard the message of Jesus, who understood it and now sought to live and teach it constituted these communities. It seems, therefore, that within the symbolic universe of the Matthean narrative, the character group called "disciples", who may have been characterized in certain streams of the tradition as historically male, functioned as an inclusive symbol.

Such an explanation of ambiguity and conflicting traditions does not represent a unique situation for the evangelist. We have already seen that a similar situation had to be addressed in relation to the gentile mission.[56] Just as with that question, an early tradition which may even have been historical is tempered by other memories which have more profoundly shaped subsequent practice. Therefore, if an early tradition, even an historical memory, was preserved which linked the specific term μαθητής only with οἱ

---

56 See also William R. Farmer, "The Post-Sectarian Character of Matthew and Its Post-War Setting in Antioch of Syria," *Perspectives in Religious Studies* 3 (1976): 235-247, in which he demonstrates how Pauline and anti-Pauline as well as other conflicting traditions are placed side by side so as to "mitigate against extreme interpretations of any one particular point of view."

δώδεκα (twelve male followers) or even male followers generally, this could
not have functioned exclusively since early memories of others who accompanied Jesus have also been preserved. Moreover, the practice of the
early church in which both women and men quickly became believers and
were involved in both missionary activity and the care of local house
churches was activated by an inclusive rather than exclusive memory of discipleship within the Jesus movement. This finds particular expression in
the Matthean tradition in the vocation-story of a woman, the commission
to proclaim the resurrection given to the women at the tomb, and the final
commission of the risen Jesus to make disciples [μαθητεύσατε] of *all* nations
[πάντα τὰ ἔθνη]. The term μαθητής is not, therefore, representative of founding members of the various missionary churches, nor of their successors,
and gender does not seem to have been constitutive of its representational
function through the history of the tradition. The term could function,
therefore, as an 'inclusive' symbol for discipleship within the Matthean
narrative world.

A similar argument could follow for the Petrine traditions. Perhaps at
their core is an historical memory regarding Peter's place within the disciples of Jesus. Such a memory may well have been nurtured and developed
within the Matthean community, especially if it were situated at Antioch,
given Peter's role in the community surrounding the dispute with Paul and
the negotiations with the Jerusalem church (Gal 2:11-14). If he had a leadership role at that time, it seems that it was as a representative of the disciples
of Jesus[57] and that this role was extended to include all within the
community (18:18-20; 28:19-20). Moreover, the tradition in 23:8-12 speaks
strongly against a hierarchical model of leadership which singles out offices
and titles exclusively from the community.[58] Thus the Petrine traditions
along with those of the "disciples" could be seen to have functioned inclu-
sively within the world view the gospel establishes while also being in a

---

57   Hans Dieter Betz, *Galatians: A Commentary on Paul's Letter to the Churches in
      Galatia*, Hermeneia (Philadelphia: Fortress, 1979), 99, discusses the Pauline reference to
      Peter together with James and John as στῦλοι, claiming that it was an "honorific
      epithet."
58   Crosby, *House of Disciples*, 98, points out that this passage while supporting the non-
      hierarchical vision of the evangelist also addresses abuses in the contemporary house
      churches: "Any teaching, leadership, title, or role that elevated anyone above the rest of
      the brothers and sisters in the believing community was to be rejected as undermining
      the way *exousia* was to be lived by the brotherhood and sisterhood in the house
      churches."

tensive relationship with other traditions that were more specifically inclusive.

This vision of inclusive discipleship is blurred, however, by the silencing of women's voices, the only ones to be heard directly being the Canaanite woman (15:22, 25, 27), the mother of the sons of Zebedee (20:21), and the women in the courtyard during Jesus' trial (26:69, 71). The words given to the Canaanite woman affirm women's participation in the liturgical and theological life of their communities, but the absence of other women's voices renders women absent from or insignificant to the construction of the communities' ideological world view.[59] Hence, the confessional titles and liturgical formulae are found predominantly on the lips of men proposing, therefore, that this was their exclusive domain. What, however, were the words of women in the Matthean community? Also, since women are presented in discipleship terms within the world of the narrative and a remnant of one woman's call story has been preserved, we are lead to ask what other stories of women's discipleship have been omitted from the final text or have been lost in the process of transmission, and how many voices have been silenced. These very hints and questions, however, may point to the destabilizing function of these stories within the narrative world of the gospel.

A further blurring of the vision of inclusive discipleship results from the fact that each time that the narrative specifies the name of a householder, that householder is male: Joseph (2:11); the centurion (8:6); Peter (8:14); the ruler (9:23); and Simon the leper (26:6). In each of their households, however, except for that of the centurion, a woman is present; and in three of them, the woman together with Jesus is the principal actor in the events which take place there. It is within the house of Peter that the story is told of the healing of his mother-in-law and her call to ministry. A young woman is raised to life within the house of the ruler, Jesus being for her a direct channel of salvation. The prophetic and compassionate ministry of the woman who anoints Jesus takes place within the house of Simon the leper. This may be intended to support a growing tendency within the community toward male leadership of households while still affirming women's significant ministerial roles within those households.[60]

---

59   Of the silence of women in literature Rabinowitz, "Female Speech," 128, says that it "acts out the misogynist's denial of the active pole for the female protagonist."
60   Crosby, *House of Disciples*, 36, makes the observation that a good many of the gatherings in private homes were in the homes of women, but has failed to note that there is

Such a tendency may have been countered by those stories in which we find women seeking access to the fruits of the βασιλεία outside the household in the public arena. In the first half of the gospel, the women whose stories are situated here are those who are outsiders to the patriarchal household: the woman with the haemorrhage and the Canaanite woman (9:20-22; 15:21-28). Free from the restrictions of this type of household, they approach Jesus directly on their own behalf and through the power of Jesus are incorporated into the new household based on new kinship structures. One of these women is Jewish and the other is gentile and their stories challenge any exclusive ethnic or gender-based practices that may have developed within the households of faith. This challenge is supported by the teaching of Jesus regarding the new household (10:35-36; 11:28-30; 12:46-50). The very households that have been established as constitutive of the Matthean community will be continually challenged by the vision of the new household for which the life story of Jesus is paradigmatic. It contains women and men, Gentile and Jew, all as full participants in the gifts of the βασιλεία; and it is constituted according to the radical freedom of the βασιλεία vision contained in the preaching of Jesus. That this vision is not just for the present but for the future is suggested by the fact that young women as well as young men, Jewish and gentile, become recipients of the fruits of this βασιλεία (8:5-13; 9:18-19, 23-26; 15:21-28; 17:14-18) and therefore share in its vision.

In summary, therefore, it can be seen that in relation to the symbolic function of gender and the characterization of women within the Matthean narrative world, we find values and norms in tension and this tension is not resolved even though the final redaction strives for what Meier calls an "inclusive synthesis".[61] Women's ministry and participation in the liturgical and theological life of the community is affirmed and the possibilities for this are opened up because of the emphasis on response to Jesus rather than position in patriarchal familial or kinship structures as the basis for such participation and ministry. Women also mirror faithful discipleship and missionary endeavour. Their inclusion at the centre of the Jesus movement and hence of the life of the Matthean church advances the goal

---

no mention of a woman householder in Matthew's gospel. This could mean that it was so much a part of the community's consciousness that it was taken for granted or it could also be explained, as has been done above, in terms of a growing trend toward patriarchalization of the egalitarian practices of their house churches.

61   Meier, *Antioch and Rome*, 57.

of inclusion which characterizes the entire gospel: inclusion of poor and rich; Jew and Gentile; good and bad; female and male.[62] This inclusion has been established by the systematic development of the theme of women's inclusion in and centrality to the life of Jesus, finally arriving at the climactic point where they alone remain faithful to the dying Jesus and are the first to witness the empty tomb and encounter the risen Jesus. The world which they symbolize, however, is in tension with the patriarchal norms and values which exalt male leadership and discipleship and affirm patriarchal familial structures. There is an ambivalence with regard to gender and the characterization of women in the narrative world of Matthew. It may be the necessary ambivalence which leads to the survival of an ideal, namely, that of the βασιλεία, or it may be the ambivalence associated with the demise of that ideal. Only a closer examination of the world of the Matthean communities will allow us to decide between these alternatives.

III. Women in the Matthean Communities

Significant studies of the Matthean *Sitz im Leben* accompany much of the research on Matthew's gospel, and in drawing some conclusions regarding the contribution of women to this *Sitz im Leben* as a result of this study, it will be necessary to rely upon some of the generally accepted opinions in areas outside our specific focus, especially date and place of composition. At the present time in Matthean scholarship, it is commonly held that the "final redaction" of the gospel to which I have referred throughout this study took place in the closing decades of the first century, probably between 80 and 90 CE. There is less consensus regarding location, but the majority opinion tends toward Syria, and even more specifically, Antioch.[63]

---

62 Fred W. Burnett, *The Testament of Jesus-Sophia: A Redaction-Critical Study of the Eschatological Discourse in Matthew* (Lanham/New York/London: University Press of America, 1981), 178, 181, who, as a result of a study of Matt 24, draws the conclusion that the community was egalitarian and hence inclusive. Here, however, I have applied this conclusion to the narrative rather than the historical world of the Matthean gospel.

63 For a survey of the various opinions of scholars, see Meier, *Antioch and Rome*, 15-27; Senior, *What are They Saying about Matthew?* 5-15; Benedict T. Viviano, "Where was the Gospel according to St. Matthew Written?" *CBQ* 41 (1979): 533-540; and most

Even though it has not always been given specific attention in studies of the gospel communities, it has been one of the foundational assumptions in relation to early Christianity that the christian communities of particular cities or locations during the first two centuries consisted of "house churches".[64] This seems understandable given the centrality of the household in the political and socio-economic world of both Hellenistic and Roman society wherein the household unit was the microcosm of the city and the state, and the stability of the latter two depended on the stability of the former.[65] Such a system was patriarchal since its root model was the authority and domination of the *paterfamilias* over both the persons and resources belonging to his household.[66]

> While imperial Rome made its presence felt directly through the contract system, the imperial household was primarily reinforced indirectly through a culture of patriarchy which cyclically extended from it to the community and local household and back from the household and community to the Principate. Thus the patriarchal connection between the *politeía* and the *basileîa* as [sic] ultimately grounded in the *oikîa/oikos*.[67]

Since, however, many of the beliefs and attitudes of the Jesus movement and therefore of the early christian communities were egalitarian and in conflict with the social structure of Palestinian Jewish society at the

---

recently, W. D. Davies and Dale C. Allison, *The Gospel according to Saint Matthew*, Vol I, ICC (Edinburgh: T. & T. Clark, 1988), 138-147, who conclude their analysis thus: "So while, in our judgement, the First Gospel was probably put together for the church of Antioch, this conclusion remains no more than the best educated guess."

64   Filson, "Early House Churches"; Schüssler Fiorenza, *In Memory of Her*, 175-184; Abraham J. Malherbe, *Social Aspects of Early Christianity*, 2nd ed., (Philadelphia: Fortress, 1983), 60-91; Meeks, *First Urban Christians*, 75-77; John H. Elliott, *A Home for the Homeless: A Sociological Exegesis of 1 Peter, Its Situation and Strategy* (Philadelphia: Fortress, 1981); John E. Stambaugh and David L. Balch, *The New Testament in Its Social Environment*, Library of Early Christianity (Philadelphia: Westminster, 1986), 138-140; and Crosby, *House of Disciples*, who gives serious consideration to this structure as a basis for examining economics in the Matthean church. Glanville Downey, *A History of Antioch in Syria: From Seleucus to the Arab Conquest* (Princeton: Princeton University Press, 1961), 277, draws attention to the excavations at Dura-Europos which witness to early house churches in the region of Antioch. For details of this excavation, see Graydon F. Snyder, *Ante Pacem: Archaeological Evidence of Church Life before Constantine* (Macon, Ga.: Mercer University Press, 1985), 68-71. In our use of the term "house *churches* ", we should, however, heed the warning given by E. A. Judge, "The Social Identity of the First Christians: A Question of Method in Religious History," *JRH* 11 (1980): 212, that "it is hard to see how anyone could seriously have related the phenomenon of Christianity to the practice of religion in its first-century sense. ... Without temple, cult statue or ritual, they lacked the time-honoured and reassuring routine of sacrifice that would have been necessary to link them with religion."

65   Crosby, *House of Disciples*, 21-32.

66   Ibid., 26-29; and David L. Balch, *Let Wives Be Submissive: The Domestic Code in 1 Peter*, SBLMS 26 (Chico: Scholars, 1981), 23-62.

67   Crosby, *House of Disciples*, 26.

beginning of the first century and of Graeco-Roman society generally, it seems that the household model generally adopted by the early christians was not that of the patriarchal familial household but that of the *collegia* or voluntary association.[68] Crosby points out that the structures of authority represented in the Matthean gospel indicate that the Matthean church was no exception.[69] Kraemer, however, would critique and extend such assumptions on the basis of evidence for women's leadership and active participation in Jewish synagogues. She suggests that house-synagogues may well have been the model used by early christian communities,[70] and her suggestion would accord well with the strong Jewish foundation to the Antioch christian communities. We do not, however, have specific evidence for women's leadership or participation in the synagogues of Antioch,[71] nor has the research been undertaken which would gather and analyze inscriptional, papyrological and other archaeological and literary data relating to the lives of women in Syria and Antioch during the first century of the Common Era.[72] Until such evidence is available which may modify the present reconstruction, the voluntary association seems to provide a model for foundational christian communities.

The various types of voluntary associations which existed at the time and which may have influenced house-synagogues as well as "house churches" were generally characterized by more egalitarian structures which afforded greater opportunities for leadership and participation to all,

---

68 Schüssler Fiorenza, *In Memory of Her*, 180, 183-184; Meeks, *First Urban Christians*, 76; Crosby, *House of Disciples*, 29-31; and E. A. Judge, "'Antike und Christentum': Towards a Definition of the Field: A Bibliographical Survey," *ANRW* II.23.1, 15.
69 Crosby, *House of Disciples*, 104-111.
70 Ross S. Kraemer, "Review Essay of *In Memory of Her: A Feminist Theological Reconstruction of Christian Origins* by Elisabeth Schüssler Fiorenza," *RSR* 11 (1985): 8.
71 See Brooten, *Women Leaders*, for such evidence in diverse centres.
72 Sarah B. Pomeroy, *Women in Hellenistic Egypt: From Alexander to Cleopatra* (New York: Schocken, 1984), has carried out such research in relation to women in Hellenistic Egypt, and Lilian Portefaix, *Sisters Rejoice: Paul's Letter to the Philippians and Luke-Acts as Received by First-Century Philippian Women*, CB.NT 20 (Stockholm: Almqvist & Wiksell, 1988), focusses specifically on Philippi. A similar study in relation to Syria or specifically to Antioch would provide a necessary complement to this current research. One aspect of such research which may provide some explanation for what seems to be significant participation of women in the socio-religious life of the Matthean communities situated in Antioch or more broadly within Syria is the strong presence of female symbols and feminine deities within Syriac religions: see D. S. Wallace-Hadrill, *Christian Antioch: A Study of Early Christian Thought in the East* (Cambridge: University Press, 1982), 15, 167-168; Susan Ashbrook Harvey, "Women in Early Syrian Christianity," in Cameron and Kuhrt, *Images of Women*, 288-298; and Frederick W. Norris, "Isis, Sarapis and Demeter in Antioch of Syria," *HTR* 75 (1982): 189-207. Female symbols and feminine deities do not necessarily, however, mean improved social status for women.

especially women and slaves.[73] They were, however, still incorporated into the prevailing culture, and hence shared in many of its patriarchal assumptions.

> Although many of these voluntary associations functioned in a more egalitarian form than the patriarchal mode of household (especially in their treatment of women), they shared in common with the patriarchal model the same basic organizing principle of the households. To the extent that the *koina/collegia* were households they fit within the wider bureaucracy, but to the extent they were alternate, they served as a *potential subversive element* in society, especially in their stress on the equality of women.[74]

Such dissonance would not, however, have been surprising to citizens of the first-century Mediterranean world whose life was permeated with what Malina calls "recognized and acknowledged inconsistency."[75]

The model, therefore, of a number of different house churches, some of which would have been structured according to collegial principles but situated within a society that was fundamentally patriarchal, provides us with an understanding of the Matthean church in which the gospel and women's place within it can be adequately explained. The androcentric world view and its attendant acceptance of patriarchy which was seen to be almost constitutive of the gospel's narrative world can be explained in terms of the cultural world in which the Matthean church existed and the appropriation within some of the house churches of the structures and values belonging to that world.[76] On the other hand, the alternative vision of a discipleship of women which is carefully developed in the text points towards the implementation of subversive egalitarian practices within at least some of the Matthean house churches. These practices, however, seem to have been in

---

73   Stambaugh and Balch, *Social Environment*, 124-126. A similar phenomenon has been noted within Gnostic communities by Kurt Rudolph, *Gnosis: The Nature and History of Gnosticism*, trans. Robert McLachlan Wilson (San Francisco: Harper & Row, 1983), 211-214, who suggests that such communities may have been modelled on the "cult associations". He locates them predominantly in large cities especially in the East, p. 291, and one of their early leaders, Menander, is linked with Antioch in Syria, p. 298. At this point, however, any claim regarding the influence of early Gnostic communities on the Matthean community would be sheer speculation .

74   Crosby, *House of Disciples*, 30. The italics is my emphasis. Judge, "Social Identity," 213, also notes in relation to early christians "their distinctive style of life which marked them out, and left them in potential conflict with the public community."

75   Bruce J. Malina, "Normative Dissonance and Christian Origins," *Semeia* 35 (1986): 38-39.

76   Luise Schottroff, "Das geschundene Volk und die Arbeit in der Ernte Gottes nach dem Matthäusevangelium," in *Mitarbeiter der Schöpfung: Bibel und Arbeitswelt*, ed. Luise and Willy Schottroff (München: Chr. Kaiser, 1983), 196, says of the Matthean evangelist that he has "kein kritisches Bewußtsein gegenüber einer massiv patriarchalischen Ordnung."

conflict or tension not only with the surrounding culture and the belief system of some of the house churches,[77] but also with certain patriarchalizing
tendencies which were gaining support perhaps even within those house
churches whose structures were more egalitarian.

The situation, therefore, that the Matthean gospel may well have
addressed was one in which women were active in ministry and leadership
within at least certain house churches which constituted the gospel's recipients.[78] The well-developed narrative theme of women's discipleship within
the gospel story provided the pattern against which the community could
recognize its present practice and structure its future. This aspect of the story
was a part of the overall inclusive vision which the evangelist wished to
place before the communities.[79] Moreover, many of the traditions which we
have examined would seem to be women's traditions, traditions which they
preserved and developed in order to give expression to their needs within
the house churches and their aspirations and visions for the future of the
communities to which they belonged.[80] Jo Ann McNamara makes a similar
point in general when she says:

> Female evangelists contributed their memories and experiences to the
> making of that story, as it was repeated and transmitted to a new generation
> of listeners. Naturally, no one can claim to have a secret key for separating

---

77   Schüssler Fiorenza, *In Memory of Her*, 180, seems to suggest rightly that "many dissen-
      sions and disagreements which are usually interpreted theologically or ideologically
      might have their concrete roots in the diversity of house churches within a city or
      region."
78   Such would not be a unique phenomenon within the early christian churches since
      there is evidence of such ministry and leadership within the Pauline literature, see
      Rom 16:1-5, 6, 7, 12, 13, 15; Phil 4:2-3. The research of Brooten, *Women Leaders*, has
      illustrated that as early as the first century, women may have exercised leadership in
      certain synagogues of the diaspora and Kraemer, "Hellenistic Jewish Women," has
      pointed to the active roles in family and society exercised by Jewish women of Asia
      Minor. Inscriptional evidence also points to priestesses within Graeco-Roman reli-
      gions: see Kraemer, *A Sourcebook*, 37-38, § 21-23, and Mary R. Lefkowitz and Maureen
      B. Fant, eds., *Women's Life in Greece and Rome: A Source Book in Translation*
      (Baltimore: Johns Hopkins University Press, 1982), 113, § 113-114; 259-260, § 255-259.
79   Burnett, *Testament of Jesus-Sophia*, 178, 181, by way of his study of the Wisdom theme
      in the Matthean eschatological discourse, concludes that the gospel community is in-
      clusive and egalitarian. Also Smith, "Were the Early Christians Middle-Class?" 275, as
      quoted in n. 25 above.
80   Crosby, *House of Disciples*, 47, says of the special M material used in the Matthean
      redaction that it "evolved from the various viewpoints found within the groupings
      which were part of the various households in the Matthean church." That these vari-
      ous viewpoints also influenced the shaping of traditions like Q and Mark received by
      the community is imaged by Meier, *Antioch and Rome*, 55, when he says that "M was
      the living sea of oral tradition in which Mark and Q floated and were steeped." There is
      nothing to suggest that women were not active participants in the development of the
      communities' traditions, especially those which touched their own lives most
      intimately.

gospel material with a feminine origin from that with a masculine origin. Yet, in one sense, at least, women were active collaborators in the writing of these books. The gospels, or that oral tradition from which they were constructed, reflect the teaching heard in early Christian assemblies, a teaching that can hardly have been uniform. All the witnesses to Jesus' life must have been questioned repeatedly and the contradictions in their stories heatedly discussed. ... Though we cannot accurately distinguish the voices of women, it is unmistakably clear that the Gospels deliberately address auditors of both genders.[81]

One place where it has been suggested that we find women's contribution to the gospel is in relation to the tradition of the four women from the Hebrew Scriptures. These women were paradigms for the women who were incorporated into the life of the house churches, not according to their place in a patriarchal family but because of their commitment to the βασιλεία vision of Jesus as it was lived in the Matthean community. The scriptural models were both Jewish and gentile and hence could encompass all women whether they had belonged to the Jewish community of Antioch[82] and its surrounding districts before becoming members of the christian community or whether they had come to the community from the state religion or one of the mystery cults.[83] They also represented the courage and initiative which enabled women to challenge the norms and structures of patriarchal culture by demonstrating alternative values. These stories, therefore, functioned symbolically for the women of the Matthean churches who had embraced a community whose value system was counter-cultural.[84]

---

81   Jo Ann McNamara, *A New Song: Celibate Women in the First Three Christian Centuries* (New York/Binghamton: Harrington Park Press, 1985), 24-25.

82   Many scholars give witness to the fact that there had been a Jewish community in Antioch almost since the city's foundation in 300 BCE by Seleucus Nicator. See Robert R. Hann, "Judaism and Jewish Christianity in Antioch: Charisma and Conflict in the First Century," *JRH* 14 (1987): 342; Wayne Meeks and Robert L. Wilken, *Jews and Christians in Antioch in the First Four Centuries of the Common Era*, SBLSBS 13 (Missoula: Scholars, 1978), 2-3; and Carl H. Kraeling, "The Jewish Community at Antioch," *JBL* 51 (1932): 130-160.

83   Wallace-Hadrill, *Christian Antioch*, 14-18; Franz Cumont, *The Oriental Religions in Roman Paganism* (New York: Dover, 1956), 103-134; and Zumstein, "Antioche sur l'Oronte," 124-125.

84   Crosby, *House of Disciples*, 29, notes that the non-patriarchal form of households based on the model of the associations represented a particular threat to "the patriarchal constitution of the empire" and he says later, p. 105, that "a more egalitarian constitution of the house churches would be one case wherein a direct challenge to the wider patriarchal system existed since egalitarianism, by definition, supports political and social equality." See also Elliott, *Home for the Homeless*, 180. Elisabeth Schüssler Fiorenza, "Response to "The Social Functions of Women's Asceticism in the Roman East" by Antoinette Clark Wire," in *Images of the Feminine in Gnosticism*, ed. Karen L. King, Studies in Antiquity and Christianity (Philadelphia: Fortress, 1988), 327, says in this regard: "It seems that women in antiquity could not overthrow the patriarchal institution of the household and the roles derived from it. They could, however, reject and

The preservation of other traditions surrounding women and their participation in the Jesus movement and its βασιλεία vision may also have occurred primarily, but certainly not solely, among women members of the house churches or among those house churches in which women's participation and leadership was significant. We can, therefore, also claim them as women's traditions. This does not mean, however, that women did not participate in the shaping of other important traditions in the Matthean community, but for the purpose of this study, it is the traditions in which women are significant characters and what they reveal of women's participation in and aspirations for the community that are our concern.

The retention of the story of Peter's mother-in-law in the form of a vocation story would seem to be foundational for the strong tradition of women's discipleship that was central to the ethos of the Matthean communities. It raises questions regarding the origin of this strong tradition in Antioch. Were some of the women disciples of Jesus or some of the women missionaries of the Easter message among those who were scattered following the persecution of Stephen and who arrived in Antioch to preach Jesus' message there (Acts 11:19-20)?[85] If so, it would be understandable that they would have brought with them vocation stories of the women who were his followers, including this story of Peter's mother-in-law. These stories, along with those of the women's commissioning on the resurrection morning, would, indeed, have been foundational both for their own missionary activity and for the discipleship of women which they would have engendered in and modelled for the community. This would provide an adequate explanation also for the community's retention of this vocation story while leaving open the question of the existence of other vocation stories of women that may have been lost.

Both Acts 15 and Gal 2:11-14 record the tension in Antioch surrounding the Jewish and gentile mission and both associate it with the male protagonists: Peter, Paul, Barnabas, James and members of the Jerusalem council. This same tension is evidenced throughout the Matthean gospel but the story which is central to its resolution in the community's symbolic

---

supplant these by creating alternatives to the patriarchal institution of the household based on sexual control and relationships of dominance and subordination."

85   With regard to this early missionary activity of women, Luise Schottroff, "Women as Followers," 421, says: "The fact that Mary of Magdala and other women actively joined in the prophetic proclamation of the Jesus movement is shown also in their role after Jesus' death."

universe is that of the Canaanite woman. Her story has been significantly developed within the Matthean communities and these developments point to its importance among the growing body of women's traditions. For the women, it was not legal questions of circumcision or non-circumcision, nor the debate about who eats with whom that were determinative of the extension of the mission beyond a Jewish constituency, but rather the needs of gentile women to share in the healing power of the Jesus story and to participate in the egalitarian structures that resulted from his βασιλεία vision. This story claims a gentile women and not Peter or Paul as the founder of this gentile mission in Antioch. As gentile women became full participants in the life of the community the story was augmented to reflect this.[86]

An earlier claim that this same story also reflects the tension in the community in relation to women's participation in its liturgical life and its theological reflection gives rise to significant questions. According to the Matthean vision of discipleship, *all* are to be discipled in the resurrection era (28:19), and hence all face the central discipleship question: "Have you understood all this?" (13:51). Each person is then addressed by the following statement of Jesus: "Therefore *every* scribe who has been trained for the βασιλεία τῶν οὐρανῶν is like a householder who brings out of their* treasure what is new and what is old" (13:52). Were women, therefore, participants in the type of scribal school that was suggested by Stendahl[87] and supported by Meier as centrally significant to the shaping of the gospel story?

> The development of traditions does not happen in a vacuum. With so many complicated strands of tradition circulating and growing in the Antiochene church, it was only natural that a group of teachers or scribes should arise to formulate, study, comment on, and teach the expanding Christian tradition. Acts 13:1 states that the earliest leaders of the Antiochene church were prophets and teachers, ... who also conducted public worship. ... This interaction between powerful, charismatic preaching (prophecy) and Spirit-filled study of Scripture and catechesis (teaching), all in the context of liturgical

---

86 Such participation would not be at all surprising given the egalitarian structures of the house churches; the experiences of both Jewish and gentile women during the Hellenistic era of much greater participation in the public arena; and women's participation in the religious rituals in worship of female deities which were especially strong in Syria. See Ross Kraemer, "Hellenistic Jewish Women," 194-199, who draws on inscriptional material from Asia Minor which indicates that Jewish women played active roles in both "the public affairs of their communities and in the public lives of their families"; Brooten, *Women Leaders*, who discusses titles given to women in synagogal inscriptions which point to their leadership role; S. Kelly Heyob, *The Cult of Isis among Women in the Graeco-Roman World*, EPRO 51 (Leiden: Brill, 1975), whose study of the Isis cult reveals its significance for women and also their participation in its priestly offices alongside men; and Norris, "Isis, Sarapis and Demeter," 189-208, who points to strong evidence of the presence of Isis worship in Antioch.

87 Stendahl, *School of Matthew*.

celebration, would be the perfect matrix for what Stendahl has dubbed "The School of St. Matthew." One need not agree with all of Stendahl's thesis about Matthew's use of OT citations and the parallels with the Qumran literature to assent to his basic insight that Matthew's gospel comes out of a lengthy Jewish-Christian scribal tradition in Matthew's church. ... It would be in this group of Christian scribes that the OT prophecies in their varied textual forms would have been studied and applied to Christian catechesis, apologetics, and polemics. ... In a larger sense, of course, Matthew inherits not just the work of the scribal school but of all the bearers of tradition at Antioch. [88]

How did women participate in this process of theological reflection that gave rise to the Matthean traditions and gospel?

The complexity of the question in relation to women's study of the scriptures (Torah) within first and second century Judaism cannot be solved here,[89] but it can be pointed out that while it was not commanded that women study Torah as it was commanded for men which may have excluded them from the official houses of study,[90] such study was not forbidden them.[91] Rather, it was expected that they have a sound knowledge of the laws by which they were bound,[92] and they would also have heard the scriptures read in the synagogue on the Sabbath. Therefore, we can presume that the women in the Matthean community whose background was in Judaism could certainly have participated in the community's reflections on the life of Jesus in the light of their own scriptures as is manifest throughout the gospel. To the degree that such reflection took place in a "scribal school" distinct from the house churches, women may have been excluded, but this cannot be claimed with absolute surety. To the extent that the locus of this aspect of the community's life was, in fact, the house churches and their

---

88   Meier, *Antioch and Rome*, 55-57.
89   See, Meiselman, *Jewish Woman in Jewish Law*, 34-42; Anne Goldfeld, "Women as Sources of Torah in the Rabbinic Tradition," in Koltun, *Jewish Woman*, 257-271; Rachel Biale, *Women and Jewish Law: An Exploration of Women's Issues in Halakhic Sources* (New York: Schocken, 1984), 29-40; and Wegner, *Chattel or Person?*, 161-162, to point to but a few of the discussions of this question among Jewish scholars.
90   Ibid., 161. Brooten's study of synagogal references to women as *presbytera* has, however, led her to ask whether Jewish women actually had been scholars, *Women Leaders*, 55; and the example of the Therapeutrides whose lifestyle is described by Philo in *De Vita Contemplativa*, especially § 24-33, points to women who studied the scriptures and allegorical interpretations in the solitude of their contemplative life as well as composing hymns and psalms all of which presume on ready access to the traditions. There is no sure evidence to suggest, however, that these latter groups of women functioned outside Egypt.
91   The famous example of a woman steeped in knowledge not only of the scriptures but also of halakhic law is the second century woman, Beruriah. For further discussion of the traditions surrounding her, see Goldfeld, "Women as Sources," 263-267; Swidler, "Beruriah"; and Goodblatt, "Beruriah Traditions".
92   Biale, *Women and Jewish Law*, 29.

liturgical gatherings, then women may well have participated fully.[93] In relation to women from a gentile background, their participation in their own religious rituals[94] and the growing possibility of their having received some education owing to the more widespread acceptance of the education of girls as well as boys[95] would support the possibility of their participation in the liturgical life of the house churches, in its catechetical activity and therefore subsequently in the theological reflection taking place there.

Women's independent access to resources which could be reordered in favour of the βασιλεία vision at the heart of the Matthean church's lifestyle is affirmed as central to the continued preaching of the gospel in the story of the woman who anoints Jesus.[96] As women participated in leadership functions within certain house churches and brought their own resources to the service of the communities' gospel lifestyle based on the Jesus story in which service, especially of the most needy (11:5; 20:28; 25:31-46), and compassion (9:36; 14:14; 15:32) were central values, this story of a woman's direct service of Jesus in his greatest need out of her own resources would have supported and empowered them.

---

93   Crosby, *House of Disciples*, 43-48.
94   See nn. 78 and 86 above.
95   Eva Cantarella, *Pandora's Daughters: The Role and Status of Women in Greek and Roman Antiquity*, trans. Maureen B. Fant (Baltimore/London: Johns Hopkins University Press, 1987), 97; Leonard Swidler, "Greco-Roman Feminism and the Reception of the Gospel," in *Traditio - Krisis - Renevatio aus theologischer Sicht. Festschrift Winfried Zeller zum 65. Geburtstag*, ed. B. Jaspert and R. Mohr (Marburg: Elwert Verlag, 1976), 49; Sarah B. Pomeroy, "Technikai kai Mousikai: The Education of Women in the Fourth Century and in the Hellenistic Period," *AmJAH* 2 (1977): 51-68. Susan G. Cole, "Could Greek Women Read and Write?" in *Reflections of Women in Antiquity*, ed. Helene P. Foley (New York: Gordon & Breach, 1981), 230, warns that this increase in educational opportunity should not obscure the fact that a good part of the population still remained illiterate. Such educational opportunities may also have been available to Jewish girls in the Diaspora.
96   The greater economic power and even independence of women in the Hellenistic and Roman era based on legal and inscriptional evidence is illustrated by Kraemer, "Jewish Women in Rome and Egypt," 95-96; idem, "Hellenistic Jewish Women," 194-195, which treats of women in Asia Minor; Marilyn Arthur, "'Liberated' Women: The Classical Era," in *Becoming Visible: Women in European History*, ed. R. Bridenthal and C. Koonz (Boston: Houghton Mifflin, 1979), 75-76, where she deals with the economic situation of women in the Hellenistic era; and David M. Schaps, *Economic Rights of Women in Ancient Greece* (Edinburgh: Edinburgh University Press, 1979), especially 75 and 96. For documentary evidence, see also Kraemer, *A Sourcebook*, 90, § 47; Lefkowitz and Fant, *Women's Life*, 24, § 48, and 157, § 158; Brooten, *Women Leaders*, 157-165; and Yigael Yadin's description of the archive of Babata, "Expedition D - The Cave of Letters," *IEJ* 12 (1962): 227-257, and *Bar Kokhba: The Rediscovery of the Legendary Hero of the Last Jewish Revolt against Imperial Rome* (London: Weidenfeld & Nicholson, 1971), 222-253. Unfortunately, the documents of this archive have not yet been published.

As well as being supported in the teaching of Jesus, women's status as historical subjects within their house churches, independent of the patriarchal familial structures, is remembered and celebrated in their traditions. It is paradigmatic in the women from the Hebrew Scriptures whose memory they have preserved and it is manifest in the gospel stories. The woman who is healed of her flow of blood approaches Jesus directly on her own behalf as does the Canaanite woman on behalf of her daughter and both participate directly in Jesus' ἐξουσία. The woman who anoints him offers her own independent resources and the women at the cross and the tomb act independently of any males and they become the first missionaries of the resurrection kerygma. Their stories firmly establish women's full participation in the life of their house churches within the gospel story of Jesus.

The traditions surrounding women characters would have been one of the sources of women's empowerment and they also give witness to other sources of such power. The first of these was women's direct relationship with Jesus as illustrated above. They had direct access to Jesus' ἐξουσία in the liturgical and catechetical life of their house churches and in the retelling, reshaping and remembering of the Jesus story. Their fidelity, symbolized both in word and deed in the gospel story, was now able to be manifest in the living of the βασιλεία vision in the new situation of a cosmopolitan community in the large Hellenistic city of Antioch. It was a fidelity empowered by compassion and learned discipleship (26:6-13) and carried out with the support of one another (27:55-56; 28:1-10). They remembered also in the story of Herodias and the wife of Pilate the lack of authority and power accorded women within the structures of patriarchy and the trickery to which this could lead in order to achieve a goal. As Naomi Steinberg suggests, such stories give expression to the "ambiguity of power and the social problem of order and disorder."[97] This would have been highlighted

---

97 Naomi Steinberg, in her article "Israelite Tricksters, Their Analogues and Cross-cultural Study," *Semeia* 42 (1988): 1-13, especially 6, 9-10 (this whole issue of *Semeia* being devoted to a study of female wit in a world of male power), says of trickery in general: "Evidence from the social sciences suggests that individuals resort to the use of trickery under certain social conditions. In particular, when individuals lack authority--they resort to strategies which allow them to achieve their goals and gain compliance with their wishes. I understand trickery to be a kind of power available to persons in a subordinate position. ... The figure of the trickster suggests the vulnerability of those in power. ... Through trickery, by both women and men, the underdog plays the part of power broker and the one expected to wield authority is under the thumb of the weak. This analysis suggests that stories of the use of deception by one individual against another are concerned with the ambiguity of power and the social problem of order and disorder."

for women in the Matthean house churches who experienced there more possibilities for full inclusion and participation in the exercise of authority and power than was available to them in the *polis*. Emerging patriarchalizing tendencies in the community, however, would have also emphasized the ambiguity of their power.

Within the context of such tendencies, the Petrine tradition and that of an exclusive group of male disciples may have operated as a powerful corrosive of the inclusive vision which the gospel sought to establish. These traditions could have been used to support a hierarchical form of leadership and an attendant institutionalization which would have functioned to exclude women more and more from leadership and ministerial roles which would then have been conceived of as the domain of men. Such a trend may well have been growing within the communities given the contrast within the narrative between the character group called "disciples"and a number of the women characters, and the tension which the presence of the disciples introduces into the women's stories. The women, in many of these instances, act as foils for the disciples' lack of faith or failure and they represent true discipleship but they must overcome the obstacles posed by the disciples.

The miracle stories involving women characters may also point to obstacles which women in the community were struggling to overcome. As Schüssler Fiorenza says,

> Miracle-faith in Jesus is best understood as protest against bodily and political suffering. It gives courage to resist the life-destroying powers of one's society.[98]

If attempts to exclude women from ministry and leadership were mounting within the Matthean communities, then the vocational/healing story of a woman within the house of Peter would have offered strong protest against such exclusion. The remembering of Jesus' healing of the woman with a haemorrhage may have empowered women to resist laws and structures which rendered them outsiders on the basis of gender, while the story of a woman's struggle with Jesus on her own behalf and on behalf of her daughter may have strengthened women's faith in the face of what seemed like a

---

98   Schüssler Fiorenza, "Toward a Feminist Biblical Hermeneutics," 98. See also
      Antoinette Wire, "Ancient Miracle Stories," 77-84.

long struggle into the future to retain their access to the power of Jesus and their participation in the communities' ritualization of that power.

As symbols of power and sources of empowerment, the traditions which I have called "women's traditions" gave expression to the spirit and vision of women members of the Matthean house churches. They were not anomalous in their own right but rather expressed a firm belief in the centrality of women to the βασιλεία vision of Jesus. They became anomalous when included within patriarchal traditions and narratives. Within the patriarchal world view of the dominant culture and even of the house churches, these stories of women were anti-structural and represented liminality,[99] a liminality which is, in fact, the meeting ground of the divine and the human. Their function was, however, two-edged. On the one hand, the presence of these stories of women at the centre of the patriarchal narrative and at the heart of the life of the house churches offered a constant critique of patriarchy and all its attendant structures and world view. On the other hand, their incorporation into such a narrative co-opted their very subversive power for the support of patriarchy so that woman, idealized as "the other" or "the faithful one", was removed from the realm of concrete structures and values where men struggled and failed and where patriarchy prevailed.[100]

Exactly how the final Matthean narrative was read and heard within the various house churches is beyond our grasp. It seems clear, however, that in the final analysis, the evangelist and the community has not sought to eliminate anomaly from the gospel especially in relation to women.[101] Rather it has been allowed to remain as one aspect of the dissonance which Malina suggests was "typical of early Christian movement groups" and which "best accounts for the survival and growth of those groups."[102] Women and their traditions were at the centre of the survival and growth of the Matthean

---

99   For a discussion of this terminology as employed by Victor Turner and in relation to the female imagery of the Book of Proverbs, see Claudia V. Camp, "Wise and Strange: An Interpretation of the Female Imagery in Proverbs in Light of Trickster Mythology," *Semeia* 42 (1988): 14-36, especially 30-32.

100 Ibid., 33. Camp asks the question: "Is it all too convenient for the patriarchal power structure to give liminality its due in order to draw on its power for themselves?" This two-edged nature of women's stories or female gender within the Matthean gospel has already been noted by Anderson, "Gender and Reading," 21; and Schaberg, *Illegitimacy of Jesus*, 77.

101 Mieke Bal, "Tricky Thematics," *Semeia* 42 (1988): 133-155, especially 149, says: "... cultures cannot afford to exclude "anomaly"--deviation from their own imposed norms, like patriarchal power--without ultimately being overwhelmed by it."

102 Malina, "Normative Dissonance," 39.

church, but their centrality was both threatening and threatened. There remained, therefore, an ambiguity within this particular expression of the early christian tradition, an ambiguity which was at the heart of the survival of the βασιλεία vision of Jesus which the Matthean evangelist preached for the house churches.[103] This ambiguity must be embraced by women in the christian tradition today if they are to move their churches beyond patriarchy to the inclusive vision of the βασιλεία that the Matthean gospel envisages.

---

103 Brooten, "Jewish Women's History," 26, says in this regard that "differentiated, detailed historical research on women's history and on understandings of the female in both Judaism and Christianity is the first step towards acknowledging and working with the ambiguity in our religious tradition."

Conclusion

Tension, ambiguity and anomaly mark the Matthean gospel at the points where women function as significant characters in the narrative. This discovery has raised many feminist critical, literary and historical questions during the course of this study, and these have led to the formulation of certain hypotheses regarding the symbolic function of gender within the gospel text and its history of compilation, as well as towards tentative conclusions regarding the participation of women within the socio-religious life of those communities constituting the Matthean church. The study has provided us, therefore, with theoretical constructs and conclusions for consideration within the academy of biblical scholars and has opened up areas for further research. The work of feminist biblical scholarship, however, is not only at the service of the academy but of the "church of women" or "women-church". Hence, the insights gained from this study are also available for appropriation within that church as it seeks the implementation of the βασιλεία vision of inclusion.

As a result of the feminist critical and hermeneutical considerations undertaken in the opening chapter, a model was proposed for a feminist reading of a gospel text. In subsequent chapters this model was applied, yielding significant results. An initial gender reading of the gospel brought to light some of the patriarchal constructs and androcentric perspectives which shaped the compilation of the gospel and its history of interpretation. It also enabled a re-reading of the text "against the grain" whereby women characters were able to function significantly at the centre of the narrative in accordance with many of the hints and suggestions in the text which have generally been overlooked. In relation to the history of those traditions which were concerned with women in the life of the historical Jesus, important trends emerged within the Matthean community. Some traditions had been preserved with little change being made to what seemed to be early memories or early records. Others had undergone considerable development within various communities constituting the Matthean church in response to questions and problems that they faced. Both trends, however, pointed to the significance of those traditions for the life of that church but also the challenge they provided as they were brought together with counter-traditions. The reconstruction of the gospel's historical subtext highlighted women's inclusion within the life of the Matthean church in its various manifestations as an expression of the inclusive discipleship which was constitutive of its vision of the βασιλεία based on the preaching and practice of Jesus. Such inclusion was, however, under threat as a result of the trend toward patriarchalization also evident within that historical subtext.

The model itself and the results it has yielded make their contribution and will need to be evaluated within the context of feminist biblical scholarship in particular and Matthean and biblical scholarship generally.[1] They are, however, but the beginnings of a feminist reading of the gospel of Matthew. The inclusive re-reading of the text and re-visioning of its historical subtext must guide all future readings of the gospel so that women are no longer excluded from the text or its historical subtext. The feminist reading begun here must be extended until all the patriarchal constructs and androcentric perspectives evident in the text are uncovered. Other texts and groups of texts within the gospel also deserve detailed examination to determine whether they support or challenge the hypotheses which have emerged from this particular study which focussed exclusively on those texts in which women function as significant characters. Many of these have already been listed according to categories at the beginning of Chapter One, but during the course of this study it has become clear that particular attention needs to be directed to the "Father" imagery of the gospel,[2] the christological image of Jesus-Sophia and the effect of both within the community's symbolic universe.

Such studies of the text must be accompanied by ongoing research into the lives of women in the Graeco-Roman world generally and in particular in Antioch and Syria. Further literary, epigraphical, papyrological and archaeological research may provide some of the data that we need to draw firmer conclusions regarding the religious, familial, social and cultural lives of Syrian women within Judaism, Gnosticism, Christianity and the Graeco-Roman religions. This would greatly assist our reconstruction of the

---

1   At present, it is within the specific field of feminist biblical scholarship that most careful attention has been given to the development of theoretical or hermeneutical models for a feminist reading of scripture. If, however, our work is to contribute to the contemporary paradigm shift in biblical scholarship generally, it needs to be given due attention in that wider arena also. See Hackett, "Women's Studies," especially 146.

2   Such a study is already being undertaken by Robin Mattison at Vanderbilt University.

historical subtext of the Matthean gospel as well as provide knowledge of our historical foresisters.

Questions raised and insights gained during this study have far-reaching implications for any articulation of the theology of the Matthean gospel. It has already been indicated above that a feminist study of the almost exclusive "Father" imagery within the text as well as research into its source or sources within the community may shed new light on the symbolic universe the gospel seeks to create and the influence of this on its readers, especially women. A more extensive study of the image of Jesus-Sophia throughout the entire text and the relationship between this and other images and titles used in relation to Jesus may supplement our understanding of the gospel's christology. Furthermore, any articulation of the soteriology contained within the gospel must now take account of the explicit presentation of Jesus as direct source of salvation for both women and men. The gospel's theology, christology and soteriology must therefore be reconsidered in the light of the inclusive βασιλεία vision which it proclaims.

It is in the area of the gospel's ecclesiology, however, that the most significant challenges have been provided by this study. The Matthean vision of *ekklēsia* has been shown to be inclusive, legitimating, therefore, structures and practices within the community that allowed for women's participation together with men in a way that was not always possible in the prevailing patriarchal culture. Such a vision was supported by a non-hierarchical view of leadership which facilitated women's full and active participation in the community's liturgical and theological life and its prophetic ministry together with an understanding of discipleship that was inclusive. This vision was challenged, however, by the patriarchal trend towards male hierarchical leadership and discipleship. Perhaps the very inclusive nature of the gospel's ecclesiology was enhanced by the incorporation within the text of both visionary traditions and their corresponding counter-traditions and it is on the basis of fidelity to this inclusion that subsequent ecclesiological interpretations need to be critiqued.

A final aspect of the gospel's theology which needs serious reconsideration and articulation is that of the family. Within the course of this study it has become clear that the inclusive βασιλεία vision that the gospel proposes and a number of the stories which we have considered provide a profound critique of the patriarchal family, especially the role and status assigned to both women and children within it. Further investigation is needed, however, to determine the actual theology of family that the gospel presents in light of its βασιλεία vision and, as seen in relation to ecclesiology above, this may need to incorporate both tradition and counter-tradition as well as being faithful to the profound critique of patriarchal structures contained within the gospel.

Such theological considerations are not only of concern to the academy but also to the "church of women", that church which seeks to make the inclusive and liberating vision of the βασιλεία of Jesus a reality in our contemporary world.[3] Here the gospel vision and its attendant theological articulation are brought into dialogue with the experience of women and men who are struggling to recognize God's salvific purpose for inclusion and liberation in their own lives and world. They too will contribute to the reshaping and re-articulation of Matthean theology, christology, soteriology and ecclesiology. It is in this context also that the liberating vision of the *ekklēsia* can be most fully appropriated so that it shapes the lives of its members.

As the stories we have considered in this study are told and retold within the "church of women" in new and creative ways, they will provide the church's members with a new vision which will break old boundaries. Many of the stories will critique the patriarchal family structure under whose domination many women live and provide them with a vision which will free their own initiative and creativity, allowing the βασιλεία vision of Jesus to find expression in their lives and relationships. Other stories will legitimate women's solidarity in the struggle against oppressive forces that would destroy all who oppose them. Questions will be raised about structures which are non-inclusive or which deny the inclusion and liberation of any person. The re-telling of certain stories, however, will empower women of faith to cross all boundaries and limitations that have been erected to exclude or diminish them. In our anamnesis of these women's stories perhaps we can name those who have not been given a name, remember them within the calendar of "women-church", and give voice to those who are silent within the text. These are but a few possibilities towards which the conclusion of this study points. The life-giving appropriation and

---

3   Schüssler Fiorenza, *In Memory of Her*, 344, says of this church: "Since women in a patriarchal church cannot decide their own theological-religious affairs and that of their own people--women--the *ekklēsia* of women is as much a future hope as it is a reality today. Yet we have begun to gather as the *ekklēsia* of women, as the people of God, to claim our own religious powers, to participate fully in the decision-making process of church, and to nurture each other as women Christians."

creative articulation of the traditions considered in this study will, in fact, take place within "women-church".

The women, the memories of whom are retained within the text of the Matthean gospel, and those who participated at the heart of the Matthean church have left us a legacy. Their stories and their lives point to the tension and the ambiguity which arise when a vision of an inclusive, liberated and liberating community as promulgated by Jesus seeks concrete expression in a society which is patriarchal and oppressive, especially of women and children. They remind us that tension and ambiguity must be embraced if we are to move our contemporary churches and society beyond patriarchy, but they also provide us with stories of solidarity, courage, initiative and deep faith for the journey. The women of the Matthean community and the stories of women in the life of Jesus which they have preserved for us are truly our heritage as women, as biblical scholars, and as biblical christians.

Bibliography

Abel, E. L. "The Genealogies of Jesus O XPICTOC." *NTS* 20 (1973-74): 203-210.

Abrams, M. H. *A Glossary of Literary Terms*. 3rd ed. New York: Holt, Rinehart & Winston, 1971.

Adler, Rachel. "The Jew Who Wasn't There: *Halakhah* and the Jewish Woman." In *On Being a Jewish Feminist: A Reader*, edited by Susannah Heschel, 12-18. New York: Schocken, 1983.

Aland, Kurt, ed. *Synopsis of the Four Gospels. Greek-English Edition of the Synopsis Quattuor Evangeliorum*. 3rd ed. Stuttgart: United Bible Societies, 1979.

Albright W. F. and C. S. Mann. *Matthew. Introduction, Translation, and Notes*. AB 26. Garden City, New York: Doubleday, 1971.

Allen, Willoughby C. *A Critical and Exegetical Commentary on the Gospel according to S. Matthew*. ICC. Edinburgh: T. & T. Clark, 1907.

Alsup, John E. *The Post-Resurrection Appearance Stories of the Gospel Tradition*. CThM A:5. Stuttgart: Calwer, 1975.

Alter, Robert. *The Art of Biblical Narrative*. New York: Basic Books, 1981.

Amaru, Betsy Halpern. "Portraits of Biblical Women in Josephus' Antiquities." *JJS* 39 (1988): 143-170.

Anderson, Janice Capel. "Matthew: Gender and Reading." *Semeia* 28 (1983): 3-27.

----------. "Matthew: Sermon and Story." In *SBL 1988 Seminar Papers*, edited by David J. Lull, 496-507. Atlanta: Scholars, 1988.

----------. "Mary's Difference: Gender and Patriarchy in the Birth Narratives." *JR* 67 (1987): 183-202.

----------. *Over and Over and Over Again: Studies in Matthean Repetition*. Ph.D. diss., University of Chicago, 1985.

Argyle, A. W. *The Gospel according to Matthew*. CNEB. Cambridge: University Press, 1963.

Arthur, Marilyn. ""Liberated" Women: The Classical Era." In *Becoming Visible: Women in European History*, edited by R. Bridenthal and C. Koonz, 60-89. Boston: Houghton Mifflin, 1979.

360 Bibliography

Bacci, Carol. "First-wave Feminism: History's Judgement." In *Australian Women: Feminist Perspectives*, edited by Norma Grieve and Patricia Grimshaw, 156-167. Melbourne: Oxford University Press, 1981.

Bal, Mieke. "Tricky Thematics." *Semeia* 42 (1988): 133-155.

Balch, David L. *Let Wives Be Submissive: The Domestic Code in 1 Peter.* SBLMS 26. Chico: Scholars, 1981.

Balsdon, J. P. V. D. *Roman Women: Their History and Habits.* London: Bodley Head, 1962.

Bamberger, Joan "The Myth of Matriarchy: Why Men Rule in Primitive Society." In *Woman, Culture, and Society*, edited by Michelle Zimbalist Rosaldo and Louise Lamphere, 263-280. Stanford: Stanford University Press, 1974.

Barrett, C. K. *A Commentary on the First Epistle to the Corinthians.* 2nd ed. BNTC. 1971. Reprint. London: Black, 1979.

Bass, Dorothy C. "Women's Studies and Biblical Studies: An Historical Perspective." *JSOT* 22 (1982): 6-12.

Batey, Richard A. *New Testament Nuptial Imagery.* Leiden: Brill, 1971.

Bauer, David R. *The Structure of Matthew's Gospel: A Study in Literary Design.* JSNTSup 31. Sheffield: Almond, 1988.

Bauer, W., W. F. Arndt, F. W. Gingrich and F. W. Danker. *A Greek-English Lexicon of the New Testament and Other Early Christian Literature.* 2nd ed. Chicago: University of Chicago Press, 1979.

Beare, Francis Wright. *The Gospel according to Matthew: A Commentary.* Oxford: Blackwell, 1981.

Beauvoir, Simone de. *The Second Sex.* Edited and translated by H. M. Parshley. New York: Knopf, 1952.

Beek, M. A. "Rahab in the Light of Jewish Exegesis." *AOAT* 211 (1982): 37-44.

Behm, Johannes. *Die Handauflegung im Urchristentum nach Verwendung, Herkunft und Bedeutung in religionsgeschichtlichem Zusammenhang untersucht.* Leipzig: Deichert, 1911.

Benoit, P. *L'évangile selon saint Matthieu.* La sainte Bible de Jérusalem. 3rd ed. Paris: Cerf, 1961.

----------. "Marie-Madeleine et les disciples au tombeau, selon Jn 20,1-18." In *Exégèse et Théologie 3*, 270-282. CFi 30. Paris: Cerf, 1968.

Benoit, P. and M.-E. Boismard. *Synopse des quatre évangiles en français.* Tome II. Commentaire par M.-E. Boismard avec la collaboration de A. Lamouille et P. Sandevoir. Preface de P. Benoit. Paris: Cerf, 1972.

Bergeant, Diane. "Exodus as a Paradigm in Feminist Theology." *Concilium* 189 (1987): 100-108.

Berlin, Adele. *Poetics and Interpretation of Biblical Narrative.* Bible and Literature Series 9. Sheffield: Almond, 1983.

Best, Ernest. *Following Jesus: Discipleship in the Gospel of Mark.* JSNTSup 4. Sheffield: JSOT Press, 1981.

----------. *Disciples and Discipleship: Studies in the Gospel according to Mark.* Edinburgh: T. & T. Clark, 1986.

Betz, Hans Dieter. *Galatians: A Commentary on Paul's Letter to the Churches in Galatia.* Hermeneia. Philadelphia: Fortress, 1979.

Beyer, Hermann Wolfgang. "διακονέω, κτλ." *TDNT* II:81-93.

Beyer, Klaus. *Die aramäischen Texte vom Toten Meer.* Göttingen: Vandenhoeck & Ruprecht, 1984.

Biale, Rachel. *Women and Jewish Law: An Exploration of Women's Issues in Halakhic Sources.* New York: Schocken, 1984.

Birch, Bruce C. "A Response to Elisabeth Schüssler Fiorenza, "Toward a Feminist Biblical Hermeneutics: Biblical Interpretation and Liberation Theology"." Unpublished Paper for the Working Group on Liberation Theology, AAR/SBL, Feminist Hermeneutic Project, 1982.

Bird, Phyllis A. "The Harlot as Heroine: Narrative Art and Social Presupposition in Three Old Testament Texts." *Semeia* 46 (1989): 119-138.

Blank, Josef. "Frauen in den Jesusüberlieferungen." In *Die Frau im Urchristentum*, edited by G. Dautzenberg, H. Merklein and K. Müller, 9-91. QD 95. Freiburg/Basel/Wien: Herder, 1983.

Blass, F., A. Debrunner, and R. W. Funk. *A Greek Grammar of the New Testament and Other Early Christian Literature.* Chicago: University of Chicago Press, 1961.

Bleicher, Josef. *Contemporary Hermeneutics: Hermeneutics as Method, Philosophy and Critique.* London/Boston/Henley: Routledge & Kegan Paul, 1980.

Bloch, Renée."'Juda engendra Pharès et Zara, de Thamar" Matt., 1.3." In *Mélanges bibliques rédigés en l'honneur de André Robert*, 381-389. TICP 4. Paris: Bloud & Gay, 1957.

Bloem, H. *Die Ostererzählung des Matthäus: Aufbau und Aussage von Mt 27,57-28,20.* Rome: Zeist, 1987.

Bode, Edward Lynn. *The First Easter Morning: The Gospel Accounts of the Women's Visit to the Tomb of Jesus.* AnBib 45. Rome: Biblical Institute Press, 1970.

Boismard, M.-E. and A. Lamouille. *Synopsis Graeca Quattuor Evangeliorum.* Leuven/Paris: Peeters, 1986.

Bonnard, Pierre. *L'Évangile selon Saint Matthieu.* Commentaire du Nouveau Testament 1. Deuxième Série. Genève: Labor et Fides, 1982.

Boomershine, Thomas E. "Mark 16:8 and the Apostolic Commission." *JBL* 100 (1981): 225-239.

Bornkamm, Günther, Gerhard Barth, and Heinz Joachim Held, eds. *Tradition and Interpretation in Matthew.* 2nd ed. Translated by Percy Scott. London: SCM, 1982.

Bossman, David M. "Authority and Tradition in First Century Judaism and Christianity." *BTB* 17 (1987): 3-9.

Boulding, Elsie. *The Underside of History: A View of Women through Time.* Boulder, Colorado: Westview Press, 1976.

Brooks, Stephenson H. *Matthew's Community: The Evidence of His Special Sayings Material.* JSNTSup 16. Sheffield: JSOT Press, 1987.

Brooten, Bernadette J. "Early Christian Women and Their Cultural Context: Issues of Method in Historical Reconstruction." In *Feminist Perspectives on Biblical Scholarship,* edited by Adela Yarbro Collins, 65-91. SBL Centennial Publications 10. Chico: Scholars, 1985.

----------. "Jewish Women's History in the Roman Period: A Task for Christian Theology." In *Christians Among Jews and Gentiles: Essays in Honor of Krister Stendahl's Sixty-Fifth Birthday,* edited by George W. E. Nickelsburg with George W. Macrae, 22-30. Philadelphia: Fortress, 1986.

----------. *Women Leaders in the Ancient Synagogue.* Brown Judaic Studies 36. Chico: Scholars , 1982.

Brown, Raymond E. *The Birth of the Messiah: A Commentary on the Infancy Narratives in Matthew and Luke.* Garden City, New York: Doubleday, 1977.

----------. "Gospel Infancy Narrative Research from 1976 to 1986: Part I (Matthew)." *CBQ* 48 (1986): 468-483.

----------. "Rachab in Mt 1,5 Probably is Rahab of Jericho." *Bib* 63 (1982): 79-80.

Brown, Raymond E. and John P. Meier. *Antioch and Rome: New Testament Cradles of Catholic Christianity.* New York/Ramsey: Paulist, 1983.

Brown, Raymond E., Karl P. Donfried, and John Reumann, eds. *Peter in the New Testament: A Collaborative Assessment by Protestant and Roman Catholic Scholars.* Minneapolis: Augsburg/New York: Paulist, 1973.

Brown, Raymond E., Karl P. Donfried, Joseph A. Fitzmyer, and John Reumann, eds. *Mary in the New Testament: A Collaborative Assessment by Protestant and Roman Catholic Scholars.* London: Geoffrey Chapman, 1978.

Brown, Schuyler. "The Matthean Community and the Gentile Mission." *NT* 22 (1980): 193-221.

----------. "The Mission to Israel in Matthew's Central Section (Mt 9,35-11,1)." *ZNW* 69 (1978): 73-90.

----------. "The Two-fold Representation of the Mission in Matthew's Gospel." *StTh* 31 (1977): 21-32.

Brueggemann, Walter. *The Prophetic Imagination.* Philadelphia: Fortress, 1978.

----------. "A Shape for Old Testament Theology, I: Structure Legitimation." *CBQ* 47 (1985): 28-46.

----------. "A Shape for Old Testament Theology, II: Embrace of Pain." *CBQ* 47 (1985): 395-415.

----------. "Trajectories in Old Testament Literature and the Sociology of Ancient Israel." *JBL* 98 (1979): 161-185.

Bultmann, Rudolf. "Is Exegesis without Presuppositions Possible?" In *Existence and Faith: Shorter Writings of Rudolf Bultmann*, selected, translated and introduced by Schubert M. Ogden, 342-351. The Fontana Library Theology and Philosophy. London/Glasgow: Collins, 1960.

----------. *The History of the Synoptic Tradition.* Translated by John Marsh. Oxford: Blackwell, 1963.

Burger, Christoph. *Jesus als Davidssohn: Eine traditionsgeschichtliche Untersuchung.* FRLANT 98. Göttingen: Vandenhoeck & Ruprecht, 1970.

----------. "Jesu Taten nach Matthäus 8 und 9." *ZThK* 70 (1973): 272-287.

Burkill, T. A. "The Syrophoenician Woman: The Congruence of Mark 7.24-31." *ZNW* 57 (1966): 23-37.

----------. "The Syrophoenician Woman: Mark 7,24-31." *StEv* IV=*TU* 102 (1968): 166-170.

Burnett, Fred W. "Παλιγγενεσία in Matt. 19:28: A Window on the Matthean Community?" *JSNT* 17 (1983): 60-72.

----------. *The Testament of Jesus-Sophia: A Redaction-Critical Study of the Eschatological Discourse in Matthew.* Lanham/New York/London: University Press of America, 1981.

364 Bibliography

Buttrick, George A. "The Gospel according to St. Matthew. Exposition. Text." *IntB* VII:250-625.

Cady Stanton, Elizabeth. *The Woman's Bible: The Original Feminist Attack on the Bible.* Introduced by Dale Spender. 2 parts. New York: European Publishing Co, 1895/1898. Reprint (2 parts in 1). Edinburgh: Polygon, 1985.

Cady, Susan, Marian Ronan, and Hal Taussig. *Sophia: The Future of Feminist Spirituality.* San Francisco: Harper & Row, 1986.

Cameron, Averil and Amélia Kuhrt, eds. *Images of Women in Antiquity.* Detroit: Wayne State University Press, 1983.

Camp, Claudia V. "The Wise Women of 2 Samuel: A Role Model for Women in Early Israel." *CBQ* 43 (1981): 14-29.

----------. "Wise and Strange: An Interpretation of the Female Imagery in Proverbs in Light of Trickster Mythology." *Semeia* 42 (1988): 14-36.

Campbell, Edward F. *Ruth: A New Translation with Introduction, Notes, and Commentary.* AB 7. Garden City, New York: Doubleday, 1975.

Cantarella, Eva. *Pandora's Daughters: The Role and Status of Women in Greek and Roman Antiquity.* Translated by Maureen B. Fant. Baltimore/London: Johns Hopkins University Press, 1987.

Carroll, Berenice A., ed. *Liberating Women's History: Theoretical and Critical Essays.* Urbana/Chicago/London: University of Illinois Press, 1976.

Cerfaux, Lucien. "La section des pains: (Mc vi,31-viii,26; Mt xiv,13-xvi,12)." In *Synoptische Studien: Festschrift A. Wikenhauser,* 64-77. München: Karl Zink, 1953. Reprinted in *Recueil Lucien Cerfaux,* I, 471-485. Gembloux: Duculot, 1954.

Charlesworth, James H., ed. *The Old Testament Pseudepigrapha: Apocalyptic Literature and Testaments.* Vol. 1. London: Darton, Longman & Todd, 1983.

Chatman, Seymour. *Story and Discourse: Narrative Structure in Fiction and Film.* Ithaca/London: Cornell University Press, 1978.

Christ, Carol P. *Laughter of Aphrodite: Reflections on a Journey to the Goddess.* San Francisco: Harper & Row, 1987.

Clark, Elizabeth A. *Women in the Early Church.* Message of the Fathers of the Church 13. Wilmington, Del.: Michael Glazier, 1983.

Cohn, Haim Hermann. "Witness," *EJ* 16:583-590.

Cole, Susan G. "Could Greek Women Read and Write?" In *Reflections of Women in Antiquity,* edited by Helene P. Foley, 219-245. New York: Gordon & Breach, 1981.

Collins, Adela Yarbro, ed. *Feminist Perspectives on Biblical Scholarship*. SBL Centennial Publications 10. Chico: Scholars, 1985.

Collins, Raymond F. *Introduction to the New Testament*. London: SCM, 1983.

Conn, Joann Wolski, ed. *Women's Spirituality: Resources for Christian Development*. New York/Mahwah: Paulist, 1986.

Cope, O. Lamar. *Matthew: A Scribe Trained for the Kingdom of Heaven*. CBQMS 5. Washington: Catholic Biblical Association of America, 1976.

Craven, Toni. "Tradition and Convention in the Book of Judith." *Semeia* 28 (1983): 49-61.

Crosby, Michael H. *House of Disciples: Church, Economics, and Justice in Matthew*. Maryknoll: Orbis, 1988.

Culham, Phyllis. "Ten Years After Pomeroy: Studies of the Image and Reality of Women in Antiquity." In *Rescuing Creusa: New Methodological Approaches to Women in Antiquity*, edited by Marilyn Skinner, 9-30. Lubbock, Texas: Texas Tech, 1987.

Culpepper, R. Alan. *Anatomy of the Fourth Gospel: A Study in Literary Design*. Foundations and Facets: New Testament. Philadelphia: Fortress, 1983.

Cummings, J. T. "The Tassel of his Cloak: Mark, Luke, Matthew - and Zechariah." In *Studia Biblica 1978: II. Papers on the Gospels*, edited by E. A. Livingstone, 47-61. JSNTSup 2. Sheffield: JSOT Press, 1980.

Cumont, Franz. *The Oriental Religions in Roman Paganism*. New York: Dover, 1956.

Dahl, N. A. "Die Passionsgeschichte bei Matthäus." *NTS* 2 (1955-56): 17-32.

Daly, Mary. *Beyond God the Father: Toward a Philosophy of Women's Liberation*. Boston: Beacon, 1973.

----------. *The Church and the Second Sex: With a New Feminist Postchristian Introduction by the Author*. Harper Colophon Books. 1968. Reprint. New York: Harper & Row, 1975.

----------. *Pure Lust: Elemental Feminist Philosophy*. London: The Women's Press, 1984.

Danby, Herbert., trans. *The Mishnah: Translated from the Hebrew with Introduction and Brief Explanatory Notes*. 1933. Reprint. Oxford: Oxford University Press, 1985.

Daniélou, Jean. *Les évangiles de l'Enfance*. Paris: Seuil, 1967.

Daube, David. "Jesus and the Samaritan Woman: The Meaning of συγχράομαι." *JBL* 69 (1950): 137-147.

----------. "Anointing at Bethany." Part F of Chapter VIII in *The New Testament and Rabbinic Judaism*, 312-324. Jordan Lectures in Comparative Religion 2. London: Athlone Press, 1956.

Dautzenberg, Gerhard, Helmut Merklein, and Karlheinz Müller, eds. *Die Frau im Urchristentum*. QD 95. Freiburg/Basel/Wien: Herder, 1983.

Davies, Stevan L. *The Revolt of the Widows: The Social World of the Apocryphal Acts*. Carbondale: Southern Illinois University Press, 1980.

Davies, W. D. *The Sermon on the Mount*. Cambridge: University Press, 1966.

----------. *The Setting of the Sermon on the Mount*. 1963. Reprint. Cambridge: University Press, 1966.

Davies W. D. and Dale C. Allison. *The Gospel according to Saint Matthew*. Vol I. ICC. Edinburgh: T. & T. Clark, 1988.

Davis, Charles Thomas. "Tradition and Redaction in Matthew 1:18-2:23." *JBL* 90 (1971): 404-421.

Deaux, Kay and Mary E. Kite. "Thinking about Gender." In *Analysing Gender: A Handbook of Social Scientific Research*, edited by Beth B. Hess and Myra Marx Ferree, 92-117. Newbury Park, Ca.: Sage, 1987.

Denis, Albert-Marie. "La section des pains selon s. Marc (6,30 - 8,26), une théologie de l'eucharistie." *StEv* IV=TU 102 (1968): 171-179.

Dermience, Alice. "La péricope de la Cananéenne (Mt 15,21-28): Rédaction et théologie." *EThL* 58 (1982): 25-49.

Derrett, J. Duncan M. "The Anointing at Bethany and the Story of Zacchaeus." Chapter 12 in *Law in the New Testament*, 266-285. London: Darton, Longman & Todd, 1970.

----------. "Law in the New Testament: The Syro-Phoenician Woman and the Centurion of Capernuam." *NT* 15 (1973): 161-186.

----------. "Mark's Technique: The Haemorrhaging Woman and Jairus' Daughter." *Bib* 63 (1982): 474-505.

Descamps, Albert. "Rédaction et christologie dans le récit matthéen de la passion." In *L'Evangile selon Matthieu: Rédaction et théologie*, edited by M. Didier, 360-415. BEThL XXIX. Gembloux: Duculot, 1972.

Didier, M., ed. *L'Evangile selon Matthieu: Rédaction et théologie*. BEThL XXIX. Gembloux: Duculot, 1972.

Dockx, S. *Chronologies néotestamentaires et vie de l'église primitive: Recherches exégétiques*. Paris/Gembloux: Duculot, 1976.

Douglas, Mary. *Purity and Danger: An Analysis of Concepts of Pollution and Taboo*. London/Boston/Henley: Routledge & Kegan Paul, 1966.

Downey, Glanville. *A History of Antioch in Syria: From Seleucus to the Arab Conquest*. Princeton: Princeton University Press, 1961.

Doyle, B. Rod. "Matthew's Intention as Discerned by His Structure." *RB* 95 (1988): 34-54.

----------. *Matthew's Wisdom: A Redaction-Critical Study of Matthew 11:1-14:13a*. Ph.D. thesis, Melbourne University, 1984.

Driver, Anne Barstow. "Religion: Review Essay." *Signs* 2 (1976): 434-442.

Driver, G. R. "Two Problems in the New Testament." *JTS* 16 (1965): 327-337.

Duling, Dennis C. "The Therapeutic Son of David: An Element in Matthew's Christological Apologetic." *NTS* 24 (1977-78): 392-410.

Durand, Alfred. *Evangile selon saint Matthieu*. VSal 1. Paris: Beauchesne, 1924.

Ebeling, Gerhard. "Jesus and Faith." Chapter VII in *Word and Faith*, 201-245. Translated by James W. Leitch. London: SCM, 1963.

Edwards, Richard A. "Uncertain Faith: Matthew's Portrait of the Disciples." In *Discipleship in the New Testament*, edited by Fernando F. Segovia, 47-61. Philadelphia: Fortress, 1985.

Eisenstein, Hester. *Contemporary Feminist Thought*. London/Sydney: Unwin, 1984.

Elderkiln, G. W., ed. *Antioch-on-the-Orontes I. The Excavations of 1933-1936*. Princeton: Princeton University Press, 1934.

Elliger, K. and W. Rudolph, eds. *Biblia hebraica stuttgartensia*. Stuttgart: Deutsche Bibelgesellschaft, 1966-67.

Elliott, J. K. "The Anointing of Jesus." *ET* 85 (1973-74): 105-107.

Elliott, John H. *A Home for the Homeless: A Sociological Exegesis of 1 Peter, Its Situation and Strategy*. Philadelphia: Fortress, 1981.

Exum, J. Cheryl. ""Mother in Israel": A Familiar Story Reconsidered." In *Feminist Interpretation of the Bible*, edited by Letty M. Russell, 73-85. Philadelphia: Westminster, 1985.

----------. "The Mothers of Israel: The Patriarchal Narratives from a Feminist Perspective." *Bible Review* 2 (1986): 60-67.

----------. ""You Shall Let Every Daughter Live": A Study of Exodus 1:8-2:10." *Semeia* 28 (1983): 63-82.

Farmer, William R. "The Post-Sectarian Character of Matthew and Its Post-War Setting in Antioch of Syria." *Perspectives in Religious Studies* 3 (1976): 235-247.

Fascher, Erich. *Das Weib des Pilatus (Matthäus 27,19). Die Auferweckung der Heiligen (Matthäus 27,51-53). Zwei Studien zur Geschichte der Schriftauslegung.* HM 20. Halle: Niemeyer, 1951.

Fenton, J. C. *The Gospel of St. Matthew.* PNTC. 1963. Reprint. Harmondsworth, Middlesex: Penguin, 1980.

Fetterley, Judith. *The Resisting Reader: A Feminist Approach to American Fiction.* Bloomington: Indiana University Press, 1978.

Feuillet, André. "Les deux onctions faites sur Jésus, et Marie-Madeleine. Contribution à l'étude des rapports entre les synoptiques et le quatrième évangile." *RThom* 75 (1975): 357-394.

Fewell, D. N. "Feminist Reading of the Hebrew Bible: Affirmation, Resistance and Transformation." *JSOT* 39 (1987): 77-87.

Filson, Floyd V. "Broken Patterns in the Gospel of Matthew." *JBL* 75 (1956): 227-231.

----------. *A Commentary on the Gospel according to St. Matthew.* BNTC. London: Black, 1960.

----------. "The Significance of the Early House Churches." *JBL* 58 (1939): 105-112.

Fitzmyer, Joseph A. *The Genesis Apocryphon of Qumran Cave I: A Commentary.* 2nd ed., rev. BibOr 18A. Rome: Biblical Institute Press, 1971.

Flannery, Austin, ed. *Vatican Council II: The Conciliar and Post Conciliar Documents.* Dublin: Dominican Publications, 1975.

Flusser, David. "Healing through the Laying-on of Hands in a Dead Sea Scroll." *IEJ* 7 (1957): 107-108.

Fowler, Robert M. "Reading Matthew Reading Mark: Observing the First Steps toward Meaning-as-Reference in the Synoptic Gospels." In *SBL 1986 Seminar Papers,* edited by K. H. Richards, 1-16. Atlanta: Scholars, 1986.

----------. "Who is "The Reader" in Reader Response Criticism?" *Semeia* 31 (1985): 5-23.

Frankemölle, Hubert. *Jahwebund und Kirche Christi: Studien zur Form-und Traditionsgeschichte des "Evangeliums" nach Matthäus.* NTA N.F. 10. Münster: Aschendorff, 1974.

----------. "Zur Theologie der Mission im Matthäusevangelium." In *Mission im Neuen Testament*, edited by Karl Kertelge, 93-129. QD 93. Freiburg/Basel/Wien: Herder, 1982.

Freed, Edwin D. "The Women in Matthew's Genealogy." *JSNT* 29 (1987): 3-19.

Freund, Elizabeth. *The Return of the Reader: Reader-Response Criticism.* New Accents. London/New York: Methuen, 1987.

Freyne, Sean. *Galilee, Jesus and The Gospels: Literary Approaches and Historical Investigations.* Philadelphia: Fortress, 1988.

----------. "Our Preoccupation with History: Problems and Prospects." *Proceedings of the Irish Biblical Association* 9 (1985): 1-19.

----------."Vilifying the Other and Defining the Self: Matthew's and John's Anti-Judaism in Focus." In *"To See Ourselves as Others See Us": Jews, Christians, Others in Antiquity*, edited by E. Frerichs and J. Neusner, 117-144. Studies in Humanities. Chico: Scholars, 1985.

Fridrichsen, Anton. "Einige sprachliche und stilistische Beobachtungen." *AMNSU* 2/CNT 1 (1936): 8-13.

Friedan, Betty. *The Feminine Mystique.* Harmondsworth, Middlesex: Penguin, 1965.

Fuchs, Albert. "Entwicklungsgeschichtliche Studie zu Mk 1,29-31 par Mt 8,14-15 par Luke 4,38-39. Macht über Fieber und Dämonen." *SNTU* A/6-7 (1981-82): 21-76.

Fuchs, Esther. "The Literary Characterization of Mothers and Sexual Politics in the Hebrew Bible." In *Feminist Perspectives on Biblical Scholarship*, edited by Adela Yarbro Collins, 117-136. SBL Centennial Publications 10. Chico: Scholars, 1985.

Fuller, Reginald H. *The Formation of the Resurrection Narratives.* Philadelphia: Fortress, 1980.

Funk, Robert W. "The Form of the New Testament Healing Miracle Story." *Semeia* 12 (1978): 57-96.

Furman, Nelly. "His Story versus Her Story: Male Genealogy and Female Strategy in the Jacob Cycle." In *Feminist Perspectives on Biblical Scholarship*, edited by Adela Yarbro Collins, 107-116. SBL Centennial Publications 10. Chico: Scholars, 1985.

Gadamer, Hans-Georg. *Truth and Method.* 2nd ed., edited by John Cumming and Garrett Barden, and translated by William Glen-Doepel. London: Sheed & Ward, 1979.

Gaechter, Paul. *Das Matthäus-Evangelium: Ein Kommentar.* Innsbruck: Tyrolia-Verlag, 1963.

370 Bibliography

Gailey, Christine Ward. "Evolutionary Perspectives on Gender Hierarchy." In *Analysing Gender: A Handbook of Social Scientific Research*, edited by Beth B. Hess and Myra Marx Ferree, 32-67. Newbury Park, Ca.: Sage, 1987.

Gardner, Jane F. *Women in Roman Law and Society*. London/Sydney: Croom Helm, 1986.

Garland, David E. *The Intention of Matthew 23*. NT.S 52. Leiden: Brill, 1979.

Gatzweiler, K. "Un pas vers l'universalisme: La Cananéenne. Mt 15,21-28." *ASeign* 2/51 (1972): 15-24.

----------. "Les récits de miracles dans l'Evangile selon saint Matthieu." In *L'Evangile selon Matthieu: Rédaction et théologie*, edited by M. Didier, 209-220. BEThL XXIX. Gembloux: Duculot, 1972.

Gaudemet, Jean. "Le statut de la femme dans l'empire Romain." *RSJB* 11 (1959): 191-222.

Gaventa, Beverly Roberts. "Response to Elisabeth Schüssler Fiorenza, "Toward a Feminist Biblical Hermeneutics: Biblical Interpretation and Liberation Theology"." Unpublished paper for the Working Group on Liberation Theology, AAR/SBL, Feminist Hermeneutic Project, 1982.

Geller, Stephen A. "Through Windows and Mirrors into the Bible: History, Literature and Language in the Study of the Text." In *A Sense of Text: The Art of Language in the Study of Biblical Literature*, 3-40. JQR Supplement 1982. Winona Lake: Eisenbrauns, 1983.

Gerber, Uwe. "Feministische Theologie: Selbstverständnis - Tendenzen - Fragen." *ThLZ* 109 (1984): 561-592.

Gerhardsson, Birger. *The Mighty Acts of Jesus according to Matthew*. Lund: Gleerup, 1979.

Giblin, Charles Homer. "Structural and Thematic Correlations in the Matthean Burial-Resurrection Narrative (Matt. xxvii.57-xxviii.20)." *NTS* 21 (1974-75): 406-420.

Gilligan, Carol. *In a Different Voice: Psychological Theory and Women's Development*. Cambridge, Mass./London: Harvard University Press, 1982.

Ginzberg, Louis. *The Legends of the Jews*. Vol 2. Translated by H. Szold. Philadelphia: Jewish Publication Society of America, 1910.

----------. *The Legends of the Jews*. Vol 5. Notes to Volumes 1 and 2. Philadelphia: Jewish Publication Society of America, 1925.

Gnilka, Joachim. *Das Matthäusevangelium*. Teil I and II. HThK. I,1-2. Freiburg: Herder, 1986/1988.

Goldfeld, Anne. "Women as Sources of Torah in the Rabbinic Tradition." In *The Jewish Woman: New Perspectives*, edited by Elizabeth Koltun, 257-271. New York: Schocken, 1976.

Goldin, Judah, trans. *The Fathers according to Rabbi Nathan*. YJS X. New Haven: Yale University Press, 1956.

----------. "The Youngest Son or where Does Genesis 38 Belong." *JBL* 96 (1977): 27-44.

Goodblatt, David. "The Beruriah Traditions." *JJS* 26 (1975): 68-85.

Greene, Gayle and Coppelia Kahn. "Feminist Scholarship and the Social Construction of Woman." In *Making a Difference: Feminist Literary Criticism*, edited by Galyle Greene and Coppelia Kahn, 1-36. London/ New York: Methuen, 1985.

Greenlee, J. Harold. "Εἰς μνημόσυνον αὐτῆς, 'For her Memorial': Mt xxvi.13, Mk xiv.9." *ET* 71 (1959-60): 245.

Grob, R. "ἅπτω." In *The New International Dictionary of New Testament Theology*. Vol. 3, edited by Colin Brown, 859-861. Exeter: Pater Noster, 1978.

Gross, Rita M. "Androcentrism and Androgyny in the Methodology of History of Religions." In *Beyond Androcentrism: New Essays on Women and Religion*, edited by Rita M. Gross, 7-22. American Academy of Religion Aids for the Study of Religion. Missoula: Scholars, 1977.

Grundmann, Walter. *Das Evangelium nach Matthäus*. ThHK I. 2nd ed. Berlin: Evangelische Verlagsanstalt, 1971.

----------. "κράζω." *TDNT* III:898-903.

Gryson, Roger. *The Ministry of Women in the Early Church*. Translated by Jean La Porte and Mary Louise Hall. 1976. Reprint. Collegeville: The Liturgical Press, 1980.

Gundry, Robert. *Matthew: A Commentary on His Literary and Theological Art*. Grand Rapids: Eerdmans, 1982.

----------. *The Use of the Old Testament in St. Matthew's Gospel with Special Reference to the Messianic Hope*. NT.S 18. 1967. Reprint. Leiden: Brill, 1975.

Hackett, Jo Ann. "Women's Studies and the Hebrew Bible." In *The Future of Biblical Studies: The Hebrew Scriptures*, edited by Richard E. Friedman and H. G. M. Williamson, 141-164. SBL Semeia Studies 16. Atlanta: Scholars, 1987.

Haddad, George M. *Aspects of Social Life in Antioch in the Hellenistic-Roman Period*. Chicago: University of Chicago Press, 1949.

Hahn, Ferdinand. *Das Verständnis der Mission im Neuen Testament.* WMANT 13. Neukirchen-Vluyn: Neukirchener, 1963.

Haines, Richard C. *Excavations in the Plain of Antioch II: The Structural Remains of the Later Phases.* Chicago: University of Chicago Press, 1971.

Hann, Robert R. "Judaism and Jewish Christianity in Antioch: Charisma and Conflict in the First Century." *JRH* 14 (1987): 341-360.

Harrington, Daniel J. *The Gospel according to Matthew.* Collegeville Bible Commentary New Testament Series 1. Collegeville: Liturgical Press, 1983.

Harrington, Wilfrid. *Mark.* New Testament Message 4. Dublin: Veritas, 1979.

Hartlich, Christian. "Is Historical Criticism out of Date?" In *Conflicting Ways of Interpreting the Bible,* edited by Hans Küng and Jürgen Moltmann, 3-8. Concilium 138. New York: Seabury, 1980.

Harvey, Susan Ashbrook. "Women in Early Syrian Christianity." In *Images of Women in Antiquity,* edited by Averil Cameron and Amélia Kuhrt, 288-298. Detroit: Wayne State University Press, 1983.

Hauptman, Judith. "Images of Women in the Talmud." In *Religion and Sexism: Images of Woman in the Jewish and Christian Traditions,* edited by Rosemary Radford Ruether, 184-212. New York: Simon and Schuster, 1974.

Havener, Ivan. *Q: The Sayings of Jesus. With a Reconstruction of Q by Athanasius Polag.* Good News Studies 19. Wilmington, Del.: Michael Glazier, 1987.

Hayes, John H. and Carl R. Holladay. *Biblical Exegesis: A Beginner's Handbook.* Atlanta: John Knox, 1982.

Heil, J. P. "Significant Aspects of the Healing Miracles in Matthew." *CBQ* 41 (1979): 274-287.

Heiler, F. *Die Frau in den Religionen der Menschheit.* TBT 33. Berlin/New York: de Gruyter, 1977.

Heine, Susanne. "Eine Person von Rang und Namen: Historische Konturen der Magdalenerin." In *Jesu rede von Gott und ihre Nachgeschichte im frühen Christentum: Beiträge zur Verkündigung Jesu und zum Kerygma der Kirche. Festschrift für Willi Marxsen zum 70. Geburtstag,* edited by Dietrich-Alex Koch, Gerhard Sellin and Andreas Lindeman, 179-194. Gütersloh: Gerd Mohn, 1989.

----------. *Women and Early Christianity. Are the Feminist Scholars Right?* Translated by John Bowden. London: SCM, 1987.

Held, H. J. "Matthew as Interpreter of the Miracle Stories." In *Tradition and Interpretation in Matthew*, edited by G. Bornkamm, G. Barth and H. J. Held, 165-299. 2nd ed. Translated by Percy Scott. London: SCM, 1982.

Hendrickx, Herman. *The Infancy Narratives*. Manila: East Asian Pastoral Institute, 1975.

----------. *The Passion Narratives of the Synoptic Gospels*. Manila: East Asian Pastoral Institute, 1977.

----------. *The Resurrection Narratives of the Synoptic Gospels*. Manila: East Asian Pastoral Institute, 1978.

Hengel, Martin. *The Charismatic Leader and His Followers*. Translated by James Greig. New York: Crossroad, 1981.

----------. "Maria Magdalena und die Frauen als Zeugen." In *Abraham unser Vater: Festschrift für Otto Michel zum 60. Geburtstag*, 243-256. AGSU V. Leiden/Köln: Brill, 1963.

Herzog, William R. II. "Interpretation as Discovery and Creation: Sociological Dimensions of Biblical Hermeneutics." *American Baptist Quarterly* 2 (1983): 105-118.

Heschel, Susannah, ed. *On Being a Jewish Feminist: A Reader*. New York: Schocken, 1983.

Hess, Beth B. and Myra Marx Ferree, eds. *Analysing Gender: A Handbook of Social Scientific Research*. Newbury Park, Ca.: Sage, 1987.

Heyob, S. Kelly. *The Cult of Isis among Women in the Graeco-Roman World*. EPRO 51. Leiden: Brill, 1975.

Heyward, Carter. "Ruether and Daly: Theologians--Speaking and Sparking, Building and Burning." *Christianity and Crisis* 39 (1979): 66-72.

----------. "An Unfinished Symphony of Liberation: The Radicalization of Christian Feminism Among White U.S. Women." *JFSR* 1.1 (1985): 99-118.

Hill, David. *The Gospel of Matthew*. NCB Commentary. Grand Rapids: Eerdmans, 1972.

Hoet, Rik. *"Omnes autem vos fratres estis"*: *Etude du concept ecclésiologique des "frères" selon Mt 23,8-12*. AnGr 232. Roma: Università Gregoriana, 1982.

Holst, Robert. "The One Anointing of Jesus: Another Application of the Form-Critical Method." *JBL* 95 (1976): 435-446.

Horton, Fred L. "Parenthetical Pregnancy: The Conception and Birth of Jesus in Matthew 1:18-25." In *SBL 1987 Seminar Papers*, edited by K. H. Richards, 175-189. Atlanta: Scholars, 1987.

Hutter, Manfred. "Ein altorientalischer Bittgestus in Mt 9,20-22." *ZNW* 75 (1984): 133-135.

Hyman, Paula. "The Other Half: Women in the Jewish Tradition." In *The Jewish Woman: New Perspectives*, edited by Elizabeth Koltun, 105-113. New York: Schocken, 1976.

Iser, Wolfgang. *The Implied Reader: Patterns of Communication in Prose Fiction from Bunyan to Beckett*. Baltimore/London: Johns Hopkins University Press, 1974.

----------. *The Act of Reading: A Theory of Aesthetic Response*. Baltimore/London: Johns Hopkins University Press, 1978.

Jameson, Fredric R. "The Symbolic Inference; or, Kenneth Burke and Ideological Analysis." In *Representing Kenneth Burke*, edited by H. White and M. Brose, 68-91. Baltimore: Johns Hopkins University Press, 1982.

Jeremias, Joachim."Beobachtungen zu neutestamentlichen Stellen an Hand des neugefundenen griechischen Henoch-Textes." *ZNW* (1939): 115-124.

----------. *Jerusalem in the Time of Jesus: An Investigation into Economic and Social Conditions during the New Testament Period*. Translated by F. H. and C. H. Cave. London: SCM, 1969.

----------. *Jesu Verheissung für die Völker*. Stuttgart: Kohlhammer, 1956.

----------. "Mc 14,9." *ZNW* 54 (1952-53): 103-107.

----------. *The Prayers of Jesus*. Philadelphia: Fortress, 1978.

----------. "Die Salbungsgeschichte Mc 14,3-9." *ZNW* 35 (1936): 75-82.

Johnson, Marshall D. *The Purpose of the Biblical Genealogies: With Special Reference to the Setting of the Genealogies of Jesus*. MSSNTS 8. Cambridge: University Press, 1969.

Johnson, Sherman E. "The Gospel according to St. Matthew. Introduction and Exegesis." *IntB* VII: 229-625.

Jones, Alexander. *The Gospel according to St Matthew: A Text and Commentary for Students*. London: Geoffrey Chapman, 1965.

Judge, E. A. "'Antike und Christentum': Towards a Definition of the Field: A Bibliographical Survey." *ANRW* II.23.1, 3-58. Berlin/New York: de Gruyter, 1979.

----------. "The Social Identity of the First Christians: A Question of Method in Religious History." *JRH* 11 (1980): 201-217.

----------. "St. Paul as a Radical Critic of Society." *Interchange* 16 (1974): 191-203.

Kaehler, Else. *Die Frau in den paulinischen Briefen.* Zürich: Gotthelf, 1960.

Kaplan, Zvi. "Beruryah." *EJ* IV:701.

Käsemann, Ernst. "The Problem of the Historical Jesus." In *Essays on New Testament Themes*, 15-47. Translated by W. J. Montague. London: SCM, 1964; Philadelphia: Fortress, 1982.

Keck, Leander. "Will the Historical Critical Method Survive? Some Observations." In *Orientation by Disorientation: Studies in Literary Criticism and Biblical Criticism*, edited by R. A. Spencer, 115-127. Theological Monograph Series 35. Pittsburg: Pickwick Press, 1980.

Kee, Howard Clark. *Miracle in the Early Christian World: A Study in Sociohistorical Method.* New Haven/London: Yale University Press, 1983.

Keegan, Terence J. *Interpreting the Bible: A Popular Introduction to Biblical Hermeneutics.* New York: Paulist, 1985.

Kelber, Werner H. "Gospel Narrative and Critical Theory." *BTB* 18 (1988): 130-137.

----------. *The Passion in Mark: Studies on Mark 14-16.* Philadelphia: Fortress, 1976.

King, Karen L., ed. *Images of the Feminine in Gnosticism.* Studies in Antiquity and Christianity. Philadelphia: Fortress, 1988.

Kingsbury, Jack D. "The Developing Conflict between Jesus and the Jewish Leaders in Matthew's Gospel: A Literary-Critical Study." *CBQ* 49 (1987): 57-73.

----------. "The Figure of Peter in Matthew's Gospel as a Theological Problem." *JBL* 98 (1979): 67-83.

----------. *Matthew as Story.* 2nd ed. Philadelphia: Fortress, 1988.

----------. *Matthew: Structure, Christology, Kingdom.* London: SPCK, 1975.

----------. "Observations on the "Miracle Chapters" of Matthew 8-9." *CBQ* 40 (1978): 559-573.

----------. "The Title "Kyrios" in Matthew's Gospel." *JBL* 94 (1975): 246-255.

----------. "The Verb *AKOLOUTHEIN* ("To Follow") as an Index of Matthew's View of His Community." *JBL* 97 (1978): 56-73.

Klein, Michael L., ed. *The Fragment-Targums of the Pentateuch according to Their Extant Sources.* Vol. 2. AnBib 76. Rome: Biblical Institute Press, 1980.

Klostermann, Erich. *Das Matthäusevangelium.* HNT 4. 3rd ed. Tübingen: Mohr, 1938.

376   Bibliography

Kolodny, Annette. "Dancing through the Minefield: Some Observations on the Theory, Practice and Politics of a Feminist Literary Criticism." *Feminist Studies* 6 (1980): 1-25.

----------. "A Map for Rereading: Or, Gender and the Interpretation of Literary Texts." *New Literary History* 11 (1980): 451-467.

----------."Turning the Lens on "The Panther Captivity": A Feminist Exercise in Practical Criticism." *Critical Inquiry* 8 (1981): 329-345.

Koltun, Elizabeth, ed. *The Jewish Woman: New Perspectives.* New York: Schocken, 1976.

Koontz, Gayle Gerber and W Swartley, eds. *Perspectives on Feminist Hermeneutics.* Occasional Papers No. 10. Elkhort, Ind.: Institute of Mennonite Studies, 1987.

Kraeling, Carl H. "The Jewish Community at Antioch." *JBL* 51 (1932): 130-160.

Kraemer, Ross S. *Ecstatics and Ascetics: Studies in the Function of Religious Activities for Women in The Greco-Roman World.* Ann Arbor: Xerox University Microfilms, 1976.

----------. "Hellenistic Jewish Women: The Epigraphical Evidence." In *SBL 1986 Seminar Papers,* edited by K. H. Richards, 183-200. Atlanta: Scholars, 1986.

----------, ed. *Maenads, Martyrs, Matrons, Monastics: A Sourcebook on Women's Religions in the Greco-Roman World.* Philadelphia: Fortress, 1988.

----------. "Non-Literary Evidence for Jewish Women in Rome and Egypt." In *Rescuing Creusa: New Methodological Approaches to Women in Antiquity,* edited by Marilyn Skinner, 85-101. Lubbock, Texas: Texas Tech, 1987.

----------. "Review Essay of *In Memory of Her: A Feminist Theological Reconstruction of Christian Origins* by Elisabeth Schüssler Fiorenza." *RSR* 11 (1985): 6-9.

----------. "Women in The Religions of the Greco-Roman World." *RSR* 9 (1983): 127-139.

Krentz, Edgar. *The Historical-Critical Method.* Guides to Biblical Scholarship. Philadelphia: Fortress, 1975.

Krieger, Murray. *A Window to Criticism.* Princeton: Princeton University Press, 1964.

Kroeger, Catherine C. "A Classicist Looks at the Difficult Passages." In *Perspectives on Feminist Hermeneutics,* edited by Gayle Gerber

Koontz and W. Swartley, 10-15. Occasional Papers No. 10. Elkhort, Ind: Institute of Mennonite Studies, 1987.

Kroeger, Richard and Catherine "An Inquiry into Evidence of Maenadism in the Corinthian Congregation." In *SBL 1978 Seminar Papers*, edited by Paul J. Achtemeier, 331-338. Missoula: Scholars, 1978.

Kuhn, Thomas S. *The Structure of Scientific Revolutions*. 1962. Reprint. Chicago: University of Chicago Press, 1968.

Kümmel, Werner Georg. *Introduction to the New Testament*. Rev. ed. Translated by Howard Clark Kee. London: SCM, 1975.

----------. *The New Testament: The History of the Investigation of its Problems*. Translated by S. McLean Gilmour and Howard C. Kee. 1972. Reprint. London: SCM, 1978.

Küng, Hans and Jürgen Moltmann, eds. *Conflicting Ways of Interpreting the Bible*. Concilium 138. New York: Seabury, 1980.

Lachs, S. T. *A Rabbinic Commentary on the New Testament: The Gospels of Matthew, Mark and Luke*. Hoboken, NJ.: KTAV, 1987.

Lacks, Roslyn. *Women and Judaism: Myth, History and Struggle*. Garden City, New York: Doubleday, 1980.

Laffey, Alice L. *An Introduction to the Old Testament: A Feminist Perspective*. Philadelphia: Fortress, 1988.

Lagrange, M.-J. *Evangile selon saint Matthieu*, EtB. 3rd ed. Paris: Gabalda, 1927.

----------. "Jésus a-t-il été oint plusieurs fois et par plusieurs femmes? Opinions des anciens écrivains ecclésiastiques (Luc, 7,36-50; Matthieu, 26,6-13; Marc, 14,3-9; Jean, 12,1-8; cf. Jean, 11,2)." *RB* 9 (1912): 504-532.

Lamarche, Paul. "La guérison de la belle-mère de Pierre et le genre littéraire des évangiles." *NRTh* 87 (1965): 515-526.

Lambert, Jean C. "An "F Factor"?: The New Testament in Some White, Feminist, Christian Theological Construction." *JFSR* 1.2 (1985): 93-113.

Lambrecht, Jan. *The Sermon on the Mount: Proclamation and Exhortation*. Good News Studies 14. Wilmington, Del.: Michael Glazier, 1985.

Langlamet, François. "Rahab." *DBS* IX:1065-1092. Fasc. 52. Paris: Letouzey et Ané, 1979.

Lapide, Pinchas. *The Sermon on the Mount: Utopia or Program for Action?* Translated by Arlene Swidler. Maryknoll: Orbis, 1986.

Lategan, Bernard C. and Willem S. Vorster, eds. *Text and Reality: Aspects of Reference in Biblical Texts*. SBL Semeia Studies 14. Atlanta: Scholars, 1985.

Lattke, Michael. "New Testament Miracle Stories and Hellenistic Culture of Late Antiquity." *Listening* 20 (1985): 54-64.

Leenhardt, Franz J. *La place de la femme dans l'église d'après le Nouveau Testament.* ETR 23/1. Montpellier, 1948.

Lefkowitz, Mary. "Influential Women." In *Images of Women in Antiquity*, edited by Averil Cameron and Amélia Kuhrt, 49-64. Detroit: Wayne State University Press, 1983.

Lefkowitz, Mary R. and Maureen B. Fant, eds. *Women's Life in Greece and Rome: A Source Book in Translation.* Baltimore: Johns Hopkins University Press, 1982.

Legasse, S. "L'épisode de la Cananéenne d'après Mt 15,21-28." *BLE* 73 (1972): 21-40.

Legault, A. "An Application of the Form-Critique Method to the Anointings in Galilee (Lk 7,36-50) and Bethany (Mt 26,6-13; Mk 14,3-9; Jn 12,1-8)." *CBQ* 16 (1954): 131-145.

Leipoldt, Johannes. *Die Frau in der antiken Welt und im Urchristentum.* Gütersloh: Gerd Mohn, 1962.

Leonard, E. A. "St. Paul on the Status of Women." *CBQ* 12 (1950): 311-320.

Lerner, Gerda. *The Creation of Patriarchy.* Women and History 1. New York/Oxford: Oxford University Press, 1986.

----------. "Placing Women in History: Definitions and Challenges." *Feminist Studies* 3 (1975): 5-14.

Léon-Dufour, Xavier. "La guérison de la belle-mère de Simon-Pierre." In *Etudes d'évangile*, 123-148. Parole de Dieu 2. Paris: Seuil, 1965.

----------. "Vers l'annonce de l'église: Etude de structure (Mt 14,1-16,20)." In *Etudes d'évangile*, 231-254. Parole de Dieu 2. Paris: Seuil, 1965.

Levi, Doro. *Antioch Mosaic Pavements.* 2 Vols. Princeton: Princeton University Press, 1947.

----------. "Mors Voluntaria: Mystery Cults on Mosaics from Antioch." *Berytus* 7 (1942): 19-55.

Lohmeyer, Ernst. *Das Evangelium des Matthäus.* KEK. Revised by W. Schmauch. Göttingen: Vandenhoeck & Ruprecht, 1956.

Lohr, Max. *Die Stellung des Weibes zu Jahwe-Religion und Kult.* BWAT 1/4. Leipzig: Hinrichs, 1908.

Longstaff, Thomas R. W. "The Women at the Tomb: Matthew 28:1 Re-examined." *NTS* 27 (1981): 277-282.

Luz, Ulrich. "The Disciples in the Gospel according to Matthew." In *Interpretation of Matthew*, edited by Graham Stanton, 98-128. Issues in Religion and Theology 3. Philadelphia: Fortress/London: SPCK, 1983.

----------. *Das Evangelium nach Matthäus, 1.* Teilband: Mt 1-7. EKK I,1. Zürich: Benziger/Neukirchen-Vluyn: Neukirchener, 1985.

Malbon, Elizabeth Struthers. "Fallible Followers: Women and Men in the Gospel of Mark." *Semeia* 28 (1983): 29-48.

Malherbe, Abraham J. *Social Aspects of Early Christianity.* 2nd ed. Philadelphia: Fortress, 1983.

Malina, Bruce J. *The New Testament World: Insights from Cultural Anthropology.* London: SCM, 1983.

----------. "Normative Dissonance and Christian Origins." *Semeia* 35 (1986): 35-59.

----------. "Patron and Client: The Analogy behind Synoptic Theology." *Forum* 4 (1988): 2-32.

Marin, L. "Les femmes au tombeau: Essai d'analyse structurale d'un texte évangélique." *Langages* 22 (1971): 39-50.

Marshall, Ian Howard, ed. *New Testament Interpretation: Essays on Principles and Methods.* Exeter: Paternoster, 1977.

Martin, Francis. *Encounter Story: A Characteristic Gospel Narrative Form.* 3 vols. DSS Diss., Pontifical Biblical Institute, Rome, 1977.

Martin, François. "Parole écriture accomplissement dans l'évangile de Matthieu." *Semiotique et Bible* 50 (1988): 27-51.

Marx, Alfred. "Ecriture et prédication. 25 - Rahab, prostituée et prophétesse. Josue 2 et 6." *ETR* 55 (1980): 72-76.

Matera, Frank J. *Passion Narratives and Gospel Theologies: Interpreting the Synoptics through Their Passion Stories.* Theological Inquiries. New York: Paulist, 1986.

----------. "The Plot of Matthew's Gospel." *CBQ* 49 (1987): 233-253.

März, Claus-Peter. "Zur Traditionsgeschichte von Mk 14, 3-9 und Parallelen." *SNTU* A/6-7 (1981-82): 89-112.

McFague, Sallie. *Metaphorical Theology: Models of God in Religious Language.* Philadelphia: Fortress, 1982.

McKnight, Edgar V. "The Contours and Methods of Literary Criticism." In *Orientation by Disorientation: Studies in Literary Criticism and Biblical Criticism*, edited by R. A. Spencer, 53-69. Theological Monograph Series 35. Pittsburg: Pickwick Press, 1980.

380   Bibliography

McNamara, Jo Ann. *A New Song: Celibate Women in the First Three Christian Centuries.* New York/Binghamton: Harrington Park Press, 1985.

----------. "Wives and Widows in Early Christian Thought." *IJWS* 2 (1979): 575-592.

McNeile, Alan Hugh. *The Gospel according to St. Matthew. The Greek Text with Introduction, Notes, and Index.* London: Macmillan, 1915.

Meeks, Wayne A. *The First Urban Christians: The Social World of the Apostle Paul.* New Haven/London: Yale University Press, 1983.

----------. "Understanding Early Christian Ethics." *JBL* 105 (1986): 3-11.

Meeks, Wayne and Robert L. Wilken. *Jews and Christians in Antioch in the First Four Centuries of the Common Era.* SBLSBS 13. Missoula: Scholars, 1978.

Meese, Elizabeth A. *Crossing the Double-Cross: The Practice of Feminist Criticism.* Chapel Hill/London: The University of North Carolina Press, 1986.

Meier, John P. "John the Baptist in Matthew's Gospel." *JBL* 99 (1980): 383-405.

----------. *Law and History in Matthew's Gospel: A Redactional Study of Mt. 5:17-48.* AnBib 71. Rome: Biblical Institute Press, 1976.

----------. *Matthew.* New Testament Message 3. Dublin: Veritas, 1980.

----------. "Matthew 15:21-28." *Interp.* 40 (1986): 397-402.

----------. *The Vision of Matthew: Christ, Church, and Morality in the First Gospel.* Theological Inquiries. New York/Ramsey/London: Paulist, 1979.

Meiselman, Moshe. *Jewish Woman in Jewish Law.* New York: KTAV/New York: Yeshiva University Press, 1978.

Metzger, Bruce. *A Textual Commentary on the Greek New Testament. A Companion Volume to the United Bible Societies' Greek New Testament.* 3rd ed. New York: United Bible Societies, 1975.

Meyers, Carol. "The Roots of Restriction: Women in Early Israel." *BA* 41 (1978): 91-103.

Michaelis, Wilhelm. "ὁράω κτλ." *TDNT* V:315-381.

Michel, Otto. "μνημονεύω." *TDNT* IV:682-683.

Miller, John W. "Depatriarchalizing God in Biblical Interpretation: A Critique." *CBQ* 48 (1986): 609-616.

Milligan, Mary. ""Give us a Double Share of Your Spirit" (cf 2 Kings 2:9)." *UISG* 74 (1987): 47-58.

Minear, Paul S. "The Disciples and the Crowds in the Gospel of Matthew."
    AThRS 3 (1974): 28-44.

Moiser, Jeremy. "The Structure of Matthew 8-9: A Suggestion." *ZNW* 76
    (1985): 117-118.

Moloney, Francis J. *Woman First Among the Faithful: A New Testament
    Study.* Blackburn, Vic.: Dove, 1984.

----------. *Woman in the New Testament.* Sydney: St. Paul Publications, 1981.

Moltmann-Wendel, Elisabeth. "Christentum und Frauenbewegung in
    Deutschland." In *Frauenbefreiung: Biblische und theologische
    Argumente,* edited by Elisabeth Moltmann-Wendel, 13-77. München:
    Chr. Kaiser, 1978.

----------. *A Land Flowing with Milk and Honey: Perspectives on Feminist
    Theology.* Translated by John Bowden. London: SCM, 1986.

----------. *The Women Around Jesus.* Translated by John Bowden. New York:
    Crossroad, 1982.

Moore, Stephen D. "Are the Gospels Unified Narratives?" In *SBL 1987
    Seminar Papers,* edited by K. H. Richards, 443-458. Atlanta: Scholars,
    1987.

Morgenthaler, Robert. *Statistik des neutestamentlichen Wortschatzes.*
    Zürich/Frankfurt am M.: Gotthelf, 1958.

Mortley, Raoul. *Womanhood: The Feminine in Ancient Hellenism,
    Gnosticism, Christianity, and Islam.* Sydney: Delacroix, 1981.

Moulton W. F. and A. S. Geden, eds. *A Concordance to the Greek Testament
    according to the Texts of Westcott and Hort, Tischendorf and the
    English Revisers.* 5th ed. Edinburgh: T. & T. Clark, 1978.

Muilenburg, James. "Form Criticism and Beyond." *JBL* 88 (1969): 1-18.

Munich, Adrienne. "Notorious Signs, Feminist Criticism and Literary
    Tradition." In *Making a Difference: Feminist Literary Criticism,*
    edited by Gayle Green and Coppelia Kahn, 238-259. London/New
    York: Methuen, 1985.

Munro, Winsome. "Women Disciples in Mark?" *CBQ* 44 (1982): 225-241.

Murphy-O'Connor, Jerome. "The Structure of Matthew XIV-XVII." *RB* 82
    (1975): 360-384.

Nations, Archie L. "Historical Criticism and the Current Methodological
    Crisis." *SJT* 36 (1983): 59-71.

Neill, Stephen. *The Interpretation of the New Testament. 1861-1961.* The
    Firth Lectures, 1962. London: Oxford University Press, 1964.

382 Bibliography

Neirynck, Frans. "Les femmes au tombeau: étude de la rédaction matthéenne (Matt. xxviii. 1-10)." *NTS* 15 (1968-69): 168-190.

Neirynck, Frans and Frans van Segbroeck. *New Testament Vocabulary: A Companion Volume to the Concordance.* BEThL LXV. Leuven: University Press, 1984.

Nestle-Aland. *Novum Testamentum Graece.* 26th rev. ed. Stuttgart: Deutsche Bibelgesellschaft, 1979.

Neusner, Jacob. "From Scripture to Mishnah: The Origins of Mishnah's Division of Women." *JJS* 30 (1979): 138-153.

----------. *A History of the Mishnaic Law of Purities.* SJLA 6. Parts 15 and 16. Leiden: Brill, 1976/1977.

----------. *The Idea of Purity in Ancient Judaism.* SJLA 1. Leiden: Brill, 1973.

----------. *Method and Meaning in Ancient Judaism.* Brown Judaic Studies 10. Missoula: Scholars, 1979.

Niditch, Susan. "The Wronged Woman Righted: An Analysis of Genesis 38." *HTR* 72 (1979): 143-149.

Nineham, D. E. "The Genealogy in St. Matthew's Gospel and Its Significance for the Study of the Gospels." *BJRL* 58 (1975-76): 421-444.

Nolan, Brian M. *The Royal Son of God: The Christology of Matthew 1-2 in the Setting of the Gospel.* OBO 23. Friborg Suisse: Éditions Universitaires/Göttingen: Vandenhoeck & Ruprecht, 1979.

Norris, Frederick W. "Isis, Sarapis and Demeter in Antioch of Syria." *HTR* 75 (1982): 189-207.

O'Faolain, Julia and Lauro Martines. *Not in God's Image: Women in History from the Greeks to the Victorians.* New York/Hagerstown/San Francisco/London: Harper & Row, 1973.

Offen, Karen. "Defining Feminism: A Comparative Historical Approach." *Signs* 14 (1988): 119-157.

Ortner, Sherry B.. "Is Female to Male as Nature Is to Culture?" In *Woman, Culture and Society*, edited by Michelle Zimbalist Rosaldo and Louise Lamphere, 67-88. Stanford: Stanford University Press, 1974.

Osiek, Carolyn. *Beyond Anger: On Being a Feminist in the Church.* New York/Mahwah: Paulist, 1986.

----------. "The Feminist and the Bible: Hermeneutical Alternatives." In *Feminist Perspectives on Biblical Scholarship*, edited by Adela Yarbro Collins, 93-105. SBL Centennial Publications 10. Chico: Scholars, 1985.

Otwell, J. H. *And Sarah Laughed: The Status of Women in the Old Testament.* Philadelphia: Westminster, 1977.

Palmer, Richard. *Hermeneutics: Interpretation Theory in Schleiermacher, Dilthey, Heidegger and Gadamer.* Evanston Ill.: NorthWestern University Press, 1969.

Pannenberg, Wolfhart. "Hermeneutic and Universal History." Chapter 4 in Vol. 1 of *Basic Questions in Theology,* 96-136. Translated by George H. Kehm. Philadelphia: Fortress, 1970.

Patai, Raphael. *Sex and Family in the Bible and the Middle East.* Garden City, New York: Doubleday, 1959.

----------. *The Hebrew Goddess.* New York: KTAV, 1967.

Patte, Daniel. *The Gospel according to Matthew: A Structural Commentary on Matthew's Faith.* Philadelphia: Fortress, 1987.

Paul, André. *L'Evangile de l'enfance selon saint Matthieu.* Lire la Bible 17. Paris: Cerf, 1968.

Peradotto, J and J. P. Sullivan, eds. *Women in the Ancient World. The Arethusa Papers.* Albany: State University of New York Press, 1984.

Perkins, Pheme. *Resurrection: New Testament Witness and Contemporary Reflection.* Garden City, New York: Doubleday, 1984.

Perkins, Pheme, John Koenig, Rosemary Radford Ruether, and Beverly W. Harrison. "Review Symposium - *In Memory of Her. A Feminist Theological Reconstruction of Christian Origins.* By Elisabeth Schüssler Fiorenza." *Horizons* 11 (1984): 142-157.

Perrin, Norman. "The Evangelist as Author: Reflections on Method in the Study and Interpretation of the Synoptic Gospels and Acts." *Biblical Research* 17 (1972): 5-18.

----------. *Rediscovering the Teaching of Jesus.* London: SCM, 1967.

----------. *The Resurrection Narratives: A New Approach.* London: SCM, 1977.

Pesch, Rudolf. "Die Heilung der Schwiegermutter des Simon-Petrus: Ein Beispiel heutiger Synoptikerexegese." In *Neuere Exegese - Verlust oder Gewinn?* 143-176. Freiburg: Herder, 1968.

----------. *Das Markusevangelium.* Teil I and II. HThK II,1-2. Freiburg/Basel/Wien: Herder, 1976/1980.

Peters, Ted. "The Nature and Role of Presuppositions: An Inquiry into Contemporary Hermeneutics." *IPQ* 14 (1974): 209-222.

Petersen, Norman. *Literary Criticism for New Testament Critics.* Guides to Biblical Scholarship. Philadelphia: Fortress, 1978.

----------."Literary Criticism in Biblical Studies." In *Orientation by Disorientation: Studies in Literary Criticism and Biblical Criticism,*

384 Bibliography

edited by R. A. Spencer, 25-50. Theological Monograph Series 35. Pittsburg: Pickwick Press, 1980.

----------. *Rediscovering Paul: Philemon and the Sociology of Paul's Narrative World*. Philadelphia: Fortress, 1985.

----------. "When is the End not the End? Literary Reflections on the Ending of Mark's Narrative." *Interp.* 34 (1980): 151-166.

Plaskow, Judith. "Blaming Jews for Inventing Patriarchy." *Lilith* 7 (1980): 11-12.

----------. "Christian Feminism and Anti-Judaism." *Cross Currents* 28 (1978): 307-309.

Pleket, H. W., ed. *Epigraphica. Vol 2. Texts on the Social History of the Greek World*. Leiden: Brill, 1969.

Plummer, Alfred. *An Exegetical Commentary on the Gospel according to S. Matthew*. London: Scott, 1915.

Polag, Athanasius. *Fragmenta Q. Textheft zur Logienquelle*. Neukirchen-Vluyn: Neukirchener, 1979.

Polzin, Robert M. "Literary and Historical Criticism of the Bible: A Crisis in Scholarship." In *Orientation by Disorientation: Studies in Literary Criticism and Biblical Criticism*, edited by R. A. Spencer, 99-114. Theological Monograph Series 35. Pittsburg: Pickwick Press, 1980.

Pomeroy, Sarah B. *Goddesses, Whores, Wives and Slaves: Women in Classical Antiquity*. New York: Schocken, 1975.

----------. "Selected Bibliography on Women in Classical Antiquity." In *Women in the Ancient World. The Arethusa Papers*, edited by J. Peradotto and J. P. Sullivan, 345-392. Albany: State University of New York Press, 1984.

----------. "Technikai kai Mousikai: The Education of Women in the Fourth Century and in the Hellenistic Period." *AmJAH* 2 (1977): 51-68.

----------. *Women in Hellenistic Egypt: From Alexander to Cleopatra*. New York: Schocken, 1984.

Portefaix, Lilian. *Sisters Rejoice: Paul's Letter to the Philippians and Luke-Acts as Received by First-Century Philippian Women*. CB.NT 20. Stöckholm: Almqvist & Wiksell, 1988.

Potin, Jean. "Guérison d'une hémorroïse et résurrection de la fille de Jaïre. Mc. 5,21-43." *ASeign* 2/44 (1969): 38-47.

Preaux, Claire. "Le statut de la femme à l'époque hellénistique principalement en Egypte." *RSJB* 11 (1959): 127-175.

Quinn, J. D. "Is 'ΡΑΧΑΒ in Mt 1,5 Rahab of Jericho?" *Bib* 62 (1981): 225-228.

Rabinowitz, Nancy Sorkin. "Female Speech and Female Sexuality: Euripides' *Hippolytos* as Model." In *Rescuing Creusa: New Methodological Approaches to Women in Antiquity*, edited by Marilyn Skinner, 127-140. Lubbock, Texas: Texas Tech, 1987.

Rad, Gerhard von. *Genesis*. 3rd rev. ed. OTL. 1961. Reprint. London: SCM, 1972.

Rahlfs, A., ed. *Septuaginta*. Stuttgart: Deutsche Bibelgesellschaft, 1979.

Ranck, Shirley Ann. "Points of Theological Convergence between Feminism and Post-Modern Science." *IJWS* 2 (1979): 386-397.

Rawson, Beryl, ed. *The Family in Ancient Rome: New Perspectives*. London/Sydney: Croom Helm, 1986.

Reiter, Rayna R., ed. *Toward an Anthropology of Women*. New York/London: Monthly Review Press, 1975.

Rhoads, David and Donald Michie. *Mark as Story: An Introduction to the Narrative of a Gospel*. Philadelphia: Fortress, 1982.

Rich, Adrienne. "When we Dead Awaken: Writing as Re-vision." *College English* 34 (1972): 18-30.

Ricoeur, Paul. *Essays on Biblical Interpretation*. Edited with an introduction by Lewis S. Mudge. London: SPCK, 1981.

----------. *Interpretation Theory: Discourse and the Surplus of Meaning*. Fort Worth, Texas: Texas Christian University Press, 1976.

----------. *Time and Narrative*. 2 vols. Translated by Kathleen McLaughlin and David Pellauer. Chicago: University of Chicago Press, 1984/1985.

Rieger, Renate. "Half of Heaven Belongs to Women, and They Must Win it for Themselves: An Attempt at a Feminist Theological Stock-Taking in the Federal Republic of Germany." *JFSR* 1.1 (1985): 133-144.

Riekert, S. J. P. K. "The Narrative Coherence in Matthew 26-8." *Neot* 16 (1982): 118-137.

Rigaux, Beda. *Témoignage de l'évangile de Matthieu*. Pour une histoire de Jésus 2. Louvain: Desclée de Brouwer, 1967.

Rimmon-Kenan, Shlomith. *Narrative Fiction: Contemporary Poetics*. London/New York: Methuen, 1983.

Ringe, Sharon H. "A Gentile Woman's Story." In *Feminist Interpretation of the Bible*, edited by Letty M. Russell, 65-72. Philadelphia: Westminster, 1985.

Ritt, Hubert. "Die Frauen und die Osterbotschaft. Synopse der Grabesgeschichten (Mk 16,1-8; Mt 27,62-28,15; Lk 24,1-12; Joh 20,1-18)." In *Die Frau im Urchristentum*, edited by Gerhard Dautzenberg,

386   Bibliography

Helmut Merklein and Karlheinz Müller, 117-133. QD 95. Freiburg/
Basel/Wien: Herder, 1983.

Robbins, Vernon K. "The Woman who Touched Jesus' Garment: Socio-
Rhetorical Analysis of the Synoptic Accounts." *NTS* 33 (1987): 502-515.

Robinson, Robert B. "Literary Functions of the Genealogies of Genesis." *CBQ*
48 (1986): 595-608.

Rochais, Gerard. *Les récits de résurrection des morts dans le Nouveau
Testament.* MSSNTS 40. Cambridge: University Press, 1981.

Rosaldo, Michelle Zimbalist and Louise Lamphere, eds. *Woman, Culture
and Society.* Stanford: Stanford University Press, 1974.

Rubin, Gayle. "The Traffic in Women: Notes on the "Political Economy" of
Sex." In *Toward an Anthropology of Women,* edited by Rayna R.
Reiter, 157-210. New York/London: Monthly Review Press, 1975.

Rudolph, Kurt. *Gnosis: The Nature and History of Gnosticism.* Translated by
Robert McLachlan Wilson. San Francisco: Harper & Row, 1983.

Ruether, Rosemary Radford. "Feminist Interpretation: A Method of
Correlation." In *Feminist Interpretation of the Bible,* edited by Letty
M. Russell, 111-124. Philadelphia: Westminster, 1985.

----------. *Sexism and God-Talk: Toward a Feminist Theology.* Boston:
Beacon, 1983.

----------, ed. *Religion and Sexism: Images of Woman in the Jewish and
Christian Traditions.* New York: Simon and Schuster, 1974.

Ruether, Rosemary Radford and Eleanor McLaughlin, eds. *Women of Spirit:
Female Leadership in the Jewish and Christian Traditions.* New York:
Simon and Schuster, 1979.

Russell, E. A. "The Canaanite Woman and the Gospels (Mt 15.21-28; cf. Mk
7.24-30)." In *Studia Biblica 1978: II. Papers on the Gospels,* edited by E.
A. Livingstone, 263-300. JSNTSup 2. Sheffield: JSOT Press, 1980.

Russell, Letty M. , ed. *Feminist Interpretation of the Bible.* Philadelphia:
Westminster, 1985.

----------. *The Future of Partnership.* Philadelphia: Westminster, 1979.

----------. *Household of Freedom: Authority in Feminist Theology.* The 1986
Annie Kinkead Warfield Lectures. Philadelphia: Westminster, 1987.

----------. *Human Liberation in a Feminist Perspective--A Theology.*
Philadelphia: Westminster, 1974.

----------. "In Search of a Critical Feminist Paradigm for Bibilical
Interpretation." Paper presented to the Working Group on Liberation
Theology, AAR/SBL, Feminist Hermeneutic Project, 1983.

Ruthven, K. K. *Feminist Literary Studies: An Introduction*. Cambridge/New York: Cambridge University Press, 1984.

Sabourin, Leopold. *L'Evangile selon saint Matthieu et ses principaux parallèles*. Rome: Biblical Institute, 1978.

Sakenfeld, Katharine Doob. "Feminist Uses of Biblical Materials." In *Feminist Interpretation of the Bible*, edited by Letty M. Russell, 55-72. Philadelphia: Westminster, 1985.

Sanders, James A. *Canon and Community: A Guide to Canonical Criticism*. Guides to Biblical Scholarship. Philadelphia: Fortress, 1984.

Sasson, Jack M. *Ruth: A New Translation with a Philological Commentary and a Formalist-Folklorist Interpretation*. The Johns Hopkins Near Eastern Studies 11. Baltimore/London: Johns Hopkins University Press, 1979.

Schaberg, Jane. *The Illegitimacy of Jesus: A Feminist Theological Interpretation of the Infancy Narratives*. San Francisco: Harper and Row, 1987.

Schaps, David M. *Economic Rights of Women in Ancient Greece*. Edinburgh: Edinburgh University Press, 1979.

Schlatter, Adolf. *Der Evangelist Matthäus: Seine Sprache, sein Ziel, seine Selbständigkeit. Ein Kommentar zum ersten Evangelium*. Stuttgart: Calwer, 1948.

Schlier, Heinrich. "ἀλείφω." *TDNT* I:229-232.

Schnackenburg, Rudolf, ed. *Die Bergpredigt: Utopische Vision oder Handlungsweisung?* Düsseldorf: Patmos, 1982.

Schoedel, William R. *Ignatius of Antioch: A Commentary on the Letters of Ignatius of Antioch*. Hermeneia. Philadelphia: Fortress, 1985.

Schottroff, Luise. "Das geschundene Volk und die Arbeit in der Ernte Gottes nach dem Matthäusevangelium." In *Mitarbeiter der Schöpfung: Bibel und Arbeitswelt*, edited by Luise and Willy Schottroff, 149-206. München: Chr. Kaiser, 1983.

----------. "Maria Magdalena und die Frauen am Grabe Jesu." *EvTh* 42 (1982): 3-25.

----------. "Women as Followers of Jesus in New Testament Times: An Exercise in Social-Historical Exegesis of the Bible." In *The Bible and Liberation: Political and Social Hermeneutics*, edited by Norman K. Gottwald, 418-427. Maryknoll: Orbis, 1983.

Schüssler Fiorenza, Elisabeth. *The Book of Revelation: Justice and Judgment*. Philadelphia: Fortress, 1985.

----------. *Bread Not Stone: The Challenge of Feminist Biblical Interpretation.* Boston: Beacon, 1984.

----------. "Breaking the Silence - Becoming Visible." *Concilium* 182 (1985): 3-16.

----------. "Emerging Issues in Feminist Biblical Interpretation." In *Christian Feminism: Visions of a New Humanity,* edited by Judith L. Weidman, 33-54. San Francisco: Harper & Row, 1984.

----------. "The Ethics of Interpretation: De-Centering Biblical Scholarship." *JBL* 107 (1988): 3-17.

----------. "A Feminist Critical Interpretation for Liberation: Martha and Mary: Lk. 10:38-42." *Religion and Intellectual Life* III:2 (1986): 21-36.

----------. "Feminist Theology and New Testament Interpretation." *JSOT* 22 (1982): 33-46.

----------. "Feminist Theology as a Critical Theology of Liberation." In *Woman: New Dimensions,* edited by Walter J. Burghardt, 29-50. New York/Ramsey/Toronto: Paulist, 1977.

----------. "'For the Sake of our Salvation ...'": Biblical Interpretation as Theological Task." In *Sin, Salvation and the Spirit,* edited by D. Durken, 21-39. Collegeville: Liturgical Press, 1979.

----------. *In Memory of Her: A Feminist Theological Reconstruction of Christian Origins.* New York: Crossroad, 1983.

----------. "Remembering the Past in Creating the Future: Historical-Critical Scholarship and Feminist Biblical Interpretation." In *Feminist Perspectives on Biblical Scholarship,* edited by Adela Yarbro Collins, 43-63. SBL Centennial Publications 10. Chico: Scholars, 1985.

--------. "Response to Antoinette Clark Wire, Bruce Birch, Beverly Gaventa, Drorah Setel." Unpublished paper prepared for Discussion at the AAR Meeting, New York City, December, 1982.

----------. "Response to "The Social Functions of Women's Asceticism in the Roman East" by Antoinette Clark Wire." In *Images of the Feminine in Gnosticism,* edited by Karen L. King, 324-328. Studies in Antiquity and Christianity. Philadelphia: Fortress, 1988.

----------. "Rhetorical Situation and Historical Reconstruction in 1 Corinthians." *NTS* 33 (1987): 386-403.

----------. "The Study of Women in Early Christianity: Some Methodological Considerations." In *Critical History and Biblical Faith: New Testament Perspectives,* edited by Thomas J. Ryan, 31-58. College Theology Society Annual Publication Series. Villanova: College Theology Society, 1979.

----------. "Toward a Feminist Biblical Hermeneutics: Biblical Interpretation and Liberation Theology." In *The Challenge of Liberation Theology: A First World Response*, edited by Brian Mahan and L. Dale Richesin, 91-112. Maryknoll: Orbis, 1981.

----------. "Towards a Liberating and Liberated Theology: Women Theologians and Feminist Theology in the USA." *Concilium* 115 (1979): 22-32.

----------. "The Twelve." In *Women Priests: A Catholic Commentary on the Vatican Declaration*, edited by Leonard and Arlene Swidler, 114-122. New York: Paulist, 1977.

----------. "'Waiting at Table': A Critical Feminist Theological Reflection on Diakonia." *Concilium* 198 (1988): 84-94.

----------. "The Will to Choose or to Reject: Continuing Our Critical Work." In *Feminist Interpretation of the Bible*, edited by Letty M. Russell, 125-136. Philadelphia: Westminster, 1985.

----------."'You are not to be called Father": Early Christian History in a Feminist Perspective." *Cross Currents* 29 (1979): 301-323.

Schweickart, Patrocinio P. "Reading Ourselves: Toward a Feminist Theory of Reading." In *Gender and Reading: Essays on Readers, Texts, and Contexts*, edited by E. A. Flynn and Patrocinio, P. Schweickart, 31-62. Baltimore: Johns Hopkins University Press, 1986.

Schweizer, Eduard. *The Good News according to Matthew*. Translated by David E. Green. Atlanta: John Knox, 1975.

----------. *The Good News according to Mark: A Commentary on the Gospel*. Translated by Donald H. Madvig. Atlanta: John Knox, 1970.

----------. *Matthäus und seine Gemeinde*. SBS 71. Stuttgart: KBW Verlag, 1974.

Segal, J. B. "The Jewish Attitude toward Women." *JJS* 30 (1979): 121-137.

Selvidge, Marla J. *Daughters of Jerusalem*. Scottdale, Penn./Kitchener, Ont.: Herald Press, 1987.

----------. "Mark and Woman: Reflections on Serving." *Explorations* 1 (1982): 23-32.

----------. "Violence, Woman, and the Future of the Matthean Community: A Redactional Critical Essay." *USQR* 39 (1984): 213-223.

Senior, Donald. "The Death of Jesus and the Resurrection of the Holy Ones (Mt 27:51-53)." *CBQ* 38 (1976): 312-329.

----------. "Matthew's Special Material in the Passion Story: Implications for the Evangelist's Redactional Technique and Theological Perspective." *EThL* 63 (1987): 272-294.

390 Bibliography

----------."The Ministry of Continuity: Matthew's Gospel and the Interpretation of History." *BiTod* 82 (1976): 670-676.

----------. *The Passion Narrative according to Matthew: A Redactional Study.* BEThL XXXIX. 1975. Reprint. Leuven: University Press, 1982.

----------. "The Passion Narrative in the Gospel of Matthew." In *L'évangile selon Matthieu: Rédaction et théologie,* edited by M. Didier, 343-357. BEThL XXIX. Gembloux: Duculot, 1972.

----------. *The Passion of Jesus in the Gospel of Matthew.* Wilmington, Del.: Michael Glazier, 1985.

----------. *What Are They Saying About Matthew?* New York/Ramsey: Paulist, 1983.

Senior, Donald and Carroll Stuhlmueller. *The Biblical Foundations for Mission.* Maryknoll: Orbis, 1983.

Setel, T. Drorah. "Feminist Insights and the Question of Method." In *Feminist Perspectives on Biblical Scholarship,* edited by Adela Yarbro Collins, 35-42. SBL Centennial Publications 10. Chico: Scholars, 1985.

----------. "A Jewish-Feminist Response to Elisabeth Schüssler Fiorenza's "Toward a Feminist Biblical Hermeneutics: Biblical Interpretation and Liberation Theology"." Unpublished Paper for the Working Group on Liberation Theology, AAR/SBL, Feminist Hermeneutic Project, 1982.

----------. "Prophets and Pornography: Female Sexual Imagery in Hosea." In *Feminist Interpretation of the Bible,* edited by Letty M. Russell, 86-95. Philadelphia: Westminster, 1985.

Shuler, Philip L. *A Genre for the Gospels: The Biographical Character of Matthew.* Philadelphia: Fortress, 1982.

Skinner, Marilyn, ed. *Rescuing Creusa: New Methodological Approaches to Women in Antiquity.* Lubbock, Texas: Texas Tech, 1987.

Smith, Robert H. "Were the Early Christians Middle-Class? A Sociological Analysis of the New Testament." *Currents in Theology and Mission* 7 (1980): 260-276.

Snyder, Graydon F. *Ante Pacem: Archaeological Evidence of Church Life before Constantine.* Macon, Ga.: Mercer University Press, 1985.

Soares Prabhu, George M. *The Formula Quotations in the Infancy Narrative of Matthew: An Inquiry into the Tradition History of Mt 1-2.* AnBib 63. Rome: Biblical Institute Press, 1976.

Soulen, Richard N. *Handbook of Biblical Criticism.* 2nd ed. rev. and enl. Atlanta: John Knox, 1981.

Spencer, R. A., ed. *Orientation by   Disorientation: Studies in Literary Criticism and Biblical Criticism*. Theological Monograph Series 35. Pittsburg: Pickwick Press, 1980.

Stagg, Evelyn and Frank. *Woman in the World of Jesus*. Philadelphia: Westminster, 1978.

Stambaugh, John E. and David L. Balch. *The New Testament in Its Social Environment*. Library of Early Christianity. Philadelphia: Westminster, 1986.

Stanton, Graham. *The Interpretation of Matthew*. Issues in Religion and Theology 3. Philadelphia: Fortress/London: SPCK, 1983.

----------. "The Origin and Purpose of Matthew's Gospel: Matthean Scholarship from 1945 to 1980." In *ANRW* II.25.3, 1889-1951. Berlin/New York: de Gruyter, 1985.

Stegemann, Hartmut. ""Die des Uria": Zur Bedeutung der Frauennamen in der Genealogie von Matthäus 1,1-17." In *Tradition und Glaube: Das frühe Christentum in seiner Umwelt. Festgabe für Karl Georg Kuhn zum 65. Geburtstag*, edited by G. Jeremias, H.-W. Kuhn and H. Stegemann, 246-276. Göttingen: Vandenhoeck & Ruprecht, 1971.

Steinberg, Naomi. "Israelite Tricksters, Their Analogues and Cross-cultural Study." *Semeia* 42 (1988): 1-13.

Stendahl, Krister. *The Bible and the Role of Women: A Case Study in Hermeneutics*. Translated by Emilie T. Sander. Facet Books - Biblical Series 15. Philadelphia: Fortress, 1966.

----------. "Biblical Theology, Contemporary." *IDB* I:418-432.

----------. "Matthew." In *Peake's Commentary on the Bible*, 769-798. 2nd ed. London: Nelson, 1962.

----------. "Quis et Unde? An Analysis of Matthew 1-2." In *The Interpretation of Matthew*, edited by Graham Stanton, 56-66. Issues in Religion and Theology 3. Philadelphia: Fortress/London: SPCK, 1983.

----------. *The School of St. Matthew and Its Use of the Old Testament*. Philadelphia: Fortress, 1968.

Sternberg, Meier *The Poetics of Biblical Narrative: Ideological Literature and the Drama of Reading*. Indiana Literary Biblical Series. Bloomington: Indiana University Press, 1985.

Stillwell, Richard. *Antioch-on-the-Orontes II. The Excavations of 1933-1936*. Princeton: Princeton University Press, 1938.

Stock, Augustine. *Call to Discipleship: A Literary Study of Mark's Gospel*. Good News Studies 1. Wilmington, Del.: Michael Glazier, 1982.

----------. "The Limits of Historical-Criticial Exegesis." *BTB* 13 (1983): 28-31.

Strack, H. L. and P. Billerbeck. *Kommentar zum Neuen Testament aus Talmud und Midrasch*. Vol. I. München: Beck, 1922.

Strecker, Georg. *Der Weg der Gerechtigkeit: Untersuchung zur Theologie des Matthäus*. FRLANT 82. Göttingen: Vandenhoeck & Ruprecht, 1962.

Suggs, M. Jack *Wisdom, Christology, and Law in Matthew's Gospel*. Cambridge, Mass.: Harvard University Press, 1970.

Summers, Anne. *Damned Whores and God's Police: The Colonization of Women in Australia*. Pelican Books. Harmondsworth, Middlesex: Penguin, 1975.

Swarte Gifford, Carolyn de. "American Women and the Bible: The Nature of Woman as Hermeneutical Issue." In *Feminist Perspectives on Biblical Scholarship*, edited by Adela Yarbro Collins, 11-33. SBL Centennial Publications 10. Chico: Scholars, 1985.

Swidler, Leonard. "Beruriah: Her Word Became Law." *Lilith* 1.3 (1977): 9-13.

----------. *Biblical Affirmations of Women*. Philadelphia: Westminster, 1979.

----------. "Greco-Roman Feminism and the Reception of the Gospel." In *Traditio - Krisis - Renovatio aus theologischer Sicht. Festschrift Winfried Zeller zum 65. Geburtstag*, edited by B. Jaspert and R. Mohr, 41-65. Marburg: Elwert Verlag, 1976.

----------. *Women in Judaism: The Status of Women in Formative Judaism*. Metuchen, NJ.: Scarecrow Press, 1976.

Tavard, George H. *Woman in Christian Tradition*. Notre Dame/London: University of Notre Dame Press, 1973.

Taylor, Vincent. *The Gospel according to St. Mark. The Greek Text with Introduction, Notes, and Indexes*. London: Macmillan, 1952.

Tetlow, Elizabeth M. *Women and Ministry in the New Testament*. New York/Ramsey: Paulist, 1980.

Theissen, Gerd. *Miracle Stories of the Early Christian Tradition*. Edited by J. Riches and translated by Francis McDonagh. Studies of the New Testament and Its World. Edinburgh: T. & T. Clark, 1983.

Thiering, Barbara. *Created Second? Aspects of Women's Liberation in Australia*. Adelaide: Griffin Press, 1973.

----------, ed. *Deliver Us from Eve: Essays on Australian Women and Religion*. Sydney: Australian Council of Churches, 1977.

Thiselton, Anthony C. *The Two Horizons: New Testament Hermeneutics and Philosophical Description with Special Reference to Heidegger, Bultmann, Gadamer and Wittgenstein*. Forward by J. B. Torrance. Exeter: Paternoster, 1980.

Thomas, D. Winton. "Kelebh 'Dog': Its Origin and Some Usages of It in the Old Testament." *VT* 10 (1960): 410-427.

Thompson, Mark C. "Expository Articles - Matthew 15:21-28." *Interp.* 35 (1981): 279-284.

Thompson, William G. *Matthew's Advice to a Divided Community: Mt. 17,22-18,35.* AnBib 44. Rome: Biblical Institute Press, 1970.

----------. "Reflections on the Composition of Mt 8:1-9:34." *CBQ* 33 (1971): 365-388.

Thompson, William G. and Eugene LaVerdiere. "New Testament Communities in Transition: A Study of Matthew and Luke." *TS* 37 (1976): 567-597.

Thraede, Klaus. "Frau." *RAC* 8:227-242.

Tischleder, P. *Wesen und Stellung der Frau nach der Lehre des heiligen Paulus: Eine ethisch-exegetische Untersuchung.* NTA 10/3-4. Münster: Aschendorff, 1923.

Todd, Alexander Dundes and Sue Fisher, eds. *Gender and Discourse: The Power of Talk.* Advances in Discourse Processes XXX. Norwood, NJ.: Ablex, 1988.

Tolbert, Mary Ann. "Defining the Problem: The Bible and Feminist Hermeneutics." *Semeia* 28 (1983): 113-126.

Tompkins, Jane, ed. *Reader-Response Criticism: From Formalism to Post-Structuralism.* Baltimore/London: Johns Hopkins University Press, 1981.

Tracy, David. *The Analogical Imagination: Christian Theology and the Culture of Pluralism.* London: SCM, 1981.

Trible, Phyllis. "Depatriarchalizing in Biblical Interpretation." *JAAR* 41 (1973): 30-48.

----------. "Feminist Hermeneutics and Biblical Studies." *Christian Century* 99 (1982): 116-118.

----------. *God and the Rhetoric of Sexuality.* Overtures to Biblical Theology 2. Philadelphia: Fortress, 1978.

----------. *Texts of Terror: Literary-Feminist Readings of Biblical Narratives.* Overtures to Biblical Theology 13. Philadelphia: Fortress, 1984.

Trilling, Wolfgang. *Das wahre Israel: Studien zur Theologie des Matthäus-Evangeliums.* 3rd ed. StANT 10. München: Kösel-Verlag, 1964.

Vanhoye, Albert. "Structure et théologie des récits de la passion dans les évangiles synoptiques." *NRTh* 89 (1967): 135-163.

394   Bibliography

Veyne, Peter, ed. *A History of Private Life: 1. From Pagan Rome to Byzantium.* Translated by Arthur Goldhammer. Cambridge, Mass./London: Belknap, 1987.

Via, Dan O. "Narrative World and Ethical Response: The Marvelous and Righteousness in Matthew 1-2." *Semeia* 12 (1978): 123-149.

----------. "Structure, Christology, and Ethics in Matthew." In *Orientation by Disorientation: Studies in Literary Criticism and Biblical Criticism,* edited by R. A. Spencer, 199-215. Theological Monograph Series 35. Pittsburg: Pickwick Press, 1980.

Viviano, Benedict T. *Study as Worship: Aboth and the New Testament.* SJLA XXVI. Leiden: Brill, 1978.

----------. "Where was the Gospel according to St. Matthew Written?" *CBQ* 41 (1979): 533-546.

Vögtle, Anton. *Messias und Gottessohn: Herkunft und Sinn der matthäischen Geburts-und Kindheitsgeschichte.* Düsseldorf: Patmos, 1971.

Waetjen, Herman C. "The Genealogy as the Key to the Gospel according to Matthew." *JBL* 95 (1976): 205-230.

Wainwright, Elaine M. "In Search of the Lost Coin: Toward a Feminist Biblical Hermeneutic," *Pacifica* 2 (1989): 135-150.

----------. *"Like Treasure Hidden in a Field": A Literary-Critical Analysis of Key Pericopes Concerning Women in the Matthean Gospel.* Master's thesis, Catholic Theological Union, Chicago, 1985.

Walker, Rolf. *Die Heilsgeschichte im ersten Evangelium.* FRLANT 91. Göttingen: Vandenhoeck & Ruprecht, 1967.

Wallace-Hadrill, D. S. *Christian Antioch: A Study of Early Christian Thought in the East.* Cambridge: University Press, 1982.

Walter, Nikolaus. "Eine vormatthäische Schilderung der Auferstehung Jesu." *NTS* 19 (1972/73): 415-429.

Weeden, Theodore J. *Mark: Traditions in Conflict.* Philadelphia: Fortress, 1971.

Wegner, Judith Romney. *Chattel or Person? The Status of Women in the Mishnah.* New York/Oxford: Oxford University Press, 1988.

Weidman, Judith L., ed. *Christian Feminism: Visions of a New Humanity.* San Francisco: Harper & Row, 1984.

Weinfeld, Moshe. "Ruth, Book of." *EJ* 14:518-524.

Weiss, K. "πυρέσσω/πυρετός." *TDNT* VI:956-959 .

Welch, Sharon D. *Communities of Resistance and Solidarity: A Feminist Theology of Liberation.* Maryknoll: Orbis, 1985.

Westermann, Claus. *Genesis 37-50: A Commentary.* Translated by John J. Scullion. Minneapolis: Augsburg, 1986.

White, Hayden. "The Value of Narrativity in the Representation of Reality." *Critical Inquiry* 7 (1980): 5-28.

----------. "Historicism, History and the Figurative Imagination." *History and Theory* 14 (1975): 43-67.

Wilkins, Michael J. *The Concept of Disciple in Matthew's Gospel as Reflected in the use of the Term Μαθητής.* Leiden/New York/København/ Köln: Brill, 1988.

Williams, James G. *Women Recounted: Narrative Thinking and the God of Israel.* Bible and Literature Series 6. Sheffield: Almond, 1982.

Wilson, Robert. R. *Genealogy and History in the Biblical World.* Yale Near Eastern Researches 7. New Haven/London: Yale University Press, 1977.

Wink, Walter. *The Bible in Human Transformation: Toward a New Paradigm for Biblical Study.* Philadelphia: Fortress, 1973.

----------. *Transforming Bible Study.* London: SCM, 1981.

Wire, Antoinette Clark. "Ancient Miracle Stories and Women's Social World." *Forum* 2 (1986): 77-84.

----------. "On Elisabeth Schüssler Fiorenza's "Toward a Feminist Biblical Hermeneutics"." Unpublished Paper for the Working Group on Liberation Theology, AAR/SBL, Feminist Hermeneutic Project, 1982.

----------. "The Social Functions of Women's Asceticism in the Roman East." In *Images of the Feminine in Gnosticism*, edited by Karen L. King, 308-323. Studies in Antiquity and Christianity. Philadelphia: Fortress, 1988.

----------. "The Structure of the Gospel Miracle Stories and Their Tellers." *Semeia* 11 (1978): 83-113.

Witherington, Ben III. *Women in the Ministry of Jesus: A Study of Jesus' Attitudes to Women and Their Roles as Reflected in His Earthly Life.* MSSNTS 51. 1984. Reprint, Cambridge: University Press, 1988.

----------. *Women in the Earliest Churches.* MSSNTS 59. Cambridge: University Press, 1988.

Yadin, Yigael. "Expedition D - The Cave of Letters." *IEJ* 12 (1962): 227-257.

----------. *Bar Kokhba: The Rediscovery of the Legendary Hero of the Last Jewish Revolt against Imperial Rome.* London: Weidenfeld & Nicholson, 1971.

Zakowitch, Yair. "Rahab als Mutter des Boas in der Jesus-Genealogie (Matth. I.5." *NT* 17 (1975): 1-5.

Zappone, Katherine E. "A Feminist Hermeneutics for Scripture: The Standpoint of the Interpreter." *Proceedings of the Irish Biblical Association* 8 (1984): 25-38.

Zerwick, Maximilian. *Biblical Greek.* SPIB 114. Translated by J. Smith. Rome: Biblical Institute Press, 1963.

Zikmund, Barbara Brown. "Feminist Consciousness in Historical Perspective." In *Feminist Interpretation of the Bible,* edited by Letty M. Russell, 21-26. Philadelphia: Westminster, 1985.

Zinserling, Verna. *Women in Greece and Rome.* Translated by L. A. Jones. New York: Schram, 1973.

Zumstein, Jean. "Antioche sur l'Oronte et l'évangile selon Matthieu." *SNTU* A/5 (1980): 122-138.

----------. *La condition du croyant dans l'évangile selon Matthieu.* OBO 16. Friborg Suisse: Éditions Universitaires/Göttingen: Vandenhoeck & Ruprecht, 1977.

Index to Citations of Ancient Sources

I. Hebrew Scriptures and Apocrypha

II. Pseudephigraphical and other Jewish Literature

III. Christian Scriptures

Acta Conciliorum Oecumenicorum

Iussu atque mandato Societatis scientiarum Argentoratensis
Edenda instituit Eduardus Schwartz

Continuavit Johannes Straub

Quart, Kartoniert

Das monumentale Werk liegt seit 1984 abgeschlossen vor (Series Prima). Diese Ausgabe der
Akten der ökumenischen Konzile von Ephesus 431 bis Konstantinopel 553 (die Akten der
Konzile von Nicäa 325 und Konstantinopel 381 sind nicht erhalten, sondern nur deren
Kanones) gehört zu den Arbeitsgrundlagen eines jeden, der sich mit der Kirchengeschichte
und der Geschichte der frühen Jahrhunderte beschäftigen will. Im Jahre 1914 hatte Schwartz
den ersten Band vorgelegt, bis kurz vor seinem Tode, 1940, hat er daran gearbeitet und die
Ausgabe tatsächlich bis auf einen Band abgeschlossen. Dessen Druckmanuskript wurde
Johannes Straub übergeben, der den Band IV,1 1971 vorlegte und auf dessen Initiative die
Registerbände zurückgehen. Bis zum Erscheinen der Ausgabe von Schwartz war die
wissenschaftliche Welt auf die Ausgabe der Konzilsakten von Mansi angewiesen, die ihrerseits
Ausgaben aus dem ausgehenden 17. Jahrhundert reproduziert. Die staunenswerte Leistung
von Eduard Schwartz bedeutet einen Fortschritt der Wissenschaft um 300 Jahre; es wäre
sehr zu wünschen, wenn künftig nur noch nach den ACO zitiert würde.
Eine Übersicht über den Aufbau des Werkes (mit bibliographischen Daten und aktuellen
Ladenpreisen) kann beim Verlag angefordert werden.

Acta Conciliorum Oecumenicorum

Sub auspiciis Academiae Scientiarum Bavariae edita
Series Secunda

Diese Reihe wurde 1984 eröffnet.

Volumen Primum

Concilium Lateranense a. 649 celbratum

Edidit Rudolf Riedinger

Quart. XXVIII, 467 Seiten. 1984. Kartoniert DM 434,— ISBN 3 11 008235 7

Volumen Secundum, Pars Prima

Concilium Universale Constantinopolitanum Tertium

Concilii Actiones I—XI

Edidit Rudolf Riedinger

Quart XIII, 513 Seiten. 1990. Kartoniert DM 520,— ISBN 3 11 011758 4

Preisänderungen vorbehalten

Walter de Gruyter Berlin · New York

HERAUSGEGEBEN IM AUFTRAG DER
KIRCHENVÄTER-KOMMISSION DER
PREUSSISCHEN AKADEMIE DER
WISSENSCHAFTEN

ITALA

Das Neue Testament in altlateinischer Überlieferung

Nach den Handschriften herausgegeben von Adolf Jülicher
durchgesehen und zum Druck besorgt von
Walter Matzkow und Kurt Aland

Band I: Matthäus-Evangelium
Zweite verbesserte Auflage
Quart. VIII, 214 Seiten. 1972. Kartoniert DM 245,–
ISBN 3-11-002256-7

Band II: Marcus-Evangelium
Zweite verbesserte Auflage
Quart. VII, 160 Seiten. 1970. Kartoniert DM 225,–
ISBN 3-11-001244-8

Band III: Lucas-Evangelium
Zweite verbesserte Auflage
Quart. VII, 282 Seiten. 1976. Kartoniert DM 365,–
ISBN 3-11-002255-9

Band IV: Johannes-Evangelium
Quart. X, 230 Seiten. 1963. Kartoniert DM 280,–
ISBN 3-11-001243-X

Preisänderung vorbehalten

Walter de Gruyter Berlin · New York